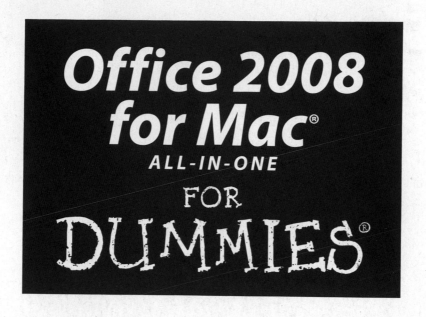

Office 2008 for Mac®
ALL-IN-ONE
FOR DUMMIES®

by Geetesh Bajaj and James Gordon

WILEY

Wiley Publishing, Inc.

Office 2008 for Mac® All-in-One For Dummies®

Published by
Wiley Publishing, Inc.
111 River Street
Hoboken, NJ 07030-5774

www.wiley.com

For general information on our other products and services, please contact our Customer Care Department within the U.S. at 877-762-2974, outside the U.S. at 317-572-3993, or fax 317-572-4002.

For technical support, please visit www.wiley.com/techsupport.

Wiley also publishes its books in a variety of electronic formats. Some content that appears in print may not be available in electronic books.

Library of Congress Control Number: 2009935234

ISBN: 978-0-470-46041-2

Manufactured in the United States of America

10 9 8 7 6 5 4 3 2

WILEY

About the Authors

Geetesh Bajaj has been creating Microsoft Office documents, presentations, and templates for over a decade now. Geetesh heads Indezine, a presentation design studio based out of Hyderabad, India, and he also runs the popular indezine.com Web site. Geetesh is a Microsoft-awarded Most Valuable Professional (MVP) and author of four other computer books (two of them published by Wiley).

James Gordon is a lead programmer/analyst at the University at Buffalo and the State University of New York where he also teaches workshops on Microsoft Office and other technologies. Microsoft has presented its Most Valuable Professional (MVP) award to James for his contributions to technical communities. James has written several programs, including the popular InsertPicture add-in that runs in PowerPoint for Mac, and is a member and past-president of ProMac Users Group, Inc.

Dedication

To Steve Jobs and Bill Gates.

Authors' Acknowledgments

We thank the divine, and other mere mortals with divine abilities.

Special thanks to everyone at Wiley for helping us put this book together. Acquisitions editor Kyle Looper and project editor Mark Enochs kept everything on track. Thanks go to the editorial team, including copy editors Jen Riggs and John Edwards, and technical editor James Russell.

Thanks go to our families and friends for allowing us to focus on our writing without deserting us. We express our appreciation to them all.

Geetesh wishes to thank his office staff who helped him take the time off to write this book as well as the amazing bunch of other Microsoft MVPs who are too numerous to be listed here.

Jim wishes to extend special thanks to the University at Buffalo for allowing leave to work on the book. The University at Buffalo is truly one of the best places to work or attend.

We thank the Macintosh Business Unit of Microsoft, who created the subject matter of the book, and Microsoft Corporation for the awesome MVP program, without which it is unlikely the authors would have been able to meet and collaborate. And we also thank Apple for creating an enriching OS platform.

Finally, both the authors thank each other!

Publisher's Acknowledgments

We're proud of this book; please send us your comments through our online registration form located at http://dummies.custhelp.com. For other comments, please contact our Customer Care Department within the U.S. at 877-762-2974, outside the U.S. at 317-572-3993, or fax 317-572-4002.

Some of the people who helped bring this book to market include the following:

Acquisitions, Editorial, and Media Development

Senior Project Editor: Mark Enochs

Acquisitions Editor: Kyle Looper

Copy Editors: Jennifer Riggs, John Edwards

Technical Editor: James Russell

Senior Editorial Manager: Leah Cameron

Media Development Project Manager: Laura Moss-Hollister

Media Development Assistant Project Manager: Jenny Swisher

Media Development Assistant Producers: Angela Denny, Josh Frank, Shawn Patrick, and Kit Malone

Editorial Assistant: Amanda Graham

Sr. Editorial Assistant: Cherie Case

Cartoons: Rich Tennant (www.the5thwave.com)

Composition Services

Project Coordinator: Patrick Redmond

Layout and Graphics: Samantha K. Cherolis, Joyce Haughey, Christine Williams

Proofreaders: ConText Editorial Services, Inc., Caitie Copple

Indexer: BIM Indexing & Proofreading Services

Special Help

Tonya Cupp, Laura Miller, and Beth Taylor.

Publishing and Editorial for Technology Dummies

Richard Swadley, Vice President and Executive Group Publisher

Andy Cummings, Vice President and Publisher

Mary Bednarek, Executive Acquisitions Director

Mary C. Corder, Editorial Director

Publishing for Consumer Dummies

Diane Graves Steele, Vice President and Publisher

Composition Services

Gerry Fahey, Vice President of Production Services

Debbie Stailey, Director of Composition Services

Contents at a Glance

Table of Contents

Introduction

Welcome to *Microsoft Office 2008 for Mac All-in-One For Dummies*. We set out to make this book specifically for Mac users who for one reason or another spend a fair amount of time working in Office. Long-time Mac aficionados, recent switchers, and newbies will find valuable tips, advice, and how-to instruction throughout.

Office 2008 has more features than ever before. The only problem is you might not know where to find them! Plenty of workarounds and shortcuts exist, and this book explains everything in the language you converse in each day: plain English.

With this book, you can broaden your own expertise with Office. As you discover new aspects of Office products, you'll create better documents and you can accomplish more tasks in less time.

We also offer simple, straightforward explanations to help you quickly understand in-depth topics, such as performing mail merge using Word and exporting a PowerPoint presentation as a movie, without feeling overwhelmed. We want *Microsoft Office 2008 for Mac All-in-One For Dummies* to be an enjoyable experience, and we hope you grow your knowledge in a friendly, helpful way.

About This Book

We start with all the basic information that you'd expect, such as a look at the interface and options. We then go beyond the basics, providing you with new, quicker ways to do what you do all the time and helping you discover valuable tools that you may have been unaware of.

This book is organized as a series of self-contained minibooks, with each one focusing on a particular application or component in Office 2008. You'll discover that the tricks you use in one application can be used in other Office applications as well. In addition, the valuable Cheat Sheet can be downloaded from the Web site (`www.dummies.com/cheatsheet/office2008formacaio`) and printed out to be used as a portable reference for shortcuts and common tasks.

We realize that some might have worked in one of the various versions of Microsoft Office for Windows. Throughout this book, we endeavor to highlight Office features that are available only on the Mac. We don't do that to make Windows users go green with envy; our reasons are infinitely nobler. In fact, we highlight these differences for several reasons:

✦ **Mac owners might not be aware that Office 2008 for Mac isn't identical to the Windows version.** Since the earliest versions of Office, Microsoft introduced many new features on the Mac long before the features were brought to the Windows version. As hardware and operating systems have improved, Microsoft has updated the Mac version of Office to incorporate new functionality, speed, file sharing, document delivery, and file formats. Microsoft's *Macintosh Business Unit* (or *MacBU*) is proud of this fact and strives to continue to bring new features to its Macintosh customers.

✦ **Mac users need to be aware that if they use Office for Windows, some features used every day simply aren't on the Windows platform.** The topics in this book with Mac Only indicators have no equivalents in Windows Office.

✦ **We provide help for the many people who have recently switched from Windows to Mac OS X.** Such users may find comfort in the fact that most of the options in Microsoft Office applications, such as Word, Excel, and PowerPoint, work in the same way on both the Windows and Macintosh platforms. However, the Mac operating system has features not found in Windows. MacBU often incorporates Mac OS X–specific features wherever they make sense in Office for Mac. Many times such features have no equivalent on the Windows version of Microsoft Office.

✦ **All the content in this book is very important for users who work on both Windows and Macintosh versions of Office.** Nowadays, a lot of businesses use both Macintosh and Windows computers. Maybe you use a Windows computer at work and a Macintosh at home. Or maybe you have a Macintosh that dual boots to Windows. Indeed, we've often worked in situations stranger than this! The world is changing so fast — who knows what will happen next? But for now and the near future, this book has you covered!

The success of Office for Mac is due to Microsoft's continuous process of innovation. As hardware and operating systems improve, Microsoft updates the Mac version of Office to incorporate new functionality, speed, file sharing, document delivery, and file formats. Competition keeps MacBU on its toes. Apple has iWork, Google has Google Apps, and Sun has OpenOffice. With such strong competition from several other products in word processors, Microsoft has continued to innovate and provide a product that Mac users want to use over competing products. That in itself is no average achievement.

How to Use This Book

This book has basic and in-depth information organized by major applications in Microsoft Office. Turn to the Table of Contents or the index to get right to the information on a specific topic. However, that doesn't mean that we discourage you from reading cover to cover; you just don't have to!

Throughout this book, you see step-by-step instructions, which are based on Mac OS X version 10.5 Leopard. If you're using 10.4 Tiger (or 10.6 Snow Leopard), some of our steps that involve using Mac OS X Finder may not match your screen. But don't worry; these changes are small, and you shouldn't have any problems following any of these steps.

How This Book Is Organized

Each of the six minibooks in *Microsoft Office 2008 for Mac All-in-One For Dummies* stands alone. We start with a general introduction to Office 2008 and then move on to the big applications you'll use the most. The following sections provide an overview of each minibook.

Book I: Introducing Office 2008

Many tools and features are common to all or more than one of the Office applications. For example, pictures, charts, and diagrams work in exactly the same way across the applications. Rather than repeat these common features for each application, we save you time, pages, and book weight by covering these in depth in the first part of the book.

Book II: Word 2008

In this minibook, we show you how you can use Word's amazing capabilities to do everything from writing letters to printing envelopes. On the way, you'll discover how to mail merge hundreds of documents and format your fonts. We also show you how you create newsletters in Word and make notes of your meetings, including audio notes! Have fun.

Book III: Excel 2008

The Excel minibook is chock-a-block full of interesting stuff you can do with this program. We cover all the basics and then show you how to do some advanced stuff with easy step-by-step instructions. We also show you how to go on a journey of cell hopping, and look at data validation, lists, forms, and charts. Truly mesmerizing, numeric stuff!

Book IV: PowerPoint 2008

Okay, this is the minibook that lets you enjoy yourself and work at the same time, and then get paid for it, too! Figure out how you can use PowerPoint basics to create structured presentations and then add the pizzazz with the umpteen new options that Microsoft bestowed upon this latest version of PowerPoint.

Book V: Entourage 2008

So do you e-mail? And do you need a place to store your contacts and organize your calendar? Then you need Entourage, and this minibook covers more ground on this program than you'll find anywhere else. Determine how you can set up your e-mail accounts; invite others to events you organize; and use the cool, new My Day feature.

Book VI: Entourage's Project Center

Wouldn't it be nice to have someone manage your projects and all the paraphernalia associated with those projects? Entourage's Project Center is even better than that, and this minibook shows you how you can create, implement, and share projects. You also read about how you can integrate these projects with other programs on your Mac including Word, Excel, and PowerPoint.

Bonus Chapters

Don't forget to check out the book's Web site at www.dummies.com/go/office2008formacaiofd for two bonus chapters. Bonus Chapter 1 looks ahead to the next version of Office for Mac while Bonus Chapter 2 covers new features in Service Pack 2, such as Document Connection and PowerPoint path animations.

Conventions Used in This Book

For Dummies books are accessible and easy to read, but sometimes you have to type commands and click menu items. To keep these actions as simple as possible, we have some conventions to indicate what needs to be done or what you might see onscreen.

Stuff you type

We use **bold** to tell you what to type. For example, if we say, "Type **22** and then press the Return key on your keyboard," type the number 22 and then immediately press the Return key. (Remember, you must always press the Return key to process the command or enter text.)

Menu commands

When we give you a specific set of menu commands to use, it appears like this: Choose File⇔Send To⇔Microsoft Word. In this example, click the File menu, choose the Send To item, and then choose the Microsoft Word option in the submenu.

Key combinations

With keyboard commands, press two or more keys in sequence, hold down each key until all the keys in the sequence have been pressed, and then you release all the keys. We use the hyphen sign (–) to chain together these combinations. Press Shift-⌘-3 means to hold down the Shift key, then the ⌘ key, and then the number 3 key. (Incidentally, if you do that, a picture of your current screen will be saved to your computer's Desktop.)

Note: On a Mac, the ⌘ key and the key are the exact same key on your keyboard. Your keyboard may have either of these symbols or both on this key, which is usually located next to the spacebar. We use the newer ⌘ symbol throughout this book.

Right-click versus Control-click

Applications for the Mac use context-sensitive pop-up menus extensively. To see a context-sensitive menu, hold down the Control key and click something. And yes, for those wondering, right-clicking and Control-clicking do exactly the same thing.

Display messages

Whenever we mention a message or any text that you see onscreen, it appears like this: `This message is displayed by an Office application.`

Icons Used in This Book

The icons in this book are important visual cues for information you might not want to miss.

This icon indicates special timesaving advice and other items of note.

This icon alerts you to pay close attention because every once in a while we might discuss a topic that could cause problems.

Of course, we expect you to remember everything you read in this book. You'll have to take part in a written exam that's held twice a year in 265 cities across the world, and we read every single paper you write. Just kidding! We use this icon to point out important info for you to keep in mind.

We know. Sometimes things can get pretty complicated. We use this icon when we've taken extra care to simplify something we think most users might find daunting. Just keep in mind that this information is optional and isn't critical to your understanding of the topic. We still provide all the necessary how-to coverage for the application features you need to know about.

Microsoft doesn't keep the Windows and Macintosh versions of Office in lock step with each other. Several excellent features of Office are available only in the Macintosh version. If you're new to the Mac and are already familiar with the Windows version of Office, look for this icon to help you identify features that may be new to you.

Like every new release of Office, Office 2008 has introduced several amazing features that make working with the Office programs easier and more intuitive. This icon highlights these new features in Office 2008.

Where to Go from Here

Start reading this book in any minibook, chapter, or even section. You can dive in anywhere to get the info you need. When appropriate, we add cross-references to other parts of the book for more information.

The first place to find information (aside from this wonderful book) is to look in Office Help, which is completely new. Throughout the book, we also mention additional resources for help. Many of the resources are Web pages created and maintained by Microsoft *MVPs, Most Valuable Professionals.* The MVP program was established by Microsoft to highlight "a worldwide network of exceptional technical community leaders," according to the Microsoft MVP Web site at `http://mvp.support.microsoft.com`.

We've received MVP awards for many years, including 2009. We encourage you to participate in online communities and user groups. People who regularly contribute high-quality information to the technical community may eventually become candidates to receive MVP distinction.

When you come across MVP-supplied content on the Web, be assured that it's reliable. MVPs are volunteers. MVPs don't receive compensation from Microsoft and are independent from Microsoft Corporation.

Book I

Introducing Office 2008

The 5th Wave   By Rich Tennant

"The odd thing is he always insists on using the latest version of Office."

Contents at a Glance

Chapter 1: Oscillating in the Office 2008 World

*L*ike most people, you might already be exposed to Microsoft Office in some way, or perhaps you just got started with this suite of business programs from Microsoft. Either way, be prepared to go on a journey of discovery through this book as we show you how you can work better with Office 2008 for Mac.

You might already know that Microsoft Office can do umpteen things, but maybe you don't know where to find those umpteen things! That's where the good news starts for Microsoft Office 2008 users. The new Project Gallery, which we explain in Chapter 2 of this minibook, makes Office far less intimidating by showing you at a glance all the things you can do.

You might have heard about the changes to Office file formats; we show you how easy it is to work with old and new formats. Getting along with users of other Office versions on Mac and Windows is very easy with Office 2008. Although we still can't say that Office for Mac has every feature available in Office for Windows, you won't want to live without some of the compelling Mac-only Office features.

Fascinatingly, the latest Mac version of Microsoft Office retains Office 2004's familiar menus and interface. For example, although the Windows version exposes not-so-conspicuous Office 2007 features to Windows users via the new Ribbon interface, Office for Mac solved the same problem years ago by introducing floating context-sensitive palettes.

Office 2008 has many galleries and introduces the new *Elements Gallery,* borrowing some of the better aspects of the Windows Office 2007 Ribbon. We cover Elements Gallery in Chapter 3 of this minibook.

Whether you've used Office 2004 for Mac or you're brand new to Office 2008 for Mac, we address all information in an easy-to-grasp manner so that you can understand it. To make sure that we're all on the same level as far as terminology and concepts go, we start this chapter with an overview of each of the Office applications. Office 2008 has exciting new interface improvements, new file formats, and some completely new features to discover and get acquainted with. You'll find that Office 2008 brings most of the suite into the future with its emphasis on helping you get organized, manage your documents, create and manage projects, and collaborate by using the very latest Web technologies. This is going to be so much fun!

Getting Familiar with Office 2008

Wouldn't it be great if there were a central place where you could find all your favorite wizards, templates, and recently used files as well as oversee the projects you're working on? Wouldn't you like to see more than just a handful of recently used files? How about if the same place had an incredible search capability that took advantage of Mac OS X's Spotlight search?

You can stop dreaming because Office 2008 indeed has just such a place — *Project Gallery,* which is a fantastic way to get started whenever you open an Office application, oversee your projects, or find documents.

Getting started in Project Gallery

Lots of things are important to everyone. Here's a quick list of some of common goals:

✦ Saving time by creating just the right document the first time you do it.

✦ Making your work have a consistent look and feel so that you feel good.

✦ Having confidence in managing your affairs.

✦ Feeling that you can confidently find the documents you need quickly.

✦ Finding a way to stop working and start making billions.

Office 2008 makes it easy to achieve everything in that list — except maybe the last part about making billions! Project Gallery is a one-stop shop that allows you to open new or existing documents, projects, and documents within a project as well as effectively search for a document even if you can't remember much about it.

Choose File➪Project Gallery to open the Project Gallery window. Figure 1-1 shows what Project Gallery looks like.

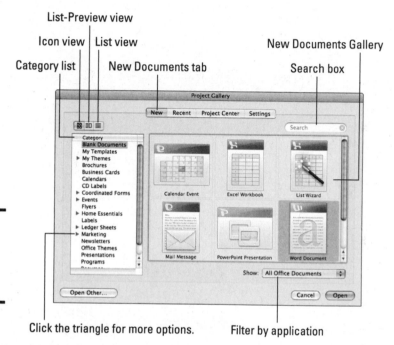

List-Preview view

Icon view | List view

Category list | New Documents tab

New Documents Gallery

Search box

Figure 1-1:
Project Gallery in Microsoft Office 2008.

Click the triangle for more options. | Filter by application

The Project Gallery interface has four tabs: New, Recent, Project Center, and Settings. We first look at the New tab.

The New tab

Many moons ago you'd choose File➪New in an Office application to start a new document or a spreadsheet. A simple folder structure would display a plain blank document option that you could click to start working on a new Word document, Excel spreadsheet, or PowerPoint presentation. In addition, you'd see folder tabs containing templates and wizards. This same simple folder concept is on steroids with Project Gallery. Office 2008 enhances this concept by enabling you to see all the Office wizards, templates, recently used files, and projects in a single, integrated, well-designed interface.

Want to start a fresh document from scratch? Click the New tab to display a list of all the templates and wizards available to you (refer to Figure 1-1). You can access your own templates or your organization's templates right here, too!

As you work through this book, you might wonder why some of the figures in this book don't look exactly the same as what you see in your copy of Office for Mac. That's okay. Some interfaces can look different, especially if you have a custom installation of Office that didn't use the default installation options. Don't worry. This book still covers all the features you'll need to know about.

New in Office 2008, Project Gallery allows you to start a blank document based on a style or a theme. As you'd expect, you can use the new styles and themes provided with Office 2008, or you can use your own saved themes and styles. And if you don't know much about themes and styles, no problem — we cover how to apply themes and styles in Word, Excel, and PowerPoint and even explain how to create your own custom themes and styles throughout this book.

The Recent tab

Looking for a recently used file? Click the Recent tab, as shown in Figure 1-2. A list of recently opened documents appears. You can set the number of recently used files to be displayed to 100 if you want, though that's probably not the most efficient use of the feature. You can also filter documents by application. Office 2008 includes an amazing new search feature based on *Spotlight,* the Mac built-in search technology. Many of the Recent tab options, such as the number of recently opened documents, have to be selected in the Settings tab of Project Gallery. More on that shortly.

The Project Center tab

Click the Project Center tab of Project Gallery to instantly access documents associated with projects created with Project Center (see Figure 1-3). Project Center documents can be any kind of document, not just Office documents. Pictures, e-mail, PDFs, movies, MP3s, PowerPoint presentations, you name it! They're all fair game for Project Center.

In Figure 1-3, you see an empty Project Center tab. Don't panic if your Project Center looks like this. An empty Project Center tab merely means that you haven't created any new projects in it!

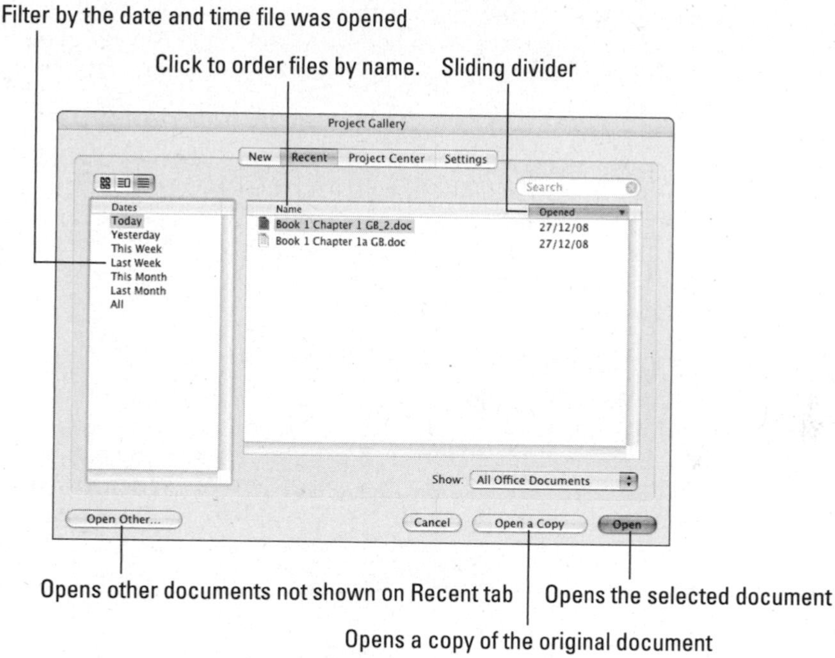

Filter by the date and time file was opened

Click to order files by name.   Sliding divider

Figure 1-2:
The Recent
tab.

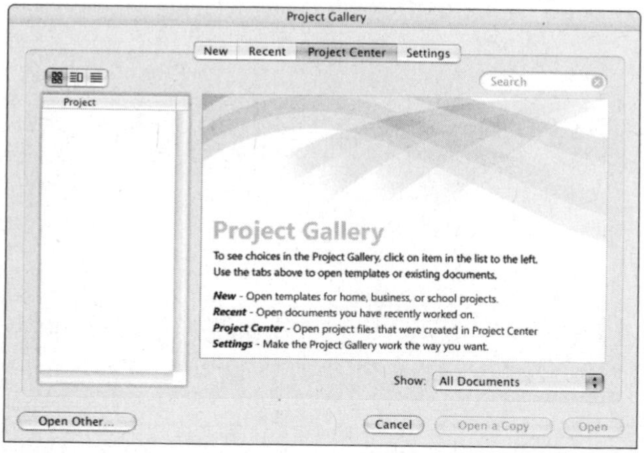

Opens other documents not shown on Recent tab   Opens the selected document

Opens a copy of the original document

Figure 1-3:
The Project
Center tab.

The Settings tab

The final tab of Project Gallery is the Settings tab, and true to its name, this tab is the place to control various settings for the other three tabs in Project Gallery. Heck, this tab also lets you decide whether you want Project Gallery to open when you launch any Microsoft Office application. Figure 1-4 shows the Settings tab in all its glory.

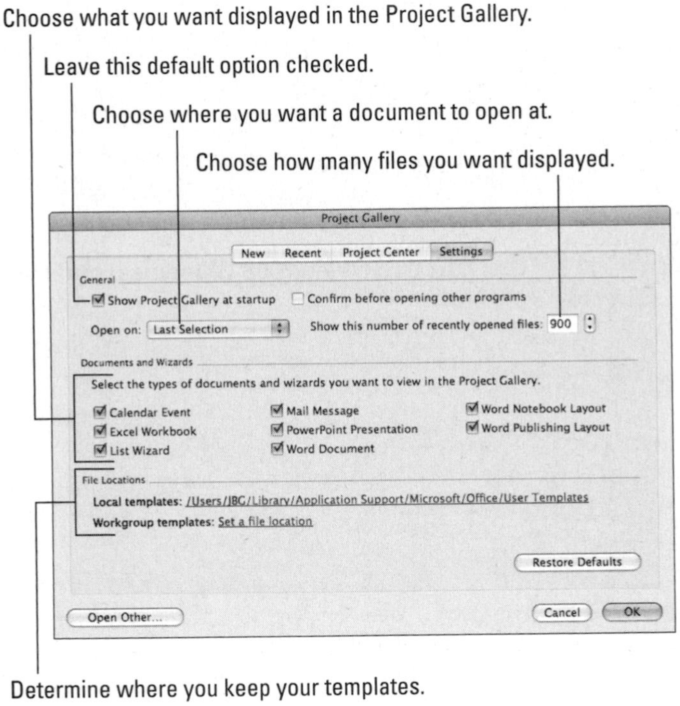

Choose what you want displayed in the Project Gallery.

Leave this default option checked.

Choose where you want a document to open at.

Choose how many files you want displayed.

Figure 1-4:
The Settings
tab.

Determine where you keep your templates.

Helping Word veterans make the transition

Great software is like a fine wine. Software comes in vintages (or versions), some of which are appreciated by computer users the way wine is appreciated by connoisseurs. When an experienced user uncorks Word 2008, the bouquet has new elements and familiar scents. Here are some of the new improvements:

✦ **Themes:** Word's old themes were getting stale. But new themes and the ability to use those themes in Excel and PowerPoint are definite improvements in Word 2008.

✦ **Styles:** You can use Word styles throughout the Microsoft Office suite.

✦ **Elements Gallery:** The new Elements Gallery enhances your ability to apply designs, add elements, and apply formatting styles.

✦ **Draw:** A new drawing engine that encompasses new graphs, organization charts, WordArt, and drawing tools for enhanced appearance. Also adds the new SmartArt graphics to show logical relationships.

✦ **AppleScript:** The sweetest AppleScript automation ever. AppleScript dictionary updates are included as well as completely new support for Automator Actions so that you can automate common workflows.

✦ **Mail Merge Manager:** We think the 2008 version of Mail Merge Manager is the best ever, Mac or PC, because you can control everything from a single palette and merging to e-mail works so well.

✦ **XML file format:** This is a new default file format that's based on XML (eXtensible Markup Language), which is based on the file format that was introduced with Office 2007 for Windows. The default file format for Office 2007 (Windows) and Office 2008 (Mac) is identical. The XML format is new compared to Office 2003 (Windows) and Mac (2004).

Did Microsoft achieve its goal of creating a better version of Word in Word 2008? Depending on how you use Word, the answer veers between perhaps and certainly. Word 2008 is certainly an excellent version despite not having VBA.

Exploring all that Microsoft Word has to offer can be satisfying. We help you discover the nice, new nuances of tables, styles, graphs, charts, and sharing on the Web.

Looking for Visual Basic for Applications (VBA)

Alas, an ingredient is missing from Microsoft Office 2008 that some can't do without: *Visual Basic for Applications (VBA)*. VBA is a programming language that's been built into Microsoft Office for both Mac and Windows since the last few versions, and it lets geeks program and integrate Microsoft Office applications in amazing ways, such as in automating everyday tasks. Unfortunately, VBA was left out when Microsoft Office 2008 was being created. As we write this book, Microsoft is busy adding it in so that the next version of Office for Mac will have this complex enhancement restored. For those who must have VBA, Office 2004 will have to do until the next version of Office.

De-mystifying Excel

If Word is like a fine wine, Microsoft Excel is like having a super bright, quiet, know-it all kid around. Excel sits waiting quietly for someone to ask it to do something, but far too often people are afraid to give it a task. That's because lots of users just find Excel too scary with all its neatly arranged cells and numbers!

Excel 2008 banishes the scary stuff by making huge improvements in the interface.

You don't have to be an accountant or an engineer to use Excel 2008. Excel 2008 doesn't act like a brat, either. Book III is all about Excel; there you'll figure out how to make good use of easy-to-use features, such as the List Wizard, budget and finance tools, and even travel tools.

Even experienced Excel users tend to get comfortable with one or two Excel features and then hesitate to explore additional uses. That's a shame because Excel can do a lot with just a small amount of effort.

Among the top reasons for people to use Excel is to manage lists. Excel 2008 makes it easy to arrange data into rows and columns. Using mailing lists as data sources for Word mail merge is easy. Excel is great because it's simple to sort data alphabetically and numerically. You can instantly sort a list of thousands alphabetically or by postal code. Excel doesn't care if your list is just a few rows, a thousand, or even a million rows; Excel's just happy to crunch those numbers and to arrange the alphabet for you.

Having an easy tool to use is always a good thing, and Excel 2008 offers a lot of new and improved features, as well as old favorites:

✦ **List Manager:** In Excel, List Manager helps you create, organize, maintain, and update your lists. With a few mouse clicks, you can use List Manager to help you locate records, count the number of entries, and even do fancy mathematics on data within your lists. If you want to use List Manager straightaway, navigate to Book III.

✦ **Themes and styles:** Whatever your area of work, organizing data in lists is important, as is how polished your data looks when it's presented. Both onscreen and when printed, Excel is a champ at presenting data in useful ways. Excel 2008 has support for new office-wide themes and styles (except for font styles) much like Word 2008 and PowerPoint 2008 so that you can easily create great looking reports.

✦ **Ledger sheets:** Keeping track of business activities is easier now with brand-new Mac-only ledger sheet Excel worksheets. We explore this new feature along with all the other features we discuss here in Book III, Chapter 1.

✦ **Graphical reports:** Now for some more Excel-lent stuff related to all the data present in your Excel spreadsheets. You don't have to wonder how to make a good impression with your data. Data analysis is something Excel is famous for. Macs are noted for ease of use and the best graphics around. Put that together in Excel 2008, and you're making the best year-end reports ever. Even if the economy tanks, at least your data will look great and uplifting. Hopefully, you'll use Excel to make better forecasts than your competition and smoothly sail your company out of a recession.

✦ **Graphs and charts:** Beautiful expository graphs can be created in Excel 2008. These can be used in other applications and shared in many ways. Researchers and students find that Excel 2008 can help them prepare lab reports and display tables and graphs in ways that make complex concepts easy to visualize and understand. You can draw figures and flow charts with new Excel 2008 drawing tools. Enhance your reports with pictures and illustrations. You can even include a movie to illustrate a point. Excel 2008 has the ability to import data from many sources, including other computers, the Internet, networks, and co-workers.

✦ **Forms:** The Excel forms go beyond anything that can be created in Microsoft Word or Adobe Acrobat. Sure, you can make nice looking forms in the other applications, but only Excel can perform logical operations and calculations, enforce business rules, and carry out complex calculations within a form.

✦ **Database features:** Excel has always had extraordinary, though often ignored, database features, and sometimes their very existences are underplayed for reasons not known to us. If you need fewer than a few hundred thousand or so records in a table, Excel may be all you need. We go into depth in all things Excel in Book III to show you how to take advantage of Excel 2008's surprisingly complete database capabilities.

✦ **Document sharing:** The documents you create in Excel often need to be shared. Excel 2008 has a couple tricks up its sleeve in the sharing department, too, such as the ability to do live sharing of a workbook on a network. You can save an Excel workbook as a Web page that even has working sheet tabs. Sometimes you need to share only part of a workbook. We show you simple ways to save a graph or any other part of a workbook as a picture. You can send an Excel workbook directly from Office via e-mail, Microsoft Messenger, or one of the brand new Microsoft file-sharing services.

Whether you need a simple database or a state-of-the-art spreadsheet program, Excel is competent for the task. This book is the one place you're likely to find everything you need to take advantage of these tools that Excel provides.

Slide shows with PowerPoint

Of all the Office 2008 applications, PowerPoint is probably the most fun to use. PowerPoint 2008 comes with lots of interesting templates, and thousands more are available. And you can also create some of your own. All you have to do is open a template; mix in your words, pictures, movies, and graphs; and you're well on your way. Because PowerPoint takes care of the look and feel, you can productively use the time saved to create a compelling message and story for your presentation. If you have a multimedia message to present, PowerPoint 2008 helps you deliver that, too.

When you need to put something together in a hurry, built-in content and design templates are at your fingertips. You can build new presentations based on old ones very quickly. But don't forget that no PowerPoint template will ever take care of the hard part for you: You still have to refine your presentation message all by yourself.

What's great about PowerPoint is that most people can make truly professional presentations with very little effort thanks to many new and improved features:

✦ **Presenter tools:** Improvements in this area give presenters current time information to help them stay on track.

✦ **Toolbox:** The new Toolbox combines the Formatting Palette, Scrapbook, Reference Tools, ClipArt, and more into a single palette that saves screen real estate. Having everything in one place also lets presenters and presentation creators be more efficient while creating better looking presentations.

✦ **Elements Gallery:** Formatting your presentations has never been easier. With the new Elements Gallery, you can apply slide themes, slide layouts, transitions, new table styles, charts, new SmartArt graphics, and WordArt. You can even add your own elements to this Gallery.

✦ **Multiple masters and layouts:** New in PowerPoint 2008, you now have the power of design control. You can use and create multiple slide masters as well as control over multiple slide layouts.

✦ **iPhoto integration:** PowerPoint has new ways to interact with your iPhoto albums. You can send slide shows directly to iPhoto, and with our help, you can bring iPhoto albums into PowerPoint.

✦ **Working with Web 2.0:** We guide you through the process of getting YouTube videos into PowerPoint and offer pointers on how to get your PowerPoint presentations into YouTube.

✦ **Special effects:** The special effects you can apply to pictures are all new in PowerPoint 2008.

✦ **Drawings, shapes, SmartArt, WordArt, charts, and graphs:** The inner workings of PowerPoint that make all these things were completely redone for 2008. You'll notice niceties, such as the new reflection feature, because of this improvement.

✦ **Document themes and styles:** There's a whole new way to work with document themes and styles, and special places to save them.

✦ **New gradient fill formatting:** Now you can add multiple colors to gradient fills to add interest to filled shapes.

Flip to Chapter 3 of this minibook to read about the common core of Office features before moving on to Book IV, which is devoted to features exclusive to PowerPoint.

Also, PowerPoint offers a speaker confidence by being a tool to organize your thoughts and to express them electronically in a beautiful and/or business-like way. You can easily rehearse your presentation with PowerPoint using the Rehearse Timings feature.

Beyond business presentations, PowerPoint slide shows are also a great way to share photographs with family and friends. You can add your own personal touch by narrating the slide show. You can e-mail smaller presentations right from within PowerPoint. Larger slide shows can be saved on inexpensive CDs and sent via regular mail, or uploaded to file-sharing sites.

If you're a teacher or a student, you probably have found PowerPoint to be an indispensable tool. No longer do students have to put up with ancient chalk technology that's hard to see. Projectors have become inexpensive enough that most schools can afford to install them and display PowerPoint presentations on them.

Today, PowerPoint can help even more. You can easily share your PowerPoint presentations with individuals, specific groups, or the entire world. With Web 2.0 technologies, such as iChat, Microsoft Messenger, YouTube, Yahoo!, Microsoft Office Live, Facebook, and MySpace, presentations can be distributed to audiences inexpensively.

You may not have thought of some of the ways to use PowerPoint. If you're looking for a tool that creates flash cards for your computer, use PowerPoint. Not only that; PowerPoint can make flash cards for cellphones and iPods. We explain the basics of how you can do this in the PowerPoint chapters that you find in Book IV.

Making your day with Entourage

The first time you encountered the PIM acronym, you might have said, "What's a PIM?" *PIM* is one of the few acronyms that sounds good when pronounced. PIM stands for *Personal Information Manager,* which is a great description of Microsoft Entourage.

Entourage is probably the best application to manage, store, archive, and search e-mail on the Mac. Organizing mail into categories is an efficient way to save time because using categories helps you set priorities.

For those switching to Office 2008 from a Windows Office version, think of Microsoft Entourage as Microsoft Outlook. Integration with Microsoft Exchange is included in all bundled packages of Microsoft Office 2008 except the Home and Student edition, just like the Windows product lineup.

If you've been using Apple applications, think of Entourage as a super-charged combination of Apple Mail, Address Book, and iCal. And throw in a project management system and clipping organizer. And of course, better integration with Microsoft Office applications.

Even users of open source find Entourage hard to resist. Imagine having Thunderbird, Sunbird, a contact manager, a project manager, an *LDAP (Lightweight Directory Access Protocol)* client, a security certificate manager, and more all rolled into one. That's the power of Entourage 2008. Among the new and improved features are the following:

✦ **Rules:** PowerPoint isn't the only application that lets you have fun. Believe it or not, you can easily do amazing things with the Rules feature of Entourage. By creating and bending your own mail rules within Entourage, you automate your inbox entirely. Rules are both powerful and playful, and can move and/or copy messages to folders on your hard drive.

✦ **Project tagging:** It's fun (well, sometimes) and easy to manage e-mail, tasks, Calendar events, your to-do list, and even your documents. In Entourage, you can tag all these things with categories and/or assign them to projects. When you create projects in Entourage, they're accessible throughout the Microsoft Office 2008 suite. In Word, Excel, and PowerPoint a Projects tab in the new Toolbox lets you have instant access to your projects. Your project documents are available on the Project Center tab of Project Gallery. We devote Book VI to the Entourage Project Center application and dive into the niceties of this powerful set of tools.

✦ **Junk mail filter:** Entourage can help control junk mail from becoming a crisis through a built-in junk mail filter that's kept up-to-date automatically when Office updates are installed.

✦ **Address Book:** Keeping track of your contacts has become an essential activity for everyone. Everything you'd expect in a Contact Manager or an Address Book is in Entourage. Just wait 'til you see the many ways you can print your Address Book.

✦ **LDAP compatibility:** Large organizations, businesses, and universities often have institution-wide address books that use an LDAP standard. If your institution uses LDAP, you can use Entourage to look up people in the institution's LDAP directory and to add contacts from LDAP into your Entourage contacts. Entourage can auto-complete e-mail addresses from the institution's directory without you having to add people to your contact list.

✦ **Calendar:** A great Calendar is built right into Entourage. You can create and manage your Calendar by making Calendar events. Planning meetings or other activities is a cinch; reminders can be set. Your entire daily schedule can appear in the new Entourage My Day feature, which gives you access to your Calendar even when Entourage 2008 is closed. Entourage users who also use Microsoft Exchange can see each other's free/busy information — even with Outlook users on the same server. Because Entourage uses industry standard Calendar events, you can share them with other Entourage users and with other standards-compliant Calendar programs. For example, open-source Sunbird Calendar users can share Entourage Calendar events.

✦ **Task Manager:** You probably have many tasks to do. Whether you have to write a report or complete an assignment, you can add your task to the Entourage Task Manager. The new My Day feature reminds you of your tasks as the day progresses and lets you manage your tasks on the fly during the work day.

✦ **Notes:** Maybe you just need to make a quick note about something lest you forget. Use the Entourage Notes feature. Notes is better than regular Stickies or tying a thread on your finger because Entourage Notes can be linked to just about anything and can be tagged in categories and projects. Get more familiar with linking in Entourage in Book V.

✦ **Project management:** Organizing your activities into discrete projects is a great way to keep track of your busy office or home lifestyle. Project Center is a major application within Microsoft Entourage that integrates with all the Office 2008 applications. Project Center supports organizing and linking and sharing of document files from all applications on your Mac. We cover the Entourage Project Center in complete detail in all of Book VI.

✦ **Customizable toolbars:** At last! Entourage 2008 allows you to customize the toolbars of every single window in Entourage.

Mingling instantly with Messenger

Communicating and collaborating with peers, co-workers, classmates, your boss, your parents, and your kids is all the rage. Whether you use a computer, an iPhone, or another mobile device, instant messaging is a priority. Microsoft Messenger allows for live communication and collaboration. For those who abhor instant messengers because they let others interrupt your work, Microsoft Messenger has plenty of features to keep unwanted elements away!

In addition to its instant messaging functions, Messenger also provides text and document sharing. The latest update of Messenger on the Mac integrates with *Microsoft Office Communications Server 2007,* a unified communications server package, to provide new live video and audio chat in addition to text messages. Quite possibly by the time you read this, live video and audio will be available without having to use Microsoft Office Communication Server.

Lighting the future with Silverlight

The Internet may be getting older, but new technologies for it are emerging. *Silverlight* is one such technology that gives Web browsers new capabilities.

All the apps working together

Imagine a large, happy family in an ideal world where each person's personality and skills meshed together so that the whole family benefits. Now imagine that each member of this family communicates and interacts with other families in friendly ways. Office 2008 is very much like an ideal family. Each application within Office 2008 is designed to work together with the other Office applications, the Internet, and the Mac OS X applications as well as to interface with Office 2007 for Windows.

Word can be coupled with Excel to generate professional quality, personalized custom brochures, letters, and e-mail sent to a small group of friends or to hundreds of thousands of people.

The Excel graphs can be displayed in Word, Excel, and PowerPoint. The results of Excel formulas can be displayed in Word or PowerPoint or even on the Web. Mac and PC users can work on the same Excel document at the same time.

You often hear *seamless* used to describe applications that work together as well as Office 2008 applications. The same powerful drawing tools are available in Word, Excel, and PowerPoint. The documents you create from any application can be organized and shared with Project Center in Entourage.

Some interesting specialty features are built into Office 2008. Maybe even some you wouldn't expect, such as a special, large capacity Clipboard — the *Scrapbook*. Within Office, you're not limited to just one thing on the Clipboard at a time. In Office 2008, Word, Excel, PowerPoint, and Entourage all share the same Scrapbook, which is a common multiple-item clipboard that can be used to share content between one application and another.

Many people are familiar with Adobe Flash and its associated player. If you've ever watched a cartoon on your Mac, played a game online, or watched a Google or YouTube video, you've most likely used the Flash Player. And if you're like most people, you might wish that the presentation quality was better. In comes Silverlight, which provides a much richer visual and interactive experience than Flash, and is competing head-to-head with Adobe's new Adobe AIR product.

Even though it's a small Web browser plug-in, Silverlight allows you to play an enormous amount of rich PC content on a Mac.

When it comes to Web 2.0, Silverlight ensures that Macs aren't second-class citizens when it comes to taking advantage of new Web content, such as watching movies online at Netflix, zooming almost infinitely in and out of a map. In the near future, you most likely will be able to run some Microsoft Office applications online in Silverlight on your Mac.

What's New Office-Wide for 2008?

If you're upgrading from an older version of Office for Mac, you immediately see new elements in the user interface, such as the new Elements Gallery, when you open any Office application. Yet often, you don't see the things that get changed the most because these changes affect what goes on behind the scenes, as with the revamped graphics engine that draws boxes that still look like boxes, but now they have some new formatting options.

Elation from Elements Gallery

Perhaps the most visible change from earlier versions of Microsoft Office is the new Elements Gallery in Microsoft Word, Excel, and PowerPoint.

To display this handy new feature, click any of the buttons on the new Elements bar, which is located just under the Standard toolbar. Figure 1-5 shows how Elements Gallery looks in Microsoft Word 2008.

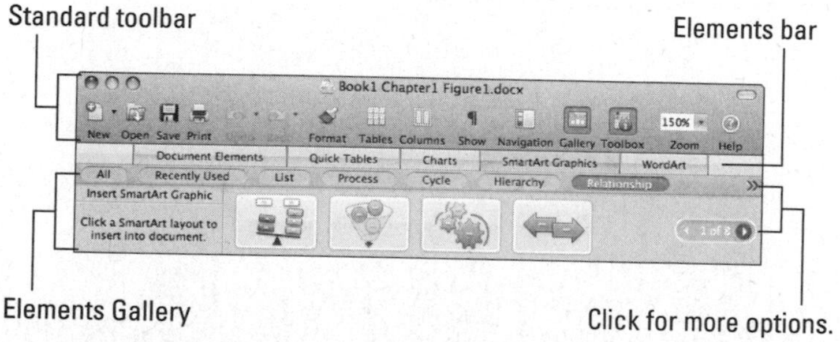

Standard toolbar

Elements bar

Figure 1-5:
Elements
Gallery in
Word.

Elements Gallery

Click for more options.

To display Elements Gallery, which in Figure 1-5 shows the SmartArt Graphics elements, follow these steps:

1. **Click the Word icon in the Dock.**

A new blank document opens, or you're taken to Project Gallery, where you open a new blank Word document.

2. **In Word's View menu, choose any of the following views:**

- Print Layout View

- Web Layout View

- Publishing Layout View

Elements Gallery is not available in other views in Word.

3. **Click any of the buttons, such as the SmartArt Graphics button on the Elements bar, or click the Gallery button on Word's Standard toolbar.**

   Elements Gallery reveals itself in the document window.

4. **Click the Relationship button in Elements Gallery.**

If your screen is wider than the one shown in Figure 1-5, you may see more SmartArt graphics elements from which to choose.

To hide Elements Gallery, click the SmartArt Graphics button on the Elements bar a second time, or click the Gallery button on Word's Standard toolbar.

All buttons on the Elements bar are toggle buttons that alternate between showing and hiding Elements Gallery.

Another way to show and hide Elements Gallery is to click the Gallery button on the Standard toolbar.

Getting smart with SmartArt Graphics

You could always easily make attractive graphics in Microsoft Office. But with the new SmartArt Graphics, professional pizzazz is only a few clicks away.

One of the behind-the-scenes aspects of Office 2008 is that the way shapes and graphics are drawn has been completely overhauled. One of the Mac Microsoft MVPs has dubbed them with a cute nickname, *squeezy graphics*.

Whatever you call them, they give Office added capabilities, including true 3D perspectives and a realistic reflection effect for pictures and shapes.

Discovering new Office-wide themes

Word used to have its own themes, and PowerPoint had different themes. There was no coordination.

The new *Office document themes* (color combinations and other formatting aspects) are now Office-wide. Themes made in PowerPoint can be shared with Word and Excel. Themes are portable between Mac and Windows platforms and are saved in files with .thmx extensions.

You can save and manage themes in entirely new ways with Formatting Palette, Elements Gallery, and Project Gallery. We get you up to speed on themes in Chapter 6 of this minibook.

Comparing Office 2008 for Mac with Office for Windows

The team who developed the Macintosh Business Unit (MacBU) wanted to be able to incorporate features of Mac OS X in its version of Microsoft Office. They succeeded in creating a very Mac-like product. Consequently, Office for Mac has many features not found in Windows Office and vice versa. This is also the reason why version numbers often alternate between Mac and Windows Office — each version has unique features.

Picking the products

Microsoft sells Office in various bundles at various prices. Home and student users can save a lot of money by purchasing special packages. Businesses and educational institutions can save money by purchasing under a volume license agreement. Details about these packages can be found on Microsoft's Web site, Mactopia, for Mac products:

www.microsoft.com/mac

Both Mac and PC platforms

All bundles for both Apple Macintosh and Microsoft Windows include these applications:

✦ Microsoft Word

✦ Microsoft Excel

✦ Microsoft PowerPoint

We break it down a little further though. Here we list which applications are unique to Mac or PC versions of Office. If similar functionality is offered by Office for Mac, we tell you which Office for Mac feature to explore as a possible substitute for the missing Windows application.

Just on Windows

Office Home and Student 2007 for Microsoft Windows comes with an additional program called OneNote 2007, which is not available for Mac.

Word 2008 on the Mac has Notebook View, which offers similar functionality to OneNote without having to install an additional application. OneNote files aren't compatible.

Office Professional 2007 for Microsoft Windows comes with four additional applications that aren't included Microsoft Office 2008 for the Mac:

✦ **Microsoft Access 2007:** In Office for Mac, use Microsoft Query with Excel 2008 for relational database capabilities. Data from Access databases can be queried by Mac's Microsoft Query application.

✦ **Accounting Express 2009:** Yes, that 2009 suffix was not a typo. Current shipments of Office 2007 now include Accounting Express 2009 because Microsoft changes the software to keep the bundle up to date. No equivalent is found in Office for Mac.

✦ **Outlook 2007 with Business Contact Manager (BCM):** Microsoft Entourage 2008 is the most similar application in Office for Mac. Entourage includes most features of Outlook including Microsoft Exchange Server support. The following explains two differences:

  • *Project Center:* Outlook doesn't include Project Center, which is Mac only, and is included in Entourage.

  • *Outlook BCM:* The Outlook BCM feature is Windows only. Entourage doesn't support BCM.

✦ **Publisher 2007:** In Office for Mac, use the Microsoft Word Publishing Layout View for similar functionality without installing a separate application.

Just on Macintosh

The following list describes features found only in Office for Mac:

✦ **Project Gallery:** This application lets you prioritize, organize, share, and search for and launch documents.

✦ **Project Center:** Project Center in Office 2008 for Mac is project management software targeted toward businesses and home and student users. Project Center is what most people are looking for when they seek software that helps them manage their everyday projects.

  Project Center in Office 2008 for Mac isn't the same as a similar sounding but entirely different Microsoft product for Windows called Microsoft Project, which is marketed to professional project managers.

✦ **My Day:** The new My Day Entourage feature keeps you on top of things while it stays on top of all the application windows on your screen. Calendar events and tasks pop on and off as your day progresses.

Microsoft Office 2008 Home and Student edition for Mac comes with Word, Excel, PowerPoint, and Entourage. Like the Home and Student edition of Office 2007 for Windows, Entourage (the Mac e-mail program) doesn't have support for Microsoft Exchange Server.

Comparing Office 2008 for Mac package bundles

Table 1-1 compares what comes in the box with each of the three available Office 2008 for Mac package bundles:

Table 1-1	Office 2008 for Mac Packages		
Feature	*Home and Student Edition*	*Office 2008 for Mac*	*Special Media Edition*
Microsoft Word	X	X	X
Microsoft Excel	X	X	X
Microsoft PowerPoint	X	X	X
Microsoft Entourage	X	X	X
Support for Microsoft Exchange	N/A	X	X
Support for Automator Actions	X	X	X
Sample Automator Actions	N/A	X	X
Entourage Project Center	X	X	X
Project Gallery	X	X	X
Microsoft Expression Media 2	N/A	N/A	X

Understanding file format compatibility

Newer file formats for Windows and Macintosh versions of Word, Excel, and PowerPoint are identical. You can freely pass these files between Macs and PCs.

Microsoft Access MDB files (.mdb) can be queried with Microsoft Query in Office 2008 for Mac, but Query is read-only. Tables and records can't be modified by Office for Mac. Reading Access files requires a third party driver called an ODBC (Open DataBase Connectivity) driver, which isn't supplied with Office 2008.

Microsoft SQL Server databases can be queried with Microsoft Query in Office 2008. The same limitations regarding Microsoft Access apply.

The following applications aren't supported, and their files can't be opened in Office 2008:

✦ Microsoft OneNote

✦ Microsoft Project

✦ Microsoft Publisher

✦ Microsoft Visio

Navigating the interface

Although Microsoft Office applications for Macintosh and Windows started from similar code bases many years ago, the two platforms have diverged in their approach to the Desktop and in how application windows behave.

Launching applications

You can launch Office 2008 applications in any one of several ways. The first two are the ones you're likely to use most often:

✦ Double-click the document icon of any document previously made by any Office 2008 application.

✦ Click an application icon on the Mac OS X Dock.

✦ If the application has been launched recently, click the Apple Menu, choose Recent Items, and then select a recently used file or application from the Recent Items submenu.

✦ Open the Applications Folder and then open the Microsoft Office 2008 folder. You can double-click an application's icon to open the application.

✦ Right-click or Control-click any document and choose Open With from the pop-up menu to specify which application to use to open a file.

✦ Drag a document's icon to the appropriate Dock icon.

For those used to Microsoft Windows, there's no taskbar in Mac OS X. Instead, Mac OS X provides a Dock that you can easily customize. If you hold down the Option key while you open an application, other applications that are running will be hidden. This is more like the way Windows works, so you might be more comfortable opening applications and documents this way.

Figure 1-6 shows the Office 2008 Dock icons. Of course, Dock icons can be arranged in any order by dragging them, so yours may not be in the same order that ours are. You won't see Microsoft Messenger or Expression Media unless you install them separately. Expression Media is included only with certain product bundles, as we mention earlier in this chapter.

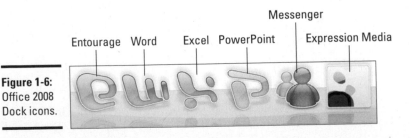

Figure 1-6:
Office 2008
Dock icons.

Entourage   Word   Excel   PowerPoint   Messenger   Expression Media

Opening Spaces

Apple has a new Mac OS X feature for people who like to keep things in neat compartments on their screens. In Mac OS X Leopard and Snow Leopard, this feature is Spaces. You can put one document in each space if you like.

To turn on Spaces, follow these steps, as shown in Figure 1-7:

1. Click the Apple Menu in the menu bar.

2. Click System Preferences and then double-click Exposé and Spaces.

3. Click the Spaces tab and then select the Enable Spaces check box.

You see that you have a number of customization possibilities.

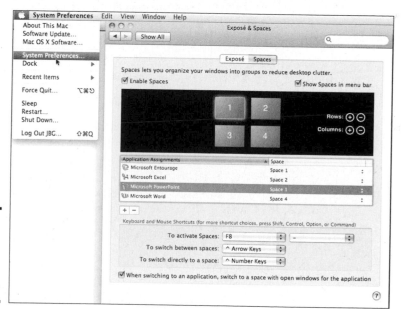

Figure 1-7: Turning on Spaces in System Preferences.

Switching from one document to another

Several different methods can be used to switch from one document to another while using Microsoft 2008 for Mac. Here are some common ways to switch from one open document to another:

✦ **Click the Window menu.** Select an open document from the bottom of the menu. Tried and true.

✦ **Click any visible window.** You may see other windows behind the active window. If you can see even a little piece of window, click it to make it the active window.

✦ **Press F8 (or FN-F8 on some laptops) to switch to Spaces (if you turned on Spaces in the preceding section).**

✦ **Click and hold an application icon in the Dock, and then select a document from the top portion of the pop-up menu.** Each application's icon in the Dock is also a document switcher. Figure 1-8 shows what you'd see if you had five Word documents open. In this figure, we want to switch to the document Book 1 Chapter 1, which we selected in the pop-up menu.

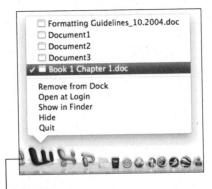

Figure 1-8: Use the Dock icons to switch among documents.

Dock icons

Switching from one application to another

Here are the two easy ways to switch between applications:

✦ **Press ⌘-Tab on the keyboard.**

✦ **Click any application icon in the Dock.**

Coping with Office automation incompatibility

Office 2008 for Mac doesn't have support for a very popular programming language — Microsoft Visual Basic for Applications (VBA). Previous versions of Office for Mac did have VBA support. This means that

✦ VBA scripts, macros, and add-ins no longer run at all in Word, Excel, or PowerPoint 2008.

✦ Office 2008 doesn't ship with the popular Solver add-in for Excel. You can download a new, free AppleScript version of Solver from Solver's creators at the Frontline Systems Web site:

    www.solver.com/mac

✦ RealBasic, another popular programming language, is no longer supported.

Office 2008 does include extensive support for Apple's system-wide scripting language, AppleScript. Although you can use AppleScript as a substitute for VBA, unlike VBA, AppleScript isn't cross-platform. Unfortunately, Windows versions of Office don't support AppleScript.

The incompatibility will go away when VBA returns to Office for Mac in the next major release of it, but no plans are in the works to include VBA as an update to Office 2008. Office 2004, the previous version before Office 2008, does support VBA on the Mac.

If you need to be able to run VBA on the Mac, you're limited to Office 2004 (or earlier). Other options include

✦ Running a Windows version of Office in the Apple Boot Camp or in a Windows virtual machine with Parallels or VMWare Fusion.

✦ Running Office 2007 for Windows directly in Mac OS X with the NTFS product for Mac OS X from Paragon software.

Co-existing with Office 2004 and earlier

Office 2008 by default creates new Word, Excel, and PowerPoint documents in the new XML-based file format. The new XML formats have the same file extensions as the old ones plus the letter x appended to the file extension, such as .docx, .xlsx, and .pptx. When you're using Office 2008, you can save files in the new XML format documents or in the old format. Choose File➪Save As in any of the Office 2008 applications to find an option to save in the old format in the Format list box. Then your documents can be opened in any version of Office from Office 97 to Office 2004, both Mac and Windows. You definitely should do this when sharing documents with people using versions of Microsoft Office prior to Office 2004 on the Mac and Office 2003 on Windows.

Alternatively, you don't have to save in the old file format for users of Office 2004 (Mac) or Office 2003 (Windows) in one scenario. Microsoft has provided updates and converters (which we describe later in this chapter) so that these older program versions can open and save files in the new XML file format. Although the older programs can't work with any of the new Office 2008 feature content in XML format documents, updated Office 2003 and 2004 programs retain the new feature content and the new XML file format. Notice how the following section differs in this regard.

Saving from 2008 to the old format

Before you save in the old format (without an x at the end of the file extension), realize that saving in the old format permanently removes or changes many things including SmartArt Graphics, organization charts, drawings, and graphs. If you open your document in Office 2008 after saving it in the old format, your document opens in Compatibility Mode, which we discuss earlier in this chapter. Be sure to save a copy in the new XML format before you follow these steps to save in the old format. Note that we're using Word in this example:

1. **Choose File➪Save As within any Office 2008 program.**

   A Save As dialog opens.

2. **Click the Format drop-down list and choose the Word 97–2004 Document (.doc) format.**

3. **Change the filename if you desire, and then click the Save button.**

Choosing a default save format

Office 2008 lets you change the default so that you can always save in the old Office 97 through Office 2004 format if you choose to do so. Each application has a slightly different way to set this, so the following are the instructions for each application.

To change Microsoft Word 2008 to always save in the pre-Office 2007/2008 format:

1. **Click the Word menu and choose Preferences.**

   The Word Preferences dialog opens.

2. **Click the Save button.**

   The Save dialog appears.

3. **Below Save Options, click the Save Word Files As drop-down list, choose Word 97–2004 Document (.doc) without an *x* at the end and click OK.**

To change Excel 2008 to always save in the old Excel 97 through 2004 XLS format:

1. **Click the Excel menu and choose Preferences.**

   The Excel Preferences dialog opens.

2. **Click the Compatibility button.**

3. **Below Transition, click the Save Files in This Format drop-down list, choose Excel 97–2004 Workbook (.xls) without an *x* at the end, and click OK.**

To change Microsoft PowerPoint 2008 to always save in the old PowerPoint 97 through 2004 PPT format:

1. **Click the PowerPoint menu and choose Preferences.**

   The PowerPoint Preferences dialog opens.

2. **Click the Save button.**

3. **Below Save options, click the Save PowerPoint Files As drop-down list, choose PowerPoint 97–2004 Presentation (.ppt) without an *x* at the end, and click OK.**

Saving from 2004 to the new XML format

To further enhance compatibility with the new file formats, Microsoft did the following:

✦ **Save feature:** Updated Microsoft Office 2004 so that it can save in the new XML file format.

✦ **Open feature:** Updated Microsoft Office 2004 so that it can automatically open documents that were saved in the new XML file format (requires Open XML Converter).

✦ **Open XML Converter:** Released *Open XML Converter,* a free application that converts files made in the new file format into 97–2004 formats. This application can covert multiple documents at once. See the following section, "Using Open XML Converter."

Copies of Office 2004 need to be updated to at least the 11.5.1 update. To update Office 2004, choose Help⇨Check for Updates in Word, Excel, Entourage, or PowerPoint versions of Office 2004 for Mac.

In Office 2004 (with updates installed), to save a currently active document to the new XML Mac and Windows format in Word, Excel, or PowerPoint, follow these steps:

1. **Choose File⇨Save As.**

   A Save As dialog opens.

2. **Click the Format pop-up menu and choose one of the following 2008 formats:**

   • Word 2008 Document

   • Word 2008 Macro Enabled Document

   • Excel 2008 Workbook (.xlsx)

   • Excel 2008 Binary Workbook (.xlsb)

   • Excel 2008 Macro-Enabled Workbook (.xlsm)

- Excel 2008 Macro-Enabled Template (.xltm)
- Excel 2008 Add-In (.xlam)
- PowerPoint 2008 Presentation
- PowerPoint 2008 Template
- PowerPoint 2008 Show

3. **Change the filename if desired and then click the Save button.**

When sharing documents with users of both 2004 and 2008 versions of Office, it's usually best to keep the documents in the older non-XML file format. Your documents will work fine in Office 2004, and in 2008, they will open and can be worked on in Compatibility Mode. When users of Office 2004 open documents created in the new XML file format, they should keep them in the new format unless they have to save the files for someone with an even older Office version.

Simply adding an *x* to a file extension doesn't turn an old format document into a new XML format document. Likewise, deleting the *x* from a new XML format document doesn't turn the new XML format into the old format. Doing either of these things causes problems with your document. Use the procedures we discuss in this chapter or use the Open XML Converter to change the file formats.

Using Open XML Converter

Installing the Open XML file provides the following capabilities:

✦ **Gives updated Office 2004 applications the ability to open and work with files in the new XML file format.**

✦ **Acts as a standalone application that converts Office for Mac 2008 and Office for Windows 2007 files from the new XML format to the old format.**

To obtain the Open XML Converter application (see Figure 1-9), follow these steps:

1. **Go to the Mactopia Web site:**

   www.microsoft.com/mac

2. **Click Downloads and below the Browse for Downloads and Products headings, click Additional tools.**

   A list appears below the Downloads heading.

3. **Click the Open XML File Format Converter for Mac 1.02 link and then follow the instructions that appear below the Details pane in the lower right of the page.**

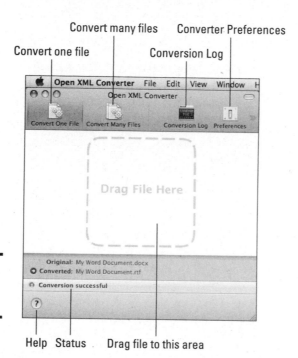

Figure 1-9:
Open XML
Converter.

Here are at least four different ways to use Open XML Converter after you install it:

✦ The converter works automatically in the background if you have Office 2004 with the 11.5.1 or later update already installed. After you've installed the converter, you can open the new XML format files just like the old ones.

✦ Right-click or Control-click a new XML format Word, Excel, or PowerPoint document and then choose Open XML Converter from the pop-up menu.

✦ Open the Open XML Converter application in your Applications folder. Choose Convert One File from the Open XML Converter menu and drag a file into the converter window, as shown in Figure 1-9.

✦ Open the Open XML Converter application, choose Convert Many Files from the Open XML Converter menu, and then drag files into the converter window. Click the + sign to navigate to a Finder window that allows you to select files to add to the list. After the files are selected, click the Convert button.

As shown in Figure 1-10, Open XML Converter preferences let you

✦ Choose where to save the converted files.

✦ Choose whether to automatically open the files after they've been converted.

Figure 1-10:
Open XML
Converter
preferences.

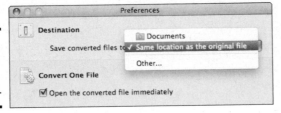

Chapter 2: Project Gallery — The Natural Starting Point

In This Chapter

✔ Getting started with Project Gallery

✔ Starting with the right wizard or template

✔ Looking at content in galleries

✔ Searching for your things in Project Gallery

✔ Organizing and sharing projects in Project Center

✔ Tweaking your settings

*I*f you've ever been to a museum with lots of galleries filled with art or fossils, you know that a gallery can be both overwhelming and awe-inspiring. The good news is that Office 2008 galleries, such as Project Gallery, make the software less intimidating by showing the types of things you can do at a single glance, which is still pretty awe-inspiring but not so overwhelming. In this chapter, we show you how Project Gallery helps you get started with all kinds of new documents and then we help you even more by assisting you in finding your saved work.

Most are more akin to the other people around us than we like to believe. For starters, we all want to be more organized, but most don't have enough time in the day to take care of all the details. Project Gallery saves you time by searching for those documents you lost track of. Better yet, Project Gallery automatically organizes and displays all the documents that you've associated with projects you create in Project Center, a fantastic project organizing feature we detail fully in Book VI. In this chapter, we focus entirely on Project Gallery, which is a gallery consisting of

✦ Blank documents

✦ Templates

✦ Wizards

✦ Office themes

✦ Recently used documents

✦ Documents associated with Project Center projects

Project Center is a completely different animal from Project Gallery. We cover the former in Book VI, and this chapter discusses the latter.

Starting off on the right foot can make your life easier, which is precisely what Project Gallery does. Project Gallery is one of the many exciting features of Office that may be new to you, especially if you're new to the Mac, because Project Gallery has never been available in a Windows version of Office.

Launching Project Gallery

Project Gallery is available within every Office application and can be set to always appear whenever an Office application begins. In fact, that's the default behavior unless you want to change it. If you open Project Gallery by launching an Office application, Project Gallery will default to a new, blank document for the application that was used to launch Project Gallery.

In addition, you can launch Project Gallery on demand, even if you've turned off automatic launching of Project Gallery when an Office application opens. Here are more ways to launch Project Gallery:

✦ **From the File menu of Word, Excel, PowerPoint, or Entourage, choose the first item, Project Gallery.**

✦ **Press Shift-⌘-P when an Office application is running.**

You can also put the Project Gallery icon in your Dock so that it's always accessible with one click, even when no other Office 2008 application is running. First, check if you already have an icon for the Microsoft Project Gallery in the Dock. If you don't, follow these steps to put the Project Gallery's icon in the Dock:

1. **Launch the Mac OS X Finder and locate the Microsoft Project Gallery application.**

   Look in the Mac OS X Applications folder; then look inside the Microsoft Office 2008 folder, and you should find an icon for the Microsoft Project Gallery there.

2. **Drag the icon for Microsoft Project Gallery, drop it into your Dock, and then let go.**

   From now on, you can click the Dock icon for Project Gallery to launch it.

Time to start exploring Project Gallery's interface. The Project Gallery contains four tabs — New, Recent, Project Center, and Settings. In Figure 2-1, we illustrate the New tab of Project Gallery.

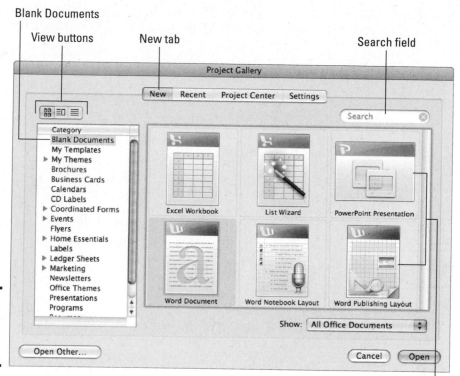

Figure 2-1:
Project
Gallery's
New tab.

Blank Documents

View buttons · New tab · Search field

Large icons

Opening Blank Documents from Project Gallery

As you can see from Figure 2-1, many categories are available for you
to choose the type of new document you want to create. When Project
Gallery opens, the default category is Blank Documents. From here, you
can choose from several types of blank documents , which we cover in the
following sections.

Opening blank new documents

When Blank Documents is selected in the Categories list, you can choose to
start a new blank document from any one of the several kinds of documents
shown in the gallery. Office suggests a blank document type by selecting it
for you.

The type of new document that Project Gallery selects by default depends
on how you open Project Gallery. If you automatically open Project Gallery
from Word, Excel, or PowerPoint, a blank document for the corresponding
application is selected by default.

As shown in Figure 2-1, a Word document is what you would see if you launch Project Gallery from Word. To create the selected blank document, you can do any of the following:

✦ Press Return or Enter on the keyboard.

✦ Double-click the blank document's icon in the gallery.

✦ Click the Open button at the bottom of the gallery.

When Project Gallery is open, you aren't limited to the helpful options that are pre-selected for you. Indeed, you're free to select any kind of document, template, Office theme, or wizard from any category on the New tab, or you can switch to another tab of Project Gallery. We explain the other tabs later in this chapter.

Opening other blank documents

Project Gallery is chock full of many different kinds of documents that we hope you'll explore. In the Blank Documents category, you find other kinds of documents besides the traditional plain Word document, Excel workbook, or PowerPoint presentation. We explore the additional document types in this section.

Starting an Excel list

Other than a conventional Excel spreadsheet, the Blank Documents category shown in Figure 2-1 allows you to choose the List Wizard option. The List Wizard lets you create an Excel List sheet, a special kind of Excel object that lets you organize data in rows and columns as well as sort, filter, and/or calculate them with several dynamic options. For more on the List Wizard, see Book III, Chapter 7.

Start taking notes in Word Notebook Layout View

Word Notebook Layout View is for typing (and recording audio notes) in meetings and classes. This offers much of the functionality of the Microsoft OneNote product for Windows without installing (or buying) another application. When you choose this option, a new blank Word document opens in Notebook Layout View. We explain how to use Notebook Layout View in Book II, Chapter 1.

Creating a new Word Publishing Layout View document

Word Publishing Layout View is for creating newsletters, magazines, and other documents in which text flows through stories in page layout. Book II, Chapter 7 explains how to work with Word's Publishing Layout View.

Writing a new e-mail message

Mail Message in Project Gallery's Blank Documents category lets you open a new, blank e-mail message in Entourage. Book V, Chapter 3 has the information you need to know about using e-mail in Office.

Creating a new Calendar event

In Project Gallery, use Calendar event to open a new blank Calendar event in Entourage. Book V, Chapter 6 covers how to use Calendars and Calendar events.

Exploring More Project Gallery Categories

We worked with the Blank Documents category in the preceding section. However, as you look through the list of categories in Project Gallery (refer again to Figure 2-1), you can see that you have many more category selections from which to choose. In this section, we highlight particular categories. Keep in mind that whenever you're on the New tab of Project Gallery, you create a new document based upon the kind of document you select.

Using My Templates to open new documents

Sometimes the best things in life are your own creations or your favorite templates. The My Templates category in Project Gallery starts out empty. As you use Office, you'll probably create your own templates or use established company templates. When you save those templates in the My Templates folder, which we explain in the following section, your templates appear automatically in Project Gallery below the My Templates category so that you can launch new documents from them.

Saving a document as a template for My Templates

You can easily save a Word, Excel, or PowerPoint file as a template in the My Templates folder so that it shows up thereafter in the My Templates category within Project Gallery. Follow these steps:

1. **Create a document that has all the basic formatting you want to reuse.**

   For example, a letterhead document in Microsoft Word.

2. **Choose File⇨Save As.**

   The Save As dialog appears, as shown in Figure 2-2.

3. **Type a filename for your template in the Save As text box.**

4. **In the Format drop-down list, choose the appropriate template option from the pop-up list and then click Save.**

   The appropriate format is one of the following, depending upon which application you use to create the template:

   - Word Template (.dotx)

   - Excel Template (.xltx)

   - PowerPoint Template (.potx)

To make it easy for you, Office saves your template in My Templates folder by default, which is convenient for most users. If your Save As dialog looks different from Figure 2-2, click the Show/Hide Full Dialog toggle button, which is the triangle to the right of the Save As field. That changes your screen's appearance to match Figure 2-2. For those who want to use alternative locations for templates, we explain how to do this in detail when we discuss Project Gallery's settings at the end of this chapter.

Name your template   Show/Hide full dialog

Choose template format   My Templates folder

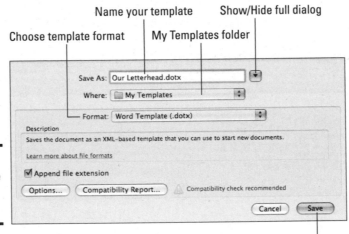

Figure 2-2:
Saving a file
as a Word
template.

Save the template.

Digging deeper into templates

You can save templates anywhere in your file system, but if you decide to put them someplace other than the default My Templates folder, they might not be available within the My Templates category within Project Gallery.

If you have a template in a location other than the default, you can make an alias of the template and put the alias into the My Templates folder.

To open the default My Templates folder, follow these steps:

1. **Double-click the hard drive icon on your Mac Desktop.**

   The Finder appears and shows you a list of files.

2. **In the left panel, below Places, click the User icon.**

   The User icon looks like a little house and is typically named after you or your computer.

3. **Below the User icon, click Library, Application Support, Microsoft, Office, User Templates, and My Templates successively.**

   This takes you to a folder where you can save your own templates.

To use templates stored on network drives, make aliases for template files and drag the aliases into the My Templates folder. Alternatively, you can choose a different location for templates on the Settings tab in Project Gallery. (See Chapter 1 of this minibook for more on the Settings tab in Project Gallery.)

To make an alias in Finder, select a template file or folder icon and press ⌘-L.

Opening new documents based on My Themes

Themes have been part of Word for many years, but the new themes in Office 2008 aren't limited to Word alone. In Office 2008, themes received a major overhaul with the introduction of Office-wide themes. Now Word, Excel, and PowerPoint can work with the same themes. This means that if you save your PowerPoint formatting choices, such as fonts, colors, and backgrounds, as a theme, you can re-create that to some extent in your Word and Excel documents as well. This is a great feature because now all your documents can have a consistent look no matter which application was used to create them. We cover themes in more detail in Chapter 6 of this minibook.

Themes control the font family, colors for lines, and fills for objects and shapes. In addition, themes can hold PowerPoint slide backgrounds and layouts. You can use the several pre-built themes that are included within Office 2008, or you can create and save your own.

The Office theme files are compatible across Office 2008 for Mac and its Office 2007 cousin on Windows. That's great news if you want to share the theme files you create or customize. We cover customizing and creating themes in Chapter 6 of this minibook.

We also discuss creating your own customized themes in Books II, III, and IV in relation to Word, Excel, and PowerPoint, respectively.

Starting with the right template, theme, or wizard

The Project Gallery's New tab is filled with a variety of professionally pre-pared templates, themes, and wizards. (Yes, your license for Office allows you to make and distribute documents based on what you find and use from Project Gallery.)

When you open Project Gallery (see the section, "Launching Project Gallery," earlier in this chapter), be sure to click the small, black disclosure triangles in the Category list on the left to display additional content, as shown in Figure 2-3. Scroll bars are available automatically in categories that have more content than will fit into the standard Project Gallery window.

New tab   Search Project Gallery

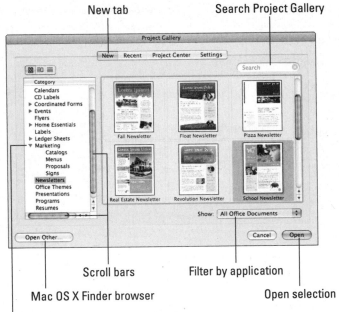

Figure 2-3: Click disclosure triangles to see more categories for new documents.

Scroll bars   Filter by application

Mac OS X Finder browser   Open selection

Click triangles to see more content.

Filtering results by application

If you find it disconcerting to have all sorts of possibilities shown in the Category list with no distinction between the programs you used to create, we have some good news. You can filter the content that Project Gallery displays by the application used to create the new document.

Click the Show button in the lower-right portion of Project Gallery to view a pop-up menu (as shown in Figure 2-4) that limits the display to Word, Excel, PowerPoint, or Entourage files.

Figure 2-4:
Filter Project
Gallery
results.

Finding the Fab Four (Wizards, That Is)

Sick of manually aligning your lists? Do you dread preparing mailing labels and envelopes every time you send out a business letter? Dread no more. Amid all the templates in Project Gallery's New tab, you'll discover four Office wizards that help you take care of these common tasks.

Making lists with the List Wizard

In Project Gallery, select Blank Documents in the Category list (refer to Figure 2-1) and then select the List Wizard option to get started on any kind of list in Excel 2008. Book III, Chapter 7 has deep-dive information on using this wizard. Some examples of content that would benefit from using the List Wizard are

✦ Class lists

✦ Employee lists

✦ Item inventories

Making labels and name badges

In Project Gallery in the Category list, select Labels and then select Mailing Label Wizard. You can use this wizard to create a variety of labels, such as:

✦ Mailing labels

✦ Name badges

✦ Shipping labels

✦ Tent cards

You can also start a mail merge with the Mailing Label Wizard. The Mailing Label Wizard uses Word along with a data or address sources to do its magic. Book II, Chapter 6 is where you'll find what you need to know to get started making labels and doing mail merges.

Designing with the Envelope Wizard

In Project Gallery, in the Category list, select Stationary and then select Envelope Wizard to print envelopes. This wizard is great for holiday cards, invitations, and business envelopes. Like the Mailing Label Wizard, this also uses Word.

Making perfect business letters

In Project Gallery under the Category list, select Stationary and then select Letter Wizard. You'll make perfect business letters every time with this wizard, which also uses Word.

Viewing What's in the Galleries

The View buttons on the New tab are in a new place in the Office 2008 version of Project Gallery — above the Category list (see Figure 2-5). The following are the traditional views, including one new view, List with Kind, in Office 2008. We explain each of the views as they appear in the New tab of Project Gallery from left to right:

✦ **Icon:** This is the default view that shows large icons for all the templates and wizards.

✦ **List with Preview:** This view typically has a preview that's almost the same size as the icon, but to its credit, you can figure out which application any selected template or wizard belongs to thanks to the use of miniature application icons next to the filenames and the descriptive information provided in the Details section. You can sort the list alphabetically by name by clicking Name at the top of the list of names. Click a second time to reverse the order. To group the list by Kind, click Kind at the top of the list. Click Kind again to reverse the order. Again, refer to Figure 2-5 to see where to click.

✦ **List with Kind:** This view, new to Office 2008, is the same as the List with Preview option but without the preview. List with Kind shows you what kind of document is in the list, such as Word Wizard or Word Template, as shown in Figure 2-5. You can sort the list alphabetically by clicking Name at the top of the list of names. Click a second time to reverse the order. To group the list by Kind, click Kind at the top of the list. A second click to Kind reverses the order. Again, refer to Figure 2-5 to see where to click.

In most cases, you can order any sort of list alphabetically or numerically in the Office interface by clicking on the headings of the list. A second click reverses the sort.

List with Kind view

List with Preview view

Icon view

Click to sort by Name.

Click to sort by Kind.

Search for templates by name.

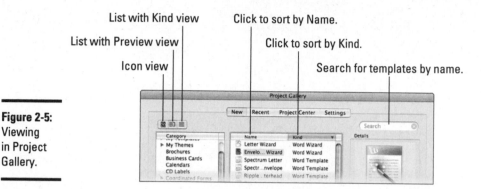

Figure 2-5:
Viewing
in Project
Gallery.

Finding Your Things in Project Gallery

You don't want to spend a lot of time trying to locate your documents and spreadsheets on your computer. Project Gallery offers a few ways to search for your misplaced files.

Searching fast within Project Gallery

New in Project Gallery is a special search field. While you type in the Search field located in the top right of the Project Gallery window (refer to Figure 2-5), Project Gallery instantly narrows the items displayed for the currently selected tab while you type each character. This is a small but extremely powerful thing. Try it and you'll be hooked right away.

Finding things with Open Other

Project Gallery can present a regular Mac OS X Finder Open File browsing dialog, as shown in Figure 2-6. Simply click the Open Other button in the lower-left corner of Project Gallery, as shown in Figure 2-3, to open the familiar Open window in the Finder.

In the Open window, you can browse all of Mac OS X or search by filename to locate the content you seek.

Spotlight is the search technology built inside Mac OS X. If you use the Search feature in Office 2008, the Mac OS X Spotlight feature conducts the search.

Finding recently used files

What's that you say? Four recently used files at the bottom of the File menu aren't enough? No need to worry in this new Mac version of Microsoft Office. In Project Gallery, you can have hundreds of recently opened files!

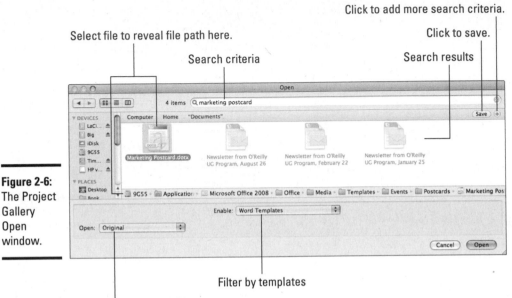

Select file to reveal file path here.

Click to add more search criteria.

Click to save.

Search criteria

Search results

Figure 2-6:
The Project
Gallery
Open
window.

Filter by templates

Open the original or a read-only copy.

To display recently used files, click the Recent tab in Project Gallery (see the section, "Launching Project Gallery," earlier in this chapter, for more on opening Project Gallery). Figure 2-7 shows the Recent tab displayed in List with Kind view.

You can finally find recently used files easily. If you know even part of the filename you're searching for, just start typing it in the Search box. While you type each character, Mac OS X Spotlight narrows the list.

What's really amazing about this search is that you don't have to know the exact filename. Just type a few consecutive letters from anywhere within the filename, and the list magically narrows. Instantly! While you type!

We think this is one of the best Office features of all time: It exemplifies the benefits of Office working with Macintosh technologies.

Remembering misplaced filenames

Okay, so you completely forgot the filename. You might be thinking, "I'll know it when I see it!" The Recent tab can help you in the following ways:

✦ If you have a rough idea of the timeframe regarding the last time the document you're seeking was opened, click one of the date ranges in the Dates menu.

✦ To order the list by the date each document was last opened, click Opened at the top of the column of dates.

✦ Click the Show drop-down list to narrow the choices by the application that was used to create the document.

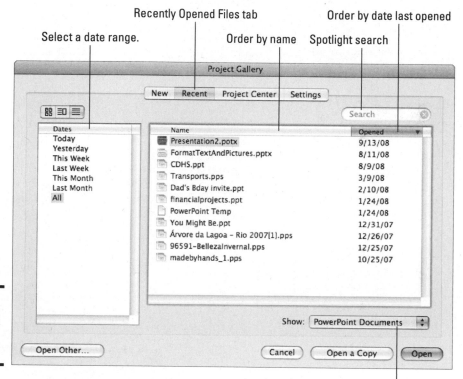

Figure 2-7:
The Project
Gallery
Recent tab.

Being aware of network connections

The Recent tab in Project Gallery is aware of your network. The Recent tab displays files that are accessible only on your hard drive and currently connected network drives.

The Recent tab doesn't display recently used filenames located on networks unless the network drive is currently connected and available to the Mac OS X Finder. If the recently used file

you were expecting isn't on the recent list, you may need to check if the network volume (or other device such as flash drive or additional hard drive) is still available in Finder. It's also possible that the file you're looking for is no longer within the number of recent files you have set the limit to on the Project Gallery Settings tab.

Getting another chance to find a file

You can open a copy of any file without opening the original version. To open a copy of a document without disturbing the original, click the Open a Copy button at the bottom of the Project Gallery Recent tab (refer to Figure 2-7).

Prospecting the Project Center Tab

Project Center is a major feature of Office for Mac. Book VI is devoted to Project Center as an integral part of Entourage. Project Gallery plays host to just the documents portion of the entire Project Center feature through its Project Center tab, as shown in Figure 2-8.

If that sounds confusing, here are some facts to help you understand Project Center better:

✦ The Project Center tab of Project Gallery (see Figure 2-8) provides a quick way to find and launch documents that are associated with Project Center projects.

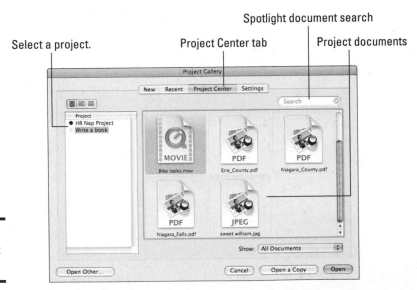

Spotlight document search

Select a project.   Project Center tab   Project documents

Figure 2-8: The Project Center tab.

✦ The Project Center tab is empty until you create some projects (or even just one project) with Entourage. You might wonder why you create projects in Entourage. That's because Project Center is a part of Entourage, and whenever you create a new project in Project Center, you're essentially using Entourage. As soon as you create projects in Entourage, they're added automatically to the Projects listing in the Project Center tab. Whenever you associate a document with an existing project, the document will be available on the Project Center tab of Project Gallery. Of course, you can also open Project Center documents from within the Project Center application.

✦ The Project Center tab of Project Gallery has all the same features as the Recent tab (which we describe earlier in this chapter). The difference between the Recent and Project Center tabs is that the Project Center tab limits the content to files associated with projects, which means any kind of file can be displayed and searched for. The Recent tab limits you to documents created by Office applications.

✦ The documents shown in Project Center aren't limited to Office documents. You can locate and launch any kind of file.

✦ Documents that you associate with your projects in Entourage are displayed in the Project Center tab.

Customizing Project Gallery

Do you wish the tabs in Project Gallery and what you see within those tabs worked a little differently? What if you could make them behave just the way you want? To do that, click the Project Gallery Settings tab to open the preferences headquarters (as shown in Figure 2-9).

Choose how many recently opened files you want to view.

Project Gallery Settings tab

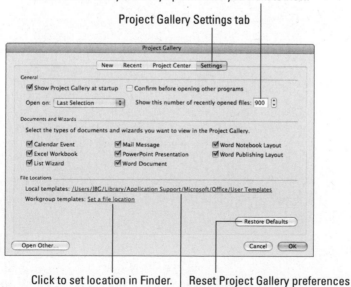

Figure 2-9:
The Project
Gallery
Settings tab.

Click to set location in Finder.   Reset Project Gallery preferences

Click to open location in Finder.

General settings

The topmost section of the settings tab has General Project Gallery settings. If you want Project Gallery to open whenever you start Word, Excel, and PowerPoint, select the Show Project Gallery at Startup check box.

If you select the Confirm before Opening Other Programs check box, you get an alert every time you click a document from an application other than the one used to activate Project Gallery. We recommend that you don't select this check box.

From the Open On drop-down list, choose which tab Project Gallery activates when it's launched. You may choose from:

+ **One of the four Project Gallery tabs:** New, Recent, Project Center, and Settings.

+ **Last Selection:** This activates the tab that was used last.

The Show This Number of Recently Opened Files drop-down list lets you crank the number of files that are displayed on the Recent tab. We used 900 and didn't notice any performance problems on an iMac. Be brave. Go large!

Documents and wizards settings

The default is that each and every preference setting is turned on (checked). We recommend that you leave them all selected because this allows Project Center to take advantage of all the documents and wizards in the Gallery. If there is a particular reason you don't want Project Gallery to use a document type, deselect the check box next to it.

File location default settings

Earlier in this chapter, we pointed out that when you save a template from Word, Excel, or PowerPoint, the default file location is the My Templates folder. The default location of the My Templates folder for Office 2008 has changed from previous versions of Office. In previous versions, the My Templates folder was in the Applications folder. In Office 2008, the folder is the Mac OS X's Application Support folder. The new default location offers several advantages over the old location. Among the most important advantages are

+ Your templates won't be affected if you upgrade or uninstall Microsoft Office.

+ Each user of the computer has his own My Templates folder. One user can't see or use another user's templates, thereby greatly improving privacy for sensitive templates.

+ Office 2008 conforms to Apple's excellent privacy and security recommendations. Office now uses the recommended Mac OS X Application Support Folder for user templates.

Most readers don't need to change the default file location settings or add additional locations for keeping templates. Unless you want to know more about this subject, please feel free to move on to another chapter or enjoy doing something else.

If you need to use templates that are shared, the rest of this section is written with you in mind and is a bit on the technical side.

Changing file location settings for templates

The very first time you start your Mac or if you have to reinstall Mac OS X, you're presented with a nice Welcome dialog and asked to configure a user account and give it a name. You'll find that same name in the Mac OS X System Preferences menu under the Accounts list in the left menu. In Figure 2-10, we have several user accounts. A Mac OS X file path begins with the user account of the currently selected user in the Mac OS X Accounts pane. To figure out how to add new users, start from your computer's Desktop and use the Help menu. Choose Mac Help and then search for the topic Creating a New User Account. Another relevant Help topic is How Your Computer Is Organized.

User Accounts

Current User Name

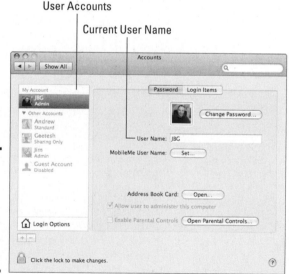

Figure 2-10:
Examining
the
Accounts
pane in
System
Preferences.

Local templates

Take a look at the File Locations settings near the bottom of the Project Gallery Settings tab, as shown in Figure 2-9. The first setting is Local Templates. This setting displays the current file path to your My Documents folder. Your path is different from Figure 2-10, but the structure of your file path is the same as ours.

To change the location for your local templates:

1. **Open Project Gallery to the Settings tab.**

2. **In the File Locations section, click the Local Templates filename.**

   A Mac OS X file-locating dialog opens.

3. **Navigate to the desired folder or use the dialog to create a new folder.**

4. **Click the Choose button.**

Workgroup templates

This setting lets you choose a shared location, usually on a shared network drive, for additional templates to appear in Project Gallery. To set or change the location for your local templates, do the following:

1. **Open Project Gallery to the Settings tab.**

2. **In the File Locations section, click Set a File Location for Workgroup Templates or click the filename if you've already set one that you wish to change.**

   A Mac OS X file–locating dialog opens.

3. **Navigate to the desired folder or use the dialog to create a new folder.**

4. **Click the Choose button.**

The anatomy of a pathname

If you already know what a file pathname is, you can skip ahead. The terms *file path, file pathname, directory, file directory,* and *Finder path* all mean essentially the same thing. A file path is a statement listing the folders to a particular file on your computer. The pathname is read from left to right. A colon (:) separates each folder name from the next one in the hierarchy. The hierarchy begins with the User folder.

Here we dissect the example file pathname displayed in the Local Templates portion of the Settings tab of Project Gallery, as shown in Figure 2-9:

- `/Users/`. Every file path starts with the Users folder.

- `/JBG/`. The name of the current user. In Figure 2-10, JBG appears in the User Name field.

- `/Library/`. Every user has a Library folder where important system and user information resides. Don't mess around with any of these settings unless you know what you're doing.

- `/Application Support/`. This is the folder that applications are supposed to use for user-generated files, such as templates and themes, and other application support files and folders.

- `/Microsoft/`. This is the folder that Microsoft uses for supporting its applications.

- `/Office/`. This folder is for Microsoft Office support files.

- `/User Templates/`. This is the folder that contains both your My Themes and My Templates folders in addition to other support folders.

Chapter 3: Menus and Toolbars

In This Chapter

✔ Finding what's new in Elements Gallery

✔ Summoning a pop-up menu

✔ Customizing your menus and toolbars

When you face the challenge of trying something new in Office 2008, you probably think about what you already know to see whether you can use that knowledge to complete the new task. After all, most Office applications such as Word, Excel, and PowerPoint do work with similar commands, features, and options. So it's not out of the ordinary to expect that your Word skills may help you use PowerPoint or Excel, or the other way around. When you realize that most of your knowledge is applicable, you feel good and gain self-confidence. That's precisely the whole point of this chapter and Chapters 4–6: We show you tools and skills that help you while using *all* the Office applications. In fact, if you figure out how to use these skills in one application, you'll know how to use them in the others too.

Understanding how to use the tools and features in this chapter and Chapters 4–6 of this minibook is particularly rewarding. You might even have the confidence to venture out of your comfort zone and try other new things in the Office 2008 for Mac suite. For instance, after you know how to draw in Word, you'll be pleased to discover that Excel and PowerPoint use the same drawing tools the very same way. You save so much time figuring out things only once.

Cruising Elements Gallery

You know that excited feeling you get when you buy some new high-tech accessory for your car or a new peripheral for your computer? At first, your new gadget is very shiny and showy, perhaps too fancy looking to be of any use, but soon it becomes part of your every day life, and you can't live without it. The brand new Office 2008 Elements Gallery (as shown in Figure 3-1) is like that. Elements Gallery is a new way to quickly insert a wide variety of often-used elements, such as tables, charts, diagrams, and so on into your documents. Elements Gallery is a great new feature that works the same way in Word, Excel, and PowerPoint.

Standard toolbar

Menu bar   Gallery bar   Elements Gallery button

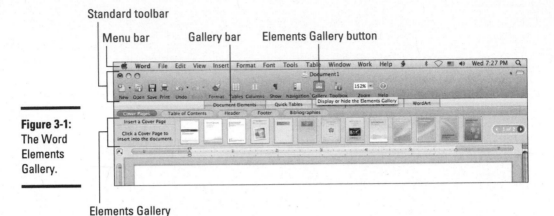

Figure 3-1:
The Word
Elements
Gallery.

Elements Gallery

We know you want to get started right away with Elements Gallery, but first you need to turn it on. You can do any one of the following to toggle Elements Gallery on or off in Word, Excel, and PowerPoint:

+ **From the menu, choose View⇨Elements Gallery.**

    If the Elements Gallery option is grayed out in the View menu, then try a different view. In Word 2008, you must be in Web Layout View, Print Layout View, or Publishing Layout View to use Elements Gallery. All these views can be turned on from Word's View menu. The Elements Gallery is always available in Excel and PowerPoint, except while running a PowerPoint slide show.

+ **Click the Gallery button on the Standard toolbar.**

+ **Click once on any item in the Elements bar to turn it on and click a second time to turn it off.**

    The Elements bar is the thin strip with options, such as Document Elements, Quick Tables, and so on.

As soon as you turn on Elements Gallery, you'll have an impulse to click the different kinds of elements. Don't resist the temptation! Go ahead and try some of the elements. They're very easy to use — just click an element to activate it. Experienced users might recognize some elements, but everyone will find lots of new elements to experiment with. In fact, so many wonderful elements are in Elements Gallery that we have room to discuss only the most commonly used elements.

If you look at Elements Gallery (refer to Figure 3-1), you'll notice that sometimes so many elements are in a single group that they don't all fit in one row. In that case, click the scroll arrow at the right side of the row (see Figure 3-2). After you click that arrow, the next group of elements slides into Elements Gallery. In the leftmost part of Elements Gallery, the descriptions change as the mouse hovers over the elements.

Figure 3-2:
Expanding
the
elements.

The description area   Click here to display more elements.

As the Office 2008 timesaving accessory, the new Elements Gallery is *très* cool. You use it just about every time you work. You might even find it fun to explore the many different kinds of elements. Not only can you add elements to your documents, but you can also easily apply themes and styles from Elements Gallery. Your documents are sure to look more professional.

Summoning Pop-Up Menus

When you use Office applications, menu choices change depending upon what you're doing. If you've selected an object, say a graph, a new menu option may appear in the menu bar at the top of the screen. Choices in black are available, and choices grayed out aren't available.

In Office 2008, you can sometimes right-click or Control-click something to bring up a pop-up menu. For example, in Word, Excel, or PowerPoint, when you see a red squiggly line under a word, that word might be misspelled. Sure, you could highlight the misspelled word and manually type the correction, but it's so much easier to right-click or Control-click the word and summon a pop-up menu, as shown in Figure 3-3. Click any of the suggested word replacements (if you find the one you're looking for), and the application saves you the trouble of typing anything at all!

Office 2008 has tons of such helpful features, and if you love to explore and discover new things, you're in for so much fun. Office 2008 has plenty of right-clicking or Control-clicking secrets to reveal. Almost everything in the interface has a pop-up menu associated with it — even toolbars and white space. A word of caution, though: Don't right-click or Control-click all over the interface when you're squeezed for time — it's so addictive that you may lose track of your original work purpose!

One of the greatest things about owning a Mac is that Apple publishes *User Interface Guidelines* for any software vendor that creates applications for the Mac. Of course, this includes Microsoft and its Office 2008 applications. With these guidelines, you get a consistent look and feel for all your applications. Standard Mac menus have been popular consistently for over 20 years. You might think it's crazy, but in Office 2007 for Windows, Microsoft got rid of the menus and replaced them with tabs. Thankfully, Office 2008 for Mac still has good, old-fashioned, dependable menus.

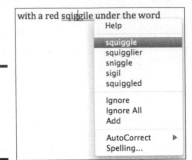

Figure 3-3:
Right-
clicking
to correct
spelling.

Traversing the Menus and Toolbars

Office 2008 looks good right out of the box, but that's only a starting point — what you see in the interface isn't all there is. Just like you can rearrange the furniture in a room to suit your taste, feel free to rearrange the toolbars (and menus) to suit the way you work in Office 2008. One of the Office 2008 best features is the incredibly easy-to-work-with range of customization options. The following sections tell you how.

First, we discuss toolbars because they're so much fun to work with. Existing users of Office for Mac recollect that toolbars used to be right under the menu bar; but new in Office 2008, the Standard toolbar and the Formatting toolbar are now incorporated in the document window (see Figure 3-4). New Office 2008 toolbars are now replicated in each document window and can't be moved, dragged to other places, or docked to the screen borders. This lets you save and close a document, and then open it again with all your customizations intact and saved as part of the document. In many ways, this is in keeping with the popular, simple Web browser design, which Apple adopted in its applications. As wonderful as simplicity may be, Office 2008 certainly isn't as basic in its capabilities as a mere Web browser! The simplicity we refer to here has more to do with the way the interface looks and works rather than the actual aptitude of the applications in Office 2008.

Figure 3-4:
Standard
and
Formatting
toolbars are
replicated
in each
document
window.

To be fair, Microsoft must perform a balancing act when deciding which controls to place on the toolbars. If Microsoft provides toolbar icons for too many options, the interface gets busy and confusing. Whatever your preference, we show you how to get all the tool icons you want on your own toolbars, without making your interface cluttered. And you can use the same process to remove the tool icons you don't want!

When you first start an Office application, the Standard toolbar is displayed directly below the document name at the top of the document window. Entourage has only one toolbar; but Word, Excel, and PowerPoint each have several additional built-in toolbars.

To toggle these toolbars on and off:

1. **Choose View⇨Toolbars.**

2. **Choose a toolbar from the submenu.**

    A check mark appears next to the toolbars that you've toggled *on,* or made *visible.* Simply remove the check mark to toggle off the toolbar.

Customizing Word, Excel, and PowerPoint toolbars and menus

The Customize Toolbars and Menus dialog is a super-powerful dialog in Word, Excel, and PowerPoint. Whenever that dialog is open, you have total control over all the toolbars and menus. You also have easy access to all kinds of wonderful hidden features — brilliant jewels in the form of off-the-beaten-path commands kept secret from mere mortals, but not from you!

Adding a jewel of a command

The Fit to Window command is a Word feature that's so handy you might wonder why it's not always on by default. The Fit to Window command automatically keeps the document proportionally sized to the size of the document window. After you try this command, you'll probably use Fit to Window a lot; it's a great example for discovering how easy it is to add commands to any toolbar.

To add the Fit to Window command to a Word toolbar:

1. **In Word, choose View⇨Customize Toolbars and Menus.**

    The Customize Toolbars and Menus dialog appears, as shown in Figure 3-5.

2. **Click the Commands tab.**

3. **In the Categories list (on the left), choose the View category.**

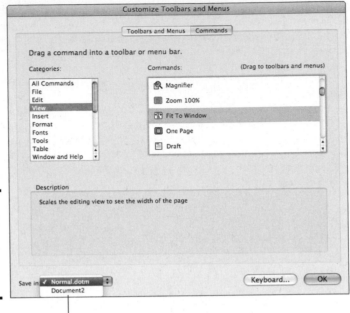

Figure 3-5:
The magical
Customize
Toolbars
and Menus
dialog.

Click where you want to save your changes to.

4. **In the Commands list (on the right), scroll down to the Fit to Window command and choose it.**

   Notice that when you choose a command, its description appears in the Description area. This is very handy for finding out more about commands you may have never seen before.

5. **Drag the Fit to Window command from the dialog to any toolbar and then release the mouse button.**

   When the Customize Toolbars and Menus dialog is open, you can move any toolbar command or menu item by dragging it to any toolbar or menu.

   You can rearrange the commands within a toolbar or menu by dragging the commands into the order you want.

6. **Click OK to close the Customize Toolbars and Menus dialog.**

   You can use this same general steps to add other commands in Word, Excel, and PowerPoint.

Of course, after you get into the magical Customize Toolbars and Menus dialog, you'll want to try hundreds of commands that you never knew about.

Don't delete the Customize Toolbars and Menus command. If you do, you can't go to the Customize Toolbars and Menus dialog unless you right-click or Control-click an empty area within any visible toolbar and select the Customize Toolbars option in the context menu that appears.

Ditching a dud command

Believe it or not, you can add too many commands to your toolbars. Soon, it might look like your toolbars are infested with more icons than mosquitoes in a jungle! Sometimes a command that sounds perfect turns out not to be at all what you'd hoped it'd be. You can easily get rid of an unwanted or little used command. For Mac diehards, it's akin to removing a Dock icon without the *poof!*

Follow these steps to clean your toolbars:

1. **From the menu bar, choose View⇨Customize Toolbars and Menus.**

This brings up the Customize Toolbars and Menus dialog (refer to Figure 3-5).

2. **Click and drag any unwanted commands off the toolbars and let go anywhere.**

You could drag it back to the open dialog or just into empty space!

3. **Click OK to close the Customize Toolbars and Menus dialog.**

Now you can get back to your non-infested jungle . . . er, program interface.

Rolling your own

You might think that you could design much better toolbars than the ones the Microsoft folks provided. Maybe you noticed that having the same toolbar repeat over and over again in each window is less of a convenience and more like a waste of valuable screen real estate. Not everyone has a gorgeous Apple 30-inch cinema display or two placed in a dual screen setup. And even if you do, you paid good money for that and have every right to design your own toolbar!

You'll be pleased to know that you can make your own toolbars, fresh from scratch. They're healthier for your computing environment because they're homemade with only the finest commands that you select. While you're at it, you can make your own menu choices, too! If only growing organic vegetables was this easy.

Also keep in mind that your new customized toolbars aren't prisoners of the document window. Instead, they *float* — they can be moved by your mouse to any screen position. You can change their shape by clicking and dragging the lower-right corner of the toolbar. They're also *dockable* — they gently stick to the top, bottom, left, or right edge of the screen and out of your way like well-behaved children drinking hot soup on a winter night.

To make a new toolbar in Word, Excel, or PowerPoint:

1. **From the menu bar, choose View➪Customize Toolbars and Menus.**

   The Customize Toolbars and Menus dialog appears (refer to Figure 3-5).

2. **On the Toolbars and Menus tab, click the New button.**

   The Add a Toolbar pane, as shown in Figure 3-6, opens.

3. **In the Add a Toolbar pane, type a name for your new toolbar and click OK.**

   A very small box with an empty space on it appears onscreen. This small box is your new toolbar.

4. **Click the Commands tab, choose any of the categories from the list on the left, drag commands to the new toolbar, and click OK to close the Customize Toolbars and Menus dialog.**

Figure 3-6:
Naming a
new toolbar.

Your new toolbar appears in the toolbars list. You can view the new toolbar by choosing View➪Toolbars, or choosing View➪Customize Toolbars and Menus and then clicking the Toolbars and Menus tab.

Okay, your new toolbar looks nice, but not all the new commands on the toolbar have nice icons. You can control whether to display a command's icon, text description, or both. To see the command controls, right-click or Control-click over a newly added command button and choose Properties. The Command Properties dialog, as shown in Figure 3-7, opens. In this dialog, you can do quite a bit from changing the icon/button of the command to assigning keyboard shortcuts, as we show you next.

Changing the command button icon

After you're in the Command Properties dialog, which we explain in the preceding section, follow these steps to change the icon:

1. **Click the Customize Icon downward-pointing arrow, as shown in Figure 3-7 to open a fly-out menu with plenty of options.**

2. **Choose from any of the available icons in this fly-out menu.**

Alternatively, if you copied a picture from any other application to the Mac OS X Clipboard, you can use the Paste Button Image option as the command button icon or button.

Run Command
Reset Command
Delete Command
Properties...

Figure 3-7:
Making toolbar buttons look just right.

Customize icon   Set a keyboard shortcut

Icon display option

Remember that the Paste Button Image option works only with pictures copied to the Mac OS X Clipboard. You can't copy text characters and paste them as a button/icon for any command.

Assigning keyboard shortcuts to new command buttons

As if that weren't enough customization, you can set or change the keyboard shortcut for any command. Remember that it's possible to do this customization in Word and Excel only, not PowerPoint. To proceed with assigning keyboard shortcuts, follow these steps:

1. **Make sure you followed steps in the preceding section to access the Command Properties dialog, as shown in Figure 3-7.**

2. **Press the Keyboard button.**

A dialog opens that shows you any existing keyboard shortcuts for the selected command. In addition, it lets you type a new shortcut for the command in the Press New Keyboard Shortcut text box. Also see the following chapters for more:

- Book II, Chapter 1
- Book III, Chapter 1
- Book IV, Chapter 3

3. **Click OK when done to get back to the dialog, as shown in Figure 3-7.**

At this point, you can work with other options or click OK to get back to your program interface.

Resetting, renaming, or trashing toolbars and menus

Maybe you got a little carried away with all this moving and customizing of toolbars and menus, and now you're not so keen on some of the changes you made. Maybe you moved a command from the Standard toolbar and now you want the Standard toolbar restored the way it was originally. No need to worry; resetting is easy. Follow these steps:

1. **From the menu bar, choose View⇨Customize Toolbars and Menus.**

The Customize Toolbars and Menus dialog appears (refer to Figure 3-5).

2. **Click the Toolbars and Menus tab.**

This brings up the dialog, as shown in Figure 3-8.

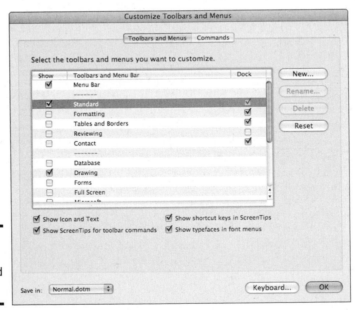

Figure 3-8:
Resetting
toolbars and
menus.

3. **Reset your toolbar or menu:**

- *To reset a toolbar,* select a toolbar and click the Reset button.
- *To reset a command,* right-click or Control-click a menu and from the pop-up menu that appears, choose Reset Command (see Figure 3-9).

4. **Click OK to close the Customize Toolbars and Menus dialog.**

You can't delete built-in toolbars.

Figure 3-9:
Resetting
menus in
Office 2008.

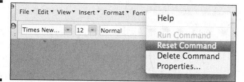

Sharing toolbars and menus

Customizing your toolbars and interface is really cool, but what's even cooler is that you can share these customizations with other folks. However, make sure that you advise people that you've done this before you share your documents with them; otherwise, they might be surprised when they open your document and see a different toolbar layout than what they're used to.

Instead of saving your customizations just for your own computer, save them in the current document. Then, when your customized document is opened on another computer, your customized menus and toolbars will appear while that particular document is open.

To do this, follow these steps:

1. **From the menu bar, choose View⇨Customize Toolbars and Menus.**

   The Customize Toolbars and Menus dialog (refer to Figure 3-5) appears.

2. **In the lower-left corner of the dialog in the Save In list, save your changes to either the currently opened document or the template.**

   - If you see the name of your file in this list, you can choose that option to save the customizations as part of the file.

   - If you see an option similar to Normal.dotm, that refers to the default settings template.

   - If you see something like Document2, Presentation1, or similar, you haven't saved the file you are working on yet.

If you want to have a variety of settings, each with its own customized toolbar and menus, make several documents and customize each one differently. Before you start your customizations, change the setting to keep the customizations within the current document, which we describe in the preceding step list. When you're done customizing, choose File⇨Save As⇨Template. Save your customized documents into the My Templates folder, and your customizations are available in Project Gallery. Remember that any documents you make from this sort of template carry your customized toolbars and menus with them wherever they go.

Customizing Entourage and Project Center Toolbars

Before Office 2008, Entourage and Project Center were less powerful programs without the ability to customize toolbars and menus. This is partly because Entourage and Project Center are much younger applications than Word, Excel, and PowerPoint and also because these programs have different windows, which you discover in this section. When it came to implementing toolbar customizations in Entourage, MacBU (Macintosh Business Unit) at Microsoft who are responsible for the development of Microsoft Office for Mac platform decided to introduce a new way to customize the interface. Thus, the toolbar customization procedures in these programs aren't exactly the same as in Word, Excel, and PowerPoint.

In Entourage and Project Center, the toolbars are based on types of windows instead of on the entire application. Each different kind of window has its own toolbar customization possibilities. For example, a New Mail message window is different from a Calendar event window. Each kind of window has one toolbar that's locked in that window. Within Entourage and Project Center, the windows on each tab can have their own customizations. Toolbar customizations aren't global to the entire application in Entourage or Project Center like they are in other applications.

Getting started with toolbar customizing in Entourage and Project Center is easy as pie. To get at the customization box (see Figure 3-10), follow these two steps in any window:

1. **Right-click or Control-click anywhere on the toolbar.**

2. **Choose Customize Toolbar from the pop-up menu.**

   This brings up the dialog that you see in Figure 3-10.

3. **When the customization box is open, you can drag commands to and from the toolbar.**

   Figure 3-10 shows you the options available when you customize the New Event toolbar in Entourage. Because each different kind of window has its own customization options, you can expect to see different options depending upon which kind of window you're customizing.

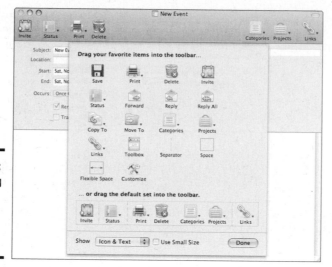

Figure 3-10:
Customizing
the New
Event
toolbar in
Entourage.

Chapter 4: Busting Out Your Toolbox

In This Chapter

✔ Taking hold of the Toolbox

✔ Working with the Object Palette

✔ Using the all-mighty Scrapbook

✔ Working with Reference Tools

✔ Checking compatibility

✔ Managing the Project Palette

In this chapter, we explore the things you can do with Office 2008's Toolbox. In addition to the Toolbox, Office 2008 is blessed with many Mac-only floating context-sensitive palettes. Many new palettes have been added to the Toolbox, and the Toolbox organization has changed from previous Office editions. With Office 2008's new ability to customize the Toolbox, you'll love palettes now more than ever.

Taking a Look Inside the Toolbox

Seven is a lucky number, so it's fitting that Toolbox in Office usually has seven distinct tabs chock-full of options, ready at a moment's notice for you to use. And if you're wondering what the *Toolbox* is, it's the floating tools palette that provides you with umpteen options. The exact tools you see at any given time are context-sensitive and vary depending upon what's currently selected, what view you're using, and which application you're currently using. Figure 4-1 shows Excel's default Toolbox when turned on in a new, blank workbook (access the Toolbox by clicking the Toolbox button on Excel's toolbar). The title of the Toolbox displays the name of the currently selected tool. Each tab represents a different tool in the Toolbox palette.

Turning the Toolbox on and off is a simple matter. Click the red Close button in the upper left just as you would with any other Mac window or click the Toolbox button on the application's Standard toolbar to toggle the Toolbox on and off.

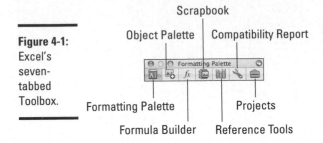

Figure 4-1:
Excel's
seven-
tabbed
Toolbox.

Scrapbook

Object Palette   Compatibility Report

Formatting Palette   Projects

Formula Builder   Reference Tools

 If you can't see the Toolbox, choose View➪Toolbox➪Formatting Palette or any of the other Toolbox tabs, as shown in Figure 4-2. You can also click the Toolbox button on the Standard toolbar of Word, Excel, or PowerPoint. You can then see the Toolbox icons across the top of the window just under the title bar. The leftmost icon shows the Formatting Palette, which appears by default.

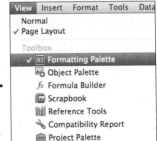

Figure 4-2:
Summoning
the Toolbox.

 Much like your mechanic's toolbox at the local auto shop, Office's Toolbox is like having seven different toolboxes together, each with a custom toolset to take care of a specific job.

Introducing the Toolbox palettes

This chapter explores the Toolbox tabs (except for one used in Excel; see a little later in this section). By the time you're done, you'll be an expert mechanic, but we're not going to give you a certificate. Not yet!

The seven tabs of Excel's Toolbox, as shown in Figure 4-1 are

✦ **Formatting Palette:** This tab lets you apply formatting options to selected objects.

✦ **Object Palette:** This tab lets you add shapes, clip art, symbols, and photos.

✦ **Formula Builder:** A helpful formula tool unique to Excel that we discuss in Book III, Chapter 2.

✦ **Scrapbook:** This tab is the regular clipboard on steroids.

✦ **Reference Tools:** A collection of reference materials, such as a dictionary, a thesaurus, and more.

✦ **Compatibility Report:** Find out how compatible your presentations are with older PowerPoint versions on both Mac and Windows.

✦ **Project Palette:** A mini–Project Center within the Toolbox.

We explore them all except Formula Builder in this chapter. The Toolbox is great because it floats, so you can drag it out of the way whenever you want. Later, we show you how to make the Toolbox slowly fade away from your field of view or you can even roll up the Toolbox like a window shade. You'll find this fantastic feature in Word, Excel, and PowerPoint.

We can't resist pointing out that Mac-only palettes make task panes in Office for Windows versions obsolete.

Using palettes in the Toolbox

The palettes all have different features, but essentially they work the same way. For this section, we're using the Excel Formatting Palette in our examples, as shown in Figure 4-3. The Formatting Palettes in Word and PowerPoint look similar but not identical.

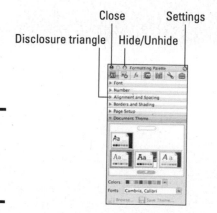

Figure 4-3:
The new
Excel
Formatting
Palette.

To use the Formatting Palette, click the disclosure triangles to expose and hide various palette panels (see Figure 4-3). Within each panel, you're offered relevant options and actions to take, depending upon what's currently selected in your document (Word), sheet (Excel), or slide (PowerPoint).

But even more is new in Office 2008. The Formatting Palette has a couple of really neat tricks up its sleeve, or rather on its upper-left corner. First, if you look closely at the top left of the Formatting Palette, you see a new button. In addition to the red Close button is a new green Hide button (the button with a small plus sign). Go ahead; give it a click, and the Formatting Palette now slides discreetly away so that it takes hardly any screen space.

Take a look at the top-right corner of the Formatting Palette and you see a tiny arrow button. Click that arrow button, and the Formatting Palette turns around so you can see its backside. That's where you'll find the Toolbox Settings dialog, as shown in Figure 4-4.

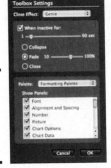

Figure 4-4:
The new
Toolbox
Settings
feature.

No Objections to the Object Palette

Russian nesting dolls are noted for their beauty and the thrill of discovering something smaller inside something larger. Like a nesting doll, the Object Palette has many sub-objects inside, categorized in various ways. As you traverse the subsets of the Object Palette, you continually discover new things.

Choose View⇨Toolbox⇨Object Palette to toggle the Object Palette on and off in Word, Excel, and PowerPoint. In Entourage, choose Tools⇨Toolbox⇨ Object Palette to toggle the palette on and off. Notice right away that you see four sub-tabs, each containing distinct kinds of objects, with the pop-up menu extended so that you can see each of the distinct sub-object choices:

✦ **Shapes:** This tab allows you to add shapes to the active document, sheet, or slide.

✦ **Clip Art:** From this tab, you can add cut-out images.

✦ **Symbols:** Add symbols such as keyboard controls, registered and copyright symbols, and so on.

+ **Photos:** This displays the content of your Apple iPhoto albums. iPhoto is a photo-viewing and -editing program that's part of Apple's iLife suite of programs. Most new Macs include iPhoto by default.

 You won't see the Shapes tab in Entourage, and that's perfectly okay as long as you see the Clip Art, Symbols, and Photos tabs within the application. All other Office programs show the Shapes tab in addition to the other three tabs.

Squeezing shapes

 An audience appreciates shoring up a document with an interesting or instructive shape. With the Shapes tab, you can find and insert just the right shape and then customize its appearance. Click the Object Palette Shapes tab to display the built-in shapes available to you, as shown in Figure 4-5.

Hide/Unhide

Close   Settings

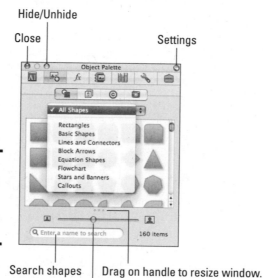

Figure 4-5:
The Shapes
tab of the
Object
Palette.

Search shapes   Drag on handle to resize window.

Resize shapes with the slider.

If you look closely at the shapes, you might notice some new ones. A brand-new, high-tech drawing engine in Office 2008 called OfficeArt draws practically everything you see on the screen except for text.

Before you actually insert a shape, look at the shiny new Shapes tab in the Object Palette itself. Just below the selector tab is a pop-up menu that comes preset to All Shapes. Click the pop-up menu (see Figure 4-5) to see your options for filtering the shapes by categories, such as Basic Shapes, Lines and Connectors, Block Arrows, and so on (again, see Figure 4-5).

At the bottom edge of the Shapes tab are three little dots, which you can drag up and down to adjust the size of the Shapes palette. Under the three dots is a slider control, which you can drag left and right to zoom in on and out of the shapes in the palette. Lastly, you see a search field where you can type the shape name you're looking for, and the search filters the shapes accordingly.

You're probably itching to get your hands on one of these shapely shapes, but here's the procedure for inserting shapes first:

1. **Click inside your document in the approximate place you want to insert the shape.**

2. **In the Toolbox, select the Object Palette tab, and then select the Shapes palette. Click a shape in the Shapes palette.**

3. **Hold down the left mouse button and drag across the document to draw a shape at the size you want.**

   Alternatively, click once on the shape in the Shapes palette and then once again in the document to place the selected shape.

4. **Let go of the mouse when you're done.**

Before you start customizing your new shapes, we take a moment to point out some of the new features your shapes have thanks to the new OfficeArt drawing engine. Compared with shapes from previous Office versions, 2008 shapes now have nice soft shadows by default and more of a 3D appearance.

Here's some more info on manipulating shapes:

✦ **Rotating a shape:** In Excel and PowerPoint rotating a shape is accomplished by dragging the green dot at the top of the shape.

✦ **Shape controls:** Most shapes have one or more yellow diamonds that act as shape controls (see Figure 4-6), which can be dragged to alter the shape's appearance.

✦ **Resizing handles:** Each shape has eight resizing handles, as shown in Figure 4-6. The corner handles resize the shape proportionately in the direction you drag whereas the other handles resize the shape by either altering only the width or the height.

✦ **Adding text to shapes:** Solid shapes such as circles, rectangles, and triangles are secretly text boxes. If you want to add text to a solid shape, or edit existing text, do the following:

   1. *Right-click or Control-click the shape.*

   2. *Choose Add Text or Edit Text from the pop-up menu.*

   3. *Start typing.*

Resizing handle

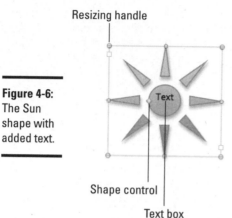

Figure 4-6:
The Sun
shape with
added text.

Shape control

Text box

After you insert a shape, click the Formatting Palette and try all the neat new controls, such as the shadow controls, transparency, and themes. You can also right-click or Control-click a shape and choose Format to perform precise fine-tuning.

Clamoring for clip art

No question about it: People love to decorate their documents. Art and graphics can add visual appeal, and there's truth to the old expression that a picture's worth a thousand words. For most documents that picture is some kind of clip art.

Clip art is most often small drawings or pictures added to documents for interest or pizzazz. The Object Palette's new Clip Art tab specializes in this kind of artwork.

The Clip Art tab in the Object Palette is different from the Clip Art option in the Insert⇨Picture⇨Clip Art menu.

You can easily use the clip art found in the tab of the same name within the Object Palette. Simply drag the piece of clip art you want from the Object Palette into your document.

Like the Shapes tab, which we discuss earlier in this chapter, you can filter the type of clip art you see within the palette using a similar pop-up menu. Choices include All Images, Animals, Business, and so on (see Figure 4-7).

Clip art is great, but lots of people go through clips as if they're free. Actually, most of them are! We know people who want new clips for every document and every possible purpose.

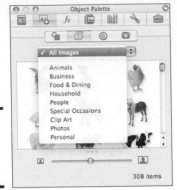

Figure 4-7:
The Object Palette's Clip Art tab.

The Object Palette's Clip Art tab shows only a very limited collection of pictures and drawings that belong to the larger Office Online Clip Art collection, which includes millions of pictures, drawings, sounds, and animations. Office Online is a part of the Microsoft Web site, and before you launch your browser and start looking for the clip art, we suggest you read the rest of this section.

As the proud owner of Microsoft Office, you're entitled to use the content available from Office Online:

`http://office.microsoft.com`

If you visit that site, you might find it entirely Windows-centric. But don't worry, because all the clips that download from this site will work within Office applications. Also, you really don't have to visit that site to get the clips, as we show you next.

You can download as many clips as you want to your computer and use them however you want. As long as you have a Web browser, grabbing clip art from Office Online is a breeze. What's more, you can also do this from right within your Office application without using a web browser. Follow these steps:

1. **From the menu of any Office application, choose Insert⇨Picture⇨ Clip Art.**

   This summons the Clip Gallery (see Figure 4-8).

2. **At the bottom of the Clip Gallery, click the Online . . . button.**

   Your default Web browser opens and connects to the Office Online Clip Art tab. If your Office application asks you for permission to launch your default browser, click the Yes option.

3. **Search or browse the collection by entering keywords in the Search text box.**

   We don't show you the actual interface because Microsoft updates this site fairly often, and the location of the Search text box may change.

Clip Gallery

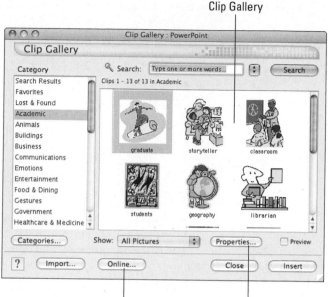

Figure 4-8:
The Clip
Gallery.

Click here to change tags and categories.

Click here to access Office Online.

4. **After the search is finished, select the check boxes next to the clips you want to download.**

   Unless you searched for an exotic keyword that yields no results, you'll end up with some or many results. Each result is actually a thumbnail with a check box.

   As you select the check boxes in your browser, you'll see a Selection Basket that shows the number of clips you have opted to download.

5. **When you are ready to download your clips, click the Download # Items link.**

6. **Agree to the service agreement.**

   You have to agree to the service agreement to download any clips. If you have lots of time or if you love legal gobbledygook, go ahead and read each word, and then accept the agreement.

7. **Click the Download Now button.**

   Your browser downloads the clips as a single file.

8. **Select the Save option when you're prompted by a dialog.**

   The same dialog that provided the Save option also lets you choose an Open With option. Make sure you don't choose Open With.

9. **Make sure the saved file name has the `.cil` file extension.**

Apple Safari does it right, but you have to manually type **.cil** in Mozilla Firefox and some other browsers that save the file without the `.cil` extension.

10. **Click the Save button and wait for the download to complete.**

11. **In the Web browser's Download window, double-click the CIL file.**

This automatically loads your clips into Clip Gallery.

If your Web browser's Download window is hidden or not turned on, use your Web browser's menus to open the Download window. Firefox users can choose Tools⇨Downloads, and Safari users should choose Window⇨Downloads.

Now that you have your clips in Clip Gallery, you can tag your clips so that they can be searched, and you can categorize them so they can be filtered.

The clips you download from Office Online enter into Clip Gallery with default keyword tags already, and are also categorized by default into the Favorites category. However, you can change the categories and keyword tags to suit your own needs. To change the category of a clip:

1. **Select the clip in the Clip Gallery (refer to Figure 4-8).**

2. **Click the Properties button to open the Properties window, as shown in Figure 4-9.**

3. **Click the Categories tab, as shown in Figure 4-9.**

4. **Select and deselect categories as desired.**

You can also create a new category by clicking the New Category . . . button. In the New Category window, type a name for your new category and click OK to return to the Categories tab of the Properties window.

5. **Click OK to exit the Properties window and go back to the Clip Gallery.**

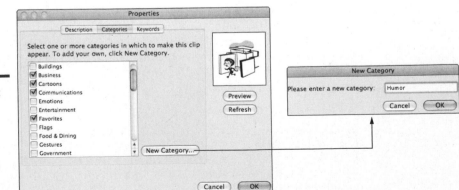

Figure 4-9: The Category tab in the Clip Art Properties window.

Follow almost the same steps if you want to set or change the keyword tags for a selected clip:

1. **Select a clip in the Clip Gallery (refer to Figure 4-8).**

2. **Click the Properties button to open the Properties window.**

3. **Click the Keywords tab to view the window that you see in Figure 4-10.**

Figure 4-10:
The
Keywords
tab in the
Clip Art
Properties
window.

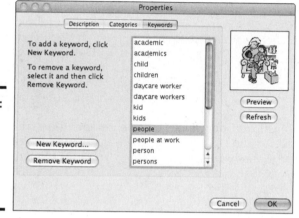

4. **Add and remove keywords as desired.**

Any new keywords that you add with the New Keyword . . . button are available in the keyword list that you see in this window.

5. **Click OK to exit the Properties window and go back to the Clip Gallery.**

By now you're probably wondering how to get clips from Clip Gallery into a document. That's easy. Select the clip you want, and do one of the following:

✦ **Double-click a piece of clip art.** You might think that nothing happened. Actually every time you double-click a piece of clip art, it's placed behind the scenes (and behind the Clip Gallery window) in your document. Double-click more than one piece of clip art to place them all the same way.

✦ **Click the Insert button.** This option exits the Clip Gallery window and places the piece of clip art in your document.

✦ **Drag the piece of clip art from the Clip Gallery to your document.** If the Clip Gallery is covering your document, you need to drag the Clip Gallery window a wee bit so that you can see both this window and your document at the same time, but the drag and drop works, especially if you have a large monitor!

As nice as Clip Gallery is, it's no substitute for a full-featured media browser, such as Expression Media, which comes with the Media Edition of Microsoft Office 2008. If you have a reasonable number or photos or other digital assets, you might want to give Expression Media Edition a try if you have a reasonable number of photos or other digital assets.

Showing the way with symbols

In the old days, Mac users often growled under their breaths — and sometimes out loud — when they had to insert symbols into documents because the dialog required a magnifying glass. But that was then, and this is now. The new Symbols tab in the Object Palette of the Toolbox has come to the rescue. You can see it in all its glory in Figure 4-11. One particularly wonderful improvement is that now you can control how big the symbols look before you commit to inserting them.

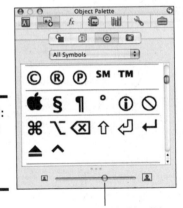

Figure 4-11: The Object Palette's Symbols tab.

Size symbols with this slider.

Symbols are elegant and oh, so simple! And they're useful, too, because you really need to insert things like symbols for keyboard characters, foreign languages, registered and copyright symbols, currency, and so on. Just position your cursor where you want the symbol inserted in your document and click the symbol to insert it in.

Picking the perfect photo

Having a bunch of high-quality images handy is a great thing. Maybe you have some CDs of stock photos that you bought years ago lying around and gathering dust. Or you may have just returned from a vacation with tons of new high-res digital pictures. The Object Palette's Photos tab (see Figure 4-12) can bring these digital photo assets to life because you can select any folder to populate the palette. By default, the Photos tab on the Object Palette shows the content within your iPhoto folder. This is one of the ways in which Office coexists and adds synergies to your Mac's built-in applications. As long as the iPhoto folder contains pictures in popular formats, such as JPEG, the Photos tab makes it easy for you to put the photos into Office documents.

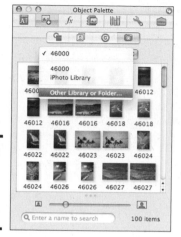

Figure 4-12:
The Object Palette's Photos sub-tab.

Photos on the Object Palette work just the way you'd expect. Drag a picture from the palette into a document, and there it is. After a photo is in your document, it's a great time to click over to the Formatting Palette and experience the fun stuff on the Picture section. We explain more about this in the "Perfecting your pictures" section, later in this chapter.

One of the best resources for finding photos is the Flickr photo-sharing Web site. We show you a specific part of the Web site in Figure 4-13.

Free and not-so-free photos

You have a lot of exciting ways to get high-quality pictures, but you do always have to be respectful of the picture owner's rights. We thank our local librarian friend for providing this handy link:

```
www.librarycopyright.net/
    digitalslider
```

This site lets you ascertain the copyright status of most work available in the U.S., including photographs.

Libraries are great sources of images. The vast majority of books haven't been digitized, and libraries certainly have plenty of books with pictures that are no longer under copyright, so you can scan and use them. Packages of stock photos are sold in computer stores and online, but make sure that you understand copyright restrictions when using these. They don't all offer completely unrestricted photo use.

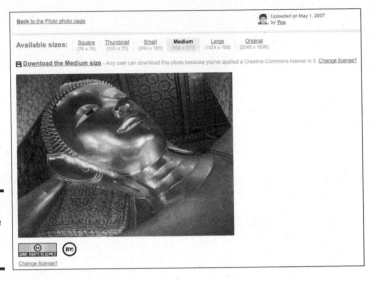

Figure 4-13:
Flickr online
photo
resource.

www.flickr.com

At Flickr, you can search through millions of photos. Almost all photos are of excellent quality. Flickr is a photo-sharing site — anyone who wants to can upload pictures into Flickr and share them with their friends or the entire world. When you visit Flickr for the first time, you can either use keywords to search for photos or you can browse through a user's collection. Click any of these thumbnails to access the page for a particular picture, where a larger preview of the selected thumbnail appears. The secret to using Flickr is to click the small All Sizes button above most of the larger picture previews because this allows you to find and download the picture you want in all available resolutions. Flickr then displays the picture, and if the owner of the picture allows you to, you can download the picture. To ascertain whether the owner allows download and use of uploaded pictures, Flickr uses the Creative Commons guidelines. You can read more about these guidelines at:

www.flickr.com/creativecommons

Follow these steps to download a picture:

1. **Type www.flickr.com in the Web browser and then search for pictures by typing in the keywords for the picture subjects you want to find.**

   You end up with pages filled with thumbnails of search results.

2. **Click any thumbnail to get to that particular picture's page.**

3. **Click the All Sizes button above the picture.**

If the All Sizes button isn't available, the picture's owner doesn't want other users to download and use her pictures. In that case, look for another picture that does have the All Sizes button available.

4. When you're ready, click Download the Large Size link (see Figure 4-13) to save the best quality picture to your computer.

The picture in Figure 4-13 is of the Reclining Buddha at one of Bangkok's amazing temples, taken using a digital camera by Geetesh Bajaj, one of this book's authors.

Perfecting your pictures

Getting the photos into your document is just the beginning. After you find the perfect picture and put it in your document, you may decide that the picture could look better. Here's where the Formatting Palette comes into play again. The Formatting Palette is smart and provides formatting options based on what you have selected in your document, spreadsheet, or slide. Select a picture in your document, switch to the Formatting Palette (see Figure 4-14) in your Toolbox, and then choose from many traditional photo-editing controls, plus some brand-new ones in Office 2008, such as

✦ **Recolor:** Changing the color of a picture affects the mood. Click the Recolor button, and you'll see a menu with choices that let you add a duotone-like effect, or make a picture warmer or colder by changing its color. In addition to some beautiful preset color choices, a More Options submenu gives you access to your document theme colors, and still another nested More Color option lets you use the standard Mac OS X color picker so that you can choose any color you like.

✦ **Crop:** When you click the Crop tool, the picture's border changes and displays several handles that you can drag inside the picture area to cut off the parts of the picture you don't want to see. Click the Crop tool a second time to turn off the crop handles.

✦ **Shape:** If you want to make your picture stand out, you can experiment with the new Shape tool. You can end up using the selected picture as a fill for a cookie cutter shape. Imagine a picture that's enclosed within a heart shape, and of course, you can play with hundreds of other shapes!

✦ **Transparent Color:** Sometimes you may want to create a see-through picture. If you want to create a mask or perhaps a special effect, use the Transparent Color tool to turn a color in the picture transparent. Here's how:

1. *With your picture selected, click the Transparent Color button on the Formatting Palette.*

   The cursor changes into a pointer.

2. *Click an area of the picture that contains the color you want to turn transparent.*

The original

Figure 4-14:
Making a
dramatic
daffodil in
just two
steps.

The formatted copy

The color disappears from your picture. Where color was before, you now see through the picture. This effect may not work sometimes, especially with illustrated clip art, such as line drawings. However, it works very well with photographs.

✦ **Brightness, Contrast, and Transparency:** Fine-tuning the looks of a picture is easy with Brightness, Contrast, and Transparency controls. You have your choice of sliders or value controls. These controls are *live,* so you can see the changes take effect while you adjust the controls.

✦ **Replace:** The Replace button is the *Oops* button. Imagine you added just the shape you wanted and recolored the picture to the exact shade you like. You then realize that you needed to use another picture. Rather than do all the edits all over again, you can click the Replace button to replace the current picture with another one while preserving styles and certain effects.

✦ **Effects:** Don't be afraid to click the Effects button. This Mac-only feature offers a totally new set of effects. See Figure 4-15. If you have a good graphics card, you don't have to wait forever for the effects to draw anymore. Many draw instantaneously now. You see these same effects in other Mac applications because they are generated by Mac OS X and therefore available to all applications. Each effect has different controls. Some have yellow diamonds that you can drag to control the effect's centering point. (See Figure 4-15.) Yes, there are even blurs, including Gaussian blur!

Effects list

Preview

Centering diamond

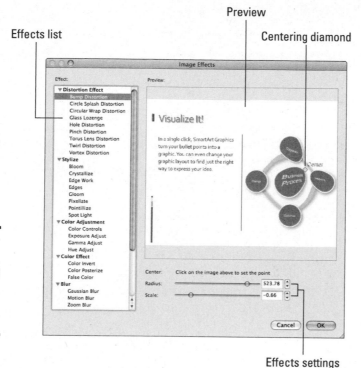

Figure 4-15:
Using Mac
OS X special
effects on
pictures in
Office.

Effects settings

✦ **Format:** Detailed formatting is available with a click of the Format button, as we mention earlier in this chapter. In the Format dialog, you can fine-tune various controls.

✦ **Reset:** Sometimes you realize you messed up the picture while formatting it. If you want to restore it to the way it looked when you first downloaded it, click the Reset button.

✦ **Quick Styles and Effects:** And just one more feature . . . You can do dramatic things with the Quick Styles and Effects panel in the Formatting Pane. You'll find new reflection effects, 3D effects, and true rotation effects within this section of the palette. Enjoy!

To show you how easy it is to make changes in a picture, look at Figure 4-14. The original picture (top) was copied and pasted, and then we clicked one of the options in the Quick Styles and Effects panel (bottom). After you select an inserted picture, the dramatic formatting is accomplished with these short steps:

1. **Select the picture you want to format.**

2. **In the Formatting Palette, access the Quick Styles and Effects panel and choose the Soft Edge Rectangle preset.**

3. **Click the Shapes button on the Formatting Palette.**

4. **In the submenu that appears, choose Basic Shapes⇨Oval.**

Scrapbook: The Clipboard Evolves

Every once in a while you might wonder why the Mac OS X Clipboard can't remember what was on it after you restart your computer. Someone in Microsoft obviously wondered the same thing and came up with *Scrapbook,* a multiple-item Clipboard with a memory, as shown in Figure 4-16. And did we mention that Scrapbook is handily accessed with a Toolbox tab? If you can't see the Scrapbook tab on the Toolbox, choose View⇨Toolbox⇨Scrapbook.

To put Scrapbook to work, you have to do a little setup. A setting makes Scrapbook as automatic as the Mac OS X Clipboard. Here's how to toggle Scrapbook's automatic setting:

1. **Make sure the Scrapbook tab is selected in your Toolbox.**

If you can't see the Toolbox, choose the View⇨Toolbox/Scrapbook.

2. **Click the down arrow next to the big, green Add button (see Figure 4-16) to summon a pop-up menu.**

3. **From the pop-up menu that appears, choose the Always Add Copy option.**

That's all you need to do, and the Scrapbook setting is now set to automatic.

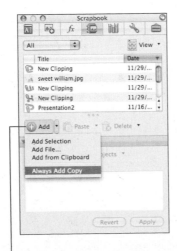

Figure 4-16:
Scrapbook,
the super
Clipboard.

The Add button

That's all there is to it. Well, almost. The automatic Scrapbook setting must be configured individually in Word, Excel, PowerPoint, and Entourage, so you have to perform this little ritual in each application's Scrapbook if you want uniform behavior throughout Office. Even though the setting isn't global, the clips you put into Scrapbook are available in all the Office applications. Pop a picture into Scrapbook in Word, for example, and it's available to you in all the other applications.

Now all you have to do is get some stuff into Scrapbook. If you follow the preceding steps, adding items to Scrapbook happens automatically every time you copy something in Office with the Copy command. After you have a bunch of clips in Scrapbook, the pop-up menu buttons at the top of the Scrapbook palette become useful. The Find Clips button on the top left allows you to filter the contents of Scrapbook by date, category, keywords, and so on. The View pop-up button toward the top right changes the way clips are displayed in the Scrapbook palette in three views: List, Detail, and Large Preview views.

You can get clips out of Scrapbook almost as easily as you can get them in. Here's a quick rundown of the ways to get your selected clip out of Scrapbook:

✦ **Press Shift-⌘-V to paste the currently selected clip in the Scrapbook palette into the active, open document.**

✦ **Right-click or Control-click, and choose Paste in the resultant pop-up menu.**

✦ **Click the Paste button on the Scrapbook palette.**

✦ **Click the triangle to the right of the Paste button for special paste options.**

✦ **Drag a clip from Scrapbook to a document.**

If you have a special fondness for a particular clip and want to change its name, double-click the name of the clip and then type a name in the resulting input field, just like you rename anything in Mac OS X Finder. Quite a few people like the Organize panel of the Scrapbook palette, which lets you tag clips with categories and assign them to specific projects. When you assign a clip to a specific project, the clip gets added to the Project Center Clippings feature, which we discuss in Book VI, Chapter 4.

Getting Serious with Reference Tools

Going to the library is a great experience. Who doesn't like all the books and journals, the people, and even that book smell? Little pleasures are there to be discovered, and a librarian is there to help you. Even if you don't visit a library often, you'll want to take a look at the improved Reference Tools (see Figure 4-17) in Office 2008. You may not need to look up the same kinds of things anymore, but plenty of new things are there waiting for you to find.

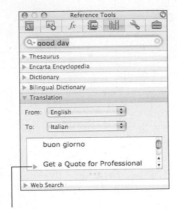

Figure 4-17:
The
Reference
Tools.

Disclosure triangle

Access Reference Tools by clicking the Reference Tools tab in the Toolbox. If you can't see the Reference Tools tab in the Toolbox, choose View➪Toolbox/Reference Tools.

Within Reference Tools, you can access a dictionary, a thesaurus, an encyclopedia, and a bilingual dictionary. Here's how:

1. **Type a word or phrase into the search field at the top of the Reference Tools tab of the Toolbox.**

2. **Click the disclosure triangles in the panels that represent the kind of results you want; choose from Dictionary, Thesaurus, and Encarta Encyclopedia.**

3. **Press Return or Enter on the keyboard to see the results.**

If you're connected to the Internet, you get your results almost instantly. You can select small parts of the results and drag the text into your document. The whole thing is pretty nifty, but we couldn't help notice and react to the hard sell in the Translation section, where you might often be invited to get a quote for a professional translation! We hope a real librarian would never do that. Overall, Reference Tools is a great feature, so don't let that stop you. Reference Tools works only while you're connected to the Internet.

You don't have to type anything into the search field to use Reference Tools. In any document, all you have to do is right-click or Control-click a word or phrase, and choose Lookup or Translate from the pop-up menu. Reference Tools does the rest. In fact, if the desired result appears as a pop-up suggestion, all you have to do is choose it to accept the suggestion.

Making Compatibility Checking a Snap

Hard to believe, but a lot of people are still working in organizations that require them to use Windows versions of Office instead of Office 2008 for Mac. What's not at all hard to believe is that some of your best friends may still be running very capable 10-year-old Macs. Yet here you are with your fancy new Office 2008, making documents that might not play well with older, but still serviceable hardware and software.

Aside from the file compatibility issues we discuss in Chapter 1 of this mini-book, it's really hard to predict what you may have done in a document that might not look right in an older Office version. Perhaps you're a sucker for soft shadows, especially in PowerPoint. Soft shadows look great on a Mac, and they've been around for years, but play the same presentation on a Windows PC running Office 2003, and it's a recipe for one ugly slide show.

This is where Compatibility Report (see Figure 4-18) comes to the rescue. Compatibility Report knows almost every aspect of each Office version since Office 97 (that's the last nine versions of Office collectively on Windows and Mac platforms!), and it can tell you whether things in your document might not play nice with an older version. Not only can Compatibility Report give you a report; it might be able to fix some aspects of your document so that what you see in Office 2008 is what your co-workers or friends see when they open your file in their older software.

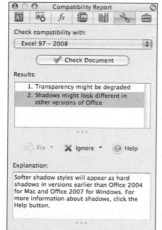

Figure 4-18:
The
Compatibility
Report.

Before you start using Compatibility Report, it's a good idea to save your document: Choose File⇨Save As and give the compatible document a new name. This way if you use the Fix feature, you won't have changed your original document.

Peeking at Your Projects in the Project Palette

Artists sometimes paint from a palette that has just about every square inch covered with different colors and blends of colors. A palette small enough to fit in an artist's hand can produce a painting as large as a wall mural. Like a colorful artist's palette, the Project Palette (see Figure 4-19) gives you a different result just about anywhere you touch it. This feature has more choices per square inch of screen space than any other we can think of.

Project Palette is a succinct interface for Project Center. We recommend that you create a project by following the examples in Book VI, Chapter 1 where we thoroughly describe each of the Project Center features that are represented by the Project Palette. If you don't already have an existing project and some understanding of the Project Center features, Project Palette may not make much sense to you. Book VI, Chapter 1 is the place to get started with Project Center.

The number of controls and features packed into Project Palette is astonishing — not even one pixel is wasted. Every tiny thing in the palette does something when you click it. This creates a challenge for your authors because it's difficult to outline each click's response in Figure 4-19. Almost every feature and action that can be taken in Project Center has been condensed into the Project Palette. After you have explored Book VI, we encourage you to click every single part of the Project Palette to explore what everything does. Each tiny square or dot is a button. Even the bands that divide its sections offer things to do when you click them. You'll be dazzled.

Figure 4-19:
The dazzling
Project
Palette.

Chapter 5: Graphing, Drawing, and Making Art

In This Chapter

✔ **Introducing new graph and chart applications**

✔ **Graphing and charting with flair**

✔ **Inserting new SmartArt graphics**

✔ **Organizing your organization chart**

✔ **Learning how to create shapes and drawings**

✔ **Getting font-fancy with WordArt**

✔ **Working with layers**

Among the many things people use Office for are creating graphs, charts, and other types of art. With Office 2008, you find a new engine under the hood that controls how Office draws things onscreen, and this OfficeArt is running whenever you use graphs, charts, organization charts, SmartArt, and WordArt. This chapter covers all the bases so that you can discover ways to make Office 2008's improved features work for you.

Getting the Nitty-Gritty on Graphs and Charts

Your Mac can make pretty much any graph and can do so superbly. You're especially lucky when you have a Mac coupled with Office 2008, which offers three superb graphing programs from which to choose. Call it an embarrassment of riches, call it smart planning, but whatever you call it, you can make amazingly beautiful and rich graphs with your Mac.

Each of the three graph applications that you have access to provides particular strengths that make it attractive, and we want you be able to choose the one that's right for the particular graphing need you have at any moment. The three applications are

✦ **Apple Grapher:** This application draws graphs of mathematical equations.

✦ **Elements Gallery:** Create bar charts, pie charts, and other graphs from tabular data. This feature launches Excel chart tools from Elements Gallery.

✦ **Microsoft Graph:** Similar to Elements Gallery charts, this application is included with Office primarily to provide backward compatibility while you transition to the new Excel charts.

Whenever we talk about graphs and charts, we remind you that Microsoft uses *graph* and *chart* interchangeably. Both refer to the same thing. We explore each of the applications mentioned in the following sections.

Graphing an equation with Grapher

Often people have math equations that they want to graph. In grade school, teachers used to foist the task of drawing graphs onto students. Today some teachers even require students to buy expensive graphing calculators. But rarely do they point their students to *Grapher* (see Figure 5-1), the built-in graphing program that comes with Mac OS X, and that's a shame.

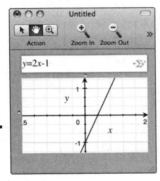
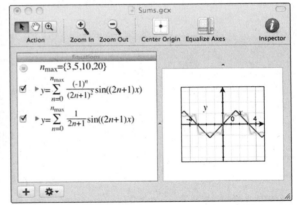

Figure 5-1: Examples of graphs in Grapher.

Use Grapher if you have an equation of some sort and want to convert it into a graph. Find Grapher in the Utilities folder inside the Mac OS X Applications folder. Although Grapher isn't part of Microsoft Office, you can copy the graphs you make in Grapher and paste them into Office applications. As you can see in Figure 5-1, Grapher can handle a wide range of graphing tasks from simple line graphs all the way to calculus, and it can even animate graphs for you.

Graphing data using Elements Gallery

Researchers, business people, students, and others often start with a data set that'd be much more understandable in graphical form rather than presented as a table-like collection of data arranged in columns and rows. The new Charts feature in Elements Gallery specializes in turning dull data into eye-poppingly great graphs.

Office 2008 handles graphs and charts in a completely new way. Even the way Office draws what you see onscreen is brand new. Also new is how you create a graph or chart. To make life easier for you, the tools and formatting options are consistent across Word, Excel, and PowerPoint. To give you all the power of Excel, the new default graphing application uses Excel to graph for other Office applications. Even if you're creating graphs in Word or PowerPoint, Excel is doing it all behind the scenes. With regard to making spectacular looking graphs the easy way, the new graphs take full advantage of the new Elements Gallery and the new Office-wide themes and templates.

Graphing in Word or PowerPoint

In the olden days, if you wanted to help someone escape from prison, you'd bake a cake, embed a file in it, and give it to your imprisoned friend. Okay, we carried this metaphor a little too far, but the concept of embedding applies to graphs in Word and PowerPoint. Graphs are embedded into Word and PowerPoint much like a file baked in a cake. Each graph is actually an Excel worksheet embedded in Word or PowerPoint. You format the graph to make it look the way you want in Word or PowerPoint, but the data lives and breathes in an Excel spreadsheet.

This is important to realize because when you create a graph by clicking a graph type from Elements Gallery in Word or PowerPoint, the first thing you see is an Excel workbook with some sample data in it. Perhaps you expected a graph but instead you got an Excel worksheet. Don't worry! Just drag the Excel window a little to the side, and underneath the Excel window, you see your graph is already in Word or PowerPoint. Your graph is just patiently waiting for you to put data into the Excel worksheet. After you paste or enter the data you want to replace the sample data, you can close Excel. When you go back to your Word or PowerPoint document, you see your new chart.

To make a chart in Word or PowerPoint, follow these steps:

1. **On the Elements bar, click the Charts tab.**

If Elements Gallery isn't visible, choose View➪Elements Gallery. The Elements Gallery isn't available in all views. You may have to choose a different view from the View menu to be able to use Elements Gallery.

2. **Choose your chart type by clicking any of the types in the gallery.**

If you can't find an exact chart type, select one that's closest in appearance to what you want.

This opens a Microsoft Excel 2008 worksheet with some sample data already filled in.

3. **Enter or paste data to replace the sample data.**

4. **Close Excel to get back to Word or PowerPoint.**

You don't have to save any data at this point in Excel if you're adding a chart in Word or PowerPoint.

You can make formatting changes to charts while you're working in Word, Excel, or PowerPoint. We explain how to make these formatting changes a little later in this chapter. If you want to view or change the data upon which your chart is based, take one of the following actions to access your data:

✦ **Right-click or Control-click a graph series:** Move the mouse pointer over the chart area to see the name of the chart element that is under the pointer. A *series* is the data in a column or row represented by a bar, area, line, or other graphical element of a chart

✦ **Choose Edit Data from the pop-up menu (as shown in Figure 5-2):** This brings up the Microsoft Excel data worksheet for this chart, and you can change or edit data as required. You can also increase or decrease the number of series and categories.

Figure 5-2:
Choose Edit
Data from
the pop-up
menu in
Excel.

Graphing in Excel

In this section, we discuss how to create a graph or chart from scratch when you are starting from Excel (not Word or PowerPoint). Excel is so smart at times, it's almost scary. For example, Excel can take your data and convert it into a beautiful chart that you can customize in your worksheet. Follow these steps:

1. Select any cell within a continuous row and column data set in Excel.

See Book III, Chapter 1 for tips for working in worksheets.

2. On the Elements bar, click the Charts tab.

If Elements Gallery isn't visible, choose View⇨Elements Gallery. If Elements Gallery isn't available, choose a different view from the View menu.

3. Click the chart type you want.

If you can't find the exact chart type you want, select the one closest in appearance. After you select your chart type, Excel places your chart in the current worksheet.

Excel has a special kind of worksheet — a *chart sheet,* which is just a sheet completely dedicated just to the presentation of your chart but is linked to the data on your worksheet. For more information about chart locations, see Book III, Chapter 5. To move a chart to or from a chart sheet, do the following:

1. **Click anywhere in the chart within your worksheet.**

As soon as a chart is selected, the menu bar shows a new menu option: Chart.

2. **From the Chart menu, choose the Move Chart option.**

The Move Chart dialog opens, as shown in Figure 5-3.

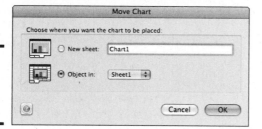

Figure 5-3:
Moving
charts in
Excel.

3. **Choose where you want to put the chart.**

As you can see in Figure 5-3, you have two choices:

a. Save as a chart in a new chart sheet.

b. Save as a chart object in one of the existing sheets.

4. **Click OK.**

Formatting charts in Word, Excel, and PowerPoint

If you've started a chart, you're probably a bit proud of yourself for doing it so quickly and easily. However, your chart might be very plain-looking at this stage, but you're using a Mac, and Mac users are noted for making graphics look outstanding. A Mac user can't be satisfied with just a default graph. People will think you're using Windows, which would just be embarrassing. (Okay, one of this book's authors uses Windows a lot, but he's going to leave that statement alone and let Mac users feel superior anyway!)

Get excited about the new chart-formatting options available in Office 2008. The new options are almost like taking your chart to a department store and letting it try on new clothes. The following headings show you ways you can customize how your chart looks.

Changing chart types with Elements Gallery

You can easily change the chart type just by clicking a new chart type in Elements Gallery. If you don't like the type, try on another. Try various chart types and pick the one that you think best represents your data.

Formatting chart elements with the Formatting Palette

The Formatting Palette is your friend when formatting charts and graphs. Be sure it's turned on by clicking its tab in the Toolbox. If the Toolbox isn't visible, click the Toolbox button on the Standard toolbar.

One thing you'll notice right away is that if you're following along on your computer, you have to click the Formatting Palette's disclosure triangles to expose and hide various sections of the Formatting Palette. The palette and its various panes are simply too long to fit onto the screen all at once. The number of panes you can display at one time is determined by the size of your screen and its resolution. It took three figures (see Figures 5-4, 5-5, and 5-6) just to show you all the panes!

The Formatting Palette changes depending upon what chart element is selected at any given moment and the formatting options you have applied, so your palette will probably never exactly match the figures in this section.

Starting at the top and working our way down the palette, here we go!

Select different elements of your chart and then explore the available options on the Formatting Palette. We encourage you to create a chart and experiment with the various options in the Formatting Palette to see what the controls do. We start at the top of the Formatting Palette and work our way down, describing each section as we move down the palette.

✦ **Font:** This section appears only when text is selected.

✦ **Alignment and Spacing:** As with Font, this section appears only when text is selected.

✦ **Number:** This pop-up menu lets you select the format of numbers. It appears only when text and/or numbers are selected.

✦ **Chart Options:** This is further divided into these sections:

  • *Titles:* From the pop-up menu, you can choose the entire graph, the horizontal (X) axis, or the vertical (Y) axis. Use the input field located beneath the pop-up to enter a title for the item chosen in the pop-up menu.

Text options

Click here to access
the Font Color Palette

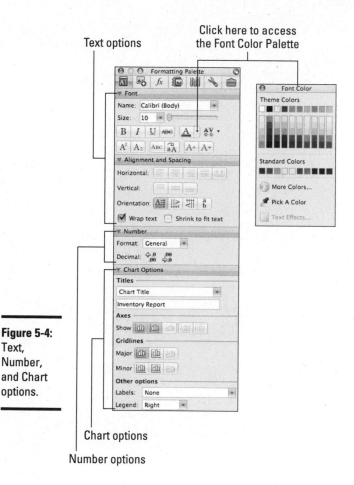

Figure 5-4:
Text,
Number,
and Chart
options.

Chart options

Number options

- *Axes:* Click the buttons in this section to toggle various axes on and off. Hold the mouse cursor over each button to determine what it controls.

- *Grid Lines:* Click the buttons in this section to toggle various axes on and off. Hold the mouse cursor over each button to determine what it controls.

- *Other Options:* Use the pop-up menus to choose Labels and Legends options.

Whenever a chart or any element within is selected, the Formatting Palette undergoes a transformation and displays a brilliant array of formatting controls. Figures 5-4, 5-5, and 5-6 show these formatting controls.

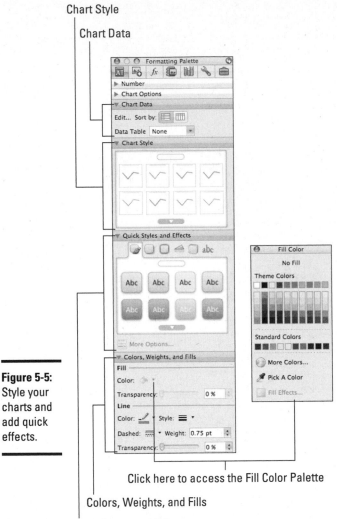

Chart Style

Chart Data

Figure 5-5:
Style your
charts and
add quick
effects.

Click here to access the Fill Color Palette

Colors, Weights, and Fills

Quick Styles and Effects

✦ **Chart Data:** This has the following options:

 • *Edit button:* This opens the Select Data Source dialog, as shown in Figure 5-7.

   The Chart Data Source dialog lets you set or modify the ranges used for chart labels and data. Here you can see that a series is a row or column of data. If you click the Switch Row/Column button in the middle of the dialog, you exchange rows with columns as presented in the chart. We recommend that you copy our simple data into a workbook and try this yourself so that you can see what happens. Experiment by adding a row called **March** and enter some data, or adding a column called **Shoes** and adding some data.

Click here to access the
Shadow Color Palette

Shadow

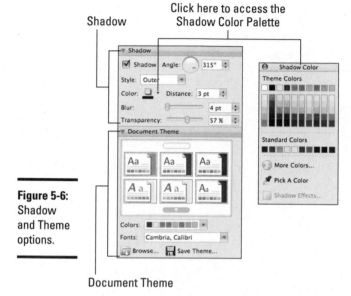

Figure 5-6:
Shadow and Theme options.

Document Theme

X-axis category labels (Column A)

Y-axis values (Range B2:C2)   Chart data range A1:C3

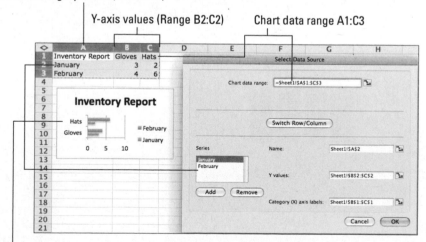

Figure 5-7:
Editing the data source.

Series

- *Sort By:* This button on the Formatting Palette does the same thing as the Switch Row/Column button does in the Chart Data Source dialog.

- *Data Table:* This feature lets you display the data range in the chart area. The pop-up is None by default, but you can choose to display the source data right on the chart either with or without a legend. This can be useful if your chart's on a chart sheet. If your chart's on a worksheet, you may have to drag the chart box to make it larger if it appears to be jumbled.

After you select an element on a graph, repeatedly press the left arrow (←) or right arrow (→) key on your keyboard to cycle through the graph so that you can select format individual elements for formatting.

✦ **Chart Style:** Getting dramatic effects for your graph data is amazingly simple to do in the Chart Style section of the Formatting Palette. Some really nifty styles have black backgrounds for the latest look. Click a style to apply it to a chart.

✦ **Quick Styles and Effects:** But that's not all! In the Formatting Palette, find the Quick Styles and Effects section (as shown in Figure 5-8). Before you start clicking the options, remember that the style you click is applied to whatever you've currently selected. For example, if you click the background that surrounds the chart, your style will be applied to the outer background of the chart. If you click a bar or pie section, that's what the formatting will be applied to. In certain chart types, notice that different parts of the chart are selected when you click a second time on a chart element, such as a bar or a pie slice.

✦ **Colors, Weights, and Fills:** Select various chart elements and apply these as desired.

✦ **Shadow:** Add shadows and control the shadow appearance with this section.

Figure 5-8:
The Chart Style and Quick Styles and Effects sections.

✦ **Document Theme:** Apply themes and save them from this portion of the Formatting Palette. We have a full discussion of themes in Chapter 6 of this minibook.

TIP

Users of previous versions of Office may notice commands have been rearranged on the Formatting Palette. Some options have moved to new or different sections and subdivisions.

Applying multiple formatting options

Alright, now have some fun and discover even more ways to format charts. First, some chart types let you drag slices of your chart. For example, in a 3D pie chart, you can grab individual slices and pull them out. Next, you can apply various formatting options in succession to achieve highly customized results. For example, when you turn on the shadow control and add a nice blur, you really bring out the pie slices. See Figure 5-9 where we applied the following formats to a 3D pie chart to make quite a striking difference!

1. First we selected the piece of the chart labeled B and then dragged that slice of the pie away from the center.

2. We selected an attractive document theme from the Document Themes on the Formatting Palette.

   We cover themes in more detail in Chapter 6 of this minibook.

3. We selected the entire pie and then used the Shadow control on the Formatting Palette to give the pie a nice soft shadow.

   You may be able to make out the shadow settings we used in Figure 5-9, but even if you can't, be sure to experiment with the Shadow controls on your own.

4. We used the Chart Options section of the Formatting Palette to toggle off the grid lines.

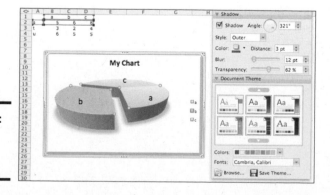

Figure 5-9:
A sleek-looking chart.

Discovering even more chart-formatting options

Amazing, isn't it? There's so much stuff you can do to make your charts look their best! The Formatting Palette allows you to do most of the formatting you need, but if you're really hard-core and want absolute control over your graph's fine-tuning, you can still do more. Follow these steps:

1. **Right-click or Control-click the chart area.**

2. **From the pop-up menu that appears, choose Format Chart Area or 3-D Rotation.**

   Either way, the Format Chart Area dialog opens (see Figure 5-10).

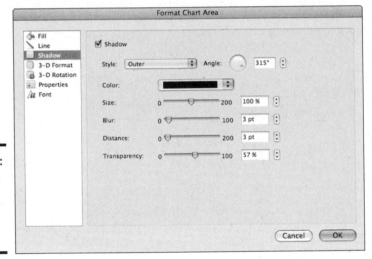

Figure 5-10:
Fine-tuning with the Format Chart Area dialog.

Each section of the Format Chart Area dialog allows minute fine-tuning of every aspect of every element of your graph.

Graphing the old-fashioned way in Microsoft Graph

Right about now, a few of you might be thinking, "Bah! Humbug to all this change!" Maybe you tried using some of Office 2008's new features, but the inability to twirl 3D bar graphs like a baton has you discouraged about all things "new." Or maybe you miss true old-fashioned vector-based patterns (like earlier Excel versions had); for many, they're essential for publishing graphs.

Aside from your personal preference in how you edit graphs or charts, another reason you might want the old charts back may be because you need to share files with users who are using older versions of Office, and they can't edit the graphs you send them!

Well, we have good news: The old interface is alive and well in Office 2008. Microsoft Graph (as shown in Figure 5-11) is still available just like it was in previous versions, and it sports the same old interface.

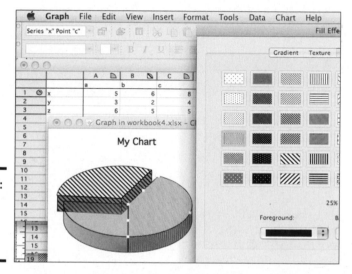

Figure 5-11:
Old school with Microsoft Graph.

Although Graph is still around for *backward-compatibility* reasons (so that charts made in older Office Graph versions continue to work in Office 2008), its future isn't promising. During the Office 2008 development, Microsoft made a huge investment in Excel graphing but didn't make any improvements to Microsoft Graph. The writing appears to be on the wall.

For the time being, Mr. and Mrs. Procrastinator and those frustrated by the new 3D charts can still use Graph. Here's how you get to Graph from Word, Excel, and PowerPoint:

1. **From the main menu, choose Insert⇨Object⇨Microsoft Graph Chart.**

2. **Click OK.**

   Microsoft Graph opens, and you can get busy creating your chart here. You'll miss all the cool effects that the new charting improvements in Office 2008 provide, but the upside is that your charts will be backward compatible with older versions of Office, both on Mac and Windows.

Making an Organization Chart with SmartArt Graphics

If you like the new look of charts in Office 2008, wait until you come face to face with new OfficeArt and see how it improves the appearance of diagrams. And that brings us to a quick question: How are charts and diagrams different? The easy answer is that whereas *graphs* crunch numbers and percentages and represent data values as points on a graph, *diagrams* show logical relationships, such as President, Vice-President, and Secretary of State. Another example of a diagram would show the relationships among parent, child, and sibling.

Like a new engine in your car makes it run a lot better, this new engine makes Office 2008 run better. One aspect of the new Office-wide engine is SmartArt Graphics. With the new SmartArt Graphics feature, you have lots of choices and many new customization features for everything that appears as a graphic onscreen. And yes, these graphics are smart, as you see in this section!

Organizing the organization chart

Usually you show who's in charge within an organization with an organization chart (as shown in Figure 5-12). With SmartArt Graphics, you can produce visually interesting organization charts, so everybody knows exactly who employees report to. The place to find the completely new and improved Organization Chart feature is the leftmost position of the Hierarchy graphics on the SmartArt tab of Elements Gallery.

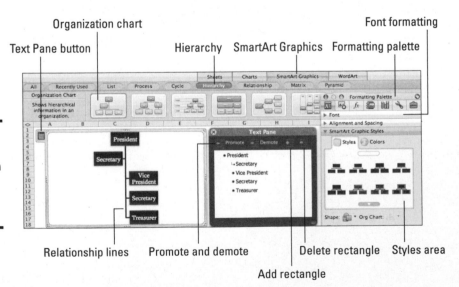

Figure 5-12: Creating an organization chart with SmartArt Graphics.

You don't have to be nervous anymore about trying to get the little boxes all lined up and having problems with connecting the lines in a clean and sensible way. If you've ever made an org chart in older versions of Office, you'll appreciate how SmartArt Graphics allows you to drag, drop, resize, and format the way you'd expect to. Getting an organization chart is now easier — follow these steps:

1. **Click the SmartArt Graphics tab of the Elements bar.**

   The Elements Gallery opens. If the Elements bar isn't visible, choose View⇨Elements Gallery.

2. **Click the Hierarchy category and then click the first item, Organization Chart.**

   A new organization chart is placed in your document (Word), sheet (Excel), or slide (PowerPoint).

3. **Replace the text in organization chart rectangles with your own text by clicking inside the rectangles and typing, or by entering text in the Text pane.**

You can work freely both in the Text pane and in the chart. You can turn the Text pane on and off by clicking the Text Pane button (see Figure 5-12). We take a look at how to work with the Text pane and then cover how to work within the chart. Notice that in this version of Organization Chart, *Assistant* has replaced *Subordinate*.

Working in the Text pane

Here are some tips for working in the Text pane:

✦ Replace the default text placeholders with your own text.

✦ The text in the lines of the Text pane is synchronized automatically with the shapes in the organization chart.

✦ Each time you press Return or Enter at the end of a line in the Text pane, an Assistant rectangle is created.

✦ Select a line of text; then click the Promote and Demote buttons to change the relationships.

✦ To add a new rectangle, click the Add Rectangle button (the one with the green plus symbol next to the Demote button).

✦ To remove a rectangle, select it in the chart and then click the red Delete Rectangle button, which is the minus sign – next to the right of the Add Rectangle button.

Working with Organization Chart

An *organization chart* is the graphical representation of relationships between positions, roles, and/or people. Now you can easily drag the shapes around, which is a vast improvement over previous versions of Organization Chart where this was nearly impossible. Here are some of the things you can do inside the chart:

✦ **Click a rectangle to select it.** You can add, edit, and delete text while a rectangle is selected. These shapes behave like ordinary text boxes, so you can also apply formatting to a shape while it's selected.

✦ **Drag shapes and the relationship lines are maintained.**

✦ **Add Assistants.** You can add Assistants (subordinates) using the Org Chart pop-up on the SmartArt Graphics Styles section of the Formatting Palette.

✦ **To delete a shape, select it and then press the Delete key.**

✦ **Change relationships.** To change the relationships, click the relationship lines to select them and then use the Org Chart pop-up on the SmartArt Graphics Styles section of the Formatting Palette to set the desired relationship. Experiment with this after you add Assistants to see how it works. The trick is to be sure that relationship lines are selected instead of the boxes.

Formatting your organization chart

Click the border of your OfficeArt-based chart to select the entire chart. Notice that the Formatting Palette offers a new section — SmartArt Graphic Styles — in addition to the other sections. Have fun experimenting with the Styles and Colors tabs.

Creating Your Own Shapes

You'll feel like a kid in a candy store as you explore the explosion of new SmartArt shapes in Elements Gallery. Each of them can be customized and formatted in endless ways so that you can get just the right look. Be sure to experiment with them all. Right-click or Control-click individual shapes and then choose Format Shape from the pop-up menu to fine-tune the shape precisely. Make sure you pay attention to the Formatting Palette at all times because options in this corner of the Toolbox change dynamically to reflect whatever's selected in your document, sheet, or slide.

Even with the plethora of new shapes to choose from in Elements Gallery, you may have a hankering for some good old-fashioned simple shapes, or maybe you want to try your hand at creating your own shapes.

Early in Chapter 4 of this minibook, we discuss the Shapes panel of the Object Palette in Toolbox. There you find the traditional shapes. Mixed in with the shapes are three special tools that you can use to create your own lines and shapes. The three most interesting of all of the tools in this section are Curve, Freeform, and Scribble.

Making a curvy line

Try using the Curve tool first, and after you get the hang of that one, try Freeform and Scribble. For our examples here, we focus on the Curve tool:

1. **From the main menu, choose View⇨Toolbox⇨Object Palette.**

2. **Click the Shapes panel and then choose Lines and Connectors from the drop-down list (see Figure 5-13).**

Shapes

Object Palette | Lines and Connectors

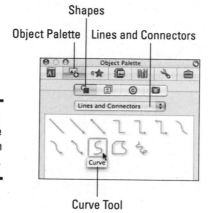

Figure 5-13:
Locating the Curve tool in the Toolbox.

Curve Tool

3. **Click the Curve tool.**

   The Curve tool is the one that looks like a handwritten S (see Figure 5-13). When you select the Curve tool, the cursor changes into a plus sign (+) to signify it's ready to start drawing a line as soon as you drag in the document.

4. **Drag a line into your document and click the mouse button as you drag; then drag the line in another direction and click again.**

   Your line continuously gets longer as you move the cursor around, until you double-click the mouse, which signifies the end of the line you're drawing. Each time you click while you drag, you create a point, which behaves as an axis for your line's curves.

This sort of drawing creates Bézier curves, as shown in Figure 5-14. Don't worry too much about where the name Bézier comes from, but do remember that this is the same technology that forms the foundations of mighty drawing programs, such as Adobe Illustrator and the like!

Figure 5-14:
A wavy line and a solid shape.

Drawing a solid shape

By doing a variation on the steps in the preceding section to create a curvy line, you can end at the same point you started and then double-click at the end the line, which results in a closed path. When you create a loop, or closed path, you get a solid shape, as shown in the right side of Figure 5-14.

Formatting your lines and shapes

Now the fun begins. After you draw a line or a solid shape, right-click or Control-click your line or shape and choose Format Shape in the pop-up menu.

If you right-click or Control-click a solid shape, it can be formatted with the Format Shape dialog. You can apply the new gradient fills that we discuss in Book IV, Chapter 3. If you simply select a line or solid shape, you have many formatting options offered to you on the Formatting Palette.

Lines and curves can be formatted with arrow and dot beginnings and endings, making the Curve tool ideal for drawing arrows and pointers to meet any need. Look for the Arrows section on the Formatting Palette whenever you select a line, and then Choose Style Begin and Style End options to format the beginning and ending points of your line.

If you know the name of a shape or line, you can use the Search box to find shape and line types easily.

If you want to read about the differences among vector shapes and pictures, look at this site:

www.indezine.com/articles/bitmapvectors.html

Editing points on a line or shape

For the ultimate in precision control of your lines and shapes:

1. **Right-click or Control-click your line or shape.**

2. **Choose Edit Points from the pop-up menu to display the Edit Points menu, as shown in Figure 5-15.**

   You get the same menu if you're working with a line.

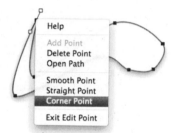

Figure 5-15: Editing a point on a solid shape.

When Edit Points is active, you can drag, add, and delete points as well as control exactly how the line behaves while it passes through each point. There's still more! Right-click or Control-click right on top of a point. Notice the little handles that appear at the point, as shown in Figure 5-16. Drag the handles to control how the line passes through the point.

Drag the handles.

Figure 5-16: Working the handles of a point on a line.

Making an Impression with WordArt

It's easier than ever to turn plain text into a work of art. The WordArt feature allows you to draw attention to the look of text as well as to the text itself, so be judicious in its use. If your purpose is to shout, WordArt can help you do that, but in most cases, WordArt can turn your text into something beautiful.

Creating WordArt

To use WordArt in Word, Excel, and PowerPoint:

1. **Click the WordArt button on the Elements bar of Elements Gallery.**

   The WordArt button is immediately to the right of the SmartArt Graphics button (refer to Figure 5-12).

2. **Click one of the styles in the Gallery.**

   A text box opens.

3. **Type some text in the text box, as shown in Figure 5-17.**

Formatting WordArt

If you have the time, you can get some really spectacular results by exploring the secrets of WordArt. In Figure 5-17, you see a little diamond beneath the letter *e* in *get.* In WordArt, you can drag the diamond to change the WordArt shape.

Figure 5-17:
Drag the diamond to change the WordArt shape.

Drag the diamond.

Here are some other ways to format WordArt while the WordArt text box is selected:

✦ Click a different WordArt style button on the WordArt tab in Elements Gallery.

✦ Apply any available formatting from the hundreds of options available to you on the Formatting Palette.

✦ Double-click the border of the WordArt text box and choose from the options in the Format Shape dialog.

✦ Right-click or Control-click the WordArt text box, and then choose Convert to SmartArt to radically change the nature of the text box. You'll have to select a SmartArt graphic from Elements Gallery, which changes automatically to SmartArt when you choose this option.

When it comes to formatting WordArt, Word offers formatting options and tools that are different from Excel and PowerPoint. You'd think there was a contest to see which set of formatting tools is better, and the decision was to go with both. In all three applications (Word, Excel, and PowerPoint), you can use the Formatting Palette to apply changes immediately to selected WordArt, and you can also right-click or Control-click, and then choose Format WordArt from the pop-up menu. So don't be worried when you see that Word's formatting tools appear to be completely different from Excel's and PowerPoint's. The formatting options are very different in Word.

Working in Layers

When you sit in a theater to watch a show production, the experience is very three-dimensional. As you sit facing the stage, your depth perception tells you that the objects placed closer to you appear larger, and objects that appear far away are generally smaller. Behind all these objects is the background. Sometimes it's a set, and sometimes it's just a curtain. Now while you sit in front of your computer, Office documents offer the same sort of 3D experience.

Starting at the back

Everything you see in Office is on a layer. Some things are closer to you than others. The layer that's furthest to the back is the background layer.

Whether it's Word, Excel, PowerPoint, or even an HTML e-mail in Entourage, there's a background layer that's like the back wall of a stage. This background layer is a thing unto itself that can be formatted independently, and everything else is in front of it. The background is accessed by the following four methods:

- ✦ **Word:** Choose Format⇨Background.
- ✦ **Excel:** Choose Format⇨Sheet⇨Background.
- ✦ **PowerPoint:** Choose Format⇨Slide Background.
- ✦ **Entourage:** Choose Format⇨Background Color.

Moving on to the layers on top

The next layer closest to you from the background is the text layer; and any additional objects, such as pictures, WordArt, shapes, or text boxes that are added are placed in layers closer to you with each additional object. Except for HTML mail, you can control the order of the layers of selected objects, and you can group objects together in the Formatting Palette in the Size, Rotation, and Ordering section.

You'll find that layers on top of other layers can make it hard to see everything sometimes. A shape can be on top of a picture, for example, and the shape can hide all or part of the picture. In Book II, Chapter 7, we explain how to control text flow in Microsoft Word so that shapes can be in front, in-line, or behind text. Realizing that objects are on layers helps when you read Book IV, Chapter 7 when you set up custom animations in PowerPoint.

In Figure 5-18, we finally answer the age old question: "Why did the chicken cross the road?" The answer, of course, is to be the top layer in our PowerPoint slide! In this figure, the road is the background to a PowerPoint slide. On top of the road are two text boxes. On top of the two text boxes is a SmartArt object. The chicken is at the front of everything.

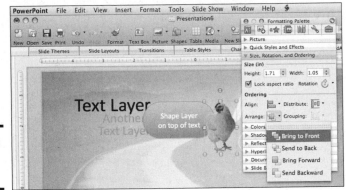

Figure 5-18: Layering text.

Chapter 6: Common Tools That Make Your Life Easier

In This Chapter

✔ Checking your spelling and grammar

✔ Working on your themes and templates

✔ Creating your own document themes

✔ Saving your work in various formats

✔ Equating figures and formulas with Equation Editor

✔ Programming and automating options

This chapter covers an eclectic collection of tools shared by Office 2008 applications, ranging from everyday features, such as spell checking, themes, and styles to specialized tools, such as Equation Editor, AppleScript, and Automator.

Proofing Your Spelling and Grammar

Fat fingers get a lot of the blame for spelling errors, and good grammar is as much a good habit as it is a skill. Clear communication with the right words, correct spelling, and richer command over language is essential at home, office, or school.

Running spelling and grammar checks

As we mention in Chapter 3 of this minibook, spelling errors are indicated by a red squiggly line under the misspelled word. You can rectify such errors by Control-clicking or right-clicking the word, and then choosing the correct spelling from the resulting pop-up menu. With the same procedure, you can also get help with grammar by Control-clicking or right-clicking words with green squiggly lines in Microsoft Word. Office 2008 also has *AutoCorrect,* which fixes spelling errors for you while you type; it's excellent, but you still need to know your homonyms because spelling and grammar can't tell the difference between words such as to, two, and too.

Even with all the squiggles, you might accidently overlook an error. A good idea is to always run the spell and grammar checkers before you share a document with someone. The most common way to fire up the spell and grammar checker is

✦ **In Word, choose Tools⇨Spelling and Grammar.**

Notice Word has both spell and grammar checking, but other Office applications have only spell checking.

✦ **In Excel, PowerPoint, and Entourage, choose Tools⇨Spelling (see Figure 6-1).**

In this chapter, we focus on aspects of spell checking that all the Office applications have in common. Be sure to visit Book II, Chapter 4 for details about spell and grammar checking; AutoText details are in Book II, Chapter 6; AutoCorrect settings are explained in detail in Book IV, Chapter 5; and dictionaries are covered in Book II, Chapter 4.

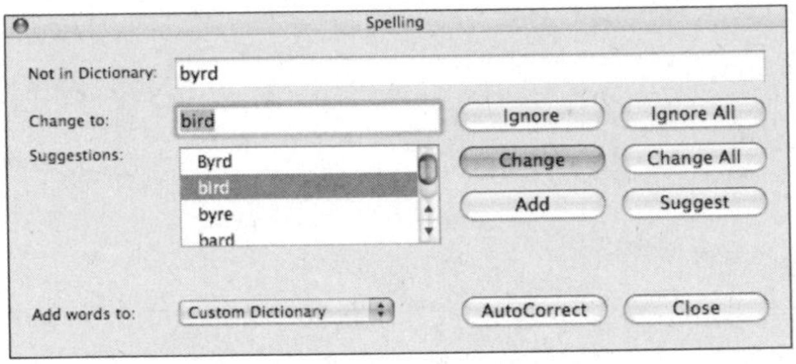

Figure 6-1:
Spell checking in PowerPoint.

Controlling the AutoCorrect feature

Every word you type is compared with at least two lists of words. One list is Word's built-in Dictionary, and the other is Word's built-in AutoCorrect list. You have control over both lists. For example, you can customize your dictionary however you want, and you can add additional dictionaries. You can even make your own dictionary in Word. If you want to create your own dictionary, check out the Create Dictionaries topic in Word's Help feature. In addition to regular dictionaries, you can create a dictionary to exclude from spell check so that it doesn't flag misspelled words when more than one spelling is acceptable, such as *color* and *colour*.

The mysterious blue flash that briefly underlines a word after you mistype for a second or two is AutoCorrect at work. This flash is Office's way of alerting you that what you typed was changed automatically based on a rule in the AutoCorrect preferences. Most people like the way AutoCorrect works by default, but it drives some people crazy to have their typing "corrected" for them in ways they don't want. If that sounds like something that irritates you as well, go to the menu bar, and choose Tools⇨AutoCorrect to get at these preferences, as shown in Figure 6-2.

AutoCorrect Preferences

Exceptions to the AutoCorrect rules

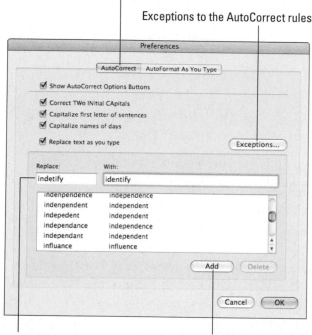

Figure 6-2:
Adding
a new
AutoCorrect
entry.

Replace spelling

Add new rule to the list

Notice the Exceptions button in Figure 6-2. Say you often abbreviate *University at Buffalo* as *UB,* and you don't want Office to change it to *Ub.* Do the following:

1. **Click the Exceptions button in the Preferences dialog, as shown in Figure 6-2.**

The AutoCorrect Exceptions dialog opens, as shown in Figure 6-3.

2. **Type your abbreviation in the Don't Correct box, click Add, and then click OK (see Figure 6-3).**

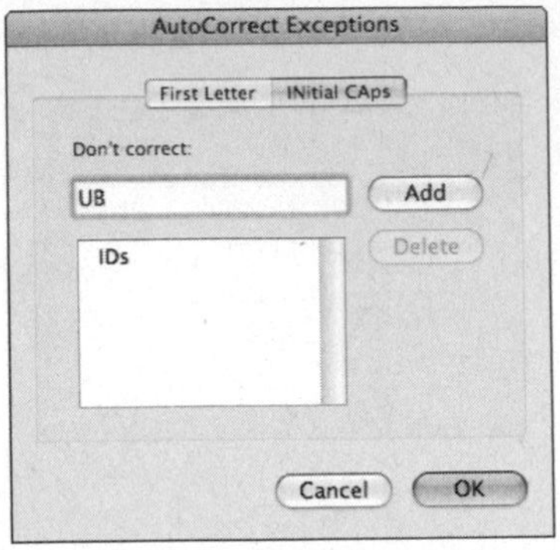

AutoCorrect Exceptions

First Letter | INitial CAps

Don't correct:

UB | Add

IDs | Delete

Cancel | OK

Figure 6-3:
Telling
AutoCorrect
to just let
UB be.

Configuring spelling and grammar preferences

Whenever you see green squiggly lines (in Word only), the grammar checker suggests you revise your words. Like AutoCorrect, the grammar checker has plenty of interesting settings. To get at these settings, do the following:

1. **In Word, choose Preferences and under the heading Authoring and Proofing Tools, click the Spelling and Grammar button.**

   The Spelling and Grammar Preferences dialog appears, as shown in Figure 6-4.

2. **Be sure that the Check Grammar as You Type check box is selected in the Grammar section of the dialog (see Figure 6-4).**

3. **Choose other grammar settings as desired.**

   For most people, we suggest checking all the boxes.

4. **Choose a writing style.**

   Click the pop-up menu and choose one of the following styles:

   - Casual
   - Standard
   - Formal
   - Technical
   - Custom

5. **Click the Settings button to fine-tune the selected writing style or create a custom writing style.**

   See Book II, Chapter 4 for more information about writing style settings.

Make sure these are checked.

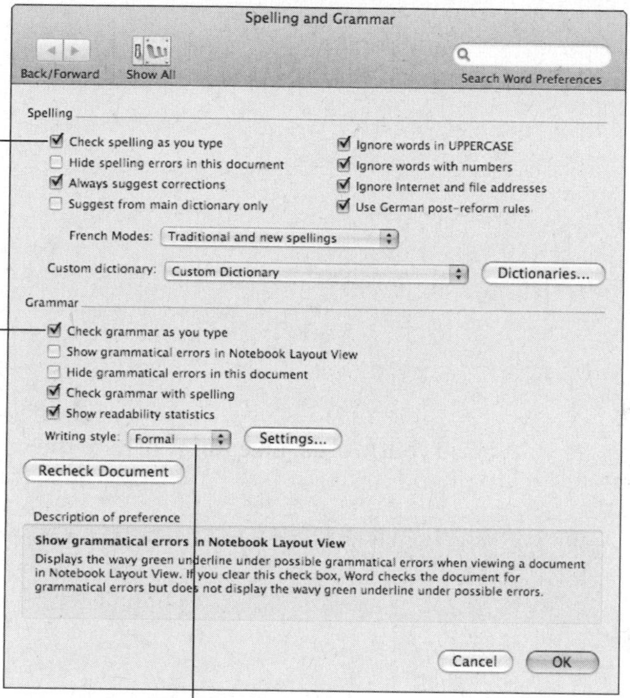

Spelling and Grammar

Back/Forward   Show All   Search Word Preferences

Spelling

☑ Check spelling as you type   ☑ Ignore words in UPPERCASE
☐ Hide spelling errors in this document   ☑ Ignore words with numbers
☑ Always suggest corrections   ☑ Ignore Internet and file addresses
☐ Suggest from main dictionary only   ☑ Use German post-reform rules

French Modes: Traditional and new spellings

Custom dictionary: Custom Dictionary   Dictionaries...

Grammar

☑ Check grammar as you type
☐ Show grammatical errors in Notebook Layout View
☐ Hide grammatical errors in this document
☑ Check grammar with spelling
☑ Show readability statistics

Writing style: Formal   Settings...

Recheck Document

Description of preference

Show grammatical errors in Notebook Layout View
Displays the wavy green underline under possible grammatical errors when viewing a document
in Notebook Layout View. If you clear this check box, Word checks the document for
grammatical errors but does not display the wavy green underline under possible errors.

Cancel   OK

Figure 6-4:
The spelling
and
grammar
settings in
Word.

Writing Style pop-up

Understanding Themes and Templates

Office has various ways that you can save formatting and document information so that it can be reused easily. Among the available file formats you
can use to open new documents are templates and themes. We discuss templates and themes throughout this book, but here we wish to introduce you
to these two concepts.

Themes can store a lot of information. The general idea of a *theme* is that
you can maintain a consistent look for your documents by applying a font
family and color formatting from a particular theme. Themes can be applied
to Word documents, Excel spreadsheets, and PowerPoint presentations.
Office comes with built-in themes, and you can edit and save your own
themes.

If you use Project Gallery to open a new document based on a theme, a new PowerPoint presentation opens with the theme that you select, even if the theme you chose was created by Word or Excel. PowerPoint is a special case in this regard because it has the most complete implementation of the entire theme concept. We expect that future versions of Word and Excel will have more theme-aware possibilities.

Themes can be saved from Word, Excel, or PowerPoint. When a theme has been saved from PowerPoint, it can have much more than just a font family and a color scheme. PowerPoint themes can include the formatting and content on slide masters and layout masters. We discuss slide and layout masters in detail in Book IV, Chapter 4, so for now just be aware that PowerPoint lets you put a lot more stuff in your themes than Word or Excel.

Themes can be applied and saved with the Formatting Palette in Word, Excel, and PowerPoint. In PowerPoint, slide themes are applied with Elements Gallery. We refer you to Book IV for more details about themes in PowerPoint.

You might think of themes as a sort of super style. For example, if you applied a text style in Word and then applied a document theme, the theme's font will override the text style. If you were to apply a QuickStyle to a shape in PowerPoint, when you apply a document theme, the QuickStyle is overridden. Even if you don't know what QuickStyles and shapes are, just remember that document themes can override other formatting that's applied already.

We want to point out some noteworthy quirks about the behavior of themes. Themes don't work the same way in each application. Themes can be applied to different elements depending upon which application you're using. Here are some of the differences:

+ **Word:** After you apply a style to text, themes can be used to change the styled text's appearance. Themes don't affect AutoShapes or WordArt. Themes do affect QuickTables.

+ **Excel:** This is almost the opposite of Word. Styled text isn't affected by themes, but AutoShapes, Graphs, and Charts do take on theme formatting. Tables and lists aren't affected by themes.

+ **PowerPoint:** You can apply themes to almost everything in PowerPoint.

+ **Office 2008:** Themes can be applied only to newer file formats such as DOCX, XLSX, and PPTX. If you open an older DOC, XLS, or PPT file, you won't find the Document Theme section in the Formatting Palette!

Applying a theme

The Formatting Palette in Word, Excel, and PowerPoint contains a Document Theme section at or near the bottom. You can turn on the Formatting Palette, if it isn't already visible, by clicking the Toolbox button on the Standard toolbar and then clicking the Formatting Palette button. See Figure 6-5.

Document Themes

Formatting Palette   Click arrows for more themes

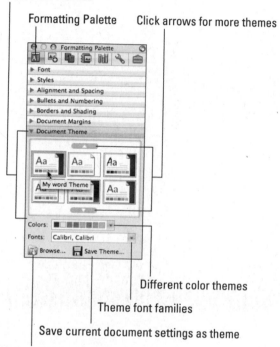

Figure 6-5:
Using
Document
Theme
on the
Formatting
Palette.

Different color themes

Theme font families

Save current document settings as theme

Browse Finder for more themes

To apply a theme to the current document, all you need to do is to click one of the document themes. This is slightly different in PowerPoint, where you use Elements Gallery as we discuss in Book IV, Chapter 3.

To use a different color scheme, click the Colors control on the Formatting Palette. A pop-up menu will be displayed, and you can select a different theme color scheme from the pop-up. See Figure 6-6.

To apply a different font family, similarly click the Fonts control on the Formatting Palette to display a list of available font families.

Click here for different color themes

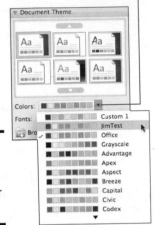

Figure 6-6:
Applying
a different
theme color
scheme.

As you work in Office applications, you'll most likely decide to format the colors of various things, such as text boxes, WordArt, Shapes, chart elements, and more. In various dialogs and on the Formatting Palette, you're presented with a color palette that looks like Figure 6-7.

Figure 6-7:
Document
theme color
variations.

The colors in the top row are the actual Theme Colors currently applied to the active document. The rows and columns of colors beneath the Theme Colors are lighter (tints) and darker (shades) values of those colors so that you can apply variations but still stay within your basic Theme Colors palette.

Saving your own theme

It's quite easy to make your own document themes. When you have colors and fonts formatted the way you like them, use the Document Theme section of the Formatting Palette (refer to Figure 6-5). Here are the steps to take:

1. **In the Document Theme section of the Formatting Palette, click the Save Theme button (see Figure 6-5).**

   The dialog in Figure 6-8 opens.

2. **Click the Expand Dialog button if the full version of the dialog isn't displayed.**

   Notice that the default option for this dialog is to display the My Themes folder.

3. **Give your theme a name.**

   Themes use the `.thmx` file extension.

4. **Click the Save button to finish saving your theme.**

Themes that are saved in the My Themes folder can be used by Project Gallery to open new PowerPoint presentations based upon theme colors and font families. Themes saved in this location also become available in the Formatting Palette, but you have to quit the application and then reopen it before you see freshly saved themes in the Formatting Palette. If you save themes in the My Themes subfolders, they become available to use in PowerPoint's Elements Gallery on the Slide Theme tab.

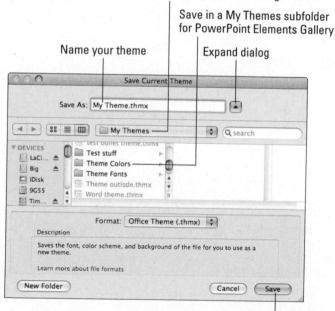

Figure 6-8: Saving your own document theme.

Save in My Themes for Project Gallery and Formatting Palette

Save in a My Themes subfolder for PowerPoint Elements Gallery

Name your theme

Expand dialog

Save your theme

Getting to know more about themes

In Book IV, Chapter 3, we explain how you can set precise colors for each of the color blocks of a document theme. For even more information complete with a practice document, you can take a free, online course about themes. To take the course:

1. **Open PowerPoint and click the Help button (the question mark) on the Standard toolbar.**

2. **Search for *themes*.**

3. **Select the Design Great Looking Documents with Themes topic.**

4. **Click the big Start Course button.**

Saving Everything as a Template

A *template* is a special file that remains unchanged when you open it. When you open a template, a copy of the template is opened with a new filename so that the template file itself remains unchanged. That way you can reuse the template repeatedly. When you save a document as a template from Word, Excel, or PowerPoint, your document is saved with the entire contents intact as a Word, Excel, or PowerPoint template. A template includes everything, such as the document's words, formatting, objects, pictures, graphs, charts, and content. Typically, people save a document that has room for additional content, such as a business letterhead, as a template.

Project Gallery has many built-in templates. You can also make your own templates for Project Gallery's My Templates category. The following section explains how to create your own templates.

The letter *t* in the file extensions `.dotx`, `.xltx`, and `.potx` alerts you that you're creating a template.

You can easily save Word, Excel, or PowerPoint files as templates in the My Templates folder. Here's a step-by-step procedure to follow:

1. **Create a document that has all the basic formatting you want to reuse**

   For example, a letterhead document in Microsoft Word.

2. **From the File menu, choose File⇨Save As.**

   The Save As dialog appears, as shown in Figure 6-9.

3. **Type a filename for your template in the Save As text box.**

4. **In the Format drop-down list, choose the appropriate template and then click the Save button.**

Depending upon which application you're using to create the template, the appropriate Format is one of the following:

- Word Template (.dotx)
- Excel Template (.xltx)
- PowerPoint Template (.potx)

To make it easy for you, Office automatically saves your template in the My Templates folder by default, which is convenient for most users. If your Save As dialog looks a lot different from Figure 6-9, click the Show/Hide Full Dialog toggle button, which is the triangle to the right of the Save As field. That changes your screen's appearance to match ours. For those who want to use alternative locations for templates, we explain how to do this in detail when we discuss Project Gallery's settings at the end of Chapter 2 in this minibook.

Choose your template format

Save in My Templates folder

Name your template   Show/Hide full dialog

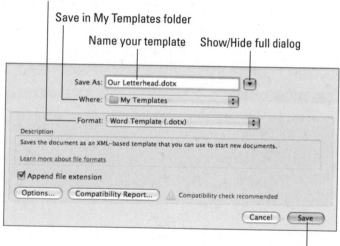

Figure 6-9:
Saving a file
as a Word
template.

Save your template

Sharing Files in Other Formats

Although Office uses the latest XML file formats, not everyone has the latest version of Microsoft Office. Office programs offer various file formats; choose File➪Save As➪*[Format]* to accommodate various compatibility needs. We feature examples specific to each application in other minibooks.

Saving as an Adobe PDF

Adobe's *Portable Document Format (PDF)* has long been a popular way to distribute documents, especially to people who don't have Microsoft Office.

PDF documents keep the look and feel of the original document even if the recipient doesn't have the needed fonts. You can also use PDFs to make it less convenient for others to edit a document.

One great new development in Office 2008 is that you no longer have to go through the Print dialog to make a PDF. Now you can choose File➪Save As➪PDF.

Saving as a Web page

A few years ago this was a really hot feature. You can turn your documents into Web pages that can be uploaded to a Web server to be delivered via a network or on the Internet. Although you can still do this, Google Docs and other online office products made Web-saving capabilities in Office almost obsolete.

Saving as a 97 to 2004 document

This is the format to use if you know your recipient has an older version of Microsoft Office or other older software products that know .doc, .xls, and .ppt file extensions. Before saving in this format, be sure to run Compatibility Report. You find this tool in the Toolbox:

1. **If the Toolbox isn't visible, click the Toolbox button on the Standard toolbar.**

2. **Click the Compatibility Report button (see Figure 6-10).**

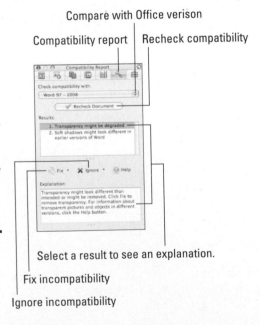

Compare with Office verison

Compatibility report | Recheck compatibility

Figure 6-10:
Checking compatibility with other Office versions.

Select a result to see an explanation.

Fix incompatibility

Ignore incompatibility

3. **Click the pop-up button to compare the current document against features available in specific Office versions.**

4. **Click the Recheck Document button to update the report.**

Getting Mathematical with Equation Editor

Teachers, students, scientists, and other academicians need occasionally to represent numeric equations that ordinarily aren't possible to type from the keyboard. The solution to this dilemma is Equation Editor, which comes with Office 2008. Equation Editor (see Figure 6-11) works in Word, Excel, and PowerPoint. Equation Editor included with Microsoft Office lets you type mathematical symbols and equations; it's made by Design Science. Equation Editor is a *light* version of MathType, which has more symbols and fonts. For information about the complete MathType package, please visit the Design Science Web site:

`http://snipurl.com/mathtype`

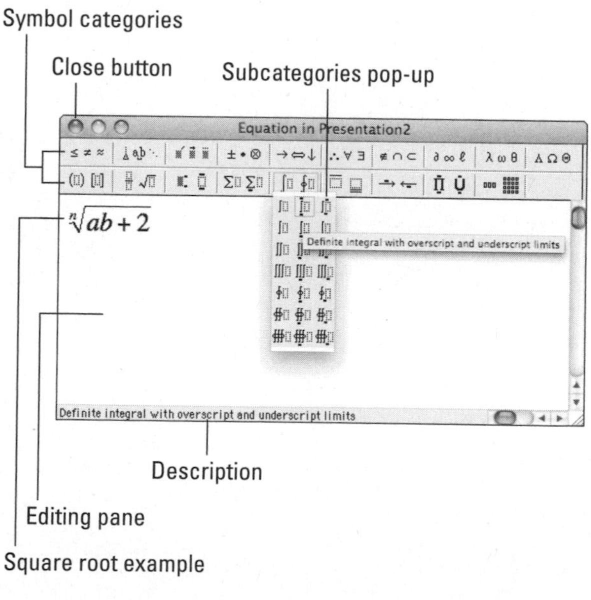

Symbol categories

Close button   Subcategories pop-up

Figure 6-11: Microsoft's Equation Editor.

Description

Editing pane

Square root example

Although Equation Editor looks complicated, it's actually quite easy to use. Follow these steps to create a symbol or a formula (see Figure 6-11):

1. **Position the cursor in your document, spreadsheet, or presentation where the symbol, formula, or equation is to be placed.**

2. **Choose Insert⇨Object⇨Microsoft Equation.**

   Equation Editor opens in its own window.

3. **Click a formula template from the symbols categories.**

   Some categories have submenus from which to choose. Descriptions appear when you mouse over the various symbols.

4. **Click inside dotted boxes to type numbers or text.**

   You can add text by simply typing in the Editing pane. For example, you can take a formula and turn it into an equation by typing **y=** in front of the formula.

5. **Click the red Close button when done.**

The result is an Equation Editor object in your document. To reopen Equation Editor to make additional edits to your object, just double-click the Equation Editor object in the document.

Programming and Automation Options

Not having Visual Basic for Applications (VBA) as standard with Office 2008 is no doubt a problem for many Office users. Microsoft did enhance AppleScript support tremendously for Office 2008, and it ships with *Automator Actions* (cool automation scripts) in all but the Home and Student edition.

Coping without VBA

We wish we could tell you some magical way to still have Office 2008 and VBA together. The best we can do is describe various strategies, none of them ideal, to help you cope without VBA. Here's a rundown of some common scenarios:

✦ **Stick with Office 2004 and tough it out until the next version of Office comes out.**

   If you've kept Office 2004 updated and also installed *Open XML Converter*, a free download from Mactopia, you can open and work with new Office XML file format documents right in Office 2004. You can also save in the new file formats from Office 2004. Documents that go back and forth between 2004 and 2008 will most likely lose formatting and some objects might be converted into pictures, so this isn't always a smooth ride. You don't get any of the new 2008 features this way except for the ability to use the new XML (eXtensible Markup Language) file format.

✦ **Install Office 2004 and 2008 side-by-side.**

Before you do this, consider using just one version of Entourage. Be advised: If you switch back and forth between Entourage 2004 and 2008, your mail could get split up between the two versions, and each version will have its own calendars, tasks, reminders, and so on.

✦ **Run Windows Office on your Mac.**

This is admitting defeat, but it's a viable option. We know of four different products, two of which are virtual machines that let you install and run Microsoft Windows on your Mac, and then subsequently install and run a Windows version of Microsoft Office.

- *Parallels Desktop for Mac Windows virtual machine:* Parallels lets you run Microsoft Windows and Mac OS X simultaneously. You need to purchase Microsoft Windows and a Windows version of Microsoft Office to use this product.

- *VMware Fusion Windows virtual machine:* Parallels lets you run Microsoft Windows and Mac OS X simultaneously. You need to purchase Microsoft Windows and a Windows version of Microsoft Office to use this product.

- *Paragon NTFS for Mac OS X:* NTFS for Mac OS X allows you to install and run Windows versions of Microsoft Office directly in Mac OS X without installing Microsoft Windows.

- *Mac OS X Boot Camp:* Boot Camp lets you boot directly into Microsoft Windows, completely bypassing Mac OS X. You need to purchase Microsoft Windows and a Windows version of Microsoft Office to use this product.

✦ **Run a Windows PC remotely.**

With Microsoft's free Remote Desktop Connection Client, you can run a networked PC right from your Mac. Doing so requires that you use a PC that's been configured to let you log in remotely. That PC has to have Windows and Microsoft Office installed on it as well before you could use it in place of Office for Mac. Remote Desktop Connection Client is a free download from Mactopia at

        www.microsoft.com/mac

✦ **Substitute AppleScript for VBA.**

Because AppleScript is Mac only, this isn't a cross-platform solution. Paul Berkowitz authored *VBA to AppleScript 2004 Migration Guide,* which helps VBA developers convert existing VBA code into AppleScript:

        www.mactech.com/vba-transition-guide

Being savvy with AppleScript

Deep down inside your computer is a scripting language — *AppleScript* — that's extremely powerful. Some applications on your computer support AppleScript just a little bit, but Office 2008 was designed to offer excellent AppleScript support. Great AppleScripts are waiting on the Internet for you to find them, particularly for Entourage, so you don't have to become a scripter to take advantage of Office's AppleScript capabilities. Apple has a Web site devoted to helping people figure out AppleScript. The URL is

```
developer.apple.com/applescript
```

Automating with Automator

An even easier way to automate your Mac than with AppleScript is with the Automator application. Automator allows you to create workflows from actions available for various applications. Office 2008 supports Automator, and with the exception of the Home and Student edition, Office 2008 comes with some Automator workflows (see Figure 6-12).

The secret to using Automator workflows is to look in the menu bar of any Office application, and just to the right of the Help menu is a script symbol. Click the Script Symbol menu to reveal a submenu that contains an About This menu, followed by Automator workflows.

In Book IV, Chapter 6, you find a great example of how to create an Automator workflow that imports a batch of pictures into PowerPoint. You can use that chapter as a boilerplate example for creating workflows in other applications.

Figure 6-12:
The Automator menu in Word 2008.

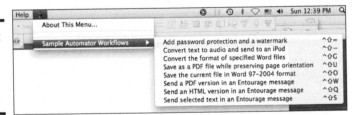

Chapter 7: Getting Help!

In This Chapter

- ✔ Getting familiar with the new Help interface
- ✔ Looking into newsgroups and community resources
- ✔ Checking for updates
- ✔ Finding helpful Office Web sites
- ✔ Getting some MVP assistance
- ✔ Joining the club
- ✔ Helping legal and medical professionals

*H*elp has changed! Really. In the past when you searched Microsoft Office Help, you'd enter some keywords and get results from a database on your hard drive. Today, searching for help happens online unless you don't have an Internet connection.

Now everyone has *Web 2.0*, which allows the entire world to communicate interactively with everyone else. Office 2008 is the first version of Office for Mac to take advantage of interactive Web technologies. Interactive Web technologies are often called Web 2.0 technologies. Office 2008 Help allows you to interact with the people who provide Help at Microsoft as well as to interact with other users who have the same products that you do. Suddenly, a community can help you, and you may not be aware but you're already connected to it. Just open the door!

Helping You with New Help

People at Microsoft have been listening to Office customers for more than 25 years. In that long time, they've heard their fair share of complaints and praise for their help and product support. The people of the Macintosh Business Unit (MacBU) at Microsoft in particular have gone out of their way to find, listen to, and change the way they provide help. As a result, the Help feature in Office 2008 has been completely restructured. No longer does Help simply search a fixed database file saved on your computer. Help now defaults to search a robust database that's continuously updated and located on Microsoft's online servers. Instead of taking months or years for customer feedback to be incorporated into Help, the Help database is continually updated with new content, maybe even while you read this chapter!

When you use Help from any Office application, you're actually starting a specialized Web Help browser. This opens many new possibilities, including the ability to provide sound, animation, and user feedback. The Help browser allows you to choose help from a variety of sources, including traditional Help searches, community forums, and specialized training. You're no longer limited to simply searching for keywords.

Of course, you may not always be connected to the Internet, so Help continues to have a database of Help topics right on your computer so that you can use Help no matter where you are, albeit in a more limited way.

Browse Help to discover more about Office. Figure 7-1 shows the new Microsoft Word Help interface. Be sure to explore Help in all the Office applications. When browsing Help topics, click the triangles that are sprinkled throughout Help to expose additional content. In Figure 7-1, we clicked the triangle next to Word Training in the Contents list so that we can get at the free Training Courses and free training videos.

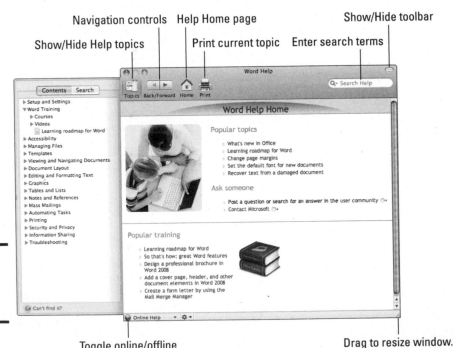

Figure 7-1: The Word Help feature.

Sending feedback to Microsoft

If you've ever wished you could talk to the people who write the Help topics, you'll be pleased to discover that your wish has been granted. We've already noticed a remarkable improvement in the content of Help topics, but ample room is there for further progress. That's why it's so important for you to lend a hand by offering your thoughts about Help topics.

And you can easily lend that hand. At the bottom of most Help topics, you see this question: "Was this information helpful?" Click one of the three buttons: Yes, No, or Somewhat and then fill in the small form, an example of which is shown in Figure 7-2. Doing so takes only a moment, and you can be sure that one of the people who authors these Help topics will read your comments.

MacBU is a small, but passionate group within the large expanse of Microsoft, and the people in it pay attention to your feedback.

If Microsoft nailed a topic just right, good for them! Please, let them know. If Office Help missed the boat partially or completely, don't lambast. Instead, explain exactly what you're seeking and how the Help topic could be improved. The person who reads your comments has devoted her professional career to helping people. Be polite and instructive in your commentary, and the Help topics will evolve and get better and better as time passes.

> Please help us improve by providing more feedback.
>
> ○ Information is wrong
> ○ Needs more information
> ○ Not what I expected
> ○ Other
>
> [   ]
>
> Characters remaining: 850
>
> (Back) (Submit)

Figure 7-2:
Sending
feedback in
Help.

Asking someone for help

The Help database covers almost every common topic that comes up, but at times, you might be doing something complex or new that's not addressed in Help yet, or you just can't wait around for the Help topic to be updated. In these situations, search the user community to see whether your question has been asked and answered already in a public question and answer forum. After all, Office has been around 25 years, so a huge body of knowledge is in these communities. First, search with keywords to see whether somebody's already answered it. Then, if you don't find what you're looking for, go ahead and post your question to a forum.

Before posting a question, be sure to look up the product version and include this information in the question that you post. You can find the version number in the first menu item under the application name in the upper-left corner of your screen. Figure 7-3 shows you where to find this information for Word, by choosing the About Word option from the application menu. Figure 7-3 also shows the resulting information window where you will find the version number and the number of the latest update that has been installed. The user community consists of other computer users ranging from novice to expert. We can't guarantee that someone will respond to your inquiry, but usually within a few days (or even a few minutes if you're lucky), you see a response to your message.

Click on the application menu.

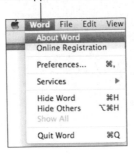
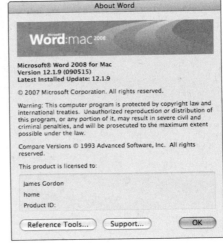

Figure 7-3:
Click here
to find a
program
version.

Occasionally Microsoft employees respond to postings, but that's rare. If you see an unanswered question while searching or browsing the user community, feel free to jump right in and offer your thoughts if you know the answer. The community is a two-way street that relies on people like you to help with answers and to ask questions.

If you'd prefer to contact Microsoft for help, click the Contact Microsoft link in the Help window's home page (see Figure 7-1) to be taken to a Web page with many options, such as Learn More About, How-To, Training, and more. This is also a good choice for IT experts to click if they wish to find deployment information.

Getting online training for free

In the past, Help has been pretty bland. Not anymore! Now you can get free online training courses and free training videos about popular topics right from Help. Refer to Figure 7-1 and follow these instructions to find these new resources in Word, Excel, PowerPoint, and Entourage.

1. **Open Help (see Figure 7-4).**

   You can use any one of the following methods:

   - From the menu bar, choose Help⇨[*Application*] Help.
   - Press the Help button (if available) on your keyboard.
   - Click the question mark icon (if available) on any toolbar.
   - Right-click or Control-click and then choose Help (if available) from the pop-up menu.

2. **Click the Topics button on the Help toolbar to display the Help drawer.**

3. **Click the Contents tab on the drawer.**

4. **Click the second triangle down on the left next to [*Application*] Training to disclose the subtopics.**

5. **Click subtopic triangles to disclose individual courses and videos.**

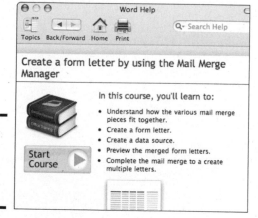

Figure 7-4: Help offers free online training courses.

Utilizing Newsgroups and Community Resources

Using Post a Question or search for an answer in the user community in the Ask Someone section of Help (refer to Figure 7-1) is an uncomplicated, new way to view and participate in a traditional online community resource, *newsgroups*. Thousands of queries are posted on these newsgroups, and most have detailed responses with resolutions and workarounds.

Go to any archive in these newsgroup postings and you'll find a treasure trove. One great advertising-supported resource for searching archived newsgroup posts is Google Groups. In particular, give the Advanced Groups

Search link a try. You can easily keep the results Mac-focused by including *Macintosh* in your search. Find Google Groups at this URL

`groups.google.com`

We highly encourage you to join the global community and give back something rather than simply take from it. Believe it or not, you know things that are of value to others, so why not share your knowledge with them? Look for recent postings you can answer or look for posted answers that you could improve upon. People who are willing to take this extra step typically install specialized newsgroup-reading software on their computer. Head to our Entourage minibook, Book V, Chapter 4, where we explain how to configure and use Entourage with newsgroups.

Checking for Updates

Checking for updates and installing them can be a pain; believe us, we know. But you need to do it anyway. Please. And with the improvements made in the update process, updating is less of a pain these days than it used to be.

Your Mac is more than just a mere computer. Apple has invested heavily in making it a complete user experience. This experience relies upon a complex interaction of your hardware, the operating system, and the application software. Both the operating system and the application software are updated routinely to keep them running like well-oiled machines.

And people at Apple and Microsoft really do talk to each other, which is a good thing because it means that both companies can rely on each other to resolve problems, whether hardware- or software-related. Nobody likes when a problem affects Microsoft Office, and both companies have worked very hard to provide corrections for any problems via automatic application and operating system updates.

Your job in all this is to make sure that you keep both your operating system and Microsoft Office updated. Fixes made by Apple may not have an effect unless you update Office, and fixes by Microsoft may not take effect until you update Mac OS X.

Here are the two key ways to keep up to date:

✦ **Apple Software Update:** Use the Apple Software Update program, which is the best way to keep your operating system and all your Apple applications up to date. To run it, choose Apple Menu➪Software Update.

✦ **Microsoft Office update:** The other half of the equation is to keep Microsoft Office up to date. From any Office application, choose Help➪Check for Updates (see Figure 7-5). Just click the Check for Updates button. We recommend that you leave the automatic setting at Check for Updates Weekly.

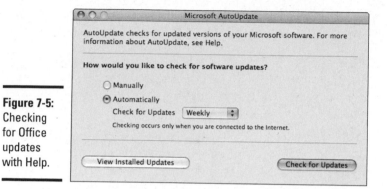

Figure 7-5:
Checking
for Office
updates
with Help.

Even if you don't run the updates for your Mac OS X and Microsoft
Office from the menus we list on your own, don't be surprised if the
update engine appears on its own as a dialog or a window and then asks
you to download and install new updates. Pay heed to these suggestions
and do what's needed.

Getting Help from Office Web Sites

Although *many* groups at Microsoft seem to have gotten the message to
build standard Web pages that look as good on non-Windows machines
(read: *Mac*) as they do on Windows machines, not *every* group has gotten
the message. We help steer you to some excellent resources outside
Redmond. MacBU has created an entire Web site — *Mactopia* — just for Mac
users. This is one place on Microsoft's site that really does get it right. Visit
the site at www.microsoft.com/mac.

Mactopia is *the* place to get the latest downloads of templates and additional software products, such as Microsoft Messenger and Remote Desktop
Connection Client, as well as Office updates that can be saved as files so you
can install them from CDs or flash drives.

Getting freebies from Mactopia

More Office is to be had than what comes with the install discs. You can also
get hundreds of great templates for Word, Excel, and PowerPoint from the
Mactopia site.

Figure 7-6 shows the Mactopia templates site. One good thing is that
most of the older templates still work in Office 2008. For example,
templates for Office 2003 for Windows and Office 2004 for Mac are available
on the Microsoft Web site. You can download Office 2004 templates from
www.microsoft.com/mac/templates.mspx.

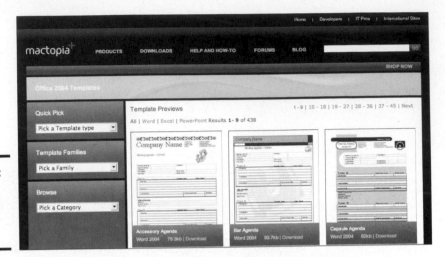

Figure 7-6:
The
Mactopia
templates
site.

Getting freebies from the Microsoft Office Web site

Use Microsoft's main Office Online Web site (http://office.microsoft.com). What's really great is that all the clip art works with Office 2008. We explain how to use clip art from the Microsoft Office site with Clip Gallery in Chapter 4 of this minibook.

Also pretty good is that most of the templates on the Microsoft Office Web site work just fine with Office 2008. You are likely to run across two obstacles when using this site to obtain templates.

✦ Because Office 2008 doesn't support Visual Basic for Applications (VBA), any template with macros doesn't work.

✦ Due to the incompatible design of the Microsoft Office Web site, you can't download most templates using standard Web browsers. The only remedy is to download Office 2007 templates using Microsoft's Internet Explorer Web browser in Microsoft Windows on a PC that also has Microsoft Office 2007 installed. Then move the template files from the Windows PC to your Mac using email, a flash drive, CD, file sharing, Mesh.com, OfficeLive, or other means. This whole rigmarole is supposed to ensure that templates are downloaded only by licensed users of Microsoft Office. For Mac users, the Microsoft Office site's draconian digital rights management (DRM) policies prevent licensed Microsoft Office users from getting the content. Granted, it's a freebie, but the Microsoft Office Web site deserves a raspberry for a policy of intentional incompatibility.

As we explain in Chapter 2 of this minibook, templates work best in the My Templates folder.

Making the Most of MVP Sites

An exceptional group of independent experts, not Microsoft employees, take commitment to the community very seriously. Every year Microsoft recognizes exceptional contributors to technical communities by presenting to them the Most Valuable Professional (MVP) award. We're proud to say that we've been recipients of the MVP award for several years.

In addition to their personal Web sites and blogs, MVPs have gone to the trouble of assembling Web sites that deal with each Office application. At each site, you find a treasure trove waiting for you to explore. We've listed the best of the best!

Welcome to Word:mac

An astounding amount of information about Microsoft Word is on this site (`http://word.mvps.org/Mac/WordMacHome.html`). The site is arranged so that you can browse or search. We give you the URL to the main site, but if you're writing professionally, find the "Bend Word to Your Will" document by Mac MVP Clive Huggan. We highly recommend that you search for his article and download it.

Excelling with Excel MVPs

We did mention that MVPs are independent experts, right? As it turns out, the Excel MVPs haven't put together a combined MVP site. Rather, each of them has contributed to the community in various ways. And to be honest, the Excel MVPs are partial to the Windows version of Excel. Nonetheless, you'll find some valuable insights and free templates that can be garnered from their Web sites. A link that lists the Web sites of the Windows Excel MVPs can be found at `http://mvps.org/links.html#Excel`.

One Excel MVP makes a daily video podcast on iTunes. Excel MVP Bill Jelen, or *Mr. Excel,* provides amazing content for free in highly enjoyable segments. This is one podcast you're sure to want to subscribe to. You can get to his podcasts easily in iTunes; follow these steps:

1. **Open a Web browser.**

2. **Go to this URL:**

   ```
   http://phobos.apple.com/WebObjects/MZStore.woa/wa/
   viewPodcast?id=82989468
   ```

3. **When prompted, allow the Web browser to open iTunes.**

   Wait while iTunes opens and then locates the Mr Excel podcasts. After a short wait, you see the list of available podcasts.

4. **When you see the list of podcasts, double-click any that seem interesting.**

Another Excel MVP, Jon Peltier, has made a specialty of working with charts and graphs. His Web site has everything you could possibly imagine about charts and graphs and explains how to make charts and graphs from the simplest to the most complex. His site is Windows-centric, so remember that add-ins, EXE files, and VBA don't work with Excel 2008. To get a complete list of Jon's chart links, visit http://peltiertech.com/Excel/Charts/ChartIndex.html.

PowerPointing MVPs

PowerPoint MVPs are much more fun than the other MVPs. We think the very social and showy nature of PowerPoint attracts people who are outgoing and friendly, so their Web sites tend to be livelier than the rest. Like other MVP sites, you don't have a shortage of generosity from PowerPoint MVPs. You'll find boatloads of templates, how-to articles, and more at these sites.

Steve Rindsberg, a brilliant and friendly man hosts a famed Web site known as the PowerPoint Frequently Asked Questions site, or PowerPoint FAQ (www.pptfaq.com/index.html). You're fortunate because Steve goes out of his way to make sure his site is Mac-friendly. If a question about PowerPoint hasn't already been answered authoritatively on his site, we'd be quite surprised.

Geetesh Bajaj (who modestly didn't write this part of the book because it's about his own Web site) is an MVP with the site Indezine (as shown in Figure 7-7) found at www.indezine.com. This Web site is a lively, ever-changing mix of magazine-style articles; free design templates; free background templates; links to an amazing array of resources, how-to articles, reader comments, training, photos to download, clip media, sound stuff, RSS feeds, and interviews — everything you could possibly expect to find in an online magazine. Whew!!

You'll also find product reviews and articles about hardware, such as projectors and remotes, for presenters. Be sure to click the Info link to subscribe to the mailing list so that you'll receive via e-mail free templates and interesting articles on a regular basis.

Connecting with Entourage MVPs

Collaboration is key with Entourage, and the MVPs have put together a superb, collaborative site for this Office application. The Entourage Help Page, as shown in Figure 7-8, (www.entourage.mvps.org) offers more than just help; it's a dynamic site updated regularly. Whether you have a special configuration problem, need synching instructions, or want to explore in more depth how Entourage works with Microsoft Exchange, you'll find useful information here. The range of topics discussed is very large. Click the Search A–Z Index link or the Site Navigation Map link, and you have access to everything you could possibly know about Entourage.

Figure 7-7:
The
Indezine
magic
carpet ride.

Figure 7-8:
Getting
help from
MVPs for
Entourage.

Entourage has supported AppleScript for a long time. Consequently, many scripts are available to help you. Be sure to check out the many popular scripts available for download. For example, use the search term *duplicates* in the search box in the upper-left part of the site's window to list the site's content relating to this popular topic.

It only makes sense that one of the principal methods of keeping up to date with Entourage goings-on is by e-mail. Before there was a Web site and an online community, there was a mailing list. Now there's a special, free list — *YouTalk*. Subscribe and help comes to you, rather than you going to a Web site to get assistance. You can participate or simply sit back and learn. Look for the Subscribe to the Entourage YouTalk List link near the top right of The Entourage Help Page.

Join the Club!

If you're not impressed with all the electronic collaboration and communication, you might just be a people person rather than a virtual-people person. Sharing stories about your latest software find or hardware configuration, or just sharing a cup of coffee with friends might be the best way for you to interact with real, live people!

Joining a user group

User groups have regular in-person meetings with presentations and parties. Novices and geniuses are all in the room together, sharing their experiences.

Some user groups get big discounts and free stuff from manufacturers. You can almost always get free books from user groups if you're willing to write short reviews.

Apple and MacBU are strong user group supporters. Get involved. Visit the Apple User Groups Web site (www.apple.com/usergroups) to search for a group and to get answers to these questions:

+ Why join a user group?

+ Who joins user groups?

+ What groups are near me?

Joining the Customer Experience Improvement Program

Well, the Customer Experience Improvement Program (CEIP) isn't actually a program to improve Microsoft's customers. The customers are fine. What Microsoft really means is that customers can help improve Office by sending feedback directly while using the programs. This is a non-intrusive way to help Microsoft track down and fix serious software problems. Usually, this comes into play when an Office application crashes and you see a dialog asking whether it's okay to send an error report to Microsoft.

Joining the program is completely voluntary. Find a setting in the [*Application*] menu⇨Preferences⇨Feedback dialog for Word, Excel, PowerPoint, and Entourage that allows you to join the program of each application individually. You may also be asked whether you want to join during the install process (see Figure 7-9).

When the CEIP kicks in on your computer, Office gathers information about itself and what was happening at the time of the problem. Microsoft Error Reporting Program (MERP 2.0) creates a log file and presents a small form where you describe step-by-step the actions you took just prior to the problem event. You can take a look at the log file and decide for each event whether you wish to submit a report.

MacBU gathers the log files and analyzes the reports sent by program members. The goal is to fix serious bugs as soon as possible. Often, a substantial number of reports are needed to discern a trend or detect something in common. Some bugs are very esoteric, pertaining to a specific brand or model, and affect only a few users working on particular hardware. We encourage you to join and participate in the CEIP.

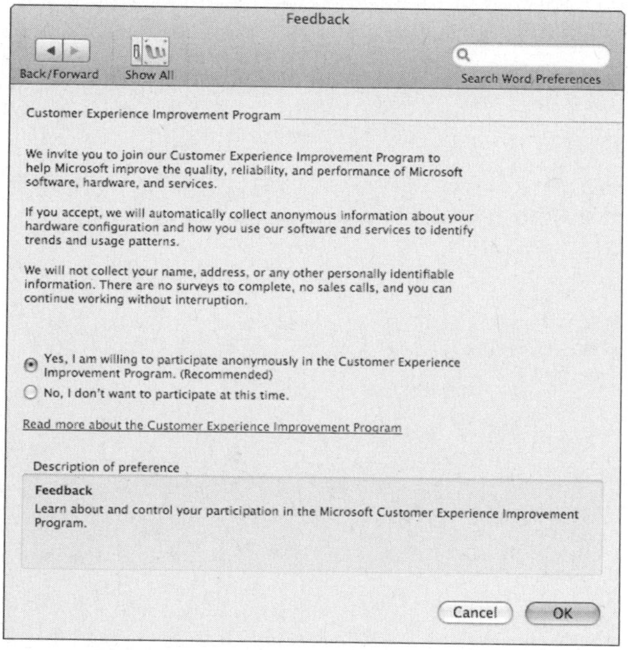

Figure 7-9:
Joining
CEIP from
Preferences.

Getting Help for Legal and Medical Professionals

A good attorney is worth her weight in gold, and many lawyers prefer Macs. Likewise physicians who know how to use a Mac and an iPhone together can save lives. Each professional should consider running a professional practice on Apple hardware and software. Macs might be the better choice to track billable hours, keep records, and maintain privacy and security, which are high priorities. In Book II, Chapter 6, we include instructions on how to create a Table of Authorities, which is of interest to legal professionals.

We worry that sometimes people are misled into thinking that Microsoft's Mac version of Office is unsuitable for professionals. No matter what your profession is, you'll find tips and suggestions on the Internet. Here we provide three links for professions that we think are prime candidates for using Macs:

✦ Attorneys

   www.themaclawyer.com

✦ Medical Practice

   www.macpractice.com/mp
   www.primarypsychiatry.com/aspx/articledetail.
      aspx?articleid=1099

Book II

Word 2008

The 5th Wave   By Rich Tennant

"It says, 'Seth — Please see us about your idea to wrap newsletter text around company logo. Signed, the Production Department.'"

Contents at a Glance

Chapter 1: Getting to Know Word's Interface

In This Chapter

✔ Opening new Word documents

✔ Understanding the Word views

✔ Viewing your document in Print Layout View

✔ Taking notes in Notebook Layout View

✔ Engaging an audience in Publishing Layout View

✔ Taking a toolbar moment

✔ Customizing Word the way you want it

To think that less than 30 years ago, the mere idea of having a computer with a word processor in most homes, much less most businesses, was just a prediction by idealists. Back then you were really high-tech if you had an IBM electric typewriter. Here you are today with Microsoft Word, an utterly amazing tool, just about everywhere.

Welcome to the Word minibook. We start by going over the various layouts you'll find in Microsoft Word. From there, we encourage you to explore and customize as you go. For information on any Office 2008 features that work the same in Word, Excel, PowerPoint, and Entourage, check out Book I.

So much is new in Word 2008. Along the way, we point out some exceptionally useful features that you may have missed, or perhaps heard about but haven't investigated yet.

Opening Blank Word Documents

Before we describe Word's interface, launch Word. The most sensible way is to click Word's icon from the Dock. When you click Word's Dock icon, one of two different things happens, depending upon the settings you've chosen in Project Gallery. (We describe Project Gallery's settings in Book I, Chapter 2.)

✦ **If Project Gallery does not launch when applications are opened,** Word opens a new, blank document in the view that was last used. (We describe views in the following section.)

✦ **If Project Gallery launches when applications open,** follow these steps:

1. *Click the New tab, if it isn't selected already.*

2. *In the Category list on the left, choose Blank Documents.*

3. *Set the Show filter to Word documents, as shown in Figure 1-1.*

After you follow these steps, you can choose from the following (see Figure 1-1):

- *Word Document:* Opens a new, blank Word document in the last used view.

- *Word Notebook Layout:* Opens a new, blank Word document in Word Notebook Layout View.

- *Word Publishing Layout:* Opens a new, blank Word document in Word Publishing Layout View.

Blank documents

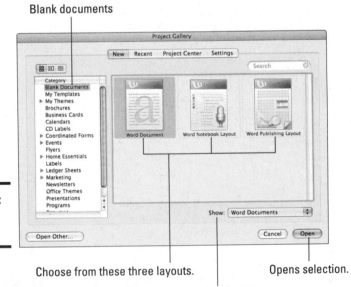

Figure 1-1:
The Word
layouts.

Choose from these three layouts.   Opens selection.

Set Show filter to Word Documents.

You can double-click one of the layouts in Project Gallery, or you can select a layout and then click the Open button to open it. If you click the Cancel button, a new, blank Word document opens in the most recently used view.

If Word is already running, you can open a new, blank document in the most recently used view. Choose from the following:

✦ **Click the New button on Word's Standard toolbar.** When you click the small triangle next to the New button, a submenu appears from which you can choose a layout.

✦ **Choose File⇨New Blank Document.**

✦ **Press ⌘-N.**

Looking at Word's Views

Word's View menu is a good place to start examining Word's interface. When you choose View, the topmost section lists all the available Word views (as shown in Figure 1-2). You can choose from the following:

✦ **Draft:** Shows a simplified view of your document along with the names of text styles that have been applied. Content isn't displayed the way it will look when you print.

✦ **Web Layout:** Word approximates what your document will look like if you save it as a Web page and then open it in a Web browser.

✦ **Outline:** With heading levels, (which we explain in Chapter 3 of this minibook), you can organize your document into an outline. Text can be promoted and demoted in levels that you specify with the Outline toolbar, which turns on automatically when you choose Outline view.

✦ **Print Layout:** Print Layout View shows you how your document will look when you print. See the section, "Working in Print Layout View," later in this chapter for more.

Book II
Chapter 1

Getting to Know
Word's Interface

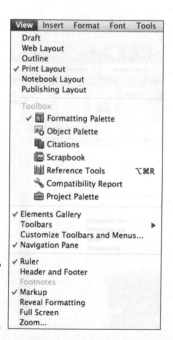

Figure 1-2:
View menu
options.

✦ **Notebook Layout:** Notebook Layout View enables you to take notes and record audio that's synchronized with your text while you type. We discuss this in the section, "Taking notes in Notebook Layout View," later in this chapter.

✦ **Publishing Layout:** Newsletters, brochures, flyers, and even small magazines can be created in Publishing Layout View. Publishing Layout View is a new Word 2008 feature, which we discuss in the section, "Designing in Publishing Layout View," later in this chapter.

Figure 1-2 shows Word's complete View menu. In addition to using the View menu, you can switch from one view to another by clicking the view buttons, as shown in Figure 1-3, in the lower-left corner of the document window.

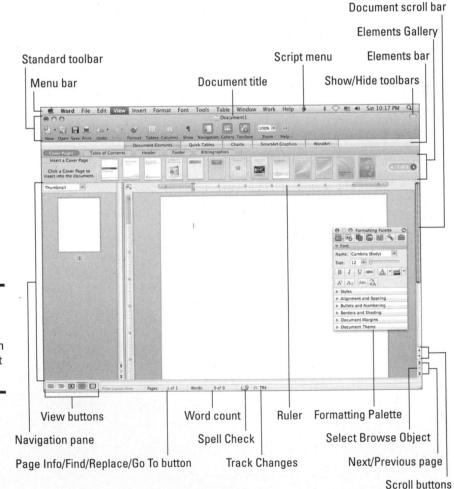

Figure 1-3:
A blank
Word
document in
Print Layout
View.

You get a chance to explore all Word's views and make up your mind about how you want to use them. The goal of this book is to help you create documents not only quickly, but also to create documents that look fantastic and communicate your message to your audience. And in case you're wondering, we wrote this book in Word 2008!

Although the figures in this chapter have a plain-Jane look, that doesn't mean that you have to accept Word's default appearance. We recommend that you customize Word's interface to fit your needs. Everyone's Word should look and work differently, at least a bit.

You have a lot of choices in how you can view your Word documents. In Figure 1-2, we toggled on options, such as the Formatting Palette, Elements Gallery, and Ruler. In the View menu, simply click an option to toggle it on and click it again to toggle it off. When an option is toggled on, a check mark appears.

Menus and toolbars are *context-sensitive:* Office knows what layout you're using and what's currently selected in your document. The options you see while using menus and toolbars in Office are updated automatically to offer what's appropriate at any given moment. Right-clicking or Control-clicking in the interface produces a context-sensitive pop-up menu that relates to wherever you click.

Working in Print Layout View

Print Layout View is a good starting point for beginners because it's closest to what you see onscreen compared with what you get when you print. We use this view as an example to explain the general layout of Word's interface. Figure 1-3 shows a document in Print Layout View after enabling most of the options in the View menu. (See the previous section for more.)

The following views in Word have the same basic interface characteristics as Print Layout View. Although each has minor variations, information regarding Print Layout View also applies to the following views:

- ✦ **Draft**
- ✦ **Web Layout**
- ✦ **Outline**

The Notebook Layout View and Publishing Layout View interfaces are significantly different, so we discuss them separately later in this chapter.

We draw special attention to specific interface elements (see Figure 1-3):

- ✦ **Blinking insertion cursor:** When you type, insert something, or paste, this is the place in your document where it happens. After you have text in your document, you can click anywhere in the text to set the cursor's location.

✦ **Document title:** This is the filename of your document. A new document has a generic name, such as Document #, until you save it.

✦ **Ruler:** You have horizontal and vertical rulers. Adjust margins and indents by dragging ruler elements. Click in the horizontal ruler to add tab stops. Double-click rulers for additional options. Toggle the ruler on and off in the View menu.

✦ **Script menu:** Here you find the Word Automator Actions that come with all Office package bundles except the Home and Student edition. (For more on Automator, see Book I, Chapter 6.)

✦ **View menu:** In Figure 1-2, the View menu is highlighted to help you find the menu.

✦ **Show/Hide Toolbars:** This button is near the upper-right corner of the window and toggles toolbars on and off.

✦ **Standard toolbar:** Figure 1-3 shows the default toolbar buttons for Page Layout View. Different buttons appear when you switch views.

✦ **Elements bar:** This bar is always visible. Click the tabs to activate Elements Gallery.

✦ **Elements Gallery:** Allows you to do all kinds of things, from inserting a cover page to adding charts, SmartArt graphics, WordArt, and more!

✦ **Navigation Pane:** Can be toggled on and off in the View menu or you can click the Navigation button on the Standard toolbar. This pane helps you move around in multiple page documents. A scroll bar appears when there are more pages than what fits on the screen. A pop-up menu at the top of the Navigation Pane allows you to choose one of these two Navigation Pane operating modes:

• *Thumbnail:* A small thumbnail of each page is visible with the page number for that thumbnail. Click a thumbnail to instantly view that page.

• *Document Map:* This option shows a map of your document based upon the heading levels you've used within your document. Right-click or Control-click in the Document Map to limit the map to specific headings. This view doesn't show a map until you apply heading styles to text in your document. You can apply text heading styles with the Styles section of the Formatting Palette or choose Format⇨Styles. We discuss styles in Chapter 3 of this minibook.

✦ **Scroll bar:** Scroll bars automatically appear whenever needed. Drag scroll bars with your mouse. You can customize your scroll bars by modifying the Appearance settings in Mac OS X preferences.

✦ **Toolbox:** Toggle the Toolbox on and off with the Toolbox button on the Standard toolbar or in the View menu, choose one of the Toolbox options.

✦ **Scroll buttons:** Click or click and hold these buttons to scroll through your document.

✦ **Next/Previous Page buttons:** Click these buttons to view the next or previous page.

✦ **Select Browse Object button:** This button is between the Next/Previous Page buttons. When you click this button, a pop-up menu offers various ways to browse your document. See Figure 1-4.

**Book II
Chapter 1**

Getting to Know
Word's Interface

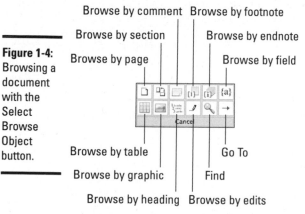

Figure 1-4: Browsing a document with the Select Browse Object button.

Browse by comment   Browse by footnote
Browse by section   Browse by endnote
Browse by page   Browse by field

Browse by table   Go To
Browse by graphic   Find
Browse by heading   Browse by edits

✦ **View buttons:** Click these to switch from one view to another, which is the same as choosing a different view in the View menu. Hover the cursor over each button to see what it does.

✦ **Page Information and the Find/Replace/Go To button:** To view page information that updates automatically, glance at this. This same spot is also a button that you can click to make the Find/Replace/Go To window open.

✦ **Word Count button:** The number of words in your document is updated on this button while you type. Click this spot to display the Word Count dialog, as shown in Figure 1-5. (***Note:*** This figure isn't for a blank document, so you can get an idea of what you'll see.)

✦ **Spell Check button:** Click this button to initiate a spell check from the current cursor location or check the spelling of text you selected.

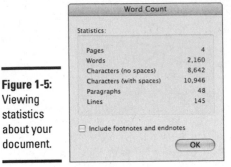

Figure 1-5:
Viewing statistics about your document.

✦ **Track Changes button:** Click the Track Changes button to toggle the Track Changes feature on and off. The small dot changes colors to indicate when track changes are activated. This button activates the Reviewing toolbar if it isn't visible already when you use this button to turn on track changes.

Taking notes in Notebook Layout View

Word's Notebook Layout View (see Figure 1-6) has so many uses; where should we begin? Notebook Layout View is great for students who jot notes, office workers who attend meetings, assistants who track tasks, or professionals who need to record meetings with clients. What's more, if you get an adapter, you can annotate telephone conversations that you have with business people or clients. Word Notebook Layout View allows you to record sound while you type. What you type is linked to the audio so that Word annotates the audio. You can play back the audio that was recorded when you typed the text by clicking anywhere in the text of the document and then clicking the speaker icon that appears.

Notebook Layout versus Microsoft OneNote

For those who work on both Macs and PCs, you have some platform limitations. Notebook Layout View in Word for Mac offers the core functionality of the Microsoft OneNote Windows program, but without the requirement of a different file format. On Word for Mac, audio and typed annotations are stored in standard Word documents. Word for Mac can't open Windows OneNote files. Word for Windows can open files made in Word for Mac Notebook Layout View, but can't use any of the Notebook Layout View features. Word for Windows will display only the typed text. Word Notebook Layout View is Mac-only.

Audio Record stop and play

Scribble and Erase   Show/Hide Audio controls

Document appearance

Input volume   Timeline slider control

Document section tabs

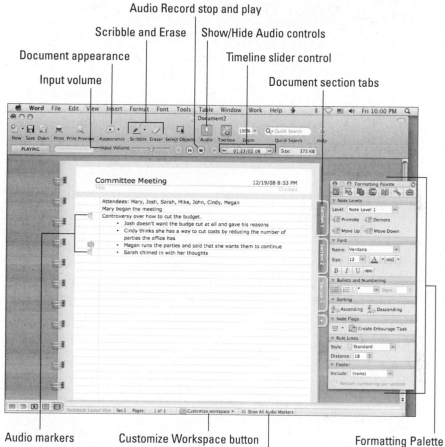

Book II
Chapter 1

Getting to Know Word's Interface

Figure 1-6:
Word
Notebook
Layout
View for
meetings.

Audio markers   Customize Workspace button   Formatting Palette

Show Audio Markers button

MAC ONLY

Time to see how Word Notebook Layout View looks and works. To start, make a new, blank document in Notebook Layout View from Project Gallery. To open new, blank Word document in Notebook Layout View:

1. Choose File⇨Project Gallery.

Project Gallery opens with the New Documents category selected.

2. Double-click Word Notebook Layout.

You may have to scroll to see this option.

Right away you can see that Notebook Layout View is very interesting; it looks just like a notebook, complete with (optional) spiral bindings and (optional) lined notebook paper (refer to Figure 1-6). The Formatting Palette looks different, too; it has all sorts of new controls on it, just for Notebook Layout View. Take a quick peek at the Word menus and you'll see that many of the menu items have changed. You can use most, but not all, of Word's Print Layout features in Notebook Layout View.

You may find it easier to figure out how to use Notebook Layout View when you really have to use it, such as while taking notes in an actual meeting or class. (Of course, if necessary, be polite and let everyone know that you're recording the session. Make sure you're following the policies of your organization.) All Mac laptops and iMacs are equipped with built-in microphones that offer surprisingly good sensitivity in meetings. Other Macs require a microphone to record audio notes. To get started with a little recording session:

1. **Click the Audio button.**

This displays the Audio Notes toolbar (as shown in Figure 1-7).

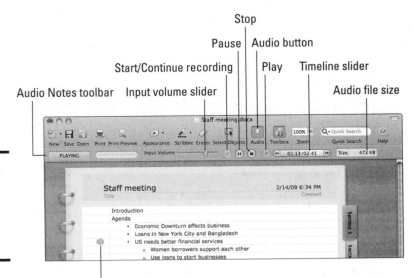

Figure 1-7: Recording audio in Notebook Layout View.

2. **Adjust the Input Volume slider.**

Try starting with the Input Volume slider adjusted so that the sound input level indicator shows the volume is about $3/4$ of the way from full volume. Take a sound sample before you do your real recording to get the best level for the meeting room.

3. **Click the red Start Recording button and then type notes while you record the session.**

   Audio is synchronized automatically with your typed notes as you type. Press Return or Enter as you type while recording to make it visually apparent in your document when a new topic or something noteworthy you want to differentiate appears. Keep an eye on the sound input level indicator and try to keep it at about $3/4$ volume with the Input Volume slider. You can adjust indenting levels later with the Formatting Palette.

4. **Click the highlighted blue and black Stop button to stop recording the audio.**

   The Start Recording button becomes a Continue Recording button.

After you record some audio, you can have some fun playing it back. If you move your mouse over the margin to the left of anything you typed, an audio icon appears. Click that icon to hear the audio that was recorded while the text on that line was being typed. You can use the Timeline Slider control to play back audio for any given moment; click into the Timeline and drag and then click the light blue Play button to the left of the Timeline.

TIP

If you want to listen to Notebook Layout View audio from a Word document in iTunes, you can export the audio as an MP4 file; choose Tools⇨Audio Notes⇨Export Audio. Drag the file into iTunes and you're in business!

Some things in Notebook Layout View are there mostly to make it enjoyable to use. In the Notebook Layout View Standard toolbar, you can click the Appearance button to reveal a fly-out menu, as shown in Figure 1-8, that can adjust how the notebook looks. You can choose from a range of looks with or without notebook rings, all the way from Simple Contemporary to Beige Plastique!

**Book II
Chapter 1**

Getting to Know Word's Interface

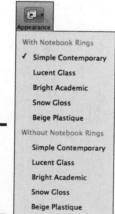

Figure 1-8: Change looks for your Word Notebook!

In addition to the Appearance button, you can customize the blank space that surrounds your document. At the bottom of the document window, on the status bar, click the Customize Workspace button (refer to Figure 1-6) to choose an attractive workspace background (see Figure 1-9). And if you get bored at your meeting or class, you can always use the Scribble and Erase buttons (see Figure 1-6) on the Notebook Layout View Standard toolbar to entertain you. Now, get back to work!

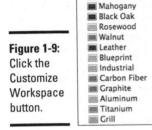

Figure 1-9: Click the Customize Workspace button.

Perhaps you prefer to use generic section names, such as Section 1, in your notebook. But if you want to use something more descriptive, double-click a section tab to the right of the document and then type to change the section name.

If you want to see something really nice for a document that's long and in sections, when you press ⌘-F to find text, section tabs that contain your search criteria light up if a match to the search criteria is in that section.

Designing in Publishing Layout View

Welcome to Word Publishing Layout View! We could scream and shout: Extra! Extra! Read all about it! The headline reads, "Ordinary computer user discovers complete publishing program in Office for Mac." But we'd rather be as understated about Word's publishing capabilities as Microsoft has been!

Headlines aside, Office for Mac contains a publishing program that you can use to create and publish your own newspaper, newsletter, or any story-based communication periodical. With Word Publishing Layout View, you can design and create professional-looking publications that can be distributed via e-mail or print. The best part is you don't need special skills, a different program, or a special file format. Word 2008 does it all in standard Word documents with the traditional Word tools you're used to.

Yes, Publishing Layout View doesn't come close to Adobe InDesign or QuarkXPress, but you probably don't need to print 5,000 brochures that have been created with four-color separations! If you don't understand the language of *color separations,* you'll love Word's Publishing Layout and the ability to use a language most can understand.

Word includes professionally designed templates that help you with layout. The templates available on the Publishing Templates tab of Elements Gallery, such as Newsletters, Brochures, Flyers, and Invitations to name a few, hint at the wide variety of tasks that Word Publishing Layout View is designed for. Because Elements Gallery is highly interactive and so easy to use, if you want to create a document that falls into any of these categories, go to the Publishing Templates tab of Elements Gallery and click any that catch your fancy.

To create a new, blank document in Word Publishing Layout View, as shown in Figure 1-10, follow these steps:

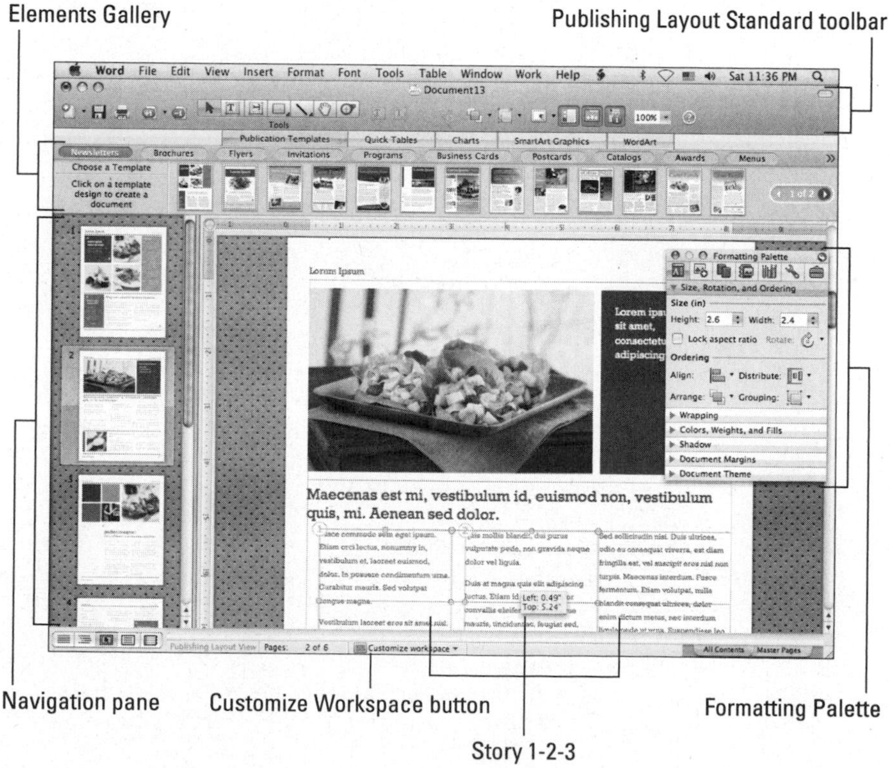

Book II
Chapter 1

Getting to Know
Word's Interface

Elements Gallery   Publishing Layout Standard toolbar

Figure 1-10: A newsletter in Word Publishing Layout View.

Navigation pane   Customize Workspace button   Formatting Palette

Story 1-2-3

1. In Word, choose File⇨Project Gallery to bring up Project Gallery.

2. Click the New tab if it isn't selected already.

3. Select Blank Documents in the Category list if it isn't already selected.

4. Double-click the Word Publishing Layout View option.

   At this point, your interface looks similar to Figure 1-10.

5. If Elements Gallery isn't already visible, click the Publication Templates button on the Elements bar.

6. In Elements Gallery, click the Newsletters tab if it isn't already selected.

7. Hover your cursor over the thumbnail previews and read the descriptive text that changes on the left side of Elements Gallery as you move over the templates until you get to Advantage Newsletter.

   The Advantage Newsletter template is likely to be the leftmost template, unless you've rearranged the templates in Elements Gallery.

8. Click the Advantage Newsletter template.

   The Advantage Newsletter template opens to page 1. Your screen looks even more like Figure 1-10.

9. Choose View⇨Navigation Pane, and in the resultant Navigation Pane on the left, click the thumbnail for page 2 to make it the active page.

   Your interface looks almost exactly the same as Figure 1-10.

Publishing Layout versus Microsoft Publisher

Publishing Layout View in Word for Mac offers the core functionality of the Microsoft Publisher Windows program, but without the requirement of a different file format. On Word for Mac, Publishing Layout View documents are stored as standard Word documents. Word for Mac can't open Windows Publisher files. Word for Windows can open and work with files made in Word for Mac Publishing Layout View, but Word for Windows doesn't have the Publishing Layout View's Standard toolbar or Publishing Layout View. Publishing Layout View is Mac-only.

When you distribute documents made in Publishing Layout View in Word for Mac, consider using the PDF format to preserve the formats and layouts that you create. To create a PDF from your document, choose File⇨Save As. In the Format section, choose PDF. This way people using Word for Windows, other versions of Word for Mac, or those who may not have the same fonts that you do will still enjoy the full fidelity of your published documents.

Touring the menus

No matter which layout you choose, Word menus are worth exploring. We think Word users in particular tend to be more keyboard-centric in their thinking and behavior and will really appreciate that the Macintosh Business Unit (MacBU) at Microsoft decided to stick with the Apple User Interface Guidelines. Office for Mac has retained menus instead of going all the way to tabs splattered with icons of assorted sizes.

People who prefer to use the keyboard over the mouse will appreciate this: We're about to show you a way to navigate menus for all applications in Mac OS X, dubbed *full keyboard access*. When you use full keyboard access, you can use menus without having to use a mouse or a trackpad, and you'll find that you'll speed through your work much faster.

To navigate menus using just the keyboard (*Note:* Before you get started, if you're on a laptop, hold down the Fn key in combination with the following keyboard combinations):

First, there is one simple bit of setup that you need to perform so that you can use Mac OS X's full keyboard access feature. Press Control-F7 once to toggle on the full keyboard access setting. Nothing happens onscreen when you do this. If you ever need to toggle this feature off, press Control-F7 again.

- Whenever you wish to use the Menu, press Control-F2.

  When you do so, in the upper-left corner of your screen, the Apple icon is highlighted.

- Press up-, down-, left-, and right-arrow keys to navigate through the menus.

- Press Return or Enter to select a menu item.

- Press Esc to cancel.

Of course, if you're used to using the mouse, this keyboard stuff might seem a bit strange to you at first. But if you like to type fast and are comfortable with your fingers flying over the keyboard, or if you're on an airplane where you're squished in with a shoehorn, you'll appreciate this feature a lot.

That might be a lot of steps, but page 2 of this particular template shows off the story characteristics of Word Publishing Layout View. A newsletter will be distributed to an audience, so it has to look really good. An important part of looking good is a great layout, which this newsletter template has. We explain how to customize templates in Chapter 7 of this minibook. For now, we focus on the interface.

Notice that the Standard toolbar is different in Word Publishing Layout View. (See Chapter 7 of this minibook for more information about the Standard toolbar.) You can't customize the Standard toolbar in Word

Publishing Layout View. You can, however, customize the workspace with the Customize Workspace button in the status bar at the bottom of the document window.

Text boxes in Word Publishing Layout View are very interactive. Just hover the mouse over the story text boxes, as shown in Figure 1-10, and you'll notice 1, 2, and 3 appear and disappear as the mouse passes over the text boxes. These numbers tell you that the text boxes are part of a story in which text flows from one text box to another. If you click inside box 1 and start typing, when box 1 fills up, the text continues into box 2, and then into box 3. If you drag a story text box, you see guides and measurements that appear to help you precisely lay out your publication. Also notice that different toolbar buttons become active depending upon which story box you click. The first text box and the last text box within a story have different options from text boxes that are between them. After you read more examples in Chapter 7 of this minibook, you'll see how easy it is to make newsletters and other publications in Word Publishing Layout View.

This is one of those times in which we can't do a better job explaining things than Word's built-in Help. Reading about using the grid lines and the Master Pages feature (the tabs in the lower-right corner of the document window, as shown in Figure 1-10) is as easy as searching Help for *Lay out a newsletter in Publishing Layout View.*

Making the Most of Toolbars

If you read Book I, Chapter 3 about customizing toolbars, you know that we encourage you to add and remove commands as well as to make your own toolbars. The more you use Word, the more you'll want to experiment with the commands in the Customize Toolbars and Menus dialog that you access from Word's View menu. Remember to visit this feature regularly.

Just about everyone can use the Fit to Window command in Word's Print Layout View. Follow the instructions in Book I, Chapter 3 and choose View➪Customize Toolbars and Menus to put the Fit to Window command into a toolbar or a menu. See Figure 1-11. After you put the Fit to Window toolbar button onto a toolbar, click the Fit to Window button and then resize the document window by dragging the lower-right corner of the document window. Watch as the document adjusts itself to fit the current window size.

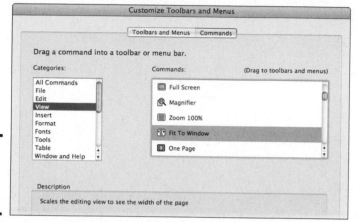

Figure 1-11:
The Fit to Window command.

Making Word Behave the Way You Want It To

Wouldn't it be great if you could force your unruly teenager to behave just the way you want by saying a few special words? Well, Word can't make your teenager act any better, but you can do some simple things to make Word behave the way you want it to.

Finding Word's new Preferences pane

Do you get irritated when Word corrects spellings and formats bulleted lists without being asked? That's the AutoCorrect feature working more than you want it to. Word's Preferences pane is where you head when you wonder why Word is doing what it's doing, and it's where you can change the settings. To make it easier for you to access Word's settings is a redesigned Preferences pane (see Figure 1-12) in Word 2008 that you access by choosing Word⇨Preferences.

As you work in Word, changes to various preferences are made without visiting the Preferences pane. Options that you choose from pop-up menus, widgets, toolbars, and Toolbox controls sometimes affect preferences without making a big deal about it. We visit various preference panes and offer suggestions for settings throughout chapters in this book.

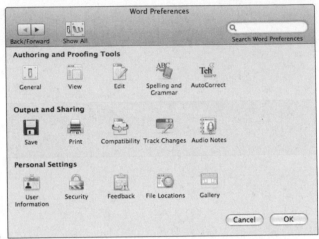

Figure 1-12: Checking out Word's new Preferences pane.

Turning AutoCorrect on and off

A lot of people wish Word wasn't so presumptuous about how things ought to be. In particular, when Word is autocorrecting things, maybe it'd be better if Word started by asking you what you want done. Unfortunately, Word isn't a talking context-sensitive robot. You have to turn correction features on or off on your own.

Now there just happens to be a simple setting in AutoCorrect that allows you to turn off the entire AutoCorrect feature. Choose this magical sequence: Word⇨Preferences and then click the AutoCorrect button and deselect the Automatically Correct Spelling and Formatting as You Type check box.

Setting compatibility preferences

In addition to the AutoCorrect preferences, take a peek at the compatibility preferences, as shown in Figure 1-13. A wide variety of specific behaviors can be turned on and off here, such as

✦ **Font Substitution:** If you open a document that used a font that isn't available on your computer, Word substitutes a font that you do have for the font that you don't have. If you'd rather choose the font, click the Font Substitution button and then choose the font you want.

✦ **Option Sets:** The Recommended Options For pop-up menu has pre-configured combinations of settings from the behavior options. You can change Word 2008 to behave like older versions of Word or even WordPerfect.

✦ **Behavior Options:** You can turn individual Word behaviors on and off in this section. The choices are eclectic. As you make choices, the Option Sets button changes to let you know which set an individual choice you check belongs to. You can make your own custom options by selecting and deselecting the options you desire.

✦ **Compatibility Report:** This setting affects the Compatibility Report feature of the Toolbox.

✦ **Default button:** Click this button to use the settings you've made as the default behavior for Word from now on. If you click this button, you must allow the Normal.dotx template to be modified in order to permanently change Word's behavior.

✦ **OK:** Click OK to apply the options you've chosen to the currently active Word document.

✦ **Cancel:** Click Cancel to not make changes to Word's preferences. If you changed Word's default behavior, the Cancel button won't undo new default settings that you made.

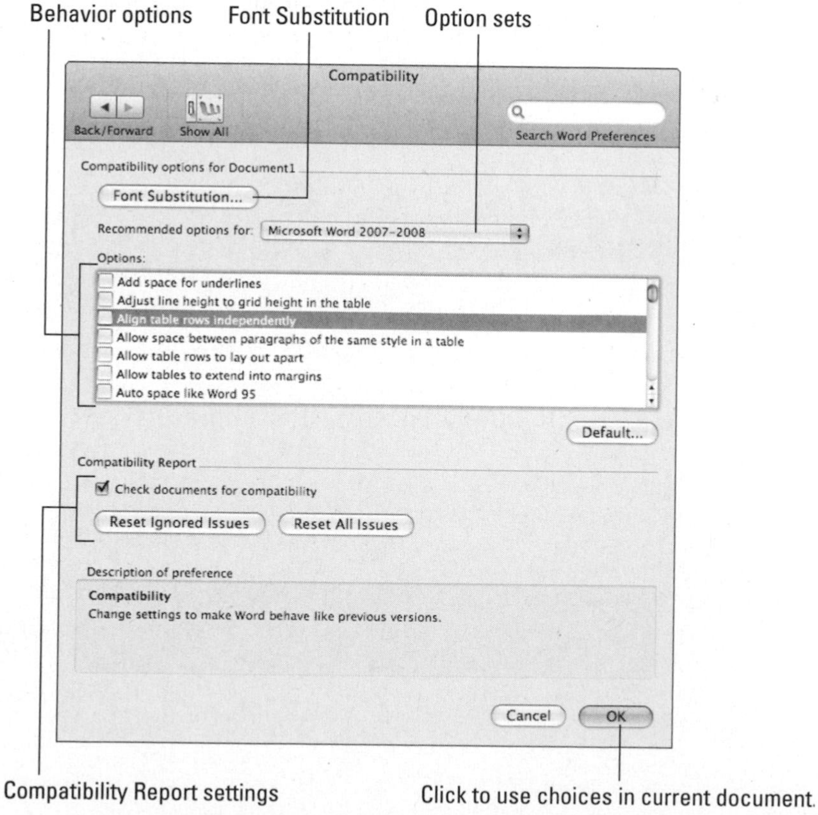

**Book II
Chapter 1**

Getting to Know
Word's Interface

Behavior options   Font Substitution   Option sets

Figure 1-13:
A mixed bag
of Word
behaviors.

Compatibility Report settings   Click to use choices in current document.

Customizing Word's keyboard shortcuts

Being able to speed up your work is always a good thing. Keyboard short-cuts are one of the best ways to increase your productivity, and customizing those shortcuts makes your computer more personalized.

Mac OS X has its own keyboard shortcuts in addition to Word's keyboard shortcuts. When you press a key or a key combination, Mac OS X searches to see whether a task is assigned to that shortcut in Mac OS X system pref-erences. If Mac OS X has a shortcut defined for what you pressed, the key-board shortcut is carried out by the operating system. However, if Mac OS X keyboard shortcuts aren't defined for what you pressed, Mac OS X tells Word what you pressed on the keyboard. You have to check to make sure that if you want to use a particular keyboard shortcut in Word, your desired shortcut isn't already assigned to do something else by Mac OS X. Apple has a lot of nice keyboard shorcuts already defined for Mac OS X, and you can easily get a complete list of them:

1. **In Finder (the Desktop), choose Help⇨Mac Help.**

2. **In the Ask a Question search box, type** shortcuts **and then press Return or Enter.**

   Help responds with a list of relevant topics.

Likewise, Word also has a generous assortment of keyboard shortcuts right from the start. If you switched to the Finder application in the preceding steps, switch back to Word. The shortcuts in Word are available by search-ing Word's Help for Keyboard Shortcuts. You can set up Word so that it automatically displays keyboard shortcuts in menus and toolbar ScreenTips:

1. **In Word, choose View⇨Customize Menus and Toolbars.**

2. **In the resultant dialog, select the Show Shortcut Keys in Screen Tips check box.**

3. **Click OK to make the change.**

Yes, you can assign keyboard shortcuts to Word commands and change the ones that Microsoft assigned. Word doesn't force you to stick with the default shortcuts. You can assign and reassign shortcuts as you wish. You can change the settings for just a single document and even save that docu-ment as a template so that when you open that template, the keyboard shortcuts you customized apply to the documents created from that tem-plate. Figure 1-14 shows the Customize Keyboard dialog that allows you to reassign a keyboard shortcut so that Word will speak the selected text. To access the Customize Keyboard dialog and set a keyboard shortcut:

1. **Choose View➪Customize Menus and Toolbars.**

2. **In the resultant dialog, click the Keyboard button.**

   This opens the Customize Keyboard dialog (see Figure 1-14).

3. **In the Categories list, select a category, and in the Command list, choose a command,**

4. **To assign (or reassign) a keyboard shortcut for the selected command, type in a customized keyboard shortcut combination for the selected command and then click the Assign button.**

5. **Click OK twice in succession to get back to your open document.**

Current Keys list

Categories list

Commands list

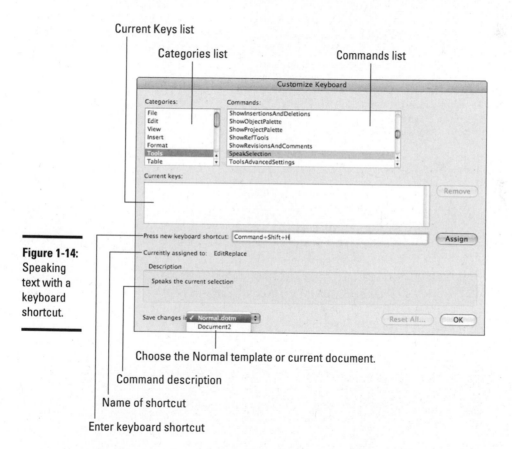

Figure 1-14:
Speaking
text with a
keyboard
shortcut.

Choose the Normal template or current document.

Command description

Name of shortcut

Enter keyboard shortcut

As shown in Figure 1-14, we're assigning a new shortcut to Word's Speak Selection command:

✦ **Categories:** Lists general categories of Word commands that can accept keyboard shortcut assignments.

✦ **Commands:** Lists of commands within Categories that can accept keyboard shortcut assignments.

✦ **Current Keys:** If the selected command already has a keyboard assignment, it's displayed here.

✦ **Press New Keyboard Shortcut:** Decide which keys to press for your keyboard shortcut.

✦ **Currently Assigned To:** If the keyboard combination you pressed has been assigned already to something in Word, the command that it's assigned to is displayed. This feature doesn't check to see whether what you pressed has already been assigned to a shortcut in Mac OS X. If a conflict exists, the Mac OS X shortcut is executed, not Word's.

✦ **Description:** Describes the currently selected command in the Commands list.

✦ **Assign button:** Press this button to assign the keyboard shortcut that's in the Press New Keyboard Shortcut box to the currently selected command in the Commands list.

✦ **Save Changes In pop-up menu:** Determines whether the keyboard shortcut you assign when you press the Assign button is saved in the current Word document or in Word's Normal.dotx template:

- *If you save to a document,* the assignment works only for that particular document.

- *If you save to Normal.dotx,* the assignment works from now on whenever you use the Normal template in Word.

Note: You can transfer shortcuts from one document template to another and to the Normal.dotx template with the Organizer tool. We explain the Organizer tool in Chapter 3 of this minibook.

Chapter 2: An Open and Shut Case

In This Chapter

✔ **Opening Word documents**

✔ **Using templates and wizards**

✔ **Making your Web pages**

✔ **Finding and recovering files**

✔ **Saving documents**

✔ **Sending Word docs everywhere**

Word has some pretty slick ways of dealing with a wide variety of file formats, from the unknown to the mysterious. As you'd normally expect, Word can open and save its own files, but Word can work with other kinds of files as well. Every once in a while you might receive a document that you just can't get to open. Word can often help with this problem. Some file formats are widely shared, such as RTF (Rich Text Format) files. Word can open and save files as RTFs and in other formats as well. You also have ways to protect the information inside your Word files. And of course, Word has a master Normal.dotx template that can make styling your text a breeze. And if you don't know what that is, don't worry because we explain it all in this chapter.

Opening the World in Word

You'd think that opening files would be an old hat to most everyone who has ever touched a computer by now, but a lot of people still don't know about some ways to open files in Word. You might use some of these methods all the time, whereas you might use others once in a blue moon, but it's good to know they're available just in case!

Trying out templates

A plethora of Word templates come pre-built in Project Gallery. With these templates, you can create great-looking documents for specific purposes or audiences without going to a lot of trouble. And even if some of them aren't exactly what you're looking for, remember that they're easy to customize to your own taste and can save you lots of time.

To get to the templates quickly, follow these steps:

1. **In Word, choose File⇨Project Gallery.**

   Project Gallery appears.

2. **Click the New tab, if it isn't selected already.**

   See Figure 2-1.

3. **Choose Word Documents from the Show pop-up menu.**

   This filters Project Gallery to show only Word documents, templates, and wizards.

4. **Click each different category in the Category list.**

   Be sure to click the disclosure triangles to expose sub-categories.

5. **Double-click a template to open it in Word.**

   Project Gallery closes, and Word automatically attaches the template to your document. Your template is now ready for you to customize or use in Word.

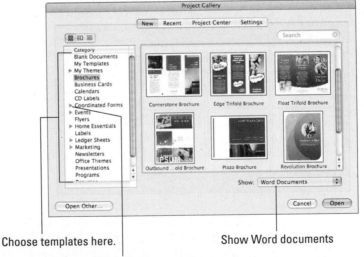

Figure 2-1:
Picking a great Word template.

Choose templates here.

Show Word documents

Click triangles to see subcategories.

Now that you've opened a template, you might want to visit Chapter 7 in this minibook to read more about how to customize them.

Being normal with Normal.dotx

Perhaps you've suspected that Word must have a special template somewhere that you can use as a default when you create that seemingly plain, blank document. Well, you're right; this special template is Normal.dotx, and it has all the settings that control what you see when you create a new, blank document. In Chapter 7, we explain how to save a customized Word document as the Normal.dotx template so that by default, Word opens your customized template instead of Word's default Normal.dotx template.

Becoming a whiz with wizards

Three of the most common tasks you're likely to do with Word can be accomplished quickly with Word's Envelope, Letter, and Mailing Label Wizards. *Wizards* are a series of dialogs with choices to make at each step. They've been designed with the intention to help you create certain kinds of documents in a jiffy. To get at these three Word wizards, head to Project Gallery and type **wiz** in the Search box. The Word wizards appear, as shown in Figure 2-2. To launch one of the wizards, just double-click the one you want.

Book II
Chapter 2

**An Open and
Shut Case**

You come across other wizards in this book, but these three can open new documents, which is why they're in Project Gallery (and why they're in this chapter). Here's a brief description of each wizard (see Chapter 6 in this minibook for more on mail merge):

✦ **Envelope Wizard:** Use Envelope Wizard to print envelopes. You can use it to print just one envelope or thousands. Because envelopes come in many sizes, you can configure the wizard to print any envelope size that fits into your printer.

✦ **Letter Wizard:** You have 124 different Word templates just waiting for your customization in the Letter Format tab's Page Design pop-up menu. Even though it's called Letter Wizard, not all the formats are letters. In fact, the Letter Wizard templates are the same 124 Word templates that you find in Project Gallery's New tab and in Elements Gallery. The Letter Wizard gives you a step-by-step ways to customize these templates.

If you're looking for the Resume Wizard, it's been rolled into the Letter Wizard. You'll find Simple, Blocks, Initials, Grayscale, and Vitae résumé templates in the Page Design pop-up menu found in Step 1 of the Letter Wizard.

✦ **Mailing Label Wizard:** The Mailing Label Wizard can also open a new document. Although the name implies that it's just for making sheets of mailing labels, you can actually use it to make all sizes and shapes of stick-on labels, and for other things, such as tent cards and name badges.

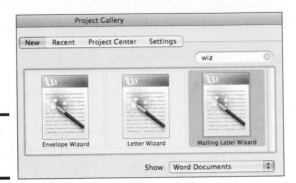

Figure 2-2:
The Word
wizards.

Opening Web pages

Surfing the Web is great, but at times, you may want to edit those Web pages in Word. Several approaches bring all or part of a Web page into Word. Remember, Word is all about words. Web browsers can have all sorts of content that Word can't deal with, so don't expect Word to faithfully reproduce a Web page. Be happy if you get the text you want.

Copying and pasting

This is a fast, easy way to get Web page content into Word. To do so:

1. **Select what you want in your Web browser and then choose Edit⇨Copy.**

2. **Switch to Word and choose Edit⇨Paste.**

   If the result isn't good enough, try the following suggestion.

Saving and opening a Web page

Word can open Web pages that have been saved as `.htm`, `.html`, or `.mht` (Web archives). For example, say you're using a Web browser and you find a Web page that you want to edit in Word. Use the Web browser to save the Web page as a file on your computer and then open the saved file in Word. Here's how:

1. **In the Web browser, choose File⇨Save As.**

   The Web browser's Save dialog opens.

2. **Choose a location.**

   Remember the filename or give the file a name of your choosing.

3. **Save the file.**

After you save your Web page in Word, you need to know how to open it. To open your saved Web page in Word, follow these steps:

1. **In Word, choose File⇨Open.**

   The File Open dialog appears.

2. **Choose All Files from the Enable pop-up menu.**

3. **Navigate to and select the file you saved in the preceding steps.**

4. **Click the Open button or double-click the filename.**

   Word does its best to open the Web page you saved. Bear in mind, many Web page elements, such as Flash, Silverlight, style sheets, and various scripts are ignored by Word. Just the same, you may be able to get the content you want into Word so that you can take it from there and do your own editing magic in Word.

**Book II
Chapter 2**

**An Open and
Shut Case**

TIP

If your first attempt didn't turn out well, you can try using a different Save As format in your Web browser. Web browsers and Web pages vary widely. In Word, a Web page saved by one browser, such as Safari, may look completely different from the same page saved by a different Web browser, such as Firefox. Each Web browser has different Save As formats from which to choose, so don't give up after just one attempt. Try saving the page again with a different browser and/or format. Word can open any format that your Web browser can Save As. Sometimes the results just aren't good no matter what format or browser you choose. This is a limitation of opening Web pages in Word.

Saving a document as a Web page

Fifteen years ago, the Internet was something exciting and new to most people. Everyone wondered how the Internet would shake out, and Microsoft wanted to be a leader in the field. At that time, the best way to distribute Word documents on the Web was to save them as *HyperText Markup Language (HTML)* files, the native file format understood by Web browsers. The idea was to save a Word document in HTML and upload it to a Web server; then anyone with access to the server could download the file, and his Word copy would reconstruct the document exactly as it was before.

Recently, new Internet technologies have made this scenario passé. Also, depending on a particular scenario, you have better ways to share documents online, which we discuss in Book VI, Chapter 2.

However, it's good to know that Word can open and create Web pages just in case you ever need to make a Web page from a Word document. In Safari, choose File⇨Save As and save the Web page. Then in Microsoft Word, choose File⇨Open and then choose Enable⇨All Files. Select the Web page you saved from Safari and you can work with it in Microsoft Word. Keep in mind that Word is designed to handle text and pictures, and this feature was designed to give faithful reproduction of Word documents. Other design elements, such as Flash, video, and complex Web pages, either don't render well or don't render at all in Word. However, with simple Web pages, or if you just want to use the text in a Web page, this approach can be a lifesaver. Also, if someone sends you a file with the .mht file extension, it's probably a Web Archive saved from Microsoft's Internet Explorer browser. Word 2008 can open this type of file.

Word is better at creating Web pages from scratch than it is at rendering Web pages made with other tools. To turn a Word document into a Web page, follow these steps:

1. **In Word, choose Print Layout view by clicking the View button.**

2. **From the View menu, choose Web Layout to preview of how your document will look as a Web page.**

3. **When you're satisfied with the way your document looks, choose File⇨Save as Web to save your changes.**

Extracting text from any file

Every so often you might come across a mystery file that you can't figure out what it contains or maybe even which file format it uses. Maybe the file was corrupted before you got it, or maybe it's in a Microsoft Windows format that has no equivalent on the Mac side. Don't worry. Even if you don't know what application created the file, Word might be able to help. If text is in a file, Word can extract the text no matter what application created the file. To do so, follow these steps:

1. **Choose File⇨Open.**

   The Open dialog appears.

2. **Choose Recover Text from Any File in the Enable pop-up menu.**

3. **Select the file that you want to extract the text from and then click Open.**

   Alternatively, you can double-click the file you want to extract the text from.

   A new Word document opens. The Word document contains the text, if any, that was in the file you selected. You might now know what the mystery document was, have a hint about what kind of file it was, or you may have rescued the text from a corrupt file and can now use the rescued text.

Finding files in Finder

Your file's gone! You knew right where that file was a minute ago, but now it's gone. Now is the time to use Spotlight. Whether you use the Word Open command or you're browsing your files with Finder, find the Spotlight Search box with its little magnifying glass icon in the upper-right corner of the window. Type a search term into the Search box, and Spotlight instantly displays the files containing that term.

If you're browsing in Finder, turn Cover Flow view on (keyboard shortcut ⌘-4). Select a document and press the spacebar to enlarge the Cover Flow preview and then scroll through your entire document with the Mac OS X QuickView without even having to open the file, as shown in Figure 2-3. Of course, you can use any of Mac OS X's more than 20 different ways to open the file at this point, including double-clicking the QuickView window.

Book II
Chapter 2

An Open and
Shut Case

Press spacebar to enlarge.

Cover Flow view   Enter search term.

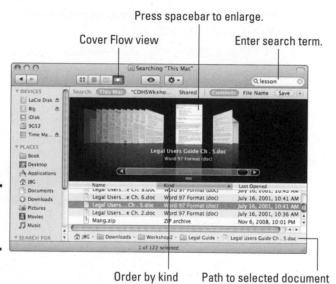

Figure 2-3:
Finding a
missing file.

Order by kind   Path to selected document

Comparing two Word documents

Now you've done it. You have two documents, and both might be the same, but you're not sure. One document is newer than the other, but still you have doubts. The Compare Documents tool allows you to compare the two documents and find out what the differences are.

Before you can use the Compare Documents tool, you have to add the Compare Documents button to one of your toolbars:

1. **In Word, choose View⇨Customize Toolbars and Menus.**

The Customize Toolbars and Menus dialog appears.

2. **Near the top of the dialog, select the Commands tab.**

3. **In the Categories list, choose Tools, and in the Commands list, choose Compare Documents in the middle of the list.**

4. **Drag the Compare Documents icon onto the toolbar you want it to appear on.**

When you release the mouse, the icon turns into a command button on your toolbar. You can now use this tool anytime you need to.

5. **Click OK to close the Customize Menus and Toolbars dialog.**

See Book I, Chapter 3 for more on customizing your toolbars and menus.

After you place the Compare Documents button on your toolbar, to use the feature to compare two Word documents:

1. **Open one of the Word documents that you want to compare.**

2. **Click the Compare Document button.**

The Open dialog appears.

3. **Select the second Word document that you wish to compare with the document that you opened in Step 1 and click Open.**

Word highlights the differences between the two documents with the Reviewing and Track Changes feature, which we cover in Chapter 4 of this minibook.

Recovering AutoRecover files

Uh oh. Crash time! Microsoft Word quits unexpectedly, and you hold your breath (which isn't too helpful as far as the poor document is concerned). If that ever happens to you, and we hope it never does, all you have to do is open Microsoft Word again. In normal circumstances, Word looks for and opens any AutoRecover files for the document(s) that you were working on when the crash occurred. Your document(s) open with Recovered appended to the filename. Choose File⇨Save As to restore the original filename and location. Word can recover files that were open because by default, Word saves your document(s) every ten minutes while you're working on it. You can change the save time interval within the AutoRecover setting in the Word Preferences. Here's how to find and change the AutoRecover setting:

1. **Choose Word⇨Preferences.**

The Word Preferences dialog opens.

2. Choose Save.

Word's Save preferences are displayed, as shown in Figure 2-4.

3. Change the number of minutes in the Save AutoRecover Info Every: [X] Minutes setting.

Deselect this setting if you don't want Word to save an AutoRecover file. You might do this for extremely large documents that take a long time to save.

You don't need to select the Always Create Backup Copy check box. With AutoRecover and Time Machine, the bases are covered. The option is only there for backward compatibility.

4. Click OK when you're finished.

Search Word preferences

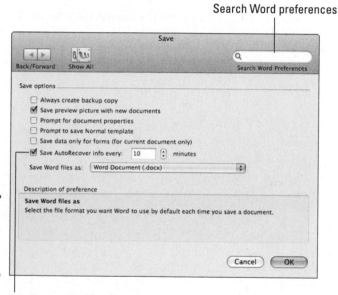

Figure 2-4:
Finding your Save options!

AutoRecover preference

Rarely, Word might not automatically display the AutoRecover file for the document(s) you were working on the next time you open Word. In that case, do the following in Word to open the AutoRecover file:

1. In Word, choose File⇨Open.

The Open dialog appears.

2. **Type** AutoRecover **in the Spotlight Search box on the top right of the Open dialog.**

   Spotlight lists all AutoRecover files on the selected volume. Click Computer if you don't see one or more AutoRecover files. Of course, if your Word document had been open before changing your settings in AutoRecover preferences or if you deselected AutoRecover in Word Preferences, you won't have anything to recover.

3. **Double-click the most recently saved AutoRecover file, or select the file and click Open.**

   If the file you want is grayed-out, choose All Files in the Enable pop-up menu, which allows you to open any file type that was previously restricted.

 You can also use Mac OS X Time Machine to recover any file that you've saved at least once. When you use Word for Mac, it's nearly impossible to lose more than a few minutes worth of work thanks to AutoRecover and Time Machine.

Saving Word Documents

Most of the time saving a file in Word is a very simple task. But at times, you may want to limit access to a particular file. Or maybe you want to save a document so that it's compatible with older versions of Word; or perhaps you want to save your document in a format that's compatible with other programs. Or maybe you want to send a document via e-mail or Microsoft Messenger; or put it online as a Web page. The Word Save As options accommodate all these needs and more.

Just close me

This may seem somewhat obvious, but Word keeps track of whether a document's been changed since it was opened last. If you close a document after making any changes at all, Word displays a dialog asking whether you want to save changes.

✦ **If you click Save,** Word replaces the old version of your document with the current version.

✦ **If you click Don't Save,** well, Word doesn't save your changes (and yes, at times, you don't want your changes made and would rather start over with the original document). Word closes your document, and any changes you made since the last save are discarded.

✦ **If you click Cancel,** Word thinks you really didn't mean to close the window and keeps the document open just as it was before you tried to close the window.

Giving a document a new name, a new location

When you open a new, blank document, it starts off with a generic name, such as Document 1. That's not much help when you want to find your file again later, but it's easy to fix:

1. **Choose File⇨Save As.**

   The Save As dialog appears. By default Word uses whatever you typed in the first line of the document as the filename.

2. **(Optional) In the Save As field, type in a new name.**

3. **Navigate to the desired location and click Save.**

   A good place to store documents is in the Documents folder. Save As dialogs have a New Folder button in the lower-left corner in case you want to create a new folder in which to save your document.

TIP

If you want to save time typing a filename, we have a little trick you can use. While the Save As dialog is open, you can navigate to a file and then click it. Your current document takes the name of the document you click. Keep that name if you want to replace the document you clicked with the current document, or modify the name a little to make a new version of the document. Of course, this trick isn't Word-specific; it works with any other program!

Securing Word documents

Sometimes you absolutely don't want everyone, including Aunt Millie and her 16th nephew opening or editing a document. You can control who can do what with a particular document by using the helpful Options button in the Save As dialog. This brings up the Save preferences dialog, as shown in Figure 2-4.

Now, we realize that what we're going to tell you isn't necessarily the fastest way to get at the settings, but we think it certainly is the coolest way to get there. If you normally choose File⇨Save As and then click the Options button; you might prefer our method because it's more fun. For the record, these settings are in Word's Preferences on the Security panel. Sure, you can get there by using the menus, but follow along and watch what happens:

1. **With your Word document open, choose File⇨Save As.**

   The Save As dialog opens.

2. **Click the Options button.**

   The Save preferences dialog is displayed (refer to Figure 2-4).

3. **Click in the Search Word Preferences Search field.**

   The Save preferences dialog magically turns into the Word Preferences dialog — so cool!

4. **Type** pass **in the Search Word preferences field.**

   The Security option is highlighted — also cool! (See Figure 2-5.)

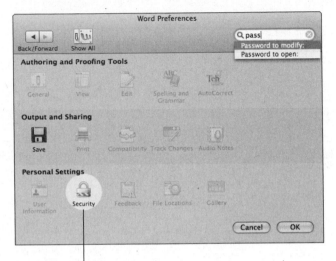

Figure 2-5:
Getting
to your
document's
security
settings.

The Security option is highlighted.

5. **Press Return, Enter, or click Security.**

   The Security preferences dialog opens. See Figure 2-6.

When you're in Word's Security preferences dialog, Security Options for "*Document Name*" section apply only to the currently active Word document. The Privacy Options section includes settings that are retained by Word for all documents. We look at the settings in Figure 2-6 more closely in the following sections.

Security Options for "Document Name"

✦ **Password to Open:** If you type a password here, a password must be used whenever that saved document is opened. Be sure to keep a record of the password somewhere. Five years from now, you might not remember what it is. Better yet, choose File➪Save As to save a protected version and keep a version without protection, just for you.

✦ **Password to Modify:** If you type a password here, you require someone to enter that password to modify a document that's been opened already. Password to Modify is independent from Password to Open.

Set file to be read-only.

Set password to make changes.

Set password to open document.

Protection for tracked changes, bullets and numbering, and forms

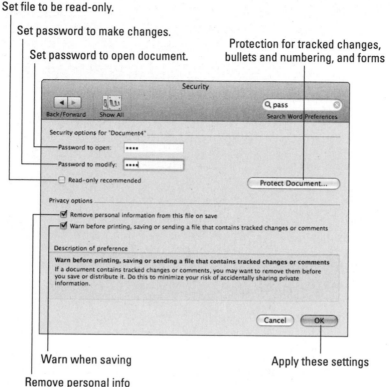

Figure 2-6:
Setting
document
security
options.

Warn when saving

Apply these settings

Remove personal info

✦ **Read-Only Recommended check box:** When this is selected, the file is marked as Read-Only in the document title whenever it's opened. Choose File⇨Save As (not Save) to save a document that was opened as read-only.

✦ **Protect Document button:** This button is the same as using Protection from Word's Tools menu. A document can be protected against changes for any one of the following:

• Tracked changes (see Chapter 4 in this minibook)

• Bullets and numbering (see Chapter 3 in this minibook)

• Forms (see Chapter 7 in this minibook)

✦ **Remove Personal Information from This File on Save.** Check this option to remove all your personal information from being saved with the file.

Privacy Options

✦ **Remove Personal Information from This File On Save check box:** Select this to stop Word from including personal information, such as your name and your computer's name, within the Word document when you save it.

✦ **Warn before Printing, Saving or Sending a File that Contains Tracked Changes or Comments check box:** People put all kinds of private remarks into comments and then set Word so the comments don't display. When they send the document to someone who should never see the comments, that person can turn on comments, and there they are! Word can't stop you from saying things that might prove embarrassing later, but it can warn you that your document has comments or tracked changes.

✦ **Save Preview Picture with New Documents check box:** Wait! This setting is on the Save preferences dialog, as shown in Figure 2-4. If there's a chance the File icon could reveal something personal or private, deselect this.

✦ **Prompt for Document Properties check box:** This setting is also in the Save preferences dialog, as shown in Figure 2-4. Every Word document has a Properties dialog that hardly anyone knows about or uses. Well, in Windows Vista, some of the information in the Properties dialog, such as Author, is displayed along with the File icon. Select this and take a peek at what's on the Summary tab of the Properties dialog and make sure nothing's there that could come back and bite you later.

Turning your document into a template

A lot of work is involved in creating a special document that has the layout, the fonts, and the design you want. You can reuse that special document as a starting point for new documents, which saves you the time of doing it all from scratch again. In Word, these special documents are *templates*. Whether the template is a form, a business letter, an invitation, a tent card, or simply a document formatted in a way that you plan to use again, you can save your work as a template so that identical copies can be made on demand without altering the original by mistake!

Say you do volunteer work at the local Humane Society and you regularly make a flyer about found animals. Project Gallery has a built-in Lost and Found template that you can customize for your local society. After you make customizations (see Chapter 7 of this minibook) to the template, you can save your customizations as a template. Do the following:

1. **In Word, Choose File⇨Save As.**

The Save As dialog appears.

2. **In the Save As text box, enter a filename.**

3. **In the Format drop-down list, choose Word Template (.dotx).**

   Word automatically switches to the My Templates folder.

4. **Click Save.**

   Your template is saved and will show up in Project Gallery.

To use your customized templates, go to Project Gallery, click the New tab, and choose My Templates from the Category list, as shown in Figure 2-7.

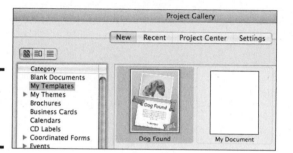

Figure 2-7: Locating saved templates.

TIP

We just showed you an Office-specific way of saving a document as a template. There's another way using Mac OS X instead of Office. Mac OS X allows you to turn any document file from any application into a template. To turn a document into a template in Finder, choose File⇨Get Info. In the General section, select the Stationery Pad check box. Templates made this way aren't in Project Gallery. To turn a Stationery template back into a regular document, repeat the procedure and deselect the Stationery Pad check box.

Being compatible with others

Being aware and respectful of other people's tastes is key to getting along with everyone in this world. Microsoft promotes this concept well in Word by giving you a lot of file format choices.

You have Office 2008, but remember, not everyone else does. At times, you may need to save your files in a format that people with other software can open. Knowing the software capabilities of the people you're communicating with helps you choose the most appropriate format. Fortunately, almost every word processor can use certain file formats.

Word 2008 launches the newest file format for Microsoft Word documents on the Mac. The new files have an *x* at the end of the filename to signify that they're eXtensible Markup Language (XML) documents. Table 2-1 gives a rundown on the various extensions you find in the Save As dialog:

Table 2-1   **Save As Formats and Compatibility**

File Type	Extension	Compatibility
Word Document	.docx	Fully compatible with Word 2008 (Mac) and Word 2007 (Windows). This format has good compatibility with Word 2004 (Mac) and Word 2003 (Windows) when the latest 2003 and 2004 updates and converters are installed (available for free from the Microsoft site). New 2007 and 2008 features aren't supported fully by 2003 and 2004, but you can open the DOCX format with older versions and still view and print the DOCX documents — but you can't edit them with the same capabilities. OpenOffice version 3 and Apple Pages (part of iWork) can open these documents, but their conversion process changes how the documents look and work.
Word Template	.dotx	Same compatibility benefits and issues as explained for Word Document (DOCX).
Word Document Stationery	.doc	When you choose Word Document Stationery in Word's Save As dialog, your document is saved as a Stationery file in Word 97–2004 file format. This is the same as using Finder's Get Info command to turn a document into a Mac OS X Stationery template. To turn a (DOCX) format document into a Stationery template, flip back to the section, "Turning your document into a template," earlier in this chapter.
PDF (Portable Document Format)	.pdf	The PDF format is a great way to distribute a Word document when you want the recipient to be able to view and print your document just the way you saved it, regardless of what fonts the recipient has installed on her Mac. Your document retains its fonts and formatting on just about every computer. This is also a good file format when you don't want anyone editing or changing your document in any way.
Word Macro–Enabled Document	.docm	If you receive a Word document that has Visual Basic macros from Windows Word 2007, you can open, work on, and save the document body while keeping the macros intact, even though Word 2008 can't edit or use the macros.
Word Macro–Enabled Template	.dotm	Same compatibility characteristics as Word Macro–Enabled Document (DOCM).

File Type	Extension	Compatibility
Word 97–2004 Document	`.doc`	All versions of Microsoft Office from 97 to 2004 for both Mac and Windows can open this format, but new 2007 and 2008 features aren't supported fully.
Word 97–2004 Template	`.dot`	Same compatibility as Word 97–2004 (DOC).
Rich Text Format	`.rtf`	This is the best choice to use when you want to cover the widest possible audience. Although RTF isn't a formal standard, most word processors do a decent job of working with this format. Do remember, though, that after you save to the RTF format, you lose the editing ability for Word-specific features, such as WordArt, Picture Styles, and so on.
Word 4.0–6.0/95 Compatible	`.rtf`	This RTF variant has support for specific features of Microsoft Word versions 4, 6, and 95. Use this format if you know your recipient is using one of these older versions of Microsoft Word, either Mac or Windows.
Plain Text	`.txt`	Saves only the text portion of the Word document. Everything else is discarded.
Web Page	`.htm`	Turns your Word document into a Web page (HTML) document and also creates a supporting folder of linked objects, such as pictures or movies. Web browsers, such as Safari and Firefox, can open the result.
Single File Web Page	`.mht`	Similar to Web Page (HTM), Single File Web Page creates a single file also known as a Web archive. Web browsers, such as Safari and Firefox, can open the result.
Word 2003 XML Document	`.xml`	Creates an XML document without compressing it, specifically for Word 2003.
Speller Custom Dictionary	`.dic`	A custom dictionary is a list of words. Each word is followed by a carriage return. After saving a custom dictionary, use Word's Spelling and Grammar preferences to enable it.
Spelling Exclude Dictionary	`.dic`	Similar to a Speller Custom Dictionary, this is a list of words, each followed by a carriage return. Create an Exclude list for alternate correct spellings, such as *colour* for *color*. Use Word's Spelling and Grammar preferences to enable your Spelling Exclude Dictionary.

Book II Chapter 2

An Open and Shut Case

New format XML Word documents are zipped folders that contain XML files, which are simply text files containing HTML and XML. If you're really into this sort of thing, you can unzip and open the actual XML files by using a utility, such as Smith Micro's StuffIt or StuffIt Expander (free).

Sending copies everywhere — fast!

No need to wait for a special moment to send a Word document. You can do it right from Word: Choose File➪Send To, and you even have choices about how the document can get to where it's going. Here are your options:

✦ **Send to Mail Recipient as HTML:** This method takes advantage of Word's ability to create HTML documents, and most modern e-mail programs do a decent job of interpreting HTML mail. Use this method when exact reproduction isn't critical, and the recipient doesn't need to edit the document. However, do remember that e-mail sizes can be considerably larger if you use this option. To get a better idea of how your document will look when received, choose View➪Layout before sending.

✦ **Send to Mail Recipient as Attachment:** When you want the recipient to get an exact copy of the Word document, use this option to send the active document as an e-mail attachment.

✦ **Send to Microsoft Messenger Contact:** This option becomes available when Microsoft Messenger is open at the same time Word is open. The contact instantly receives a copy of the Word document in Word format.

✦ **Send to Microsoft PowerPoint:** PowerPoint as a possible recipient might seem odd, but that's not exactly the case. The purpose of this option is to allow you to use Microsoft Word to create an outline. Then you send the outline to PowerPoint, which can turn it into a presentation.

Chapter 3: Working with Text, Words, and Paragraphs

In This Chapter

↙ **Taming text**

↙ **Formatting the easy way**

↙ **Applying, creating, and organizing styles**

↙ **AutoFormatting while you type**

↙ **Numbering your lines automatically**

After you have your document underway, you discover how important formatting and fine-tuning your document are. Although the type of formatting and fine-tuning you do is related to your personality, some things are surprisingly universal. Foremost among these similarities is an observation: It's one thing to get down words, but as a Mac user, you want them to look their best. Readers appreciate the time that writers spend to make their work readable. Some writers enjoy creating documents that pay attention to finer details, such as the spacing among lines and characters, as well as kerning and paragraph formatting. This chapter covers Word's ability to help you create documents with style.

Triumphing Over Text

Before we begin the discussion about working with text, we want to mention the single most important feature in all of Office: the Undo button. The ability to easily back out of document changes makes it easy to be daring, but not reckless. Some things, such as file operations, can't be undone. But most of the changes you make in your Word documents aren't set in stone.

Most people know that each time you click the Undo button, the most recent change is undone. Some people even know that each successive click of the Undo button reverts the next most recent change, and you can keep clicking the Undo button until you've undone all the changes in the document's Undo history. But only a select few know that you can click the down arrow next the Undo button (see Figure 3-1). This reveals the Undo history with the most recent action on top. And if you like, you can undo multiple actions all at once with one click.

Figure 3-1:
Undoing
multiple
actions at
once.

Click here to undo several changes at once.

Formatting deftly with the Formatting Palette

Plain old text can be monotonous, ineffective, and boring all at the same time. If this book had just one font and no illustrations, you might have left it on the shelf at the store — and we're so very happy that you didn't. We show you how you can make your documents more interesting and readable by judicious use of fonts and formatting. Word has an amazing context-aware Formatting Palette that pays attention to what you've selected so that you can quickly apply formatting. (To read more about the Formatting Palette, head to Book I, Chapter 4.)

To change text, you first have to select it. Table 3-1 lists the various ways you can select text in Word. After you select text, the Formatting Palette shows style and formatting settings for the selected text.

Table 3-1	Selecting Text
To Select This . . .	*. . . Do This*
A string of text	Drag over the text.
One word	Double-click the word.
An entire paragraph	Triple-click anywhere in the paragraph.
A single line	Move the mouse cursor into the left margin. When the cursor turns into an arrow, click the mouse.
Contiguous lines	Move the mouse cursor into the left margin. When the cursor turns into an arrow, drag the mouse.
The entire document	Press ⌘-A.

While we're on the subject of selecting things, Word has a default When Selecting, Automatically Select Entire Word option in preferences. Fortunately though, you can change this setting. By default, when you drag over text in Word, the cursor selects entire words at a time. This might bother you when you're trying to select only a portion of a word, but you can tell Word to knock it off. Here's how:

1. **In Word, choose Preferences.**

   The Preferences window appears.

2. **Click the Edit button in the Preferences window.**

   The Edit dialog appears.

3. **Deselect the When Selecting, Automatically Select Entire Word check box.**

4. **Click OK to implement the change and close the dialog.**

Nobody wants to be seen as lazy, apathetic, or boring just because his document is lifeless and unexciting. To avoid that, select some text and apply a new font. The Formatting Palette has some new features in the Font section. New in Word 2008, fonts are now organized by Font Collections, Document Theme, and then by a list of fonts. This arrangement makes it easier to pick fonts for special occasions, fonts that match a specific purpose, and fonts that are compatible with Windows versions of Microsoft Office. (See Figure 3-2.)

Book II
Chapter 3

Working with Text, Words, and Paragraphs

Figure 3-2:
Finding the Windows Office Compatible Font Collection.

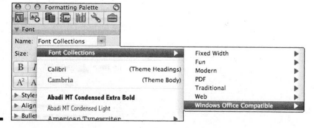

The next item on the Formatting Palette is font size control (see Figure 3-3). As in previous versions, you can click the Size pop-up menu and then choose a font size, or you can type the specific point size that you want into the Size box. But with the new slider feature, you can adjust the font size by dragging the slider. This new slider is a small thing, yet it makes using the Formatting Palette dynamic and interactive.

Other handy formatting options are also at your fingertips on the Formatting Palette. These include

✦ **Bold:** Applies bold to the selected text.

✦ **Italics:** Applies italic to the selected text.

✦ **Font Color:** Applies the color you choose to the selected text.

✦ **Highlight Color:** Applies a color background to the selected text.

✦ **Superscript:** Raises the selected text and shrinks it. Also dubbed a *power* or a *superior*.

Click arrow for pop-up.

Type an entry.

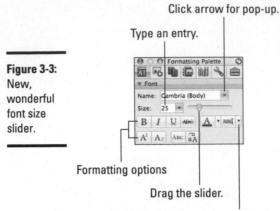

Figure 3-3:
New,
wonderful
font size
slider.

Formatting options

Drag the slider.

Move cursor over buttons to see option names.

✦ **Subscript:** Lowers the selected text and shrinks it.

✦ **Small Caps:** Makes selected text all capitals, but not all one size. Notice the first letter of the sentence is taller.

✦ **All Caps:** Makes selected text all capitals of the same size.

In addition to these options, you have other formatting categories on the Formatting Palette to consider. Click the disclosure triangles to expose the options available in each of these categories:

✦ **Styles:** Apply pre-configured combinations of formatting options, in particular heading styles. See the section, "Writing with Style," later in this chapter.

✦ **Borders and Shadings:** Apply border lines and shading to selected text.

Each option in the Borders and Shading section of the Formatting Palette is a pop-up menu. Borders appear at paragraph marks, and using this section is simple and straightforward. Select some text, click the pop-up menus, and choose from the available options. The text shown in Figure 3-4 has two different shadings applied.

✦ **Bullets and Numbering:** Toggle on or off automatic indenting with special character or ordered numbers for lists. See the section, "Shooting bullets and numbing numbers," later in this chapter.

Simplicity is a good rule to follow. Use one or two fonts in your documents, and use them in a couple sizes only, such as a large font for headings and a small font for regular text.

Figure 3-4:
Text with borders and shading.

The quick brown fox jumps over the lazy dog.

The quick brown fox jumps over the lazy dog.

Borders and Shading

Borders

Type: ☐ ▾ Style: ——— ▾

Color: ✎ ▾ Weight: 1/2 ▾

Shading

Pattern: ☐ 20% ▾

Color: 🎨 ▾ Fill color: 🎨 ▾

Book II Chapter 3

Working with Text, Words, and Paragraphs

Dropping a cap

The Drop Cap feature isn't about losing your hat; it's just about adding beauty to your text with an option that's more familiar to print designers. In the days of yore, a typesetter would painstakingly use wooden blocks and then drop in a large, fancy capital letter at the beginning of the first sentence of a new chapter. In typesetting jargon, this embellishment is a *drop cap*. To make a drop cap, select the first character of the first paragraph in a document and then choose Format⇨Drop Cap. Figure 3-5 shows a drop cap for T.

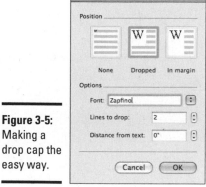

Figure 3-5:
Making a drop cap the easy way.

*T*he quick lazy dog. jumps over the

As shown in Figure 3-5, the first character that comprises the actual drop cap doesn't have to be the same font as the rest of the paragraph. You can find special, embellished fonts that work very well as drop caps.

When you create your drop cap, you can set the number of lines of text that the drop cap uses, and whether the cap will appear dropped, as shown in Figure 3-5, or in the left margin. The None option restores a drop cap to the character that it was before you turned it into a drop cap.

Spacing sweetly

Sometimes you want your text on a page to be aesthetically pleasing. Consider how important it is to have a poem look just right to create the right ambience on the page. In these situations, you might need to adjust the text spacing to make things look nice. Word 2008 enables you to make adjustments to the spacing between the letters, or *kerning,* as well as control line spacing and paragraph spacing. When working with the Alignment and Spacing section, the settings apply to entire paragraphs (see Figure 3-6). Click anywhere in a paragraph or select multiple paragraphs when you apply these formatting options.

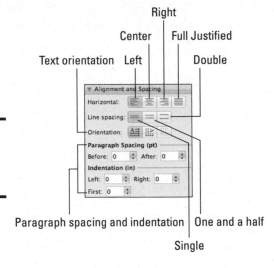

Figure 3-6:
Adjusting
paragraph
properties.

Although using the Formatting Palette is quick and easy, Word offers an older version of the same controls over the spacing and indentation of your text. To get at the old-style line and paragraph spacing controls:

1. **Select the text you want to fine-tune and then choose Format⇨Paragraph.**

The Paragraph dialog appears, as shown in Figure 3-7.

2. **Make adjustments as desired and click OK when you're finished.**

You can use negative numbers for negative indentation.

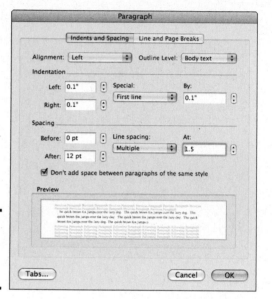

Figure 3-7:
Spacing out in a good way.

Kicking in kerning

We know; kerning sounds like jargon. However, *kerning* is a fancy word for the space between two letters. Usually kerning comes into play when dealing with text in large point sizes, such as in a headline, for example. A capital letter, such as *W*, can look too far away from a small *a* or the rest of the letters in a word, especially when a large point size is used. Adjusting the kerning can make it "look right." Figure 3-8 shows the same text without kerning (top) and with kerning (bottom). Notice that the bottom one looks "right," whereas the *W* and the *a* are too far apart in the top one.

Not all fonts support kerning, but the ones you get from professional typesetting companies, such as Monotype or Adobe, normally do. Because support for kerning isn't a given, check your font's specifications with the font's vendor or manufacturer to ascertain whether any given font supports kerning.

Water — Without kerning

Figure 3-8:
Comparing without and with kerning.

Water — With kerning

Assuming that the font you choose in Word supports kerning, follow these steps to kern:

1. **Select the word, sentence, or paragraph you want to kern and then choose Format⇨Font.**

   The Font dialog appears.

2. **Select the Character Spacing tab, as shown in Figure 3-9.**

3. **Select the Kerning for Fonts option and type** 20 **in the Points and Above number box.**

   Most of the time, Word doesn't allow you to type any number lower than eight in the Points and Above number box.

4. **Click OK to return to the selected text.**

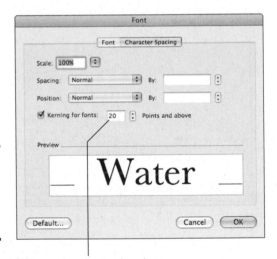

Figure 3-9: Character Spacing options for kerning.

Make your kerning settings here.

Spacing the characters

A companion concept to kerning is *tracking,* or *character spacing.* Kerning comes into play only with individual characters, whereas character spacing controls the amount of space among all the selected letters in your document.

Think of kerning as spacing based on the shapes of the letters, and character spacing as spacing just based on the distance between the letters, whatever their shapes might be.

Word allows you to increase or decrease character spacing to pack the letters tighter or stretch them out more. To increase or decrease the spacing between the letters of the selected text, follow these steps:

1. **Select the word, sentence, or paragraph you want to adjust the character spacing for and then choose Format⇨Font.**

The Font dialog appears.

2. **Select the Character Spacing tab (see Figure 3-9).**

3. **Choose from the following options:**

- *Scale:* Scales the selected text larger or smaller by the percent indicated. Type a number or click the down arrow to select from a menu of options.

- *Spacing:* Click the Normal, Expanded, or Condensed pop-up menu. This controls the amount of space between words based on these parameters by increasing or decreasing the By *[number]* in points. Although you can go down to 1 point with the Decrease option button to the right of the input field, you can type in any figure in the By *[number]* box, even something as low as 0.05 point.

- *Position:* See the following section.

- *Kerning:* See the preceding section.

Making friends with subscript and superscript

When you get thirsty for a glass of good old H_2O, it better be crystal clear and the *2* better be a subscript between the H and the O. Otherwise, it won't taste like water because it's not water; it's some other chemical composition. Of course you can do fancy stuff, such as use the Equation Editor, which we explain in Book I, Chapter 6, but most of the time all you have to do is select a character and then click the Subscript (or Superscript, depending on what you're doing) button on the Formatting Palette, as appropriate.

Using special characters for special occasions

Deep inside each font are special characters that can be used as long as you know how to find them. For example, the new Symbols section of Formatting Palette offers several choices and replaces the Symbol option on the Format menu from previous Word versions.

Still, many more interesting characters are living within your fonts. Mac OS X has a nifty Characters Palette to put these characters to work. Before you can use the Characters Palette, you have to turn it on in Mac OS X System Preferences. Follow these steps to turn on the Characters Palette:

1. **Choose Apple Menu⇨System Preferences.**

The System Preferences pane appears.

2. **In the Personal category, click the International button to change the sheet to a multi-tabbed interface.**

3. **Click the Input Menu tab.**

4. **Select the Character Palette option to turn it on.**

   By default, the Character Palette option also selects the Show Input Menu in Menu Bar option at the bottom of the sheet.

   The Input menu is the flag for your computer's default language and appears on the right in the menu bar. See Figure 3-10.

5. **Click the red Close button to close System Preferences.**

With the Characters Palette turned on, it's time to put it to work. To use the Characters Palette, follow these steps:

1. **In Word, position the cursor in your document at the point you want to enter a special character.**

2. **Click the Input Menu in your menu bar. (See Figure 3-10.)**

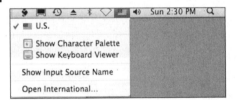

Figure 3-10: Finding Character Palette on the Input menu.

3. **Choose the Show Character Palette option from the Input menu to bring up the Characters Palette, as shown in Figure 3-11.**

4. **Select a character to insert into your document; then click Insert.**

   The selected character is inserted into your Word document at the insertion cursor.

5. **Click the red Close button to close the Characters Palette.**

The Characters Palette depicts special characters, and when you choose one in the Category list, it shows you all the existing glyph variants in the Collections pop-up menu. (A *glyph* is the artistic drawing, or shape, that comprises an individual character within a character set.) Simply select a symbol and then click the Insert or Insert with Font button in the lower-right corner. (The Characters Palette decides which option to offer based upon the fonts in your document.) Notice the options in the lower left and also the Search box to help you find symbols quickly. The example in Figure 3-11 shows how to find a slashed zero that doesn't look like a capital O. The Characters Palette is extraordinarily interactive, so your screen might not look exactly like this figure.

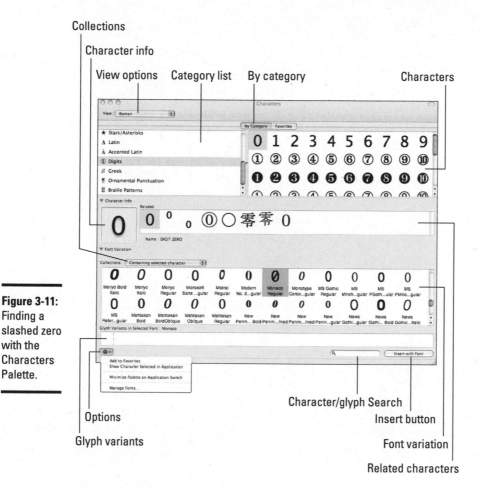

Collections
Character info
View options   Category list   By category   Characters

Book II
Chapter 3

Working with
Text, Words, and
Paragraphs

Figure 3-11:
Finding a
slashed zero
with the
Characters
Palette.

Options

Glyph variants

Character/glyph Search
Insert button
Font variation
Related characters

Shooting bullets and numbing numbers

For the most part, Word's bullets and numbering features work like seamless
magic. Select a range of text or an outline, click a button on the Formatting
Palette, and in a flash, you have a great looking list.

Creating a list with the Formatting Palette

Turning a list into a bulleted or numbered list is easy as pie with the
Formatting Palette. Try this simple example (see Figure 3-12):

1. **Type a simple list.**

   For example, enter this text:

> **First item**
>
> **Next item**
>
> **Last item**

2. **Select the list or a sequence of small paragraphs.**

3. **Click the appropriate bullet or number type on the Formatting Palette.**

   Your list has either the bullet style or number style you chose. If you chose a numbered list, it looks much like Figure 3-12, with consecutive numbers in front of each item.

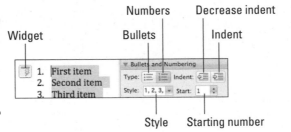

Figure 3-12: Applying bullets or numbers to a list.

You can fine-tune the formatting of your bullets and numbers right on the Formatting Palette, as shown in Figure 3-12. Your options are

✦ **Type:** Choose bullets on the left or numbers on the right.

✦ **Indent:** Click the left button to decrease indentation or the right button to increase indentation.

✦ **Style:** Choose from available bullet and number styles. We show you how to customize these styles in the following sections.

✦ **Start:** In a numbered list, choose the starting number.

If your document already has a numbered list somewhere, Word may display a small widget, as shown in Figure 3-12. Click the widget and you can start the numbering over. Of course, you could always change the Start number on the Formatting Palette to restart at any number you choose.

Starting a numbered list automatically

Word's default AutoCorrect setting detects automatically when you're starting a numbered list. To make Word think you're starting a numbered list, do the following:

1. **Type some text and then press Return or Enter.**

2. **Type 1 followed by a period, a space, and some text.**

3. **Press Return or Enter.**

Word indents the number and the text, turns on numbering, and displays a widget. Click the widget for the following options:

- *Undo Automatic Numbering:* Undoes the automatic number format that was just applied.

- *Stop Automatically Creating Numbered Lists:* Tells Word to stop using the Automatic Numbering feature.

- *Control AutoFormat Options:* Displays the AutoFormat as You Type tab in the AutoCorrect preferences dialog. See the section, "AutoFormat as You Type," later in this chapter.

**Book II
Chapter 3**

**Working with
Text, Words, and
Paragraphs**

Telling Word to stop adding bullets or numbers

The easiest way to turn off bullets and numbering is to select the text you don't want formatted with bullets or numbers and click the appropriate Bullets or Numbers button on the Formatting Palette to turn it off.

If you are typing a bulleted list and you want to tell Word that you've typed the last entry for the list, simply press Return or Enter twice after the last entry in the list. Word returns to normal text.

Starting over in the middle of a list

You may need to start over your numbering in the middle of a list. Follow these steps to start over your numbering in the middle of list (see Figure 3-13):

1. **Select the text where you want numbering to restart.**

2. **Right-click or Control-click, and then choose Restart Numbering from the pop-up menu.**

   Word starts the numbers from the first number that you have in the Start field of the Bullets and Numbering section of the Formatting Palette.

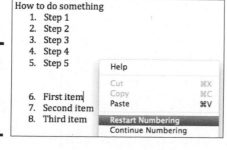

Figure 3-13: Restarting numbers in a numbered list.

Making special bullets and numbers

In the "Using special characters for special occasions" section, earlier in this chapter, we talk about using special characters. You may be wondering whether you can use these characters to make your bulleted and numbered lists more interesting. Well, yes you can. Word allows you to take advantage of special characters, and you can even use pictures (although it's best to use very tiny ones) as bullets or numbers. After you create something you're happy with, you can create new styles based on your customized bulleted and numbered lists so that you can apply them to other lists later.

Word supports seven indent layers of bullets and numbers (which are probably way more layers than you'll ever need, but it's good to know the depth is there if you ever do need it). The current formatting for each of the layers can be viewed and then customized. Choose Format⇨Bullets and Numbering. This brings up the Bullets and Numbering dialog (see Figure 3-14). This dialog allows you to customize each level of bullet or number. Across the top of the dialog are four tabs:

✦ **Bulleted:** Customize a bullet for each of the layers.

✦ **Numbered:** Set style and formatting options for numbered lists.

✦ **Outline Numbered:** Customize options for working in Outline View.

✦ **List Styles:** Create and save list customizations as styles.

Each of the four tabs of the Bullets and Numbering dialog, as shown in Figure 3-14, has its own special customization options. The first two, Bulleted and Numbered, work similarly, so we start with them. In Figure 3-14, you can see the bulleted list styles, and we've selected the first indent, which is a dot by default.

Loving legal beagles and authors of long documents

Some of our readers might spend a lot of time working in Outline view, in particular those in the legal profession and writing long documents, such as books and manuscripts. The Outline Numbered tab of the Bullets and Numbering dialog will be of particular interest to you. On this tab, you can choose from different styles that apply to the entire bullets and numbering scheme. Of the eight choices presented, legal professionals will be most interested in the bottom-left style, Article 1. Follow these steps to turn on legal formatting for long documents:

1. **Select the sentence, text, phrase, or paragraph that you want to format the numbers for.**

   Alternatively, place your insertion point in that block of text.

2. **Choose Format⇨Bullets and Numbering.**

   The Bullets and Numbering dialog opens (refer to Figure 3-12).

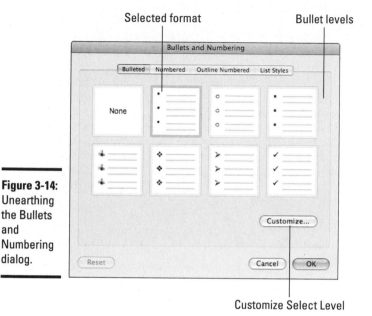

Selected format

Bullet levels

Figure 3-14:
Unearthing
the Bullets
and
Numbering
dialog.

Customize Select Level

3. **Click the Outline Numbered tab.**

4. **Choose an option:**

   - For legal customizations, select the Article I option.

   - For long documents, select the Chapter 1 option.

5. **Click the Customize . . . button.**

   The Customized Outline Numbered List dialog opens.

6. **Click the arrow button in the lower-left corner.**

   The dialog expands to reveal more options.

7. **To enable legal-style customizations, select the Legal Style Numbering check box for each level.**

   Use this check box only for legal-style documents.

8. **Make other adjustments as desired and click OK.**

Painless paragraph formatting

Whether prose or poetry, a business report or a science project, you can have a paragraph call attention to itself by changing the paragraph's formatting. Conversely, you have a potential problem on your hands when a paragraph unintentionally calls attention to itself when it crosses a page boundary.

Dealing with widows and orphans

Earlier in this chapter, we discuss indents and spacing paragraph controls. Here we delve into different aspects of paragraph control. A paragraph that starts with a single line at the bottom of a page and then continues onto the next is a *widow;* its counterpart, the *orphan,* occurs when the last line of a paragraph ends at the top of a page.

Widows and orphans aside, it's good to know that Word allows you to control paragraph formatting so that you can call attention to paragraphs when you want to, and to avoid unhappy problems like widows and orphans. To get at these paragraph formatting controls:

1. **Choose Format⇨Paragraph.**

   The Paragraph dialog opens.

2. **Click the Line and Page Breaks tab.**

   Line and page break settings become available, as shown in Figure 3-15.

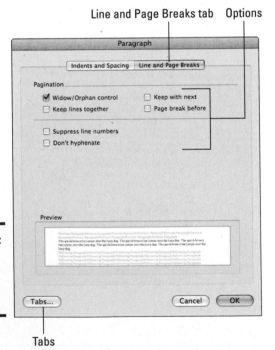

Figure 3-15: Keeping paragraphs under control.

Although widow and orphan control is the main claim to fame of the Line and Page Breaks tab, here's a rundown regarding what happens when you put a check into its check boxes:

Pagination

These check boxes affect paragraphs:

✦ **Widow/Orphan Control:** Prevents widows and orphans.

✦ **Keep Lines Together:** Sometimes Word's paragraph spacing can cause text that ought to stay together to get separated. For example, you might have a heading near the end of a page and you want the heading to stay associated with the paragraph that follows. Word wants to put the heading at the bottom of a page and then the associated text winds up all by itself at the top of the next page. To prevent this problem, select both the heading and the following paragraph, and then select this check box. Word keeps the text and the heading together.

✦ **Keep with Next:** You may wish to make sure two paragraphs are always kept together. Select both paragraphs and then select this check box. Word won't allow a page break to come between them.

✦ **Page Break Before:** If you have a paragraph that you want to always start at the top of its page, select a paragraph and then select this check box. Word makes sure a page break always occurs before the selected paragraph.

Other options

Here are some other options you can choose from the Paragraph dialog:

✦ **Suppress Line Numbers check box:** This works if you've turned on line numbering, which we discuss in the section, "Automatically Number Lines," later in this chapter. The lines that are selected when you choose this option aren't included in the page count.

✦ **Don't Hyphenate check box:** This check box does what it says. Select paragraphs that you don't want Word to use hyphenation with and then select this check box.

✦ **Tabs button:** Click this button to display the Tabs dialog (see the section, "Precision tab placement," later in this chapter), which we discuss in the following section.

Tinkering with tabs

The old-fashioned idea of a basic *tab stop* is that when you press the Tab key, the cursor jumps to the next tab stop that's set on the ruler and then you start typing. In Word, this kind of tab stop is the left tab stop. These days, tabs do a lot more than just act as a position to stop the cursor. Read on!

Working with the Tabs menu

Word has five types of tab stops. To see the list of tabs, you must use a view that supports rulers. Follow these steps:

1. **Choose either View⇨Draft or View⇨Print Layout View.**

   Both views support rulers.

2. **Choose View⇨Ruler if the ruler isn't turned on already.**

   You can see Word's rulers.

3. **Click the Tabs menu to the far left of the horizontal ruler.**

   The Tabs menu, as shown in Figure 3-16, appears.

Click for Tabs menu.   Horizontal Ruler

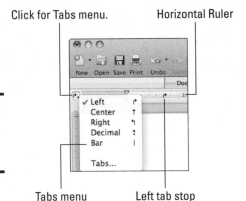

Figure 3-16: Displaying the Tabs menu.

Tabs menu   Left tab stop

Notice the five kinds of tabs in Figure 3-16, each with its own icon. Left is the default tab. If you choose a different kind of tab, the Tabs menu displays the selected kind of tab.

When you work with tabs, be sure to toggle paragraph marks on and off with the Show All Non-Printing Characters button on the Standard toolbar. This button is simply labeled Show on the toolbar. When paragraph marks are turned on, they look like the icon in the margin. Whenever you press the Tab key, an arrow pointing to the right appears.

Setting a tab stop

Tabs work at the paragraph level; when you set tab stops, they work with the currently selected paragraphs. You can select an entire document before you set tabs if you want your tab stops to work for the whole thing. The actual steps to set a tab stop are simple:

1. **Select one or more paragraphs.**

   If you want to select the entire document, choose Edit⇨Select All or press ⌘-A.

2. **Click the Tabs menu (see Figure 3-16) and choose one of the five tab stops.**

   See the following section for more detail about each tab stop option.

3. **Click in the horizontal ruler wherever you want a tab stop.**

   Each time you click, the symbol for the tab stop you chose is placed into the ruler.

The five kinds of tab stops

Your paragraph behaves differently for each of the five kinds of tab stops. Here's a description of each kind of tab stop:

✦ **Left:** By default, each document has a left tab stop every ½ inch, unless you click in the ruler to add your own stops. If you press the Tab key, the cursor advances to the next tab stop. If you start typing at a left tab stop, your text begins at that tab stop. See Figure 3-17.

Figure 3-17:
Typing from
a left tab
stop (Draft
View).

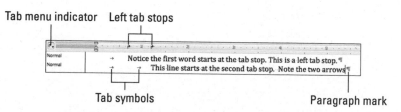

✦ **Right:** After you set a right tab stop, press the Tab key to move to the right tab stop and start typing. Use a right tab to right-align text, perhaps when making a column. See Figure 3-18.

Figure 3-18:
Typing at
a right tab
stop (Draft
View).

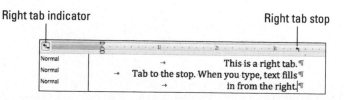

✦ **Center:** After you set a center tab stop, press the Tab key to move to the stop. When you start typing, your text is centered below the tab stop. See Figure 3-19.

Figure 3-19:
Typing at a
center tab
stop (Draft
View).

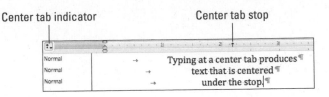

Center tab indicator   Center tab stop

+ **Decimal:** As the name implies, use this tab stop when you're typing decimal numbers. Word lines up the numbers at the decimal point. Even if you don't type an actual decimal point, Word assumes the decimal point.

+ **Bar:** Danger: Using a bar tab stop may cause inebriation. Okay, not really. A bar tab stop is much the same as a left tab stop, except Word puts a vertical bar at the tab stop. After you set a bar stop and start typing, your text is to the right of the bar. See Figure 3-20.

Bar tab indicator   Bar tab stop

Figure 3-20:
Typing at a
bar tab stop
(Draft View).

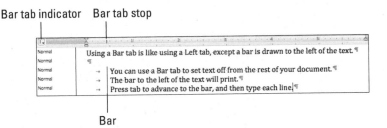

Bar

Precision tab placement

Although clicking in the ruler to place tabs is fast and easy, you may have a need for precise tab positioning. You can approach this in several ways, but we suggest you try to click into the ruler to place your tab stop(s) first. You can drag tabs in the ruler to reposition them. If that placement isn't precise enough for you, choose Tabs . . . from the Tabs menu (see Figure 3-16) to open the Tabs dialog, as shown in Figure 3-21, where you can fine-tune to thousandths of an inch.

The Tabs dialog has lots of tab settings that you can control. When working with this dialog, your changes aren't committed until you press OK. Here's the run down:

+ **Default Tab Stops:** When you open a new, blank document, a tab stop exists every ½-inch — even though there's no tab stop marker to show this in the ruler. You can press the Tab key in a blank document if you don't believe us. You can adjust the default setting, but we can't think of any particular reason to do so.

List of tabs in this paragraph   Set default interval for tab stops.

Position

Alignment of selected tab

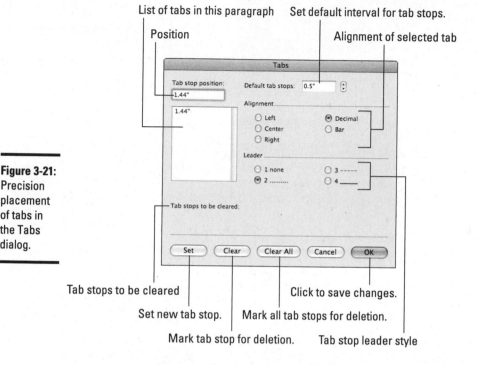

Figure 3-21:
Precision
placement
of tabs in
the Tabs
dialog.

Tab stops to be cleared

Set new tab stop.

Mark tab stop for deletion.

Click to save changes.

Mark all tab stops for deletion.

Tab stop leader style

✦ **Tab Stop Position:** Enter a position in inches, and then

  • *To clear the entered tab stop position,* click the Clear button.

  • *To create a new stop at the entered tab stop position,* select the Alignment and Leader settings and then click the Set button.

  • *To modify a stop at the entered tab stop position,* click the Alignment and Leader settings and then click the Set button.

✦ **List of tabs:** Clicking tab stops here enters the stop into the Tab Stop Position field so you don't have to type.

✦ **Clear button:** Adds the entered tab stop position to the Tabs Stops to be Cleared area. The tabs clear when you click OK.

✦ **Clear All button:** Marks all tab stops for the current paragraph and notes this in the Tab Stops to be Cleared area. The stops clear when you click OK.

✦ **Leader:** For left, right, center, and decimal tab stops, selecting one of these adds the selected style as a fill between the tab stops.

Clearing tab stops

To remove a tab stop, you can simply drag a tab stop from the ruler and then release the mouse anywhere. This works only about half the time, though. Use the Tabs dialog (see Figure 3-21) if you come across a stubborn tab that won't go away.

Formatting an Entire Document

When you think of a document as a whole, elements such as columns, margins, and page breaks come to mind. Knowing how to manage these elements helps you create a better, more consistent layout. In this section, we discuss controls that when applied, affect the entire document.

Ruling margins by the Ruler

Most people are accustomed to seeing a perimeter style margin surrounding the text in documents. You'd have a hard time reading a book if the type went from edge-to-edge on each page. In a book or magazine in which the sheets are bound, you need extra white space, or *gutter,* in addition to a margin. Even normal documents that need to be printed and filed need that gutter.

Paper can become tattered, which is one more reason to keep the text away from the edges. Even when reading on a computer screen or a handheld device, your eyes seem to prefer the definition a clean margin provides.

 You can adjust the margins by dragging the margin sliders in the rulers. Of course, the rulers must be turned on first by choosing View➪Ruler when in Draft View or Print Layout View. This turns on the rulers at the top and left edge of the document area in Word.

Even then, many users find it easier to adjust margins with a dialog. Follow these instructions to display the margin settings in the Document dialog:

1. **Choose Format➪Document.**

2. **Click the Margins tag.**

The Document dialog (as shown in Figure 3-22) opens. You can type in exact values for the margins so that you can keep consistent margin values in all your documents.

The Margins tab of the Document dialog is straightforward. Enter decimal values for distances in inches or use the up/down buttons next to the input fields. You need to know about the following other aspects of the Margins tab:

Header and footer settings

Margin settings

Preview

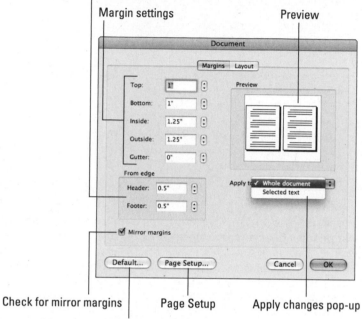

Figure 3-22:
Managing
margins
with ease.

Check for mirror margins

Page Setup

Apply changes pop-up

Make these settings Word's default.

✦ **Mirror Margins:** Select this check box to use mirror margins and a gutter when you set up a document to be printed with facing pages, such as a book or a magazine. If a regular physical book is open, the extra gutter on the page to your left is mirrored on the page to your right so that the text is kept away from the binding by an equal amount on both pages.

✦ **Apply To:** Choose from the following:

 • *Whole Document:* The settings apply to the entire document.

 • *Selected Text:* The settings apply to whatever text you selected before opening the Document dialog.

✦ **Default:** Default turns the current settings into Word's default settings to be used from now on when creating new, blank documents. This setting is stored in Word's Normal (.dotx) template.

✦ **Page Setup:** Displays the Page Setup dialog (see Chapter 8 of this minibook).

✦ **Cancel:** Closes the Document dialog without applying changes to the document. If you click the Default button, those changes are done.

✦ **OK:** Applies the changes.

The Document Margins section of the Formatting Palette also enables you to manually set the margins for your document.

Breaking up things

As documents grow, they need to be broken into manageable parts. The longer a document gets, the more parts it's likely to have. We focus on three specific kinds of breaks — page breaks, section breaks, and column breaks — to achieve manageable parts.

Click the Show button on the Standard toolbar to toggle on and off your ability to see breaks in your document.

Page breaks

Page breaks are points in your document where one page ends and the next page starts. Most of the time Word can handle these breaks automatically, but at times, you want to force a page break — to begin a new chapter, for example. This is accomplished easily: Click in your document where you want to force a break and then choose Insert⇨Break⇨Page Break.

To remove a page break, make sure that you've enabled the Show All Non-Printing Characters option. Then double-click the page break so that it's highlighted and press the Delete key on your keyboard.

Section breaks

Section breaks are points in your document where formatting changes, such as margin settings, header and footer formatting, styles, and page setup, occur. To create a section break:

1. **Click where you want the desired break to occur and then choose Insert⇨Break (see Figure 3-23).**

2. **Choose one of the following options:**

   - *Section Break (Next Page):* Creates a section break and a page break at the same spot.

   - *Section Break (Continuous):* Creates a section break at the insertion cursor without forcing a new page.

   - *Section Break (Odd Page):* Sets a section break that's always at the top of the next odd-numbered page.

   - *Section Break (Even Page):* Sets a section break that's always at the top of the next even-numbered page.

If you choose to display non-printing characters (see the section, "Working with the Tabs menu," earlier in this chapter), you can see the break indicator at the beginning or end of a section. Break formatting information is contained within the indicator, so you can copy and paste breaks as a way to copy and paste formatting within a document, or even from one document to another.

Figure 3-23: Sectioning a document.

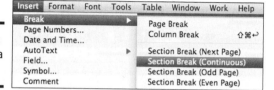

**Book II
Chapter 3**

Working with
Text, Words, and
Paragraphs

Making columns

You can put text into columns in Word. Follow these steps (see Figure 3-24):

1. **Select the text you wish to put into columns and then click the Columns button on the Standard toolbar.**

    A submenu appears.

2. **Move the mouse cursor over the submenu.**

    As your mouse cursor moves over the submenu, the number of columns lights up. When you move to the right, the submenu grows.

3. **Click the number of columns you want.**

    Word automatically turns your text into the number of columns you chose. Word inserts a continuous section break (see the preceding section) before and after the text that's now in columns.

After you have text in columns, you can adjust the width between the columns by dragging column width indicators in the ruler. Section break indicators are visible when you click the Show All Non-Printing Characters button on the Standard toolbar. To restore multiple columns to a single column, select the column text and follow the steps you used to create the columns, but choose to make one column.

Tickling footers and watching your header

People seem to really enjoy customizing headers and footers because they're versatile and can be used to contain page numbers, dates, and logos for formal stationery. Word 2008 has a completely new interface for working with headers and footers. You can work with headers and footers in Print Layout View or Web Layout View. To work with the new interface:

Show non-printing characters

Columns   Columns submenu

Adjust column width   Number of columns

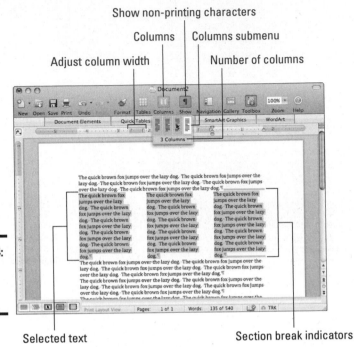

Figure 3-24:
Putting
text into
columns.

Selected text   Section break indicators

1. **In the Elements bar, choose Document Elements.**

This activates the Document Elements Gallery.

2. **Click either the Header or Footer tab.**

This displays lots of fancy new header and footers that you can customize (see Figure 3-25).

3. **From the Insert As pop-up menu, choose one of the following:**

- *Odd Pages:* Inserts the element on odd pages only.
- *Even Pages:* Inserts the element on even pages only.
- *All Pages:* Inserts the element on every page.

4. **Choose one of the header or footer elements.**

The selected header or footer element is inserted into your document.

The Formatting Palette's Header and Footer options are available whenever you edit a header or footer. Eagle-eyed readers may notice that the Table section may also become available because the header and footer layout is done with tables in some elements. We discuss tables in Chapter 5 of this minibook. Here we focus on just the header and footer controls.

After you insert a header or a footer, you can click into the element to insert the following from the Formatting Palette (see Figure 3-26):

Document elements tab

Header elements

Insert As pop-up

Footer elements

Elements Gallery   Click for more elements.

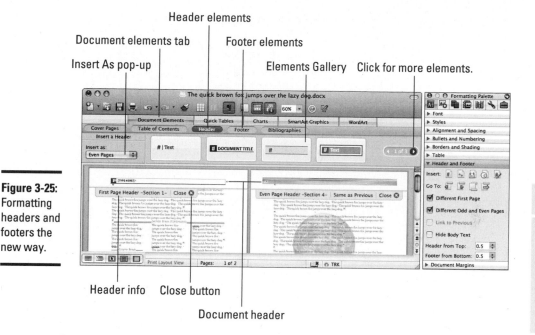

Figure 3-25:
Formatting headers and footers the new way.

Book II
Chapter 3

Working with
Text, Words, and
Paragraphs

Header info   Close button

Document header

Current date

Page number   Format page number

Figure 3-26:
Header and footer insert items.

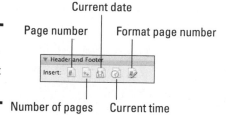

Number of pages   Current time

✦ **Page Number:** Displays the current page number.

✦ **Number of Pages:** Displays the document page count.

✦ **Current Date:** Displays today's date (not the date inserted).

✦ **Current Time:** Displays the current time.

✦ **Format Page Number:** This button doesn't actually insert anything; it displays the Page Number Format dialog, as shown in Figure 3-27, which you can use to format not only page numbers, but chapter numbers as well.

As shown in Figure 3-27, you can control the following:

✦ **Number Format:** Choose a format in this pop-up menu.

✦ **Include Chapter Number:** Select this check box to activate automatic chapter numbering, chapter starts with style options, and separator options.

Number formats pop-up

Chapter number styles and separators

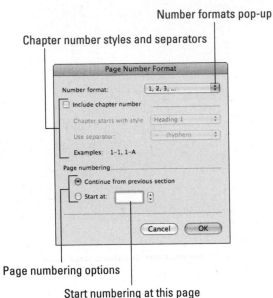

Figure 3-27:
The Page
Number
Format
dialog.

Page numbering options

Start numbering at this page

◆ **Chapter Starts with Style:** Choose from heading styles.

◆ **Use Separator:** Choose a separator from the pop-up menu.

◆ **Page Numbering:** Choose one of the following options in this section:

• *Continue from Previous Section:* The numbering will continue in the same format as whatever has come before it in the document.

• *Start At:* Enter a number to start page numbering at for this section of the current document.

The Formatting Palette's Go To section allows you to move about your document's headers and footers (see Figure 3-28). This section has the following options:

Figure 3-28:
Getting to
headers and
footers.

◆ **Show Previous:** Displays the previous section's header or footer.

◆ **Show Next:** Displays the next section's header or footer.

✦ **Switch between Header and Footer:** Switches you to the current section's footer if you're currently viewing the header or vice-versa.

✦ **Go to Section:** A pop-up menu from which you can choose to edit any section's header or footer.

Getting around with bookmarks

You have a lot of ways to get from one place to another in a long document. One of the best ways is to create *bookmarks,* electronic markers that you can use to identify specific places, throughout your document. Follow these steps to create a bookmark:

1. **Click at the point in the document where you want to create a bookmark and then choose Insert⇨Bookmark.**

The Bookmark dialog opens.

2. **In the Bookmark Name field, type a name that makes sense to you later (no spaces are allowed) and click the Add button.**

Your bookmark is added to the list of bookmarks for that document. You can view these at any time by summoning the Bookmark dialog.

Follow these steps to go to your bookmarks:

1. **Press ⌘-G.**

The Find and Replace dialog appears. (See Figure 3-29.)

2. **Click the Go To tab if it isn't selected already.**

3. **In the Go to What list, choose Bookmark.**

4. **To the right of the Enter Bookmark Name field, click the pop-up menu to choose a bookmark or type a name of a bookmark in the field if you already know it.**

5. **Click the Go To button or press Return.**

Word takes you to the place in your document where the bookmark resides. Click the red Close button to close the Find and Replace dialog.

Book II
Chapter 3

Working with Text, Words, and Paragraphs

Figure 3-29:
Working with bookmarks.

Writing with Style

Styles are like fine wines: You have an almost unlimited variety; different kinds are best for different occasions; they're fun to use; and you don't have to be a connoisseur to appreciate a good one. We think that homemade styles can be the best of all.

A *style* is the way in which content is formatted, and the format is made up of a collection of attributes. The Formatting Palette is where the most popular formatting attributes and characteristics of style are applied. In fact, the Formatting Palette could have just as accurately been called the Styling Palette.

Applying slick styles

It's great that styles, one of the most powerful features in Word and Office, are so easy to work with. You'll find that styling your document is as intuitive as 1–2–3. Follow these steps to apply a style:

1. **Select some text to apply a style to.**

2. **In the Formatting Palette, click the Styles disclosure triangle to reveal all style options if they aren't visible already.**

3. **In the Pick a Style list, choose a style that you want to apply to the selected text.**

    The style is applied to your selection.

After you've applied some styles, click into the text of various portions of your document. Notice that the Formatting Palette tells you which particular style has been applied to that selection. The current style of selected text is kept constantly refreshed. You'll see this displayed as the first thing in the Styles section of the Formatting Palette.

Applying document themes to styles

After you've applied some styles to your text, you can change the theme of your entire document by clicking a document theme within from the Document Theme section of the Formatting Palette. While you apply different document themes, watch the styles you applied in your document instantly adopt the new theme colors and fonts. Notice that the Formatting Palette Style's section also updates to match the document theme you apply.

Can't see the Document Theme section in the Formatting Palette? Some new features, such as document themes, work only with the new XML-based file formats, such as DOCX and DOTX. If you're working with older DOC or DOT files, or even RTF files, the Document Theme option isn't active and won't show up in the Formatting Palette.

Making a homemade style

The real power of styles comes from creating your own. Word has a fast and easy way to save a new style.

Create a new style from formatted text

Say you spent some time formatting text just the way you want it and you want to save that format as a style so you can use it again in another document. Here's what you do:

1. **Select the formatted text.**

2. **In the Styles section of Formatting Palette, click the New Style . . . button.**

This button is oversized, green, and has a plus sign so you can't miss it!

The New Style dialog opens, as shown in Figure 3-30. The attributes of your selection display in this dialog.

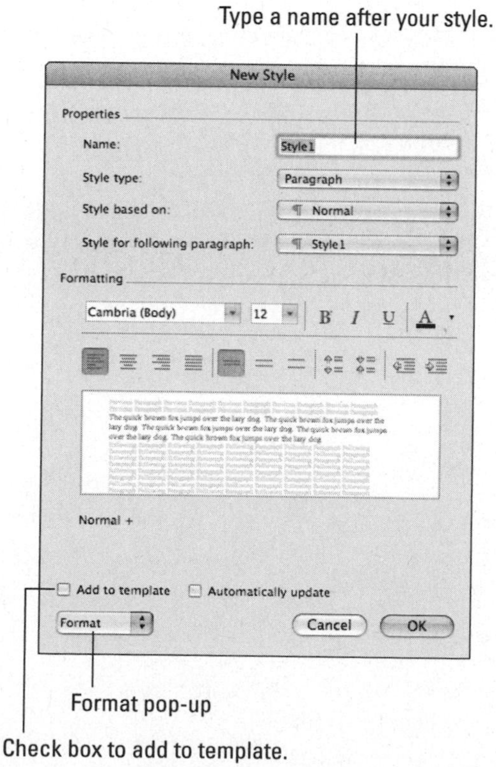

Book II Chapter 3

Working with Text, Words, and Paragraphs

Type a name after your style.

Figure 3-30: Making a new text style.

Format pop-up

Check box to add to template.

3. **Below Properties, in the Name field, type a name for your style and then select the Add to Template check box.**

   If you leave this deselected, your style is saved only with the current document. If you select the check box, the changes are saved to Word's Normal (.dotx) template.

4. **Click OK.**

   Your style appears in Formatting Palette in the Styles section in Pick Style to Apply.

For the style connoisseur, Word enables you to see an overview of styles within an entire document. To do this, switch the view in the View menu to either Draft or Outline. If you drag the divider between the style information and your document's body all the way to the left edge of the window, you can't see the style information, and you'll lose the divider. To get the divider back:

1. **From the Word menu, choose Preferences.**

2. **Choose View.**

3. **Below the Window section, find the section for style area width. Enter a number or use the up/down control to enter a value greater than zero.**

Working with the Style dialog

The Style dialog allows you to create new styles, modify existing styles, delete styles, and organize styles. To create new styles from scratch or from existing styles, follow these steps:

1. **Choose Format⇨Style.**

   The Style dialog opens. Here you see a list of the styles you already have.

2. **Click the New button.**

   The New Style dialog opens (see Figure 3-30).

When you open the New Style dialog, notice that you can create styles from one of four style types:

✦ **Paragraph:** Affecting entire paragraphs, these are the most commonly used styles.

✦ **Character:** Affects any character attribute, such as font, size, and italics.

✦ **Table:** Creates new styles for tables.

✦ **List:** Creates styles for bulleted or numbered lists.

Notice as you change style types in the New Style dialog's Style Type pop-up menu, the other options in the New Style dialog change as well. Click the Format pop-up menu in the lower-left corner of the New Style dialog, as shown in Figure 3-30, to find specialized formatting tools. Following is a list of formatting customizations that are saved with a style:

+ **Font Formatting:** Displays the Font dialog.

+ **Paragraph Formatting:** Displays the Paragraph dialog.

+ **Tabs:** Displays the Tabs dialog.

+ **Border:** Displays the Borders and Shadings dialog.

+ **Language:** Displays the Language dialog.

+ **Frame:** Displays the Frame dialog.

+ **Numbering:** Displays the Bullets and Numbering dialog.

+ **Shortcut Key:** Displays the Customize Keyboard dialog.

You can save your styles in Word's *Normal* template (the default template used when Word opens), a custom template, or within your individual documents. If you save a style in Normal (.dotx), it's available to all documents from then on.

Copying styles

If you have a custom style that was saved in the document you're working on, you can copy the style to other documents (usually templates) or to the Normal (.dotx) template with the Organizer dialog, which we discuss in the following section.

Using Organizer

Organizer can copy styles, AutoText (which we cover in Chapter 6 in this minibook), and toolbars (which we cover in Chapter 1 of this minibook) from one Word template or document to another. Organizer can also be used to rename or delete styles, AutoText, or toolbars, but copying styles seems to be the most common use for Organizer.

Opening Organizer

Use the Styles dialog to fire up Organizer. Follow these steps:

1. **Choose Format⇨Style.**

   The Style dialog opens.

2. **Click the Organizer button.**

   The Organizer dialog, as shown in Figure 3-31, opens.

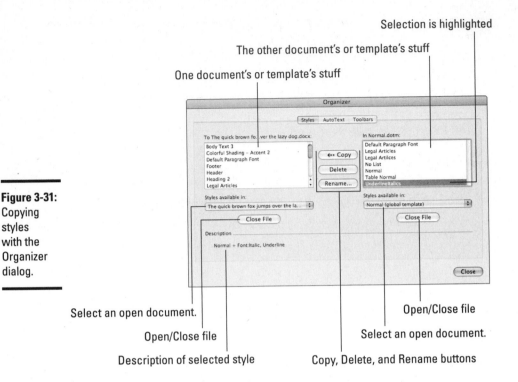

Selection is highlighted

The other document's or template's stuff

One document's or template's stuff

Figure 3-31:
Copying
styles
with the
Organizer
dialog.

Select an open document.

Open/Close file

Description of selected style

Open/Close file

Select an open document.

Copy, Delete, and Rename buttons

Copying styles, AutoText, and toolbars

Organizer is quite simple. You can copy styles, AutoText, and toolbars from one open document or template and put them in another. In Figure 3-31, Document 2 has a custom style that we wish to copy to our Normal (.dotx) template so we can use it whenever we open a new, blank Word document.

Here's how to copy styles, AutoText, and toolbars:

1. **On either the left or right side of Organizer, select an open document or template from the pop-up menu.**

2. **On the opposite side, select a different document or template from the pop-up menu.**

3. **On either side, select something (a style, AutoText, or a toolbar) to copy to the other document or template.**

    The Copy button arrow will always point at the document that will be copied to.

4. **Click the Copy button to copy your selection to the destination.**

    The item list of the destination document or template will automatically update to show that the item was added.

Copying formats

It's not a big topic, but it's important because it is so popular. To copy formatting in Word:

1. **Select something — anything! Text, tables, anything that has formatting associated with it.**

2. **Click the Format button on Word's Standard toolbar.**

3. **Click an object you want to apply the formatting to.**

   This applies the formatting of the object from Step 1.

   Be sure to copy formatting from similar objects. For example, you can copy the formatting of a table and apply that formatting to another table.

Word's Normal (.dotx) template is the template that determines all formatting aspects when opening new, blank Word documents. Styles, AutoText, and toolbars saved in Normal (.dotx) are always available to you in Word. In Organizer, the Normal (.dotx) template is referred to as Normal (global template).

AutoText copy works only between two Word templates (.dotx). AutoText can't be copied to or from regular Word documents. Of course, you can use Save As to turn an ordinary Word document into a template and then copy the AutoText.

Renaming or deleting items

In addition to copying, you can select an item from either side of Organizer and then click either:

✦ Delete: Deletes the selected style, AutoText, or toolbar from the document or template that is selected in that side's pop-up menu.

✦ Rename: Causes a small window to open that lets you type a new name for the selected style, AutoText, or toolbar.

AutoFormat as You Type

By default, most of Word's AutoFormat options are turned on. You can get at the list of AutoFormat options by taking these two steps:

1. **From Word's Tools menu, choose AutoCorrect.**

   The AutoCorrect preferences dialog opens.

2. **Click the AutoFormat as You Type tab.**

   The AutoCorrect options appropriate for automatic formatting display.

The preferences shown in Figure 3-32 are just options with check boxes that you can turn on and off at will. Most people probably don't need to adjust these, but if Word is automatically formatting something as you type and you don't want it to, this is the place to look first to look to see whether you need to turn off a setting. Moving the mouse cursor over the items updates the description. Click OK to tell Word to use your new preference settings or click Cancel to leave without making changes.

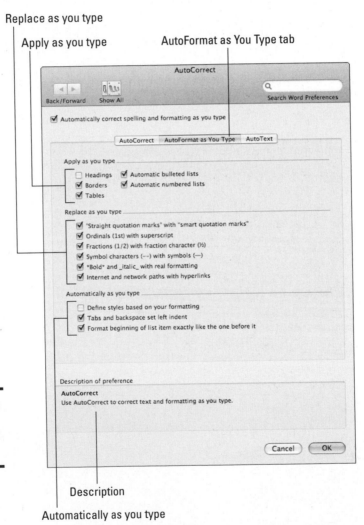

Replace as you type

Apply as you type

AutoFormat as You Type tab

Description

Automatically as you type

Figure 3-32:
Displaying
AutoFormat
options.

Automatically Numbering Lines

Word can automatically number the lines in your documents. This can be handy when referring to specific places within a document without having to use bookmarks, which we discuss earlier in this chapter. To add or remove line numbers, your document must be in Print Layout View. You can turn line numbers on for an entire document or selected portions of a document. Here's how:

1. **Select a portion, section, or several sections of a document.**

   If you want to number an entire document, skip this step.

2. **From the Format menu, choose Document.**

   The Document dialog opens.

3. **Click the Layout tab.**

4. **Click the Line Numbers button.**

   The Line Numbers options appear. See Figure 3-33.

5. **Click the Add Line Numbering check box to activate the line-numbering options.**

   Choose options as desired.

6. **Click OK twice to return to your Word document.**

Book II
Chapter 3

Working with
Text, Words, and
Paragraphs

Count by setting

From text

Start numbering at field

Add line numbering

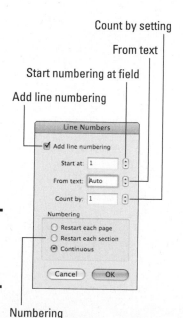

Figure 3-33:
Turning
on line
numbering.

Numbering

To remove line numbers repeat these steps, but in Step 5, deselect the Add Line Numbering check box.

You can control the following settings as you like:

✦ **Start At:** Sets the number of the first line.

✦ **From Text:** Sets the distance of the line numbers from the text.

✦ **Count By:** Skips the display of line numbers by however many you choose. If you count by two, only the numbers next to every other line will appear.

✦ **Numbering:** As shown in Figure 3-33, Continuous means the numbering won't restart at page or section breaks and will be continuous throughout the entire document or selection.

Chapter 4: Reviewing and Proofing with Word

In This Chapter

- ✔ Sharing and tracking changes
- ✔ Accepting, rejecting, and cleaning your document
- ✔ Casting spells and checks
- ✔ Working with dictionaries
- ✔ Choosing your language
- ✔ Taming the grammar checker

Sharing documents is an everyday activity in all kinds of companies and organizations, from businesses to universities and governments to churches. Sometimes you receive a document you're expected to contribute to, and other times you create a document that others need to add to and comment on. At times, multiple users are working on the same document, or maybe just one additional person is helping to edit a document. Whatever the situation may be, Word has you covered.

Make sure the text in your documents is spelled properly and is grammatically correct. Word has some nifty automatic spelling, grammar, AutoCorrect, and AutoFormat (discussed in the previous chapter) features. Time to dig into all this and more.

Keeping Track of Changes

So you're stuck on this committee at work and you have to prepare a report about something substantial. Everyone on the committee is supposed to contribute to this report, but nobody has time to meet. The solution could be a shared document. You decide to start with a Report template from Project Gallery, customize it for your committee, and then type your portion of the report.

Setting up tracking changes

This is where the Word Track Changes feature comes into play. Word keeps track of the changes made, who made them, and when the changes were made. But — and you knew there was a *but* — these changes aren't tracked automatically unless you do something to track them. Don't worry. You don't have to learn to ride a rocket or anything. All you have to do is turn on this feature; then you can send the document to your committee members, and their changes are tracked. After the members have made changes and added comments, they return the modified document to you. With this nifty feature, you can see who all made the changes in the document!

Before you turn on track changes and start sending your documents to everybody for their input, you need to tell them to check their Word preferences they open the tracked document to make sure that their names are known to Word. Check your own Word preferences to make sure your own information is accurate. Here's how:

1. **Choose Word⇨Preferences.**

Word's Preferences opens.

2. **In the Personal Settings section, choose User Information.**

The User Information preferences will be displayed. See Figure 4-1.

3. **At the top of the pane, verify that First, Last, and Initials show your actual name.**

Fill in this information and make corrections as needed. No other fields in User Information need to be adjusted in order to use track changes.

4. **Click OK to save your changes and close Preferences.**

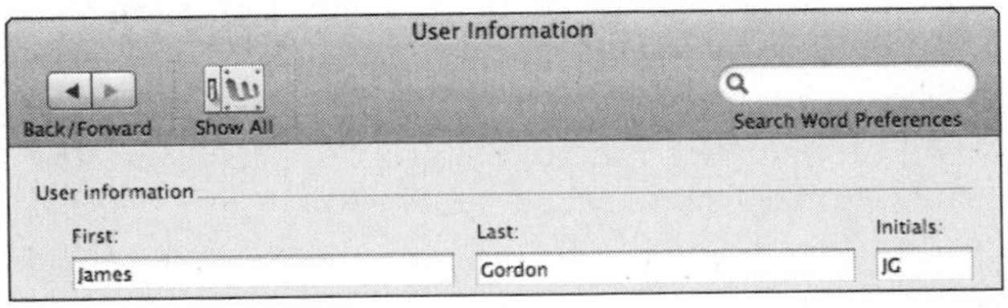

Figure 4-1: Make sure the user name is correct.

Sometimes IT departments clone Office installations, and everyone winds up with the same name or no name at all. Word can't detect different users if two or more people have the same name in the User Information preferences.

So how do you turn on the Track Changes feature for a document? There are several ways to activate track changes. Here's the first:

1. **From Word's View menu, choose Toolbars⇨Reviewing.**

Alternatively, click the TRK button visible at the bottom edge of the document window.

Either action summons the Reviewing toolbar, as shown in Figure 4-2.

2. Click the Track Changes button.

This activates track changes. Changes made to the document are recorded by the Track Changes feature.

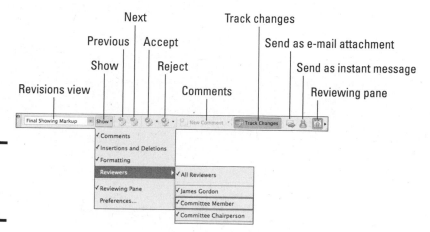

Figure 4-2:
The
Reviewing
toolbar.

Here's a second way to activate track changes:

1. Choose Tools⇨Track Changes⇨Highlight Changes.

This brings up the Highlight Changes dialog. See Figure 4-3.

2. Make sure all three check boxes are selected.

3. Click OK.

Word returns you to your document and starts tracking changes.

Figure 4-3:
Activating
Highlight
Changes.

That's all there is to it. When you're ready to distribute your document, you can use the Reviewing toolbar to send your document as an e-mail attachment or via Microsoft Messenger. This is a good time to choose Flag for Follow Up on Word's Tools menu to set a reminder to make sure the document actually does get worked on. For more about calendar, task, and reminder features of Office, visit Book V, Chapters 6 and 7.

After you receive a document with other people's changes in it, you can either accept or reject those changes — more on this in the section "Accepting and rejecting changes," later in this chapter.

You can fine-tune the Track Changes preferences, although the default settings are fine for most purposes. To access Track Changes preferences: choose Show⇨Preferences on the Reviewing toolbar. See Figure 4-4. In the Track Changes preference pane, you can change the color of each author's changes, and you can set how changes are highlighted. In fact, you can make a lot of adjustments to the way track changes displays changes and comments in Word's interface. We show you the preference pane here, but we think you should only bother with these settings if you find you're using track changes every day and you have time to experiment with various setting combinations.

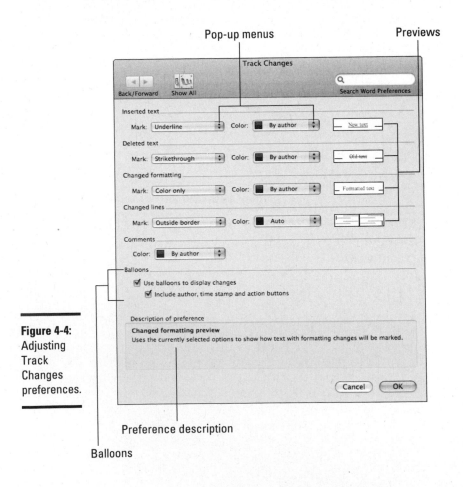

Figure 4-4: Adjusting Track Changes preferences.

If you do want to experiment (refer to Figure 4-4), click the pop-up menus for nearly endless combinations of settings. When you move the mouse cursor over preference controls, you see a description for each option.

In addition to tracking changes, the Track Changes feature also keeps track of comments for all reviewers. Any reviewer can click the New Comment button on the Reviewing toolbar to add comments for reviewers.

Working with a changed document

Picture this: You've sent out your document to two committee members, and they've made changes and returned the document to you. Now you have three copies of the same document — the original one, plus two returned documents that contain changes. You want to consolidate all the changes into the original document. In a folder that you can find easily, save the returned documents with new filenames, perhaps named after the person who worked on the revisions, so you can tell the returned files apart from each other and the original.

Merging changed versions into the original

After you save your changed documents under new filenames, you're ready to merge the changed documents into the original so that you can have a single document in which to work. Follow these steps:

1. **Open the original document you created choose Tools⇨Merge Documents.**

   The Open dialog appears.

2. **Navigate to one of the changed documents and click Open.**

   The changed document merges with the original, and you can immediately see the changes.

Repeat the preceding steps for each changed document that needs to be merged with the original. Set the Revisions View on the Reviewing toolbar to Original Showing Markup (see Figure 4-2). This way you can see the changes made to the original document (see Figure 4-5).

When using Print Layout View or Web Layout View, you see balloons on the right that describe the changes made and comments, if any, that have been added. Balloons denoting changes have Accept and Reject buttons. Comment balloons simply display comments and don't have these buttons.

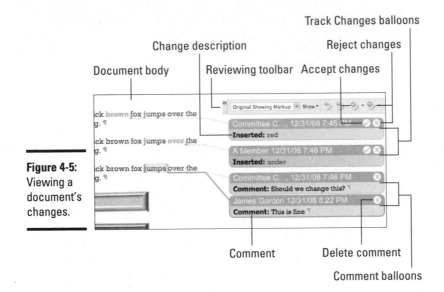

Figure 4-5:
Viewing a document's changes.

Accepting and rejecting changes

When you're ready, you can go through the changes that people made to the document and work toward creating a final document.

Keep in mind that although text changes and comments are tracked, not every change made to a document is tracked. For instance, changes made to SmartArt objects aren't tracked.

As years have passed, Microsoft has attempted to make the ideal interface to accomplish accepting and rejecting changes. Each attempt, though, has plusses and minuses. One interface works better on a large screen; another works better when there are few comments; yet another when there are a lot of comments.

Our advice is to start with balloons because they're so visible. If you find these balloons hard to read, too crowded, or clumsy to work with, try using one of the other methods, such as using the Reviewing toolbar or the Accept and Review Changes dialog that we discuss shortly. You can turn the balloons on or off by following one of these procedures:

✦ **Turn balloons on or off in preferences by following these steps:**

   1. On the Reviewing toolbar, choose Show⇨Preferences.

   Track Changes preferences opens, as shown in Figure 4-4.

   2. Select the Balloons to Display Changes option.

✦ **Switch to a view that doesn't display toolbars, such as Draft View.**

   Switch to Print Layout View or Web Layout View to see balloons again.

✦ **From Word's View menu, toggle Markup on or off.**

The Reviewing pane is an alternative to balloons for viewing changes. Toggle the Reviewing pane on and off by clicking the Reviewing Pane button on the Reviewing toolbar (see Figure 4-2). The Reviewing pane shows up as a docked window at the bottom of your Word interface so that it requires some more screen real estate than the balloons.

The Reviewing toolbar has every control needed to manage tracking changes. Hover the mouse cursor over each button to see the navigation controls to move from change to change within the document as well as buttons to accept or reject changes.

An alternative to both balloons and the Reviewing toolbar is the Accept or Reject Changes dialog, as shown in Figure 4-6. Choose Tools➪Track Changes➪Accept or Reject Changes to turn on this tool. Click its Close button to dismiss the dialog.

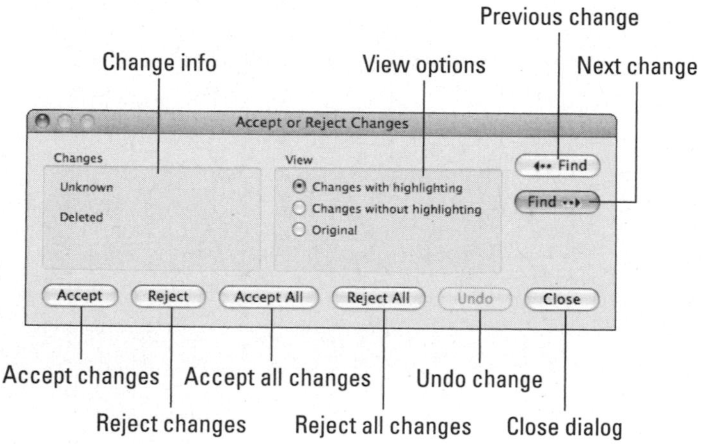

Book II
Chapter 4

Reviewing and Proofing with Word

Figure 4-6: Accepting and rejecting changes.

Finishing up

While you work on a document with track changes, Word internally keeps a history of these changes and allows you to see them via the Reviewing toolbar. Click Revisions View (see Figure 4-2) on the Reviewing toolbar to choose from the following views:

✦ **Original:** This view shows what the document looked like before any changes. Switching to this view shows the original document, but the tracked changes remain in the document, hidden from view. This view is what your document will look like if you choose to reject all changes.

✦ **Original Showing Markup:** This view shows the original text, formatting changes, and displays deleted text inline.

✦ **Final:** This view shows how the document would look if you were to accept all changes. Deleted text isn't displayed. Switching to this view hides original text that was changed or deleted by reviewers, but it's still retained within the document.

✦ **Final Showing Markup:** Shows inserted text and formatting changes. Deleted text appears in balloons.

After you have your document with everybody's changes, clean up the text by accepting or rejecting those changes. Start at the beginning of your document, and work your way to the end with balloons, the Reviewing toolbar, or the Accept or Reject Changes dialog. Decide whether to accept or reject each and every change in the document. When you accept or reject revision marks, the revision marks are removed. In the end, your final document has no revision marks at all.

After you finish going through the document accepting and rejecting changes, follow these steps to properly prepare a document for final delivery:

1. **Start with your document closed. In Finder, right-click or Control-click the file's icon; then choose Duplicate from the pop-up menu.**

   A copy of your document containing revisions is made. You now have a copy of the document in case you want to refer to the revisions later.

2. **Open the document containing tracked changes in Word.**

3. **On the Reviewing toolbar, set Revisions View to Final.**

   This is how your document will look if you complete the next step. Look through the document and make sure everything looks right. If everything is okay, proceed to Step 4.

4. **Accept all changes.**

   a. *On the Reviewing toolbar, click the small triangle to the right of the Accept Changes button to display the submenu.*

   b. *From the pop-up menu, choose Accept All Changes in Document (see Figure 4-7).*

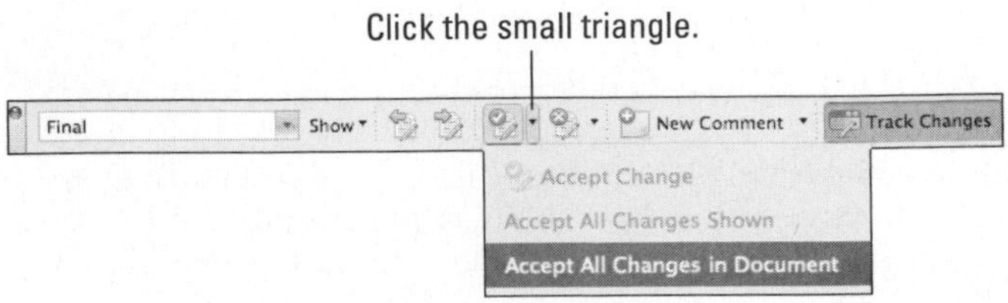

Click the small triangle.

Figure 4-7:
Accepting
all changes.

When you accept all changes, your changed text replaces the original text, and deleted text is removed from the document.

(Optional) You can reject all changes, which would restore the document to its original state before any changes were made. To reject all changes, use the Reject Changes triangle's pop-up menu.

5. **Delete all comments in your document.**

    a. *On the Reviewing toolbar, click the small triangle to the right of the Reject Changes button to display the submenu.*

    b. *Choose Delete All Comments in Document from the submenu (see Figure 4-8).*

Click the small triangle.

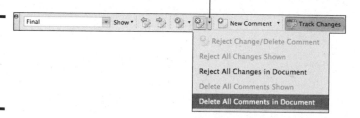

Figure 4-8:
Deleting all
comments
from your
document.

6. **Choose Word⇨Preferences.**

    Word's Preferences pane appears.

7. **Choose Security.**

    Word's Security preferences dialog appears.

8. **Select the Remove Personal Information from This File on Save check box.**

9. **Select the Warn before Printing, Saving, or Sending a File that Contains Tracked Changes check box.**

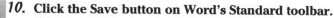

10. **Click the Save button on Word's Standard toolbar.**

    Your document is now safe for distribution. If you receive a warning that track changes are in the file, you didn't accept or reject all the revisions. Cancel the save; then repeat the steps beginning with Step 4.

Occasionally people forget to remove comments and edits, which can cause much embarrassment and even legal liability. Always make sure you have all the edits resolved by searching for track changes one last time.

Casting a Spell Check

Eye strike a key and type a word
And weight four it two say
Weather eye am wrong oar write
It shows me strait a weigh.
　　　　　— Sauce unknown

One of the miracles of Microsoft Word is spell check. By now most everyone who has ever used a word processor or typed an e-mail knows that a red, squiggly underline means you might have a spelling error; and a green, squiggly underline tells you that you might have a grammar problem. The concept is simple, yet extremely effective. When you finish typing a word, Word compares your spelling to a list of known words in a spelling dictionary. If what you typed isn't in the list, Word puts a red squiggle under your word. When you finish typing a sentence, that sentence is compared to grammar rules. If you violate a rule, Word puts a green squiggle under your sentence.

Knowing how to spell is still important!

Yes, we text message. We know that language is evolving, and our technologies are shaping it. Phonetic spellings are fine for text messages, but that's it. Sorry. It still pays off big-time to know words, their proper spellings and meanings, including nuances and context.

Consider this small example:

They are so deer.

Word shows no red or green squiggles, but you probably wanted to say

They are so dear.

As you can see, no computer substitute exists for knowing proper spelling and word usage.

Running a spelling and grammar check

Instead of going through the document one squiggle at a time, Word can check all spelling and grammar for you. If you haven't already, get in the habit of running a spell check before you finish a document. You may have missed one.

Before you run your first spelling and grammar check, Word has a great feature that's turned off by default, and you need to turn it on. The feature enables you to add new words to a custom dictionary. This dictionary allows Office to understand new words as you work on your documents. You have to set this up only once. Afterward, the Spelling feature remains available to you not just in Word, but in all Office applications. The Grammar feature works only in Word. Here's how you set up Spelling and Grammar:

1. **Choose Word⇨Preferences.**

   Word Preferences displays. (See Chapter 1 of this minibook for more on Word Preferences.)

2. **In the Authoring and Proofing Tools section, choose Spelling and Grammar.**

   The Spelling and Grammar preferences pane opens.

3. **In the Spelling section, click the Dictionaries button.**

   The Custom Dictionaries window opens.

4. **Select the Custom Dictionary check box.**

5. **Click OK to close the custom dictionary and then click OK to close the Spelling and Grammar preferences pane.**

   This activates Word's built-in custom dictionary. We'll discuss how to create and add your own custom dictionaries in just a bit!

Book II
Chapter 4

Reviewing and
Proofing with Word

After you perform these steps, the Add button in the Spelling and Grammar dialog becomes available whenever you perform a spell check, and the Add option becomes available in the pop-up menu that appears when you right-click or Control-click a word that's been flagged with a red squiggle. Now you're ready to run a spell check on the entire document. To activate spell checking, do either of the following:

+ **From the Tools menu, choose Spelling and Grammar.**

+ **Use the keyboard shortcut Option-⌘-l (lowercase L).**

Spell checker runs, and if it doesn't find errors, it gives you a clean bill of health. Yea! But more often than not, spell check reminds you that you're fallible. When that happens, the Spelling and Grammar dialog opens, highlights a word or portion of a sentence in the document, and offers several choices for correcting the perceived problem (see Figure 4-9). Most of the time the correct spelling is highlighted under Suggestions, and all you have to do is click the Change button to fix the spelling and continue to the next misspelled word.

But wait a minute! You're pretty darn sure that *allergenicity* is spelled correctly, but the spell checker says it's not. You look through the list of suggested spellings. You definitely don't want to replace *allergenicity* with *allergen city.* If this was the only time you used *allergenicity,* you'd click the Ignore button and be on your way. If you used *allergenicity* a lot in this document but don't think you'll ever use the word again, you could click the Ignore All button so that *allergenicity* doesn't get flagged again within this open document.

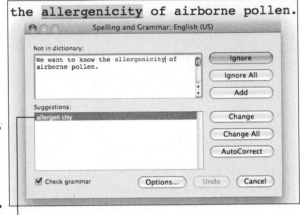

Figure 4-9:
Fixing
spelling and
grammar.

Suggested spelling

For this example, what you really want to do is add *allergenicity* to the dictionary so that Word knows from now on how to correctly spell it. To do that, all you have to do is click the Add button. If the Add button is grayed out, you haven't turned on the custom dictionary option that we covered earlier in this section.

Adding a custom dictionary

Sometimes you might need to add a dictionary. Perhaps your discipline, science, or profession uses a lot of specialized terms not found in the Word default dictionary, or maybe you need to add a dictionary for a language not supplied with Office. You can even create a dictionary and add it to Word.

A *dictionary* is simply a list of words in which the words are saved as a file with a .dic extension. Dictionary files aren't different for Mac or Windows. You can find custom dictionaries and foreign language dictionaries on the Internet by searching for them, and many are free. Word's Help system has an excellent step-by-step explanation of how you can make your own custom dictionary under Create and Use a Custom Dictionary. To tell Word to use a new dictionary file that you've found:

1. **Choose Word➪Preferences.**

   Word Preferences displays.

2. **In the Authoring and Proofing Tools section, choose Spelling and Grammar.**

   Word's Spelling and Grammar preferences pane opens.

3. **In the Spelling section, click the Dictionaries button.**

   The Custom Dictionaries dialog opens.

4. **Click the Add Button.**

   A special Add Dictionary dialog opens.

5. **Navigate to the `.dic` dictionary file and select it.**

   If the `.dic` file you want to use is grayed out, switch to Enable to All Files.

6. **Click Open.**

   Your custom dictionary appears with a check box that's selected in the Custom Dictionaries dialog.

7. **Click OK to close the Custom Dictionaries dialog and then click OK to close the Spelling and Grammar preferences pane.**

   Your new dictionary is now available to all Office applications.

**Book II
Chapter 4**

**Reviewing and
Proofing with Word**

Editing a custom dictionary

Because dictionaries are simply text files, you can open them in Word, add and remove words, and save them again. If you ever accidentally add a misspelling to a dictionary or if you want to add or remove words:

1. **In Word, use File Open to open the (`.dic`) file.**

   A list of words appears.

2. **Click the Show button on Word's Standard toolbar to toggle on the ability to see paragraph marks if they aren't showing already.**

3. **Add or remove words from the list.**

   - Type a new word to add to the list. Press Return or Enter after each new entry to add a single paragraph mark after the new word.

   - Delete misspelled or unwanted words (and their associated paragraph marks) from the list.

   Each word in the list must be followed by a single paragraph mark.

4. **Click the Save button on Word's Standard toolbar to save your changes; then click the Close button to close the document.**

If you use many medical or legal terms regularly, special Word- (and Office-) compatible dictionaries are available that include all the terms that Word might consider as spelling mistakes! Search for them online. Include a subject name, such as *medical*, the word *download*, and *.dic* as keywords in your search.

Setting a new default language for proofing

Word comes with many different language dictionaries. The default dictionary determines which language's proofing tools Word uses for spelling and grammar. You can change Word's default language dictionary easily:

1. **Choose Tools⇨Language.**

   The Language dialog opens. You see a list of languages, as shown in Figure 4-10.

   Select Spelling and Grammar language.

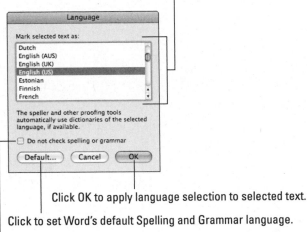

Figure 4-10: Changing Word's Spelling and Grammar language.

   Click OK to apply language selection to selected text.

   Click to set Word's default Spelling and Grammar language.

   Click to turn off Spelling and Grammar checking.

2. **Select the new language to use and click the Default button.**

   A dialog appears asking whether you're sure you want the change, and notifying you that your change will be saved in Word's Normal (.dotx) template.

3. **Click Yes to change Word's default spelling and grammar checking language to the language you selected.**

4. **Click OK to close the Language dialog.**

   The language dictionary you selected is now Word's default language for spelling and grammar.

Using a different language for proofing a selection

Be sure to check Word's Help Multilingual Features in Office 2008 topic to read more about using languages with Office. You can also use the Language feature (refer to Figure 4-10) to change the language of just the currently selected text:

1. **Select a word or passage in the text.**

2. **Choose Tools⇨Language.**

   The Language dialog opens.

3. **Select a language to use.**

4. **Click OK to close the Language dialog.**

5. **Choose Tools➪Spelling and Grammar.**

The words that have a different spelling and grammar language applied to them will be checked against the proofing tools for the language selected using the Language dialog. See Figure 4-11. The rest of the document will be checked against Word's default spelling and grammar language.

Just for fun, we selected a few words in an English sentence and set spelling and grammar to French for these words with the Language dialog. Then we ran a spell check with Spelling and Grammar from the Tools menu. The first word that the spell checker encountered that was set to French was *edited.* That set off the Spelling and Grammar dialog as expected, as shown in Figure 4-11. ***Note:*** French is shown in the title bar of the Spelling and Grammar dialog.

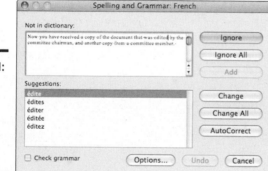

Figure 4-11:
Using French proofing tools in an English document.

Making these modifications to the Language setting doesn't change the language that's used for the Office interface. If you want the entire Office interface to be in a particular language, you have to purchase and install an Office version that's customized for the particular language you want to use.

Enabling Japanese for proofing

Japanese is a special case. Before you can use Japanese to check spelling and grammar, you must enable Japanese. To enable Japanese language features in the English version of Office, do the following:

1. **In Finder, choose Applications➪Microsoft Office 2008➪Additional Tools➪Microsoft Language Register.**

2. **Double-click the Microsoft Language Register application.**

The Microsoft Register application opens (see Figure 4-12).

3. **Switch the pop-up menu from English to Japanese and click OK to enable Japanese and close the Microsoft Register application.**

Figure 4-12:
Changing
the Office
interface
language.

Cleaning up your grammar

Good thing Word doesn't allow much bad grammar to sneak past you without flagging it. What's nice is that Word enables you to choose just how aggressive you want the grammar checker to be. You can tune the settings coarsely by choosing any of these built-in writing style preferences:

✦ **Casual:** Word lets a lot of stuff slide.

✦ **Standard:** The grammar checker gets a bit pickier.

✦ **Formal:** Word will be extremely picky.

✦ **Technical:** Grammar checking isn't as picky as Formal, but different things are looked for than with Standard.

✦ **Custom:** A set of choices that you make.

We show you how to see exactly what's scrutinized in just a bit!

Choosing a writing style

You can quickly choose one of the writing styles discussed in the preceding section by heading to Word's Spelling and Grammar preferences. Choose a writing style to be Word's default by following these instructions:

1. **Choose Word⇨Preferences.**

   Word Preferences displays.

2. **In the Authoring and Proofing Tools section, choose Spelling and Grammar.**

   Word's Spelling and Grammar preferences pane opens.

3. **In the Grammar section, click the Writing Style pop-up.**

4. **Select a writing style.**

   We mention writing styles in the previous section.

5. **Click OK to close the Spelling and Grammar preferences pane.**

Creating a custom writing style

Choosing a writing style from the pop-up menu is okay, but you don't get to see exactly what grammar rules are being checked in your document. If you want, you can fine-tune each of these writing styles to create your own totally customized writing style. All this is done in Word's Spelling and Grammar preferences pane. To see and adjust grammar settings, take the following steps:

1. **Choose Word⇨Preferences.**

   Word Preferences displays.

2. **In the Authoring and Proofing Tools section, choose Spelling and Grammar.**

   Word's Spelling and Grammar preferences pane opens.

3. **To the right of the Writing Style pop-up menu, click the Settings button.**

   The Grammar Settings dialog opens, as shown in Figure 4-13.

4. **Choose a grammar style from the pop-up menu to view the default settings for that style.**

   Feel free to modify the settings. Changing presets for a default writing style creates a custom writing style. Another way to create a custom style is to choose Custom from the pop-up menu at the top of the dialog and choose options as desired.

5. **Click OK to close the Grammar Settings pane.**

   You return to Word's Spelling and Grammar preferences pane.

6. **Select a writing style.**

   If you customized a writing style and want to use it, choose Custom.

7. **Click OK to close the Spelling and Grammar preferences pane.**

Incidentally, if you follow these steps while you have text selected that has a proofing a language other than Word's default, the grammar rules and choices will be in the language of the selected text. Each language has its own set of writing styles.

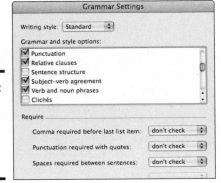

Figure 4-13:
Adjusting
how fierce
grammar
checking
should be.

Chapter 5: Making Great Tables and Charts

In This Chapter

✔ **Picking your table tools**

✔ **Making tables quickly**

✔ **Styling your tables**

✔ **Tips for working with tables**

✔ **Working with tables on the Web**

✔ **Graphing and charting your way**

✔ **Framing and anchoring**

✔ **Converting graphs to pictures and other formats**

Tables and graphs have two virtues: They look great and they help portray your information in a more visual and aesthetic style. Of course, they also have the added virtue of making a good impression on your audience while conveying important information. So what if you have to tell them your company's stock is worthless? At least you can do so with style and grace. Word 2008 makes it easier than ever before to make great-looking tables with the new Quick Tables and Charts features. Be sure to check our tips for working with tables for instructions on how to select cells and ranges of cells.

Deciding Which Table Tools to Use

Microsoft realizes that tables are one of Word's most-used features. Consequently, Word lets you work with tables using a variety of different interface tools. In the next few sections, we show four entirely different ways to create a table:

- ✦ Using Quick Tables in the Elements bar
- ✦ Using the Tables button on the Standard toolbar
- ✦ Using your mouse with the Draw Table feature
- ✦ Using Word's Insert Table dialog

Each of these methods comes with an entire set of tools that you can use when working on your tables. This presents your authors with a particular problem. If we were to cover all the possibilities, we'd need more than 1,500 bullet points just to cover the basics. Instead, we explain how most of the controls, buttons, formatting, and basic table functions appear within each interface tool grouping. You're free to use any and all these as you work. Mix, match, and work with the tools from any of the groupings. If we point out something on the Tables and Borders toolbar, chances are good you'll find the same tool on the Formatting Palette or in a dialog. No one single place has every table control.

Here's the run down on the major interface tool groupings:

✦ **Quick Tables:** You'll find these on the Elements bar. Use them to create nicely formatted basic and complex new tables.

✦ **Tables button:** Creates plain tables quickly.

✦ **Tables and Borders toolbar:** Lets you draw tables and has a full set of table formatting controls. There's lots of dragging and dropping here.

✦ **Dialogs:** Word's Table menu gives you access to table creation and formatting dialogs.

✦ **Toolbox Formatting Palette:** When you click in a table, special sections for table formatting become available.

✦ **Menus:** Word's Table menu has many options and is great for people who prefer using menus. Additional menus are available by right-clicking or Control-clicking in a table.

✦ **Keyboard shortcuts:** If you work with tables a lot, you might wish to set your frequently used table commands as keyboard shortcuts, which we describe in Chapter 1 of this minibook.

✦ **Custom toolbar:** You can create your own custom toolbars, which we describe in Book I, Chapter 3.

Here's an example of various options you can choose from to accomplish the same task: To adjust the sizes of rows, columns, or cells in a table, you can do any of the following:

✦ Drag the column and row dividers.

✦ Right-click and choose Table Properties to open the Table Properties dialog.

✦ Use the Tables section of the Formatting Palette and use the Height and Width controls.

✦ Drag the border indicators in the rulers.

We leave it up to you decide which way is best. Just remember that if we show you one way to do something, chances are you can accomplish the same thing in other ways. Find the way that works best for you.

Inserting Quick Tables in a Flash

Word allows you to make inserting a new table quick and easy. Here's how:

1. **Switch to Page Layout View or choose Insert⇨Quick Tables.**

   The Elements bar becomes available. See Figure 5-1.

2. **Click Quick Tables on the Elements bar.**

   The Quick Tables Elements Gallery appears. Quick Tables Elements Gallery has 12 basic styles and 11 complex styles from which to choose. Move the mouse cursor over Elements Gallery while looking at the left end of Elements Gallery to see the name and description for each table element.

3. **Position the insertion cursor where you want the new Quick Table to appear in your document.**

4. **Click one of the Quick Tables in Elements Gallery.**

   You have an instant, beautiful table.

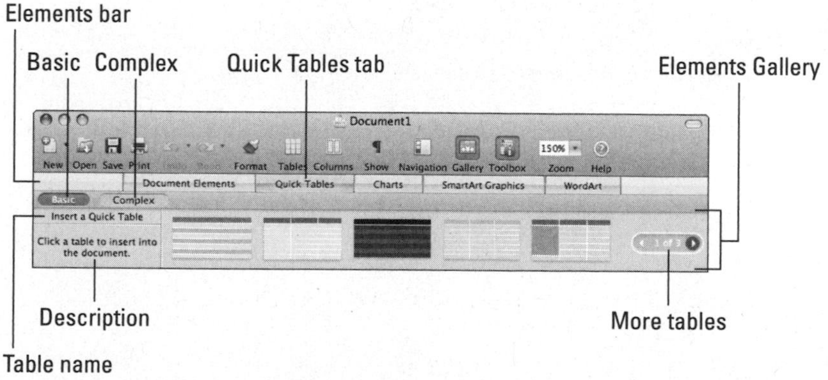

Book II
Chapter 5

**Making Great
Tables and Charts**

Elements bar

Basic Complex   Quick Tables tab   Elements Gallery

Figure 5-1:
Choosing
a Quick
Table from
Elements
Gallery.

Description   More tables

Table name

Creating Your Own Tables

Even the basic tables on Elements Gallery may have too much formatting for your purposes. You might prefer to work in Draft or Outline View and don't like switching to some other view just to insert a table. Word's Tables feature can help you.

Using the Tables button

Here's how to create a plain table with the Tables button on the Standard toolbar:

1. **Click in your document to set the insertion cursor at the place where you want the new table to appear.**

2. **Click and hold down your mouse button (the left one if you have more than one mouse button) on the Tables button while you drag the mouse down and to the right.**

   A grid appears while you drag, showing the number of rows and columns you'll get when you release the mouse (see Figure 5-2).

3. **Release the mouse to choose the number of rows and columns for your new table.**

   A new table appears in your document.

Click here and drag.

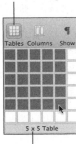

Figure 5-2:
Using the
Tables
command.

Table dimensions

Using the mouse

If you're a "mouse" person and prefer to use the mouse whenever possible, you'll love this method of creating and editing tables because it's mostly click-and-drag. Here's how to make a new table by drawing with your mouse:

1. **In Word, choose Table➪Draw Table.**

   The Tables and Borders toolbar appears (see Figure 5-3). Word might switch to Print Layout View. Word clicks the Draw Table button on the Tables and Borders toolbar for you, which makes the mouse cursor change into a pencil when it's over your document so that you can start drawing.

2. **Drag the mouse diagonally to create a dotted box shape.**

   The shape is the outside border of your new table.

3. **Release the mouse to create the table.**

The dotted lines assume the line style, color, and weight settings that you chose on the Tables and Borders toolbar. See the section, "Formatting Tables," later in this chapter.

4. **Continue drawing row and column dividers.**

Drag dividers to reposition them as desired. Click the Eraser button on the Tables and Borders toolbar to change the mouse cursor into an eraser. When the cursor is an eraser, it erases lines instead of drawing them.

5. **Click the Draw Table button on the Tables and Borders toolbar to restore the normal mouse cursor.**

Whenever you want to use the mouse to draw more rows, columns, or even another table, just click the Draw Table button. It's a toggle switch between Word's regular cursor and the table drawing cursor.

Book II
Chapter 5

Making Great Tables and Charts

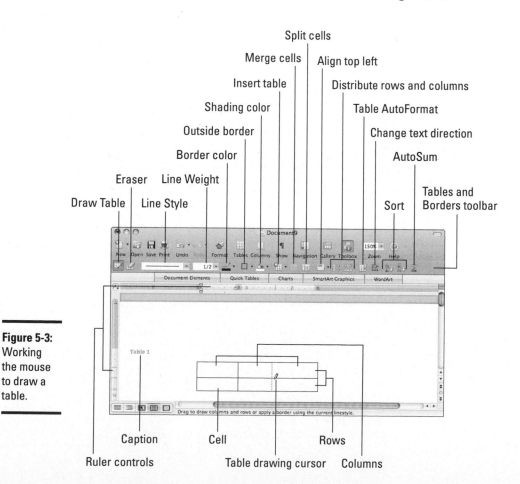

Figure 5-3:
Working the mouse to draw a table.

We explain those other buttons and terms in just a bit. We still have one more method of creating a table to discuss first.

Using the Insert Table dialog

This method is straightforward and works in all views in Word:

1. **Click in your document to set the insertion cursor at the place where you want the new table to appear.**

2. **Choose Table➪Insert➪Table.**

Word's Insert Table dialog displays. See Figure 5-4.

3. **Adjust settings as desired.**

4. **Click OK to close the Insert Table dialog.**

Your table appears in your document at the insertion cursor.

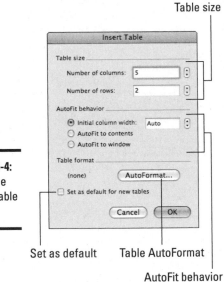

Table size

Figure 5-4:
Using the
Insert Table
dialog.

Set as default   Table AutoFormat

AutoFit behavior

With the Insert Table dialog, you can choose the following options:

✦ **Table Size:** Choose the number of rows and columns for the new table.

✦ **Autofit Behavior:**

 • *Initial Column Width:* This defaults to Auto. When Auto is chosen, the table takes up as much room as is available in the document. Alternatively, click the increase/decrease control to adjust the column width to a fixed amount. All columns will be equal width. You can resize the widths after the table is made if you decide they're not just right.

- *Autofit to Contents:* When you click inside the table and start typing, the cells will automatically size themselves to fit the contents.

- *Autofit to Window:* The same as Initial Column Width set to Auto.

✦ **AutoFormat button:** Opens the Table AutoFormat dialog (see the section, "Styling with Table AutoFormat," later in this chapter).

✦ **OK:** Makes a table with the options you chose.

Formatting Tables

Every aspect of a table's appearance can be formatted. You can merge cells together to form bigger cells, unmerge them again, change line colors, create cell shading, and more. Join us as we explore the various ways to improve the way your tables look.

Using the Tables and Borders toolbar

The Tables and Borders toolbar is a good place to begin our table formatting discussion because many of its tools are also on the Formatting Palette, the Cell Format dialog, and the Borders and Shading dialog, all of which we discuss in this chapter. Refer to Figure 5-3 earlier in this chapter as we explain the formatting tools and how they work on the Tables and Borders toolbar:

✦ **Line Style:** This is a pop-up menu from which you can choose from a variety of dotted, dashed, single, double, and triple lines for the border and dividing lines in your table.

✦ **Line Weight:** This is a pop-up menu from which you can choose from nine different line weights.

✦ **Border Color:** This control has two options:

- *Click the icon to display Word's Borders and Shading dialog.* See the section, "Using the Tables dialog," later in this chapter for more on borders and shading.

- *Click the small triangle to the right of the border color icon to display Office's color picker from which to choose a color.*

✦ **Outside Border:** This control turns border lines on or off, and it works in a specific order.

1. *Select a cell, a range of cells, or an entire table.*

2. *Click the small triangle to the right of the icon to display the Borders palette (see Figure 5-5).*

   Click a border style to apply it to the selected range. The selected range updates instantly. To tear this palette from the toolbar and make it its own floating palette, click the double-dotted part of the palette. The Horizontal Line button adds a horizontal line in the center of the range of cells.

3. *Click the Outside Border button to apply the most recently applied outside border from the small triangle.*

This makes it easy to repeat the same outside border without clicking the small triangle.

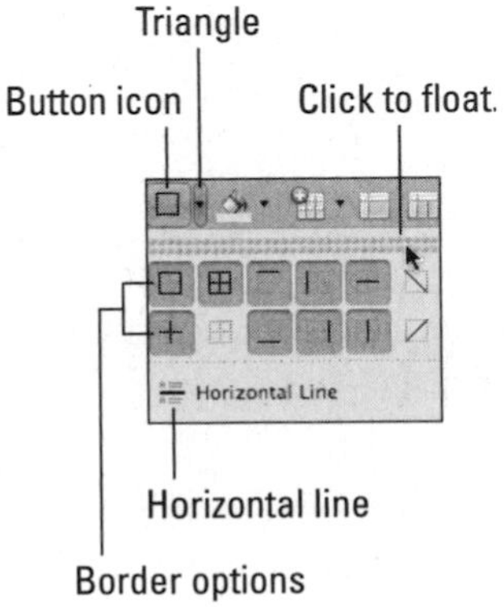

Triangle

Button icon   Click to float.

Figure 5-5:
Turning
borders on
and off with
the Borders
palette.

Horizontal line

Border options

✦ **Shading color:** This control works in a specific order:

1. *Select a cell, a range of cells, or an entire table.*

2. *Click the small triangle to the right of the icon to display the Office Shading Color palette, from which you can choose a color (see Figure 5-6).*

The color you choose is immediately applied to the selected range. The most recently chosen color is displayed by the Shading Color icon so that you can quickly reapply that color to other selections. Just click the icon instead of the small triangle to apply the most recently used color.

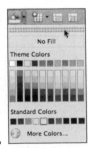

Figure 5-6:
Choosing
colors in
the Office
Shading
Color
palette.

✦ **Insert Table:** This control has two options:

• *Click the icon to display the Insert Table dialog.*

- *Position the insertion cursor within an existing table; then click the small triangle to produce a menu that offers options to insert things into your table. See Figure 5-7.*

Insert Rows

Insert Columns

Insert Table dialog

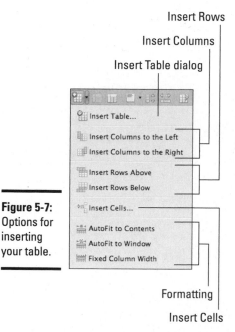

Figure 5-7: Options for inserting your table.

Formatting

Insert Cells

✦ **Merge Cells:** Select two or more cells and then click this button to remove the cell borders to create a single cell.

✦ **Split Cells:** Select one or more cells that have been merged. Click this button to unmerge the cells.

✦ **Align Top Left:** Remember this tool when formatting labels and business cards! To use this tool:

1. *Select a cell or a range of cells.*

   You must have extra height and width within the cells so that contents have room to move around. Otherwise, Align Top Left doesn't have much of a visual effect.

2. *Click the small triangle to the right of the button icon to reveal the Cell Alignment palette. (See Figure 5-8.)*

3. *Click an alignment option.*

   The selected option is applied instantly to the selected range. Click the large icon to quickly reapply the most recently applied option.

Figure 5-8:
Setting
alignment
of cell
contents.

Alignment options

✦ **Distribute Rows Evenly:** Select two or more rows, and then click this button to make the row height uniform for the selected range using the height of the bottom-most row selected.

✦ **Distribute Columns Evenly:** Select two or more columns, and then click this button to make the column width uniform for the selected range using the width of the rightmost column selected.

✦ **Table AutoFormat:** Displays the Table AutoFormat dialog. (See the section, "Styling with Table AutoFormat," later in this chapter.)

✦ **Change Text Direction:** Each click of this button changes the direction text is displayed within selected cells or range of cells. After using this tool, use the Align Top Left tool to reposition the text.

✦ **Sort Ascending:** Select one or more columns to order the contents within each column either alphabetically or numerically; it's like working in a spreadsheet.

✦ **Sort Descending:** Select one or more columns to order the contents within each column in reverse alphabetical or numerical order, as if you're working in a spreadsheet.

✦ **AutoSum:** If you have a column containing numbers that you want to add up and put the total in a cell at the bottom:

1. *Click into the empty cell at the bottom of your column containing numbers.*

2. *Click the AutoSum button.*

Word calculates the total for you automatically and inserts a Word field to perform the calculation. (We discuss Word fields and how to perform additional calculations in Chapter 7 of this minibook.)

Using the Formatting Palette

If the Formatting Palette isn't visible, click the Toolbox button on Word's Standard toolbar and then click the Formatting Palette button at the top-left corner of the Toolbox.

Notice that when you put the insertion cursor in a table by clicking in any table cell, the Formatting Palette dynamically makes the Table section available, which has table-specific controls, as shown in Figure 5-9. Move the mouse cursor over each button on the Formatting Palette to figure out what it does. Most of these are identical to the buttons on the Tables and Borders toolbar. See the preceding section for descriptions.

In Figure 5-9, we highlight certain results after applying some formatting controls with the Formatting Palette and the mouse:

✦ **Align:** We selected the cells under the Amount Paid heading; then clicked the Align button. We chose Align Top Center from the pop-up palette to center the numbers in this column.

✦ **Drag column dividers:** We dragged the column dividers to make the column widths look right.

✦ **Merge:** We selected the two bottom leftmost cells and then clicked the Merge button to make a single larger cell for Total.

✦ **AutoSum:** We clicked inside the bottom right cell and then clicked the AutoSum button so that the total of the cells above would be calculated.

Drag column divider to resize.

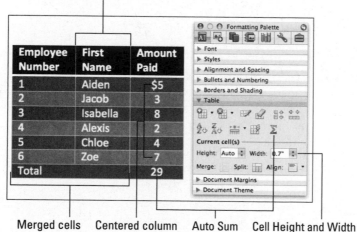

Figure 5-9:
Formatting
a table
with the
Formatting
Palette.

Merged cells   Centered column   Auto Sum   Cell Height and Width

Note that the Current Cells section of Formatting Palette has two controls not found on the Tables and Borders toolbar:

✦ **Height:** Type a value or use the increase/decrease control to adjust the height of selected cells, rows, or ranges.

✦ **Width:** Type a value or use the increase/decrease control to adjust the width of selected cells, columns, or ranges.

Applying a document theme

Because table formatting, such as shading, is actually a style and because styles can be formatted with document themes, you can apply document themes to format tables. All you have to do to apply a document theme to a table is

1. **Click anywhere within the table you want to format.**

You don't see changes unless your table has some formatting, such as shading, applied already. Tables made with Quick Tables respond nicely to document themes because they have a lot of styling.

2. **Click the Document Theme triangle to expose the Document Theme previews in the Formatting Palette.**

3. **Choose a document theme.**

Your table instantly adopts the selected theme.

If you're working with an older DOC file from before the Word 2008 era (you'll be in Compatibility Mode), you have to save the file as a DOCX file before you can use the Document Theme option.

Using the Tables Properties dialog

If you prefer working with dialogs or if you're interested in precision formatting of tables, columns, rows and cells, nothing beats the options found in the Table Properties dialog (see Figure 5-10). You can get to this dialog using one of these methods:

✦ Right-click or Control-click a table cell and then choose Table Properties from the pop-up menu.

✦ Choose Table⇨Table Properties.

In this dialog, you can control the following:

✦ **Size:** Click the check box and click the increase/decrease control to adjust the overall width of the table as measured on the ruler. Choose from inches or percentage measure with the Measure In pop-up menu.

✦ **Alignment:** Choose Left, Center, or Right alignment for a table that doesn't fill the entire width between margins. For precision, use the increase/decrease control to adjust exactly how far in from the left margin you wish the table to be placed with Indent from Left.

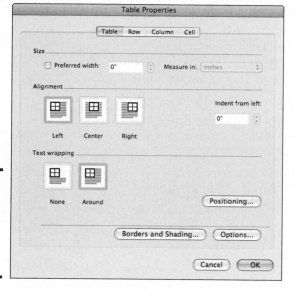

Figure 5-10:
Fine-tuning
with the
Table
Properties
dialog.

+ **Text Wrapping:** Choose None or Around. If you choose Around, the Positioning button becomes active so that you can control exactly how text flows around the table.

+ **Positioning button:** Activates the Table Positioning dialog, as shown in Figure 5-11.

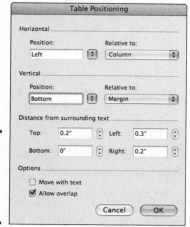

Figure 5-11:
Setting
precision
table
positioning.

The Table Positioning dialog allows precision positioning of the table within your document, either in inches or relative to other document properties in these ways:

- *Horizontal:* Click the buttons to activate pop-up menus or type a numeric value to specify a position.

- *Vertical:* Click the buttons to activate pop-up menus or type a numeric value to specify a position.

- *Distance from Surrounding Text:* Type numeric values or use the increase/decrease controls.

- *Move with Text:* When you select this check box, the table stays in the same relative position to text as you add and remove text while working in the document.

- *Allow Overlap:* Select this check box if you want the table to overlap other objects in your document.

✦ **Borders and Shading button:** Activates the Borders and Shading dialog (see Figure 5-12). You can also open this dialog by choosing Format⇨Borders and Shading.

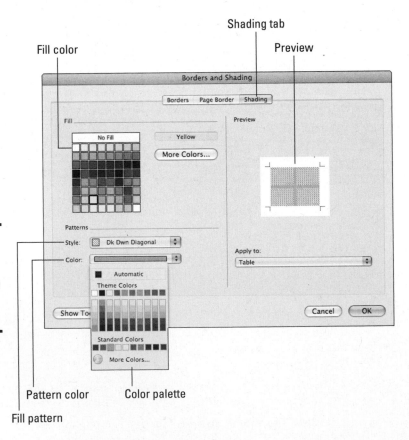

Figure 5-12: Formatting with the Borders and Shading dialog.

- *Borders tab:* This tab offers the same border-formatting options you find on the Tables and Borders toolbar and in the Borders section of the Formatting Palette. You can apply borders to tables, cells, and paragraphs.

- *Page Border tab:* This tab offers the same border-formatting options you find on the Tables and Borders toolbar and in the Borders section of the Formatting Palette. With the Page Border tab, you can apply borders to the whole document, this section, this section (the first page of the section only). and this section (all except the section's first page).

- *Shading tab (see Figure 5-12):* This lets you choose fill and pattern options that you can apply to the selected table, selected cell, and current paragraph.

  If the Tables and Borders toolbar isn't turned on when you display the Borders and Tables dialog, the Show Toolbar button is active so that you can turn on the Tables and Borders toolbar.

Back to the Table Properties dialog, as shown in Figure 5-10, to go over the remaining tabs of this dialog:

✦ **Row tab:** Allows you to adjust row settings, one row at a time.

- *Size:* Has the same size controls found on the Current Cells section of the Table portion of the Formatting Palette.

- *Allow Row to Break Across Pages:* Choose this check box, and Word allows a row to break at a page break. The default is that rows don't break at a page break.

- *Repeat as Header Row at the Top of Each Page:* Choose this check box, and Word repeats the currently selected row as the column header when a table is large enough so that a page break passes through the table. Usually you use the first row of a table for this purpose.

- *Previous Row and Next Row buttons:* These buttons allow you to navigate through the current table so you can set row options row by row.

✦ **Column tab:** Column allows you to set column widths, one column at a time. Use the Previous Column and Next Column buttons to navigate through the current table.

✦ **Cell tab:** This tab lets you set these properties for the selected cell or range of cells:

- *Width:* Set width precisely by typing a number or using an increase/decrease control. Width is measured in inches or percentage.

- *Vertical Alignment:* Choose Top, Center, or Bottom.

- *Options button:* Displays the Cell Options dialog (see Figure 5-13).

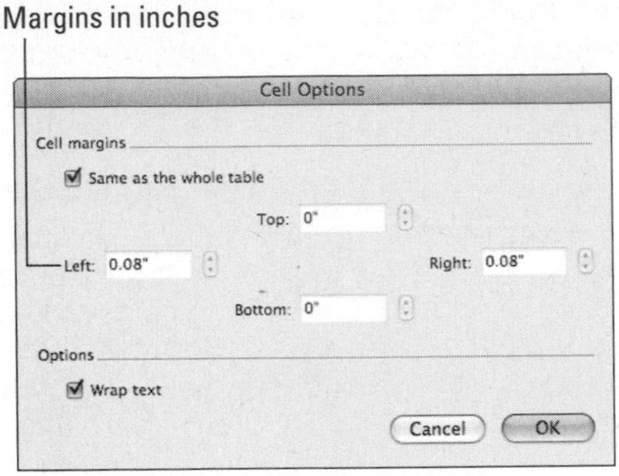

Margins in inches

Figure 5-13: Setting cell options.

Word defaults to using the same cell options for all the cells in a table, but you can deselect the Same as the Whole Table check box and format a select cell or a range of cells. By default, Word wraps text in cells, but you can deselect the Wrap Text check box to turn off wrapping.

Using styles

You have several different ways from which you can apply styles to tables. At the beginning of this chapter, we show Elements Gallery's Quick Tables feature. The Gallery gives you a total of 23 different styles from which to choose. You can up the ante a bit if you're willing to take a little extra time to work with styles.

Styling with Table AutoFormat

Table AutoFormat offers 44 (we counted them) different *formats* — actually they're styles. To activate the Table AutoFormat dialog:

1. **Click anywhere in a table.**

2. **In the Table section of the Formatting Palette, click the Table AutoFormat button.**

   The Table AutoFormat dialog, as shown in Figure 5-14, appears.

The Table AutoFormat dialog is divided into the following sections:

✦ **Formats:** It would have been more accurate to label this section Styles. Scroll through the list of Formats and click any that sound enticing.

✦ **Preview:** As you work with AutoFormat, the preview updates instantly.

✦ **Formats to Apply:** Usually you want all the check boxes selected, but deselect boxes to see if you like the formatting better that way. Use the preview as your guide.

✦ **Apply Special Formats To:** Deselect and select check boxes to see whether you like the formatting better. Use the preview as your guide.

Click OK to apply your format (style) selections and close the AutoFormat dialog.

One of the nice things about AutoFormat is that it gives a visual definition of what it means to be a style. A style has a name (as shown in the Formats section in Figure 5-14) and a bundle of formatting attributes that you can see in the preview. You can find all 44 of AutoFormat's formats in the Style dialog, which we discuss in following section.

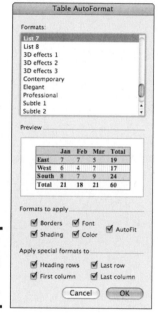

Figure 5-14:
Customizing
with Table
AutoFormat.

Styling with the Style dialog

Hang on to your hat because we're going to up the ante once again! This time we choose from more than 140 different table styles using the Style dialog, which has the 44 AutoFormats from Table AutoFormat plus many more. We also show you how to modify these built-in styles and how to add your own styles.

Applying styles

To get at all the styles Word has to offer, click anywhere within the table you want to format and then follow these steps:

1. **In Word, choose Format➪Style.**

The Style dialog opens, as shown in Figure 5-15.

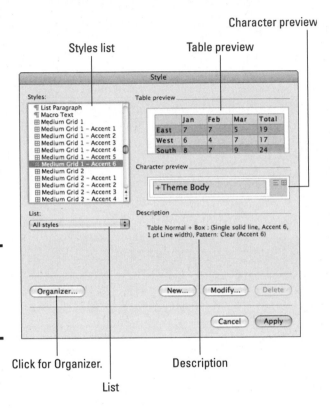

Character preview

Styles list   Table preview

Figure 5-15:
Formatting
a table with
the Style
dialog.

Click for Organizer.   Description

List

2. **In the List drop-down list, choose All Styles.**

3. **Click in the Styles list and then use ↓ and ↑ arrow keys or the scroll bar to preview a style.**

Of course, you can also manually click each of the styles!

Click any style with a description that starts with *Table* and you see a preview of the selected table style in the Table Preview area.

4. **Select the style you want to apply to your table and click the Apply button.**

The style you selected is applied to your table.

Modifying styles

If you like a style but want to tweak it just a bit or even a lot, you'll be pleased to know that table styles can be modified easily. To modify an existing table style:

1. **Click anywhere in a table.**

2. **Follow Steps 1–3 in the preceding section while referring to Figure 5-15.**

Continue here with the following Step 4:

4. **Select the style you want to modify and then click the Modify button.**

A new dialog opens, allowing you to further customize the style (see Figure 5-16).

Book II
Chapter 5

Making Great
Tables and Charts

Style based on

Style name   Style type

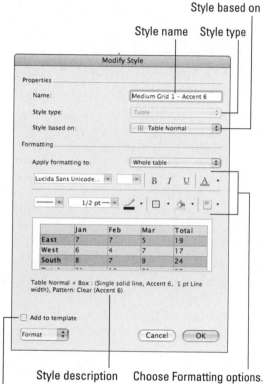

Figure 5-16:
Modifying
an existing
style.

Style description   Choose Formatting options.

Add styles to Normal template

The Modify Style dialog allows you to customize the existing style. We suggest that you always give your modified style a new name unless you specifically want to overwrite an existing style. Word doesn't allow you to overwrite built-in styles, so if you started with a built-in style, you most definitely need to type in a new name for your modified style. Time to take a look at this dialog:

✦ **Name:** This name appears in lists of styles in the Style dialog and in the Formatting Palette.

✦ **Style Type:** Table. Well, of course!

✦ **Style Based On:** Lets you select an existing style to use as the basis for your modifications. Don't change this unless you want to pick a different style to modify.

✦ **Apply Formatting To:** Click this pop-up to choose which table elements you want this table style formatting to affect. For example, you could make a style for striped row formatting that when applied doesn't affect the other table elements listed in the pop-up, such as headers.

✦ **Formatting:** A set of formatting tools for text, line, border, fill, and alignment is provided for your convenience.

✦ **Preview:** A live preview updates as you make formatting choices.

✦ **Description:** A description of the style updates as you make formatting choices.

✦ **Add to Template:** When selected, your modifications are saved as a new style in the Normal (.dotx) template. Your customized style is always available to you as a style in the Style dialog and in the Formatting Palette. If you don't select this check box, your customization remains only with the current document.

✦ **Cancel:** This closes the Modify Style dialog without making any style modifications. If you clicked Add to Template, your style will still be in the Normal (.dotx) template.

✦ **OK:** Accepts your style modifications and closes the Modify Style dialog, which returns you to the Styles dialog where you can apply your modifications to the currently active table, or click Close to close Style.

You have to click the Modify button before you click the Apply button; or you can select the table. Choose Format⇨Style to get to the same dialog.

Creating a new table style

You can create new table styles from within the Style dialog. Take these steps:

1. **In Word, choose Format⇨choose Style.**

The Style dialog opens, as shown in Figure 5-15.

2. **Click the New button.**

The New Style dialog opens, which is practically identical to the Modify Style dialog shown in Figure 5-14.

3. **Type a name for your new style in the Name field.**

4. **In the Style type pop-up menu, choose Table.**

5. **(Optional) Click the Style Based On pop-up menu to base your new style on an existing style.**

6. **In the Formatting field, choose formatting options as desired.**

7. **Select the Add to Template box if you want to use this style again.**

   When selected, your modifications are saved as a new style in the Normal (.dotx) template. Your customized style is always available to you as a style in the Style dialog and in the Formatting Palette. If you don't select the Add to Template check box, your customization remains only with the current document.

8. **Click OK to create the new style or click Cancel to close the New Style dialog.**

Working with Tables

After you have your tables created and formatted to your liking, it's time to do some actual work. Filling in a table is a snap:

✦ Just click inside any cell and start typing.

✦ To move to the next cell, press the Tab key.

✦ If you press the Tab key while in the bottom rightmost cell, a new row is added to the bottom of the table.

Basic table tips

Here are some general tips and hints for adjusting and fine-tuning your tables:

✦ **Adjusting row heights and column widths:** Double-click row and column borders to automatically size rows and columns to fit their contents. You can easily adjust column width and row height by dragging borders, or dragging the table indicator marks in rulers.

✦ **Selecting a range of cells:** You can apply formatting to cell ranges — highlight more than one cell at a time and then drag inside the table with your mouse. See Figure 5-17.

Figure 5-17:
Selecting
a range of
cells.

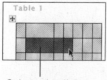

Selected cells

✦ **Selecting one or more columns at a time:** Position the mouse cursor at the top border of the table; it turns into a downward-pointing arrow. Click to select a single column, or click and drag to select multiple columns, as shown in Figure 5-18.

Cursor

Figure 5-18:
Selecting columns in a table.

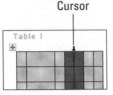

✦ **Selecting one or more rows at a time:** Position the mouse cursor at the left border of the table. It will turn into a rightward-pointing arrow. Click to select a single row or click and drag to select multiple rows. See Figure 5-19.

Table handle

Figure 5-19:
Selecting rows in a table.

✦ **Selecting an entire table:** Click the table handle, as shown in Figure 5-20, to select the entire table.

Caption

Figure 5-20:
Selecting an entire table.

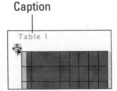

✦ **Table handle menu:** If you right-click or Control-click the table handle (see Figure 5-20), a pop-up menu lists things that you can do with or to the entire table (see Figure 5-21).

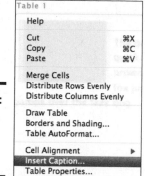

Figure 5-21:
Displaying
the table
handle
menu.

 ✦ **Repositioning a table:** Drag the table handle (see Figure 5-20) to reposition the table within the document.

 ✦ **Caption:** Word has a built-in captioning system. If you choose Insert Caption from the table handle pop-up menu, you can get a sneak peek at the table Caption dialog, as shown in Figure 5-22. For more about captions, turn to Chapter 6 in this minibook.

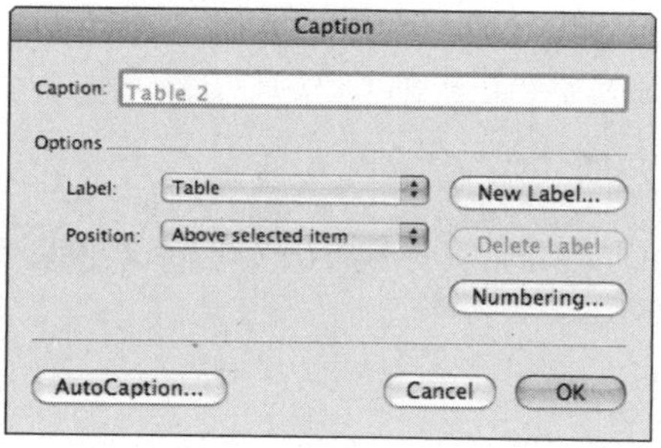

Figure 5-22:
Setting
the table's
caption.

 ✦ **Convert selected text to a table:** You can select a range of *delimited* text (in which the table elements are separated from each other by spaces, commas, or some other character) and convert it into a table. Choose Table menu➪Convert➪Convert Text to Table.

 ✦ **Convert selected table to text:** You can select a table in Word and turn it into plain old text. Choose Table➪Convert➪Convert Table to Text.

Handling tables from the Web

Word can open Web pages that you saved from your Web browser:

1. **In Word, choose File⇨Open.**

The Open dialog appears.

2. **Navigate to the saved Web page file or use Spotlight to find the page.**

Word can open Web pages in these formats: `.htm`, `.html`, `.mht`, and `.txt`.

3. **Click Open.**

Word opens the saved Web page.

If a Web page contains an *HTML (HyperText Markup Language)* table, you can use Word's Table features. You might find it easier to copy just the table portion of the Web page from the Web document into a working document.

At some point, you might come across a *PDF (Portable Document Format)* file that has valuable table information in it that you want to extract. If the table information within the PDF is text-based and not a scanned image, you can use the Mac OS X Preview application to take a stab at getting at the table information. Follow these steps:

1. **Open the PDF file in Mac OS X Preview application.**

2. **In Preview, choose Edit⇨Select All.**

3. **In Preview, choose Edit⇨Copy.**

4. **Switch to Microsoft Word by clicking Word's Dock icon or use whichever way you usually use to switch or launch applications.**

5. **Make sure you have a new or existing document open.**

6. **In Word, choose Edit⇨Paste.**

Delete extraneous information, leaving the table data untouched. If text wasn't pasted, the PDF probably doesn't contain any text, or is locked and you can't use this method to grab the data. If that's the case, you have to stop here. If not, continue on.

7. **In Word, select the pasted text that needs to be converted to a table.**

8. **Convert text selection to a table by choosing Table⇨Convert⇨Convert Text to Table.**

Word makes a table out of the data.

PDFs can contain tables that have been saved as images, as can Web pages and other documents you might find online. If that's the case, you need Optical Character Recognition (OCR) software to convert the pictures of text into actual text. OCR software isn't included with Office. Cheap scanners have been known to ship with high-quality OCR software that's worth even more than the scanner. You might find OCR software worth looking into.

Working with Charts

Hold your horses! Charts are newly revamped in Office 2008. Whether you're working in Word, Excel, or PowerPoint, Excel now handles all the charts. Because charts work the same way in all applications, we include a comprehensive section about charts in Book I, Chapter 5. In this chapter, we cover the intricacies that apply to charts specifically within Word. If necessary, read the information about charts in Book I, Chapter 5 before proceeding because we assume you already know how to create a chart in Word.

In Office, charts and graphs are the same thing. Even the dictionary agrees you can use *chart* and *graph* interchangeably. We point out this because in Office, these two words are both used to describe the same objects at times. We try to stick with *chart* unless something that we're discussing in the Office interface uses *graph*.

Whoa! It's way too big!

The first thing you're likely to notice when you start making a new chart in Word is that the chart might span the entire width of the page. Although that might be okay occasionally, at other times, you'll want to resize the chart. To resize the chart, grab any corner handle and drag it diagonally with your mouse cursor. Be careful not to make it so small that the chart distorts or loses information.

Getting unstuck

After you resize the chart, you might wonder how you can move the chart around on the page. When your chart comes in from Excel, it's locked to the left margin. If you try dragging the chart's border, it doesn't budge. Follow these steps to cure this problem:

1. **Select the border or any part of the chart and then head to the Formatting Palette Wrapping section.**

2. **Click the Style option and change the style from In Line with Text to one of the other options, as shown in Figure 5-23.**

   Now you can drag the chart and position it wherever you want on the page. Of course, this wrapping trick can work for other things, such as pictures, besides charts!

Sometimes, the Formatting Palette seems like it has too many sections, which can make finding the Wrapping section a challenge! Don't worry. Click the disclosure triangles to close each of the expanded sections until you see the Wrapping section in the Formatting Palette.

Wrapping

Style:	🔲 Square
Wrap to:	
Distance	
Left:	0
Right:	0
▶ Colors	
▶ Shadow	
▶ Docu...	
▶ Docu...	

- 🔲 In Line with Text
- ✓ 🔲 Square
- 🔲 Tight
- 🔲 Behind Text
- 🔲 In Front of Text
- 🔲 Top and Bottom
- 🔲 Through
- 🔲 Edit Wrap Boundary

Figure 5-23:
Free your chart by changing its style.

This is a frame-up!

If you read Book I, Chapter 3, you might already have the Frame button on the Standard toolbar. Even if you didn't, don't worry. A *frame* is a container that surrounds objects, such as pictures and charts. You use a frame when your text or graphics contain comments, comment marks, or note reference marks so that you can position them within a document precisely and control text flow around the frame. Follow these steps to add the Insert Frame command to a toolbar:

1. **In Word, choose View⇨Customize Menus and Toolbars.**

The Customize Menus and Toolbars dialog opens.

2. **Select the Commands tab and in the Category list on the left, select Insert.**

3. **In the Commands list on the right, scroll down until you find the Horizontal command. Drag this button to the Standard toolbar and release the mouse button when you see the insertion cursor.**

The Insert Frame button appears on the Standard toolbar. Don't worry that it's *Horizontal* in the Commands list and *Insert Frame* on the toolbar — it works just fine.

4. **Click OK to close the Customize Menus and Toolbars dialog.**

The Insert Frame command is now ready for you to use.

Frames are handy containers because you can put all sorts of stuff inside them. For example, you can put a chart into a frame, which you might want to try for several reasons:

✦ **Frames can be positioned anywhere on a page by dragging.**

✦ **You can wrap text around a frame, although you only get two of the numerous wrapping options for frames: None and Around.**

✦ **You can anchor a frame to a specific position on a page so that it doesn't move with the text.** This feature is useful for page layout, especially if you want something to stay put in Publishing Layout View.

In this example, we insert an empty frame and position it in the middle of some text. Working with a frame while it's empty is easier. After you put something into a frame, it can be nearly impossible to select just the frame. Follow these steps:

1. **Click the Insert Frame button (which you create in the preceding steps).**

Your cursor turns into a crosshair.

2. **Hold down the mouse button and drag to make the frame.**

3. **Release the mouse button when you're done.**

An empty box with a shaded border appears; this is the frame.

Before you put something inside the frame, take a moment to size and position the frame and to set its properties. Right-click or Control-click the frame and choose Format Frame. The Frame dialog appears, as shown in Figure 5-24. You can control the exact size and position of the frame with each section of the Frame dialog:

✦ **Text Wrapping:** Choose None or Around.

✦ **Horizontal:**

- Specify an exact position from the left edge of the margin, page, or column.

- Specify that the distance from the frame text will be in the horizontal direction.

✦ **Vertical:**

- Specify an exact position from the top edge of the margin, page, or column.

- Specify that the distance from the frame text will be in the vertical direction.

- *Move with Text:* Selecting this check box makes the frame's position relative to the paragraph.

- *Lock Anchor:* Selecting this check box causes text to flow around the frame instead of the frame moving as text is added or removed before the frame.

✦ **Size:**

- *Width:* Specify an exact width or let Word automatically size the frame.

- *Height:* Set a minimum height, an exact height, or let Word decide the frame's height with the Auto option.

Frames can be used as placeholders. For example, you can insert a frame into a document where you plan to put a picture later. When you're ready, you can drag a picture from the Toolbox's object palette into the frame, and the picture size adjusts to fit the frame.

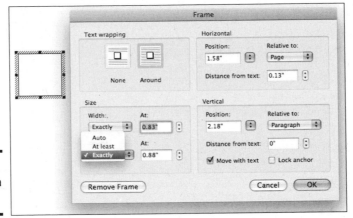

Figure 5-24: Formatting a frame.

Earlier in the chapter, we mention that by default, charts tend to fit the entire width of the document when you make them. You can avoid this problem by dragging out a frame first and then clicking in the frame before you make the chart. When your chart is made, it's inside the frame, and you can drag the frame and the chart freely within your document. As an example, follow these steps:

1. **In a Word document, click the Insert Frame button on the toolbar you put it on (see earlier in this section).**

2. **Drag a frame to a size that's large enough for a chart.**

You don't have to be exact. You can resize the frame later if it's too small or too big.

Optional: If you want to set the frame's properties, right-click or Control-click the frame's border and choose Format Frame from the pop-up menu. The Frame dialog appears, as shown in Figure 5-24. For the purpose of this exercise, you can skip the formatting and just use the default settings.

3. **Make sure the insertion cursor is blinking on and off inside the frame and click anywhere within the frame's border.**

   You can now position the insertion cursor within the frame if you don't see the blinking cursor.

4. **In Word, choose Insert⇨Chart.**

   The Charts tab of Elements Gallery displays.

5. **Click one of the chart types.**

   Excel opens with sample data. The sample data is fine for this exercise, but for your own chart, use real data.

6. **In Excel, choose File⇨Close.**

   When Office returns to Word, your chart is inside the frame. You can drag the corners of both the frame and the chart to resize them as desired. It's a good idea to keep the frame slightly larger than the chart.

Book II
Chapter 5

Making Great
Tables and Charts

Select a range of text or a picture and then click the Insert Frame button. The selection will then be contained within a frame that is easily positioned anywhere in your document.

Changing a chart into a picture

When you make a chart in Word, the chart object is a complete Excel 2008 workbook embedded inside the Word document. You can then turn the chart object into other kinds of objects. For example, you can turn the chart into a picture, making it impossible for others to edit the chart or the chart's data. However, this also makes it easier to scale the size of the chart.

To access the various options available to you, follow these steps:

1. **Select the chart.**

   Click anywhere in the chart.

2. **In Word, choose Edit⇨Cut or Copy.**

   - *Cut* removes the chart from the document.
   - *Copy* retains the chart in its present location, as is, and copies the chart to the Clipboard.

3. **Click where you want the picture of the chart to appear.**

   You can use the current document or any other open document.

4. **Choose Edit⇨Paste.**

   Your chart appears at the insertion cursor. Notice a small widget displays at the lower-right corner of the chart.

5. **Immediately click the widget (or *Smart Tag*) in the lower-right corner of the pasted chart.**

   You find various options in the pop-up menu, as shown in Figure 5-25.

6. **From the pop-up menu, choose the first option: Paste as Picture.**

   You now have a picture of your chart, not an embedded Excel chart object, at the insertion point.

Figure 5-25:
Changing a chart into an image.

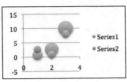

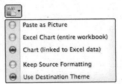

Chapter 6: Saving Time in Word

In This Chapter

- Using AutoText to make Word remember stuff
- Using mail merge the easy way
- Saving time with long document automation
- Formatting the background layer
- Using Word's new citations feature

*V*ital ingredients in the Word casserole can make your word processing faster and easier. You'll have more time to keep fit, cook, eat, and generally live life better!

An intelligence of a sort exists in Word, and yes, we're dead serious. Word can figure out how to finish typing words and phrases for you. You can give Word standard document tasks, such as captioning pictures and other objects in a long document, creating a table of contents, and generating an index. Word also has secret layers that you can use to format the background. Just don't expect Word to pay your bills. Not yet, anyway.

Automating with AutoText

Word's AutoText feature is so simple, yet so powerful; you might wonder how you got along without it. You teach Word to remember text that you use often and don't feel like typing over and over. Word can then type that text for you. If we had to choose one feature in all of Word that we think everyone should know, AutoText is the one! We start with a simple example.

Teaching Word a lesson

Before we get started, we want to remind you that you can click the Show button on Word's Standard toolbar to show or hide paragraph marks and other non-printing characters while you work. Many people find it useful to see these marks while they work.

As we drive through this section, we use five Autos:

- ✦ **AutoText:** When certain text is typed, this feature instantly inserts an AutoText entry.

✦ **AutoText name:** The name that you give to an AutoText entry. This is the specific text you type to create an AutoText entry.

✦ **AutoText entry:** The text or other object that's been saved or was built into Word so that when its name is typed, the saved entry is inserted instantly.

✦ **AutoComplete:** The processes whereby a saved AutoText entry is added to a document when its name is typed.

✦ **AutoCorrect:** The technology that the AutoText feature uses. You could consider AutoCorrect to be the parent of the AutoText feature.

Maybe you have to type your organization's name often. Maybe you have to type a word or an expression that's cumbersome, such as *Nuclear Factor-Kappa B and Placental Apoptosis.* To teach Word a word or expression, all you have to do is

1. **Type the word or expression that you use often and select it.**

   You can also select a word or expression you already have in an existing document.

   You can select as much text as you like. An entire paragraph isn't out of the question. If you select the ending paragraph mark with the text, Word knows both the text and the current text's formatting. If you want Word to know only the text, don't include paragraph marks.

2. **With the text selected, choose Insert⇨AutoText⇨New.**

   This summons the Create AutoText dialog with a suggested name for your AutoText entry, as shown in Figure 6-1.

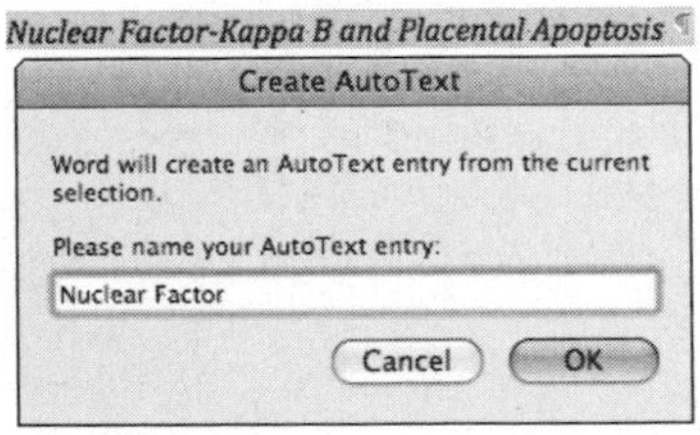

Figure 6-1:
Teaching
Word a new
expression.

3. **(Optional) If you don't want to use Word's suggestion, type a new name in the field.**

4. **Click OK to close the Create AutoText dialog and add the entry to Word.**

   Word looks for the names of AutoText entries as you type, and when you begin to type the first few letters, AutoText fills in the rest of the text for you.

In this example, whenever you type **Nuclear Factor**, Word knows you want to use the long, awful *Nuclear Factor-Kappa B and Placental Apoptosis* expression in your document. Because you included the paragraph mark, Word knows you want the paragraph formatting applied, too. You don't have to use any of the words of the saved AutoText in the name you give to AutoText. You can invent your own AutoText naming scheme.

Any AutoText entries you create in Word work in Excel, PowerPoint, and Entourage, too.

Using AutoText on a daily basis

Word always enables you to choose between accepting the AutoText displayed as a ToolTip and continuing to type. Because you taught Word the text you want and set up a name, whenever Word sees you typing that name, it displays a ToolTip (as shown in Figure 6-2) with the full or abbreviated AutoText. If you want to use the AutoText, all you have to do is press Return or Enter. Word instantly does the tough typing and inserts the full text. (This automated way of typing is *AutoComplete*.) If you don't want to use the AutoText suggestion, you can keep right on typing, and Word doesn't bother you about it.

**Book II
Chapter 6**

Saving Time in
Word

Figure 6-2:
Activating
an AutoText
prompt.

Nuclear Factor-Kappa B and Pla...
When you want to use nucl

Some people find AutoText ToolTips distracting. You can reduce the distraction by using a prefix when you give your AutoText a name. For example, you could use a prefix, such as *Atext,* for all your AutoText entries so that the AutoText appears only when you intentionally type **Atext** along with the rest of the name.

You may have noticed that we marked AutoText as a Mac-only feature earlier in this section. You may have used Word for Windows and are saying, "Hey! Wait a minute! That's available on Word for Windows, too!" Well, AutoText used to be; it was removed from Word 2007 and replaced by Building Blocks, which doesn't have the AutoText ToolTip feature so you can no longer use AutoComplete to automate your typing. No more AutoText for Windows users; it's gone. Kaput! Thankfully, AutoText is still alive on Mac.

Teaching Word even more

Turns out Word is pretty smart. You can teach Word more than just text. Word for Mac can save just about anything you come across as AutoText. The neat thing about AutoText is that you don't even have to open a template, apply a style, or even use Elements Gallery — you just keep typing, and AutoText will autocomplete for you on demand. Here's a short list of things you might want to turn into AutoText entries (these are all things you commonly use or need to type):

✦ Plain text (excluding paragraph marks)

✦ Formatted text, paragraphs, or more (including paragraph marks)

✦ Your favorite formatted tables

✦ Equations you use frequently

✦ Graphs that you've customized

✦ Pictures or logos that you use often

✦ Word fields

✦ WordArt and SmartArt

✦ A form or form letter

✦ Just about anything you want to have at your fingertips and can select within a Word document

Taming AutoText

Creating your own AutoText entries is really great. A lot of AutoText entries come with Office that you might not have much use for. In fact, many people can ditch most, if not all, of the AutoText entries that come with Word. Some would rather have just their own things in the AutoText list, thank you.

You can use the AutoText toolbar to create your own AutoText entries. After you complete your AutoText entries, you can turn off the toolbar and forget about it because AutoText is, well, automatic. From Word's View menu, choose Toolbars➪AutoText to turn on the AutoText toolbar, as shown in Figure 6-3.

You can find the same controls from the AutoText toolbar on Word's Insert menu by choosing AutoText. The controls are on the submenus.

After you turn on the AutoText toolbar, get familiar with the following three buttons:

✦ **AutoText:** Click the AutoText button (the first button on the left with a large *A*, as shown in Figure 6-3) on the AutoText toolbar to open AutoText preferences within the AutoCorrect dialog, as shown in Figure 6-4.

All Entries button   New button

AutoText button   AutoText toolbar

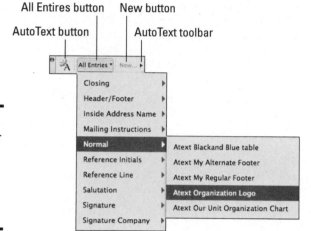

Figure 6-3:
Finding your
AutoText
entries
with the
AutoText
toolbar.

Check this box to turn AutoComplete on.   Preview

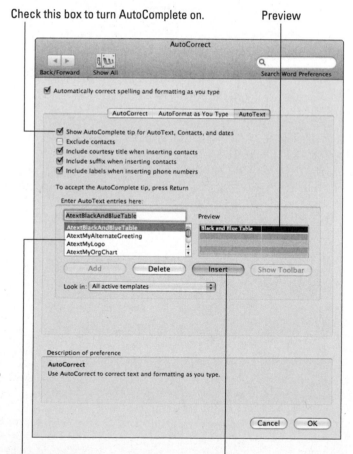

Figure 6-4:
Managing
AutoText.

AutoText entries   Insert

If you're wondering why AutoText is under AutoCorrect preferences even though AutoText has nothing to do with making corrections, it's because Word uses its AutoCorrect technology to accomplish the ability to AutoComplete AutoText entries as you type. Here you can make additional selections:

- *Automatically Correct Spelling and Formatting as You Type:* This check box is an on/off switch for all the automatic Word behaviors shown on all the tabs of AutoCorrect preferences. Deselect the box to turn off all aspects of AutoCorrect.

- *Show AutoComplete Tip for AutoText, Contacts, and Dates:* This check box is probably the most important one for AutoText because it's an on/off switch for the AutoText AutoComplete feature. Deselecting this check box pretty much defeats the purpose of AutoText unless you want to turn AutoText off for a particular demonstration. If you deselect this, you can still use the AutoText toolbar All Entries pop-up menu or Word's Insert menu to manually put AutoText entries into your document. Also, you can turn AutoComplete back on by checking the box.

   Review the other check boxes and make changes to suit your own preferences. If you write many business letters with long text entries that are often repeated, you might want to leave most of these options selected.

- *Look In:* This is a pop-up menu that lets you filter what AutoText entries are displayed in the AutoText entries list. You can choose from any currently open document template. AutoText entries are stored in templates.

- *Enter AutoText Entries Here:* Take a look at the list of entries, as shown in Figure 6-4. If you see things in the list that you want to have AutoComplete finish, leave them. Otherwise, delete the entries you don't need. Click OK when you're done cleaning AutoText entries. Click a name to see a preview of the entry.

- *Delete:* Select an AutoText entry; then click Delete to permanently remove it. AutoText entries are saved to Normal (.dotx) template. Changes to Normal template are saved when you quit Word.

- *Insert:* Inserts the selected AutoText into your document at the position of the insertion cursor.

- *Add:* If you select something before opening these preferences, you can type a name and click Add to create a new AutoText entry.

If you ever need to find your own AutoText entries, they're stored in Word's Normal template (Normal.dotx). You can use Organizer (which we discuss in Chapter 3 of this minibook) to copy AutoText entries from one template to another.

✦ **All Entries:** The All Entries button on the AutoText toolbar opens a menu (as shown in Figure 6-3) that allows you to insert an AutoText entry with one click.

✦ **New:** Select text or an object such as a chart, table, picture, or even an entire document. Click New to display the Create AutoText dialog, as shown in Figure 6-1. Give your AutoText entry a name, click OK, and you've made a new AutoText entry!

Making Magic with Mail Merge

If one major area exists in which Office 2008 for Mac beats all the others by a country mile, mail merge is it! Sending mail to a group of people in one fell swoop has never been so easy.

Your authors give two thumbs up — as well as a standing ovation — to Office 2008's Mail Merge Manager. We find OpenOffice and Windows Office Mail Merge to be little more than frustrating tests of patience and no way to get actual work done. In Word 2008, you don't have confusing field mapping, task panes, or other such gobbledygook. Mail merge is straightforward and intuitive thanks to the geniuses at Microsoft who put together the easy-to-use Mac-only Mail Merge Manager.

Mail Merge Manager is designed to be used starting at the top in Step 1, and you work your way down to Step 6. These steps are explained in the online Mail Merge course described in the following section. After you figure out how to use this handy tool, you can use it for all kinds of things, such as e-mailing forms, announcements, newsletters, and other publications; addressing envelopes; and preparing brochures. You can perform mail merges in minutes, rather than hours or days.

Getting started: Making a mail merge form letter

There is a superb, free course on making a mail merge to a form letter available to you right in Word 2008 Help. After you take the tutorial, you'll find that this book supplements the mail merge basics covered. The course takes about 20 minutes to complete. If you're new to mail merge or want to review the mail merge process, take this course before continuing further in this section. A live Internet connection is required to take this course. To take this excellent free course, do the following:

1. **Click Word's Help button on the Standard toolbar.**

Word Help opens, as shown in Figure 6-5.

Enter search terms   Course name

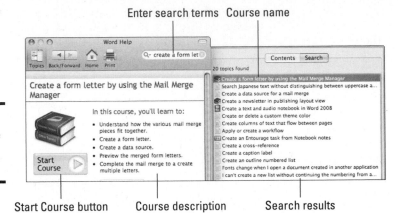

Figure 6-5:
Starting the
mail merge
course.

Start Course button   Course description   Search results

2. **In the Search box, type** create a form letter.

3. **Press Return or Enter.**

4. **Click the Create a Form Letter by Using the Mail Merge Manager topic.**

   The course description appears in Word Help, as shown in Figure 6-6.

Click disclosure triangles.

Course Navigation

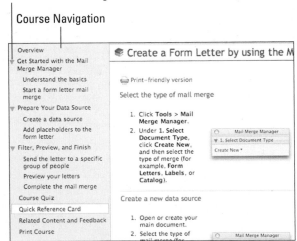

Figure 6-6:
Taking the
mail merge
course.

5. **Click the Start Course button, as shown in Figure 6-5.**

   Your default Web browser opens, and the course begins, as shown in
   Figure 6-6.

While the course is running, you can use the Navigation Pane to skip around from one part of the course to another, or to access a particular section of the course for review. Timesaver: Be sure to print the Quick Reference Card. A printer-friendly version of the course is available, as shown in Figure 6-6.

When you mail merge to send e-mail rather than conventional snail mail letters, the body of your main merge document needs to have a placeholder with e-mail addresses in it. Otherwise, Word doesn't know which e-mail addresses to send to. At times, you may not want the recipient's e-mail address to appear in the document's body. Here's a trick to keep the e-mail address from showing in an HTML format mail merge:

1. **Highlight the e-mail placeholder.**

2. **In Word choose Format⇨Font.**

   The Font dialog appears.

3. **On the Font tab of the Font dialog, in the Effects section, select the Hidden check box.**

4. **Click OK to close the Font dialog.**

   The selected e-mail field is no longer visible. This way the e-mail address doesn't show in the document, but it's still there for Word to use.

Merging to envelopes

After you print your letters, make envelopes for them. You might want to make envelopes for other purposes, too, such as cards and invitations. The general procedure is the same for merging to envelopes as for merging to a form letter, which we describe in the preceding section.

We start a fresh example with a new, blank Word document. Make sure Mail Merge Manager is visible; if not, in Word, choose Tools⇨Mail Merge Manager to turn it on. To merge to envelopes, only the first step of Mail Merge Manager needs special instructions. The rest of the steps are the same as for merging to a letter (which we describe in the preceding section). Follow these steps to choose your envelope's size for the mail merge:

1. **On Mail Merge Manager in Step 1, Select Document Type: Choose Create New⇨Envelopes.**

   The Envelope dialog appears (see Figure 6-7).

   Word creates a #10 standard business size envelope by default. If that's the envelope size you need, click OK to close the Envelope dialog, and you're done! You don't have to do any more steps to select an envelope size. You can now pick up with Step 2 of Mail Merge Manager, which we describe in preceding section.

Book II
Chapter 6

Saving Time in
Word

If you want to use an envelope size other than #10 standard business size, follow these additional steps.

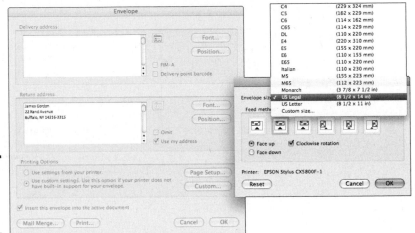

Figure 6-7:
Choosing
an envelope
size.

2. **Click the Page Setup button.**

The Page Setup dialog opens (see Figure 6-8).

Paper Size

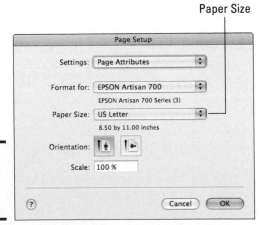

Figure 6-8:
Using Page
Setup's
paper size.

3. **Choose a paper size from the Pager Size pop-up menu.**

4. **Click OK.**

The Envelope dialog (see Figure 6-7) returns.

- If the envelope size you need is in the Paper Size pop-up menu, click OK to close the Page Setup dialog. Then click OK to close the Envelope dialog. You don't have to do any more steps to select an envelope size. Next, you complete the merge starting with Step 2 of Mail Merge Manager, as described in the preceding section.

- If the envelope size you need isn't in the Page Setup dialog, click OK to close the Page Setup dialog to return to the Envelope dialog where you can try these additional steps:

5. **In the Envelope dialog, click the Custom button.**

    The Custom Page Options dialog opens, as shown in Figure 6-9.

Envelope size

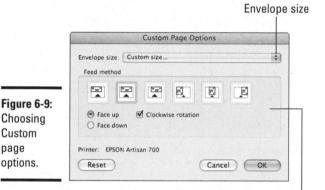

Figure 6-9: Choosing Custom page options.

Your printer's feed method

6. **In the Envelope Size pop-up menu, choose a size from the pop-up menu (move the mouse cursor to the top of the list to find the envelopes).**

    - If the envelope size you need is in the Custom Page Options Envelope Size pop-up menu, click OK to close the Custom Page Envelope dialog. Then click OK to close the Envelope dialog. You don't have to do any more steps to select an envelope size. Next, complete the merge starting with Step 2 of Mail Merge Manager, as described in the preceding section.

    - If the envelope size you need isn't in the Custom Page Options Envelope Size pop-up menu, at the bottom of the Envelope Size pop-up menu, choose Custom. Word allows you to provide width and height attributes for your envelope in the Envelope Size window, as shown in Figure 6-10. No matter what size envelope you have, Word can use it! You may have to experiment with your printer's feed method to get the custom envelope orientation the right way.

Figure 6-10:
Creating a custom envelope size.

7. **Click OK to close the Envelope Size dialog.**

8. **Click OK to close the Custom Page Options dialog.**

9. **Click OK to close the Envelope dialog.**

Complete the merge starting with Step 2 of Mail Merge Manager, as described in the preceding section.

Making labels

Generally, when it comes to creating mailing labels, you want one of two things:

✦ A sheet in which all the labels are exactly the same (to send to one person or address)

✦ To make labels from a data source in which each label has a different address obtained from the database

Word can do both kinds of labels.

Before we talk about either kind of label, we talk a little bit about label etiquette. One huge offense is cramming too much stuff onto a small label. If you're going to use labels that are 3 across and 10 down on 8½-x-11–inch paper, please don't try to put 5 or more lines of information or super long lines on these little pieces of paper. Shrinking the font to 4 or 8 points is *not* a good solution! They make bigger labels. Use them!

Making a sheet of identical labels

In this example, we start with a new, blank Word document that will contain a set of identical labels 3 across and 10 down on 8½-x-11–inch paper in less than 3 minutes! Follow these steps, and substitute your own paper size and the number of labels you want to fit on a page:

1. **In Word, choose Tools➪Labels.**

The Labels dialog appears, as shown in Figure 6-11.

Choose an address from Entourage Contacts.

Click checkbox to use your address.

Type an address.

Choose label sizes here.

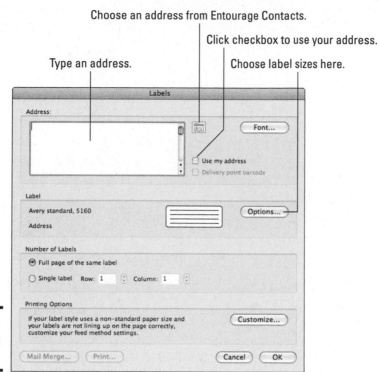

Figure 6-11:
Customizing
labels.

2. **Type a name and address into the Address field.**

Alternatively, you can click the small envelope icon to the right of the Address block to open a dialog that lets you pick a contact from your Entourage Address Book.

You could also click the Use My Address check box to use your Me contact address in your Entourage Address Book. (See Book V, Chapter 5 for information about the Me contact.)

3. **Click the Options button to bring up the Label Options dialog, as shown in Figure 6-12.**

If not already the default, choose Avery Standard in the Label Products pop-up menu, and in the Product Number list, choose 5160 — Address.

4. **Click OK to exit the Label Options dialog.**

The Labels dialog is visible again.

5. **Click OK to close the Labels dialog.**

You now have a full sheet of perfect labels!

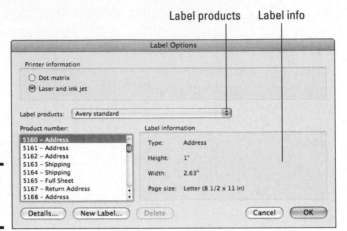

Figure 6-12:
Choosing a
label size.

It's that easy. Pretty cool, huh? The rest of this section explains how you can customize your label in just about every way imaginable. Setting up labels is handled in a single, compact pane. Another way to display the Labels dialog (see Figure 6-11) in all its glory is to, in Word, choose Tools⇨Labels.

In the Labels dialog, you can do the following:

✦ **Address your labels:** In the Address field in the upper left, type the name and address you want placed on each label. If you like, you can use an address from your Entourage contacts by following the instructions in Step 2 in the earlier steps about making identical labels.

✦ **Customize text formatting:** Use the Font button to open Word's Font dialog to customize the text formatting.

✦ **Choose your label size:** Pick a label size from hundreds of different sizes and preset labels from more than 14 different manufacturers from the Label Products pop-up menu.

✦ **Create a custom label:** As if that weren't enough, in the Label Options dialog, click the New Label button that opens the New Custom [laser or dot matrix] dialog (not illustrated because you will probably never need to do this) that allows you to create a completely customized label from scratch.

Really, 99 percent of the time all you have to do is just look on the box of labels you have and select the brand and product number from the Label Products pop-up menu in the Label Options dialog (refer to Figure 6-12).

When printing labels, try printing on a sheet of plain paper first. Hold your test sheet of labels up to the light with a sheet of blank labels to see how everything lines up. You can adjust the margins by dragging them in the ruler, or click the Customize button in the Labels dialog to fine-tune everything so your labels line up perfectly.

Making a sheet of labels fast

Here's a set of timesaving steps that produce a single sheet of identical labels:

1. **In Word, choose Tools⇨Labels.**

2. **In the Labels dialog, type the name and address you want to use.**

3. **Click the Options button to display the Label Options dialog.**

4. **Choose your brand and model label in the Label Products pop-up menu.**

   For standard 3-across-by-10-down labels, choose Avery 5160 — address.

5. **Click OK to close the Label Products pop-up and click OK again to close the Labels dialog.**

Making labels from a database

You can also use an Excel workbook as your mail merge data source. Start with a new, blank Word document. For this example, you make a set of labels 3 across and 10 down on 8½-x-11–inch paper. Make sure Mail Merge Manager is turned on by choosing Tools⇨Mail Merge Manager in Word. You also need an Excel document that's set up as a mailing list. To make labels from a database, take the following steps. In this sequence, the step numbers shown here match the step numbers of Mail Merge Manager.

1. **Select Document Type:**

   a. *Choose Create New.*

   b. *From the pop-up menu, choose Labels.*

   The Label Options dialog (see Figure 6-12) appears.

   c. *From the Label Products pop-up menu, choose Avery Standard.*

   d. *From the Product Number list, select 5160 — Address.*

   e. *Click OK to close the Label Options dialog.*

   A table appears. Don't make any adjustments to the table or click in the table. The insertion cursor should be blinking in the upper leftmost cell, which will be the only empty cell in the table. You may have to drag the bottom scroll bar to see the blinking cursor. Section 1 of Mail Merge Manager now displays the name of the Main Document and which type of merge you're performing.

2. **Select Recipients List:**

   a. *Click Get List.*

   b. *From the pop-up menu, choose Open Data Source.*

   A File Open window appears.

   c. *Navigate to the Excel (.xlsx) workbook you're using as the data source and click Open.*

A dialog appears with a pop-up menu that lists all the sheets and named ranges in the workbook.

d. *Choose the worksheet or range that has the names and addresses for the data source, and then click OK.*

Your Word mail merge document is now linked to the worksheet or data range data source in the Excel workbook. The Edit Labels dialog appears, as shown in Figure 6-13.

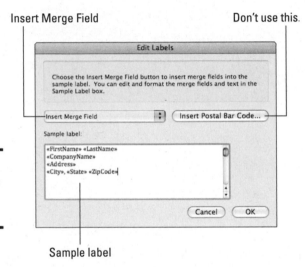

Insert Merge Field   Don't use this.

Figure 6-13: Laying out a mail merge label.

Sample label

3. **Edit Labels:**

a. *When the Edit Labels dialog opens, you see an empty Sample Label with a blinking insertion cursor. Click the Insert Merge Field pop-up, and choose the field that will be on the left of the top row of the label.*

In Figure 6-13, the first field is <<FirstName>>. Word puts chevrons surrounding the field name to indicate that they're merge fields.

b. *In this example, press the spacebar once to put a space between First Name and Last Name.*

c. *Choose Last Name from the Insert Merge Field pop-up menu.*

d. *To move the insertion cursor to the next line, press Return or Enter.*

Continue the same way to add remaining fields. You can type characters as needed, such as a comma to separate City from State. Do not use Insert Postal Bar Code because the U.S. Post Office changed how it generates postal bar codes, and Word doesn't conform to the new specification.

    e. Click OK to close the Edit Labels dialog.

You return to your Word document, and your table grid is now filled with a whole bunch of field names in chevrons. Step 3 of Mail Merge Manager opens but don't use anything from Mail Merge Manager Step 3 because the Edit Labels dialog takes care of inserting placeholders when making mail merge labels. Step 2 of Mail Merge Manager now shows the filename of the data source document.

4. (Optional) Filter Recipients:

Filter data and order records.

5. Preview Results:

See the section, "Previewing merge results," later in this chapter.

6. Complete Merge:

See the section, "Completing the merge," later in this chapter.

Done!

Merging to labels in just minutes!

With a little practice, you can get a typical mail merge to labels done in less than a minute or two. Here's a timesaving quick reference guide to speed you through the steps. Our numbering here matches the step numbers of Mail Merge Manager.

1. **Select Document Type:** Click Create New. Choose Labels. Choose a label product.

2. **Select Recipients List:** Click Get List. Choose Open Data Source. Navigate to the data source file. Select the source file and click Open. If you're using an Excel workbook as the data source, select the data source worksheet or named range when prompted.

3. **Edit Labels:** Pick fields from the Insert Merge Field pop-up menu. Arrange those fields as you want them to appear on the labels.

4. **(Optional) Filter Recipients:** Click Options to filter the data or order the records.

5. **Preview Results:** Click the <<ABC>> button and the arrow buttons to see a preview of the merge.

6. **Complete Merge:** Click Merge to Printer to make the labels. Click Merge to New Document to make a copy of the merge for your records, or in case you want to distribute the label document to others.

Merging to a catalog

In Project Gallery, you find two stunning catalogs that you can customize and use with mail merge. To access these catalogs, follow these steps:

1. **In Word, choose File➪Project Gallery.**

   Project Gallery displays.

2. **In the Category list on the left, click the disclosure triangle next to the Marketing option to reveal subcategories.**

3. **Choose the Catalogs subcategory.**

   You see at least two catalogs: Booklet and Photo. You can customize either of these templates and use them as the basis for starting a mail merge.

In Mail Merge Manager Step 1: Select Document Type, you can choose Catalog from the Create New pop-up menu. Choose this option to build custom, personalized catalogs and price sheets. For example, you could pull pictures from a database to create individualized custom catalogs based on customer purchasing volume or some other criteria.

Using different data sources

Earlier in this chapter, we used Excel as the data source for a mail merge. Word can use many different data sources to perform a mail merge. In Mail Merge Manager Step 2: Select Recipients List, you can choose the Get List option to display options, as shown in Figure 6-14.

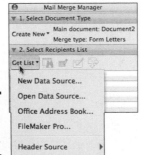

Figure 6-14:
Choosing a data source.

New Data Source

The New Data Source option (see Figure 6-14) creates a new Word document to use as the source for the mail merge. This option is fine for small, home databases, or maybe even a club's database.

You might find Word's Database toolbar to be very handy when working with the New Data Source feature. In Word, choose View⇨Toolbars⇨ Database. By default, the Database toolbar shows up as a set of buttons, but you can set the toolbar's button properties to Image and Text to see what each button does. We cover changing toolbar button properties in Book I, Chapter 3.

Be aware that using a Word document as a data source doesn't cut it for large data sources. If you find that Word becomes slow when working with the data source, move your table to Excel (you can copy from Word and paste into Excel).

Open Data Source

The Open Data Source option (see Figure 6-14) enables you to navigate in Finder to a Word document that was set up as a database using New Data Source, as described in the preceding section, or an Excel workbook containing a worksheet or named range that's already set up as a mailing list or a data source list. Open Data Source requires that you already have a list.

Office Address Book

The Office Address Book option (see Figure 6-14) allows you to use your Entourage contacts as the mail merge data source.

FileMaker Pro

The FileMaker Pro option (see Figure 6-14) allows you to navigate in Finder to a FileMaker Pro file that's already set up as a mailing list or a data source list.

Previewing merge results

Mail Merge Manager Step 5: Preview Results is a favorite step. In this step, you can see the merged data so you can decide whether your merge works as planned. In Mail Merge Manager Step 3, you put placeholders into your mail merge main document to indicate fields that would accept merge data. Those placeholders are the field names displayed with chevrons. When you see chevrons, you know you're seeing the field names. A common set of field names is

<< First Name >> << Last Name >>

This is when the magic of previewing your results comes in (see Figure 6-15). You can display your merge fields in one of three ways:

✦ If you don't press any buttons, you see the field names with chevrons.

✦ If you click the View Merged Data <<ABC>> button, Word displays the actual data that will be merged from the database instead of the field codes.

Figure 6-15:
Controlling
the preview
of our data.

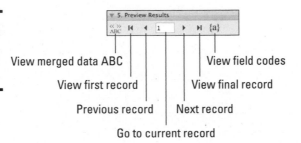

View merged data ABC

View first record

Previous record

View field codes

View final record

Next record

Go to current record

If you press the View Merged Data <<ABC>> button, you can see your document in live preview mode while you press the buttons in Mail Merge Manager (see Figure 6-15) to view the data records as they will appear when you complete the merge. You can type a specific record number into the Go to Record box and then press Return or Enter to see that particular record. The same box shows you which record is displayed currently.

✦ If you press the View Field Codes button, as shown in Figure 6-16, it overrides the View Merged Data <<ABC>> button; you see the third type of display Word has for mail merge fields. We discuss field codes in Chapter 7 of this minibook. For now, field codes look seemingly mystifying like this:

{ MERGEFIELD First Name } { MERGEFIELD Last Name }

When you are done looking at previews, just move on to the next step in Mail Merge Manager.

Completing the merge

By the time you get to Mail Merge Manager Step 6: Complete Merge, you have a very smart document on your hands; it knows what database you want to use, what fields to bring in, where to place the data within the document, and any special instructions you've given. Think of Complete Merge as having an electronic printing press, with the press ready to roll.

Performing a test run

Before you print a large merge, do a sample run. The Merge Data Range pop-up menu can help you. Doing a test run is probably a good idea, especially if you have lots of data to merge. Here are the options to control your sample run:

✦ **All:** Use this setting to complete the entire merge.

✦ **Current Record:** With the record indicated in Mail Merge Manager Step 5, this option merges only one record.

✦ **Custom:** Enter a range of records.

Doing the merge

Okay, if you've followed along so far, you're ready to do an actual merge! The question is: Where do you want the output to happen? You have three choices, as shown in Figure 6-16.

Figure 6-16:
Completing
the mail
merge.

Additional filters

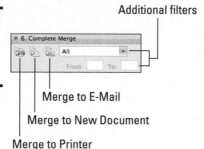

Merge to E-Mail

Merge to New Document

Merge to Printer

Merge to Printer

When you click Merge to Printer, Word sends the final product to the printer. Be sure you have plenty of paper and ink handy if you're printing a lot of pages!

Before you print your finished work to an actual paper and ink printer, first do a mail merge test run so that you don't end up wasting resources. You can save paper and ink or toner by choosing PDF in the Print dialog, or merging to a New Document (which we cover in the following section) to see the complete, final merge before you use Merge to Printer.

Merge to a New Document

When you click Merge to a New Document, Word creates a fresh, new document that has all the merged information in it. If you printed this document, it'd be the same as if you had merged to the printer. This new document is a regular Word document. This merged document doesn't have any merge fields in it — it displays the result of the merge as ordinary text. Consequently, this merged document isn't connected to the data source, and it won't change when the data source is updated. It's a good a way to make a record of the output of your mail merge and provides a merged document that you can distribute to other people.

Merge to E-Mail

Click Merge to E-Mail to send the output to your Entourage Outbox and
then to open the Mail Recipient dialog (see Figure 6-17), which offers you
the following choices:

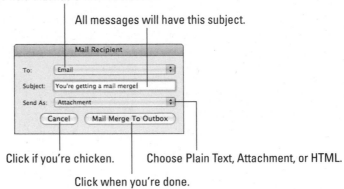

Use the field that has e-mail addresses.

All messages will have this subject.

Figure 6-17:
Making final
preparations
for merging
to e-mail.

Click if you're chicken.

Choose Plain Text, Attachment, or HTML.

Click when you're done.

+ **To pop-up menu:** You must choose the mail merge field that contains
the recipients' e-mail addresses.

+ **Subject field:** Type a subject in this field, and each message is given this
subject.

+ **Send As pop-up menu:** You have three choices:

  • *Plain Text:* Only text and numeric characters from your document
will be sent. All formatting is discarded. Text in text boxes, WordArt,
figures, charts, objects (organization charts, equations, and so on)
may be discarded.

  • *Attachment:* A copy of the Word document is sent as an e-mail
attachment. Use this to ensure the recipient gets a full fidelity
document. This is the option you'll probably use the most.

  • *HTML:* Word sends the document as HTML (the language of Web
browsers). Modern e-mail clients can render HTML, some better
than others. To see what your document might look like when it's
received, switch to Web Layout View in Word before you send in
HTML format. Due to the nature of HTML, Word, and e-mail clients,
HTML can produce widely varying appearance in e-mail programs.

Before you send the whole batch as HTML, take a moment to merge just
one record to make sure it looks okay in Entourage. Some of the gorgeous
templates in Project Gallery are too complex for Entourage and other
e-mail programs. If you're not happy with the HTML rendering, choose
Send as Attachment.

Living happily with your e-mail provider

Merge to E-Mail is a very powerful capability. If you merge 10 or 20 e-mail messages, no one will bother you. Word can merge more than one million messages at a time from an Excel database. If your merge involves hundreds of records, make sure your Entourage rules are set up sensibly. A flood of e-mails into a Sent Items box can make your account exceed your quota. Even 100 messages might cause those IT people or Internet service providers (ISP), who usually take weeks to respond to you, to be at your doorstep in minutes with fire in their eyes or your account might be shut down. Make sure your ISP or IT folks know ahead of time that you plan to send a large merge so that you don't get into trouble with them. They may have to make special arrangements to allow more than a certain number of your messages be sent and delivered.

Click the Mail Merge to Outbox button to create the mail merge documents and put them into the Entourage Outbox. The documents will go out on your next scheduled send time in Entourage, or you can click the Send/Receive button on the Entourage toolbar to send them immediately. Off they go!

Automating Long Document Chores

If you're creating a particularly long document, such as a book manuscript, you can take advantage of some clever automation features in Word 2008.

Your document may have plenty of illustrations, charts, equations, or other things that need to be labeled and kept track of. That's when Word's Index and Tables feature comes in handy.

Making an instant Table of Contents

Word 2008 features a fast, new way to make a Table of Contents (TOC). If you've been using heading styles throughout your document, the process is entirely automatic. Otherwise, select the Manual Formatting option. Follow these steps to make a TOC (see Figure 6-18):

1. **Click in the document where you want the TOC to appear.**

2. **If Elements Gallery isn't visible, choose View➪Elements Gallery.**

   If Elements Gallery is grayed out in the menu, use the View menu to switch to a view, such as Print Layout View, that supports Elements Gallery.

3. **In the Elements bar, choose Document Elements and then click the Table of Contents button just beneath the Elements bar.**

   A gallery with TOC heading samples, as shown in Figure 6-18, appears.

4. **Toward the left of these sample thumbnails, below Create With, select either the Heading Styles or Manual Formatting option.**

   • Choose *Heading Styles* if your document contains heading styles.

   • Choose *Manual* if your document does not contain heading styles.

5. **In Elements Gallery, choose a heading style.**

   Based on the heading styles you used in the document, Word creates a quick TOC for you! If you choose the Manual option, Word guesses at your document's structure and presents you with a generic TOC based on your format choice from the Gallery so that you can customize manually.

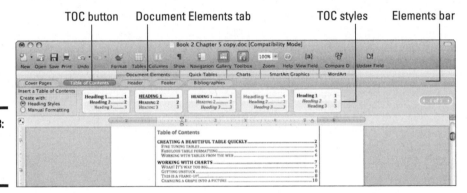

Figure 6-18:
Creating a TOC in a hurry.

How fast and easy is that? As long as your document is well-structured based on heading styles, Word's TOC feature saves you a ton of work. But what if you want more TOC style choices? No problem! Select the entire TOC that you put into your document. In Word, choose Insert⇨ Index and Tables and then select the Table of Contents tab in the Index and Tables dialog that appears, as shown in Figure 6-19.

Here you can choose from additional formatting options:

✦ **Formats:** Shows built-in and your own custom TOC format styles.

✦ **Show Levels:** Sets how many heading levels will be used in the ToC.

✦ **Show Page Numbers:** This check box shows or hides page numbers.

✦ **Right Align Page Numbers:** This check box aligns page numbers left or right.

✦ **Tab Leader:** This pop-up menu offers more choices for the type of leader line that will be inserted between headings and page numbers.

✦ **Options button:** This opens the Table of Contents Options dialog (see Figure 6-20).

TOC styles   Preview

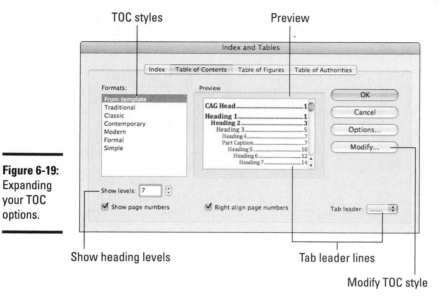

Book II
Chapter 6

Saving Time in Word

Figure 6-19:
Expanding
your TOC
options.

Show heading levels   Tab leader lines

Modify TOC style

Styles

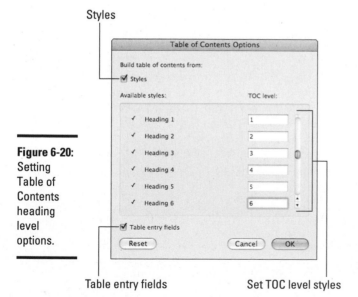

Figure 6-20:
Setting
Table of
Contents
heading
level
options.

Table entry fields   Set TOC level styles

Using Index and Tables styles

Each tab of the Index and Tables dialog represents a specific kind of index or table. Because all the Index and Tables formats use styles, you can use the same techniques to create, customize, and delete your own styles as you do for table styles in Chapter 5 of this minibook.

To enable the ability to customize any index or table, select From Template in the Index and Tables Formats list of any tab to activate the Modify button. Click Modify to open the Style dialog. In the Style dialog, click Modify Style to open the Modify Style dialog.

With the Table of Contents dialog, you can manually map styles to TOC levels by typing in TOC level values in the fields to the right of the Available Styles list. You can determine which styles to make available:

✦ **Styles:** Selecting this box allows you to choose from TOC styles from Normal (.dotx) and other open templates.

✦ **Table Entry Fields:** Select this box to allow mapping of TOC Word field codes in your document to TOC levels in a TOC. (We explain Word field codes in Chapter 7 of this minibook.)

✦ **Modify (Index and Tables dialog):** Available if you choose From Template in the Styles list.

Long Document Wizard

When you create a TOC in Word, you use the Index and Tables dialog, or as we call it, the *Long Document Wizard*. (Why Word doesn't call it a wizard is a mystery to us.) The Index and Tables dialog has four tabs (as shown in Figure 6-19), each representing a wonderful timesaving operation that Word can perform for you. The four tabs are

✦ **Index:** Automatically creates an index using marked entries.

✦ **Table of Contents:** Automatically creates a table of contents using headings.

✦ **Table of Figures:** Automatically creates a table of figures using figure captions.

✦ **Table of Authorities:** Automatically creates a Table of Authorities based on styles.

Creating an index

At times, you work on a long document in which you might want an index with page numbers. Word can automate this task for you. This procedure entails two steps:

1. **Mark the words or phrases to be used in the index.**

2. **Generate the index.**

To mark the words or phrases to be used in the index, you create a concordance file. Don't let that word scare you; a *concordance* file is a fancy name for a Word document that consists of a single- or two-column table. For information on how to create other kinds of tables, see Chapter 5 in this minibook. Follow these steps to create a concordance table:

1. **In Word, choose menu⇨New Blank Document.**

A new, blank Word document appears.

2. **Choose Table⇨Insert⇨Table.**

The Index and Tables dialog appears.

3. **In the Index and Tables dialogs, set Number of Columns to 2.**

For now, the number of rows you have is irrelevant. The other default settings are fine and don't need to be changed.

4. **Click OK to close the Index and Tables dialog.**

A two-column table appears in your document.

5. **Fill in the cells as described here (see Table 6-1):**

- *Left-hand column:* Put all the words from your document that should be marked for indexing into the left column, one word or phrase per cell.

- *Right-hand column:* Enter the appropriate document index heading corresponding to each word in the left column.

- *Don't use column headings:* Nothing else can be in the concordance file except your two-column table.

  In this example, any occurrence of *Formatting*, *Web*, *PDF*, or *Table* will appear under the Tables index heading. Any occurrence of *AutoFormat* or *Formatting* will appear in our index under the Styles index heading. You don't have to group the words or the index headings. Word figures it all out for you.

6. **Choose File⇨Save to save the table as a Word document and then click the red Close button to close the concordance table document.**

Table 6-1 shows a concordance table we made to use on a draft version of Chapter 5 of this minibook. The left column is a list of the words we want to mark for indexing. The right column is the index heading that is used for our marked words.

**Book II
Chapter 6**

Saving Time in Word

Table 6-1	Making a Simple Index Table
Formatting	Tables
Web	Tables
PDF	Tables
AutoFormat	Styles
Table	Tables
Formatting	Styles

Whenever you work with the Index and Tables dialog, work only on copies of your files. You might go through several trials before you find the result you want.

After you save your concordance file, you can use it to create an index from a long document; in this case, the draft of Chapter 5 in this minibook. Follow these steps to use a concordance file:

1. **In Word, choose File⇨Open.**

The File Open dialog displays.

2. **Select the Word document you want to index but don't open it yet.**

For this example, we select Chapter 5.

3. **In the File Open dialog, choose Copy from the Open pop-up menu and then click the Open button to open a copy of the document that you want to index.**

A copy of the document you chose opens.

4. **In the copy of your document, choose Insert⇨Index and Tables.**

The Index and Tables dialog opens (see Figure 6-21).

5. **Click the Index tab and then click the AutoMark button.**

The Choose a File dialog opens.

6. **Navigate to the concordance file you saved earlier and then click the Open button.**

Word marks the indexed words with { XE "Index" }. You have to turn on paragraph marks to see these index codes by clicking the Show button on Word's standard toolbar. The Index and Tables dialog closes. All the words in your document that will be used in the index have now been marked. The following steps create the index.

7. **Click in your document to set the insertion cursor to the place where you want to create the index.**

Use Run-in if space is tight.

Click OK after marking entries.

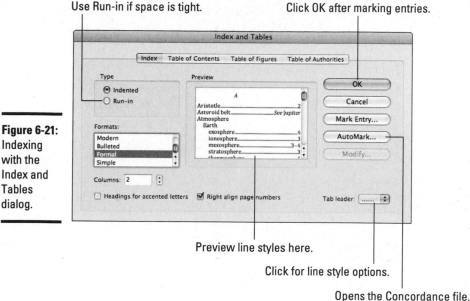

Figure 6-21:
Indexing
with the
Index and
Tables
dialog.

Preview line styles here.

Click for line style options.

Opens the Concordance file.

8. In Word, choose Insert⇨Index and Tables.

The Index and Tables dialog opens again (see Figure 6-21).

9. Click the Index tab if it isn't selected already.

10. Choose the type, format, tab leader style, and so on; or go with the default settings to format your index.

The choices you make are updated instantly in the preview.

11. After you make all your choices, click OK.

The Index and Tables dialog closes. Your index appears in your document.

Your basic index is all fine and well, but what if you want subheadings in your index? Word has that covered, too! With a colon (:), you can tell Word to create a subheading. Try this out with a new concordance table separating main headings from subheadings with a colon, as shown in the right-hand column of Table 6-2. Notice the overall main heading (*Tables* in this example) stands alone without colons so that the subheadings appear beneath the main heading. Also notice that Styles gets its own heading and is also listed as a subheading under Tables with our scheme. Look at Table 6-2 to see the headings and subheadings we used to produce the results, as shown in Figure 6-22. Figure 6-22 is in Draft View (in Word, choose View⇨Draft) with Show Hidden Marks turned on (click the Show button on the Standard toolbar).

Table 6-2	Making a Cross-Index Concordance Table for Subheadings
Formatting	Styles:Tables
Web	Tables:Web
PDF	Tables:Web
AutoFormat	Styles:Tables
Table	Tables
Formatting	Tables:Styles

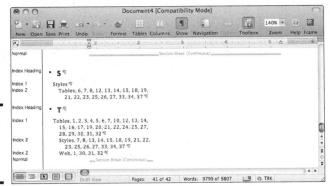

Figure 6-22: Your index inserted in Word.

When you make your index, think about how you want subheadings to work in your document. Experiment freely until you get just the right result.

Creating a Table of Figures

Many long documents have plenty of figures in them, and whether the figures are tables, pictures, graphs, drawings, SmartArt, WordArt, or embedded objects, you can list them all in one place in your document by creating a Table of Figures with the Index and Tables dialog. Before you can create a Table of Figures, you have to put a caption style onto each of the figures you want included in the table. To put a caption on a figure, follow these steps:

1. **Select a figure and then choose Insert⇨Caption in Word.**

The Caption dialog appears, as shown in Figure 6-23.

2. **Type a caption in the Caption text box and make any other changes.**

3. **Click OK when you're done and repeat the process for other figures in the document.**

Figure 6-23:
Captioning a
figure.

After you caption all the figures, take the following steps to create the Table
of Figures:

1. **In Word, choose Insert⇨Index and Tables and select the Table of
Figures tab.**

In Figure 6-24, you see the Table of Figures tab of the Index and Tables
dialog with the following options:

**Book II
Chapter 6**

Saving Time in
Word

Caption label   Preview

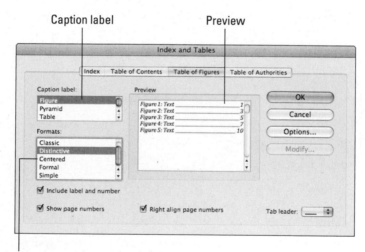

Figure 6-24:
Making a
Table of
Figures.

Table of Figure styles

- *Caption Label:* Select which objects in the document to include in the
  table.
- *Formats:* This is a list of the styles available.
- *Tab Leader:* Select a tab leader style.
- *Include Label and Number:* Select this check box to include label and
  number.
- *Show Page Numbers:* When selected, shows page numbers in the
  Table of Figures.

- *Right Align Page Numbers:* When selected, page numbers are right aligned; otherwise, they're left aligned.

- *Options button:* Displays the Table of Figures Options dialog shown in Figure 6-25, where you can modify the following:

Figure 6-25: Fine-Tuning Table of Figures Options.

- *Style:* When selected, you can choose from styles from those listed in the associated pop-up menu.

- *Table Entry Fields:* When selected, you can choose from table entry fields that you have put into your document.

- *Table Identifier:* Choose a letter of the alphabet. This allows you to identify figures when you have multiple tables of figures within a document.

2. **Select a Label in the Caption Label list.**

   For this example, we choose Figure to create a table of figures. This selection limits the output to captions labeled as Figure.

3. **In the Formats area, select a format that you like.**

   Click the various styles and check boxes, and Preview updates.

4. **Select or deselect the check boxes as desired, and when you're done, click OK.**

   Preview updates as you select and deselect options. The Table of Figures appears in your document.

Creating a Table of Authorities

If you are an attorney, lawyer, paralegal, law student, or some other sort of legal beagle, this is just for you! Creating a Table of Authorities is a two-stage process. First, you mark selected text to be indexed; then Word uses the marked text to create the table.

Marking text to include in the table

Follow these steps to mark text to include in the Table of Authorities:

1. **In Word, choose Insert⇨Index and Tables.**

   The Index and Tables dialog opens (see Figure 6-26).

2. **Select the Table of Authorities tab.**

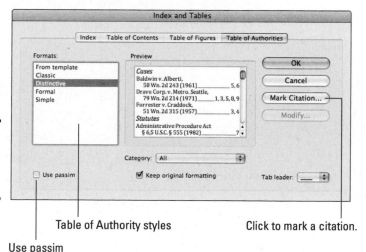

Figure 6-26:
Inserting
a Table of
Authorities.

Table of Authority styles   Click to mark a citation.

Use passim

Book II
Chapter 6

Saving Time in
Word

   In this tab, you can choose from the following to play around with Preview:

   - *Formats:* Lists format styles from which to choose.

   - *Use Passim:* If one of the citations is referenced on five or more pages, you can display the word passim instead of displaying the actual page numbers by checking this check box.

   - *Keep Original Formatting:* Select or deselect, and observe Preview.

   - *Tab Leader:* Choose from the pop-up menu and observe Preview.

3. **Click the Mark Citation button to open the Mark Citation dialog.**

   The Index and Tables dialog disappears and is replaced by the Mark Citation dialog, as shown in Figure 6-27. When this dialog is open, you can go back and forth between the dialog and the document.

4. **Click the Next Citation button.**

   Word searches the document for anything that looks like a citation; then selects the likeliest character. If you want to mark the surrounding text as a citation, drag over it in the document to select it (otherwise click the Next Citation button again to move on).

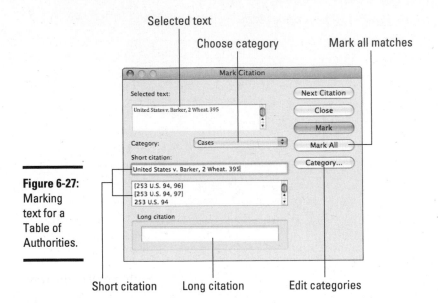

Selected text

Choose category

Mark all matches

Short citation

Long citation

Edit categories

Figure 6-27:
Marking
text for a
Table of
Authorities.

5. **Click anywhere on the Mark Citation dialog.**

The text you highlighted in your document displays in Selected Text.

6. **Choose a category from the Category pop-up menu.**

7. **Click the Mark button to mark the selected text.**

You can also click the Mark All button to tell word to mark all the matching text everywhere in the document.

8. **Click the Next Citation button to move to the next unmarked possible citation, or click Close to exit the Mark Citation dialog.**

While in the Mark Citation dialog, you can click the Category button to display the Edit Category dialog, as shown Figure 6-28. Here you can change the default category names that appear in the Category pop-up menu.

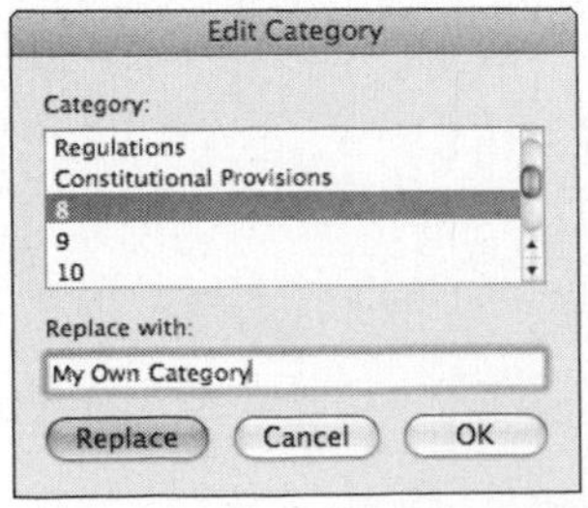

Figure 6-28:
Managing
category
names.

Building the Table of Authorities

After you finish marking the citations, follow these steps to create a Table of Authorities:

1. **Click in the document to set the insertion cursor at the place where you want the Table of Authorities to appear.**

2. **In Word, choose Insert⇨Index and Tables.**

The Index and Tables dialog opens (see Figure 6-26).

3. **Select Formats, Category, and other options as desired.**

Preview updates instantly as you make choices.

4. **Click OK to create the Table of Authorities.**

The Mark Citation dialog opens. Citations are grouped by category.

You may notice in Figure 6-27 that Word allows you to index long citations. When you use the Table of Authorities feature, you might not like the way Word uses page numbers for citations in paragraphs that extend over a page break. Word uses the page number from the end of the paragraph rather than the beginning. To fix this, manually drag the { XE... } marker to the start of the paragraph.

Creating an executive summary or an abstract

When you're in a hurry and need to create an executive summary right away, follow these steps:

1. **In Word, choose Tools⇨AutoSummarize.**

The AutoSummarize dialog, as shown in Figure 6-29, appears.

2. **In the Length of Summary area, adjust Percent of Original to control the length of the summary.**

3. **In the Type of Summary area, make your summary choice by clicking the four big buttons:**

- *Highlight key points:* Uses a highlight color to accent key points throughout your document.

- *Insert an executive summary or abstract at the top of the document.*

- *Create a new document and put the summary there.*

- *Hide everything except the summary without leaving the original document.*

The selected summary type appears either in the current document or in a new document if you choose that option.

Choose a summary type.   Slider control

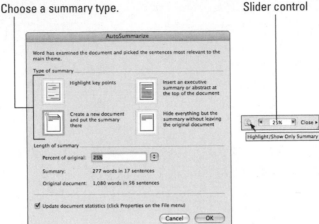

Figure 6-29:
Making an
executive
summary.

If you didn't create a new document, a nifty little slider appears (see
Figure 6-30) so you can fine-tune the summary in your document. The slider
also lets you show just the summary or the summary plus the original
document text. You can drag the slider bar, click the increase decrease
arrows, or type a value into the slider control to set percent of original.

Figure 6-30:
Adjusting
summary
percentage.

Adjust the Percent of Original control up or down to control how much of
the original content will appear in the summary. This control appears in the
dialog and in the slider.

Formatting the Background

A deep presence lurks behind the Word text. No, this presence isn't a ghost
or a snake; it's just the background. Normally the background is white, but
you can change that and even apply document theme colors to it. You have
to use Print Layout View for this to work, so if you're not already in Print
Layout View, click the Print Layout View button at the lower-left corner of
the document window to switch to it. When you modify the background
in Print Layout View, Word can convert it into Notebook Layout View and
Publishing Layout View. Word 2008 is the first Mac version of Word that can
print the background layer.

In Word, choose Format⇨Background to access the Background palette (see Figure 6-31).

Document theme colors

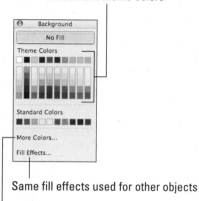

Figure 6-31:
Formatting
the
background
layer.

Same fill effects used for other objects

Mac OS X color palette

Above the background layer but still behind the text layer is a layer that you can use if you want to add a watermark. You can access the Control Panel for this feature: In Word, choose Insert⇨Watermark. The Insert Watermark dialog, as shown in Figure 6-32, appears. You can choose from two watermark types, Picture and Text. The controls speak for themselves, so we don't need to elaborate.

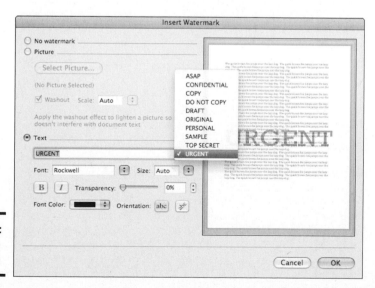

Figure 6-32:
Creating a
watermark.

Inserting a Citation

We sure wish this feature was around when we were in college! If you need to insert citations for a paper, Word 2008 has another brand-new feature to help. To activate the citation feature, follow these steps:

1. **Switch to a view that supports the Toolbox, such as Print Layout View, by clicking the Print Layout button at the lower-left corner of the document window.**

2. **If Toolbox isn't showing already, click the Toolbox button on Word's Standard toolbar to display it.**

3. **Click the Citations button (third from the left in the top toolbar) to activate the Citations dialog, as shown in Figure 6-33.**

Figure 6-33:
Inserting
citations.

Add   Delete

Edit citation or use Citation Source Manager

In the Citations dialog, you have the following options:

✦ **Citation Style:** Click this pop-up menu to choose from four different styles: APA, Chicago, MLA, and Turabian.

✦ **Citations List:** Shows Word's master citations list filtered by the selected style. Select a citation; then double-click it to insert it in your document at the insertion cursor.

✦ **Add Citation:** Displays the Add New Citation dialog for your master citations list. You can enter appropriate data for the currently selected citation style.

✦ **Delete Citation:** Removes the selected citation from Word's master citation list.

✦ **Edit Citation or use Citation Source Manager:** You have two options when you click this button:

- *Edit Citation:* Displays the Edit Citation dialog.

- *Citation Source Manager:* Displays the Citation Source Manager. Here you can copy citations to and from open documents and share citations with others.

Word maintains a master list of citations, but you have to add or copy at least one citation to your master citations list before you can insert a citation into a document.

In the Edit Citation dialog, you have these options:

✦ **Type of Source:** Click this pop-up menu to choose from a list of many source types.

✦ **Bibliography Fields:** Enter data as applicable for the citation style selected in the Toolbox pop-up menu.

✦ **Example:** Shows an example for the currently select input field.

✦ **OK:** Click OK to add your citation to Word's master citation list.

Use the Citation Source Manager dialog to set the following features:

✦ **Master List:** Your Word master list of citations.

✦ **Current List:** Citations in the currently active document.

✦ **Copy**: Copy a selected citation to or from either list. The Copy direction arrow changes depending upon which list has the currently selected citation.

✦ **New:** Opens the New Citation Source dialog.

✦ **Edit:** Opens the selected citation in the Edit Citation dialog.

✦ **Delete:** Deletes the selected source from your master list.

Chapter 7: Advanced Word Stuff

In This Chapter

- ✔ Wrapping text
- ✔ Getting text to flow like a spring brook
- ✔ Publishing your work
- ✔ Ferreting out fields
- ✔ Making smart electronic forms that look great
- ✔ Working with Web pages
- ✔ Managing several open documents at once
- ✔ Embedding objects

A lot of people call these topics *advanced,* but for the most part, these topics are better categorized as *extra stuff you could know* rather than *difficult* or *complicated.* Knowing the things in this chapter can make your experience with Word more productive and enjoyable. Who knows? Maybe you'll wind up using one of these features every day after you discover how it can help.

Wrapping Text around Objects

From pictures and graphs to SmartArt, you can easily add all sorts of objects to a Word document. But after the object is inserted in your Word document, you'll probably need to wrap your text around it.

Text wrapping denotes how text in a Word document flows around the periphery of other objects, such as pictures and graphs. Objects usually have text wrapping set to In Line with Text. *In Line with Text* is a text wrapping option that doesn't allow text to wrap on the sides of the inserted object.

Most of the time, text wrapping breaks the text so that when you insert the object into your document, the text flow is split above and below the new object. This is often just fine, but at times, you'll want to change the text wrapping style, which we show you later in this section.

The Formatting Palette has a Wrapping pane, as shown in Figure 7-1, which appears when you select any inserted objects. This pane has options that enable you to control how the text flows around, in front of, or behind the object. You can also set how close the text will be to the object and which side(s) of the object text will flow. Look at Figure 7-1; notice how the Square option allows the text to flow around the object (a picture of a gavel, in this case). To adjust Word's wrapping, take the following steps:

1. **Turn on the Formatting Palette if it isn't visible already.**

   Click the Toolbox button on Word's Standard toolbar. You may have to use the View menu and switch to a different view to enable the Toolbox.

2. **Select the object.**

   The border surrounding the object becomes prominent, usually with dots that you can drag to resize the object.

3. **In the Style pop-up menu of the Wrapping section, choose Square.**

   Text wraps around your object based on your style choice.

Word allows you to have precise control over how the text flows around an object. If you don't like the way text flows around an object, do the following:

1. **Select the object.**

   The selected indicator with resize handles displays, as shown in Figure 7-1.

2. **In the Wrap To pop-up menu in the Wrapping section of the Formatting Palette, choose from one of these four options:**

   - *Both Sides:* Text flows around the object to the left and right sides and the margins.

   - *Left:* Text flows between the left side of the object and the left margin.

   - *Right:* Text flows between the right side of the object and the right margin.

   - *Largest Side:* Text flows between the object and whichever side has more room between the object and the margin.

Now take a really close look and compare how text flows around the gavel in Figure 7-1 with Figure 7-2. Notice how in Figure 7-2, *fox* fills in the space between the gavel's handle and its head. To be able to fine-tune wrapping to this degree, you have to turn on the special Edit Wrap Boundary handles. Here's how to turn on the wrap boundary:

Drag handle to rotate the object.

Drag handle to resize object.

Wrapping style

Formatting Palette

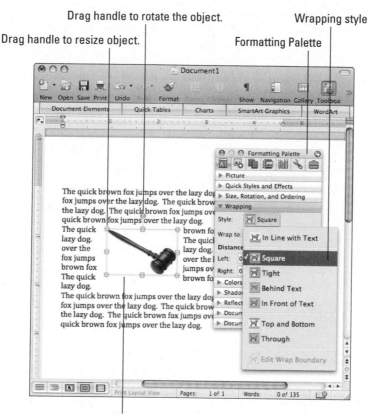

Book II
Chapter 7

**Advanced
Word Stuff**

Figure 7-1:
Wrapping
is easy
with the
Formatting
Palette.

Selected indicator

1. **Select the object.**

The selected indicator with resize handles will display as shown in
Figure 7-1.

2. **In the Formatting Palette, in the Style section, choose Tight from the
pop-up menu.**

Text will wrap closely to the object.

3. **In the Formatting Palette, in the Style section, choose Edit Wrap
Boundary from the pop-up menu.**

This turns on the wrap boundary handles, as shown in Figure 7-2. You
can drag the boundary handles at drag points to control precisely how
text flows around the object. Click a boundary line to add a drag point.

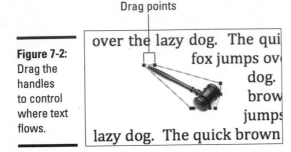

Drag points

Figure 7-2:
Drag the
handles
to control
where text
flows.

Here's another aspect about text flow that you need to know about: When
you put an object into a Word document and then add text or other stuff
earlier in the document, your object moves down along with the text in
the document. A word-processing document works that way so that your
objects stay where you place them in the document. You can change this
behavior. See Book I, Chapter 4 to read about inserting objects with the
Object Palette of the Toolbox.

If you need your object to always stay in the same spot in the document
regardless of the text it appears with, you can lock an object to an exact
position in a document. Think of this as dropping a boat anchor — water
flows by, but the boat stays in the same relative position to the shore. In
Word, if you lock an object to a margin, the object stays in the same relative
position and text flows around the object. This anchoring capability is a
basis of publishing programs and is very handy to use in Word's Publishing
Layout View and Print Layout View. Follow these steps to anchor an object
in Word:

1. **Right-click or Control-click an object.**

2. **From the pop-up menu that appears, choose Format . . .**

   The Format dialog opens.

3. **Choose Layout in the left panel and then click the Advanced button.**

   The Advanced Layout dialog opens, as shown in Figure 7-3.

4. **Click the Picture Position tab.**

5. **(Optional) Set the position of an object precisely using controls in this
   dialog.**

6. **Under Options, select the Lock Anchor check box.**

7. **Click OK to close the Advanced Layout dialog and then click OK to
   close the Format dialog.**

   Text now flows according to the settings you made, and the object is
   anchored to the position you selected.

Absolute position choices

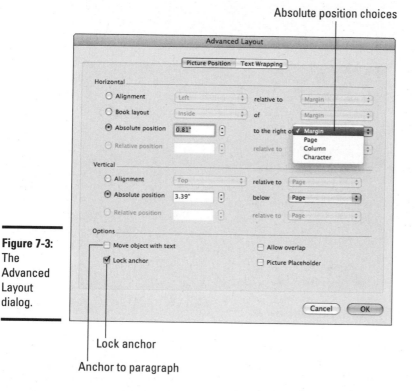

Figure 7-3:
The
Advanced
Layout
dialog.

Lock anchor

Anchor to paragraph

Flowing Text from One Text Box into Another

Text flows and behaves in certain ways around fancy objects, such as pictures and charts, placed in a Word document. We take a look at how text behaves within ordinary text boxes.

You can create plain, empty text boxes or text boxes that are formatted already with niceties and ornamentation. We start with a single, plain text box. You can make a text box by using any one of the following three methods:

✦ **In Word, choose Insert➪Text Box.**

✦ **Click the Text Box button on the Drawing toolbar.**

 If the Drawing toolbar isn't visible, choose View➪Toolbars➪Drawing.

✦ **In Publishing Layout View, click the Text Box button on the Standard toolbar.**

Each method turns the mouse cursor into a special cursor. Position the mouse where you want to start drawing and then click and hold down the mouse button while dragging diagonally in your document. Release the mouse button when the box is the shape you want (see Figure 7-4). If you hold down the Shift key while dragging, you get a perfect square.

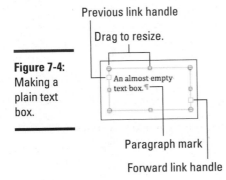

Figure 7-4: Making a plain text box.

As you start typing in the box; notice that the text inside the box wraps automatically. You may have to make the box larger or use a small font size to make the text fit the box just right. You can use hard and soft returns to control paragraph formatting in Word. Click the Show button on Word's Standard toolbar to show paragraph marks to see the difference between these two:

- ✦ **Hard return:** When you press Return or Enter, Word inserts a paragraph mark and moves the insertion cursor to the next paragraph.

- ✦ **Soft return:** When you hold down Shift as you press Return or Enter, Word moves the cursor to the next line without adding a paragraph mark. This is indicated by a little arrow symbol.

More fun with text boxes

Word 2008 sports some changes to text boxes. Notice that the resizing handles are bigger and easier to see. In Word 2008, every text box comes with two nice, new buttons: Previous Link and Forward Link. You use these to link several text boxes together so that text flows automatically from one box to another in a story. Try thinking of a chain of linked text boxes as a story in a newspaper, newsletter, or magazine.

When you create linked text boxes, if there's more text than will fit into the first box, the text overflows into the second linked text box in the story, and so on. Each chain of linked boxes has its own color and independent numbering scheme. Stories often flow to a second page or at least a second column. When you combine text boxes, text flow, and the ability to anchor text boxes, you have the foundation of page layout programs. For you, this means that you don't need an additional page layout program, such as Microsoft Publisher, if you have Word 2008.

Text boxes in Publishing Layout View

Text boxes work a little differently in Publishing Layout View than in other views. In addition to a refreshing new look for Word 2008, text boxes have new tools to help you position them on a page. Have a look at these new tools. You see the guides as you drag text box objects:

1. **Open a new, blank document in Publishing Layout View.**

   You can click the small triangle next to the New button on Word's Standard toolbar and choose New Blank Publishing Layout Document from the pop-up menu.

2. **Click the arrow next to the Show button on Word's Standard toolbar to reveal the pop-up menu, as shown in Figure 7-5, and choose whichever guides setting suits you best.**

Book II
Chapter 7

Advanced
Word Stuff

Click Show button to get pop-up menu.

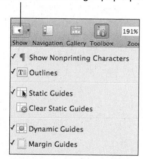

Figure 7-5:
Text box options in Publishing Layout View.

Adjusting the various settings shown in this menu can result in some fun. Follow these steps to experience this firsthand:

1. **Make sure you're in Word's Publishing Layout View.**

   If you aren't in Publishing Layout View, choose View⇨Publishing Layout.

2. **Make a text box.**

   See the section, "Flowing Text from One Text Box into Another," earlier in this chapter.

   A Text Box button is on the Standard toolbar in Word's Publishing Layout View, and this can be used to quickly insert a new text box.

3. **Click the forward link handle (as shown in Figure 7-4) on your text box.**

   The cursor changes to a crosshair when you click the forward link handle.

4. **Drag a new text box with this crosshair cursor.**

   This creates a new text box linked to the first text box.

5. **Type enough text in the first text box so that it overflows into the second box, as shown in Figure 7-6.**

Figure 7-6:
Text flowing from the first text box to the second.

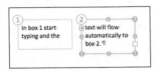

With this example, you can create text boxes that span from the second to the third, and the third to the fourth text box, and so on to create a story. Word helpfully shows you the sequence number of all text boxes in a story, as shown in Figure 7-6.

After you create a new story, the previous link and forward link handles take you instantly to the neighboring link within the story's chain. If you drag entire text boxes, guides appear to help you line up the boxes with each other.

Publishing Newspapers, Newsletters, and Periodicals

Get ready because if you read the sections before this one, you have all the elements you need to create superb publications. (If you haven't, we'll happily wait right here for you.) You know how to make text flow around objects, how to anchor objects, and how to make text flow in a story. Here we explore Publishing Layout View in more detail to see how this new feature can help you in your quest. We start with the new Standard toolbar, as shown in Figure 7-7.

Discovering new tools

As you can see, the Standard toolbar in Publishing Layout View has some familiar buttons, but this toolbar focuses on document layout and composition.

In this section, you open a template, explore some of the new Publishing Layout features, and customize your template. Then you can save your custom template as a new template for use in Project Gallery and Elements Gallery.

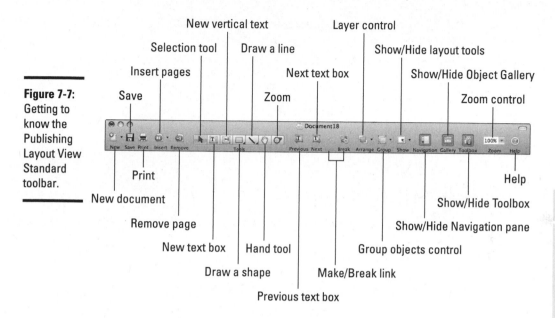

Figure 7-7:
Getting to
know the
Publishing
Layout View
Standard
toolbar.

Along the way, you also get to know the new Hand tool and the Zoom Loupe (pronounced *loop*) tool. These steps enable you to explore these two new tools:

1. **In Word, choose File⇨Project Gallery.**

   Project Gallery opens.

2. **On the New tab, in the Category list, select Newsletters, select School Newsletter, and click the Open button.**

   Alternatively, you can double-click School Newsletter.

   The School Newsletter template opens in Word's Publishing Layout View.

3. **Click the Hand tool on Word's Standard toolbar.**

   The cursor changes to a hand.

4. **Click and hold down the mouse button while dragging the mouse vertically within the document.**

   You can easily move the page without accidentally selecting individual objects and moving them!

5. **Press the Esc key.**

   The Hand tool turns off.

6. **Click the Zoom Loupe tool on Word's standard toolbar.**

   The cursor becomes loopy.

7. **Click and hold down the mouse button while dragging the mouse in various directions within the document.**

   You can easily zoom in and out.

8. **Press the Esc key.**

   The cursor returns to normal.

Customizing a template

You can easily customize your own template! Start from Project Gallery, as in the preceding section, or from Elements Gallery, which is what we do here:

1. **Open a new, blank Word document in Publishing Layout View.**

   Click the triangle to the right of the New button on Word's Standard toolbar and choose New Blank Publishing Layout Document from the pop-up menu.

2. **On the Elements bar, choose Publication Templates.**

   Publication elements display. All the publication templates are new for Word 2008.

3. **Choose an element you find interesting.**

   A new document opens based on the chosen template.

4. **Click a text box and start typing.**

   In the case of linked text boxes, type in the first text box, and the text flows to the next text box. When you click a text box, pay attention to the Formatting Palette — a new Text Box section with advanced formatting controls appears, as shown in Figure 7-8. See Chapter 2 in this minibook for details on saving your customizations as a Word Template (.dotx) file.

To replace a template's picture with one of your own:

1. **Right-click or Control-click the picture and choose Change Picture from the pop-up menu.**

2. **Navigate or use Spotlight to locate the desired replacement picture and then click Insert.**

Working with templates is easy. Use the Toolbox, menus, Elements Gallery, and toolbars that we discuss throughout this book to customize the template to your liking. This is where you unleash your creative juices to work your magic with Word's vast array of tools.

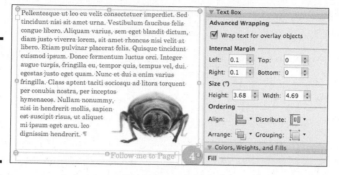

Figure 7-8:
Working in the Text Box section of the Formatting Palette.

Font formatting controls

Word 2008 Publishing Layout View has new font-formatting controls on the Formatting Palette (see Figure 7-9). You can use these controls on text that you select. These new controls include support for ligatures and baselines. Only a few fonts, such as Apple Chancery and some OpenType fonts in Mac OS X Leopard, have ligature support. Unless your font supports ligatures, the Ligatures in Document check box doesn't have any effect.

✦ **Ligature:** The blending of two characters, as shown in Figure 7-8. Ligatures are fancy and give your document special appeal. In some cases, letters that don't look clear when put in close proximity are spread apart more.

✦ **Baseline:** This is the imaginary line that text is on. You can select text and increase or decrease the baseline setting to move it slightly up or down. This increases the amount of space the line of text will use on the page.

Figure 7-9:
Using new Formatting Palette layout controls.

Mastering master pages

Word takes the concept of a master page to a new level in Publishing Layout View. A *master* page is a kind of template page within a Word document. Whatever you put on the master page is duplicated on any pages that are based on it. Master pages are a way to maintain a consistent feel throughout your document as you add new pages. If you use master pages, you can save time by not having to re-create page elements, such as page numbers, headers, and footers, with each new page as you build your publication.

The School Newsletter template we use in the section, "Discovering new tools," earlier in this chapter, makes use of these master pages. To see the master pages, click the Master Pages tab, which displays the document's master or masters, near the bottom-right corner of the window, as shown in Figure 7-10.

Master Document Page information

Ruler   Static guides

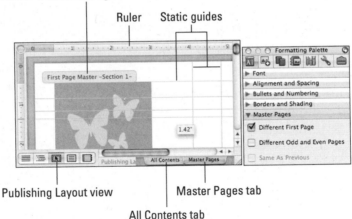

Figure 7-10:
Mastering
master
pages.

Publishing Layout view

All Contents tab

Master Pages tab

Publishing Layout View's Insert button assists you with adding pages while maintaining the layout. To insert a new page based on the Master:

1. **With a document open in Publishing Layout View, choose the All Contents tab in the lower-right corner of the document window.**

   The All Contents tab shows you the contents of the document you are building.

2. **On Word's Standard toolbar, click the small triangle to the right of the Insert button.**

   You may then choose from one of the following options:

   - *New Page:* Inserts a new page based on a master template.

- *New Master:* Allows you to create a new master page out of the current page. You can have multiple masters.

- *Duplicate Page:* Creates a duplicate page.

Switch back and forth between all contents and master pages by clicking the tabs at the lower-right corner of the document window. When you select the Master Pages tab, the Master Pages section of the Formatting Palette becomes available and offers three options:

✦ **Different First Page:** Allows the first page to be formatted independently of the rest of the master.

✦ **Different Odd and Even Pages:** Use this when setting up documents that will have pages that face each other when printed and you want to use a gutter or opposing page numbers.

✦ **Same as Previous:** Keeps formatting the same as the previous master page when you add new master pages.

Working with static guides

You can add *static guides* (see Figure 7-10), which are guide lines to help you align objects in Word's Publishing Layout View. Follow these steps to create and add static guides to your document:

1. **Make sure your rulers are visible.**

   If your rulers aren't visible, choose View⇨Ruler to toggle them on.

2. **Position the mouse cursor over a ruler and then drag a guide line from the ruler into the document.**

   It's as if there are static guides secretly waiting for you to drag them out of the rulers! While you drag, Word tells you the location of the line on the ruler. Position the static guide as desired and then release the mouse button. You can drag static guides to reposition them.

To remove static guides, click the triangle next to the Show button on the Standard toolbar and choose Clear Static Guides from the pop-up menu.

Static guides placed on the Master Pages tab appear when viewing both the Master Pages tab and the All Contents tab. Static guides placed on the All Contents tab don't appear on the Master Pages tab. When removing static guides, guides placed on the All Contents tab need to be removed independently from the Master Pages tab.

Having a Field Day

Whether you're new to Word or an old hand, Word fields can help you accomplish a wide variety of tasks, including all sorts of automation. We briefly discuss fields in relation to mail merge in Chapter 6 of this minibook. Here we take a closer look at fields and see what's going on under the Word hood.

In their broadest definition, Word *fields* are special codes between brackets that perform various tasks. We have a hard time describing them better than that because they do so many different things. Word fields are an essential part of mail merge, page numbering, and other tasks. Some fields are very simple; others are quite complex. We show you how fields work with the Time Word field as an example.

Getting to know Word fields is probably easiest if you start with a new, blank Word document in Print Layout View.

In the following steps, we collect three tools and then put them onto a toolbar so that we can use them later. You can drag them to Word's standard toolbar or any other toolbar. (Follow the instructions in Book I, Chapter 3 to create your own toolbars.) Follow these steps to drag these commands onto any toolbar of your choice:

1. **In Word, choose View⇨Customize Toolbars and Menus.**

The Customize Toolbars and Menus dialog appears.

2. **Select the Commands tab and make sure that the left pane shows All Commands.**

Click in the right panel and then press the first letter of the command to bring you to that letter of the alphabet and save time.

3. **Drag the `ViewFieldCodes`, `InsertFieldChars`, and `UpdateFields` commands to any toolbar.**

See Figure 7-11 to see part of the toolbar with these commands added.

4. **Click OK to close the Customize Toolbars and Menus dialog.**

Figure 7-11:
Adding field commands to a toolbar.

Time to find out where Word fields hide on your computer. They quietly reside in a small, but powerful dialog; choose Insert⇨Field. The Field dialog, as shown in Figure 7-12, appears. Here you can insert a special code, dubbed a *field code,* into your Word document. The field code categories are listed on the left side of the dialog in the Categories list. The Field Names list on the right side of the dialog allows you to select a field code to insert into a document.

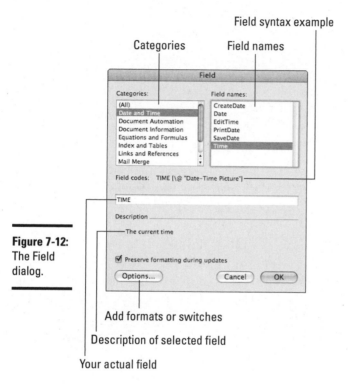

Field syntax example

Categories   Field names

Figure 7-12:
The Field
dialog.

Add formats or switches

Description of selected field

Your actual field

We're going to grab the Time Word field and put it into a blank document so we can pick it apart and see how it works. For this example, see Figure 7-12 and follow these steps:

1. **Click the New button on Word's Standard toolbar to open a new, blank Word document.**

2. **Choose Insert⇨Field.**

   The Field dialog, as shown in Figure 7-12, appears.

3. **In the Categories list, choose Date and Time.**

4. **In the Field Names list, choose Time.**

   The description in the dialog changes to The Current Time.

5. **Click OK to close the Field dialog.**

   The current time appears in the document.

After you have the time in your document, you notice that the time doesn't change. A lot of good that's going to do you. Refresh the time by updating the field code in this two-step process:

1. **Select the time in your document.**

   This tells Word that you want to do something with the time. By selecting the time (the result of the field code's action), you also select the field code. If you're really observant, you might notice that the field part of the selection looks darker, to let you know it's not just text.

2. **Click the Update Field button that you placed on a toolbar earlier in this section.**

   Alternatively, right-click or Control-click the time and choose Update Field.

   The time refreshes.

The first step in the preceding list is very important. If you don't select the field code first, nothing happens when you click the Update Field button. Here you look at the actual code. This, too, requires that you first select the field code:

1. **Select the Time field code by selecting the time in your document.**

2. **Click the View Field Codes toggle button that you placed on a toolbar earlier in this section.**

   Alternatively right-click or Control-click, and choose Toggle Field Codes.

   The actual code instead of the field's result toggles on.

You can now see the actual field code, as shown in Figure 7-13, which is always contained within two curly brackets. From left to right, this list describes a field code:

✦ **Opening bracket:** This begins the field code.

✦ **Field name:** In Figure 7-13, TIME is the field name.

✦ **Switches:** Additional items that control how the field works.

   The switches for Time allow you to control how time will be formatted in the document. Switches for other Word fields can specify file paths, hyperlinks, symbols, and all kinds of different things!

✦ **Closing bracket:** This completes the field code.

Figure 7-13:
Viewing a
field code.

{ TIME * MERGEFORMAT }

You can type inside the field code's special brackets. The brackets are *special* because they can't be typed in from your keyboard, even though they look like the regular, curly brackets. You can insert an empty pair of field code brackets into any document by clicking the Insert Field Characters button you put on a toolbar earlier in this section. In this book, we discuss these ways of inserting field codes:

✦ In Word, choose Insert⇨Field to insert any field code.

✦ Use Mail Merge Manager to insert mail merge Word fields.

✦ In Word, choose Insert⇨Tables and Indexes to insert codes related to captions and various tables.

✦ Click the Insert Field Codes button from the toolbar you placed it on earlier in this section. You can type field codes manually or paste from other codes.

✦ Double-click headers and footers, which are field codes, in a document to edit and format them.

✦ Use the Forms toolbar to insert field codes relating to forms.

Book II
Chapter 7

Advanced
Word Stuff

In Figure 7-13, the Time field is followed by the \ * MERGEFORMAT switch. This switch instructs Word to keep the previous formatting when updating the field.

Create another Word field that displays the time, but this time add some optional formatting. Start with a new, blank document:

1. **Click the New button on Word's standard toolbar to open a new, blank Word document.**

2. **Choose Insert⇨Field.**

The Field dialog, as shown in Figure 7-12, appears.

3. **In the Categories list, choose Date and Time.**

4. **In the Field Names list, choose Time.**

The description in the dialog changes to The Current Time.

5. **Click the Options button.**

The Field Options dialog opens, as shown in Figure 7-14.

6. **Choose MMMM d, yyyy in the Date-Time Formats list.**

If you live somewhere other than the United States, you have to choose d MMMM, yyyy. You'll have to drag the scroll bar down slightly to see this format. This just swaps the placement of the month and date! In the following list, *m* stands for *month, d* stands for *day,* and *y* stands for *year* (just like in Excel):

• *M* displays the number of the month.

- *MM* displays a two-digit number for the month.

- *MMM* displays a three-letter abbreviation for the month.

- *MMMM* displays the month spelled out.

- *d* displays the number of the date.

- *dd* displays the date as a two-digit number.

- *ddd* displays the date as a three-letter abbreviation.

- *dddd* displays the day of the week.

- *YY* displays a two-digit year.

- *YYYY* displays a four-digit year.

7. **Click the Add to Field button.**

\@ plus the chosen format is added to the field code. In this example, you see TIME \@ "M/d/yy".

8. **Click OK to close the Field Options dialog and then click OK to close the Field dialog.**

The current time appears in your document with the switch formatting.

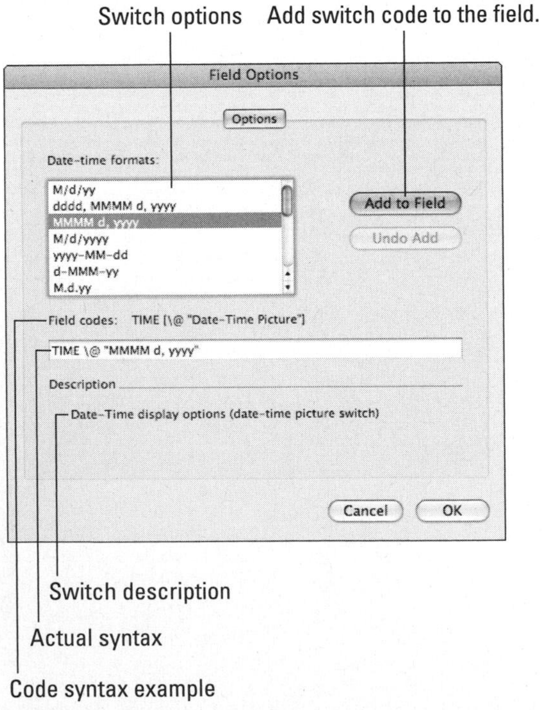

Switch options   Add switch code to the field.

Figure 7-14:
Adding an
optional
switch to a
field code.

Switch description

Actual syntax

Code syntax example

Take a look at your new field code, and compare the differences before (top) and after adding the formatting switch (bottom), as shown in Figure 7-15. You could've typed in all that formatting stuff, but Word typed it for you. Go ahead and experiment with the format code. Try the different variations that are listed in the Field Options dialog, such as M.d.yy, and notice the placement of quotation marks, if any. Quotation marks within Word fields tell Word to do certain things. In this case, they specify the formatting to apply.

Figure 7-15: Comparing Time field codes.

1:57 PM
{TIME * MERGEFORMAT} —— Original time code

January 10, 2009
{TIME \@ "MMMM d, yyyy"* MERGEFORMAT}
                                        └── Modified time code with
                                            date formatting applied

Time is a fairly typical Word field. If you've followed along so far, you know quite a bit about Word fields and can fully customize page numbers, dates, and times in headers and footers.

Creating an Electronic Form

Word can create not only paper forms, but electronic ones, too! After you figure out how to create an electronic form in Word, you can distribute the forms, and the recipients can fill them in on their computers and then return them to you. You create forms in Word's Print Layout View. You'll find that the Forms toolbar can be a great help. To access the Forms toolbar, as shown in Figure 7-16, choose View➪Toolbars➪Forms.

Figure 7-16: Making a fantastic Forms toolbar.

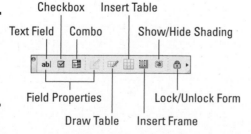

Checkbox   Insert Table

Text Field   Combo   Show/Hide Shading

Field Properties   Lock/Unlock Form

Draw Table   Insert Frame

A ground rule for forms is that you edit them in *unprotected* (or *unlocked*) mode. When the form is done and ready to be used, *protect* (or *lock*) the form to enable the form controls. You can toggle between Lock and Unlock modes for your form by clicking the Lock/Unlock Form button on the Forms toolbar (refer to Figure 7-16).

Using tables and frames in forms

The Insert Table and Insert Frame tools are on the Forms toolbar, as shown in Figure 7-16, for your convenience to help with your form's layout. They work just like any other table or frame in a Word document, and you don't have to use either of these. However, these tools can make precise placement of form controls much easier and more pleasing to the eye. You can use the Borders and Shading section of the Formatting Palette, which we describe in Chapter 5 of this minibook.

Inserting a text form field

The text box is the most common form field. You might have already filled in thousands of them in your lifetime. Name, address, and phone number are appropriate for text fields. To add one of these to a document:

ab| 1. **In an open Word document, place the insertion point where you want to insert a text form field.**

This insertion point can be within a table, in a frame, or basically anywhere in the document.

2. **Make sure that the Forms toolbar is visible.**

If it isn't, choose View⇨Toolbars⇨Forms.

3. **Click the Text Form Field button on the Forms toolbar.**

A gray box (the form field) appears in your document at the insertion cursor position, and the fun begins.

   4. **Click the gray box to select it and then click the Form Field Options button on the Forms toolbar.**

The Text Form Field Options dialog opens, as shown in Figure 7-17.

The Text Form Field Options dialog is devilishly simple, yet brilliant. When you click the Type pop-up menu and choose a selection, the rest of the Text Form Field Options dialog changes to offer appropriate choices based on your selection. Here are the six types of text form fields from which to choose:

- *Regular Text:* Word displays whatever is typed.

- *Number:* Numbers can be formatted and used in calculations.

- *Date:* Dates can be formatted.

- *Current Date:* Displays the current date in your form.

- *Current Time:* Displays the current time in your form.

- *Calculation:* Lets you calculate values based on entries made in number fields.

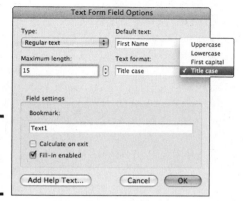

Figure 7-17:
Setting up a text box form field.

As you go through each field, notice that if you click the Type pop-up menu, you're offered a different set of formatting options depending upon the type of field you've chosen.

You can enter default text to be displayed in some fields and you can give the field a name, such as **GrossSales1**, which can be referred to in a formula calculation field (which we explain in just a bit). Always add a number to the field name and don't use special characters or spaces.

The Add Help Text . . . button of the Text Form Field Options dialog in Figure 7-17 opens the Form Field Help Text dialog that enables you to add a prompt or explanatory text about the form field. You can have this text appear in the status bar at the bottom of the document window or have it appear when the user presses the Help button on the keyboard (but not from the Help option you see when you right-click or Control-click the field). This feature is pretty obscure, and we don't recommend that you use it.

Work with form fields and set their options while the form is unprotected (or unlocked). You have to protect (or lock) a form before you can fill in the form fields.

Inserting a check box on a form

Adding a check box to a form is a piece of cake! Follow these steps:

1. **Click the Check Box Form Field button on the Forms toolbar.**

   A little square appears.

2. **Click the Form Fields Options button.**

   The Check Box Form Field Options dialog opens (see Figure 7-18).

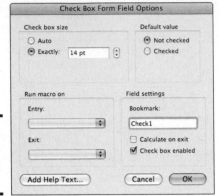

Figure 7-18:
Checking
out a check
box.

The following options in this dialog are

✦ **Check Box Size:** You have two choices here:

  • *Auto:* Let Word decide.

  • *Exactly:* Type a value or use the increase/decrease control.

✦ **Default Value:** Select Checked or Not Checked.

✦ **Run Macro On**: Word 2008 doesn't support macros, but will in the next major release of Office.

✦ **Field Settings:** Three things exist in this area:

  • *Bookmark field:* Give the check box a name ending with a number. We suggest that numbers you assign be sequential.

  • *Calculate on Exit:* If you use calculations, you can select this box to cause Word to perform the calculations after the control is used. We explain calculated form fields in just a bit!

  • *Check Box Enabled:* Deselect to disable this check box.

Upgrading to a combo

Want to upgrade to a combo meal? Yum! (Okay, so we shouldn't write a computer book while we're hungry.) In a form, a combo field is a pretty neat thing. Use a combo when you want the user to choose an entry from a list of choices. The *Drop-Down Form Field* is commonly referred to as a *combo field*. Follow these steps to create a combo field:

1. **Click the Drop-Down Form Field button on the Forms toolbar.**

A small gray box appears.

2. **Click the Properties button.**

The Drop-Down Form Field Options dialog opens (see Figure 7-19).

Figure 7-19:
Adding a
combo field.

The top half of this dialog lets you build the list of choices that will appear when the Drop-Down button is clicked in your finished, protected form.

✦ **Drop-Down Item:** Type an item to appear in the drop-down list.

✦ **Add:** Adds your typed Drop-Down item to the Items in Drop-Down List.

✦ **Remove:** Removes a selected item from the Items in the Drop-Down List.

✦ **Items in Drop-Down List:** These items appear in the drop-down list of choices that appears when the Drop-Down button is clicked in your finished, protected form.

✦ **Move:** Select an item in Items in Drop-Down List. Click an arrow to move it up or down in the list (changes the order of items in the list).

✦ **Field Settings:** Here are two of the field settings:

  • *Bookmark:* Give the check box a name ending with a number. The numbers you assign should be sequential.

  • *Calculate on Exit:* If you use calculations, you can select this box to cause Word to perform the calculations after the control is used. We explain calculated form fields in the following section!

When you're done setting up the combo box and you select it within the form, it looks something like Figure 7-20.

Figure 7-20:
Popping up
a combo
field.

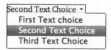

Doing the math in Word forms

One more thing! Form fields are also Word fields. Figure 7-21 shows an example of a simple calculation. The figure shows the Word document on the left side, and the Text Form Fields Options dialog on the right. Notice that 25 is highlighted, so you can tell that this is the Text Form Field Options dialog to control the calculation.

We made three text box fields named Number1, Number2, and Answer1. In Figure 7-20, you see these three fields with descriptive text to their left. Underneath the three fields, we show the Answer1 field as it looks when Display Field Codes button is clicked so that you can see the code that does the calculation is the same as the entry shown in the Field Text Form Fields Options dialog in the Expression field. You can see from the dialog that the Type is set to Calculation, and on the left side, you can see that the result of the calculation is 25.

You can modify the formula in a field code by typing it in, which we recommend if the formula is long. Table 7-1 shows the operators supported by Word fields.

Figure 7-21: Fielding a math problem.

Number1:	10
+ Plus Number2	15
= Equals Answer1	25
{ FORMTEXT { =Number1+Number2 }}	

Text Form Field Options

Type: Calculation   Expression: =Number1+Number2
Maximum length: Unlimited   Number format: 0

Field settings
Bookmark: Answer1
☐ Calculate on exit
☐ Fill-in enabled

Add Help Text...   Cancel   OK

Table 7-1	Doing Math in Word Form Fields
Operator	*Description*
+	Add
–	Subtract
*	Multiply
/	Divide
%	Percent
^	Power or root
=	Equals

Operator	Description
<	Is less than
>	Is greater than
<=	Is less than or equal to
>=	Is greater than or equal to
<>	Not equal to

Grabbing just the form field data

Word has a special feature that allows you to save just the data from forms in a document, instead of saving the entire document. This is handy when all you need to have is the data, instead of the entire form. To make this special text file, start off in Word with a filled-in form document open:

1. **Choose File⇨Save As.**

The Save As dialog opens.

2. **Click the Options button.**

Word's Save dialog opens.

3. **Select the Save Data Only for Forms (for Current Document Only) check box and click OK.**

Word's Save dialog reappears.

4. **Give your data file a name and a location and click Save.**

When you open the resulting file in Word, you see all the form answers separated by commas. You could import this file into a database as a record or even open it within Microsoft Excel.

Working Word with the Web

When the Internet was young, Microsoft thought people wanted to *round-trip* Word documents by saving them in HTML (HyperText Markup Language) format, uploading the HTML documents to a Web server, and then opening the Word pages from the Web server right in Microsoft Word. Because this scenario never really took hold, Word 2004 is the last version of Word that can open Word-based HTML Web pages directly from the Internet. Word 2008 can't directly open Web pages from the Internet. Word's File Open dialog can still open Web pages that were saved to your computer by a Web browser.

Opening Web pages in Word

Getting Web pages into Word is a two-operation process. First, you save the Web page from your Web browser to your computer. Second, you open the Web page in Word.

Saving a Web page

To save a Web page to your computer:

1. **In your Web browser, choose File⇨Save As.**
2. **Choose the Web Archive (or Web Page Complete) format if it's offered. If not, choose the HTML format.**
3. **Give the page a different filename if you like; then click Save.**

   The Web page is saved to your computer.

Opening a Web page in Word

To open a Web page in Word:

1. **In Word, choose File⇨Open.**
2. **Navigate or use Spotlight to select the saved Web page file.**

   You may have to choose All Files in the Enable pop-up menu to make the Web page file usable in Word.

3. **Click Open.**

   Word opens the Web page you just saved. The results probably don't look very good, but it's a handy way to get Web page HTML tables into Word.

Beginning with Word 2008, you can no longer edit HTML source code in Microsoft Word.

Sending Word to the Web

You can still choose File⇨Save as Web Page in Word. Although Web page designers cringe at Word's HTML capabilities, Web browsers don't seem to mind it at all, which is really all that matters here. If you have access to a Web server, you can move the files Word creates to the server, where they can be accessed by others. ***Note:*** Word 2008 no longer supports saving forms as Web pages.

Managing Multiple Open Documents

Sometimes you might work with several documents open at once; Word has some features that can help. The most common way of switching from one open document to another is simply to click from one document window to another. The document window you click comes to the front. This takes some getting used to for people switching to a Mac from a PC, in which you commonly use the Windows taskbar for this purpose. To keep Windows users from getting homesick on your Macs, you can hold down the mouse button on the Word Dock icon to get a pop-up menu that enables you to switch from one document to another, as shown in Figure 7-22.

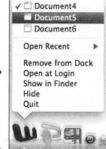

Figure 7-22:
Switching documents on the Dock.

Word's Window menu (See Figure 7-23) has a similar switching capability as well as other features:

✦ **Arrange All:** Arranges open document windows horizontally on your screen.

✦ **Split:** Divides the currently open document window into a top and bottom half so you can see and work in two portions of the document at the same time. Split is a toggle. To remove the Split, choose the Split option a second time from the Window menu.

✦ **List of open documents:** At the bottom of the Window menu, you can choose from a list of open documents to switch from one document to another.

Making Word read to you

Word 2008 has a fantastic Speak Selection feature that allows you to hear documents, which is great for proofreading. This feature is also good for when you're so tired that you can't keep your eyes open anymore but you still have to read a document. We use this tool all the time. Select the text you want to hear and then click the Speak Selection button on the Speech toolbar (if this toolbar isn't visible, choose View➪Toolbars and then choose Speech). To make Word stop speaking, click the Stop Speaking button on the Speech toolbar while Word talks (see Figure 7-24).

Figure 7-23:
Switching
documents
from the
Window
menu.

Figure 7-24:
Speaking
text out
loud.

Embedding All Kinds of Things

A Word document is a very versatile thing; so versatile that you can actually embed other kinds of object types, such as tables and charts, right inside a Word document. You can even embed another Word document.

Figure 7-25 displays a list of things you can embed in a Word document, as shown in the Object dialog. To access this dialog and insert one of the objects, take these steps:

1. **From an open Word document, choose Insert⇨Object.**

The Object dialog displays.

2. **Choose from the following options in the Display as Icon check box:**

- *Checked:* If you choose this option, the embedded object appears in your document as an icon that can be double-clicked to open the embedded object.

- *Not Checked:* The embedded object itself or a preview of the object displays in the Word document.

3. **Select an object type from the Object Type list or click the From File button:**

- *Object Type list:* Choose one of the types listed to embed it into your Word document, which is described in the Result section. Click OK to embed the object and close the Object dialog.

- *From File button:* Closes the Object dialog and Opens the Insert from File dialog where you can navigate or use Spotlight to locate a file object to embed into your Word document. Click Insert to embed the selected file. You can embed only the kinds of objects that you see listed in the Object dialog, as shown in Figure 7-25.

If you choose to open the Insert from File dialog, it has two option buttons:

✦ **Link to File:** Embeds the file path information, and a reference to the source document is created. If the source document is renamed, moved, or for some other reason, the path changes, the link breaks. If the original changes, the changes are reflected whenever the link is accessed.

If you don't choose this option, a copy of the file is embedded and the original is left untouched. If the original changes later, the embedded object isn't updated. Link to File works the same in the Object dialog as in the From File dialog.

✦ **Display as Icon:** If you choose this option, the embedded object will appear in your document as an icon that can be double-clicked to open the embedded object.

Book II
Chapter 7

Advanced Word Stuff

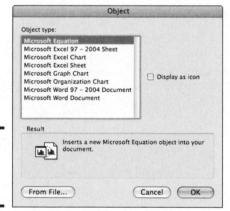

Figure 7-25:
Embedding objects in Word.

You might think that having an embedded object in a Word document, especially if it's another Word document, is confusing. If so, click the Display as Icon check box (see Figures 7-25 and 7-26) before you click OK. What if no icon appears, or the one you thought you inserted is gone? Use a picture instead of the default icon; follow these steps:

1. **Right-click or Control-click the icon (or the blank spot where the icon is supposed to be) and from the pop-up menu, choose Format⇨Object.**

The Format Object dialog appears.

2. **If not selected already, in the Format Object dialog, select the Colors and Lines tab.**

   Colors and lines formatting options display.

3. **In the Fill area, click the Color pop-up menu and choose Fill Effects.**

   The Fill Effects dialog appears.

4. **Select the Picture tab and then click the Select Picture button.**

   The Choose a Picture dialog displays.

5. **Navigate or use Spotlight to find and then select a nice, small picture (JPEG or another format) to use as the icon.**

6. **Click the Insert button.**

   The chosen picture displays in the Fill Effects dialog.

7. **Click OK to close the Insert Picture dialog and click OK to close the Format Object dialog.**

   The picture is on the icon placeholder for your embedded object. Double-click the picture to activate the embedded object.

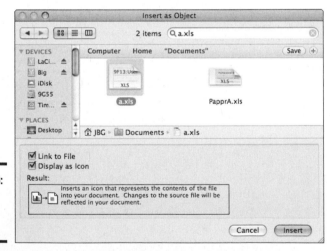

Figure 7-26:
Insert as
Object file
browser.

Chapter 8: Printing for Posterity

In This Chapter

- ✔ Setting up Page Setup
- ✔ Preparing to print
- ✔ Printing your document just right

*P*rinters are just amazing today. Not only do they print all your beautifully crafted documents, but some of them scan and fax, too. Yet others can show you previews of photos before printing them, and even some even work wirelessly without being connected physically to your computer! The good news is that whether your printer is a desktop model or a big, fancy networked behemoth, your Word documents can come out just the way you like.

When it comes to printing, Word and Mac OS X interact with each other to a high degree. When Word opens, it checks to see what the default printer is and what its capabilities are. When you open or create a document in Word, some of the Page Setup options are determined by the default printer's capabilities. The same document may have slightly different page breaks when opened on a computer with a different default printer. Some printers can print edge-to-edge, but others can't. Word is smart; it reformats your document to the current default printer, which is why a document can look a little different from one computer to another.

The choices you're offered when you print a document depend upon the printer's brand, model, and printer driver version that's installed. Certain options are available only if your printer supports them. These include *duplex* (printing on both sides of a sheet of paper), booklet layout, *full bleed* (edge to edge), collating, paper quality, print quality, and printer ink levels. And if all that printer terminology left you bewildered, don't worry because we explain each feature as we encounter them in this chapter.

Also, the figures in this chapter probably don't match exactly what you see when you use your printer. That's because every printer works with driver software to communicate with Mac OS X, and each printer brand thus has drivers that show dialogs a little differently. The good news is that all these dialogs are populated with options that generally work the same across all printers.

Sizing Up Things with Page Setup

To start with, take a look at the screen that comes up when you choose File⇨Page Setup. A very simple-looking Page Setup dialog (see Figure 8-1) appears, and most of the time you'll use it to choose Portrait or Landscape orientation only and then go on your way. But take a closer look at all the options, starting from the top.

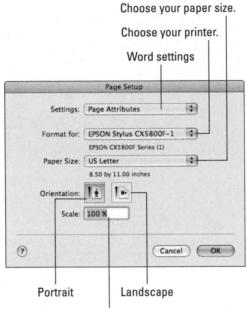

Choose your paper size.

Choose your printer.

Word settings

Portrait   Landscape

Increase or decrease the scale of your printed document.

Figure 8-1:
Setting up with the Page Setup dialog.

Configuring your settings

When you click the Settings pop-up menu, a pop-up menu appears where you have access to the following controls:

✦ **Settings:** A pop-up menu where you can choose from the following:

- *Microsoft Word:* This option takes you to Word's Margins dialog.

- *Save as Default:* If you choose this option, when you're done making adjustments to all Page Setup's settings, your saved settings become the default for Page Setup.

- *Page Attributes:* Returns you to the default Page Setup dialog (similar to Figure 8-1).

✦ **Format For:** See the following section.

✦ **Paper Size:** See the section, "Choosing a paper size," later in this chapter.

✦ **Orientation:** Choose portrait or landscape.

✦ **Scale:** You can scale the document by typing a new percentage.

Formatting for a particular printer

Word looks at the Format For setting in the Page Setup dialog (see Figure 8-1) and adjusts document formatting according to the chosen printer's capabilities. When you click Format For, a pop-up menu appears where you see a list of printers that are currently attached to your computer. If you want your documents to be formatted with a specific printer in mind, choose the printer from the list of printers in the pop-up menu.

You can set Format For to Any Printer if you want Word to use a standard set of formatting options. This is the best option to choose if you plan to share your documents with other people who may use other printer brands and models. This is also the only choice available if you don't have a printer installed and connected to your computer.

In the same Format For pop-up menu, you can choose the Print & Fax preferences option. The Print & Fax dialog, as shown in Figure 8-2, is provided by the operating system and your particular printer driver, not Microsoft Word (see Figure 8-2), so your Print & Fax preferences may look substantially different from ours unless you happen to be using the same printer brand. As shown in Figure 8-2, you can open the print queue and check the supply levels of the printer.

Book II
Chapter 8

Printing for
Posterity

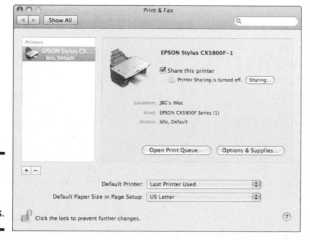

Figure 8-2:
Printing
and fax
preferences.

Choosing a paper size

The Paper Size pop-up menu has a lot to offer to a curious printing aficionado. A click of this pop-up menu offers some common size formats. Our printer can do borderless printing, but the current selection in Figure 8-3 is for US Letter size paper with a border. The Paper Size pop-up menu is nice enough to show you the border that will be used by the printer — in this case, .13 inch.

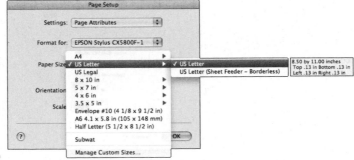

Figure 8-3:
Choosing a paper size in the pop-up menu.

At the bottom of the Paper Size pop-up menu is the Manage Custom Sizes option. This option takes you to the Custom Page Sizes dialog, as shown in Figure 8-4, where you can create a custom paper size. Keep in mind that the custom paper sizes you create here are available to all applications, not just Microsoft Word.

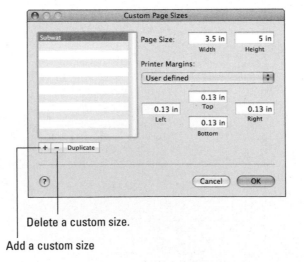

Figure 8-4:
Creating a custom paper size for your printer.

Delete a custom size.

Add a custom size

Previewing Your Document

If you have your printer settings adjusted, take an onscreen peek at how your document will look on paper.

Displaying a document preview

You might want to see how your document will look before you commit to using all that paper. Be green, you know. In an open document in Word, choose File➪Print Preview to bring up a preview window with your *document name* as the title (see Figure 8-5). The toolbar buttons in this window allow you to see one or more pages at a time, with several different options to control the preview size and the number of pages to be viewed at a time.

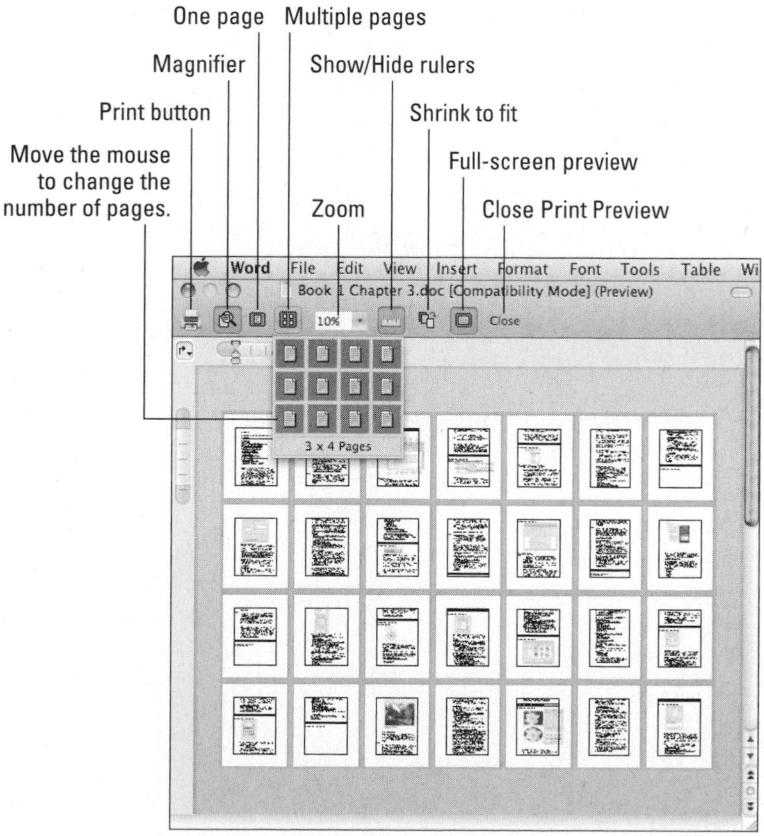

One page   Multiple pages

Magnifier   Show/Hide rulers

Print button   Shrink to fit

Move the mouse
to change the   Full-screen preview
number of pages.
Zoom   Close Print Preview

Figure 8-5:
Print
Preview
controls.

Previewing multiple pages

When you have a document that's many pages long, you can click the Multiple Pages button on the (Preview) toolbar. While you move the mouse cursor, you can increase or decrease the number of rows and columns you want to display. As you move the mouse cursor, click the mouse to choose a layout. You can also use the Magnifier and One Page buttons to do the following:

- ✦ **Magnifier:** When you click Magnifier, the mouse cursor changes to a magnifying glass. Move the mouse cursor over the document body and click the mouse to zoom the document larger. Click a second time to restore the Multiple Pages arrangement. Magnifier is a toggle switch between displaying a single page and a Multiple Pages arrangement.

- ✦ **One Page:** Switches the onscreen display between Multiple Pages and One Page.

Other preview controls

Here are more controls that can help you preview and print your Word documents:

- ✦ **Zoom:** The Zoom control has the standard zoom features you've probably become accustomed to, but at the bottom of this Zoom control, you find three special options:
  - *Page Width:* Maximizes the document to fit the window.
  - *Whole Page:* Fits the page to the window.
  - *Two Pages:* Shows two pages side-by-side.

- ✦ **Show/Hide Rulers:** Toggles Rulers on and off.

- ✦ **Shrink to Fit:** Word tries to fit your document to the *document* (Preview) window.

- ✦ **Print Preview Full Screen:** This toggles Full Screen view on and off.

- ✦ **Close:** This closes Print Preview and then returns you to the previous view.

Printing like a Pro!

Word has a couple not-so-secret secrets that can make your printing fast and easy. We show you where to look to find the printing option that's right for your situation.

Make it fast!

When you just want a printout of the current document on the default printer and you don't want to be bothered with any settings, click the Print button on Word's Standard toolbar (see Figure 8-6). You aren't pestered by any printer dialogs, and your document goes straight to the printer. Life is simple and easy!

Click to quickly print your document.

Figure 8-6:
The fastest
way to print.

Getting a few more options

When you want more than a printout with the default of everything, you can find more options by choosing File➪Print to bring up the Print dialog, as shown in Figure 8-7. You can even find an option here to expose every possible printer control. We talk more about that in just a little bit. For now, we focus on the default options.

Advanced Options

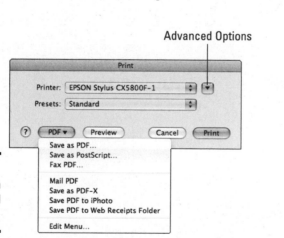

Figure 8-7:
Printing with
the standard
Print dialog.

Picking a printer

The Printer pop-up menu enables you to choose from three options:

✦ **List of printers:** All available printers are shown, and you can choose which one to use.

✦ **Add Printer:** Opens the Mac OS X printer options dialog and allows you to add a printer.

✦ **Print and Fax Preferences:** Opens the Mac OS X Print & Fax system preferences dialog.

Picking a set of preset printing options

The Presets pop-up menu enables you to choose from several different printing presets:

✦ **Standard:** Most of the time, this is the best one to use.

✦ **Last Used Settings:** Might be the one for you if you have some special customized presets.

✦ **List of Customized Presets:** If you've created customized presets in the advanced printing options (see the section, "Seeing all the possible print options," later in this chapter), you can choose one of them.

Printing to PDF

One of the really neat things about having a Mac is that every application that can print prints to PDF (Portable Document Format). Word is no exception, except that in Word, you can choose File➪Save As and in the Format pop-up menu, choose PDF. Unless you need one of the other PDF options in the following list, you don't have to go through Print to make a PDF. Here's a run down on the PDF printing options (see Figure 8-7):

✦ **Save as PDF:** Opens the Save dialog to save your document as PDF.

✦ **Save as PostScript:** Opens the Save dialog to save your document as a `.ps` postscript file. A PostScript printer is needed to print the file.

✦ **Fax PDF:** Opens the Print dialog to a Mac OS X Fax cover sheet. If your Mac has a dialup modem, you can use this option to fax your file.

✦ **Mail PDF:** Opens an e-mail message in Apple Mail, not Microsoft Entourage, and adds the PDF as an attachment.

✦ **Save as PDF-X:** This option flattens transparency and reduces colors to CYMK.

✦ **Save PDF to iPhoto:** Creates a PDF and sends the PDF to iPhoto.

✦ **Save PDF to Web Receipts Folder:** Creates a PDF and puts it into your Web Receipts folder.

✦ **Edit Menu:** Allows you to add custom PDF workflows. Click the Help button in the Print dialog for more details.

Previewing in Mac OS X Preview

The Print dialog is standard for all applications that can print. Mac OS X offers a preview of your document when you click the Preview button. If you want to use Word's fancy preview instead, which we describe earlier in this chapter, choose File➪Print Preview.

Activating advanced printing options

In the Print dialog, click the Advanced Options downward-pointing triangle to the right of the Printer pop-up menu to display the complete Print dialog, as shown in Figure 8-7. We talk about this dialog in the following section.

Seeing all the possible print options

When you click the Advanced Options button (refer to Figure 8-7), watch as the Print dialog grows and metamorphoses to offer a variety of new options from which to choose, as shown in Figure 8-8. Printer, Presets, Preview, and PDF options, which we describe in the previous sections, are the same in advanced options.

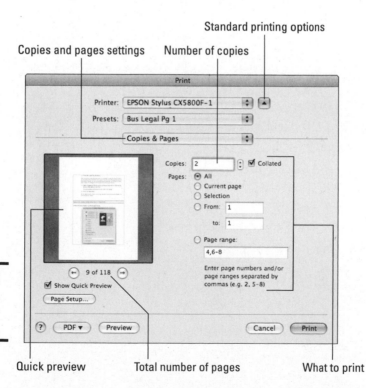

Figure 8-8:
Advanced
printing
options.

Standard printing options

Copies and pages settings   Number of copies

Quick preview   Total number of pages   What to print

Using Copies & Pages

When you open the advanced options, Copies & Pages is the default dialog. Notice in Figure 8-8, you can choose how many pages to print and which pages (or range of pages) to print.

An optional Quick Preview with forward and backward arrows is on the left to help you find specific pages in your document. Quick Preview can slow the Print dialog a bit, so you can turn off Quick Preview (just deselect the Show Quick Preview check box). You don't have to wait for Quick Preview to finish working before you click the Print button.

Using special Microsoft Word printing options

When you click the Copies & Pages pop-up menu in the advanced options dialog, you find a special Microsoft Word option. When you choose this option, which results in the dialog shown in Figure 8-9, you're offered a variety of specific printing options that you might need. For example, if your printer can't print on both sides of the paper at once (*duplex* printing), you can print all the odd pages, turn the paper over, and run it through a second time to print all the even pages.

Choose the parts of the document you want to print.

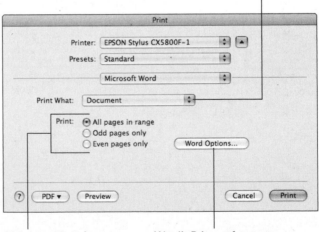

Figure 8-9:
Using special Microsoft Word printing options.

Choose which pages to print.

Word's Print preferences

The Print What pop-up menu deserves a bit of attention here. The choices in this pop-up menu enable you to print the specific parts of your document that are listed in the pop-up menu, as shown in Figure 8-10.

Figure 8-10:
The Print
What
pop-up
menu.

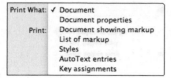

**Book II
Chapter 8**

**Printing for
Posterity**

When you click the Word Options button (refer to Figure 8-9), a Print preferences dialog (as shown in Figure 8-11) appears, where you can choose from a variety of specific printing options. The Reverse Print Order check box is a popular choice. Many printers print the first page so that it's on the bottom of the pile when you're done. This feature tells Word to print the last page first and so on so that when you're done printing, page one is on top of the page pile.

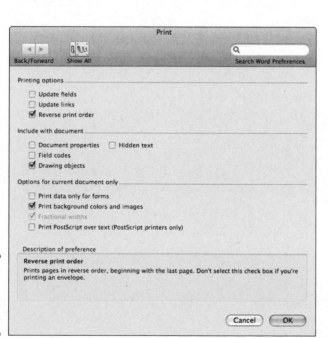

Figure 8-11:
Adjusting
Word's print
preferences.

Using special printer features

When you click the Copies & Pages pop-up menu, all the options below Microsoft Word in the menu are tailored to the brand and model printer that you choose (see Figure 8-12). The options available depend upon what capabilities your printer has and upon the skill of the folks who wrote the printer driver. We're not going to cover each feature, but we're going to point out some things most Word users want to know about:

Figure 8-12:
Finding
more
options in
Copies &
Pages.

✓ Copies & Pages
  Microsoft Word

  Layout
  Paper Handling
  Cover Page
  Scheduler

  Print Settings
  Color Management
  Page Layout Settings

  Summary

✦ **Layout:** Here you might find the duplex printing option if your printer supports this. Our printer doesn't, so the Two-Sided pop-up menu is grayed out (see Figure 8-13). Some printer drivers put duplex printing in its own Copies & Pages pop-up menu item instead of using Layout.

Layout options

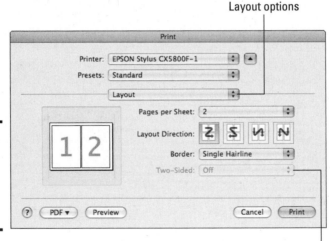

Figure 8-13:
Printing
on both
sides with
the Layout
option.

Two-sided printing

✦ **Paper Handling:** You probably don't need to adjust this one. You can use this feature to choose reverse print order instead of using Word's preferences.

✦ **Cover Page:** This adds a cover page to your document. You might choose this option if more than one person is sharing a printer (see Figure 8-14). The cover page from this Print option isn't part of the document; it's in addition to the document and doesn't affect Word's page count. This option isn't the same as adding a cover page with Elements Gallery in Word, in which the cover page becomes part of the Word document.

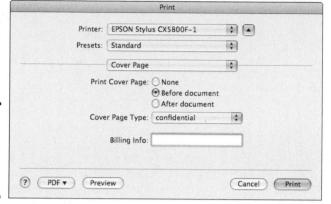

Figure 8-14:
Adding
a cover
page by the
printer.

✦ **Scheduler:** If you want to schedule your document to print at a certain time or put your print job on hold, choose this option.

✦ **Print Settings:** This dialog offers many choices. Choose a paper type, speed, and quality of the print job. For a quick draft, adjust the settings, as shown in Figure 8-15. Lately, some printers default to speed over quality. If you find that some things in your documents aren't printing right, you probably need to raise the quality setting. Your printer may have other options here.

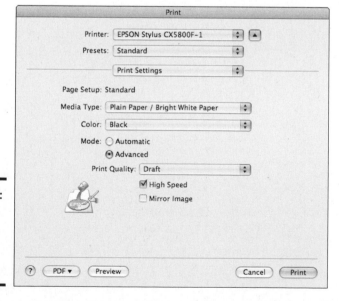

Figure 8-15:
Printing
speed,
quality,
and paper
selections.

Book III

Excel 2008

The 5th Wave   By Rich Tennant

"Well, obviously one of the cells in the navigational spreadsheet is corrupt!"

Contents at a Glance

Chapter 1: Working Every Day in Excel

*E*xcel 2008 has an entirely new kind of worksheet — a *ledger sheet* — which makes using spreadsheets fill-in-the-blank simple. Ledger sheets allow you to successfully accomplish every day tasks, such as budgeting, keeping track of your checkbook balance, tracking vehicle maintenance, recording stock portfolios, drafting expense reports, and more. In this chapter, we show you how you can use ledger sheets efficiently.

After you get your feet wet with ledger sheets, we talk about opening and saving Excel specialty file formats, and how to recover if Excel or Mac OS X crashes. Then, we reveal Excel's new interface, and how to use the Formatting Palette to alter print setup and control Page Layout View. Along the way, we explain how to customize keyboard shortcuts in Excel. Finally, we explain how to work with different sheet types and reveal Excel's special Project Gallery.

This minibook covers features unique to Excel. We talk about general Microsoft Office features — such as opening and saving files, using Project Gallery, and working with common interface components, including the new Elements Gallery, Toolbox, and palettes — in Book I.

Introducing Ledger Sheets

Ledger sheets are designed specifically to help you figure out Excel's interface and features while you work in a simplified environment. Even if you're an old hand at Excel, ledger sheets may be useful timesavers and organizers.

In our ledger sheet discussion, we use a Budget example, so you can open the same template we're using and follow along. The following sections don't really discuss budgets or budgeting — they're all about ledger sheets. And all ledger sheets work in the same basic way.

Opening a ledger sheet

You can use ledger sheets so simply; you just need to open one from the built-in collection of ledger sheets and start filling it in. You can find ledger sheets in Project Gallery and Elements Gallery. In our example, we open our ledger sheet from Project Gallery. Figure 1-1 shows the open ledger sheet.

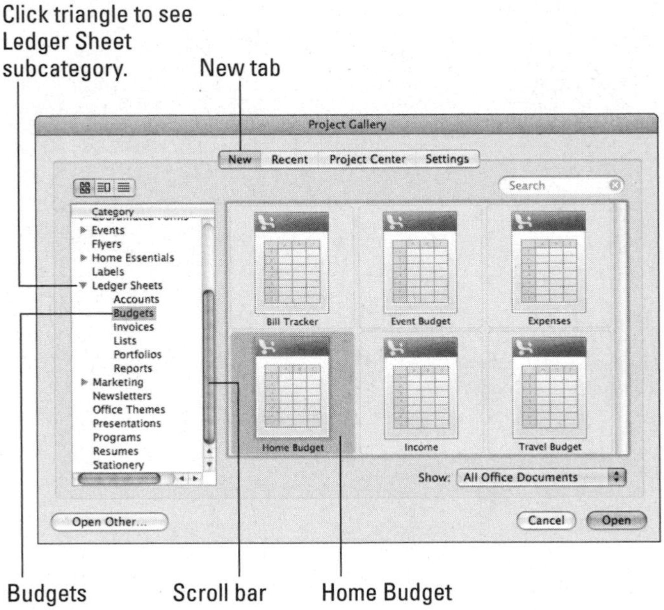

Click triangle to see
Ledger Sheet
subcategory.

New tab

Figure 1-1:
Opening a
ledger sheet
from Project
Gallery.

Budgets   Scroll bar   Home Budget

To open an Excel ledger sheet, follow these steps:

1. **If Excel is closed, click the Excel icon in your Dock to open it.**

If Excel opens Project Gallery, you're where you're supposed to be! If Excel opens directly to a spreadsheet, choose File➪Project Gallery.

Either way, you get to the Project Gallery (see Figure 1-1).

2. **In Project Gallery, click the New tab if it's not selected already.**

3. **In the Category list, click Ledger Sheets.**

A pop-up menu of built-in ledger sheets appears. This is a good opportunity to select each category. When you select a category, the ledger sheet templates in that category appear to the right of the list. You may have to drag the scroll bar to see all the subcategories.

4. **Double-click a ledger sheet template to open it in Excel.**

The ledger sheet opens, as shown in Figure 1-2; to follow our example, select the Budgets subcategory and then double-click Home Budget.

Standard toolbar

Excel menu

Formatting Palette

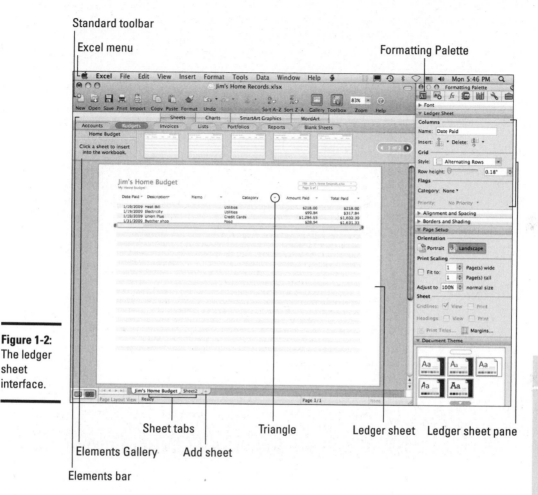

Figure 1-2:
The ledger
sheet
interface.

Sheet tabs   Triangle   Ledger sheet   Ledger sheet pane

Elements Gallery   Add sheet

Elements bar

Ledger sheets were designed so that after you open one, you only have to fill in the blanks with your own data. And you don't have a Formula Bar to worry about. (You can read more about the Formula Bar in Chapter 2 of this minibook.) Plus, you don't have to deal with any row numbers or column labels, and the formulas are invisible!

List sheets are new to Excel in 2008. They're Mac-first and Mac-only. Well, not so Mac-only that you can't share ledger sheets with Windows users. Excel for Windows can work with your ledger sheets but can't make them from scratch. When you work with other sheet types, the new Elements Gallery's Sheets tab offers the same ledger sheets that you can find in Project Gallery (see Figure 1-1). The Formatting Palette has a new section just for ledger sheets.

Entering text and data

The key to working with ledger sheets is to double-click. Double-click to edit a cell, a header, or a footer. Click outside a cell, or double-click outside a header or footer, when you're done editing.

You can work with Excel's interface in special ways when you're using a ledger sheet. See Figure 1-3, which shows these interface elements:

Figure 1-3:
Clicking
disclosure
triangles
in ledger
sheets.

✦ **Column header:** At the top of each column, a word or phrase describes the kind of entries you should put into the column. These descriptions are sometimes called *field names*. In the example in Figure 1-3, the column header is Category.

✦ **AutoFilter:** Click the AutoFilter disclosure triangle to display a pop-up menu of AutoFilter choices. Use this option to filter your column. We talk about the AutoFilter buttons in Chapter 7 of this minibook.

✦ **Cell entries:** Entries that you make to cells appear in rows and columns.

✦ **Row drag handles:** While you work in a row, drag handles appear on the left and right side of the row. You can see them up close in Figure 1-3.

✦ **Pop-up menu disclosure triangle:** When you type in some cells, a disclosure triangle appears on the right side of the cell. Click that little triangle to see the cell entry pop-up menu. You can select from this menu, as shown in Figure 1-4, so that you don't have to type.

✦ **Selected cell:** The cell you're working in. It has a different border from all the rest to indicate that it's currently active and selected. See Figure 1-4.

Figure 1-4:
Making
things easy
with the
cell entry
pop-up
menu.

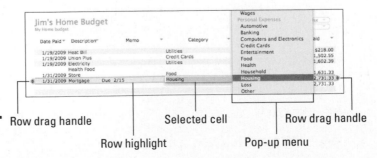

Row drag handle   Selected cell   Row drag handle

Row highlight   Pop-up menu

Of course, you're not limited to the choices in the cell entry pop-up menu. If you want something different, type what you want in cells that display disclosure triangles. Excel notices when you type something that isn't on the list and politely asks whether you want to add your new entry to the list so that you can use it again.

After you type in content in several rows into your ledger sheet, you might want to move a row up or down on the sheet. When you click into a row that's already filled in, a row drag handle appears in the margin, as shown in Figure 1-3 and Figure 1-4. You can drag the handle up or down in the list, and the entire row that's highlighted moves. Not only that, but when you release the handle, hidden formulas automatically adjust to the row's new location and then recalculate.

Working with Other File Formats

You expect Excel to open Excel files, of course, but the program can do more than that. You can actually open, work on, and save a file in several formats. Choose File➪Save As and then click Format to open the pop-up menu. Excel can both open and save in the formats listed in the pop-up menu.

Excel keeps your file in the format it has when you open it. For example, if you open an Excel binary workbook (.xlsb), it opens normally, and you can work on it. When you save the workbook, the format remains Excel binary workbook (.xlsb) unless you intentionally change the format by choosing File➪Save As and then selecting a different format from the Format pop-up menu.

**Book III
Chapter 1**

**Working Every
Day in Excel**

Default format

The Excel Workbook (.xlsx) format is the default XML format for Excel 2008 spreadsheets. Although Excel can work with a plethora of file formats, this format preserves all aspects of your workbook. Use this file format if you need to comply with open source standards requirements.

Common formats

You have several options for file formats besides Excel's default XLSX format:

✦ **Excel 97–2004 Workbook (.xls):** Save in a format usable by these earlier versions of Excel. Saving in this format doesn't preserve full fidelity (particularly charts).

✦ **Excel Template (.xltx):** Save the workbook as a template. See Book I, Chapter 2 for details about saving and opening templates.

✦ **Excel 97—2004 Template (.xlt):** Save a template in a format usable by these earlier versions of Excel. You can't preserve full fidelity (particularly charts) with this format.

✦ **Comma Separated Values (.csv):** See the section, "Delimited," later in this chapter.

✦ **Web Page (.htm):** Save the workbook in a format that Web browsers understand and can display. Excel creates a file in HTML format, along with a supporting folder. Upload both the file and folder to a Web server if you want to share your workbook via the Internet.

Excel can open and save Web pages in HTML (HyperText Markup Language) format and do great things with Web tables and data from the Web, but don't throw away your HTML (Web page) code editor. Excel isn't going to replace that.

Specialty formats

Apart from the Excel formats that are typically used the most, you have several other file formats to consider.

XML

XML (eXtensible Markup Language) are plain text files that have been zipped. You can decompress, and then read and edit by hand, files in these formats if you know how to program in this computer markup language:

✦ **Excel Macro-Enabled Workbook (.xlsm):** Workbooks in this XML format contain Visual Basic for Applications (VBA) programming language code, also called macros or macrocode. Excel 2008 can open and save files in this format. When opening this format file, Excel 2008 displays a prompt asking whether you want to remove the macros contained in the file.

We advise against removing the code because it doesn't hurt anything — and removing it can potentially cause great harm. Because Excel 2008 doesn't support VBA, macros can't run and you can't edit them. But by working in the XLSM format, you can, however, use non-VBA aspects of an XLSM workbook.

✦ **Excel Macro-Enabled Template (.xltm):** The same as XLSM, except this is a template. See Book I, Chapter 2 for details about saving and opening templates.

✦ **Excel 2004 XML Spreadsheet (.xml):** Excel 2004 and Excel 2008 can use this XML format. Excel 2008 can't preserve full fidelity (particularly charts) when you share files between Excel 2008 and Excel 2004.

✦ **Excel Add-In (.xlam):** Save a macro-enabled workbook as an Excel add-in. Excel 2008 can't run add-ins, and the macros would have to be pre-existing.

Because these files are text, even though they're compressed (zipped), they can be many times larger than when saved in binary format.

Binary

Instead of saving the computer code as words in text, Excel's *binary* formats save it in zeros and ones, known as binary numbers. Using binary numbers, rather than text, results in smaller file sizes that open and save quickly (but most humans can't read binary format):

✦ **Excel Binary Workbook (.xlsb):** This new binary format solves the bloat problem created by the new XML (.xlsx) text format by avoiding XML and text altogether. Files saved in XLSB format typically open and save faster, and are usually smaller, than XLSX files.

This file format doesn't comply with open source standards.

✦ **Excel 97–2004 Add-In (.xla):** Save a macro-enabled workbook as an Excel add-in for these earlier versions of Excel. Excel 2008 can't run add-ins, and the macros would have to be pre-existing.

Delimited

In this format type, data arranged in tables with rows and columns is saved in text files that use a specified character, called a *delimiter,* to indicate the beginning of a new column. People have mostly settled on using a comma as the delimiting character, and Comma Separated Value (CSV) is a popular file format. However, other delimited file formats can specify any character:

✦ **Tab Delimited Text (.txt):** Save row and column headers, and data, in a text file that uses the Tab character as its delimiter. This format saves only the text within cells.

✦ **Windows Comma Separated (.csv):** Save row and column headers, and data, in a text file that uses the comma character as its delimiter in a format that's slightly different from standard CSV.

✦ **MS-DOS Comma Separated (.csv):** Save row and column headers, and data, in a text file that uses the comma character as its delimiter in a format that's slightly different from standard CSV.

✦ **Space Delimited Text (.prn):** Save only the text within cells using a text file format for old dot-matrix and line printers.

Excel can deal with any delimiter, as long as you tell it which delimiter was used in the preparation of your delimited file.

Old formats

Excel still offers these formats, but it may not for long. If you have any of these files, save them in one of the current formats in case Excel stops supporting these formats:

✦ **Data Interchange Format (.dif):** Save row and column headers, along with data, in a format designed specifically for data.

This format often works better than delimited formats because it's not fussy about which characters are in the data.

✦ **Symbolic Link (.slk):** Use this old Microsoft-specific format to exchange data. It requires special handling of semicolons.

✦ **Excel 5.0/95 Workbook (.xls):** An old Excel-specific workbook format.

All the other formats

Here are the additional file formats you have to choose from:

✦ **Single File Web Page (.mht):** Save the workbook as a single-file Web page that you can upload to a Web server for distribution via the Internet and view in a Web browser.

✦ **UTF-16 Unicode Text (.txt):** Save only the text within cells using the UTF-16 standard.

✦ **Windows Formatted Text (.txt):** Save only the text within cells using Windows text file format.

✦ **MS-DOS Formatted Text (.txt):** Save only the text within cells using MS-DOS text file format.

Saving Your Workbook

The fastest way to save in the west is to click the Save button on the Excel Standard toolbar, especially if you're working on a workbook that's already been saved at least once. Although that method is quick and easy, and we encourage you to save often while you work, that's not the only way to save a workbook.

Saving for compatibility (.xls)

Be thoughtful of those who aren't using Office 2008 for Mac or Office 2007 for Windows. If you think someone may need to work in an older format, choose File⇨Save As and then choose one of the older file formats, such as Excel 97–2004 Workbook (.xls).

Be sure to click the Compatibility Report button to see what Excel might lose or modify when you save to an older file format.

Saving in Excel Workbook (.xlsx)

We know a lot of Excel types want to get deep into the blood and guts of these files, but this might not interest you unless you're super geeky. Excel XML files aren't really files; they're zipped folders that contain XML files and even more folders.

To get into the actual XML files, do the following:

1. In Finder, right-click a saved XLSX file and choose Duplicate from the pop-up menu that appears.

This makes a copy of the file so that you don't alter the original.

2. Change the file extension in Finder from .xlsx to .zip.

3. Right-click or Control-click the Zip file.

4. From the pop-up menu that appears, choose Open With and then choose Archive Utility.

A file folder appears, containing your document's XML files and additional folders.

There you go! You can open and edit XML files in Microsoft Word or any text or XML editor. If you know how to program with XML, everything about your document is now at your fingertips.

Saving small using Excel binary workbook (.xlsb)

From an efficiency point of view, Excel's new default XML file format isn't a good way to save computer files. XML is text, and text files become huge and bloated very quickly. Zipping and unzipping XML text files adds overhead and takes time. Even though XLSX files are zipped and unzipped automatically for you, they're usually much larger than when you save them in Excel binary workbook (.xlsb) file format.

Always saving in Excel binary workbook (.xlsb) format will usually result in much smaller files. After you save in Excel binary workbook (.xlsb) format, you can always choose File⇒Save As and then choose Excel workbook (.xlsx) from the Format pop-up if you want to fiddle with the XML code.

You can even make saving in Excel binary workbook (.xlsb) the default for Excel so that you always save in the most efficient file format. Follow these steps:

1. In Excel, choose Excel⇒Preferences.

The Excel Preferences dialog appears.

2. Click the Compatibility icon.

Compatibility preferences appear.

3. Click Save Files in This Format in the Transition area and choose Excel Binary Workbook (.xlsb) from the pop-up menu that appears.

4. Click OK to close Compatibility and save your preference.

Saving with AutoRecover

Excel 2008 has been out long enough so that crashes are minimal. Just the same, a crash is possible.

Setting up AutoRecover

Take a moment to make sure your preferences automatically save an emergency backup file of your work. To set up AutoRecover, follow these steps:

Save

1. **Choose Excel➪Preferences.**

   The Excel Preferences dialog appears.

2. **In the Sharing and Privacy section, select Save.**

   The Save preferences appear.

3. **Select the Save AutoRecover Information After This Number of Minutes check box.**

4. **Enter the number of minutes that you want between AutoRecover file saves, or use the increase/decrease control.**

5. **Click OK to close Save and save your preferences.**

   After you turn on AutoRecover, Excel saves your work at the specified interval so that you can recover in the event that the system or Excel crashes.

Retrieving AutoRecover

If your computer or Excel crashes, you can recover your work up to the most recent AutoRecover save, but only if you turned on AutoRecover saves (see the preceding section). Take these steps to restore any workbooks that were open at the time of the crash:

1. **Click the Excel Dock icon.**

   Excel presents any documents that you're working on that have been saved at least once. Recovered documents have (Recovered) in the title bar.

2. **To keep the recovered version, choose File➪Save As.**

   The Save As dialog appears. Take one of the following actions:

   - *To replace the existing file with the recovered version:* Navigate to the file or use Spotlight to locate the existing file. Then, click the filename to change the recovered file's name to the existing filename. Click Save to overwrite the existing file.

   - *To save the recovered file without overwriting the original:* Select a location to save the recovered file and enter a name for the file in the text box. Then, click Save.

To discard a recovered workbook, click the red Close button to close the workbook. When prompted, don't save changes.

To permanently remove AutoRecover files from your computer, follow these steps:

1. **Quit all open Office applications.**

2. **In Finder, press ⌘-F.**

The Spotlight search dialog appears.

3. **Enter** AutoRecover **in the text box.**

Spotlight displays a list of matching files, if any.

4. **Select all AutoRecover files.**

5. **Drag the files to the Trash.**

6. **Empty the Trash.**

Viewing Workbooks

A *workbook* is a container for a collection of sheets. A standard *worksheet* is a grid composed of cells arranged in columns and rows, but you can use other kinds of sheets, which we discuss in the section, "Working with Sheet Types," later in this chapter.

When you're working in Excel, you have your choice of one of two views: Page Layout View and Normal View. We discuss these views in the following sections.

If you're an Excel veteran but new to Excel 2008, Page Layout View is now the default view. Because you can use the Formatting Palette to do almost everything in Page Layout View that you did before in Page Break Preview, Excel no longer has Page Break Preview.

You can find general interface discussion about menus, toolbars, the Dock, Elements Gallery, and the Formatting Palette in Book I, as well as how to open and save files.

Using Page Layout View

Page Layout View displays your workbook so that you can see how it will look when you print it. Page breaks are clearly visible in this view, and Page Setup controls on the Formatting Palette help you see changes live while you make them.

To see Excel's interface in Page Layout View, follow these steps:

1. **Click the Excel icon in your Dock to open Excel.**

   If Excel opens directly to a worksheet, you're where you're supposed to be.

2. **If Excel opens Project Gallery, click Open.**

   A new workbook opens in Page Layout View, displaying a blank standard worksheet, as shown in Figure 1-5.

If you already have Excel open, click the New button on the Standard toolbar to open a new workbook, displaying a blank, standard worksheet, as shown in Figure 1-5.

In the interface in Figure 1-5, one sheet is brighter than the rest, and the page breaks look like physical breaks. Any sheet that has content appears bright, and sheets that contain no content are slightly grayed and display Click to Add Data. In this view, you can easily see whether text or other objects will be cut off or spill over breaks when you print the sheet.

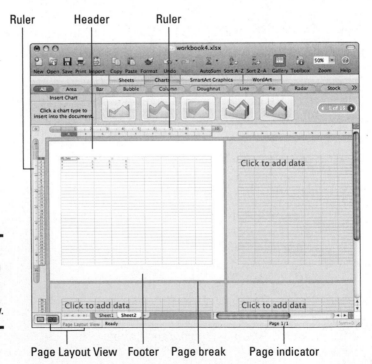

Figure 1-5: Looking at a worksheet in Page Layout View.

Figure 1-5 also shows these features of the Page Layout View interface:

✦ **Ruler:** Choose View➪Ruler to toggle the rulers off and on. You can drag rulers to resize margins. Double-click a ruler to display the Page Setup dialog, which we discuss in Chapter 8 in this minibook.

✦ **Header and footer:** Double-click the white space above and below the sheets to display header and footer controls, which we also talk about in Chapter 8 of this minibook.

✦ **View buttons:** Click the two buttons at the lower-left corner of the window to switch between Normal View and Page Layout View. The Page Layout View button is selected in Figure 1-5.

✦ **Page indicator:** As soon as you enter any data into a cell or add an object to a sheet, the page indicator updates.

Using Normal View

Experienced number crunchers and bean counters will probably prefer the traditional Normal View, as shown in Figure 1-6. Normal View is similar to Page Layout View, except the entire sheet is continuous. Instead of seeing distinct visual differentiation between pages, you see dotted lines after you select any Page Setup or Print function. Normal View maximizes the amount of worksheet that you see on the screen. You can switch to Normal View by clicking the Normal View button in the lower-left corner of the window or by choosing View➪Normal.

Using the common interface

Whether you prefer to work in Page Layout View or Normal View, most interface components are the same in both views. We highlight these common features in Figure 1-6:

✦ **Standard toolbar:** The Standard toolbar is now part of the document window in Excel 2008, a new location.

✦ **Elements Gallery:** Elements Gallery is new to Excel 2008. The Sheets tab (which we discuss in the section, "Making specific sheet types," later in this chapter) is unique to Excel.

✦ **Worksheet:** Figure 1-6 shows a standard Excel worksheet, where you can enter text and formulas, perform calculations, and store data.

✦ **View buttons:** Click these buttons to switch between Page Layout View and Normal View.

✦ **Sheet tab:** Each sheet in a workbook has a name that appears on its tab near the bottom of the window. Double-click a sheet tab to edit that sheet's name.

✦ **+ (Add Sheet):** Click the plus sign to add a new, blank standard worksheet to your workbook. You can add as many worksheets as you want until your computer runs out of memory. You could potentially add thousands of them!

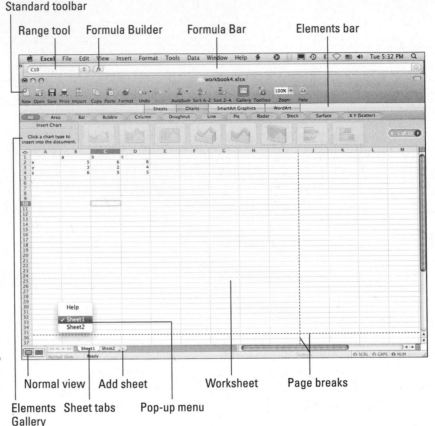

Figure 1-6:
Viewing
with Normal
View.

✦ **Range tool:** Also called the Name box. The ToolTip for this box says
Enter a Name to Assign It to a Group of Cells, or Select a Named Group
of Cells. You can assign a name (don't use spaces or special characters)
to a cell or a selected range of cells so that you can refer to that range in
cell formulas.

Select the cell(s) you want to name, type a name for the range, and then
press Return or Enter to register that name in the workbook. After you
assign a name to a cell or cell range, you can type its name into the
Range tool and then press Return or Enter to select the range.

✦ **Formula Builder:** Click this button to display Formula Builder, (see Book III,
Chapter 2 for more.

✦ **Formula Bar:** When you choose View⇨Formula Bar to toggle the
Formula Bar on, the Formula Bar now covers the entire width of the
screen to give your formulas room to stretch out.

✦ **Rows:** Excel 2008 has increased the number of rows in a worksheet to
1,048,576.

✦ **Columns:** Excel 2008 offers 16,384 columns in a worksheet.

✦ **Cells:** A worksheet in Excel 2008 has 17,179,869,184 cells. Yes, that's more than 17 billion cells per sheet!

If you find you're pushing Excel's limits and want to know exactly what they are, search Excel's Help for the Specifications and Limits for Excel 2008 topic. You can find such information as how many characters fit into one cell or how many nested levels you can have in a function.

Like other Office applications, you can find context-sensitive pop-up menus just about everywhere you right-click or Control-click in Excel.

Using the Formatting Palette

When working in Page Layout View or Normal View, you can access the Page Setup portion of the Toolbox's Formatting Palette. Follow these steps to open the Page Setup portion of the Formatting Palette, as shown in Figure 1-7:

1. **If the Toolbox isn't visible, click the Toolbox button on Excel's Standard toolbar.**

The Toolbox appears.

2. **In the Toolbox, select Formatting Palette.**

The Formatting Palette appears.

3. **Click the disclosure triangle for Page Setup.**

Page Setup options appear, as shown in Figure 1-7.

**Book III
Chapter 1**

**Working Every
Day in Excel**

Getting the perfect interface

Book I, Chapter 3 discusses how to customize Excel's menus and toolbars. Excel has its own keyboard shortcuts and shortcut organizer. The complete list of built-in keyboard shortcuts is in Excel Help; search for the Excel Keyboard Shortcuts topic to find the list.

To get to the Keyboard Shortcut dialog, choose Tools⇨Customize Keyboard. The shortcut organizer is another way to discover Excel's built-in shortcuts, as well as a way to change, add, or remove your own keyboard shortcuts. You aren't allowed to delete Excel's built-in shortcuts. Remember that if Mac OS X is already using a particular keyboard shortcut, Excel can't use it.

The ability to customize Excel keyboard shortcuts is Mac-only — Excel for Windows doesn't have this feature.

Automatic Fit To

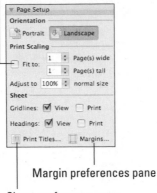

Figure 1-7:
Using Page
Setup on the
Formatting
Palette.

Margin preferences pane

Sheet preference pane

We describe using the Page Setup options, located on the Formatting Palette, in Chapter 8 of this minibook. When you have these options available instantly on the Formatting Palette, you can see your choices implemented live while you make them in Page Layout View.

Orientation

To change the orientation of your worksheet, you can select an Orientation button:

✦ **Landscape:** Display and print your sheet so that it's wider than it is tall.

✦ **Portrait:** Display and print your sheet so that it's taller than it is wide.

The page breaks change instantly in Page Layout View when you click either the Landscape or Portrait button in the Formatting Palette.

Print scaling

Below the Orientation options on the Formatting Palette, the Print Scaling options deserve some attention:

✦ **Print Scaling:** If your spreadsheet spills a little bit onto an adjacent page, select the Fit To check box in the Print Scaling section. Excel automatically adjusts page breaks for you by scaling your worksheet.

✦ **Adjust to [%] Normal Size:** Type a percentage value in this field or click the increase/decrease controls to increase or decrease the amount of scaling that you want to apply to the worksheet.

This option isn't the zoom control, which you can find on Excel's Standard toolbar.

Sheet

Sheet options appear below the Print Scaling options on the Formatting Palette:

✦ **Gridlines check boxes:** You can have the following options:

- *View:* Select to display sheet gridlines; deselect to hide them.

- *Print:* Select to have gridlines on printed sheets; deselect to print without gridlines.

✦ **Headings check boxes:** You have the following options:

- *View:* Select to display column headings; deselect to hide them.

- *Print:* Select to include column headings on printed sheets; deselect to print without column headings.

✦ **Print Titles:** Click this button to display the Page Setup dialog's Sheet tab.

✦ **Margins:** Click this button to display the Page Setup dialog's Margins tab.

We discuss Page Setup in Chapter 8 of this minibook.

Working with Sheet Types

Excel sheets can be general or dedicated to a specific purpose. You don't have to be an expert to use the various sheet types, but you should know their names and each sheet type's purpose.

You can mix different sheet types within a single workbook.

Sheet types

Here's the rundown of the kinds of specialized sheets that are available in Excel:

✦ **Ledger sheets:** We discuss ledger sheets in the section, "Introducing Ledger Sheets," earlier in this chapter.

✦ **Blank sheet:** This general-purpose worksheet has cells, rows, and columns; the cells can hold text, formulas, and data. You can place objects such as charts, WordArt, SmartArt graphics, objects from the Object Palette, pictures, sounds, and even movies in layers on worksheets. Most people are familiar with this traditional worksheet.

✦ **List sheets:** These sheets are pure gold! List sheets are one of the most useful kinds of sheets for working with data tables and lists of all kinds. We talk a lot about list sheets in Chapter 7 of this minibook.

✦ **Chart sheets:** A chart sheet contains a single graph or chart. We discuss charts in Chapter 5 of this minibook.

✦ **Excel 4.0 macro sheet:** Before VBA (Visual Basic for Applications), there was the Excel 4.0 XLM macro language. If you work in this format, Excel 2008 supports the Excel 4.0 macro language. If this applies to you, search Excel Help for *Excel 4* and then download the entire Excel 4.0 Macro Language Reference; click the Download link in the Excel 4.0 (XLM) Macro Commands topic.

✦ **Excel 5.0 dialog sheet:** VBA doesn't work in Excel 2008, so Excel must have retained this sheet type just in case VBA returns to Office for Mac, which Microsoft says will happen in the next major release.

Making specific sheet types

You don't follow the same procedure when you create each of the various sheet types.

You can easily create a worksheet by selecting which type of worksheet you want to open when you open a new workbook.

In addition to the regular Office Project Gallery described in Book I, Chapter 2, Excel has a special Project Gallery (see Figure 1-1) that you can use to create new, blank sheets of specific sheet types after you open a workbook. We describe how to use this gallery in the section, "Using Excel's special Project Gallery," later in this chapter.

Making a standard worksheet

You have several ways to create a new worksheet:

✦ Choose File⇨Project Gallery. When Project Gallery appears, click Open or Cancel.

✦ Choose File⇨New.

✦ Click the New button on Excel's Standard toolbar.

✦ If Excel isn't open, click the Excel Dock icon (or use one of the more than 18 different ways to open an application in Mac OS X).

✦ Click ⌘-N from within Excel.

✦ Right-click or Control-click any sheet tab. From the resulting pop-up menu, select Insert. In the Excel Project Gallery (see Figure 1-1) that appears, double-click Blank Sheet.

✦ Click the plus sign (+) to add a new, blank standard worksheet to your workbook (as shown in Figure 1-6).

✦ On the Sheets tab of the Elements Gallery, click the Blank Sheets button and then choose Blank Sheet.

Making a list sheet

Here's a few ways to make a sheet list:

✦ Choose File➪Project Gallery. Project Gallery appears. Double-click List Wizard.

✦ On the Sheets tab of Elements Gallery, click the Blank Sheets button and then select List Sheet.

✦ Right-click or Control-click any sheet tab. From the resulting pop-up menu, select Insert. In the Excel special Project Gallery that appears, double-click List Sheet.

We talk about additional methods of creating list sheets and how to use them in Chapter 7 of this minibook.

Making a chart sheet

Here are the two ways to create a chart sheet:

✦ Make an Excel chart; then move the chart to a chart sheet, as we explain in Chapter 5 of this minibook.

✦ Select the data range for your chart. Then, right-click or Control-click the sheet's tab. From the resulting pop-up menu, select Insert. In the Excel special Project Gallery that appears, double-click Chart Sheet.

Making an Excel 4.0 macro sheet

To make an Excel 4.0 macro sheet, right-click or Control-click any sheet tab. From the resulting pop-up menu, select Insert. In the Excel special Project Gallery that appears, double-click Excel 4.0 Macro Sheet.

Note that while you can create Excel 5.0 dialog sheets, these sheets are useless in Excel 2008. Don't bother. Wait 'til the next version.

Using Excel's special Project Gallery

Excel has Project Gallery inside each workbook. Project Gallery even has hidden features that work *only* in Excel. To expose the hidden Excel special Project Gallery, right-click or Control-click any sheet tab, and then select Insert from the resulting pop-up menu.

The Excel special Project Gallery dialog opens. In this special version of Project Gallery, everything is just for Excel. In the Category list on the left, only Excel content categories are displayed. Even in My Templates, only your Excel templates are available. The other tabs of Project Gallery are inactive.

When you access the Excel special Project Gallery, the Blank Documents category is selected by default. When Blank Documents is selected, the document templates that appear to the right of the Category list don't open new workbooks. Instead, selecting one of the templates adds a new sheet of the chosen type to the active workbook. This aspect of the Excel special Project Gallery is different from the regular Office Project Gallery. The Excel special Project Gallery can add any one of the following sheet types to the active workbook (we describe sheet types in the earlier sections):

+ Standard worksheet

+ Chart sheet

+ List sheet

+ Excel 4.0 macro sheet

+ Excel 5.0 dialog sheet

Meet MacBU's Gavin Shearer

Gavin Shearer is a Program Manager with Macintosh Business Unit (MacBU). He was kind enough to allow the authors to put a few questions to him.

Do you get razzed by the Windows Office team?

Gavin: You know, we don't. At all. If anything, they bend over backward to help us out. Back in the mists of time (before the creation of our present-day Macintosh Business Unit), Mac software was developed inside the overall Office organization, which also produced the Windows versions of our applications. A lot of the folks who work in MacBU have history with the Windows side of the house.

A huge part of my job is making sure that a Mac user can get a file created in Windows Office, double-click it, and have it "just work" on the Mac. That means we have to know what those teams are building, how it works, and make a plan to bring it to the Mac. I personally meet with the Windows Excel team on a weekly basis; if they weren't supportive of our efforts, my job would be exponentially harder, if not flat-out impossible.

What's Bill Gates really like?

Gavin: You know, I get asked this question a lot — way more than I ever would have thought possible before I joined the company. Bill's the founder, the chairman, the (former) richest man in the world . . . and for some reason, whenever I'm on airplane, once the person next to me finds out I work for Microsoft, they assume that Bill and I must be close friends. Amazing.

As it happens, I do have a "Bill" story: I've been to his house. I interned at Microsoft during the summer of 2004, and as a reward (and a way of wooing interns), the company threw a big BBQ at Bill's place on the shores of Lake Washington. In addition to being the absolute, no question, #1-with-a-bullet, best-catered barbecue I've ever attended, it was also a ton of fun. The company has a few hundred interns in any given summer, which meant there were quite a lot of us in Bill's backyard, munching on chicken and carrot sticks. Eventually, Bill came out to meet us and wound up with a ring of people around him, three or four bodies deep. He took questions, was very friendly, and basically ignored that we were trashing his lawn. Nice guy.

What's your favorite Mac thing?

Gavin: So I've been a Mac user for two solid decades now. I started using 'em in 1989, and bought my first machine — an SE/30 — when I went off to college in 1990. In the intervening years, I've used a ton of different systems: Windows, of course, but also various flavors of Unix, OS/2, even a Be. What's kept me on the Mac is that, generally speaking, the Mac (and Mac applications) works consistently, reliably, and the way I expect it to. In practical terms, it means I can get more done in less time, and my learning curve for new things is flatter. There's a thrill, a little electric "aha!" that I get sometimes with good Mac software. It may be the way I'm wired (I have plenty of friends who feel the same way about their PCs that I do about my Mac), but it doesn't really matter — the Mac just feels good. (I guess I'm addicted.)

What's the hardest part of making Office?

Gavin: Making tradeoffs. People have this impression of Microsoft being this fabulously wealthy, resource-rich company, which means they also assume we have the ability to throw an infinite number of smart people at any given problem, product, or bug. It's just not true — honestly, we don't have Scrooge McDuck's vault somewhere here on campus.

We have about 200 people working for MacBU. That's everyone — our developers, testers, marketing people, finance people, Web site people, writers, people-managers, you name it. The Windows Office team, on the other hand, employs a lot more folks (which makes sense given the relative market shares of Windows versus the Mac). As a practical matter, this means the Windows team can do a lot more in a given release than we can, and we can't do everything they do. Thus, we have to be incredibly careful and smart about picking our bets, and also be sure that the things we're doing are the right thing for our customers. We're forever having to stack-rank and trade off Thing A against Thing B, and keep our eye focused on shipping something our customers will want to buy. There's a lot of good in this process, but it can be exhausting.

Book III
Chapter 1

Working Every Day in Excel

Chapter 2: Operating Inside the Workbook

In This Chapter

✔ Selecting, editing, naming, and clearing cells

✔ Dragging text, numbers, or dates

✔ Entering things in general

✔ Using cell formulas

✔ Copying relatively and absolutely

All kinds of cells exist these days. For instance, fuel cells and stem cells have been in the news lately. As the name implies, a *cell* is a small part of a larger whole. We work with Excel *cells,* which are small rectangles that are arranged in rows and columns on a worksheet.

This chapter focuses on the things you can do in cells rows and columns. Excel conforms to standard behaviors that you're probably already used to in other applications. Even if you've spent most of your computing life using e-mail and now have to do some calculating, it's a fairly easy task to get Excel to carry out your wishes.

Interacting with Excel

Excel constantly gives you feedback as you work. You can follow the discussion in this section by simply opening Excel. Click Excel's Dock icon to see a workbook that's open to our starting point: a blank standard worksheet.

Selecting, editing, and naming cells

Here are some basics on the most common things you're apt to do with cells:

✦ **Selecting cells:** Click a cell to select it. Excel indicates the selected cell in three ways:

   • *Darkened row number and column heading:* When you open a new, blank workbook, Excel selects the cell in the upper-left corner of the worksheet, which is the intersection of column A and row 1. For convenience, we refer to that intersection as cell A1. See Figure 2-1.

- *Heavy border:* In Figure 2-1, cell B1 has a dark border to indicate it's the selected cell. In your workbook, cell A1 has the dark border to indicate it was selected by default.

- *Name box:* See the Formula Bar discussion later in this chapter.

✦ **Editing in-cell:** When you start typing in a cell, the border gets a nice, soft shadow and seems to be closer to you than the rest of the sheet, as shown in Figure 2-1, where we typed *something*. The blinking insertion cursor displays inside the cell so you can see and control where text will appear as you type or paste.

✦ **Returning to in-cell editing:** After you select something other than the cell you're editing, the cell you're editing returns to its normal appearance. To return to in-cell editing, double-click the cell you just edited. Excel displays the insertion cursor in the cell, and you can begin editing the cell's contents.

✦ **Cell range:** You can select or refer to more than one cell at a time. When more than one cell is selected or referred to at a time, it's called a *cell range*.

- To select a group of cells, drag the mouse cursor across the cells you wish to select. When you release the mouse button, the range of cells becomes highlighted, and you'll notice that the row and column headers have darkened to indicate the selected range.

- Excel uses a colon (:) to indicate a cell range. Type **A1:C5** to indicate a range of cells whose top left position is A1, and the bottom-right position is C5. Cell ranges can be named. See the Name Box entry a little later in this section.

- To select non-contiguous ranges of cells, hold down the ⌘ button as you drag the mouse cursor over cell ranges or select individual cells by clicking them.

✦ **Select all:** Near cell A1 is a diamond-shaped button that selects all the cells of a worksheet at once. This button is handy for applying formatting to all cells at once. (See Figure 2-1.) This is the same as pressing ⌘-A. This way you can apply formatting options to the entire sheet.

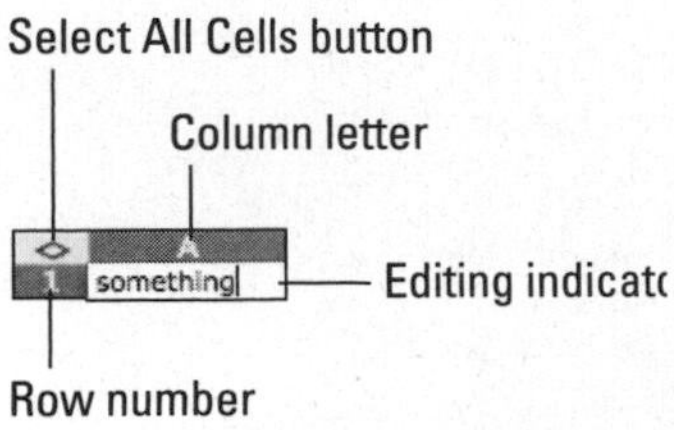

Figure 2-1:
Typing
something
in a cell.

Select All Cells button

Column letter

something

Editing indicato

Row number

Watching a Help video

Excel 2008 has a completely revamped Help system. Help now features free online training courses and movies. Check out the video *Getting Started with Excel 2008*, starring Kurt from MacBU. It's a general overview of the Excel interface. Grab the popcorn, sit back, and enjoy! It's short, so you won't need much popcorn.

Follow these steps to play the movie:

1. **Click the Help button on Excel's Standard toolbar.**

   The Excel Help dialog appears.

2. **In the Search field, type** get started **and press Return or Enter.**

   The search results open in a drawer with the Search tab selected.

3. **Double-click the Get Started with Excel 2008 topic.**

   The topic's introductory page displays in the Excel Help dialog.

4. **Click the big, amber Start Video button.**

   The movie plays in the Excel Help browser window.

5. **(Optional) Click Feedback.**

   Rate the video by taking a brief survey.

6. **Click the red Close button to dismiss Excel Help.**

Book III
Chapter 2

Operating Inside
the Workbook

✦ **Editing in the Formula Bar:** This is an alternative to in-cell editing. Before you can edit in the Formula Bar, you must turn it on. To toggle the display of the Formula Bar, in Excel, choose View⇨Formula Bar and then look at the top of the screen. The wide, skinny bar that you can see in Figure 2-2 is the Formula Bar, where you can type instead of typing in the cell. Sometimes typing in the Formula Bar is better because it doesn't cover up other cells while you type in it, and because it can show more of the cell contents at once.

✦ **Name box:** The Name box is part of the Formula Bar (see the preceding bullet). Name box can do the following:

  • *Automatically display:* The Name box displays the name or address of the currently selected cell, range of cells, or object that is currently selected. See Figure 2-2, where the selected cell is A1.

  • *Select a cell or a range of cells:* For example, type **A1:C5** in the Name box and then press Return or Enter to select the range of cells from cell A1 through C5.

- *Name the current selection:* Select a range of cells or an object. To give the selection a name, type a name into the Name box and then press Return or Enter. Don't use spaces or special characters in the name.

- *Select a named range or object:* The Name box can be used to select any object. Type the name of an existing object in the Name box and then press Return or Enter to select the object.

Figure 2-2: Editing in the Formula Bar.

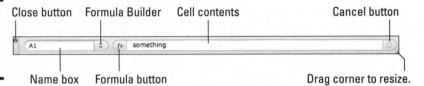

Close button   Formula Builder   Cell contents   Cancel button

Name box   Formula button   Drag corner to resize.

Clearing a cell

Want to get rid of something inside a cell? All you have to do is click that cell and press the Delete key.

That's handy for a single cell, but if you select a range of cells and press the Delete key, only the contents of the first cell in the range will be deleted. The following section explains how to clear a range of cells.

Clearing many cells at once

To clear a range of cells, select the range of cells and then hold down the ⌘ key down while you press the Delete key.

Using the Delete key method deletes cell formatting and comments along with cell contents. You can clear just formats, contents, or comments by using this method:

1. **Select the cell range you wish to clear.**

Select by dragging the mouse or entering the name of the cell range into the Name box.

2. **Choose Edit⇨Clear. From the submenu, choose one of the following:**

- *All:* Clears contents, formats, and contents.

- *Formats:* Clears formats without disturbing contents or comments.

- *Contents:* Clears contents without disturbing formats or comments.

- *Comments:* Clears comments without disturbing contents or formats.

Telling Excel you're done

Excel doesn't know when you're done typing in a cell unless you take specific action to let Excel know you're no longer working with a cell. When you're done editing in a cell or the Formula Bar, take any of the following actions to let Excel know you've finished:

- ✔ Press Return or Enter.
- ✔ Press an arrow key.
- ✔ Press the Tab key.
- ✔ Click a different cell.

Making sense of cursors

Excel is always trying to tell you what it can do. When you're in a worksheet, the cursor changes as you move the mouse around. The way the cursor looks reveals what you can do:

- ✦ **Selection cursor:** This is the dark border that surrounds a cell or range of cells to indicate what's selected, as illustrated by cell B1 in Figure 2-3, which shows the selection cursor around the cell containing *January.*

  - Press Return, Enter, Tab, or an arrow key to move the selection cursor from one cell to another.

  - Click a cell using the mouse to set the selection cursor to individual cells.

  - Drag over cells with the mouse to select a range of cells and set the selection cursor to that range.

- ✦ **Mouse cursor:** Usually this is an open cross, but it can be changed. Here are the various mouse cursors:

- ✦ **Open cross:** This is the mouse cursor you see most of the time in Excel. When you see the open cross, Excel is tired of staring at you and expects you to do something.

- ✦ **Hand:** When you see the hand, you can hold down the mouse button and drag a cell or cell range from its current location to any other location on the worksheet.

Figure 2-3:
Using a
range of
data.

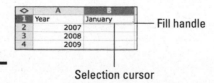

Fill handle

Selection cursor

✦ **Dark arrow:** This arrow cursor appears only if the mouse pointer moves over a column or a row indicator. Although pointing in itself is bad manners, Excel is only trying to be helpful in this case. The arrow points down when the mouse pointer is in a column indicator, or points to the right when the mouse pointer is over a row indicator (see Figure 2-4).

- Click when this arrow is visible to select the entire row(s) or column(s).

- Drag when this arrow is visible to select multiple rows or columns.

✦ **Double arrow:** The double arrow appears when the mouse pointer is over the divider between cells, between rows, and in various windows to let you know you can move pane dividers and other dividers. When you see this cursor, hold down the mouse button and drag the divider to resize, or double-click the mouse to automatically size the row or column.

Undo! If you do something by mistake, press ⌘-Z immediately!

Figure 2-4:
Selecting
two entire
rows.

◇	A	B
1	Year	January
2	2008	
3	2007	
4	2009	

✦ **Solid cross:** To see this cursor, the mouse pointer has to be positioned over the lower-right corner of the cell selection indicator, or the *fill handle*. To drag the fill handle, hold down the mouse button when you see the solid cross and then drag to copy the selection across or down. See the following section for details about special fill handle capabilities.

Dragging a Series of Text, Numbers, or Dates

Excel is pretty smart. Excel can automatically fill in a series of either numbers or dates, and can even make intelligent guesses about a series of numbers.

Filling in a series

We use an example to show how Excel can fill in a range of cells for you. Follow along on your computer to watch what happens:

1. **With Excel open, start with a blank, standard worksheet.**

2. **Fill in the worksheet.**

For this example, fill in your worksheet to match what you see in Figure 2-3 earlier in this chapter.

3. Click cell B2.

The selection cursor appears.

4. Position the mouse cursor over the lower-right corner of the selected cell (the fill handle) so that it becomes the solid cross cursor.

5. Drag the fill handle to the right and watch Excel do some magic.

As you drag across the cells, you see the ToolTip note each month in the series (compare with Figure 2-5).

Release the mouse a few cells over, and Excel types all the months for you! Your screen looks like Figure 2-5. Additionally, when you let go, a little widget appears. Resist the urge to click the widget! If you're curious about what's in the widget, look at Figure 2-5 and read the sidebar, "Wondering about widgets," but don't choose any options from the widget right now.

Month series fills in   Click the widget.

Figure 2-5:
Auto-
matically
filling in a
series.

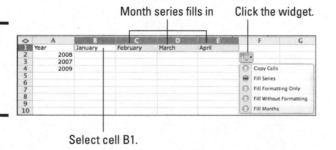

Select cell B1.

Having Excel figure out a pattern

Excel can do more than fill in a series of either numbers or dates. Excel can make intelligent guesses about a series of numbers. Follow these steps to see how Excel deduces what number values to fill in (see Figure 2-6):

1. Enter 1 in cell B2 and enter 3 in cell C2.

Typing in a cell dismisses the widget. Notice that 1 and 3 are odd numbers in sequence in adjoining cells.

2. Select B2:C2.

The trick here is to select both cells at once (drag over both cells) so that Excel notes the first two values of the series.

3. Without clicking anything else, grab the solid fill handle's cross cursor and drag it to the right.

Excel deduces from the selected cells that you want a series of odd numbers and then fills in the series.

**Book III
Chapter 2**

**Operating Inside
the Workbook**

Figure 2-6:
Making
a series
of odd
numbers.

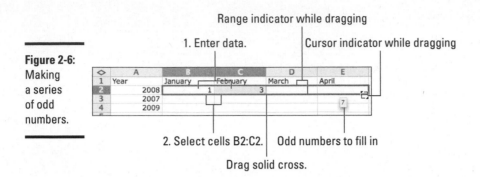

Range indicator while dragging

1. Enter data.

Cursor indicator while dragging

2. Select cells B2:C2. | Odd numbers to fill in

Drag solid cross.

Excel can figure out most series of numbers from just two or three starting numbers. Series can be in rows, such as the example we use, or in columns.

Using the Custom Lists feature

The Custom Lists feature is about making lists that Excel can use when filling in series by dragging a selected cell's fill handle (the solid crosshair cursor), which results in an automatic series fill. Custom Lists feature isn't related to the similarly named List Manager feature or the list worksheet type, which we discuss elsewhere in this book.

Not only can Excel figure out number and date series on its own; you can teach Excel to figure out just about any series. For example, say you frequently make reports that have a series of reoccurring days.

You have two easy ways to make a new series with Custom Lists:

✦ Create a custom list from scratch.

✦ Create a custom list from an existing list in a workbook.

To create a custom list from scratch:

1. **Choose Excel⇨Preferences.**

Excel Preferences displays.

2. **In the Formulas and Lists section, click Custom Lists.**

The Custom Lists preferences pane, as shown in Figure 2-7, displays. You see a handful of built-in series. You can't change these.

3. **Select NEW LIST in the Custom Lists list.**

4. **In the List Entries list, type the series entries in order.**

Press Return (*not* Enter) after each entry.

Existing lists

Make a new list.   View or edit lists.   Add or delete lists.

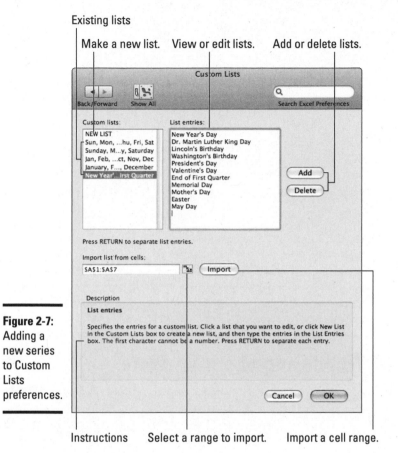

Figure 2-7: Adding a new series to Custom Lists preferences.

Instructions   Select a range to import.   Import a cell range.

5. **Click the Add button when the list is complete.**

    Your series is added to the Custom Lists list.

If you have a worksheet with a series in a range of cells that you want to add, follow these steps to add the series to Custom Lists:

1. **In the Custom Lists window (see the preceding steps), click the Import button next to Import List from Cells.**

    Custom Lists preferences pane shrinks so you can see your worksheet. The cursor changes to a plus (+) sign.

2. **Select the cell range that contains the list.**

    To do so, drag over the cells that contain the series you wish to add to the Custom Lists preferences. A dotted line indicates the selected cell range, and Excel automatically types the selected range into Custom Lists preferences pane.

3. **Press Escape or Return when you're done selecting.**

Preferences displays. Import List from Cells displays the range you selected.

4. **Click the Import button.**

The selected series appears under List Entries.

5. **Click the Add button.**

The selected series is added to Custom Lists list.

Entering in General Format

In some respects, Excel is a bit like a word processor. You can type text into a cell and format the text in much the same way as a word processor, but Excel has no concept of a sentence or paragraph. The default format for cells is *General* format. For that reason, it's important to know how Excel automatically formats what you enter into a cell. In Chapter 3 of this minibook, we describe how to change the General format to other formats.

Wondering about widgets

Occasionally Office displays little lightning-bolt widgets to offer you alternatives to the default behavior. They appear whenever Office thinks it got it right, but knows that there is an alternative behavior that you might prefer over the default behavior. You see a widget in Figure 2-5. Although Excel got it right (we wanted the default, which is Fill Series). We could have chosen an option from the pop-up menu:

- **Copy Cells:** Copies contents and formatting. This doesn't fill in the series.

- **Fill Series:** This is the default behavior and is happens in the example. Formatting is copied, and the series is filled.

- **Fill Formatting Only:** Copies just the formatting, not the contents. This doesn't fill in the series with cell content.

- **Fill Without Formatting:** Copies the selected cell's contents, not the formatting. This fills in the series without copying the formatting.

- **Fill Months:** Another way to perform Fill Series. Excel figured out we were copying months and offers it as a specific option in this case. You see this option only if you start copying the series with a month.

To dismiss a widget, click a cell away from the series and type a character.

In General format, Excel treats what you type in specific ways. Table 2-1 lists some of the common ways Excel interprets what you enter into a cell.

Table 2-1	Knowing What Excel Thinks of What You Type	
Enter This	*Excel Displays*	*Comment*
A	A	Any cell that starts with a letter of the alphabet is treated entirely as text.
1	1	Any cell that has a number is treated as the value of that number, in this case +1. The + sign for positive numbers is optional.
–1	–1	Negative numbers display the minus sign.
'15	15	When a single quotation mark starts a cell, Excel displays the characters that follow and treats them as text, not values.
$\frac{1}{2}$	2–Jan. or February 2nd, depending where in the world you live	Any / combination that could be a date is interpreted as a date and is treated as the value of that date. If a year isn't specified, the current year is assumed.
January 1	1–Jan	Any valid date is treated as the value of that date. If a year isn't specified, the current year is assumed.
.5	.5	This is the mathematical value for one-half, or five tenths.
0 $\frac{1}{2}$	$\frac{1}{2}$	Type a zero and a space before typing a fraction to let Excel know you want the mathematical fraction. This cell's mathematical value is .5.
12 o'clock	12 o'clock	Most combinations of letters and text are treated as text.
=A1	The value of cell A1	This is a *reference,* in this case to cell A1.
=SUM(A2:A5)	The mathematical sum of the values of cells in the range A2 through A5	This is a *cell formula.* If a cell begins with an equal sign, Excel assumes you want either a reference or a formula.

**Book III
Chapter 2**

**Operating Inside
the Workbook**

Making Cell Formulas

Cell formulas are equations that perform calculations or logical operations. Every cell formula starts with the = sign. An *argument* appears after the equals sign; for example, =1+1. You can enter a formula on your own, or you can use Formula Builder, which helps you build formulas using a step-by-step structured wizard-like method. We cover both ways to enter a formula in the following sections.

These words have special meaning in Excel:

✦ **Function:** A function is a specific calculation, such as SUM, MULTIPLY, or COSINE. A function can be a logical operator, such as IF. Functions are represented in uppercase in Excel documentation.

✦ **Formula:** These are the instructions that tell Excel what you want to calculate. Formulas start with the equals = sign and include functions that have arguments. A formula entered in a cell is a *cell formula*.

✦ **Argument:** An argument is a variable in a calculation or logical operation. This is the kind of argument you may remember from math class; not the kind of argument you have when someone else is being stupid.

✦ **Syntax:** These are rules that explain what should be entered and the order in which to enter arguments in a cell formula.

Entering formulas

If you're new to Excel, don't feel bad if what you type doesn't produce the expected result at first. Chances are a stray character or missing character got mixed in. Be sure to refer to the earlier section about entering formulas in General format, as chances are the clue you need about what went wrong is in Table 2-1.

For the examples in this chapter, be sure the Formula Bar is visible. Toggle the Formula Bar on from Excel's View menu and choose Formula Bar. To open a standard, blank worksheet, click the + Sheet Tab button at the bottom of the window to display a fresh worksheet. If Excel isn't open, click the Excel Dock icon to open Excel to a blank standard worksheet.

Typing a formula manually

We start with a very easy example to show you the structure of a formula and that Excel treats numbers as values within a formula:

1. **Start with a blank worksheet.**

2. **Type** =1+1 **and then press Return, Enter, Tab, or an arrow key to exit the cell.**

   Excel displays the value of the formula in cell A1 and displays the formula in the Formula Bar.

The cell's appearance changes while you type. Observe and see how the cell appears while you type and after you exit the cell. You can use the value represented in cells in formulas.

Here's another example. This time we use values from cells in the worksheet instead of using numbers in the formula. This gives you experience figuring out various ways to refer to cells and cell ranges in formulasL

1. **Start with a blank worksheet.**

2. **Type** 1 **into cells A1 and B1.**

   The value of 1 displays in cells A1 and B1, as shown in Figure 2-8.

3. **In cell C1, type** =A1+B1.

   Your screen looks exactly like Figure 2-8. Excel color-codes the cell references within your formula to match the referenced cells A1 and B1, which are now highlighted to match the color code in the formula. Your formula now displays in the Formula Bar.

4. **Press Return, Enter, Tab, or an arrow key to exit the cell.**

   Excel displays the value of the formula in cell A1 and displays the formula in the Formula Bar.

**Book III
Chapter 2**

Operating Inside
the Workbook

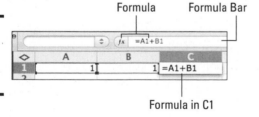

Formula   Formula Bar

Figure 2-8:
Making a
simple cell
formula.

Formula in C1

Letting Excel type a formula for you

Here's an example that shows you how to let Excel type for you so you're less likely to make a typing mistake in a formula:

1. **Start with a blank worksheet.**

2. **Type** 1 **into cells A1 and B1.**

   The value of 1 displays in cells A1 and B1, as shown in Figure 2-8.

3. **In cell C1, type the equals sign (=), click cell A1, type the plus sign (+), and then click cell B1.**

   After you type the equals sign and move the mouse, you notice the cursor changes. A cell selection indicator moves with the mouse. When you put the selection indicator over cell A1, clicking the mouse tells

Excel you want to use the value of cell A1 in the formula and types it for you. You can do the same with cell B1. Again your screen looks identical to Figure 2-8.

4. Press Return, Enter, Tab, or an arrow key to exit the cell.

Excel displays the value of the formula in cell A1 and displays the formula in the Formula Bar.

You're allowed to select ranges of cells, which is a great help when working with complicated formulas.

Entering a function manually

This example shows how to use a built-in cell function within your formula. You use the SUM worksheet function to add the values of two cells.

1. Start with a blank worksheet.

2. Type 1 into cells A1 and B1.

The value of 1 displays in cells A1 and B1, as shown in Figure 2-8.

3. In cell C1, type = SUM(A1:B1).

For the time being, ignore the pop-up menu (we discuss that in the following section). Excel displays the value of the calculation in cell C1 and the formula in the Formula Bar.

4. Press Return, Enter, Tab, or an arrow key to exit the cell.

Excel displays the value of the formula in cell A1 and displays the formula containing the SUM function in the Formula Bar.

In this example, SUM is the function, and the cell range A1:B1 is the argument. The argument of a function is placed in parentheses. Entering a function and its arguments manually may be useful when you refer to cells that are widely dispersed on a worksheet.

Letting Excel type functions and arguments

Excel has hundreds of built-in functions that you can use in cell formulas. While you type a function in a cell formula, a pop-up list appears. In the following example, we use Excel's built-in SUM function. See Figure 2-9 for this sequence.

1. Start with a blank worksheet.

2. Type 1 into cells A1 and B1.

The value of 1 displays in cells A1 and B1, as shown in Figure 2-8.

3. **In cell C1, type** =S.

Wow! While you type, a pop-up menu showing all worksheet functions beginning with the letter S displays. Look at all the functions that start with the letter S! Right now, you're interested in the SUM function.

4. **Choose SUM from within all those S options in the pop-up menu but don't type anything.**

Excel displays =SUM(|) with the vertical bar indicating the insertion cursor is ready to fill in the argument.

Figure 2-9:
Letting
Excel do the
typing.

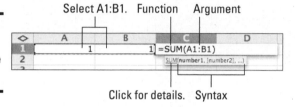

Select A1:B1.   Function   Argument

Click for details.   Syntax

5. **Drag over the range A1:B1.**

Excel enters the cell range for you and you don't have to worry about making a typing mistake (see Figure 2-9). Is that neat or what?

(Optional) You can manually type the argument.

6. **Press Return, Enter, Tab, or an arrow key to exit the cell.**

Excel displays the value of the formula in cell A1 and displays the formula containing the SUM function in the Formula Bar.

When you enter a cell formula that includes a function, Excel shows you the function's name and its syntax, as shown in Figure 2-9. The function's name is blue and is underlined like a hyperlink. That's because it's a link to the Help topic for that particular function. Each function is thoroughly documented with complete sample data and examples so that you can easily see how to use it. (See Figure 2-10.)

Using Formula Builder

Formula Builder is a tool in Toolbox designed to help you build cell formulas by walking you through your formula and its functions. Formula Builder enables you to browse all of Excel's functions. To activate Formula Builder:

1. **Click in an empty cell.**

Formula Builder puts your finished formula into the cell you choose.

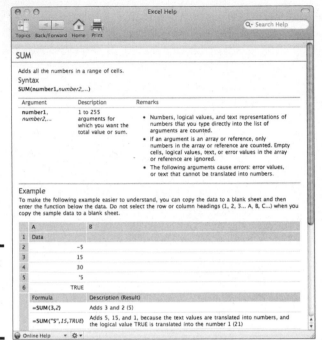

Figure 2-10:
Getting
the details
about a
function.

2. Click the Formula Builder button (as shown in the margin) on the Formula Bar.

Formula Builder opens in Toolbox (see Figure 2-11).

3. In Formula Builder, enter a search term in the search field, as shown in Figure 2-11.

You can enter the name of a function if you already know it. Otherwise, enter a term you think might be a function. Formula Builder displays the results of your search. Figure 2-11 shows the results of searching for count.

4. Click a function to select it in the search results.

You can read about the function in the Description area. If you want to read more, click the More Help on This Function link. Read the descriptions until you find the function you need. You can enter a different search term if the function you were looking for didn't turn up in the search results. If you can't find the proper function, try searching Excel Help. If that doesn't work, see Book I, Chapter 7 for additional suggestions.

5. Double-click a function in the search results list to choose it for your formula.

The function is added to your worksheet with the insertion cursor ready for your input from Formula Builder. Formula Builder displays empty fields for arguments specific to the function you selected.

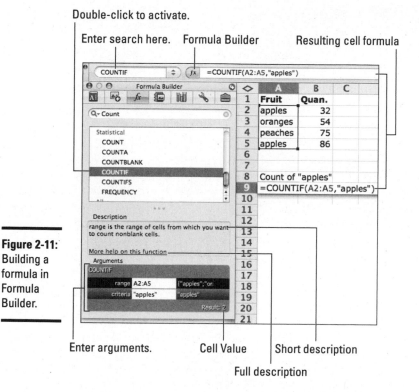

Figure 2-11:
Building a
formula in
Formula
Builder.

Double-click to activate.

Enter search here.   Formula Builder   Resulting cell formula

Enter arguments.   Cell Value   Short description

Full description

6. **Click into an argument field in Formula Builder.**

The insertion cursor blinks in the empty argument field.

7. **Do one of the following to satisfy an argument:**

- *Type text or values to satisfy the argument.*

- *Click a cell to satisfy the argument.*

- *Drag a range of cells to satisfy the argument.*

  Doing any of these methods results in the display of your argument's
  value or formula in Formula Builder. More than one argument may
  be needed for your calculation. Click More Help on This Function
  if you need specific information about the function you've chosen,
  including details about required arguments or how your function calculates its result. Some functions let you add and remove arguments
  by clicking plus or minus sign buttons to the right of argument fields.
  Formula Builder displays the current value of your function based
  upon the arguments you have provided. Don't press Return or Enter
  until you've finished satisfying all arguments unless you want to quit
  Formula Builder.

8. **After satisfying the arguments, press Return or Enter.**

The finished formula appears in the Formula Bar. The cell that you selected in Step 1 displays the formula's value or result. Double-click the cell to perform manual in-cell editing if needed, or refine your formula in the Formula Bar.

Knowing When to Be Absolute, Relatively Speaking

Usually, you simply press ⌘-C or choose Edit⇨Copy to copy things. Likewise, you press ⌘-V or choose Edit⇨Paste to paste. Copying and pasting cells and cell ranges works differently from text and other objects, so they can be a little bit puzzling if you don't know the secret about *relative* versus *absolute* references.

Using a relative reference

Say you want to use the value of cell A1 in a formula, so you type **=A1** in your formula to use the value of cell A1 and away you go. Your formula works, and all seems well.

What Excel is actually thinking when you type **=A1** is that you want to use the value of the cell that's a certain number of rows and columns away from the cell in which you're typing your formula. Your formula works as expected in its original location, but if you copy the cell containing your formula and then paste that cell somewhere else, the formula in the pasted cell no longer refers to the value in cell A1. Instead, it refers to the cell in the relative location (the same number of rows and columns away from the copied cell). This concept of relativity is why this reference style is a *relative* reference.

Here's a fun little example with a relative reference. See Figure 2-12 while you follow these steps:

1. **Click in a cell, any cell.**

For this example, we clicked in cell A1.

2. **Type something in the cell.**

For this example, we typed **Hi**.

3. **Click in any other cell.**

For this example, we clicked in cell B2.

4. **In the cell you chose in Step 3, type a formula to equal what's in the cell from Step 1 and then press Return or Enter.**

For example, assume you typed **Hi** in cell A1 in Step 2. In this new cell, you'd type =**A1**. Figure 2-11 shows =A1.

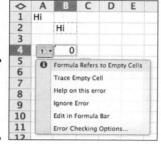

Figure 2-12:
Copying
a relative
reference.

5. **Select the cell that you just typed in, and then press ⌘-C.**

This copies the cell you just put the formula into.

6. **Click in any unused cell and choose Edit⇨Paste or press ⌘-V.**

Notice that the pasted cell doesn't show the value of cell A1. In this example, the pasted cell refers to A3 (double-click the cell to see the cell formula), which is one row up and one row over from the pasted cell. That's because we copied cell B2, which refers to A1, which is one row up and one row over from B2.

Excel noticed that we were referring to an empty cell, and put a little widget next to where we pasted to make sure that's what we wanted to do. We can click Ignore Error because we referred to an empty for demonstration purposes. If you see this warning when working for real, take a close look at your pasted formula to make sure it works as expected.

Using an absolute reference

An *absolute* reference always uses the exact cell referred to in the formula. You do this by adding a dollar sign ($) to the row, the column, or both in a formula. If you want to always refer to the value in cell A1, type =**$A$1**. A good way to remember how to make an absolute reference is to think of the dollar sign ($) as *always*. When you read =$A$1, think "equals always column A, always row 1."

In rare circumstances, you might need an absolute value reference to either a row or a column. If you want to refer to the value in column using an absolute reference A but use a relative reference for rows, type =$A1.

Comparing relative and absolute references

Follow these steps to create an absolute reference and compare how copying an absolute reference works versus copying a relative reference. See Figure 2-13.

1. **Start with a blank worksheet.**

2. **Enter the numbers exactly as shown in Figure 2-11.**

   - *In row 1, type* 1 7 8 9 10.

   - *In column A, type* 1 2 3 4 5 6.

   Make sure your values match the values shown in row A1:E1 and column A1:A6 in Figure 2-13.

3. **In cell C3, type the formula** =A1.

   As you type, cell A1 lights up to let you know you typed correctly. Notice this is a relative reference because it doesn't have any dollar signs in the formula.

4. **Press Return, Enter, Tab, or an arrow key to exit the cell.**

5. **In cell E5 type the formula** =$A$1.

   As you type, cell A1 lights up to let you know you typed correctly. Notice this is an absolute reference because it has dollar signs in the formula.

6. **Press Return, Enter, Tab, or an arrow key to exit the cell.**

7. **Drag the fill handle of cell C3 to the right to cell G3 and then release the mouse.**

   The filled-in values match Figure 2-13. Ignore the widget.

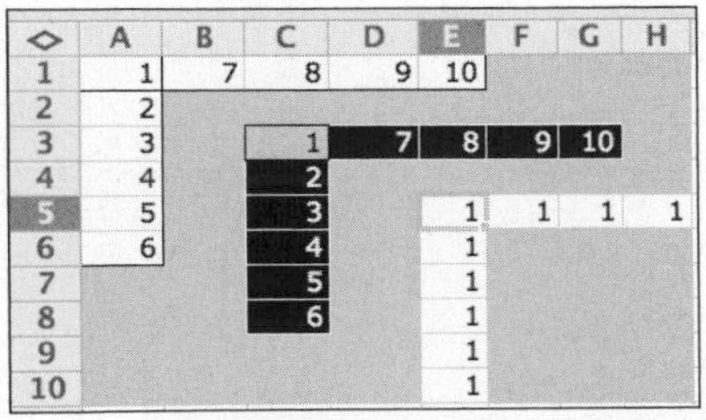

Figure 2-13:
Comparing
relative and
absolute
references.

8. **Drag the fill handle of cell C3 down to cell A6 and then release the mouse.**

   The filled-in values match Figure 2-13. Ignore the widget.

9. **Drag the fill-copy handle of cell E5 to the right to cell H5.**

   The filled-in values match Figure 2-13. Ignore the widget.

10. **Drag the fill-copy handle of cell E5 down to cell E10.**

    The filled-in values match Figure 2-13. Ignore the widget.

The point of this exercise is so that you can see what happens when you copy a relative reference to the result when you copy an absolute reference:

✦ **Relative reference:** In this case, C3 uses a relative reference, so when you fill the range, the reference changes and you get a nice replication of the original data.

✦ **Absolute reference:** Cell E5 uses an *absolute* reference, so you always get the value of cell A1.

Chapter 3: Formatting and Collaborating in Excel

In This Chapter

✔ **Taking out your formatting tools**

✔ **Coloring and shading cells for emphasis**

✔ **Figuring out dates and times**

✔ **Formatting with conditions**

✔ **Sharing your workbooks**

✔ **Protecting the history of changes**

*I*f you hold this book for five minutes in your hands each day, Excel automatically starts behaving. Jokes aside, we start this chapter by pointing out some interesting formatting options, including how to control borders, shading, and patterns. We explain the mysteries behind Excel's date and time calculations, and how Excel can apply formatting for you based on a cell's contents. Lastly, we cover Excel's unique file-sharing capabilities.

Preparing to Format

The Formatting Palette is usually the quickest way to format things in Excel (see Figure 3-1). If the Formatting Palette isn't visible, click the Toolbox button on Excel's Standard toolbar and then click the Formatting Palette button on Toolbox's small toolbar. We recommend that you leave the Formatting Palette open while you go through this chapter.

Alternatively, dialogs offer more formatting options. You can display dialogs by right-clicking or Control-clicking the interface or objects, choosing Format from the resulting pop-up menu, and selecting an appropriate formatting option from the Format dialog. You can access some dialogs by clicking buttons on the Formatting Palette.

Before you can format anything, you must first select it. In general, to select something, click it. The interface responds by changing the display to indicate your selection, usually by changing the selection's border or outline.

Formatting Cells

One of the things you might find do frequently is changing the way cells look, and you do this with the Formatting Palette. Refer to Figure 3-1 while we discuss the organization of the Formatting Palette in the following sections.

Adjusting fonts

The Font section of the Formatting Palette applies formats to fonts. When an entire cell is selected, the formatting is applied to all text within the cell. You can select individual words or letters in a cell or in the Formula Bar, and then apply formatting to only your selection. You can select text in SmartArt, WordArt, and charts to which you want to apply formatting. You can specify font name, size, and color; as well as appearance characteristics, such as boldface, superscript, subscript, and italics.

Here are some of the features you can modify:

✦ **Name:** This is a WYSIWYG (what you see is what you get) pop-up menu — simply select the font that you want from all the fonts offered. The first item in the list, Font Collections, is new in Excel 2008. Select this item to make a sublist appear, where you can select from categories including fonts compatible with Office for Windows and PDF.

✦ **Size:** Click Size to access the pop-up menu. In this menu, you can select a size from a list, type a point value, or (new for Excel 2008) drag the slider control, which is our personal favorite.

✦ **Superscript and Subscript:** Select an individual character and then click one of these two buttons to apply the format.

Applying number and text formats

General format is the default cell format. In Chapter 2 of this minibook, we provide a table that explains how General format treats characters when you enter them. Briefly, the General format applies formatting by using these simple rules:

✦ A cell that contains any text characters is formatted as text.

✦ A cell containing numbers only is formatted as a number or date.

✦ A cell that begins with an equals sign (=) is a formula.

You're allowed to override General format and apply any format that you want to a cell. If you apply text format to a cell that was formatted as a number or date, you can no longer use the number value or date in formula calculations.

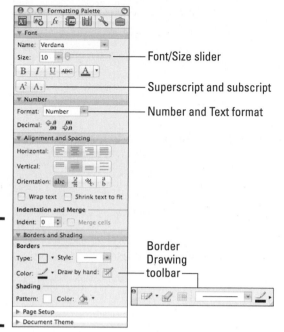

Font/Size slider

Superscript and subscript

Number and Text format

Figure 3-1:
Formatting
cells
with the
Formatting
Palette.

Border
Drawing
toolbar

The Number section of the Formatting Palette offers two options:

✦ **Format:** Click in the Format field. From the resulting pop-up menu,
select a format to apply to your cell's content. You can also scroll to the
bottom of the menu and select Customize to display the Format Cells
dialog's Number tab, as shown in Figure 3-2.

The Format Cells Number tab offers formatting options in a Category
list, as shown in Figure 3-2. Select Custom to create your own formats
by using formatting codes. You can use the existing codes shown in the
dialog as a guide.

You can find a complete list of formatting code options with examples in
Excel Help under the Number Format Codes topic.

✦ **Decimal:** Click the Decimal buttons to move the decimal point in a cell
formatted as a number either left or right.

We have a step-by-step example using Date custom formatting codes, in the
section, "Working with Dates and Times," later in this chapter.

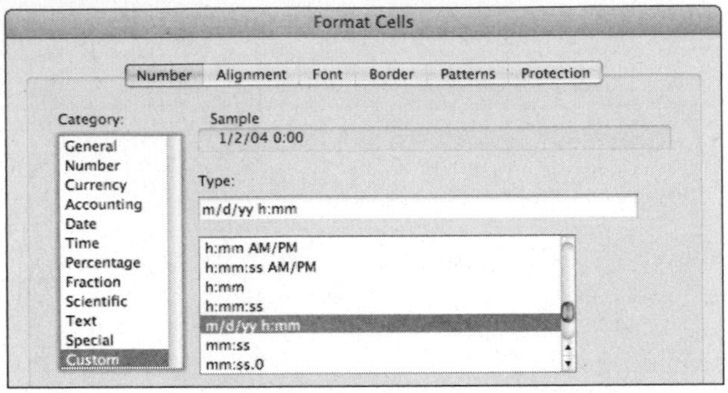

Figure 3-2:
Designing a
custom cell
format.

Fitting and positioning content

Almost like in a word processor, you can align and position cell contents:

✦ **Horizontal:** Select from left, center, right, or full justification in a cell.

✦ **Vertical:** Select top, center, bottom, or distributed evenly.

✦ **Orientation:** Tip and turn cell contents.

✦ **Wrap Text:** Allow text to wrap within a cell.

✦ **Shrink Text to Fit:** Reduce the size of the text so that it fits in the cell.

✦ **Indent:** Use the pop-up menu or type a value to indent text from the left border of a cell.

✦ **Merge Cells:** Select two or more cells, and then click this check box to merge the selection into a single cell. You retain only the content of the upper-left cell. Select an already merged cell and then deselect this check box to unmerge the merged cell.

Coloring cells and borders

You can change the format of the type, style, color, and weight of cell borders. You can fill cells with shading, colors, and patterns. Use these Formatting Palette tools:

✦ **Type:** Select Type to display a toolbar that lets you select from an assortment of line types, such as single or double lines, thick or thin, as well as which sides of the cell should have a border.

✦ **Style:** Select Style to display a toolbar from which you can select a continuous or dashed border style.

✦ **Border Color:** Choose Color to Display Excel's color picker (which we explain in the section, "Coloring and Shading," later in this chapter). Select a color that you want to apply to your border.

✦ **Draw by Hand:** Select Draw by Hand to display the Border Drawing toolbar, which lets you use the mouse to apply cell borders to the grid.

✦ **Pattern:** Select Pattern to display Excel's pattern palette.

✦ **Shading Color:** Select Shading Color to display Excel's color toolbar. Select a color with which you want to fill the cell.

Two additional formatting options that we want to mention aren't on the Formatting Palette:

✦ **Conditional formatting:** You can format cells so that the formatting changes when certain conditions are met. See the section, "Formatting Based on Conditions," later in this chapter.

✦ **Cell overlap:** When you type in one cell and then into the cell immediately to the right, the text in the second cell may cover the text in the first cell. This is normal. Adjust the column width and row heights by using the double arrow cursor, as described in Chapter 2 of this minibook. Sometimes, you can use Wrap Text or Shrink Text to Fit (both discussed in the preceding section) if you want to solve overlap problems.

Tilting your text

Quite often, people have more columns than can fit on a single screen (or page, if you want to print). Of course, you could get one or two large monitors, or invest in a printer that can output poster-size sheets.

Or you could make friends with the Formatting Palette, which thoughtfully allows you to click the Fit To button. But selecting that option causes everything to scale, which sometimes makes the stuff inside the cell too small.

In Figure 3-3, we tilted the column headers, which were much larger than the data, by clicking Fit To. We got an entire year's worth of quotas into a single sheet, without making the print too small to read. Of course, you can tilt the column headers even more by following these steps:

1. Select the cells you want to format.

2. Choose Format⇨Cells.

The Format Cells dialog opens, as shown in Figure 3-4.

Figure 3-3:
Tilting text
to make
room.

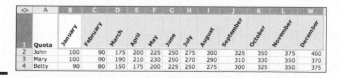

Precision alignment   Drag this line.

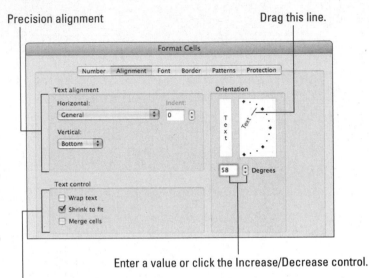

Figure 3-4:
Orienting
text angles.

Enter a value or click the Increase/Decrease control.

These options are also on the Formatting Palette.

3. Click the Alignment tab.

This tab's orientation controls enable you to tilt text to any angle. In Figure 3-4, we set the angle to 58 degrees.

4. Drag the line in the Orientation area until you get the best angle.

If you don't want to drag text to tilt it, you can type a degree angle into the field or click the Increase/Decrease control for degree angles.

Building borders

The Formatting Palette has very handy presets for borders, but you can find even more choices in the Format Cells dialog, which you can display by choosing Format⇨Cells and then selecting the Border tab. See Figure 3-5. The Format Cells dialog offers these options:

✦ **Color:** Select a color for your border from Excel's color picker.

✦ **Style:** Select a solid, dashed, thick, thin, or double-style border.

✦ **Presets:** Select one of three border options:

   • *None:* Clears borders from the selected cell or cell range.

   • *Outline:* Applies a border to the selected cell or around the outside border of a range of cells.

   • *Inside:* Applies borders to cells within a selected range, but doesn't put a border around the entire range.

✦ **Border:** Select toggle buttons to turn individual side or diagonal borders on and off.

3. Select a preset or border location. 2. Select a line style.

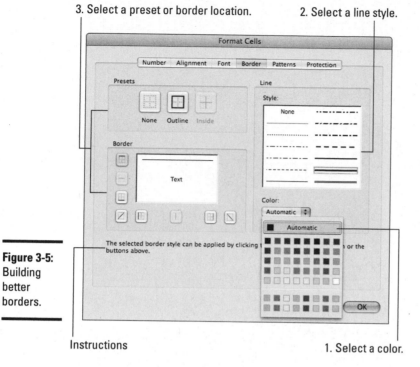

Figure 3-5:
Building
better
borders.

Instructions 1. Select a color.

Coloring and Shading

Just the other day, a rant in a newsgroup (in the "Excel Isn't a Coloring Book" post) resulted from over-the-edge colorful spreadsheets. In light of that discussion, we hope you use colors judiciously. Follow these steps to fill your cells with colors and shadings:

1. **Select the cell or range of cells you want to format.**

2. **Choose Format⇨Cells.**

The Format Cells dialog appears.

3. **Select the Patterns tab, as shown in Figure 3-6.**

4. **Select an option from the Cell Shading area.**

You can find these options:

- *Color:* Click a color from the picker, and you're done.

- *Pattern:* Click the Pattern pop-up menu and select a color from the bottom of the picker. Click the pop-up menu again and select a pattern from the top of the picker.

You can select a solid color, a pattern, or both. If you select a color from the color picker and then apply a pattern, the pattern seems like it's on top of the color you selected.

Solid fill color picker

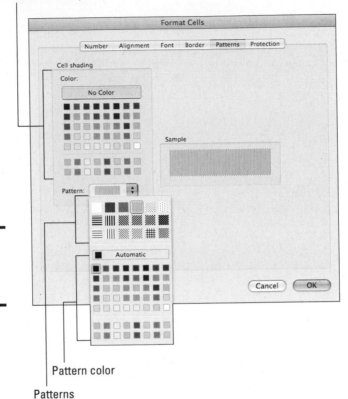

Figure 3-6:
Picking a
particular
pattern.

Pattern color

Patterns

Patterns can be difficult for some printers, so print a test page whenever you use a pattern to see whether it works. Of course, print a test page only when you need to print the final product, but it's good advice to test everything: from playing with the patterns to printing specimen sheets. Of course, we'll be blamed now for everything from wasting time to wasting paper, so do this when you have some extra time and recycled (or scrap) paper!

Changing the color picker

Eagle-eyed readers are probably wondering how they can change those 56 default colors in the color picker. Follow these steps:

1. **Choose Excel⇨Preferences to open the Preferences pane.**

2. **In the Authoring section, click the Color To button to open the Color dialog, as shown in the figure in this sidebar.**

3. **Select a color swatch in the Standard Colors area.**

4. Click the Modify button to open the Mac OS X color picker.

5. Select a new color and then click OK to close the Mac OS X color picker.

6. Repeat these steps for each color you want to change.

Each workbook has its own 56-color picker. You can copy a set of colors from one open workbook to another, but each workbook is limited to 56 different colors. If you want to use the color picker from a different, open workbook, click the Copy Colors From pop-up menu in the Color dialog. Colors that you apply to charts and SmartArt objects are controlled Office themes, which we discuss in detail in Book IV, Chapter 3.

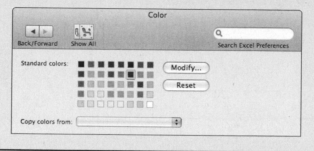

Working with Dates and Times

Excel has fantastic date- and time-calculation capabilities. You need to know just two secrets:

✦ Each day is represented by a whole number, called a *serial number*.

✦ Portions of days are represented by decimal fractions.

To follow along with our examples of how to work with date and time calculations and formats in the following sections, follow these steps to set up your Excel workbook:

1. **Click the plus sign (+) sheet tab to open a new, blank worksheet.**

2. **Choose View➪Normal.**

3. **Fill in row 1, as shown in Figure 3-7.**

Type the following text into the designated cells:

- *A1:* Today
- *B1:* Experiment
- *C1:* Date
- *D1:* Time
- *E1:* Custom Format

4. **In the Formatting Palette's Number category, click Number.**

Apply these formats to these three cells:

- *C2:* Date.
- *D2:* Time
- *E2:* Custom

When you select Custom, the Format Cells dialog, as shown in Figure 3-2 earlier in this chapter, appears.

5. **Specify settings in the Format Cells dialog.**

Use the following settings:

- *Category:* Custom
- *Type:* Enter the formatting code **mmmm d, yyyy h:mm:ss.0**.

6. **Click OK to close the Format Cells dialog.**

Finding today

Some days, you get to work and don't even know what day it is. Excel doesn't have this problem. Using the worksheet you start in the preceding section, follow these steps:

1. **In cell A2, type the cell formula =TODAY( ).**

2. **Press Return, Tab, or an arrow key to exit cell A2.**

Cell A2 displays today's date.

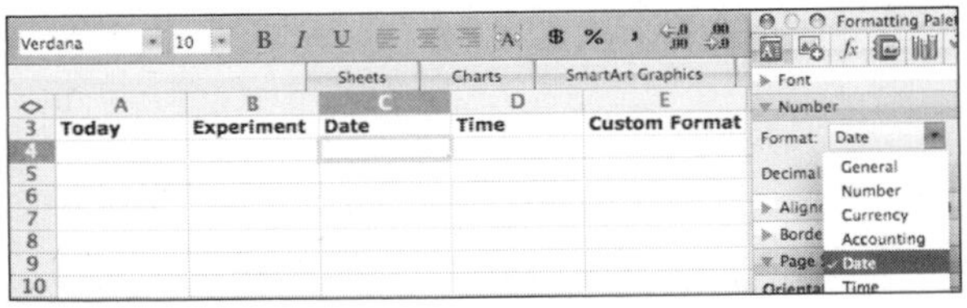

Figure 3-7: Setting up a date and time example.

Getting today's serial number

Each day has its own serial number in Excel parlance. If you follow the steps in the preceding section, you don't see the serial number in cell A2 because the default format is General, and Excel knows your formula represents a date. You can change the format of cell A1 to Number by selecting it in the Format drop-down menu (as shown in Figure 3-7), but instead, you can do something a little bit fancy by following these steps:

1. **Select cell A2.**

2. **Choose Edit➪Copy.**

   Moving dotted lines surround cell A2 to indicate that cell Excel will copy that cell.

3. **Select cell B2.**

4. **Choose Edit➪Paste Special.**

   The Paste Special dialog appears.

5. **Check the Values option in the Paste area and click OK.**

   A number larger than 38,000 appears in cell B2, under the heading Experiment.

Add more cell formulas to the worksheet (see Chapter 2 in this minibook for more on adding formulas):

1. **In cell C2, enter cell formula** =B2.

   C2 displays the date.

2. **In cell D2, enter the same cell formula** =B2.

   D2 displays the date.

3. **In cell E2, enter the cell formula** =B2 **yet again.**

   C2 displays the date.

If the hash marks appear in cell E2 or an error message appears, widen the column or check that you typed everything correctly.

Your workbook looks similar to Figure 3-8. Of course, you may not be reading this in February!

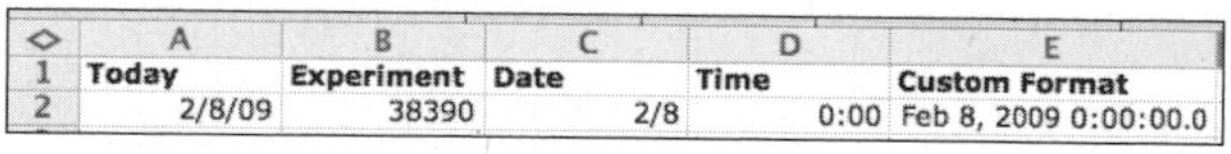

**Book III
Chapter 3**

Formatting and
Collaborating
in Excel

Figure 3-8:
Excel
recognizes
today.

◇	A	B	C	D	E
1	Today	Experiment	Date	Time	Custom Format
2	2/8/09	38390	2/8	0:00	Feb 8, 2009 0:00:00.0

Yesterday, tomorrow, and whenever

In the preceding section, we put the date serial number into cell B2. Now, change that serial number:

✦ **Subtract one from the number shown in cell B2.** Type that number into cell B2. The neighboring cells should display yesterday's date, confirming that you entered the serial number of yesterday's date.

✦ **Add two to the number now showing in cell B2.** Adding 2 to yesterday displays tomorrow's date in the neighboring cells.

The first-day mystery

The beginning of time in Excel is the date with the serial number zero. In Excel for Mac, that date is January 1, 1904; in Excel for Windows, that date is January 1, 1900. The difference is because Excel for Mac came to the market years before Excel for Windows. At the time of its introduction, Excel for Windows needed to compete in the marketplace and had to be compatible with the runaway market leader on the PC, which was Lotus 1-2-3.

Microsoft knew about a leap-year bug in Lotus 1-2-3 and had to make a choice: Be accurate but incompatible with Lotus and risk losing market share, or include the Lotus 1-2-3 error and be compatible. Microsoft chose compatibility over correctness, and the rest is history. Excel eventually eclipsed Lotus 1-2-3 to become the market leader. Excel for Windows still incorrectly computes weekdays from Jan 1, 1900 through March 1, 1900. Excel for Mac avoids the problem by starting with a later date. All subsequent leap years are computed correctly.

You can manually switch the date system in a workbook; choose Excel⇨Preferences⇨Calculation⇨Workbook Options⇨Use the 1904 Date System. Ordinarily, Excel handles the date system for you automatically, regardless of whether a workbook was created in Excel for Mac or Excel for Windows, so don't change this setting unless you need to fix a workbook in which all the dates displayed are off by four years.

Workbook options

☐ Set precision as displayed
☑ Use the 1904 date system
☑ Save external link values

In Excel, to add and subtract any number of days, just add and subtract whole numbers. You're probably wondering how Excel arrived at the serial number of today. To find out, enter **0** in cell B2. The date in the neighboring cells switches to January 1, 1904 — the first day that Excel knows about. Every day in Excel is the number of days after 1/1/1904.

Finding the time of day

Because Excel works with days as whole numbers, you might guess that portions of days are fractions. Well, you'd be right! Continuing with the example from the preceding section, append .5 (one-half day) to the number in B2. The time changes to 12:00 in cell D2. Go ahead and try some different decimals.

Excel gives times that are past noon in military-time format by default. 18:00 is 6:00 p.m. To apply civilian-time format to cell D2, follow these steps:

1. **Type the number** 38717.75 **in cell B2.**

   Cell D2 displays 18:00.

   If cell E2 displays hash marks, widen column E (see Chapter 2 of this minibook for instructions).

2. **Click cell D2 to select it.**

3. In the Number section of the Formatting Palette, select Number.

A pop-up menu appears.

4. Scroll to the bottom of the menu and select Custom.

The Format Cells dialog, as shown in Figure 3-4, appears.

5. In the Category list, select Custom.

6. In the Type field, carefully enter the formatting code h:mm AM/PM.

7. Click OK to close the Format Cells dialog.

Cell D2 displays the time in civilian format, as 6:00 PM.

8. Click the Save button in Excel's Standard toolbar.

The Save As dialog appears.

9. In the Save As field, enter Date and Time example **and then click the Save button.**

You've saved your workbook, so you can refer to it whenever you need to be reminded about dates, times, and their formatting.

10. Click the red Close button to close the workbook.

You can use your saved workbook as a resource from which to copy date and time formulas and formatting. Search for *dates* in Excel Help for more examples that use dates and times.

If you experiment with formatting codes, you may notice some patterns. Table 3-1 has some example formats that you can try.

Table 3-1	Date and Time Format Examples
Format	*Result*
h:mm	18:00
h:mm AM/PM	6:00 PM
h:mm:ss AM/PM	6:00:00 PM
yyyy	2009
yy	09
mmmm	February
mmm	Feb
mm	02
m	2

Formatting Based on Conditions

You can set Excel to change the format of any cell based on the cell's contents. Use these settings when you want a cell's appearance to change when its value changes as the result of a formula or when someone types in a form-style worksheet. The concept behind this feature is simple: Change the appearance of a cell based on the cell's current value or the formula in a cell. Excel for Mac allows up to three different formats for a cell or range of cells (see Figure 3-9).

To apply a custom conditional format, such as the one in Figure 3-9, to a selected cell or range of cells, follow these steps:

1. **Click the plus sign (+) sheet tab to open a new, blank worksheet.**

2. **Choose View⇨Normal.**

3. **Fill in row 1 and column 1.**

Type this text into these cells:

- *A1:* Time of Day

- *A2:* 8am to 11am

- *A3:* 11am to 2pm

- *A4:* 2pm to 4pm

- *A5:* 4pm to Close

- *B1:* Number of Sales

- *B2:* 5

- *B3:* 17

- *B4:* 35

- *B5:* 11

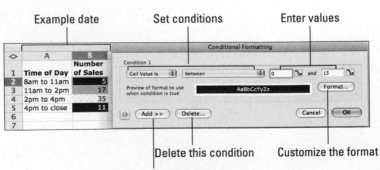

Figure 3-9: Catching reader attention with conditional formats.

Example date   Set conditions   Enter values

Delete this condition   Customize the format

Add another condition

4. **Select the cell range from B2 to B5.**

The selection cursor shades the selected range.

5. **Choose Format⇨Conditional Formatting.**

The Conditional Formatting dialog opens, as shown in Figure 3-9.

6. **From left to right, select values.**

To match the example shown in Figure 3-9, use the following settings for Condition 1 in the Conditional Formatting dialog:

- *Condition Is Popup:* Cell Value Is
- *Operator:* Between
- *Minimum value:* 0
- *Maximum value:* 15

7. **Click the Format button for Condition 1.**

The Format Cells dialog opens.

8. **Select font, border, and pattern formatting options and then click OK.**

You return to the Conditional Formatting dialog.

9. **(Optional) Click the Add button to create any additional conditions.**

10. **Click OK.**

Cells B2 through B5 display the formatting options that you chose.

Sharing Workbooks

Sharing Excel workbooks and keeping track of changes is something that Excel does better than any other application in the Office suite. Excel has three features that make collaborating easy:

✦ **Insert Comment:** This simple feature lets you put comments into comment boxes that float above your worksheet.

✦ **Track Changes:** A much more robust commenting and tracking system. When you have track changes turned on, Excel automatically records changes, who made them, and when they were made.

✦ **Share Workbook:** Two or more users can use the same workbook together in real time. Even Excel for Mac and Excel for Windows users can share a single workbook simultaneously.

Inserting a comment

You can most easily add comments to a worksheet, without disturbing contents or formatting, by using Excel's Insert Comment feature. We show you how to add a comment, edit a comment, delete a comment, and change a comment's appearance.

To insert a comment, follow these steps:

1. **Select a cell and choose Insert⇨Comment.**

A text box opens, displaying your name.

2. **Type your comment in the text box.**

You don't even have to click in the box. Just start typing. Your typed text appears in a little box with selection handles. See Figure 3-10.

3. **Click outside the text box when you finish typing.**

A red triangle appears in the upper-right corner of the cell, as shown in Figure 3-10, to indicate the cell has a comment.

TIP

Hover your mouse over a cell that has a red triangle to read the comment.

Figure 3-10:
Reading a
comment.

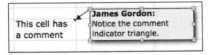

This cell has a comment

James Gordon:
Notice the comment indicator triangle.

To edit the comment, follow these steps:

1. **Select a cell that contains the red-triangle comment indicator.**

The Insert menu changes from Comment to Edit Comment.

2. **Choose Insert⇨Edit Comment.**

3. **Make your edits and then click anywhere outside the comment box.**

You can remove a comment from a cell even more easily than you can insert a comment. Select the cell that contains a comment and then choose Edit⇨Clear⇨Comments.

You might consider this feature a bit over the top, but you can format comment boxes to an incredible degree. In Figure 3-10, when you insert or edit a comment box, the selection handles turn on. When these handles are visible, double-click the comment box's border to expose the Format Comment dialog, as shown in Figure 3-11. Select from a surprisingly large number of options that you can apply to your comment box.

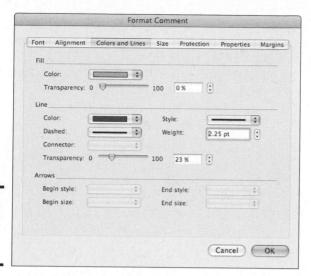

Figure 3-11: Formatting a comment box.

To change when comments appear, choose Excel⇨Preferences and click the View button. Select one of three options (as shown in Figure 3-12):

✦ **No Comments or Indicators:** The interface displays no indication that comments exist. You can still add, edit, and delete comments.

✦ **Indicators Only, and Comments on Hover:** The default behavior for inserted comments.

✦ **Comments and Indicators:** Red-triangle comment indicators and comment boxes are always visible. You don't have to hover the cursor over comment indicators to see comment boxes.

Tracking changes

Say that you want multiple people to work on a workbook that you plan to distribute via e-mail or other means. To make this situation even more fun, you're in charge of this project. You distribute a workbook to several people. Each person makes changes and then they return their changed workbooks to you. After that, you decide which changes to accept or reject for the final version. Although we use a multi-person example, the process works just as well if you're working with only one or two people.

Before you use the Share Workbook, consider turning on the Protect Shared Workbook feature so that only you have the authority to delete the change history. See the section, "Protecting a shared workbook," later in this chapter.

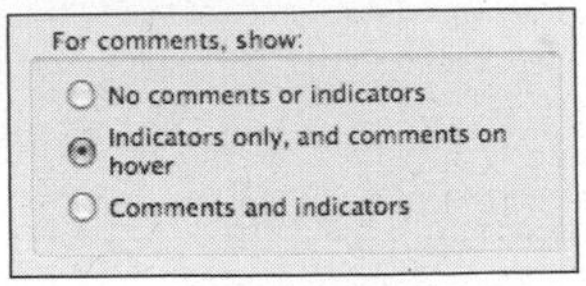

Figure 3-12:
Changing
how com-
ments are
displayed.

For comments, show:

○ No comments or indicators
◉ Indicators only, and comments on hover
○ Comments and indicators

Turning on track changes

To turn on track changes, follow these steps:

1. **Open a workbook.**

2. **Choose Tools⇨Track Changes⇨Highlight Changes.**

   The Highlight Changes dialog opens; see Figure 3-13.

3. **Select the Track Changes While Editing check box.**

   Your workbook is now in Workbook Sharing mode. Some features are disabled in Sharing mode. See the sidebar, "Workbook Sharing mode," later in this chapter, for the scoop.

4. **In the Highlight Which Changes section, click When to display a pop-up menu (as shown in Figure 3-13) and choose an option.**

   Tell Excel when to begin tracking changes. Generally, you choose All, meaning Excel tracks changes all the time.

5. **Click the Who pop-up and choose whose changes you want Excel to track.**

6. **To limit tracking to a particular range, click the Where button and select a cell range from the pop-up menu that appears, or type the name of an existing cell range into the Where field.**

7. **Click OK to close the Highlight Changes dialog.**

   Excel prompts you to save your workbook.

8. **Close your workbook by choosing File⇨Close.**

Now, you're ready to distribute your workbook. After you turn on track changes, send copies of the workbook via e-mail (or Messenger, CD, Flash drives, or what have you).

Working with track changes turned on

When the Track Changes feature is turned on and a user changes a cell, a balloon appears, telling you

✦ What was changed

✦ Who made the change

✦ When the change was made

Check to activate track changes.   When tracking options

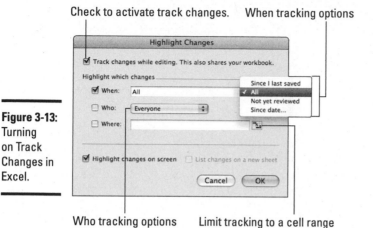

Figure 3-13:
Turning
on Track
Changes in
Excel.

Who tracking options   Limit tracking to a cell range

Granted, these balloons aren't as fancy as the ones in Microsoft Word, but they do the job, as shown in Figure 3-14.

Figure 3-14:
Making
changes to
a tracked
workbook.

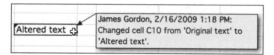

**Book III
Chapter 3**

Formatting and
Collaborating
in Excel

Merging tracked changes

After people finish doing what they need to do with your workbook, they return their edited copies to you. Now, you need to merge copies of the edited workbooks into a copy of the original. Follow these steps to merge the changes from everyone else's edited workbooks into a copy of the original workbook:

1. **Create a new folder in Finder.**

2. **Put a copy of the original workbook into the new folder.**

3. **Put copies of the edited workbooks into the same folder.**

4. **In the new folder, open the copy of the original workbook.**

Your original workbook opens.

5. **Choose Tools⇨Merge Workbooks.**

The Select File to Merge into Current Workbook dialog appears.

6. **Navigate or use Spotlight to locate a copy of an edited workbook located in the new folder that you made in Step 1, and then select that edited workbook.**

7. **Click OK.**

Repeat Steps 5–7 until you merge all the workbooks into your copy of the original workbook.

Deciding whose changes to review

You need to decide whose changes to review, what date to use as a starting point for the review, and how much of the workbook you want to review. Because Excel allows you to merge an unlimited number of workbooks, you may have changes from many individuals to deal with. Excel gives you an opportunity to filter changes before you accept or reject changes (see Figure 3-15).

Accepts a date

One person or everyone

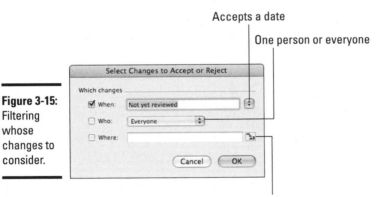

Figure 3-15:
Filtering whose changes to consider.

Entire sheet or specify a range.

You can set criteria that Excel uses when it displays changed cells before you accept or reject those changes. Follow these steps:

1. **Choose Tools➪Track Changes➪Accept or Reject Changes.**

The Select Changes to Accept or Reject dialog opens.

2. **Make any appropriate changes to the When option.**

You can accept the default, enter a date, enter All, or select various options from the pop-up menu to the right of the entry field. Excel doesn't display changes made prior to the date entered when you review the workbook.

3. **Click Who and select whose changes you want to review from the pop-up menu that appears.**

Choose Everyone to review everyone's merged changes at the same time.

4. **To limit your review to a range, click the selection button to the right of the Where field and enter a cell range or named range.**

5. **(Optional) Select the Highlight Changes on Screen option if you want Excel to highlight changed cells.**

If you select this option, Excel gives changed cells special borders and blue-triangle comment indicators that you can hover over to reveal the changes.

6. **Select List Changes on a New Sheet to create a new sheet that displays a report of the changes made.**

We talk about history reports in the section, "Generating a history report," later in this chapter.

7. **Click OK to close the Accept or Reject Changes dialog.**

Excel goes through your workbook and finds all the cells that your collaborators changed.

The settings you select in the Accept or Reject Changes dialog apply to all the merged workbooks at the same time.

Accepting and rejecting changes

If you followed our example from the preceding section, each changed cell is highlighted, and the Accept or Reject Changes dialog appears (see Figure 3-16). If Excel detects more than one change in a cell, you see a list of the cell's original content, plus all the suggested changes. When you click the Accept or Reject buttons, the dialog moves on to the next cell. The Accept or Reject Changes dialog remains onscreen until you deal with all changes. The changes you accept are retained in your final version, and the changes you reject are removed.

**Book III
Chapter 3**

Formatting and
Collaborating
in Excel

Accepting and rejecting track changes works like this:

1. **Choose Tools⇨Track Changes⇨Accept or Reject Changes.**

The Accept or Reject Changes dialog opens.

2. **Click the button that suits your needs.**

You can select

- *Accept:* Accept that change only.
- *Reject:* Disregard that change only.
- *Accept All:* Accept all changes.
- *Reject All:* Disregard all changes.

3. **Click Close when you're done.**

Excel displays the final version of your workbook.

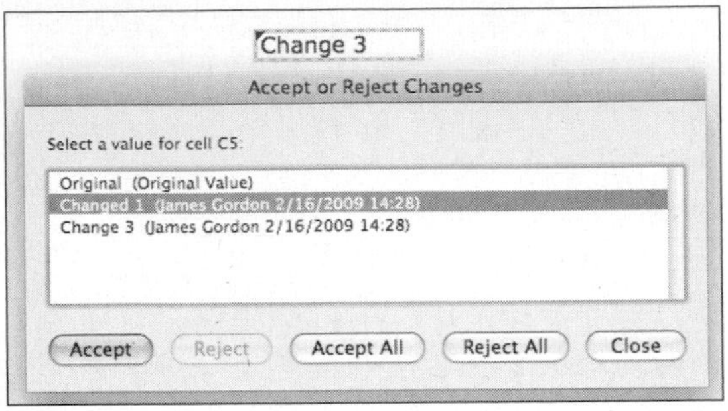

Figure 3-16: Accepting one change from several.

Finishing up

You need to turn off sharing to change your final version into a regular workbook. The following steps turn off track changes and delete the history file, as well as turn on the features that were disabled when you began sharing the workbook. To turn the shared workbook back into a regular workbook, follow these steps:

1. **Choose Tools⇨Track Changes⇨Highlight Changes.**

   The Highlight Changes dialog appears.

2. **Deselect the Track Changes While Editing check box.**

   Excel automatically saves the workbook as a fully enabled regular workbook. Excel no longer tracks changes and discards the change history.

Generating a history report

After people have made entries in the shared workbook, the question arises, "How do you see the entire change history all at the same time?" We have the answer, of course. Our favorite way is to view the changes in a separate worksheet, as shown in Figure 3-17. You can generate a history report in two ways.

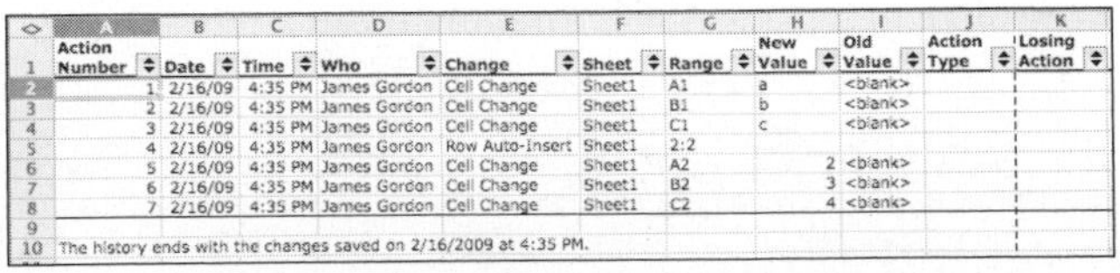

Action Number	Date	Time	Who	Change	Sheet	Range	New Value	Old Value	Action Type	Losing Action
1	2/16/09	4:35 PM	James Gordon	Cell Change	Sheet1	A1	a	<blank>		
2	2/16/09	4:35 PM	James Gordon	Cell Change	Sheet1	B1	b	<blank>		
3	2/16/09	4:35 PM	James Gordon	Cell Change	Sheet1	C1	c	<blank>		
4	2/16/09	4:35 PM	James Gordon	Row Auto-Insert	Sheet1	2:2				
5	2/16/09	4:35 PM	James Gordon	Cell Change	Sheet1	A2	2	<blank>		
6	2/16/09	4:35 PM	James Gordon	Cell Change	Sheet1	B2	3	<blank>		
7	2/16/09	4:35 PM	James Gordon	Cell Change	Sheet1	C2	4	<blank>		

The history ends with the changes saved on 2/16/2009 at 4:35 PM.

Figure 3-17: Viewing the change history report.

If you want to see a combined history, you must select the List Changes on a New Sheet option in the Select Changes to Accept or Reject dialog (which we talk about in the section, "Deciding whose changes to review," earlier in this chapter).

Workbook Sharing mode

The Track Changes and Share Workbook features put your workbook into Workbook Sharing mode. While a workbook is in Workbook Sharing mode, you can't change certain aspects of the workbook. You can use these features *before* you turn on sharing, and they work again after you turn off workbook sharing. But shared workbooks don't allow you to add or change any of the following: merged cells, conditional formatting, data validation, tables, charts, pictures, SmartArt Graphics, WordArt, subtotals, hyperlinks, scenarios, data tables, PivotTables, embedded objects, text boxes, error checking, or Excel calculator.

Before sharing your workbook, tell everyone to choose Excel➪Preferences➪General. In General preferences, each person should make sure that his name appears in the User name field. Sometimes, IT departments clone images, and everyone winds up with the same name (or no name at all). If that happens, Excel may not be able to record useful tracking and history information, or worse, you may end up with useless info.

You can't retrieve the change history from a workbook after you accept and reject changes.

You can make a history report for any individual workbook by opening it and then following these steps:

1. **Choose Tools➪Track Changes➪Highlight Changes.**

The Highlight Changes dialog appears.

2. **Select the List Changes on a New Sheet check box.**

This option isn't grayed out if changes have been made in the workbook.

3. **Click OK.**

You get an amazing report detailing exactly what changes were made, by whom, when, and a lot more, as shown in Figure 3-17.

Using Share Workbook

Excel is the first Office application to allow more than one person at a time to make changes in a shared file live, in real time. The Share Workbook feature is useful if more than one person needs to update data in a real-time environment. Excel has built-in rules you can select that decide which changes "win" in case of conflicts.

Up to 256 people can share a single workbook at one time, and they can use any mix of Macs or PCs. Not only can Excel deal automatically with conflicting information, you can tell Excel to keep a history of the changes for as many as 32,767 days (the default is 30 days). Truly amazing stuff!

Before using Share Workbook, consider turning on the Protect Shared Workbook feature so that the change history can't be deleted. See the section, "Protecting a shared workbook," later in this chapter.

Activating Share Workbook

To start sharing a workbook, follow these steps:

1. **Choose Tools⇨Share Workbook⇨Editing.**

The Share Workbook dialog opens on the Editing tab. See Figure 3-18.

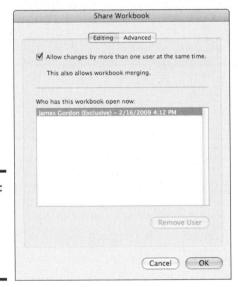

Figure 3-18: Enabling multiple-user workbook sharing.

2. **Select the Allow Changes by More Than One User at the Same Time check box.**

Selecting this box activates Share Workbook.

3. **Click the Advanced tab.**

The Share Workbook Advanced tab appears, as shown in Figure 3-19.

We usually accept the default Advanced settings, except for increasing the tracking history to 90 days.

4. **Select a Track Changes option.**

   You can select either of these options:

   - *Keep History for [Number] Days*

     Enter a number in the text box or use the Increase/Decrease control to adjust the number.

   - *Don't Keep Change History*

5. **Select an Update Changes option.**

   Here are your choices:

   - *When File Is Saved*

   - *Automatically Every [Number] Minutes.*

     Fill in the number of minutes or use the Increase/Decrease control to adjust the number. If you save automatically at regular intervals, you can select either Save My Changes and See Others; Changes or just See Other Users' Changes.

6. **For the Conflicting Changes Between Users section, select an option.**

   Choose either

   - *Ask Me Which Changes Win*

   - *The Changes Being Saved Win*

7. **In Personal View, select the Print Settings and Filter Setting check boxes to include print and filter settings.**

8. **Click OK.**

   The Save As dialog opens.

9. **Navigate to a shared network directory that's read/write accessible to all who need to share and then click Save.**

   Everyone who has permission to read and write to the directory can now open the workbook at the same time.

Everyone who needs to share a workbook simultaneously must have read/write permissions to a shared directory in Mac OS X Finder and/or Windows Explorer on a high-speed network.

Administering a shared workbook

You return to the Editing tab of the Share Workbook dialog often when you're administrating a shared workbook. To access this tab, simply choose Tools⇨Share Workbook. The Share Workbook dialog automatically opens

Book III
Chapter 3

Formatting and
Collaborating
in Excel

with the Editing tab displayed (as shown in Figure 3-18). You can see who's sharing the workbook at any given time in the Who Has This Workbook Open Now list.

The Who Has This Workbook Open Now list may indicate someone's still sharing, even if you know that she isn't (maybe her connection failed while sharing). When this happens, remove the name of the user from the list manually. Just select the user in the list and then select Remove User.

TIP

Protecting a shared workbook

Turning on protection before putting a workbook into Workbook Sharing mode prevents others from deleting the change history. Follow these steps:

1. **Open the workbook that you plan to share and choose Tools➪Protection➪Protect and Share Workbook.**

    The Protect Shared Workbook dialog appears.

2. **Select the Sharing with Tracked Changes check box, as shown in Figure 3-20.**

3. **Type a password into the Password text box and click OK to close the Protect Shared Workbook dialog.**

    If you attempt to turn off track changes, which would delete the history change log, Excel opens a dialog demanding the password. If you lose the password, you can't turn off workbook sharing.

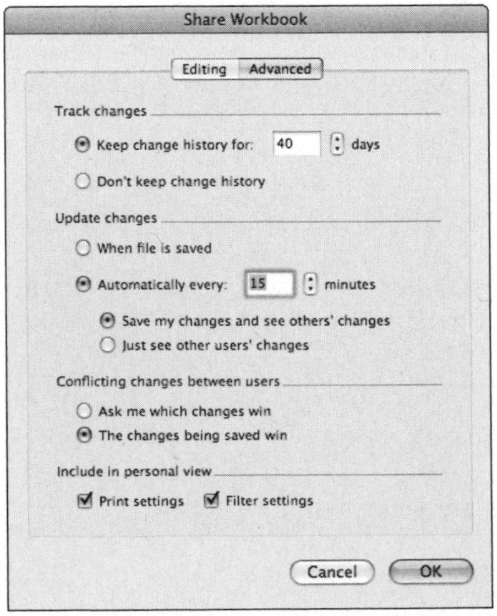

Figure 3-19: Setting up sharing rules.

Share Workbook

Editing | Advanced

Track changes

⦿ Keep change history for: 40 ⇅ days

○ Don't keep change history

Update changes

○ When file is saved

⦿ Automatically every: 15 ⇅ minutes

⦿ Save my changes and see others' changes
○ Just see other users' changes

Conflicting changes between users

○ Ask me which changes win
⦿ The changes being saved win

Include in personal view

☑ Print settings ☑ Filter settings

Cancel   OK

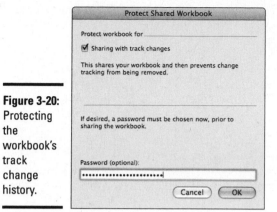

Figure 3-20:
Protecting
the
workbook's
track
change
history.

Chapter 4: Controlling Excel

In This Chapter

✔ Copying and pasting in Excel

✔ Moving and copying sheets

✔ Taking pictures with Excel's camera

✔ Nesting in Excel

✔ Curing so-called errors

Excel has some unique behaviors that enable you to do special tasks. This chapter shows you how to take advantage of Excel's ability to take ordinary features and extend them so that you have more flexibility. You also end up getting so used to these features that you might wonder how you managed without them all this time! In fact, you can twist Excel into many positions, like a rubber band. This chapter is loaded with tips on how to get Excel to work (and stretch) in special ways.

Copying and Pasting

The first thing to consider when copying and pasting in Excel is to think about the nature of what you attempt to copy. Cells, cell ranges, and formulas are treated differently from other kinds of things, such as SmartArt and graphs. We start by copying cells, formulas, and ranges. After that, we see what happens when you copy other kinds of things.

If you're not familiar with SmartArt and graphs, flip to Book I to read more about these shared Office features.

Simply copying and pasting

If you're used to copying and pasting, you know that if you select some text and then copy and paste, the default settings paste the text, along with the text format — such as blue, bold, or italic.

Follow this simple example to copy and paste in Excel:

1. **Select a cell you want to copy and choose Edit➪Copy.**

Alternatively, you can press ⌘-C or select Copy on the Standard toolbar.

2. **Click in the cell where you want to paste and choose Edit➪Paste.**

Alternatively, you can press ⌘-V or select Paste on the Standard toolbar.

When you paste the cell, Excel shows a small widget (as shown in Figure 4-1). The Paste widget handles most of your pasting requirements, but it allows you to choose only a single option.

3. Click the widget.

When copying and pasting, you have to click the widget before you start working in another cell; otherwise, the widget goes away. When you click, you can see all your pasting options. See Chapter 2 of this minibook for more about widgets.

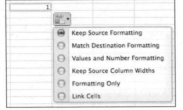

Figure 4-1:
Pasting the
special way.

Pasting special

The Paste widget handles most of your ordinary pasting requirements, but it's a one-shot deal — you can choose only a single option. On the other hand, Excel's Paste Special feature lets you pick and choose exactly what individual or combination of attributes you want to paste. You can apply and then reapply Paste Special options to a cell to get the exact combinations of options you want. Follow these steps to use Paste Special:

1. Select the cell or object you want to copy and choose Edit➪Copy.

Alternatively, you can press ⌘-C or select Copy on the Standard toolbar.

2. Click in the cell where you want to paste and then choose Edit➪ Paste Special.

If you select a cell or cell range in Step 1, the Paste Special dialog appears, as shown in Figure 4-2. If you select a different kind of object in Step 1, a different Paste Special dialog appears.

3. In the Paste section, select the option that you need.

Figure 4-2 shows these options.

4. Click OK.

The Paste Link button becomes active, depending on what you copy and which option you chose in the Paste Special dialog. The Paste Link button creates a cell formula that refers to the cell you're copying.

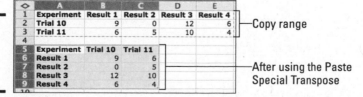

Figure 4-2:
Pasting the special way.

Turning rows into columns

Many times, you may wish you could easily change the layout of data from horizontal to vertical or vice versa. Fortunately, Excel's Paste Special Transpose option does exactly that.

To change columns into rows quickly (see Figure 4-3):

1. **Select a cell range and choose Edit⇨Copy.**

Alternatively, you can press ⌘-C or select Copy on the Standard toolbar.

2. **Select a destination cell.**

This cell becomes the upper-left cell of the pasted range.

3. **Choose Edit⇨Paste Special.**

The Paste Special dialog opens.

4. **Select the Transpose check box and then click OK.**

See Figure 4-3.

**Book III
Chapter 4**

Controlling Excel

Figure 4-3:
Turning columns into rows.

	A	B	C	D	E
1	Experiment	Result 1	Result 2	Result 3	Result 4
2	Trial 10	9	0	12	6
3	Trial 11	6	5	10	4
4					
5	Experiment	Trial 10	Trial 11		
6	Result 1	9	6		
7	Result 2	0	5		
8	Result 3	12	10		
9	Result 4	6	4		
10					

—Copy range

—After using the Paste Special Transpose

Using Paste Special with objects

If you copy an object, rather than a cell or cell range, the dialog shown in Figure 4-2 appears when you choose Edit⇨Paste Special.

In this Paste Special dialog, you can select from three different pasting formats. The Paste Link and Display as Icon buttons are grayed out, meaning you can't use them. We talk about these buttons in Chapter 5 of this mini-book. Here's a bit more about the three options from which you can choose:

✦ **PDF (Portable Document Format):** Adobe's popular vector format. Depending on what you're pasting, selecting this option might produce a vector, a low-resolution picture, or a blend of vector and picture to represent what you want to paste.

✦ **Picture:** A low-resolution picture of whatever you copied.

✦ **Microsoft Drawing Object:** Usually the same kind of object that you copied. Microsoft Drawing Object is the highest-quality Paste Special option.

Paste Special options differ, depending on what you copied. Charts, tables, and pictures all have their unique paste options.

You can Paste Special in Excel by using content that you copied from another open application, such as Word, PowerPoint, or even a Web browser.

Copying as a picture in the first place

You can easily copy a picture of an object, a cell, or a cell range, but you have to know about the secret Edit menu. Follow these steps to use the modified Edit menu:

1. **Select a cell, a range of cells, or an object on a worksheet.**

A range of cells can include a mixture of cells and objects, or just cells.

2. **Hold down the Shift key and click the Edit menu.**

Here's the secret! When you hold down the Shift key, the Edit menu offers new choices, as shown in Figure 4-4.

3. **Choose Edit⇨Copy Picture.**

A small Copy Picture pane opens.

4. **Click one of the choices:**

• *As Shown On Screen:* What you see is what you get.

• *As Shown When Printed:* The picture is formatted based on your current selections in Page Setup.

Now, you have a picture on the Clipboard that you can use in Excel or any other application that can paste pictures.

Figure 4-4:
Excel's
modified
Edit menu.

Now you know one of Office's best-kept secrets: Hold down the Shift key to modify some of the menus so that they offer more choices!

Moving and Copying Entire Sheets

Excel makes it easy to move and duplicate entire worksheets at a time, but you have to be careful with this Move or Copy tool. Don't use this tool if you're tired or distracted — you could wind up moving a whole lot of information that you don't want to move.

Before you even open the Move or Copy tool, decide which worksheet you want to move or copy. The active sheet is default, and you activate it by clicking the sheet tab. The selected sheet tabs are white. To move or copy a worksheet, follow these steps:

1. **Choose Edit⇨Move or Copy Sheet.**

   The Move or Copy dialog, as shown in Figure 4-5, opens.

2. **In the To Book pop-up menu, choose the destination for the worksheet(s) you plan to move or copy.**

   You can choose

   - *Within the Currently Active Workbook*

   - *To Any Other Open Workbook*

     The open workbooks are listed in the menu.

   - *To a Brand New Workbook*

The Before Sheet section lists all the sheets currently in the workbook. The sheets you move or copy are inserted in front of the sheet that you select.

3. (Optional) To make a copy (instead of moving the entire sheet), click the Create a Copy check box.

If you don't click this check box, Excel uses the default move behavior instead.

Click for new book or workbook.

Figure 4-5: Moving and copying entire worksheets.

Click to make copy.

If you're not copying, but instead moving, consider the cell references and hyperlinks on the sheets you're moving or copying. If you have references to other sheets, you may be creating links. When you're done with the Move or Copy tool, choose Edit⇨Links in the destination workbook. The Edit Links dialog appears. You can break unwanted links in the Edit Links dialog.

Creating Camera Magic

The Camera command creates a "picture" of a range of cells. "Picture" is in quotation marks because these pictures aren't static; they're *dynamic* — they change. Pictures are linked to the range you select, and they update when the range changes.

You can use the Camera command in a variety of ways:

✦ **Display the calculation results of numbers or charts when the calculations and charts are on hidden worksheets (but not hidden rows or columns), other worksheets, or cell ranges that are offscreen.** You can keep your formulas out of sight so unwanted visitors are less likely to tamper with them. Because the result is a linked picture, updated results are displayed automatically.

✦ **Precisely size and position the picture of the cell range.** The Camera command creates an object that you can size and format like a picture. You can position the Camera picture anywhere on a worksheet.

✦ **Position live snapshots of various ranges from distant places in a workbook.** You can make them fit close together on a worksheet.

To hide a worksheet, choose Format➪Sheet➪Hide. To unhide a sheet, choose Format➪Sheet➪Unhide. The Format menu lets you hide and unhide rows and columns, too! After you hide a row or column, you must first select the surrounding rows or columns by using the dark arrow cursor in the row or column heading before you can unhide.

Customizing the Camera tool

Before you can use this magical tool, you have to turn it on. In Book I, we explain how to customize menus and toolbars. Here's a quick refresher:

1. **Choose View➪Customize Menus and Toolbars.**

   The Customize Menus and Toolbars dialog appears.

2. **Click the Commands tab.**

3. **Drag the Camera command to any toolbar (or menu) and click OK.**

Using the Camera tool

To use the Camera tool:

1. **Drag over a range of cells with your mouse and then release it.**

   Everything within the selection range becomes part of a Camera picture. Objects (such as graphs or PivotTables) completely within the selection area are included in the resulting Camera picture.

2. **Click the Camera button on the toolbar (or select Camera from the menu if you put the command on a menu, as discussed in the preceding section).**

   The cursor changes to a plus sign (+).

3. **Move the mouse cursor to a new location and then drag the mouse to create a Camera picture.**

   The new location can be

   • On the same worksheet

   • Another worksheet in the same workbook

   • A worksheet in another open workbook (which creates a link)

When using the Camera option, the new location shouldn't overlap the original selection range.

Nesting and Nest Building

A beautiful Andorinha-dáurica bird builds nests with multiple chambers. Not unlike this bird, you can make a nest with multiple chambers right in Excel. To make your nests, use parentheses within your cell formulas.

If you want Excel to control calculation order, put what you want calculated first within parentheses (called *nesting*) inside your cell formula.

First things first

You might want to nest a formula so that you can control the order in which calculations are completed, which is *precedence*.

Here's the order in which each part of the formula is calculated:

+ Innermost parentheses to outermost parentheses

+ Multiplication and division

+ Addition and subtraction

+ Left to right

Precedence can be illustrated by the simple examples in Figure 4-6:

+ In row 2, parentheses (2×3) cause multiplication to happen first.

+ In row 3, parentheses $(5 + 2)$ force the addition to happen first.

As shown in Figure 4-6, the same numbers and operations in each formula result in entirely different values when those operations have different precedence.

Figure 4-6:
Operations in parentheses take precedence.

◇	A	B
1	**Formula**	**Valu**
2	=5+(2*3)	1
3	=(5+2)*3	2

Applying some logic

The Excel IF formula enables you to perform logical operations:

IF (a condition is met) THEN (do this) ELSE (do something else).

Figure 4-7 shows a simple example of an IF formula — =IF(A1=1,TRUE, FALSE) — which means, "If the value of cell A1 is equal to 1, the logical value of the cell is TRUE; if cell A1 isn't equal to 1, the logical value of cell A1 is FALSE." In this formula, the parentheses simply provide clarity.

Figure 4-7:
Making
simple logic.

The nested IF statement in Figure 4-8 — =IF(A2>=90,"A",IF(A2>=80, "B","C")) — wants to display a letter grade based on a student's numeric score. The formula means, "First, if the student attains a score of 80 or higher, the student gets a B; next, if the score is 90 or higher the student gets an A; finally, any score that's lower than 80 gets a C."

You can display *text* as the result of an IF formula, as long as you put quotation marks around the text.

Figure 4-8:
Nesting for
logic, clarity,
and brevity.

Book III
Chapter 4

Controlling Excel

When nesting in a formula, you need the same number of open parentheses as closed parentheses — use parentheses in pairs. Excel helps you by color-coding pairs of parentheses in your formula while you type.

You don't have a specific limit as to how many sets of parentheses you can nest within a formula, but it's usually less than 13 pairs. However, because the final ELSE can refer to another cell's value, which can have even more nesting, you really don't have a limit to the number of nests you can have in a chain.

If we take our earlier example to another nested option, it might look like this: =IF(A9>=90,"A",IF(A9>=80,"B",IF(A9>=50,"C","D"))).

Now, the formula means, "First, if the student attains a score of 50 or higher, the student gets a C; next, if the score is between 50 and 80, the student gets a B; next, if the student score is between 80 and 90, the student gets an A; finally, any score that's lower than 50 gets a D."

Correcting Errors

The idea of *errors* is a misnomer. In actuality, these so-called errors are just messages from Excel, saying it had trouble doing what you asked. We tackle the most common error messages.

Getting rid of hash marks

The error message you're most likely to see is a set of hash marks in a cell (see Figure 4-9). These marks simply mean the cell isn't wide enough to display a value that's the result of a formula. You can cure hash marks in three ways:

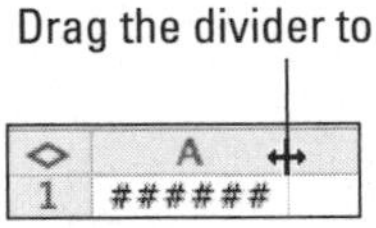

Figure 4-9:
Making a
cell larger
gets rid of
hash marks.

Drag the divider to the right.

✦ **Widen the column by dragging or double-clicking the column divider.** You use the double-arrow cursor, described in Chapter 2 of this minibook.

✦ **Merge the cell with another to make enough room.** Chapter 3 in this minibook explains merging cells.

✦ **Change the number format to show fewer decimal places by using the Formatting Palette.** Chapter 3 in this minibook tells how to change formatting.

Circular references

After working for a while within Excel, you have many formulas on sheets that take values from other formulas, which is a good thing. While you make worksheets more and more complex, you're likely to accidentally link cells so that you have an endless loop. Excel dubs this predicament a *circular reference*.

Fixing circular references

If you do accidentally make a circular reference, a warning appears, threatening you with dire consequences. Okay, we made that up, but Excel does come darn close to that!

If you do get such a warning, you may not remember where in the chain you went wrong. If you want to wait 'til later to investigate, you can continue. If you do, Excel makes a big deal about it. Excel simultaneously highlights all the cells in the chain, opens the Excel Help topic on how to get rid of circular references, and turns on the Circular References toolbar, hoping that you can analyze your formulas and get rid of the circular reference.

In Figure 4-10, we set three cells equal to each other, creating a circular reference, for your viewing pleasure! And, of course, it's so much fun to see Excel panic.

Figure 4-10:
Tracing a
circular
reference.

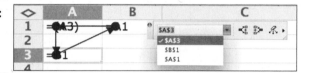

Keeping your circular reference

If you insist, we show you how you can force Excel to allow you to keep your circular reference. But you have to pay a ransom: You have to tell Excel how many times you want Excel to perform the calculation (the number of *iterations*) before it exits the endless loop.

To specify your iterations, follow these steps:

1. **Choose Excel⇨Preferences (see Figure 4-11).**

   The Preferences pane opens.

2. **Click the Calculation option.**

   Calculation preferences appear.

3. **In the Iteration area, select the Limit Iteration check box.**

4. **Set the number of iterations you want Excel to perform before exiting the loop.**

Clearing #DIV/0

You get the `#DIV/0` message if a formula is asked to divide a number by 0. Remember your math class? You can't divide by 0. You can intercept this error message and display something a bit more informative.

Finding the Analysis ToolPak

In previous versions of Excel, to activate certain functions, you had to turn on the Analysis ToolPak Excel add-ins. In Excel 2008, you don't have that bother because the functions are now built-in. A consequence of losing VBA (Visual Basic for Applications) in Excel 2008 is the loss of wizards based on the Analysis ToolPak. Mac MVPs recommend the following Web site as a replacement for some of these tools: `www.coventry.ac.uk/ec/~nhunt/oat bran`.

Say you want to test cell B7 for the `#DIV/0` error. You might put a cell formula that uses both IF and ISERROR functions into a nearby cell: `=IF(ISERROR(B7),"Please change your entry.",B7)`.

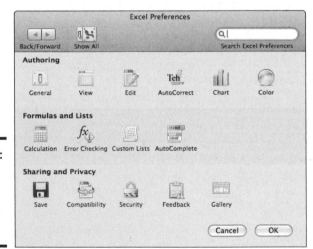

Figure 4-11: Forcing Excel to calculate a circular reference.

Other error messages

You encounter other cell messages less frequently. You can get details about them by searching Excel Help for *error messages*.

Excel puts little green triangles that have error messages associated with them into cells, and sometimes those triangles can be annoying, rather than helpful. You can turn them off entirely or select the kinds of things you want to be notified about: Choose Excel➪Preferences➪Error Checking.

Chapter 5: Heavenly Charting

In This Chapter

✔ **Making different kinds of charts**

✔ **Deciding where the chart should live**

✔ **Using error bars**

✔ **Getting a Gantt chart**

✔ **Creating histograms**

*C*harts are an Excel strongpoint. Students, businesses, scientists, news organizations, economists, and many other groups use charts. When you make charts in Office 2008, you find a brand-new charting engine that gleams with the latest Microsoft charting technology.

The terms *chart* and *graph* are interchangeable. We stick with *chart*, while acknowledging when *graph* is the preferred term.

Because the chart feature of Excel is now common to Word, Excel, and PowerPoint, we cover most aspects of charts in Book I, Chapter 5. If certain terms here seem foreign to you, we recommend that you flip to that chapter before you dive into this one. However, if you've worked with charts before, you might be familiar with chart basics. This chapter focuses primarily on aspects of charts that are unique to working with them in Microsoft Excel.

Making a Chart

In Excel, making a chart is a one-click operation after you perform a minimal amount of setup. It's hard to imagine an easier way to create charts, as shown in Figure 5-1. Follow these steps:

1. **Select a data range.**

2. **Click the Charts tab of Elements Gallery.**

If Elements Gallery isn't visible, choose View➪Elements Gallery or click Gallery on the Standard toolbar.

Select data   Charts tab   Chart button   Click a chart type.

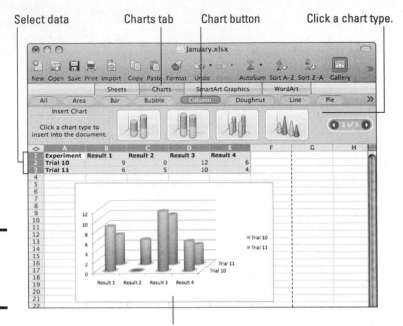

Figure 5-1:
Making a
chart in
Excel.

Chart appears on the worksheet

3. **In Gallery, click the chart type you want to create.**

4. **Click the specific chart variant.**

Each chart type has several variants available. For example, some of the variants in the bar type chart are Clustered Bar, Stacked Bar, and so on.

The chart appears on the worksheet, and the Chart menu is now activated in the menu bar at the top of the screen.

Congratulations! You made a great-looking chart in a jiffy!

If you've worked with charts in Word and PowerPoint and watched Excel appear to do the charts for those programs, you may discover you can more easily make charts in Excel, rather than Word or PowerPoint, because you don't have to keep track of which program is running. You can see your data and the chart together in Excel.

Choosing the Chart's Location

Charts can live happily on the worksheet that has the data, which is where they're born. Like other objects, you can cut, copy, and paste them to other locations; and you can add them to the Scrapbook, which we discuss in Book I, Chapter 4.

Excel also has a special kind of worksheet called a *chart sheet* that you can use to showcase a chart. A chart sheet can have only one thing: a single chart. On a chart sheet, you can format the chart by using the same tools as when you have the chart on a conventional worksheet. If you want to move the chart back onto a worksheet, you can use the Move Chart tool again.

Moving to a chart sheet

To move a chart to a chart sheet, follow these steps:

1. **Select the chart.**

   Selecting the chart activates the Chart menu.

2. **Choose Chart➪Move Chart.**

   The Move Chart dialog opens, as shown in Figure 5-2.

3. **Click the New Sheet radio button.**

4. **In the New Sheet text box, type a name for the Chart Sheet tab.**

5. **Click OK.**

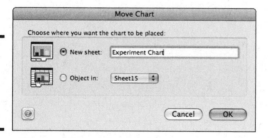

Figure 5-2: Moving a chart to a new residence.

Book III Chapter 5

Heavenly Charting

Instantly, your chart appears as a full sheet on a new tab that has the name you typed in the Move Chart dialog. The source data remains on the worksheet, and the data is still linked to the chart. If the data changes, the chart is updated instantly, even if the data is the result of a formula or a query.

Copying to Microsoft Word and PowerPoint

Because working with charts in Excel is less confusing than in Word or PowerPoint, you'll be glad to know that it's easy to move your charts to either program. Easy is good!

Using the Scrapbook

We think using the Scrapbook is the easiest way to copy charts from Excel to Word or PowerPoint. You don't have to open the destination document when you add the chart to the Scrapbook, and the chart remains in the Scrapbook, in case you want to paste it again. When you paste from the Scrapbook, the default result is a drawing object, which you can format as desired.

This is a two-stage expedition. In the first stage, you start in Excel and copy the chart to the Scrapbook. Figure 5-3 shows the copied chart in Scrapbook. In the second stage, you switch to Word or PowerPoint, and then paste your chart from Scrapbook into your Word document or PowerPoint slide. Follow these steps to perform the entire procedure:

1. **Click the Scrapbook button in the Toolbox.**

If the Toolbox palette isn't visible, click the Toolbox button on the Standard toolbar to display it.

2. **On your worksheet, select the chart you want to copy.**

3. **Click the Add button on the Scrapbook palette of the Toolbox.**

A copy of your chart appears in the Scrapbook.

4. **Open the Word document or PowerPoint slide in which you want to place the chart.**

5. **In the Scrapbook, select the chart you want to paste.**

You may have to turn on Scrapbook in Word as well. Just follow the same procedure we describe in Step 1.

6. **Click the Paste button.**

The chart is now in your destination document.

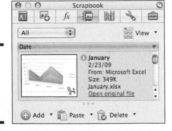

Figure 5-3:
Putting
Scrapbook
to work.

If the Scrapbook method works well for you, skip to the section "Applying Error Bars," later in this chapter. But if you need more options, or if you're just curious, go ahead and read the following sections.

Going from Excel to Word

Fortunately, the process of copying Excel charts into Word is straightforward. Follow these steps:

1. **Make sure that Word and Excel are open.**

In Excel, the currently open workbook needs to contain the chart you want to copy to Word.

2. **Select the chart in Excel.**

Click the chart's border to select it.

3. **Choose Edit⇨Copy.**

Alternatively, you can press ⌘-C or choose Copy on the Standard toolbar.

4. **Switch to the Microsoft Word document.**

Use the Dock or press ⌘-Tab.

5. **Choose Edit⇨Paste.**

Or you can press ⌘-V.

If you prefer, you can choose Edit⇨Paste Special to open the Paste Special dialog (see Figure 5-4), which offers you more paste formats and link options. Each time you select a different combination of format and paste options, the description in the Result section interactively updates so that you know what will happen when you click OK. Click OK to confirm your selection.

6. **Click the small widget in the lower-right corner of the chart.**

A drop-down menu appears, as shown in Figure 5-5.

**Book III
Chapter 5**

Heavenly Charting

Select option combinations

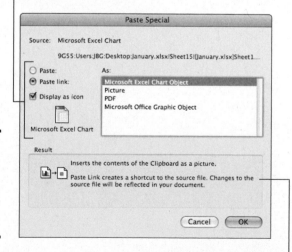

Figure 5-4:
Viewing
the Paste
Special
possibilities
in Word.

Description of operation

Figure 5-5:
Choosing
chart paste
options in
Word.

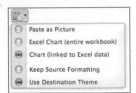

7. **Select how you want the chart to behave while it's living in your Word document.**

   You can format the chart in several ways:

   - *Paste as Picture:* Pastes a picture representation of the chart.

   - *Excel Chart (Entire Workbook):* Pastes a copy of the entire workbook as an embedded OLE object into the Word document, displaying the chart. Chart colors and fonts adopt document theme colors if you've already applied a theme to the document. See Book II, Chapter 5 for information on working with embedded charts.

   - *Chart (Linked to Data):* Pastes a chart object linked to the Excel source workbook, which remains an independent Excel file.

   - *Keep Source Formatting:* Same as the Excel Chart (Entire Workbook) option, except Word ignores existing document theme colors and retains the source colors and fonts.

   - *Use Destination Theme:* Same as Excel Chart (Entire Workbook), the chart adopts the Word document's theme.

8. **Click outside the drop-down list to close the widget.**

By default, the chart object is linked to the Excel data source, using the currently applied Office theme in Word.

Going from Excel to PowerPoint

You can copy and paste from an Excel worksheet to a PowerPoint presentation. Follow these steps:

1. **Open PowerPoint and Excel.**

   In Excel, the currently open workbook should contain the chart you want to copy to Word.

2. **Select the chart in Excel.**

   Click the chart's border to select it.

3. **Choose Edit⇨Copy.**

   Alternatively, you can press ⌘-C or select Copy on the Standard toolbar.

4. **Switch to the PowerPoint presentation and navigate to the slide on which you want to place the chart.**

   Use the Dock or press ⌘-Tab.

5. **Choose Edit⇨Paste.**

   Alternatively, you can press ⌘-V.

   Alternatively (again!), you can choose Edit⇨Paste Special. In the Paste Special dialog, you can select from every possible paste operation, as shown in Figure 5-6. The Result section of Paste Special describes what you get if you click OK. Click OK to confirm your selection.

   PowerPoint displays your chart. By default, the chart is linked to the Excel workbook as the data source.

In PowerPoint, you can open the source Excel file by selecting the chart object and choosing Edit⇨Edit in Excel. The source workbook must be closed (not already open in Excel) for this option to work.

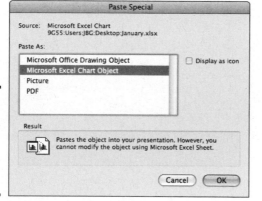

Figure 5-6: Viewing all possible paste possibilities in PowerPoint.

Applying Error Bars

The first shipments of Office 2008 didn't include error bars. If you don't have the Error Bar feature, choose Help⇨Check for Updates to bring your copy of Office up to date.

Many 2D chart types support *error bars,* which are little visual indicators of the statistically calculated error rate for a data set, although we wonder whether they'd make good candy bars!

Candy bars aside, look at Figure 5-7, where we double-clicked a bar in the chart to display the Format Data Series dialog. Yes, Excel can now compute the standard error for you and display it on your charts!

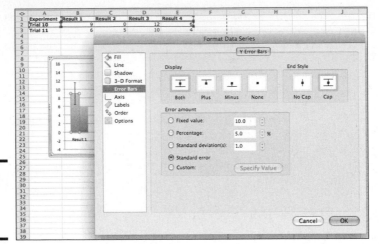

Figure 5-7:
Making
tasty error
bars.

Making a Gantt Chart

A *Gantt chart* is a special bar chart that shows the timeline of a project. We bring up Gantt charts because some people think that you need some other program besides Excel to make Gantt charts, such as Microsoft Project. Well, you don't need to have Microsoft Project to make Gantt charts — Excel can also make them, although not automatically.

Instructions that describe how to make a simple Gantt chart are in Excel Help. Just search Help for *Gantt chart*.

If you want instructions on how to make advanced Gantt charts, Excel MVP Jon Peltier has a site with all the details: `http://peltiertech.com/ Excel/Charts/GanttChart.html`.

Making a Histogram

Histograms visually show the number of occurrences (or frequency of repetition) of values proportionally in a column or a row. Because Excel no longer includes a Histogram tool, a lot of people are seeking a workaround for making histograms in Excel.

If you don't know exactly what a histogram is, you can look it up! Choose Tools⇨Dictionary. The Reference Tools dialog appears. In the search field, type **histogram** and then press Return to display results for both Encarta Encyclopedia and Dictionary. Click disclosure triangles to display additional results. Click hyperlinks for even more information. You need an active Internet connection to use the Dictionary.

You'll need to have access to the Object Palette in the Toolbox. If it's not already visible, click the Toolbox button on the Standard toolbar. Then in the Toolbox, select Object Palette.

You can make a histogram in Excel either by using cell formulas or charts. Regardless of which method you use, follow these steps to begin making your histogram:

1. **Click the plus sign (+) worksheet tab to open a new, blank worksheet in Excel.**

2. **Choose View⇨Normal.**

   The worksheet appears in Normal View.

3. **Type** Values **into cell A2 and** Frequency **into cell A3, as shown in Figure 5-8.**

4. **Fill in row 2 with the values from Figure 5-8, beginning with cell B2.**

   In this step, you can use your own data, rather than the example values.

5. **In cell B3, enter the formula** =COUNTIF($B$2:$K$2,B2).

   Be sure to type it exactly!

   This formula counts how many times the number in the cell directly above it appears in the absolute range $B$2:$K$2. In this example, that range includes the values we typed into row 2 in Step 4.

   When using your own data, substitute the rightmost column letter of your own data in row 2 for column letter K in the preceding formula. Be sure to retain the dollar signs ($). Ignore the error widget, if one appears.

6. **Select cell B3.**

7. **Drag the fill handle of cell B3 to the right until you reach the cell at the end of the range of data.**

   This cell is K3 in the example.

   The number of times each value appears in the row now appears beneath each number in the Values row.

To make your histogram by using cell formulas, check out the following section. If you want to use a chart for your histogram, skip ahead to the section, "Making a histogram by using a chart," later in this chapter.

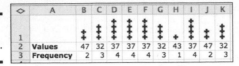

Figure 5-8:
A histogram.

Making a histogram by using cell formulas

After you complete the steps in the preceding section, follow these steps to produce a histogram by using cell formulas:

1. **Select cell B1.**

2. **Type the formula** =REPT("+",B3).

To type the ⇨ symbol, follow these steps:

a. Type the rest of the formula first.

b. Click to put the cursor between the quotation marks.

c. On the Object Palette, click All Shapes and choose Shapes from the pop-up menu that appears (see Figure 5-9).

d. On the Symbols tab, select the arrow shape.

Note: Not every shape option can be added to a formula.

Formatting Palette

Object Palette   Symbols

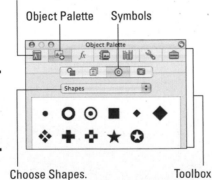

Figure 5-9:
Getting a
shape into a
formula.

Choose Shapes.   Toolbox

3. **Stop when you get to the cell at the end of the range of data, which is K1 in the example in Figure 5-8.**

The shape doesn't look right because the symbols are horizontal, rather than vertical.

4. **With the range you filled still selected, switch the Toolbox to the Formatting Palette by clicking the Formatting Palette button, as shown in Figure 5-9.**

The Formatting Palette replaces the Object Palette.

5. **In the Alignment and Spacing section of the Formatting Palette, click the Rotate Text Up button under Orientation (as shown in Figure 5-10).**

Ta da! You've just created a histogram.

You can select multiple columns by dragging over column letters. Then, double-click one of the dividers to automatically resize the columns to fit your data.

Click triangle.

Figure 5-10: Turning a cell formula sideways.

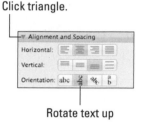

Rotate text up

Making a histogram by using a chart

This section is strictly for the serious chart maker.

Complete the steps in the section, "Making a histogram by using cell formulas," earlier in this chapter and then follow these steps:

1. **Select the entire range of cells that contains the tested data and the cell formula results.**

Include the row labels in your selection.

To follow our example, select cell range A2:K3.

2. **In Elements Gallery, choose Charts⊅Column⊅Clustered Column.**

If Elements Gallery isn't visible, choose View⊅Elements Gallery.

3. **Click any one of the bars representing values.**

The Values bars are the taller bars. All the Values bars become selected, as shown in Figure 5-11, and selection handles appear. The Values row becomes highlighted.

4. **Press the Delete key.**

The Values bars disappear, leaving the Frequency bars visible.

Now, look across the bottom of your chart. The X axis isn't right.

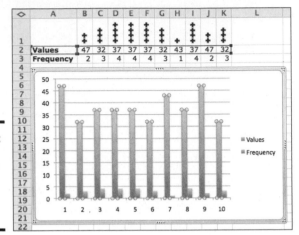

Figure 5-11:
Making a
preliminary
clustered
column
chart.

5. **On the menu bar, choose Chart⇨Source Data.**

The Select Data Source dialog opens.

The Category (X) Axis Labels field in the lower-right corner of this dialog is blank. You need to fill in that field, but Excel won't let you type in it. You have to click the selection button next to the field.

6. **Click the button next to the Category (X) Axis Labels field.**

7. **Drag over the cell range in row 2 that contains the values, but doesn't include the cell that contains the label.**

If you're following our example, select the range B2:K2.

While you drag, Excel types the cell range for you. When you're done, the entry should be similar to what you see in Figure 5-12. The ToolTip tells you what row and column you've selected. (In this case, 1R x 10C means you've selected 1 row by 10 columns.)

Figure 5-12:
Making
Excel type
the X-axis
values.

8. **Press Return after you select the range.**

The Select Data Source dialog reappears.

9. **Click OK.**

The Select Data Source dialog closes. The X-axis values now match the Values numbers in row 2 of the data source table.

The Y-axis values are correct, but we don't need the decimal values.

10. **Choose View⇨Toolbars⇨Chart.**

The Chart toolbar appears, as shown in Figure 5-13.

11. **From the Chart Objects pop-up menu on the Chart toolbar, choose Vertical (Value) Axis, as shown in Figure 5-13.**

The Y axis becomes selected.

Y-axis selector

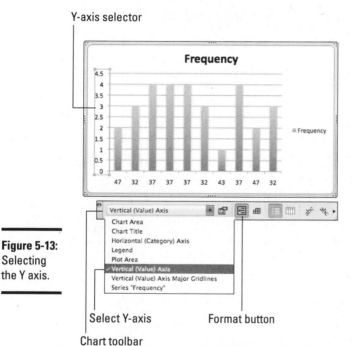

Figure 5-13:
Selecting
the Y axis.

Select Y-axis   Format button

Chart toolbar

12. **Click the Format button on the Chart toolbar.**

The Format Axis dialog, as shown in Figure 5-14, opens.

13. **Select the Scale option from the list of Format Axis options.**

Scale options appear, as shown in Figure 5-14.

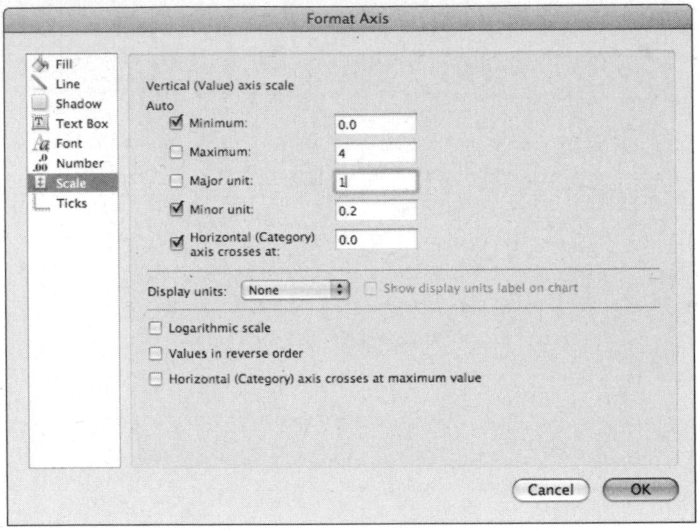

Figure 5-14:
Formatting
the Y axis.

14. **Set the Vertical (Value) Axis Scale.**

    For this example, we used these values:

    - *Maximum:* 4

    - *Major Unit:* 1

    Accept the default values for the remaining settings.

15. **Click OK.**

    The Format Axis dialog closes.

    Congratulations! For all practical purposes, the histogram chart is done at this stage. Some fussbudgets may insist that we're not done yet because we have too much space between the bars on the chart. So, we finish the job to make them happy, too. See Figure 5-15.

16. **On the Chart toolbar, click Chart Objects and choose Series "Frequency" from the pop-up menu that appears.**

17. **On the Chart toolbar, select Format.**

    The Format Data Series dialog opens.

18. **In the Format Data Series dialog, select Options from the list of options.**

19. **In the Format Data Series dialog, change the Gap Width to 10%.**

You've created a histogram that should make even the most die-hard histogram lover lust for this chart. Figure 5-16 shows your finished masterpiece.

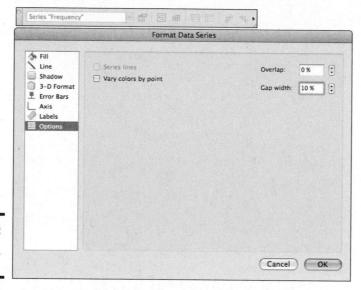

Figure 5-15:
Making the
bars wider.

Book III
Chapter 5

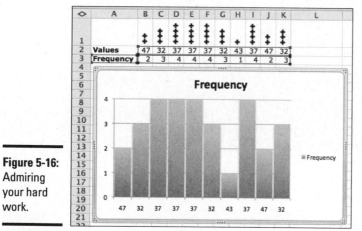

Figure 5-16:
Admiring
your hard
work.

Heavenly Charting

Apply Chart Styles formatting options from the Chart Styles section of the
Formatting Palette to further enhance the appearance of your histogram.

Chapter 6: Becoming Versatile with Excel

In This Chapter

✓ Flagging tasks for follow-up

✓ Creating forms

✓ Making and using form templates

✓ Getting Excel and the Web working together

*W*hen it comes to versatility, Excel shines very brightly. This chapter compiles a variety of very different things that Excel can do for you. Think of this as a secrets drawer that's filled with ideas and tips. We hope that you find useful and interesting things that you didn't know about. Explore this chapter just for the fun of it.

We start this chapter by showing you how to set reminders. Making input forms gets our attention next, followed by a discussion of how Excel integrates with Web technologies.

Helping You Remember

Excel is part of a powerful Office suite in which the applications are integrated with each other. The Office suite includes My Day and Entourage Calendar features in Entourage, which we talk about in Book V. Excel takes advantage of both these features with Excel's Flag for Follow Up feature.

Choose Tools⇨Flag for Follow Up to add a task to your Entourage Tasks list; see Figure 6-1. Flag for Follow Up's default prompts you to select a date and time when you want to be reminded about your workbook.

You can leave it at that, or you can switch to Entourage's Task feature and do all kinds of fancy things with your Excel reminders. Figure 6-2 shows where your Excel flags are saved in Entourage, and we hope it entices you to consider investigating our Entourage and Project Center minibooks (Books V and VI, respectively).

Figure 6-1:
Setting a
reminder
flag.

> **Flag for Follow Up**
>
> Flag for Follow Up lets you create a reminder that will alert you to follow up on this document at the date and time you specify.
>
> ☑ Remind me on 12/24/2009 at 9:00 PM
>
> Cancel   OK

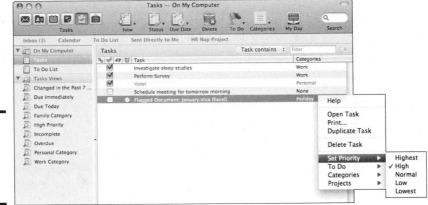

Figure 6-2:
Follow-ups
appear in
Entourage
tasks.

Preparing Your Forms

When you create a form, versatility and control are top priorities. You need versatility to precisely place words and empty fields, and you need control to make sure that entries are validated against rules that you make.

We want to point out the most important reason that Excel is a great tool for making forms: You can use the full range of Excel's powerful worksheet functions when you design your forms. The Formula Builder (which we discuss in Chapter 2 of this minibook) can help you build forms that use worksheet functions.

Customizing the Forms toolbar

When you create forms in Excel, you use the Forms toolbar extensively. You can enhance Excel's Forms toolbar. Follow these steps to add buttons to the Forms toolbar:

1. **Turn on the Forms toolbar by choosing View⇨Toolbars⇨Forms.**

The Forms toolbar appears.

2. **Choose View⇨Customize Menus and Toolbars.**

The Customize Menus and Toolbars dialog appears. See Book I, Chapter 3.

3. **Click the Commands tab.**

4. **In the Categories list, choose All Commands.**

5. **In the Commands list, scroll down until you find the Lock Cell command.**

6. **Drag the Lock Cell command to the Forms toolbar.**

    Let go when you see the insertion point indicator appear on the toolbar.

7. **Drag the Protect Sheet command to the Forms toolbar.**

    Let go when you see the insertion point indicator on the toolbar.

8. **(Optional) Drag the lower-right corner of the Forms toolbar to resize it.**

    Your toolbar now displays the Lock Cell and Protect Sheet buttons. The buttons on your toolbar may be in different positions from those shown in Figure 6-3.

Figure 6-3:
The Lock
Cell and
Protect
Sheet
buttons.

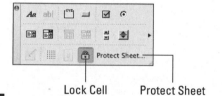

Lock Cell   Protect Sheet

9. **Click OK.**

    The Customize Menus and Toolbars dialog closes.

Tabbing in a form

Pressing the Tab key takes the cursor from one form field to the next. This is a very convenient feature for filling in forms.

To make this feature work, you need to have different conditions in place at the same time:

✦ The worksheet must be protected.

✦ The form fields must be unlocked and all other cells must be locked.

Protecting and unprotecting a worksheet

When you work with forms, you'll be turning worksheet protection on and off frequently.

You must turn off protection when you want to build a form. Turning off protection also activates the Forms toolbar and Toolbox features, and allows you to edit worksheet content. When you're done building the form, you must turn on protection so that people can tab through the *fields* (cells that you set as unlocked) and you can activate form controls (discussed in the section, "Restricting entry with form controls," later in this chapter).

Turn on protection by following these steps:

1. Click the Protect Sheet button on the customized Forms toolbar.

Clicking the Protect Sheet icon, as shown in Figure 6-3, toggles protection on and off. The Protect Sheet dialog opens when you toggle on protection, as shown in Figure 6-4.

2. Select the Contents check box.

You must select the Contents check box if you want to protect the worksheet so that the Tab key works. Usually you just leave all the check boxes selected.

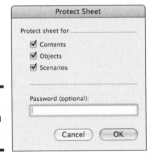

Figure 6-4:
Protecting a
worksheet.

While you're working on a form, you don't need to use a password, but if you like, you can password-protect your worksheet's forms.

Making Your Own Form Templates

Often, you can easily create a form from a tightly spaced grid. In a grid, you can easily place form elements, such as text and form controls, right where you want them.

By following these steps, you can create two grids, one landscape and one portrait, and save them as templates (which you can reuse whenever you want — look for them in Project Gallery under the My Templates category):

1. Open a new, blank workbook.

2. If you don't see the Formatting Palette, click the Toolbox button on the Standard toolbar to turn it on.

3. **Click the Landscape button.**

Clicking the Landscape button changes the orientation from Portrait to Landscape.

4. **In the Name Box on the Formula Bar, type** A1:AZ1 **and then press Return to select the cell range.**

Choose View⇨Formula Bar to open the Formula Bar, if it's not visible already.

5. **Press Return to select the cell range.**

6. **While the cell range is still selected, choose Format⇨Column⇨ Column Width.**

The Column Width dialog appears.

7. **Enter** 0.18 **in the text field and click OK.**

The value in inches is 0.18. If your system is set to use centimeters instead, use 0.46 as the value.

8. **Choose File⇨Save As.**

The Save As dialog appears.

9. **Change the Format pop-up to Excel Template (.xltx).**

The Save location automatically changes to My Templates, which is the correct location to use.

10. **Type** Form Template Landscape **in the Save As text box.**

11. **Click the Save button.**

You can save a portrait version, too. Follow these steps:

a. With the file open, click the Portrait button on the Formatting Palette.

b. Choose File⇨Save As.

The Save As dialog appears

c. Type **Form Template Portrait** in the Save As text box.

d. Click the Save button.

The Save As dialog closes.

12. **Choose File⇨Close.**

Using Your Form Templates

If you need to, you can adjust the row height and column width in your forms. By default, all the cells are locked. You need to unlock cells that you want to use as input fields.

Merge and unmerge cells by clicking the Merge Cells button on the Formatting Palette. Lock and unlock cells by first selecting them and then clicking the Lock toggle button that you can add to the customized Forms toolbar.

Making ordinary form fields

Try making a simple input form field by using one of the templates you can create in the section, "Making Your Own Form Templates," earlier in this chapter. In this example, you can make the Last Name form input field, as shown in Figure 6-5. Follow these steps:

1. **Choose File⇨Project Gallery.**

   Project Gallery appears. Select the New tab if it isn't already selected.

2. **In the My Templates category, select either form template that you save in the section, "Making Your Own Form Templates," earlier in this chapter.**

3. **Type a form field input label in the grid.**

   We typed **Last Name** in cell A2.

4. **Select a range of cells nicely sized for the input field.**

   We selected the cell range F2:N2.

5. **On the Formatting Palette, select the Merge Cells check box.**

   The Merge Cells option appears in the Indentation and Merge section under Alignments and Spacing.

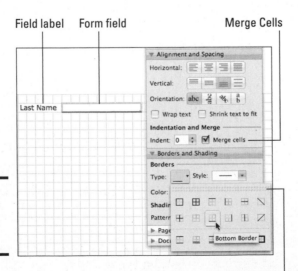

Figure 6-5:
Making an input form field.

6. On the Formatting Palette, click the Bottom Border button.

The button is below Borders and Shading, in the Borders section.

If you click the double row of dots at the top of the Borders section, the Borders toolbar becomes a floating toolbar. It's handy to use when creating forms because it's so simple to move the toolbar around.

7. Click the Lock button on the Forms toolbar.

The cell unlocks, which makes it a form field that a user can tab to, even when you have protection turned on. The Lock button is a toggle button. When it's depressed, it's locked; when it's not depressed, it's unlocked.

Restricting entry with data validation

It's always a good thing when you can help people fill out your form. One way to lend a helping hand is to make it harder for them to make mistakes when filling out the form. For example, by using data validation, you can make sure that someone enters a date into a Date field. Follow these steps to use validation:

1. Select a field (an unlocked or merged cell).

2. Choose Data➪Validation.

The Data Validation dialog opens (see Figure 6-6).

3. On the Settings tab, choose a setting from the Allow pop-up menu.

Data Validation is an interactive dialog — its options change, depending on what you decide to allow. You can allow

- *Any Value:* Allow any character, word, number, or combination.

- *Whole Number:* Apply logical operators and restrict entry to whole numbers.

- *Decimal Number:* Apply logical operators and restrict entry to decimal numbers.

- *List:* Allow entries from a cell range that you specify on the same worksheet. Click the button to the right of the Source field and then drag over the criteria list. Select the In-Cell Dropdown check box to display the list that the selected cell range contains in a drop-down list.

- *Date:* Apply logical operators and restrict entry to dates. See Figure 6-7.

- *Time:* Apply logical operators and restrict entry to time values.

- *Text-length:* Apply logical operators and restrict entry by the length of the input string.

- *Custom:* Restrict entry based on a cell formula.

If you select the Ignore Blank check box, an input field needs to be filled in before you can go anywhere else. To force an entry, deselect the Ignore Blank check box. This setting applies to all data validation Allow choices.

Book III
Chapter 6

Becoming Versatile with Excel

Allow list   Form field   In-Cell Drop-Down

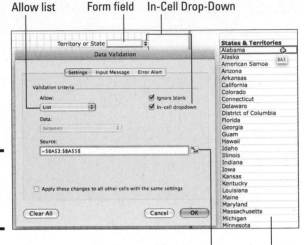

Figure 6-6:
Using a list
to restrict
entries.

Click here for source list   Source list

4. (Optional) On the Input Message tab, give your message a title and type an input message in the Input Message field (see Figure 6-8).

The input message appears in a ToolTip when you select the input field.

5. (Optional) On the Error Alert tab, select an error alert style and then type an error message in the Title and Error message field (see Figure 6-9).

The third tab of the Data Validation dialog, Error Alert (see Figure 6-9), lets you customize the error message that a user gets if he fails to follow the data validation rule you create. Try not to be sarcastic in these messages. After all, you don't want to hurt feelings or ruffle feathers.

6. Click OK to apply the validation rules and close the Data Validation dialog.

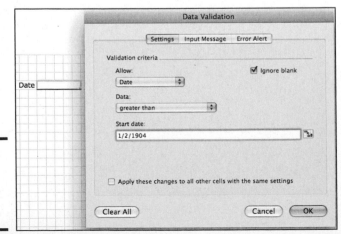

Figure 6-7:
Choosing
data
validation
settings.

Restricting entry with form controls

You can find Excel's form controls on the Forms toolbar (see Figure 6-10). The controls on this toolbar are objects that float above the worksheet in layers. Follow these general steps to use a toolbar form control on a worksheet:

1. **Select a control from the Forms toolbar.**

The mouse cursor becomes a plus sign (+).

2. **Drag the mouse on your worksheet where you want to place the control.**

The Form control that you selected appears on the worksheet.

3. **Adjust settings for the Format control in the form's dialog.**

You can now use the form control when worksheet protection is on.

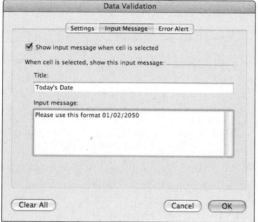

Figure 6-8:
Setting
an input
prompt.

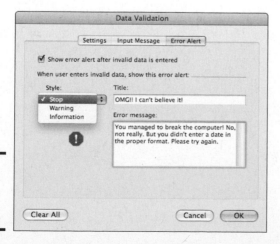

Figure 6-9:
Setting the
error alert
message.

Like with locked and unlocked cells, you must turn protection on to activate form controls and turn protection off to create and edit those controls.

You can choose from the following Forms toolbar controls:

✦ **Group Box:** Drag a group box around form controls that you want to behave as a group relative to each other.

✦ **Button:** When a user clicks this button, a macro runs. Macros created with Visual Basic for Applications (VBA) won't run in Excel 2008.

✦ **Check Box:** You can link the condition of the check box (checked or unchecked) to a cell on the worksheet. Use a check box control for multiple-choice answers to tests and surveys where the user can select more than one option within a group of suggested answers.

✦ **Option Button:** This control is better known as a radio button. You can link the condition (selected or not) to a cell on the worksheet. Use this control for multiple-choice answers to tests and surveys where the user can select only one option from a group of options. Use this control with the Group Box control.

✦ **List Box:** Drag a list box onto a worksheet, and then select a cell range from a column to populate the list box. When you click the box, a pop-up menu displays the list of inputs from the cell range. Users are restricted to choosing from the list.

✦ **Scroll Bar:** This control creates a scroll bar that you can use to select a numeric value. The value chosen is in a linked cell.

✦ **Spin Button:** Users can select a number by clicking Increase and Decrease buttons. The value chosen is in a linked cell.

✦ **Control Properties:** Select a form control and then click this button to open the control's dialog, where you can change its behavior and appearance.

✦ **Toggle Grid:** Toggles worksheet grid lines off and on.

✦ **Grayed-out controls:** You can use these controls only on Excel 5.0 dialog sheets. You can create an Excel 5.0 dialog sheet in Excel 2008, but because Excel 2008 has no VBA programming language to go along with it, you can't do anything with an Excel 5.0 dialog sheet.

The following example shows how to place radio buttons onto a worksheet and then use a group box so that Excel knows this particular group of radio buttons provide a single answer to a question. Create option buttons by following these steps:

1. **Choose View▷Toolbars▷Forms.**

The Forms toolbar opens.

2. **On the Forms toolbar, select the Option Button control.**

The mouse cursor becomes a plus sign (+).

3. **On the worksheet, drag to position the option button.**

An Option Button control includes the button itself, plus a text box into which you can type. You could fill in the text box portion with one of the choices for a multiple-choice question, for example.

4. **Repeat Steps 2 and 3 for each option button.**

You need to have at least two option buttons to be able to use them. If you have only one set of option buttons on a worksheet, you don't have to group them. If you have two or more sets of option buttons on a sheet, use group boxes to surround each group of buttons so that the groups of buttons function independently as units answering individual questions.

If you want to group buttons, go to Step 5. If you don't, you're done!

5. **Click the Group Box button in the Forms toolbar.**

The mouse cursor becomes a plus sign (+).

6. **Drag a box around each set of buttons that you want to make into separate groups.**

See Figure 6-10 for a sample arrangement. You can rename the Group Box by clicking its name. You can delete the name if you want to have just a border.

Group Box control   Option Button   Group box   Options

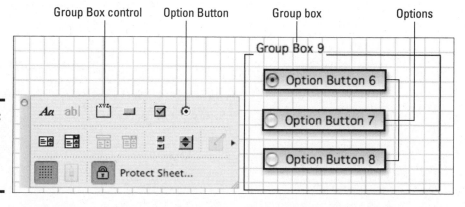

Figure 6-10:
Setting
up radio
buttons on
a form.

To assign a cell to a form control that's linked to a cell, use the Control tab of the Format Control dialog, which you display by right-clicking a control and selecting Format Control from the pop-up menu (as shown in Figure 6-11). In the Cell Link field, enter the cell that you want to display the control's state, or click the selector button to the right of the input field to select the cell by using the mouse.

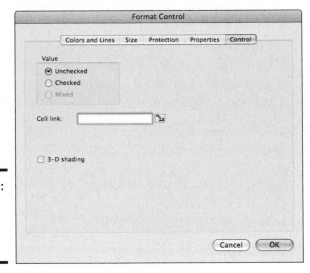

Figure 6-11: Linking option buttons to a cell.

Getting the Web into Excel

You have several ways to get information — primarily tables — into Excel. If you're a convert from Windows, you'll find that the ability to browse Web pages isn't in the Mac version of Excel. Nevertheless, you have other ways to get tables from Web pages into Excel for Mac.

Copying and pasting

The good old copy-and-paste method is the instinctive way to take Web page information from a browser and get it into Excel. See Chapter 5 of this mini-book for more information about copying and pasting (or pasting special).

Be sure to check the Web page you're working with. Many pages that have financial, census, and other tabular information offer links to download in Excel format. If the option is offered, take it!

Using a Web query

Excel can try to load tables from a Web page directly from the Internet via a *Web query* process. A Web query is simple: It's just a Web-page address saved as a text file, using the `.iqy`, rather than `.txt`, file extension.

You can easily make Web queries for Microsoft Excel in Microsoft Word. Follow these steps:

1. **Go to a Web page that has the Web tables that you want to put in Excel.**

2. **Highlight the Web address in the address field.**

3. **Choose Edit⇨Copy.**

4. **Switch to Microsoft Word and open a new document.**

   Launch Word if it's not open already.

5. **Choose Edit⇨Paste.**

   The URL is pasted into the Word document.

6. **In Word, choose File⇨Save As.**

   The Save As dialog appears.

7. **Click Format and choose Plain Text (`.txt`) from the pop-up menu that appears.**

8. **Type a filename, replacing `.txt` with `.iqy` as the file extension.**

   Don't use the `.txt` extension. The `.iqy` file extension signifies that the file is a Web query for Microsoft Excel.

   If you encounter the File Conversion dialog, as shown in Figure 6-12, click OK to accept the default settings.

9. **Select the Documents folder.**

10. **Click the Save button.**

After you save your Web query, follow these steps to run the Web query:

1. **Open Excel.**

2. **Choose Data⇨Get External Data⇨Run Saved Query.**

3. **Open the `.iqy` file you saved in Word.**

Excel attempts to open the Web page for you, which creates a query range and turns on the Database toolbar.

File Conversion - test query.iqy

Warning: Saving as a text file will cause all formatting, pictures, and objects in your file to be lost.

Text encoding:

◉ Mac OS (Default)   ○ MS–DOS   ○ Other encoding:

| Unicode 4.0 |
| Unicode 4.0 (Little–Endian) |
| Unicode 4.0 UTF–8 |
| Western (ASCII) |
| Western (Mac OS Roman) |
| Western (Windows Latin 1) |

Options:

☐ Insert line breaks

End lines with: [CR only ◆]

☐ Allow character substitution

Preview:

file:///Users/PBk/Desktop/test%20web%20page.htm

[Cancel]   (**OK**)

Figure 6-12:
Saving a
Web query.

We explain how to use query ranges and the Database toolbar in Chapter 7 of this minibook. Excel can use only HTML tables, not pictures of tables, Adobe Flash, PDF, or other formats.

Opening a saved Web page

Web browsers let you save Web pages from their File menus. Follow these steps:

1. **Save a Web page to some place on your hard drive that you'll remember.**

2. **In Excel, choose File➪Open in Excel.**

   The Open dialog appears.

3. **Navigate or use Spotlight to select the saved Web page.**

4. **Click Open to open the saved Web page in Excel.**

Opening a saved Web page in Excel has the advantage over a Web query because you save the content to your computer, so it won't disappear, like Web pages are prone to do.

Pasting HTML code into a cell

If you're good enough with HTML to know how to view the source code in a Web browser, you can copy and paste table information into any cell on a worksheet. In the Web browser, copy so that you include the beginning `<table>` tag and the final `</table>` tag. Switch to Excel and then paste the whole shebang into a cell. Excel generates the table for you.

Getting Excel onto the Web

You have several ways to distribute Excel workbooks on the Web:

✦ Share workbooks with the entire world by putting them into freely accessible Web sites.

✦ Put workbooks into more restrictive environments by using the following:

  • Limited-access Web services, such as OfficeLive, Google Docs, and Mesh.com

  • Course-management systems, such as Blackboard or Angel

Any way you do it, you need two things:

✦ An Internet-accessible file location

✦ The know-how to get your workbook to that location

Preparing a workbook for the Web

You can easily make links. However, consider whether these links will continue to work after you distribute your workbook.

In most cases, you don't want to have links in a document that you distribute in case some don't work. Resolve your links before putting them on the Web by following these steps:

1. **Open your workbook in Excel.**

2. **Choose Edit⇨Links.**

The Links dialog opens (see Figure 6-13), displaying a list of existing links. You can select a link and then click the Break Link button to remove the link. Before you distribute your workbook, be sure that anything you'd originally linked works acceptably without being linked.

Links

Source file	Item	Type	Update	
PB:Use...:Workbook1.xlsx		Worksheet	A	Update Now
				Open Source
				Change Source...
				Break Link

Source file: PB:Users:PBk:Desktop:Store:Workbook1.xlsx

Item:

Type: Worksheet

Update: ⦿ Automatic ◯ Manual

Close

Figure 6-13: Removing and resolving links.

Distributing a workbook "as is"

Probably the easiest way to distribute a workbook is to upload it to a Web server. You can use any number of Web services, including the following:

✦ OfficeLive

✦ Google Docs

✦ Blackboard

✦ Angel

Traditional Web hosting companies give you instructions about how to upload files to their Web server. Whatever service you choose, people wind up clicking a link on a Web page, and they receive your entire workbook as a file. Some Web services, including OfficeLive and Blackboard, can display the workbook in a Web browser without requiring you to save it as a Web page.

Making a Web page

TIP

Before the advent of Web services, choosing File➪Save as Web Page was the only way to get a workbook to display in a Web browser on the Internet. With the advent of Web services, making Web pages from Excel seems old-fashioned.

The Save as Web Page feature in Excel creates a workbook that, when viewed in a Web browser, looks and acts almost like a real workbook, complete with working sheet tabs. When you use this feature, Excel creates two things:

✦ A Web document with an `.htm` file extension

✦ A folder that contains pictures of the objects in your workbook, such as graphs, SmartArt, pictures, and media files

The usual method is to use an FTP program to copy the .htm file and the folder onto a Web server.

See Figure 6-14 for the options in the Save as Web Page dialog:

+ **Format menu:** Select the Web Page (.htm) option to make an .htm Web page and a folder that contains supporting documents, or single-file Web page (.mht).

+ **Workbook/Sheet/Selection option buttons:** Select the Entire Workbook button or the Currently Selected Sheet button.

+ **Web Options button:** We talk about these buttons in the following section.

+ **Compatibility Report button:** Select this button to see a Compatibility Report for this format.

+ **Automate button:** See the section, "Adding automation," later in this chapter, for a description of this button.

+ **New Folder button:** Creates a new folder in Finder.

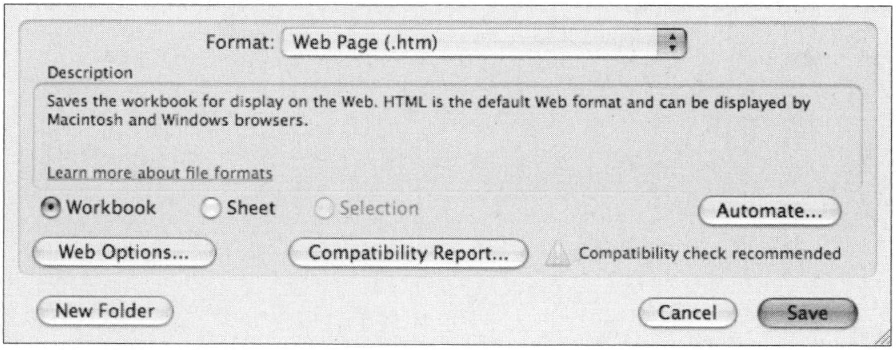

Figure 6-14:
Choosing
Save as
Web Page
options.

Web options

In the Save as Web Page dialog (choose File⇨Save as Web Page to open this dialog), click the Web Options button. In the Web Options dialog, select the General tab if it's not visible already, as shown in Figure 6-15. You have two text boxes you can fill in:

+ **Web Page Title:** Type the title for your Web page.

+ **Web Page Keywords:** Fill in content keyword tags so that Web search engines can index your workbook's Web page.

In addition to the General tab, the Web Options dialog has these tabs:

✦ **Files:** You probably shouldn't change the settings here. The defaults work great for most people.

✦ **Pictures:** You probably shouldn't change settings here, either. The defaults work great for most people.

✦ **Encoding:** Use this tab only if you want advanced control over the font encoding.

Adding automation

You might be using your Mac as a Web server. After all, Apache Web server comes with Mac OS X. Or perhaps you have a shared directory directly on a Web server.

If Excel has write access via Finder to the file location on the Web server, you can let Excel update the Web page on a predetermined schedule. For example, say you want to refresh a Web page every Monday, Wednesday, and Friday.

Click the Automate button in the Save as Web Page dialog to set a recurring schedule, as shown in Figure 6-16. You can find a wide range of possible scheduling options in the Recurring Schedule dialog.

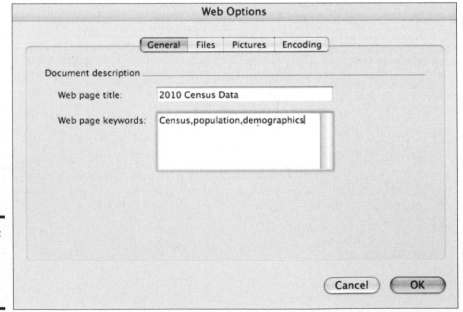

Figure 6-15:
Giving your Web page a title and tags.

Figure 6-16:
Setting an automatic Web page refresh schedule.

Chapter 7: Being Intelligent with Data

In This Chapter

✔ Cutting out the jargon

✔ Making lists and tables

✔ Working with the List Manager

✔ Taking the PivotTable course

✔ Turning Office 2008 into a fully relational database

Dealing with data is fraught with mystery and jargon, not to mention thought and anticipation. Our goal is to take the mystery away and help you use the amazingly powerful tools in Excel to analyze your data. You find data analysis and presentation features unique to Excel for Mac, and we're pleased to be able to focus on them in this chapter.

Simplifying Database Jargon

Sometimes, a word's meaning changes, depending on context. In this chapter, we use the following words with these meanings:

✦ **List:** A *list* is a collection of data arranged in rows and columns, like in a table, that you can use to display and analyze sets of data.

✦ **Database:** A *database* is a collection of lists or tables.

A list in Excel 2008 for Mac and a table in Excel 2007 for Windows are the same thing.

Listing the List Rules

Excel can figure out whether you have a table or list if your data follows these simple rules:

✦ The first row — and only the first row — includes column names. Those names are unique.

✦ The end of the table or list is the first completely empty row and/or the first completely empty column.

✦ Merged cells don't exist.

Lists can live in one of two places:

✦ **List sheet:** A sheet devoted entirely to a list.

✦ **Worksheet:** A list can be a range on a worksheet. More than one list can exist on a single worksheet.

The list shown in Figure 7-1 obeys our rules. You can use this data to follow along in our examples in the following sections by typing the table anywhere on a worksheet, or use your own data if it follows Excel's data table rules.

Think about these two questions before getting started making your own lists:

✦ Where's your data now?

✦ Where do you want the list to be when you're done?

	Experiment	Result 1	Result 2	Result 3	Result 4
Figure 7-1:	Trial 1	9	0	12	6
Typing some	Trial 2	6	9	10	4
sample data.	Trial 3	4	8	3	3

List Wizard Step 1 — Data locations

To open the List Wizard, choose View⇨Toolbars⇨List. On the toolbar that appears, click List Wizard. The List Wizard appears. The top section of the wizard asks Where Is the Data for Your List? The question presumes you have data somewhere. Your data could be on a sheet of paper, in an external database, on an Excel worksheet, or elsewhere. We show you a common case: You have a range of data on an Excel worksheet.

If you don't have a range of data to work with, type the data shown in Figure 7-1 into a blank worksheet.

Follow these steps to make a list:

1. **Select any cell in the data range.**

2. **Choose View⇨Toolbars⇨List.**

The List Manager toolbar appears, as shown in Figure 7-2.

Insert Row

Insert Column | Table Autoformat

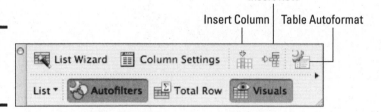

3. **On the List Manager toolbar, select List Wizard.**

Step 1 of the List Wizard appears, as shown in Figure 7-3. The List Wizard

- Figures out that a cell range contains data
- Displays the data range in the In an Open Workbook field
- Figures out that the list has headers
- Selects the My List Has Headers check box

4. **In the Where Is the Data for Your List? section, select an option.**

The question offers these choices:

- *None:* If you're new to lists and want a comprehensive step-by-step process, you can build a list from scratch by using the None option. This assumes that you're working on a worksheet that has no data, and that you plan to type the data into the wizard.

- *In an Open Workbook:* Uses data already in the workbook. Most of the time, you probably start with data already on a worksheet, so this chapter focuses on this method.

- *External Data Source:* Uses data outside the workbook. We talk about working with external data sources using ODBC (Open Database Connectivity) in the section, "Using Excel with Relational Databases," later in this chapter. You can read about Web queries in Chapter 6 of this minibook.

**Book III
Chapter 7**

**Being Intelligent
with Data**

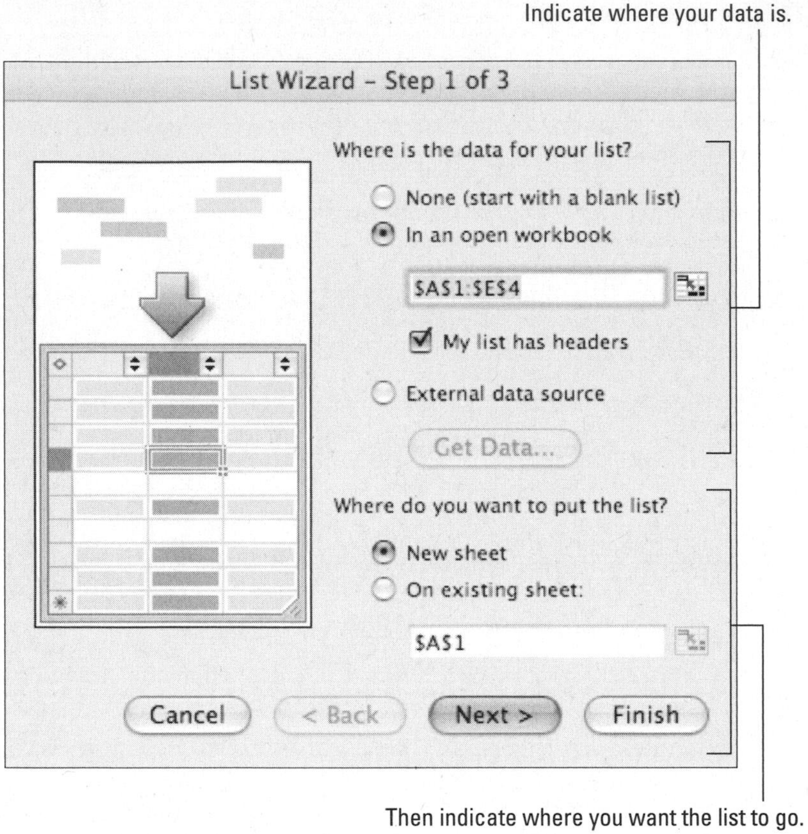

Indicate where your data is.

List Wizard – Step 1 of 3

Where is the data for your list?

○ None (start with a blank list)

◉ In an open workbook

$A$1:$E$4

☑ My list has headers

○ External data source

Get Data...

Where do you want to put the list?

◉ New sheet

○ On existing sheet:

$A$1

Cancel   < Back   Next >   Finish

Figure 7-3:
The List
Wizard —
Step 1.

Then indicate where you want the list to go.

5. **In the Where Do You Want to Put Your List? section, select an option.**

Two options appear below this question:

- *New Sheet:* Devoted entirely to a list (a list sheet). We chose this option for our example.

- *On Existing Sheet:* If you select this option, type a cell into the form field or select a cell by clicking the selection button to the right of the input field. Either way, the chosen cell becomes the upper-left cell of the new list. You can select any existing worksheet in any open workbook. If you leave the input field blank and select a data range before opening the wizard, Excel converts the current range to a list in its current place on the worksheet.

6. **Select Next to advance to Step 2 of the List Wizard.**

We discuss this step in the following section.

List Wizard Step 2 — Data types

In Step 2 of the List Wizard, you tell Excel what kind of data is in each column by selecting a data type for each column name (derived from the column headings). The wizard's default data type for all column names is Any Value.

You can set a data type for each column name, one-by-one. Follow these steps with each column name whose data type you need to change:

1. **Select a column name in the Columns list (see Figure 7-4).**

You can start with the top name in the list and work your way down. Figure 7-4 shows the last column name in the list, Result 4, selected.

Column names
(field names) Data type

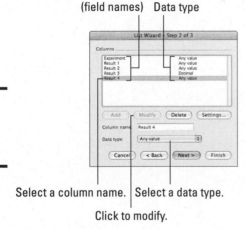

Figure 7-4:
The List
Wizard —
Step 2.

Select a column name. | Select a data type.

Click to modify.

2. **Select the appropriate data type from the Data Type pop-up menu.**

A column's entries must match the data type without exception. Choose from these data types:

- *Any Value:* Any kind of data.

- *Whole Number:* Exclusively whole numbers.

- *Decimal:* Exclusively numbers, allowing decimal values.

- *Currency:* Exclusively numbers formatted as currency.

- *Counter:* A column that assigns a number to the data row.

- *Text:* Treats all characters entered as characters and numeric values.

- *List:* Requires that all data in the column match an entry in a predetermined list of values or text for data validation.

- *Date:* All column entries are dates.

- *Time:* All column entries are times.

- *Calculated column:* You can add a column of values based on a formula by using the Add button with this option.

3. Click the Modify button.

4. Repeat Steps 1–3 for each column name until you specify the data type for each of the column names.

Setting the data type this way helps Excel do the following:

- Remember what kind of data is in each column. This is important when you're using queries to read the data.

- Enforce data validation based on the data types you choose.

- Format the list by using the data types you choose.

In Step 2 of the wizard, you can also fine-tune data types, if you want. Each column name has its own settings. To refine the data types, follow these steps:

1. Select a column name in the Columns list (see Figure 7-4).

2. Click the Settings button.

The Column Settings dialog appears, as shown in Figure 7-5.

Alternatively, double-click a column name in the Columns list to display the Column Settings dialog.

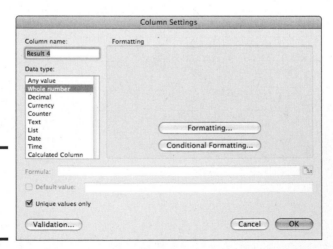

Figure 7-5:
Requiring
unique
values in
a column.

3. Select a Data Type option.

4. Choose from these options:

- *Unique Values Only:* Doesn't allow duplicate values in the column. This setting applies to many kinds of lists, such as invoices and record numbers. Many people don't realize that Excel has this capability built-in and that it doesn't require macros.

- *Default Value:* Prefills new records with the default value entered in the field. Don't use this option with the Unique Values Only setting selected.

The Column Settings dialog has three additional buttons: Formatting, Conditional Formatting, and Validation, each of which is discussed elsewhere in this book.

The settings you select in the Column Settings dialog apply to the column name you selected in Step 1 in this section, formatting and validating your database columns. The Formula field is used with the Calculated Column data type.

5. Click OK to dismiss the Column Settings dialog and return to the List Wizard Step 2.

6. When you finish making changes in Step 2 of the List Wizard, select Next.

Step 3 appears, which we talk about in the following section.

List Wizard Step 3 — List options

In the third step of the List Wizard (see Figure 7-6), you name your list and set formatting options.

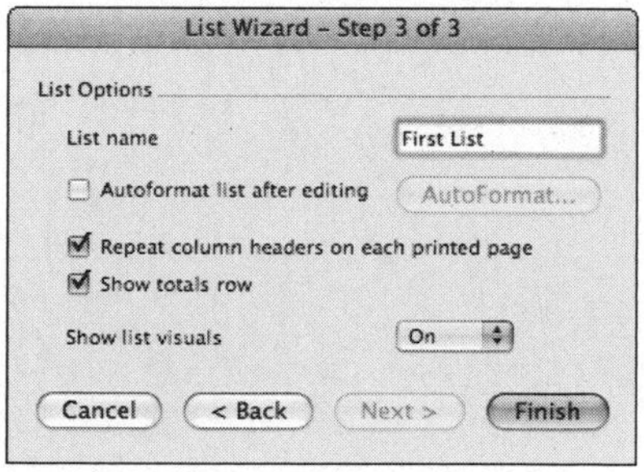

Figure 7-6:
The List
Wizard —
Step 3.

List Wizard – Step 3 of 3

List Options

List name [First List]

☐ Autoformat list after editing (AutoFormat...)

☑ Repeat column headers on each printed page
☑ Show totals row

Show list visuals [On ⇕]

(Cancel) (< Back) (Next >) (Finish)

Choose from the following options:

✦ **List Name:** If your new list will be on a list sheet, the name you type here appears on the sheet tab. If your new list will be on an existing worksheet, the name you type appears as the name of the list object on the worksheet. You can use this name to access the list object programmatically via programs like VBA. Don't use spaces or special characters.

✦ **Autoformat List after Editing:** After you select this option, click the Autoformat button to choose a list style. We like the default style best.

✦ **Repeat Column Headers on Each Printed Page:** It's usually a good idea when making a new list sheet to use repeating column heads, but it's not an option if you plan to place your list on an existing worksheet.

✦ **Show Totals Row:** If you don't need calculations, you can deselect this feature. Our example has this option turned on.

✦ **Show List Visuals:** We prefer to leave them turned on, but if you want an experience closer to Excel for Windows, turn them off or use the Auto setting.

When you're done selecting options in Step 3 of the wizard, click Finish to see your new list, as shown in Figure 7-7.

Sort, filter, and custom filter

Figure 7-7:
Viewing your new list.

Experiment	Result 1	Result 2	Result 3	Result 4	(New Column)
Trial 1	9	0	12	6	
Trial 2	6	9	10	4	
Trial 3	4	8	3	3	
Total				13	

Formula and Formula Builder

Your new list has a bevy of Excel's most powerful tools turned on and available to you:

✦ **AutoFilter buttons:** Use these buttons to sort, filter, and create custom filters for the data in your columns. Toggle AutoFilter on and off by choosing Data➪Filter➪AutoFilter.

✦ **List Manager toolbar:** One of Excel's most powerful tools. Use it to manage all your important list functions. We explore this tool in the section, "Working with Data by Using List Manager," later in this chapter.

✦ **Total row:** If you select this option in Step 3 of the List Wizard, a Total row appears. Click in any cell of the Total row to select a formula from the pop-up menu that appears. If you select Other, Excel's superb Formula Builder assists you. You're not restricted to just database formulas — you can enter your own formulas.

✦ **(New Column):** Just type a column name in this cell to add a new column.

Making a List the Fast Way

Not every list deserves the attention to detail given in the preceding section's steps. Quite often, time is of the essence. Keep in mind, however, that a list sheet made the fast way doesn't have

✦ Data types

✦ Data validation

How quickly can you make a list? Follow these steps:

1. Copy a range of data that obeys the list rules.

You can find the rules in the section, "Listing the List Rules," earlier in this chapter.

2. Click the Sheets tab of Elements Gallery.

Click the Elements button on the Standard toolbar if Elements Gallery isn't open. See Figure 7-8.

Look for List Sheet on the Blank Sheets tab of Elements Gallery. List sheets don't appear on the Lists tab. The Lists tab has preformatted lists (ledger sheets) that you can customize.

3. Choose Blank Sheets⇨List Sheet.

A blank list sheet appears.

4. Choose Edit⇨Paste.

Your data appears on a preformatted list sheet.

Figure 7-8:
Making a list sheet using Elements Gallery.

From this point, you can click the Column Settings button on the List Manager to define Column Name data types.

Working with Data by Using List Manager

After you create your list, click the List button (see Figure 7-9) in the List Manager toolbar to open a drop-down list, a one-stop shop for working with the data on your list.

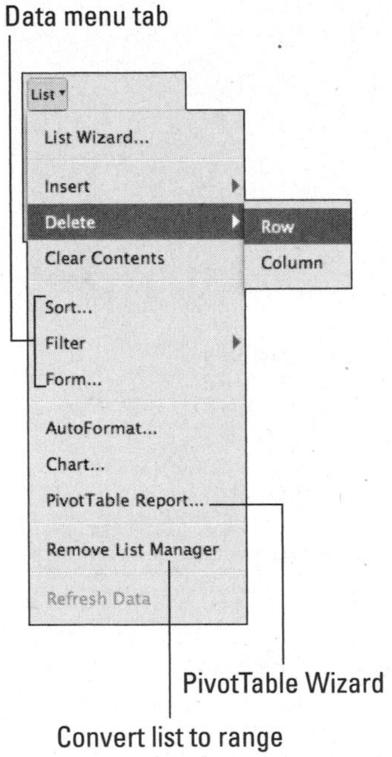

Data menu tab

List ▾

List Wizard...

Insert   ▶

Delete   ▶   Row

Clear Contents   Column

Sort...

Filter   ▶

Form...

AutoFormat...

Chart...

PivotTable Report...

Remove List Manager

Refresh Data

Figure 7-9:
Managing
your list.

PivotTable Wizard

Convert list to range

Some of the tools on the List button menu are also on the List Manager toolbar, but we don't want you to overlook these tools:

✦ **Delete Row/Column:** Available only on the List menu within the List Manager toolbar.

✦ **Chart:** Activates the Chart tab on Elements Gallery, if it's not active already.

✦ **PivotTable Report:** Turns on the PivotTable Wizard and uses your list as the data source.

✦ **Remove List Manager:** Converts the selected list into an ordinary cell range. The List toolbar remains visible, but Excel no longer considers the cell range a list.

Taking the PivotTable Course

Become familiar with the PivotTables data analysis tool. Most folks now consider PivotTables business intelligence (BI) tools, but they work for anyone with medium to large data sets.

PivotTables are a great way to present organized summaries of data.

When it comes to understanding the PivotTable feature, we're going to get you started with the excellent, 30-minute Pivot Report course that's included free with Excel 2008 for Mac. It comes complete with sample data and a review quiz at the end of the course. (You need an Internet connection to take the course.)

Access the free Pivot Report course by following these steps:

1. **Click the Help button on Excel's Standard toolbar.**

   The Excel Help dialog appears.

2. **Type** pivot report **into the search terms.**

   Search results appear in a tray below the search box.

3. **Select Analyze Your Data with PivotTable Reports.**

   A course summary appears, including a Start Course button.

4. **Click the yellow Start Course button.**

   The course starts in your Web browser.

Using Excel with Relational Databases

Experts have often said that Excel isn't a true relational database. That's flatly not true because Excel ships with a helper application — Microsoft Query — in Excel for Mac and Excel for Windows. You can use Excel workbooks as data sources in relational databases.

You might find a screen shot of the Microsoft Query interface (see Figure 7-10) helpful if you have experience using relational databases. Be reassured that indeed, you can do this sort of thing in Excel. Yes, you can use SQL (Structure Query Language), create joins, and even use calculated fields and parameter queries.

**Book III
Chapter 7**

**Being Intelligent
with Data**

Figure 7-10:
Making a join in Office 2008 for Mac.

Explaining relational databases

We need to cut through some database jargon. Database gurus talk about data this way:

✦ **Flat files:** Standalone lists and tables, such as those discussed in the earlier in this chapter.

✦ **Relational databases:** Have two or more tables in a database, and those tables are set up to reduce the total number of columns needed by relating them to each other in SQL queries.

Say that you have a list that includes the names and addresses of all employees in a company. You might also have a list that contains the attendance details of those employees.

What's common in both these lists? The employee number.

Wouldn't it be nice if the common field in these lists were linked so that you could query one list from the other? Such an arrangement would require that both lists have a relation, thus the term *relational database!* Of course, we're explaining the whole concept in a very simple way, and you can find tons of descriptions floating around in books, research papers, and online sources about these relational databases.

Installing an ODBC driver

Office for Mac doesn't ship with a special program called an ODBC (Open Database Connectivity) driver. If you want relational database capabilities in Office for Mac, you have to install an ODBC driver.

We don't go too deeply into this topic, but ODBC acts as a go-between and communicates with both Excel and the data source; see the relationship in Figure 7-11. In the figure, the database source is external to Excel. Excel's phrase for this is *external data*.

Figure 7-11:
Communi-
cating
with a
database
via ODBC.

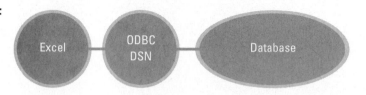

Buying an ODBC driver

We know two independent software vendors that sell ODBC drivers. Both are well-respected, Mac-friendly companies. Detailed download, installation, and operation explanations are on their respective Web sites:

✦ **ActualTechnologies:** ActualTechnologies' Microsoft Access driver can use Excel workbooks as data sources, in addition to Microsoft Access .mdb databases. This driver can work with database files located in Mac OS X Finder. Be sure to read and follow the excellent installation instructions provided.

    www.actualtechnologies.com

✦ **OpenLink:** The drivers from this company work by connecting over a network to the IP address of databases that the database administrator has preconfigured to accept your network connection.

    www.openlinksw.com

Check ODBC vendor sites for free trial offers.

Compatibility with Excel for Windows

On the Mac, Microsoft Query is read-only. It can't add or drop tables, nor can it add or remove records. This offers better security, but it reduces functionality.

If your database administrator is concerned about database integrity, Excel for Mac makes a perfect client because it can't do table or record manipulations.

**Book III
Chapter 7**

**Being Intelligent
with Data**

Reading more about relational databases

As you might have guessed by now, the topic of relational databases is a little too advanced for this book. You can find several articles about working with external data on the Web. You can download these free articles from this Web site:

        www.agentjim.com/MVP/Excel/
            ExcelHome.htm

On this site, you can find articles that explain details about how to connect to outside data sources and how to use Microsoft Office on the Mac as a relational database. The following articles are currently on the Web site:

- Macintosh, Microsoft Office, and Microsoft Access

- Microsoft Office for Macintosh Database Connectivity Overview

- Using Microsoft Office as a Relational Database

Chapter 8: Printing from Excel

In This Chapter

🖋 **Customizing your Excel Page Setup**

🖋 **Adding headers and footers**

🖋 **Creating a digital watermark**

🖋 **Deciding what print quality you want to use**

🖋 **Choosing a paper size**

*P*rinting from Excel is a bit different than the other Office applications in some respects. Excel's printing feature takes full advantage of the Mac OS X print capabilities, and Excel supplements these with some clever tricks of its own.

Using the Page Setup Dialog

Excel's Page Setup dialog lets you format your worksheet's printing output. To display this dialog, choose File➪Page Setup➪Sheet (see Figure 8-1). Alternatively, you can select Print Titles from the Formatting Palette's Page Setup section, which takes you directly to the Sheet tab.

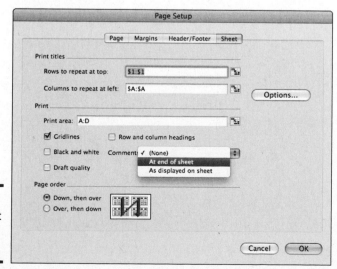

Figure 8-1:
Setting print titles and more.

Browsing the Sheet tab

You have several ways to adjust the way you print Excel files on the Sheet tab, as discussed in the following sections.

Print Titles section

This section has an Options button that we explain in the section, "Setting the Paper Size," later in this chapter. Print Titles lets you make the following decisions:

✦ **Rows to Repeat at Top:** If you want the first row (probably composed of headings) to repeat on each printed page, use this setting, as shown in Figure 8-1. You can either

- Type in a row or range of rows.

- Click the Select Range button (to the right of the Rows to Repeat at Top field); then, click the row number in your workbook, as shown in Figure 8-2. Clicking the Select Range button a second time returns you to the Page Setup dialog.

✦ **Columns to Repeat at Left:** This option is like setting a row to print, except you click a column instead. You can either

- Type in a column or range of columns.

- Click the Select Range button (to the right of the Columns to Repeat at Left field); then, click the column letters in your workbook, as shown in Figure 8-3. Clicking the Select Range button again returns you to the Page Setup dialog.

Figure 8-2:
Selecting a row that you want to print at the top of every page.

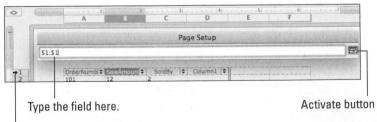

Type the field here.   Activate button

Click here to select a row.

Print section

Excel lets you limit printing to a predetermined range of cells. When you set a print area, Excel remembers this information when you save the workbook. And Excel prints this range when you click the Print button on the Standard toolbar or if you accept the defaults when choosing File➪Print.

Figure 8-3:
Selecting a column to print on the left of every page.

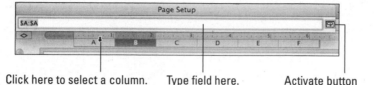

Click here to select a column.　　Type field here.　　Activate button

You have several different ways to set the print area:

✦ Choose Page Setup➪Sheet; type the cell range in the Print Area field.

✦ Choose Page Setup➪Sheet; in the Print section, click the Select Range button. Drag over the range of cells you want to print and then click the Select Range button again.

✦ Select a range directly on your worksheet; choose File➪Print Area➪ Set Print Area.

We explain comments in Chapter 3 of this minibook. The Comments menu lets you choose from these options:

✦ **None:** Don't include comments.

✦ **At End of Sheet:** Show all comments at the end of the printed sheet.

✦ **As Displayed on Sheet:** Show comments as they appear on the worksheet.

Using the Margins tab

When you click the Margins button on the Formatting Palette, the Page Setup's Margins tab appears, as shown in Figure 8-4.

You may find the Center on Page check boxes of special interest:

✦ **Horizontally:** Provides equal amounts of blank space on the left and right sides of your printed page

✦ **Vertically:** Provides equal amounts of blank space on the top and bottom of your printed page

Select both options to center printing.

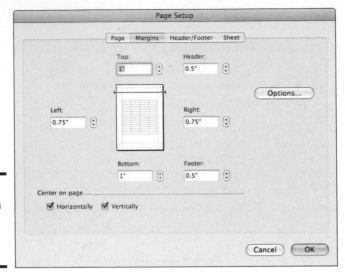

Figure 8-4:
Centering a
worksheet
on the
printout.

Working with Headers and Footers

 You can work with headers and footers in Page Layout View by choosing View⇨Page Layout or clicking the Page Layout button.

Entering a header/footer

 Formatting headers and footers adds a distinctive appearance to your printed worksheets. You can also easily include important date and time information. Follow these steps to add a header or footer:

1. **Move the cursor over the white space near the top of each page to format a header or over the white space near the bottom of each page to format a footer.**

   A prompt appears, telling you to double-click if you want to add a header (or footer), as shown in Figure 8-5.

Figure 8-5:
Excel subtly
coaxes you
to add a
header.

2. Double-click in the white space.

The Header/Footer text area opens (see Figure 8-6), and the Header/Footer toolbar becomes available (see Figure 8-7). You may have to look for the toolbar on your screen. It won't necessarily appear where you see it in the figure.

You can also use the formatting options on the Header/Footer toolbar rather than the Formatting Palette.

Figure 8-6:
Typing a header.

Type your header here

3. Type your header or footer in the text provided.

4. Click the Close button to exit the Header/Footer dialog.

Figure 8-7:
Entering page information into a footer.

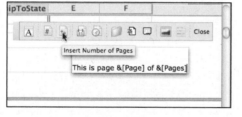

Insert Number of Pages

This is page &[Page] of &[Pages]

Finessing your footers (and headers)

When you're entering or editing a header or footer, you can use these buttons (left to right on the Header/Footer toolbar, as shown in Figure 8-8) to make things fancy:

✦ **Format Text:** Select text; then click Format Text to display the Font dialog. See Chapter 3 of this minibook for font formatting options.

✦ **Insert Page Numbers:** Inserts `&[Page]` code. When printing, the current page number appears on your printed page where you put this code.

✦ **Insert Number of Pages:** Inserts `&[Pages]` code. When printing, the number of pages in the entire document is printed with the current page number on your printed page where you put this code.

You can combine codes with text. For example, use Insert Page Numbers and Insert Page Numbers with Additional Text like this: `Page &[Page] of &[Pages]` to print Page # of #.

**Book III
Chapter 8**

Printing from Excel

✦ **Insert Date:** Inserts `&[Date]` code. When printing, the current date appears on your printed page where you put this code.

✦ **Insert Time:** Inserts `&[Time]` code. When printing, the system time appears on your printed page where you put this code.

✦ **Insert File Path:** Inserts `&[Path]&[File]` codes. When printing, the file pathname and filename of the spreadsheet appear on your printed page where you put this code.

✦ **Insert File Name:** Inserts `&[File]` code. When printing, the filename of the spreadsheet appears on your printed page where you put this code.

✦ **Insert Sheet Name:** Inserts `&[Tab]` code. When printing, the name of the worksheet appears on your printed page where you put this code.

✦ **Insert Picture:** Displays the Choose a Picture dialog, where you can navigate or use Spotlight to select a background picture. Inserts `&[Picture]` code.

✦ **Format Picture:** Displays the Format Picture dialog, where you can control the size and other formatting aspects of your picture.

Use Format Picture dialog's Picture tab. In the Image Control pop-up menu, select Watermark to format your inserted picture as a watermark.

✦ **Close:** Dismisses the Header/Footer toolbar and displays the worksheet.

Figure 8-8:
Exploring
the Header/
Footer
toolbar.

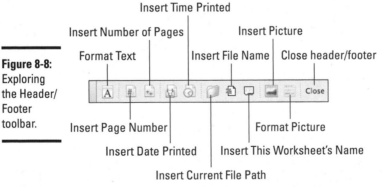

Headers and footers are divided into three distinct regions. You're in the left, right, or center region, depending on where you double-click.

If you prefer the retro look of the old Header/Footer pane from previous versions of Excel, you can still access it by choosing File⇨Page Setup and then clicking the Header/Footer tab; you can also choose View⇨Header and Footer. We think the new way — using Page Layout View — is more intuitive.

Making a Watermark

You can use the Picture feature of the Header/Footer toolbar to insert a picture as a watermark. A *watermark* gets its name from a paper-manufacturing process in which words or symbols are embedded in paper pages by wetting the paper. In an electronic environment, you create a watermark by formatting text and pictures to appear only faintly and then putting them into the background.

Follow this step-by-step process to insert WordArt as a watermark:

1. **Choose Gallery on the Standard toolbar to open Elements Gallery.**

2. **On the WordArt tab, click a style of your choice.**

3. **Type what you want to use as your watermark.**

It might be something like **Confidential**.

4. **Right-click the border of the WordArt and choose Save as Picture from the pop-up menu that appears.**

The Save dialog appears.

5. **Navigate to a handy location and click Save.**

You're now done with the WordArt you created, and you can delete it, if you want.

6. **In the workbook where you want the watermark, choose View⇨ Page Layout or click the Page Layout button.**

The workbook switches to Page Layout View.

7. **Double-click the center of the header area, where it says Double-Click to Add Header.**

8. **Click the Insert Picture button on the Header/Footer toolbar.**

9. **Go to where you saved your WordArt and select the image.**

10. **Click the Insert button in the File dialog.**

11. **Click the Format Picture button on the Header/Footer toolbar.**

Set rotation, brightness, and other settings as desired on both tabs of the Format Picture dialog.

12. **Click OK to close the Format Picture dialog and then click Close to close the Header/Footer toolbar.**

**Book III
Chapter 8**

Printing from Excel

Adjusting Print Quality

Adjusting the quality of the print jobs you get from Excel can be a two-stage (but several-step) process:

✦ In the first stage, you adjust what Excel sends to your printer.

✦ In the second stage, you tell your printer the quality level that you want.

Telling your computer what to send to the printer

The following steps determine your Excel print settings:

1. Click the Print Titles button on the Formatting Palette.

The Sheet tab opens in the Page Setup dialog (as shown in Figure 8-1 earlier in this chapter).

2. Select the appropriate settings.

You can select

- *Black and White:* Produces black-and-white printed output.

- *Draft Quality:* Prints quickly at low quality. Fine lines and details, such as gridlines, may not print, even if selected in settings.

3. Click the Page tab.

4. In the Print Quality pop-up menu, choose from options offered by your printer driver.

Options vary by brand and model of printer. See Figure 8-9. These settings affect the quality of the output that Excel sends to the printer.

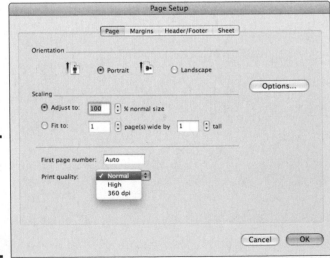

Figure 8-9: Setting print quality on the Page tab of the Page Setup dialog.

5. Click OK to close the Page Setup dialog.

Do you want it fast? Or, do you want it sharp? You have the following choices:

✦ For the fastest printing:

- Select the Draft Quality check box on the Sheet tab.
- Pick the lowest-quality option that your printer offers in the Print Quality field on the Page tab.

✦ For the highest-quality printing:

- Deselect Draft Quality on the Sheet tab.
- On the Page tab, select the highest-quality setting that your printer offers in the Print Quality field.

You can experiment with settings in between until you get the right balance of quality and speed with your printer.

Telling your printer how to do its job

The preceding section tells you how to set the quality of the output that Excel sends to the printer. This section tells you how to tell your printer what to do. Options vary by brand and model printer, so you may not see everything we illustrate available for your own printer. To tell your printer the quality level you want, follow these steps:

1. Choose File➪Print.

The first time you choose Print, a condensed Print dialog opens, much like the one pictured in Figure 8-10.

2. Click the downward-pointing triangle.

The full Print dialog opens (see Figure 8-11).

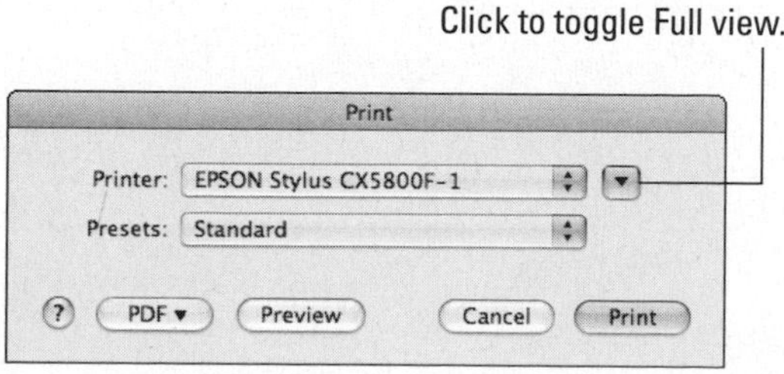

Click to toggle Full view.

Figure 8-10:
The
condensed
Print dialog.

> Print
>
> Printer: EPSON Stylus CX5800F-1
>
> Presets: Standard
>
> (?) (PDF ▾) (Preview)   (Cancel) (Print)

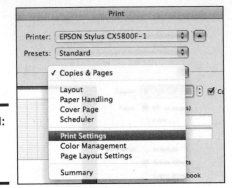

Figure 8-11:
Switching
to Print
Settings.

3. Choose Copies & Pages➪Print Settings.

You can see this option in Figure 8-12. The Print Settings dialog provided
by your printer appears.

Even if you set Excel to print top-quality output (see the preceding section),
you may need to adjust the printer's settings to get the highest-quality
print. Some printer brands default to the lowest-quality setting to
provide the highest speed.

4. Choose File➪Print.

The Print dialog opens, as shown in Figure 8-13.

Some of the Print settings also show up on the Formatting Palette and in
the Page Setup dialog.

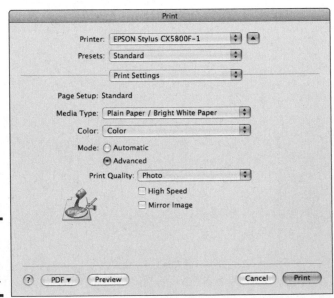

Figure 8-12:
Adjusting
the printer's
print quality.

Number of copies

Additional printer options   Set pages

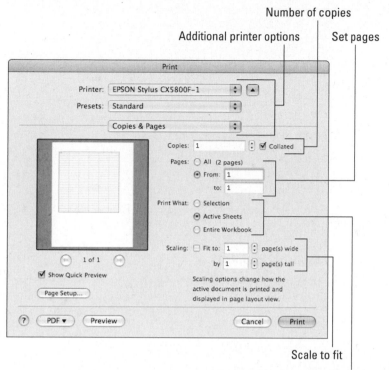

Figure 8-13:
Setting print
options.

Scale to fit

Choose what you want printed.

5. **Make any changes you want to the print options in the Printer dialog.**

   You have these options:

   - *Printer:* Select a printer from your available printers in this pop-up menu.

   - *Presets:* This pop-up menu lists the names of combinations of print settings that you've previously saved. Select one or select Standard for the default set of printing options.

   - *Copies & pages:* Choose settings provided by your printer driver.

   - *Copies:* Type or use the Increase/Decrease control to set the number of pages to print.

   - *Collated:* Select this check box to print all the pages in order for each copy.

   - *Pages:* Select All or type beginning and ending page numbers that you want to print.

   - *Print What:* You can select *Selection* (which prints what's currently selected in the workbook), *Active Sheets* (prints the currently selected sheet tabs), or *Entire Workbook* (prints all sheets of the workbook).

- *Scaling:* Scaling options change how the active document is printed and displayed in Page Layout View. For example, you can choose settings such as Fit to *[Number]* Pages Wide by *[Number]* Pages Tall.

- *Show Quick Preview:* Select this check box to display a small preview in the Print dialog.

- *Page Setup:* Select this button to display the Page Setup dialog (see Figure 8-9).

- *PDF:* Select this button to display PDF printing options, which we describe thoroughly in Book IV, Chapter 9.

- *Preview:* Select this button to display a print preview of your document in the Mac OS X Preview application.

6. After you set your print options, click the Print button.

Your spreadsheet prints with the settings you just chose.

Setting the Paper Size

Most of the time, you'll probably be happy with the default paper size settings. In case you want to change them, click the Options button on any tab of the Page Setup dialog, as shown in Figure 8-14.

The Options button displays the pane that lets you adjust paper sizes. We describe this pane in detail in Book II, Chapter 8. Changing the paper size affects the Page Layout View.

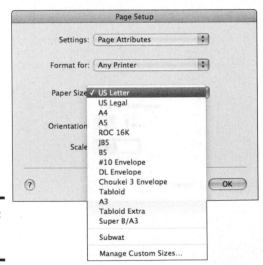

Figure 8-14:
Setting the paper size.

Book IV

PowerPoint 2008

The 5th Wave   By Rich Tennant

"Nifty chart, Frank, but not entirely necessary."

Contents at a Glance

Chapter 1: Revealing PowerPoint

In This Chapter

✔ **Getting comfortable with PowerPoint**

✔ **Showing in Presenter Tools View**

✔ **Building in Normal View**

✔ **Sorting in Slide Sorter View**

Aptly named, PowerPoint is the tool that presenters of all kinds rely on to help them communicate with their audience. Initially, PowerPoint was used to create the framework that aided presenters. Then, PowerPoint widened its scope to encompass the creation of self-running kiosk presentations. In the present scenario, PowerPoint's role has further expanded into the Web 2.0 horizons, with educators, businesspersons, students, and others incorporating Web content into PowerPoint and making PowerPoint presentations available online.

Our goal is not only to help you feel comfortable with PowerPoint, but also with yourself as a presenter. Throughout this minibook, we include advice, hopefully sage. Other times, we chirp about some of the exciting PowerPoint features.

We put you at ease and make presenting to an audience fun. At the very least, we hope to make presenting less stressful for you, even if it's your first time in front of an audience.

Getting Up and Running

Although PowerPoint can present your media content in slides, it has real value as a thought-organizing tool. We invite you to follow along in this chapter by working with the same presentation that we are. Begin by following these steps:

1. **Open PowerPoint.**

2. **Choose File⇨Project Gallery if Project Gallery doesn't open automatically when you start PowerPoint.**

    Project Gallery appears.

3. **Select the New tab if it's not already selected.**

Making PowerPoint more Windows-like

Mac users might cringe at this suggestion and can skip this sidebar. Some Windows users don't feel comfortable on a Mac because all the application windows are open at the same time — you don't have a single Application Window. You can remedy this situation if it bothers you.

Holding the Option-⌘ keys down when you click PowerPoint's Dock icon hides the other open applications so that all you see is PowerPoint. To switch to other open applications, press ⌘-Tab or click their Dock icons, similar to the old taskbar in Windows. If you hold down the mouse button on Dock icons, you can switch from one open presentation to another by using a pop-up menu, just like you can in Windows.

4. In the Category list on the left, select Presentations.

Project Gallery displays its built-in presentation templates.

5. Double-click Introducing PowerPoint 2008.

A new presentation based on the template opens in PowerPoint.

Facing Your Audience

When you work with PowerPoint, you can choose from two main operating modes. PowerPoint usually opens in Editing mode, in which you can create your presentations and work on their content. The other mode is Presentation mode, in which you actually run a presentation, playing all its content, fancy effects, timings, audio, and movies.

If you have a presentation open in PowerPoint, to get to PowerPoint's different interfaces, focus on the View menu. To start running a presentation, choose View➪Presenter Tools. Even if you don't have a projector connected, you should be able to see Presenter Tools on your monitor.

Presenter Tools View shows you the screen in Figure 1-1. Only the selected slide (not visible in Figure 1-1) is projected to your audience. You can see much more, including the elapsed time, or you can toggle to the current time. You're in complete control with an easy-to-use scroll bar in case you want to skip to any slide at any time. You can type in the slide notes pane while your presentation is running, or you can refer to slide notes you typed in previously to assist you with presenting. To leave Presenter Tools, click the End button or press the Escape key.

Start/Pause timer

Reset timer Scroll bar

Slide preview

Next

Previous

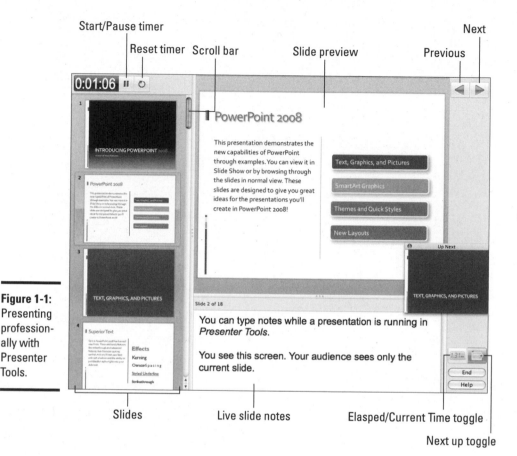

Figure 1-1:
Presenting
profession-
ally with
Presenter
Tools.

Slides

Live slide notes

Elasped/Current Time toggle

Next up toggle

Building and Editing in Normal View

Although the Presenter Tools View we explore in the preceding section is the professional presenter view, the workhorse editing view in PowerPoint is the Normal View, which you can access by choosing View➪Normal. Normal View is what PowerPoint uses by default and can be seen in Figure 1-2.

In Normal View, you build presentations by adding slides with titles, text, and rich content, and then animating them judiciously, if required. PowerPoint has other important views that you can find out more about later in this minibook. Figure 1-2 shows Normal View on a small screen, as you might see it on a 13-inch iBook. When working with a small screen, hide and display Elements Gallery and the Toolbox quickly by clicking the Elements Gallery and Toolbox buttons on the Standard toolbar. Otherwise, feel free to move things around on your screen.

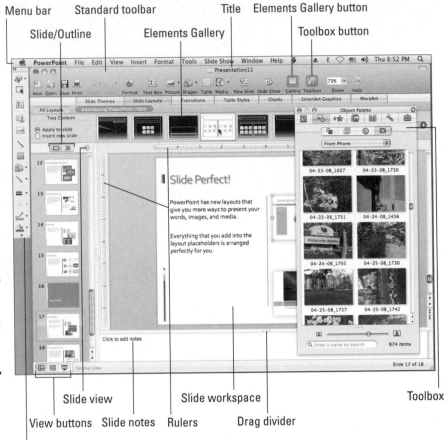

Figure 1-2:
Building
presentations
in Normal
View.

We want to let you in on a couple of minor secrets about using PowerPoint's Normal View that can make working in this view smoother for you. Refer to Figure 1-2 for the following discussion. The View buttons at the lower-left corner are only three of the possible views available in PowerPoint:

✦ **To run the presentation starting with the slide you're working on, click the miniature screen button, the rightmost View button.**

✦ **To end a running presentation, press the Escape key.**

✦ **To change to Slide View, click the Slide View button. The pane that shows the Slide/Outline selector closes.**

✦ **To restore the Slide/Outline selector pane, choose View➪Normal.**

Organizing Slides in Slide Sorter View

Shown in Figure 1-3, the Slide Sorter View (choose View⇨Slide Sorter) is used for several purposes. You can use it to do the following:

✦ Organize your slides by putting them into the proper order.

✦ Duplicate and delete slides.

✦ Multiselect sequential or nonsequential slides.

✦ Hide and unhide selected slides.

✦ Control transition effects. Transition effects play when your presentation advances from one slide to the next.

✦ Set and adjust slide timings.

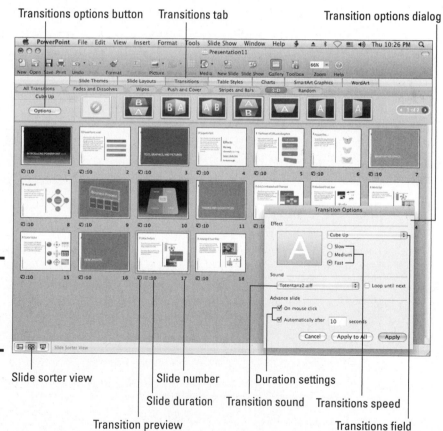

Transitions options button   Transitions tab   Transition options dialog

Slide sorter view   Slide number   Duration settings

Slide duration   Transition sound   Transitions speed

Transition preview   Transitions field

Figure 1-3: Looking over the Slide Sorter View.

Book IV Chapter 1

Revealing PowerPoint

Using slide timings is optional. You can set the amount of time a slide will be shown, and then PowerPoint advances to the next slide automatically during your presentation. Setting timings can be a consideration when setting up a self-running kiosk presentation.

Selecting slides

What you can do in Slide Sorter View depends on knowing what's currently selected. In Slide Sorter View, PowerPoint lets you know which slide or slides are currently selected by putting a small, faint, bluish border around selected slides. See Figure 1-4 (even though you can't see the blue selection around each slide in this black-and-white book) and compare the border of the slide that's selected to the slide that's not selected. The border difference is subtle, yet distinct. Selected slides may appear to be slightly larger than non-selected slides.

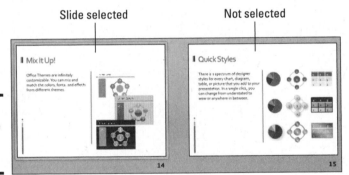

Figure 1-4: Spotting the selection indicator.

Here are some guidelines that can help you select slides in Slide Sorter View:

✦ To select one slide, click the slide.

✦ To select a range of slides, hold the (left) mouse button down while you drag across slides. Dragging in a diagonal direction can be helpful.

✦ To select multiple, noncontiguous slides, hold the Command (⌘) key down and then click the slides you want to select.

✦ To select all the slides in the presentation, press ⌘-A or choose Edit➪Select All.

Changing slide order

Changing the order is one way in which you can create a better, logical flow from slide to slide. Therefore, it's an integral part of a process that makes your presentation better each time you fine-tune and deliver it. The improvement process is a result of understanding your audience's expectations and responses better each time you give your presentation.

When you revisit a presentation that's been on the shelf for a few months, you suddenly realize that things need to be changed. You probably need to reorder some slides. Changing the slide order is drag-and-drop easy. Just drag one or more slides from where they are and position the cursor in front of the slide where you want them to be. In Figure 1-5, we're moving slides 5 and 6 to position them between slides 11 and 12.

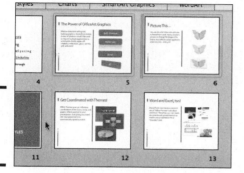

Figure 1-5: Changing the slide order.

Figure 1-5 shows the selection indicators around slides 5 and 6, and it shows that we're in the process of dragging these slides. You can see that the mouse pointer is between slides 11 and 12. The barely visible line just to the left of slide 12 indicates the insertion point.

Copying and pasting

This process is so intuitive that we almost didn't mention it. Select one or more slides, and use any common copy method, such as choosing Edit⇨Copy. Click at the desired insertion point, as shown in Figure 1-5, and then paste it by using any common paste method, such as choosing Edit⇨Paste.

Deleting the chaff from the wheat

Sometimes you just have to delete a slide. Even if you spent some time on a slide, it can go out of date or be otherwise unwanted. To delete one or more slides, select them and then press Delete.

Transitioning from one slide to the next

Applying transitions is easy. *Transitions* are effects that add animation or sound to the movement of the change between one slide and another, depending on which transition style you choose. We discuss transitions in the following sections, but first it's important to remember that when you're using transitions, you must keep both your audience and the content in mind. Think about the reason that you're adding a transition in the first place. Transitions can be overdone or underdone.

A presentation that moves from slide to slide every time with a *jump cut,* meaning without transitions, can be dull and look like it's not done yet. Appropriate transitions make presentations easier to watch. At times, you use transitions that are more visually active to help draw attention naturally to transitions in the content that you're delivering. If you use too many high-motion transitions, your audience will be reeling from motion sickness.

Like we said, it's fast and easy to apply transitions. To do so, follow these steps:

1. **While in Slide Sorter View, select one, several, or all the slides.**

2. **Click the Transitions tab of Elements Gallery.**

If Elements Gallery isn't visible, click the Gallery button on PowerPoint's standard toolbar.

The Elements Gallery displays transitions from which you can choose.

3. **Click a transition.**

A preview of the chosen transition plays in the selected slide in Slide Sorter View (it might be just a blink). A small icon appears to the lower-left to indicate a transition is applied.

In Slide Sorter View, you can fine-tune transition effects and add sounds to transitions. Click the Options button to display the Transition Options pane. (Refer to Figure 1-3.)

Setting transition options — Effect

The Effect part of the Transition Options pane has two capabilities. You find a pop-up menu that lets you select a different transition, and you have a choice of speeds: slow, medium, or fast.

Setting transition options — Sound

Sounds can act as punctuation points, exclamation points, or incidental music in your presentation. A handful of sounds are located on the Sound pop-up menu, but if you go to the very bottom of the menu, you can select Other Sound. This option causes a File browser to open, so you can choose any sound available on your system, or even sounds from your iTunes music library. Transition sounds are of short duration, only a few seconds long.

Setting transition options — Advance Slide

Here, Slide Sorter View lets you control the slide timings. You have the following options:

✦ **On Mouse Click:** When this check box is selected, you can click the mouse in a running presentation to advance to the next slide. Selecting the On Mouse Click check box doesn't affect Presenter Tools View, but it does affect presentations that run by using the other methods.

✦ **Automatically after [Number of] Seconds:** Controls slide timing. Be careful with this setting. If you have items on your slide that take a certain amount of time to run, such as animations or a movie, you should choose a time value that's longer than it takes for everything to play. Then add a few seconds because not every computer is as fast as yours, and you want your slide to finish without being cut off.

You can also add timings by choosing Slide Show➪Record Narration and Slide Show➪Rehearse Timings, features which we cover in Book IV, Chapter 8.

Chapter 2: Open Sesame and Shut Sesame

In This Chapter

✔ Opening presentations

✔ Discovering special ways to save your presentations

✔ Protecting your presentations

*P*owerPoint has some special file-handling features up its ornamented sleeve. In this chapter, we cover how to open and save files in PowerPoint. You can easily recover if your computer or PowerPoint crashes — which, of course, would never happen . . . but just in case, you can refer to this chapter. This chapter also shows you how to create a secure PowerPoint presentation that you can open on both Macs and PCs.

Opening Special File Formats

You can open PowerPoint presentations and special file formats by choosing File⇨Open. The Open dialog appears. Click Enable to open a pop-up menu, as shown in Figure 2-1, and select from the list of file types shown. If you see any file types that seem unfamiliar, don't worry. We explain the different file-type options:

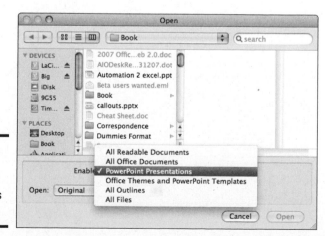

Figure 2-1:
Enabling
additional
file formats
to open.

+ **All Readable Documents:** Open any kind of file that PowerPoint understands.

+ **All Office Documents:** Open only Office documents.

+ **PowerPoint Presentations:** Open only PowerPoint presentations (.pptx) and PowerPoint shows (.ppsx). This file-type option also enables you to choose old-format PowerPoint presentations (.ppt) and PowerPoint shows (.pps).

+ **Office Themes and PowerPoint Templates:** Open only Office Themes (.thmx) and PowerPoint Templates (.potx and .pot).

+ **All Outlines:** Open documents saved in outline format from PowerPoint (.rtf).

+ **All Files:** Attempt to open any file in PowerPoint.

Regardless of which Enable option you use, PowerPoint can only open files it understands, and it lets you know if it can't open the chosen file.

When you enable the Office Themes and PowerPoint Templates option in the Open dialog (see Figure 2-1), you can browse to a template and open it as a new presentation. You use this option in the same way that you use Project Gallery or Elements Gallery to open the template.

Outlines are rich-text format (.rtf) documents that PowerPoint can create. As the name implies, they're text documents in outline form. They don't have the slide, animation, or other aspects of presentations — just the title and text placeholder content as it appears in the Outline pane of Normal View. An outline is the foundation of any well-thought-out PowerPoint presentation.

Finding out about AutoRecover

Although File Open takes care of everyday file opening, if PowerPoint or your computer crashes, you can open the AutoRecover file. Before you take advantage of AutoRecover, you first must turn this feature on by following these steps:

1. **From the PowerPoint menu, choose Preferences.**

PowerPoint's Preferences dialog appears (see Figure 2-2).

2. **Click the Save button.**

PowerPoint's Save preferences appear.

3. **Select the Save AutoRecover Info Every [Number of] Minutes check box; then click the red Close button.**

You've enabled AutoRecover and closed Preferences.

PowerPoint automatically opens the most recently autosaved version the next time you open PowerPoint after a crash or force-quit.

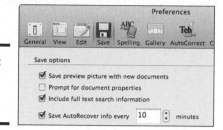

Figure 2-2:
Enabling
Auto-
Recover.

Although this feature is great, don't depend on it all the time. Make it a habit to save your presentations regularly. Pressing ⌘-S is all it takes to save changes in the presentation you're working on! Or you can choose File⇨Save As to save a new copy of your presentation.

Opening password-protected presentations

The Windows version of PowerPoint provides the ability to password-protect PowerPoint files. This feature gives PowerPoint-for-Windows users a sense of security, although some critics complain that it does little to prevent some people from opening and editing those files in PowerPoint for Windows. Unfortunately, Mac users can't open these files. If you receive a password-protected file, you can't open it in PowerPoint for Mac. Your alternative is to ask the sender to resave the presentation without password protection.

Hopefully, this annoying security feature will be removed from the next version of Office for Windows. PowerPoint for Mac has a more secure way of protecting your presentations, and the Mac method creates files that are compatible on both Mac and Windows platforms. See the "Saving with a password" section, later in this chapter.

Saving in Special Formats

Even more interesting than PowerPoint's plethora of formats that you can open is the array of Save As options. Check out Figure 2-3 and get ready to explore these options in detail.

Packaging a PowerPoint presentation

PowerPoint Package is an option that you can choose when you want to distribute a complete, editable presentation via CD, flash drive, or other media. It creates a folder that you can burn, copy, or move to whatever media you want. It's important to use this option when your presentation contains movies or any other linked content so that the presentation can actually play that linked content.

**Book IV
Chapter 2**

**Open Sesame and
Shut Sesame**

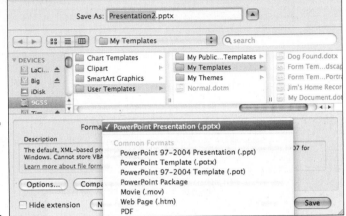

Figure 2-3:
Saving in
PowerPoint's
specialty
formats.

Saving as a movie

Choosing the Movie (.mov) option creates a QuickTime movie of your presentation. You can get the same result by choosing File➪Save as Movie. When you use the Movie option, timings are included, slide transitions may change, sound isn't included, and animations don't play.

You can add an audio track by using the Movie Options dialog. Just follow these steps:

1. **Click Options or the Movie Options button in the Save As dialog.**

The Movie Options dialog appears as shown in Figure 2-4.

2. **In the Media Settings area, click Background Soundtrack and choose Select Soundtrack from the pop-up menu that appears.**

The Choose a Soundtrack dialog appears.

3. **Navigate or use Spotlight to select the sound file that you want to include.**

If you choose your Mac OS X Media folder, you can choose non-DRM music or other audio files from iTunes.

4. **Click Choose**

The Movie Options dialog reappears and displays the name of the audio file in the Background Soundtrack pop-up button.

5. **Click OK to close the Movie Options dialog.**

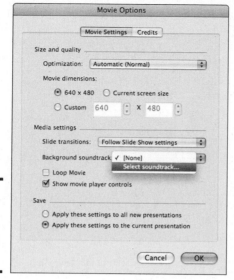

Figure 2-4:
Adding
sound to a
PowerPoint
movie.

The sound that you include by using this dialog plays across your entire movie, not just the part that comprises one or more slides.

Instead of using the File menu's Save As command and choosing Movie or using the File menu's Save as Movie command, we suggest using screen-capture software, such as Ambrosia Software's SnapZProX, to capture the presentation as a movie and get all the animations, transitions, and sound. To capture your presentation, you need to have your capturing program installed, and you'll need to play your presentation in a window. To do so, follow these steps:

1. **On the Slide Show menu, choose Set Up Show.**

2. **Under Show Type, choose Browsed by an Individual (Window).**

Set up further, as shown in Figure 2-5.

3. **Turn on the screen-capture software.**

Slide Show

4. **Click the Slide Show button on PowerPoint's Standard toolbar to start the slide show from slide 1.**

The presentation plays normally, but it appears in a window so that you can shoot screens with your screen-capture software.

A full walkthrough is available at this site: www.indezine.com/products/ powerpoint/mac/snapzpromovies.html.

**Book IV
Chapter 2**

**Open Sesame and
Shut Sesame**

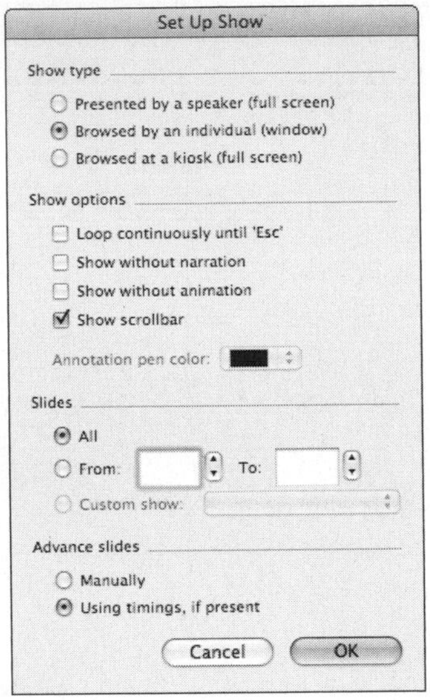

Figure 2-5:
Preparing
to play for
screen
recording.

Making a Web page

With so many new Web services, such as Office Live, Google Docs, Blackboard, and Angel, this option seems dated and nearly obsolete. It creates an HTM file and a folder for related content that you can copy to a Web server. We don't think this feature is of much use anymore, although you can try it out. It's easy enough to use and may work well for slides that contain just text.

Saving with a password

This Save As option is the fast, easy way to get your presentation into PDF format. A PDF file contains only pictures of your slides, not the notes, movies, animations, or transitions.

You can password-protect your presentation, using the PDF options from the Print dialog. Follow these steps:

1. **Choose File⇨Print.**

   The Print dialog appears.

2. **Click the PDF button in the lower-left corner of the Print pane and select the first menu item, Save as PDF, as shown in Figure 2-6.**

3. **Click in the Save As text box and enter a filename that includes the file extension .pdf.**

   The Save dialog opens, as shown in Figure 2-7.

Figure 2-6:
Setting
password
protection.

Use the PDF format.

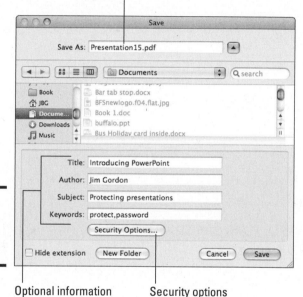

Figure 2-7:
Setting
password
protection.

Optional information   Security options

4. **Enter any optional information that you want to.**

   You can fill in Title, Author, Subject, and Keywords.

5. **Click the Security Options button.**

   The PDF Security Options dialog opens, as shown in Figure 2-8.

6. **Make any changes you want in the Security Options dialog.**

   In this dialog, you can adjust these settings:

   • *Require Password to Open Document.* If you select this check box and enter a password, the operating system requires that you enter the password to open the file.

   • *Require Password to Copy Text, Images and Other Content.* Select this check box to disable these commands in the interface.

This password protection won't stop someone from pointing a camera or cell phone at your screen and taking a picture.

- *Require a Password to Print Document.* Select this check box and enter a password if you want to use that password when you print.

7. **Click OK to close the PDF Security Options dialog.**

   You can now access the Save dialog.

8. **Click Save to save the password-protected PDF document and close the Save dialog.**

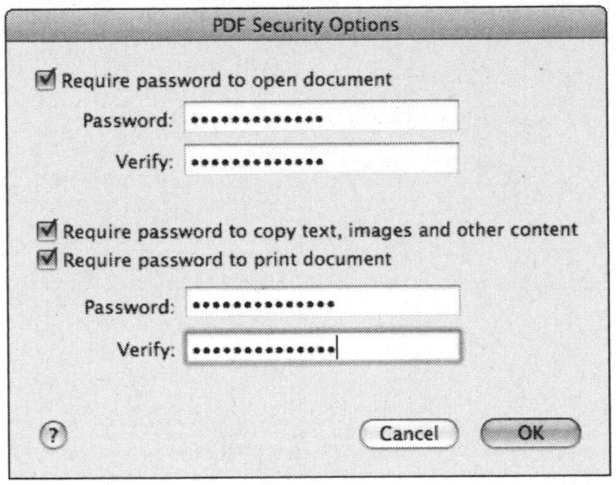

Figure 2-8: Setting password security options.

This method can create un-editable documents that are readable on both Macs and PCs. (Still, you can capture the screenshots of PDFs, so they're not entirely secure.)

Saving as a pile of pictures

The last five Save As options save the slides of your presentation as a folder full of pictures in the format that you select. JPEG, PNG, BMP, GIF, and TIFF are the supported file formats.

Pop a blank CD into your Mac and click the OK button in the Open Finder panel that appears. Use the JPEG option to save your presentation to the CD, and then eject the CD and let Finder burn the disc. Most new DVD players for television sets can play this disc as a slide show. You might have to explore your DVD player's menus a bit to discover how to turn this feature on.

Chapter 3: Working with the Whole Show

In This Chapter

✔ Getting under way

✔ Working in many views

✔ Going for broke, starting with nothing

✔ Adding new slides

✔ Dodging bullets

✔ Tempting themes

✔ Making children

In the preceding chapters in Book IV, we go over the file formats you use in PowerPoint, as well as some fundamentals. Now, it's time to let your creative juices start flowing. In this chapter, you can find out about the process of building content-rich slides that your audience will enjoy and that you can present confidently. We cover how to start from a template or start from scratch, and then introduce you to using PowerPoint's rich interface. You can discover ways to present a slide show and how to organize slides within a show.

Creating a Presentation

To create presentation slides, you need more than just good PowerPoint skills. Great slides require time and thought, and we can help you with the former by showing you how to use PowerPoint more effectively so that you can use all that saved time to create compelling stories and flows for your presentation slides.

A slide presentation is composed of two phases — the creation phase and the presentation phase. You might be responsible for either creating or presenting the slides, or maybe you play both roles. Either way, you have to know the topic of your presentation well. You may also have supplementary content from which to work, such as a Word document or an existing presentation. You may have pictures, graphs, sounds, and movies in your computer or somewhere at the back of your mind. Or you may be starting from scratch. Either way, PowerPoint has ways to help you. But remember, PowerPoint can only help you present your content well; it can't create the content.

Starting from a Microsoft Word document

Having content in a Microsoft Word document can save a lot of time. Open your document in Microsoft Word. Choose View⊅Outline to use Word's Outline View. If you think your outline is good enough to work from, you can send it right into PowerPoint from Word by choosing File⊅Send To⊅Microsoft PowerPoint. If you like working with outlines in PowerPoint, you can click the Outline button above the slide preview to use an outline to build your slide show. If you prefer working in Word, PowerPoint can send your presentation's outline directly to Word; just choose File⊅Send To⊅Microsoft Word. Another way to share an outline is to use PowerPoint's capability to save in outline format by choosing File⊅Save As; then selecting Outline/Rich Text Format (.rtf) from the Format pop-up menu.

Starting from Project Gallery

PowerPoint offers many options to help you begin a presentation; you can choose from whichever you think suits you best. If you've been following along through other chapters, by now you know we're partial to Project Gallery as a great place from which to start. If you don't know what Project Gallery is, you can get the scoop in Book I, Chapter 2.

To open Project Gallery, click PowerPoint's Dock icon. If Project Gallery doesn't open immediately, choose File⊅Project Gallery (see Figure 3-1) to open Project Gallery. Click the New tab to see the many starting points available.

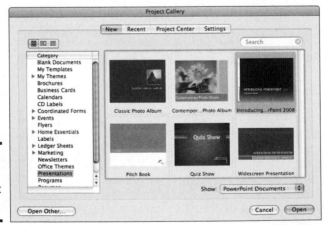

Figure 3-1:
Starting from Project Gallery.

In Project Gallery's Category list, you can explore almost 50 Office themes, presentation templates, or blank documents. If you want to follow along with our screen shots, select Presentations in the Category list; then double-click the Introducing PowerPoint 2008 presentation template.

Choosing a View

You can choose from several different view options to build slides in PowerPoint, and they are essentially equivalent. Our advice is to try building slides in all of them and then use the view you prefer. In the following sections, we explore the various views.

Using Normal View

When you open a built-in template or theme, you're in Normal View. (Refer to Book IV, Chapter 1, where we show you Normal View.) The Outline tab appears at the top of the slide thumbnails. Click the Outline tab to edit text in an outline, as shown in Figure 3-2. While you type in the outline, text in the slide updates automatically in the placeholders on the slide. Conversely, if you type in the text placeholders of the slide, the outline automatically updates. The outline and the slide pane are always synchronized.

Slide View

Outline pane   Slide

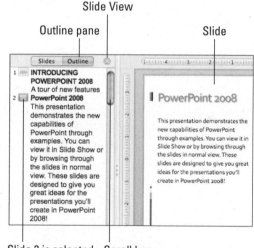

Figure 3-2:
Working
in Outline
View.

Slide 2 is selected   Scroll bar

Text placeholders are part of a slide layout and are different from the common text boxes that you add by choosing Insert⇨Text Box. Any text that you add within text boxes (as opposed to text placeholders) isn't synced with the outline.

Switching to Slide View

You work the same way in Slide View as you do in Normal View, except that in Slide View, you don't see the left pane, so you have more room in which to work directly on your slide. To get to Slide View from Normal View, click the Slide View button, as shown in Figure 3-2.

Adding notations in Notes Page View

Choose View➪Notes Page to see another PowerPoint View. Shown in Figure 3-3, Notes Page View lets you add a lot of additional material to support the slide the audience sees. You can use features similar to that of Microsoft Word in the Notes section. Notes Page View's Notes section supports bullets and numbering, as well as tables and graphs, and can include additional information you might want to have at your fingertips, such as supplemental information that can help you answer anticipated audience questions when the presentation is running. You can also print Notes Page View for your slides and use them as handouts. Instructors and students can use Notes Page View to annotate their slide shows. Notes Page View is an excellent place to properly attribute the sources of slide content.

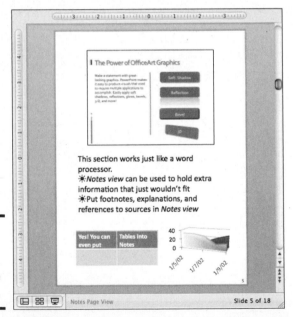

Figure 3-3: Filling in details with Notes Page View.

When you're using Presenter Tools View (see Book IV, Chapter 1) to present a slide show, you not only get to see your slide notes, but you can also edit them while the slide show is running.

Switching from one view to another

You switch from one view to another a lot when you use PowerPoint. We recommend that you create a custom toolbar and put all the view options on it. Refer to Book I, Chapter 3 for detailed information on customizing toolbars and menus. Figure 3-4 shows a toolbar that can be used to switch views.

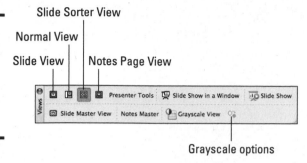

Figure 3-4: You can switch views easily with a custom toolbar.

Slide Sorter View

Normal View

Slide View | Notes Page View

Grayscale options

We're almost done with the Introduction to PowerPoint 2008 slide show example. Before we finish with it, click the Slide Show button on PowerPoint's standard toolbar to start the slide show on the first slide. While the show is running, click the mouse, press the spacebar, or use the arrow keys to advance the presentation. Enjoy just watching this nicely made presentation. When you're done, you can close this presentation.

Starting from Scratch

Even though Project Gallery has many options, you may prefer to create a project that is 100-percent your own. You have nearly infinite customization capabilities at your disposal in PowerPoint, so go ahead and use them creatively. So that you can more easily investigate PowerPoint's editing capabilities, and not always depend on PowerPoint's template offerings, in this section, we show you how you can start from scratch with a new, blank presentation. Press ⌘-N or choose File➪New Presentation to get started with a blank canvas, as shown in Figure 3-5.

Placeholders

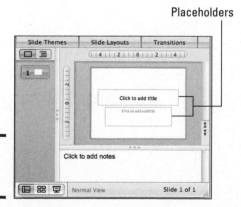

Figure 3-5: Making a title slide.

Using keyboard shortcuts in PowerPoint

Although you can customize keyboard short-cuts in Word and Excel, the keyboard shortcuts available in PowerPoint are built in and can't be customized within PowerPoint. But that doesn't mean you can't create your own shortcuts by using Mac OS X.

Click PowerPoint's Help button on the Standard toolbar and search for the term *keyboard short-cuts*. Be sure to check out each of these very nicely produced topics:

✔ **Customize Your Applications by Using Accessibility Features.** A complete, free,

20-minute course that describes how to customize Mac OS X.

✔ **PowerPoint Keyboard Shortcuts:** Lists all the keyboard shortcuts available in PowerPoint.

✔ **Common Office Keyboard Shortcuts:** Lists many keyboard shortcuts used throughout Office.

You'll be glad that PowerPoint's Help section has been completely redone for 2008. You can even have Help open while you work in PowerPoint!

Every slide show needs a beginning, so PowerPoint starts you off with a title slide. Title slides have two boxes that are text placeholders, each of which contains a prompt that urges you to click into the placeholder and start typing. When you type in a placeholder, the text you type is synchronized with the Outline pane, as we mention in the section "Using Normal View," earlier in this chapter.

Text that you put into other kinds of objects, such as Charts, SmartArt, and WordArt, doesn't appear in the Outline pane.

Adding a New Slide

Usually, only the first slide of a presentation is a title slide. You create the rest of the slides from the variety of choices waiting for you on the Slide Layouts tab of Elements Gallery. See Figure 3-6, which shows that we added a title and content slide layout. The Slide Layouts tab in Elements Gallery has several other slide layouts: 11 preset layouts of placeholders for titles, text, charts, pictures, media, and so on. If you don't see Elements Gallery, click the Gallery button on PowerPoint's standard toolbar, and then click the Slide Layouts tab to display layouts.

Insert indicators

Slide Layouts tab

Title placeholder

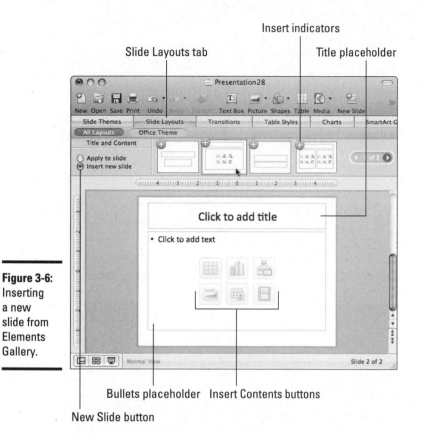

Figure 3-6:
Inserting
a new
slide from
Elements
Gallery.

Bullets placeholder   Insert Contents buttons

New Slide button

When you first start working with PowerPoint, both the All Layouts and Office Theme buttons show the same standard 11 slide layouts. We explain how to create your own, custom layouts and add them to Elements Gallery when we talk about slide masters in Book IV, Chapter 4. When you select the Insert New Slide button and click a slide layout, insertion indicators light up. They light up when Elements Gallery will add a new slide instead of changing the current slide's layout.

We discuss the title and content layout so that you can see how the new slide layout placeholders work. Inside the Bullets placeholder is an arrangement of six content buttons. You can type your own content in the placeholder and/or click a content button. Move your cursor over each button to see the kind of content you can insert. If you insert a picture by using a content button, the picture is sized to fit the placeholder. Experiment with these options to see that you can have either text or content in the placeholder.

**Book IV
Chapter 3**

Working with the
Whole Show

Formatting the Background

If the Formatting Palette isn't turned on, click the Toolbox button on the Standard toolbar and then click the Formatting Palette button. Pay attention to the Formatting Palette while you work. The available options change every time you select or click some element of the interface.

For example, to format the background, just click anywhere on the background outside the border of any placeholders. The Formatting Palette instantly changes to offer a variety of background choices, as shown in Figure 3-7.

Figure 3-7:
Formatting a background by using the Formatting Palette.

The default slide backgrounds available are based on the active Office theme applied to the presentation. We cover how you can apply an Office theme in the section "Applying a New Theme," later in this chapter. For now, be aware that these are coordinated backgrounds that always work well and look good with all sorts of foreground content. However, you're not limited to those choices. Take another look at the bottom of the Formatting Palette. Beneath the Slide Background options in Figure 3-7, you can spot a Format Background button that you can click to open the full-featured Format Background dialog, shown in Figure 3-8.

Spin the dial

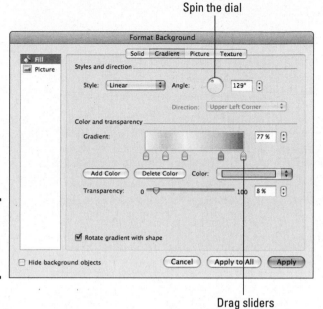

Figure 3-8:
The Format
Background
dialog.

Drag sliders

Although you've probably seen this sort of dialog in other applications in Microsoft Office, this one is different. We want to focus on the new, fun gradient fills. The new fancy fill effects are available in other shapes — even in graphs and charts!

Gradient backgrounds

To experiment with applying a gradient fill to a background, follow these steps:

1. **Make sure that you have the Slide Background pane of the Formatting Palette visible and click the Format Background button.**

   Clicking this button opens a Format Background dialog.

2. **In the left pane, click Fill. Then, click the Gradient tab.**

   The interface that you see in Figure 3-8 appears.

3. **Set the Style to Linear.**

   Other options include Radial, Rectangular, Path, and From Tile. For now, stay with Linear.

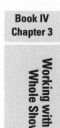

**Book IV
Chapter 3**

**Working with the
Whole Show**

4. **Spin the Angle dial by holding the mouse button down on the dial and dragging around a bit.**

   You can spin the dial only when you use the Linear style. And you don't even have to spin if you're comfortable typing at the angle value shown in the box.

5. **Click the Add Color button to add an extra color stop to the Gradient bar.**

   You can choose a color for this stop from the Color Palette pop-up menu. You can also change the transparency value for this stop by dragging the Transparency slider in the Color and Transparency portion of the dialog.

6. **Add more color stops or select the existing ones and edit as required.**

   You can drag the gradient sliders to achieve various effects. You can drag sliders over each other. Watch while your slide reflects the changes.

7. **Click the Apply button to apply your format to the current slide, or click the Apply to All button to apply your new format to all slides in the presentation.**

   You can also click the Cancel button to make no changes.

As you can see, working with gradient fills is so much fun that it can get really addictive! To see samples of gradients and more options, go to the following URL, which contains tutorials by Geetesh:

```
www.indezine.com/products/powerpoint/learn/fillslinesand
effects/gradientstops2007.html
```

Although these tutorials show PowerPoint 2007 screen shots, they explain the same things you can do in PowerPoint 2008.

Clicking for additional options

To access additional options, you can right-click or Control-click the edges of placeholders, objects, and the PowerPoint interface itself. Each time you click, a pop-up menu of context-sensitive choices appears. When you right-click or Control-click the background, for example, you can easily set guide and gridline controls, as shown in Figure 3-9.

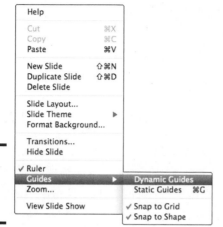

Figure 3-9:
Setting
guides and
gridlines.

Formatting Bullets and Numbers

After just a short time, the stock bullet points in PowerPoint can get tire-some. No one wants to see the same bullets over and over, and sometimes it's a great idea to just have no bullets (which we cover in the section "Living in no-bullet land," later in this chapter). One way to get around the problem of seeing the same bullets is to use custom bullets. Try to choose subdued bullets that complement your subject. We're not trying to focus attention on the bullet, but on the point!

Customizing bullet and number characters

In PowerPoint, while you're typing a bulleted list, you can use the Formatting Palette to select new characters for your bullets. Office 2008 lets you access the Mac OS X Characters Palette. Follow these steps to use this new feature:

1. **In the Bullets and Numbering section of the Formatting Palette, click the triangle to activate the pop-up Style menu.**

If the option is grayed out, it means that you don't have any text with bullet levels selected.

2. **At the bottom of the Style pop-up menu, choose Bullets and Numbering.**

This step opens the Format Text dialog, as shown in Figure 3-10.

3. **In the left pane, choose Bullets and Numbering if it's not already selected.**

If you started off formatting bullets, you can proceed to Step 4. If your list was set to numbers, you need to be on the Numbering tab of the dialog, where you can select from custom number options.

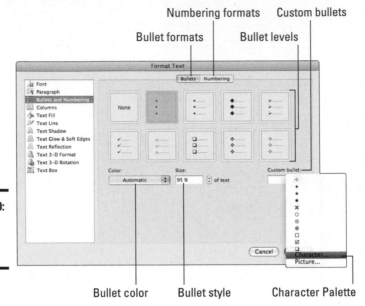

Figure 3-10:
Making
a custom
bullet.

4. **Select which bullet level you want to customize.**

   Level numbering starts at zero (None) in the top left. The highest-level number is seven, represented by the bullet-level button at the bottom-right of the series of Bullet Levels, as shown in Figure 3-10.

5. **Click the Custom Bullet pop-up menu in the lower-right corner of the Bullets and Numbering pane.**

6. **Choose Character from the Custom Bullet pop-up menu.**

   The Mac OS X Characters Palette opens, and you can select from special characters from many fonts. (See Figure 3-11.) Despite the complex appearance of the Characters Palette, you can simply choose a category from the category list, and then select a bullet you find appealing.

7. **Click Insert to choose your selection and close the Characters Palette.**

   The Format Text dialog now displays the character that you chose in Step 6.

8. **(Optional) Select a color from the Color pop-up menu and change the bullet size by using the Increase/Decrease control.**

9. **Click OK to apply the custom bullet to the selected level and close the Format Text dialog.**

   If you have any bullets in your presentation that are at the customized level, they now display the customized bullet.

Category list

View menu   Character name

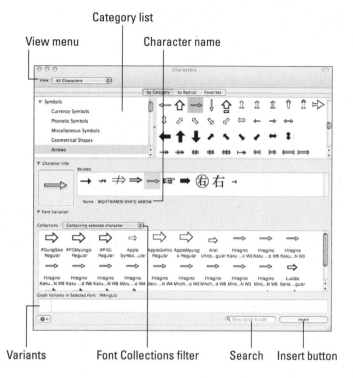

Figure 3-11:
Choosing
a custom
bullet in the
Characters
Palette.

Variants   Font Collections filter   Search   Insert button

Living in no-bullet land

We don't expect you to stop using bullets, but we want to encourage you
to experiment with slides that contain no bullets. Try a new approach: Use
phrases and add a visual on a slide with a compelling title. Try this method
for a few slides in each presentation to start with, and then evolve your own
style while you get more comfortable with a no-bullets approach.

Customizing bullets by using SmartArt graphics

Another option to foregoing bullets uses SmartArt graphics, which are new
to Office 2008, and they allow you to format your bullet points in new, attractive ways. See our vertical bullet list before-and-after example in Figure 3-12.

You start by making your points in the regular fashion. Then, follow these
steps:

1. Select the bullet points you want to format.

Click once anywhere in the text to place the insertion cursor within
that text. Then, drag the mouse to highlight all the text within the bullet
points, as shown in Figure 3-12.

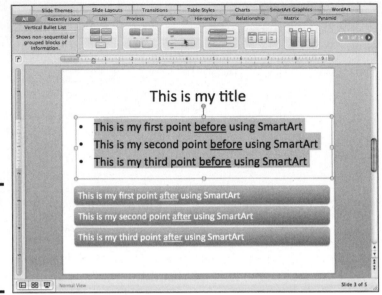

Figure 3-12:
Using new
SmartArt
graphics to
customize
bullet lists.

2. **Click the SmartArt graphics tab of Elements Gallery.**

3. **Click one of the bullet list graphics.**

   That's all you need to do! Your bullet points are instantly deleted, and SmartArt formatting takes their place.

Applying a New Theme

If you've been following along, we've built a small presentation of disparate slides that's rather plain. We can add pizzazz instantly by formatting it with one of PowerPoint's new slide themes. Elements Gallery comes with a variety of great themes, so all you have to do is click the Slide Themes tab and select one you like (see Figure 3-13).

Slide Themes tab

Figure 3-13:
Selecting
a slide
theme from
Elements
Gallery.

Click to browse.   Themes   Scroll

Getting more themes, backgrounds, and templates

Office for Mac can use all the themes, backgrounds, and templates that work in Office for Windows. The only exception is that because Visual Basic for Applications (VBA) isn't in PowerPoint 2008, templates that use VBA don't work. You can download hundreds (okay, that's thousands) of free templates and themes from Indezine at this URL:

```
www.indezine.com/powerpoint/
templates/freetemplates.html
```

Again, refer to Book I, Chapter 3 to find out where to put themes so that they appear in Elements Gallery and Project Gallery.

In Book I, Chapter 3, we explain how you can create your own themes. In that chapter, we suggest places to save themes so that you can find them in Elements Gallery and Project Gallery. In case you decided on an alternate location for your themes, you can click the Browse button in Elements Gallery to open the Choose Themed Document or Slide Template dialog and navigate in Mac OS X Finder to find them. Don't forget that you can use Spotlight in this dialog to speed your search.

Creating Smaller Versions with Custom Shows

We have a prediction to make. If you follow our tips, you'll make great slide shows. You'll wind up with one that takes three hours to present fully. People will attend and love it. You're then asked to give your presentation again, but you're offered only one hour in which to present. That's where PowerPoint's Custom Shows feature fits in. This feature lets you create smaller versions and different-order versions of your slide shows. To set up a smaller version of a slide show, sometimes called a *child version,* follow these steps:

1. **Go to the Slide Show menu and choose Custom Shows (see Figure 3-14).**

   The Custom Shows dialog opens.

2. **Click the New button to create your first custom show in the Define Custom Show dialog, as shown in Figure 3-15.**

   The Define Custom Show dialog appears. The left pane has all the slides in your existing presentation:

   • *Add:* Click Add to assign selected slides from the Slides in Presentation list (on the left side) to the Slides in Custom Show list (on the right side).

   • *Remove:* Click Remove to remove selected slides from the Slides in Custom Show list on the right side.

Book IV
Chapter 3

**Working with the
Whole Show**

3. **Click OK to close the Define Custom Show dialog, and then click OK again to close the Custom Shows dialog.**

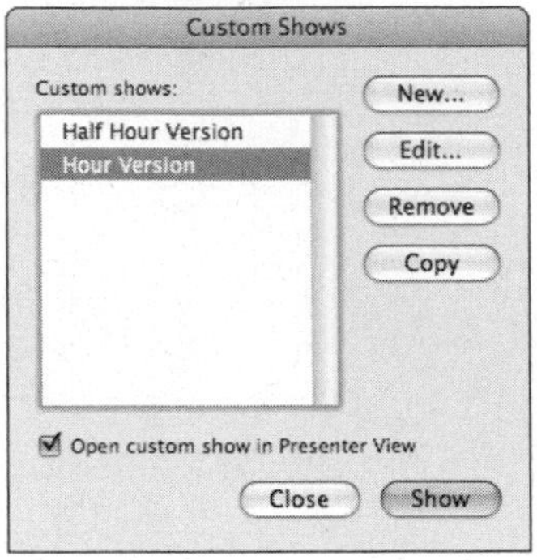

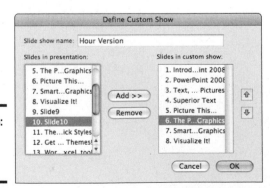

Figure 3-14:
Creating a
smaller
version
of your
presentation.

To present a custom show, again choose SlideShow⇨Custom Shows. (See Figure 3-14.) The default setting is to use the Presenter Tools View to present the show when you click the Show button. If you deselect the Open Custom Show in Presenter View check box, the slide show opens without using Presenter Tools when you click the Show button.

Another way to make subsets of slide shows is to choose SlideShow⇨Set Up Show. In the Slides portion of Set Up Show, you can choose a range of slides or default to a custom show.

You can set overrides to other slide show settings in Set Up Show. If you decide to use this dialog to override your other settings, make a note to yourself in a slide note or comment so that you don't wonder why all your slides aren't playing.

Figure 3-15:
Defining
a custom
show.

Chapter 4: Mastering the Masters

Knowing what a master is can make you seem like a PowerPoint guru, even though the subject isn't complex, as long as you follow the basics. With just a few hints from us, you can be in control of PowerPoint, using masters in ways that make your friends want to have your PowerPoint skills.

Allow us to explain what we're talking about when we use the word *master*. A master is in charge. In PowerPoint, you find several masters, each overlooking their respective domains. Using Slide Masters can save you a lot of time while you build presentations. The idea behind a master is that you put text, adjust formatting, or add objects to the master, and the changes are instantly reflected throughout the entire presentation. PowerPoint handles these masters efficiently, so your presentation's file size doesn't grow proportionately, which is important when distributing your presentations.

The neat part is that you're in charge of all PowerPoint's masters. They're here to do your bidding. And new for PowerPoint 2008, you have the ability to edit your own slide layouts. PowerPoint has several different kinds of masters (all of which we explain in this chapter):

✦ **Slide Master:** Whatever text, formatting, or objects you apply to the Slide Master are instantly applied to the entire presentation and to any layouts.

✦ **Layout (also called Layout Master or sub-master):** Masters for slide layouts.

✦ **Notes Master:** Controls the format of Notes Page View.

✦ **Handout Master:** Formats printed handouts.

Putting a Master Slide in Charge

In every presentation, one slide trumps the rest. It's called the Slide Master. It's the slide that you see when you choose View⇨Master⇨Slide Master. You can tell which one is the Slide Master because, as you can see in Figure 4-1, it's placed in a position of power in the upper-left corner, and it's bigger than the slide layouts, which fittingly appear below the Slide Master in the thumbnails pane.

The Slide Master has sub-masters called Layouts that control various slide layouts (what else?). To illustrate some of the things you can do, we'll use the Introducing PowerPoint 2008 presentation from Project Gallery (see Book IV, Chapter 3).

Getting your bearings in Slide Master View

Slide Master View is seemingly similar to Normal View in that all the regular formatting options are available. However, you can find differences if you look carefully. The thumbnail pane doesn't show the slides in your presentation (see Figure 4-1). Instead, it shows the Slide Master at the top as a larger thumbnail, followed by smaller thumbnails that represent a master for each of the layouts that appears on the Layout tab of Elements Gallery. Not surprisingly, each of these sub-masters is called a slide layout.

The Notes pane is absent from the Slide Master View because these aren't the actual slides you present — they're masters that influence those slides. Notes Page View has its own master, discussed in the section "Taking Note of Notes Masters," later in this chapter.

When working with masters and sub-masters, keep in mind the relationships between the slides and the layouts that you see in Normal View with the masters you see in Slide Master View. In particular, be aware of the following:

+ Any changes in the Slide Master affect each slide layout under it unless you format a specific slide layout differently. Changes are also applied to the slides in your presentation.

+ Any changes you make to the individual slide layouts don't affect the Slide Master. Changes made to slide layouts influence only slides in the presentation that are based on those particular layouts.

Go ahead and make changes to the Slide Master. To watch how the layouts are affected when you modify the Slide Master, first open a slide presentation. Make sure that you're in Slide Master View and click anywhere on the background of the Slide Master (in the larger pane of the window where it says Click to Edit Master Title Style). Then, choose an option from the Formatting Palette's Slide Background section to change the background.

Slide Master

Masters toolbar

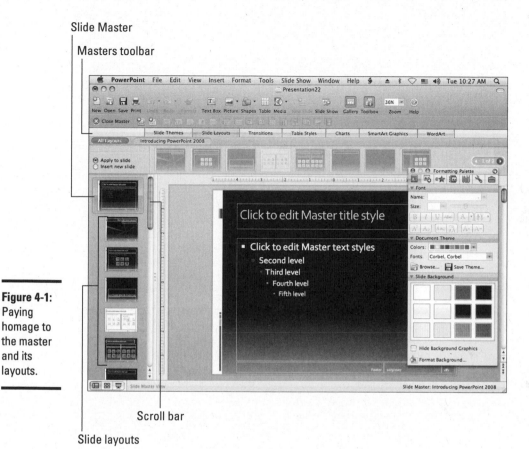

Figure 4-1:
Paying
homage to
the master
and its
layouts.

Scroll bar

Slide layouts

Your change is instantly incorporated into all the slide layouts, as well as the Slide Master slides. Choose View➪Normal to switch to Normal View, and you can see that your slide show now has the new background, as does the Slide Layouts tab of Elements Gallery. If you need to put a logo on your slide so that it appears on every slide in the presentation, you insert that logo in the Slide Master.

Looking at a new toolbar

When you visit Slide Master View, a new toolbar appears, ready to get to work. You must be in Slide Master View to see and use the Master toolbar. When in Slide Master View, choose View➪Toolbars➪Master to toggle on the Master toolbar, and you should see the toolbar that's shown in Figure 4-2.

When working with a Slide Master, only the first two buttons are available to use on the Master toolbar. The rest of the buttons come alive when you're working with slide layouts. Move the cursor over each button to see what it does or what kind of placeholder will be inserted into a slide layout when it's clicked.

Book IV
Chapter 4

Mastering the
Masters

Figure 4-2:
Laying it
out with
the Master
toolbar.

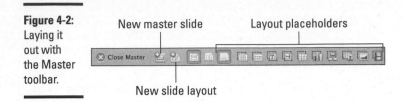

New master slide

Layout placeholders

New slide layout

Formatting Slide Layouts

Although the Slide Master is the big chief, you can format each of the built-in slide layouts independently. You should wait until you're finished formatting the Slide Master before you format any of the slide layouts for two reasons:

- ✦ The logical hierarchy is to first create a common look for all your slides and then make subtle differences in the slide layouts.

- ✦ When you format a slide layout so that it's different from its Slide Master, that particular layout, as well as slides in the presentation based on that particular layout, display the slide layout's different formatting. After you format a layout, you can get different results when you go back and reformat the Slide Master, depending on what steps you take.

Follow these steps to format a Master Slide and a layout:

1. **Click Toolbox on PowerPoint's Standard toolbar to activate Toolbox.**

2. **Select the Formatting Palette, if it isn't already visible.**

3. **Open a new, blank PowerPoint presentation by clicking the New button on the Standard toolbar.**

   A new, blank presentation appears.

4. **Choose File⇨Master⇨Slide Master.**

   The Slide Master appears.

5. **Apply a background format to the Slide Master.**

   Use any of these methods:

   - In the Slide Background section of the Formatting Palette, select a slide background.

   - In the Slide Background section of the Formatting Palette, click the Format Background button to display the Format Background dialog. In the dialog, select a format, and then click Apply to apply the format and return to the Slide Master.

- Right-click or Control-click either the background of the Slide Master or the Slide Master's thumbnail. From the pop-up menu that appears, select Format Background to open the Format Background dialog. In the dialog, select a format, and then click Apply to apply the format and return to the Slide Master.

- Choose Format➪Slide Background to display the Format Background dialog. In the dialog, select a format, and then click Apply to apply the format and return to the Slide Master.

- From the Slide Themes tab in Elements Gallery, select a Slide theme (which also affects fonts).

The backgrounds of all the slide layouts under the Slide Master take on the format applied to the Slide Master.

6. Select one or more of the layout thumbnails under the Slide Master.

Use ordinary selection techniques.

7. Choose a different background format for just the selected layouts.

Use any of the methods shown in the first four bullets of Step 5. You can't use the last option (the Slide Theme tab) in the list because Slide Theme formats affect more than just one layout.

The backgrounds of the selected slide layouts now display the formatting you chose. The Master Slide and all other layouts remain unchanged.

Your creative desires may not be fully satisfied with the background of the Slide Master. But don't worry; you can reformat that Slide Master background.

To reformat the Slide Master without affecting background changes that you made to individual layouts, select the Slide Master in the list of thumbnails, and then do any of the following:

✦ In the Slide Background section of the Formatting Palette, click the Format Background button. The Format Background dialog appears. In the dialog, select a format, and then click Apply to apply the format and return to the Slide Master.

✦ Right-click or Control-click either the background of the Slide Master or the Slide Master's thumbnail view. From the pop-up menu choose Format Background. The Format Background dialog displays. In the dialog, select a format, and then click Apply to apply the format and return to the Slide Master.

✦ Choose Format➪Slide Background to display the Format Background dialog. Make formatting choices, and then click Apply to close the dialog and apply your choices.

✦ In the Document Theme section of the Formatting Palette, click Colors and select a document theme from the pop-up menu that appears.

To reformat the Slide Master, override background changes that you made to individual layouts, and reset all the master's layouts, follow these steps:

1. **Select the Slide Master in the list of thumbnails.**

2. **From the Background section of the Formatting Palette, select a slide background.**

Any other non-background changes made to a Slide Master, such as fonts, inserting a logo, and so on, still influence its slide layouts.

When you move the cursor over a slide layout, a ToolTip tells you the name of the layout and the slide numbers that are using the layout, if any (see Figure 4-3).

Figure 4-3:
The slide layout's name and number.

Title Slide Layout: used by slide(s) 1

You can also right-click or Control-click any slide layout in Slide Master View to present an amazing array of options, including options that let you add new layouts and rename existing ones.

Just like the Slide Master, you can format all the elements on a slide layout. Any slides that use that particular layout get the changes that you make to the slide layout. But remember that when you change formatting on a layout, you're breaking the link for the changed element between that slide layout and the Slide Master.

Adding Another Set of Masters

A presentation can have more than one Slide Master, and it can have multiple slide layouts, too. In fact, you can add Slide Masters with complete sets of slide layouts that behave as independent groups. The ability to use multiple masters is very powerful stuff compared to the limited amount of customizing possible in PowerPoint 2004 and earlier versions of PowerPoint for Mac.

Adding an additional Slide Master with its hierarchical slide layouts to a presentation gives you formatting flexibility. Here's the way to do it: While working in Slide Master View, click the Insert New Master button on the Master toolbar.

That's all there is to it! See Figure 4-4. Scroll down the thumbnails pane to see a set of unformatted masters. You find a new Slide Master and a complete set of unformatted slide layouts. If you format the new Slide Master, the formatting affects the new slide layouts, but not your original Slide Master or any of its slide layouts.

Existing layouts and masters

New slide master

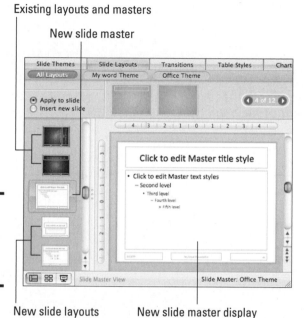

Figure 4-4:
Working with a second set of masters.

New slide layouts   New slide master display

Adding More Slide Layouts

You can create as many slide layouts as you want. Try creating a new slide layout with a subtitle placeholder and one for quotation slides. Then, you can rotate and arrange your pictures in another slide layout. To make a new, unformatted layout, follow these steps:

1. **Select any existing Slide Master in Slide Master View.**

   The selection indicator appears around the thumbnail.

2. **Click the Insert New Layout button on the Master toolbar (refer to Figure 4-2).**

   A new slide layout appears under the same Slide Master that you select in Step 1. Figure 4-5 shows the new slide layout.

3. **Use the Master toolbar to insert placeholders of various sorts into slide layouts.**

   Arrange them any way you want!

Figure 4-5:
Making a
new, custom
layout from
scratch.

If you like a particular slide layout and want to use it as a basis to create a new slide layout by editing and adding placeholders, you can duplicate that slide layout easily by selecting the layout within the Slide Master and then pressing ⌘-D. PowerPoint duplicates the layout, and you can easily rename it by right-clicking or Control-clicking the layout thumbnail and selecting Rename Layout.

Taking Note of Notes Masters

If you read this chapter from the beginning, after seeing how powerful the Slide Masters and slide layouts are, the Notes Master may seem mundane by comparison. When you choose View➪Master➪Notes Master, a view similar to what's shown in Figure 4-6 appears. Here, you can select and format the layout of the Notes Page View.

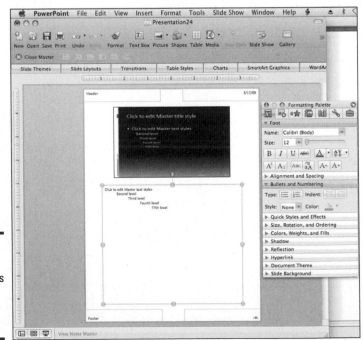

Figure 4-6:
Tuning
Notes pages
by using
the Notes
Master.

You can do the following in Notes Master View:

✦ **Add text to slide notes:** Type or paste text in the Slide Notes text box.

✦ **Format header and footer:** Choose View⇨Header and Footer to open the Header and Footer dialog (see Chapter 9 in this minibook).

✦ **Adjust the sizes of the slide preview and the slide notes boxes:** Click to select the item that you want to resize, and then drag the resize handles (see Figure 4-6).

✦ **Reposition the slide preview and slide notes boxes:** Click to select the box that you want to reposition, and then click the selection indicator that surrounds the box. The mouse turns into a special cursor (see Figure 4-6) that lets you drag the box.

✦ **Rotate the slide preview and slide notes boxes:** When a box is selected, drag the green Rotate handle, as shown in Figure 4-6.

✦ **Apply formatting:** Use the Formatting Palette.

✦ **Format the background of the Notes Page View:** Click the background and select Background Formatting Options from the Formatting Palette.

✦ **Add SmartArt and other objects:** Click the SmartArt tab of Elements Gallery and select SmartArt, or click the Object Palette of the Toolbox and select objects.

Although you can make dramatic-looking Notes pages with Notes Master, remember that if you decide to print the notes, these formatting changes will apply. A dark background uses a lot of toner and ink quickly, and complicated formatting can slow your printer. On the other hand, full-bleed fancy handouts are impressive for special audiences.

Handling Handout Masters

When you choose View⇨Master⇨Handout Master, the resulting Master affects only the background, header, and footer of slide shows when the slide shows are printed. Although you can click the positioning indicators on the Master toolbar, as shown in Figure 4-7, the positions can't be changed or resized.

Positioning indicators

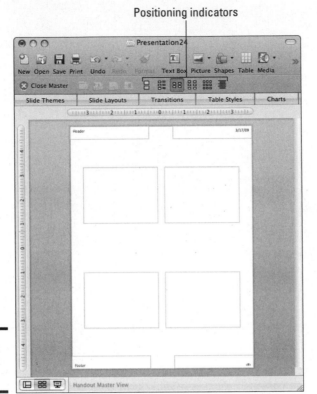

Figure 4-7:
Formatting
handouts.

Chapter 5: Proofing the Presentation

In This Chapter

✔ Dispelling spelling errors

✔ Collaborating with colleagues

✔ Flagging for follow up

*B*eing confident in the content of your presentation goes a long way to easing the worries you might have about being in front of a group. If you know that you rehearsed and proofread everything ahead of time, you feel and look authoritative and poised, and your audience is friendly and receptive. After all, they came to hear about your subject matter, and you'll have no trouble delivering content to meet their expectations. The information in this chapter can help you avoid making obvious mistakes, such as spelling errors, and helps you collaborate with others involved in the presentation.

Banishing Spelling Mistakes

PowerPoint uses the same spelling tools as Microsoft Word, which means that you get the most powerful word-processing tools right in PowerPoint. It's also important to know that when you're working in PowerPoint, at times, you work outside the reach of the spell checker. We try to steer you the right way, and we remind you that there's a dictionary, thesaurus, and language translation tools right in the Toolbox in the Reference Tools pane.

Nothing advertises ineptitude more than a spelling mistake in 44-point Helvetica projected on a large screen. Oops!

Setting spelling preferences

By default, spelling and grammar settings are turned on. You can adjust the settings by choosing PowerPoint⇨Preferences, and then selecting the Spelling tab, as shown in Figure 5-1. For most people, the default settings are fine, and you can leave them alone. In Book II, Chapter 4, we give much more detail about how spell checker works, but we repeat a few of the most common aspects in this chapter.

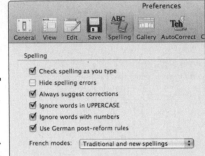

Figure 5-1:
Setting the
spelling
preferences.

Getting rid of red squiggles

If PowerPoint thinks you should check the spelling of a word, it puts a little
red squiggle under it. You can right-click or Control-click the underlined word
to make PowerPoint suggest one or more replacement words in a pop-up
window. You can select a replacement from the list and go on your way, or
you can choose one of the other options on the list, as shown in Figure 5-2.

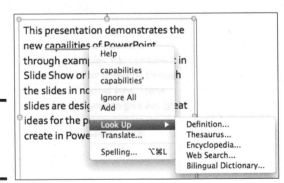

Figure 5-2:
Putting an
end to a
squiggle.

Checking the whole presentation

We've been known to overlook an occasional red squiggle, so we always
give the presentation one last thorough check before going before an audience. Choosing Tools➪Spelling sets PowerPoint on a mission to find spelling
errors and opens the Spelling pane, as shown in Figure 5-3. This tool goes
through the entire presentation looking for possible mistakes.

We want to caution you that some objects are off limits to the spell checker.
If you have a spelling error in a chart, for example, PowerPoint's spell checker
won't find it. Spell checker is only reliable when working with text in Outline
View.

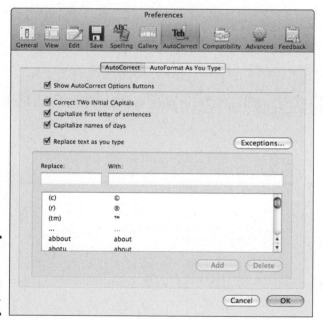

Figure 5-3:
Checking
an entire
presenta-
tion's
spelling.

Correcting automatically while you type

PowerPoint uses Word's AutoCorrect feature to fix misspellings on the fly while you type. PowerPoint has changed a word when you see a little blue flash under a word after you type it. You can adjust the AutoCorrect settings and make new AutoCorrect replacement text in PowerPoint by choosing PowerPoint⇨Preferences. Then, select the AutoCorrect tab in the Preferences dialog, as shown in Figure 5-4.

Figure 5-4:
Setting the
AutoCorrect
preferences.

Collaborating with Comments

Although PowerPoint doesn't have the big, fancy Track Changes feature of Word and Excel, it does have a nice Comment feature. You can turn commenting tools on by choosing Insert⇨Comment or Tools⇨Review Comments. Taking either action activates the Reviewing toolbar, as shown in Figure 5-5.

Previous comment

Next comment

Figure 5-5:
Reviewing
PowerPoint
comments.

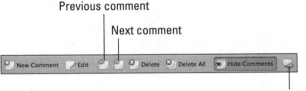

Mail Presentation as Attachment

When a new comment is inserted, a text box is created and a marker is put into the slide. You can jump through the comments in a presentation by using the Previous Comment and Next Comment buttons on the Reviewing toolbar. You may choose to edit or delete an existing comment, or make a new comment. Comments retain the name of the commentor, plus the date of the comment, as shown in Figure 5-6.

Figure 5-6:
Reviewing
a comment.

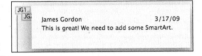

In the bonus chapter, we discuss some new ways of collaborating. If you're into the Web 2.0 philosophy that sharing is a great way to create, be sure to check out our discussion of OfficeLive and Mesh.

Remembering to Remember

You might want to remind yourself to look at any given presentation for many possible reasons. You can set a reminder by using the Task feature of Entourage. But you can also set a reminder right from within PowerPoint. Choose Tools⇨Flag for Follow Up to open a pane that lets you set a date and time that you want to be reminded to come back to the current presentation, as shown in Figure 5-7.

Flag for Follow Up works even when PowerPoint isn't running. If you want to remind yourself to look at your presentation prior to your scheduled live presentation delivery time, use Follow Up. You can also use Follow Up to remind yourself of a deadline associated with some aspect of your presentation's production. Your computer does have to be running for Follow Up to work, of course.

Figure 5-7:
Reminding
yourself
to come
back to a
presentation.

Chapter 6: Adding Text, Pictures, Tables, and Charts

In This Chapter

✔ Formatting text

✔ Bringing your pictures home

✔ Inserting a chart

✔ Creating fancy tables

In this chapter, we discuss how PowerPoint works with text, pictures, charts and tables. Each is quite different in the way it presents information on slides, but PowerPoint works with them all similarly. Most of the time, you follow a selection-and-action routine to format any of these. After you make a selection, extra options appear right on the Toolbox's Formatting Palette. We're going to unleash your creative juices and do it in a way that results in great-looking presentations. When you give your presentation, your audience will focus on the screen. That sure takes a lot of pressure off your job as a presenter, and it makes you appear more confident, consistent, and coordinated with your slides!

Before we go too far, we want to remind you that in Book I, Chapters 3 through 7, we cover the basics about many topics that we expand on in this chapter. We don't want to take your money and just repeat things, so be sure to review the earlier chapters before venturing into this one; several topics build on the basics covered in Book I.

Getting the Right Text Format

It's fast and easy to use the text that comes in PowerPoint's lavish themes and templates. You often need to customize fonts and reposition text to make the text fit and look right. Choosing a different font or making a font larger can make your presentation more readable for someone sitting at the rear of a large room. Some organizations specify that you must use a specific font to maintain consistency with their themes and templates. Sometimes, you want to customize text just for fun, which can keep your presentation interesting. This section can help you with your font-formatting needs.

Watch the Formatting Palette while you work on text. You can use its endless options to customize your text to make it interesting. Figure 6-1 illustrates many of PowerPoint's new text-formatting features.

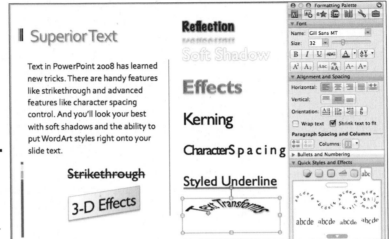

Figure 6-1:
Discovering new text-formatting possibilities.

You can get text into your slides quickly. To insert a new slide and add text, follow these steps:

1. **Click the New Slide button on the Standard toolbar.**

A new slide appears.

2. **If the new slide doesn't have placeholders, choose a slide layout that has placeholders from the Slide Layouts tab of Elements Gallery.**

3. **Click any placeholder and start typing to replace the dummy text.**

To add a text box to an existing slide, click the Text Box button on the Standard toolbar. Click the slide to place a text box, and then start typing some text.

In both the instances, you type text into a container — either a text placeholder or a text box. Note the following:

✦ When the *insertion cursor* (the blinking vertical bar) is inside a text box or placeholder, or if you highlight text characters by dragging the mouse over them, any formatting that you apply affects text that's inside the container text box or placeholder.

✦ If you click the *border* of a text box or placeholder, you have selected the box shape (the container, rather than the enclosed text), so any formatting you apply affects the text box or placeholder shape, not the text inside the box.

Compare the left text box and the right text box in Figure 6-2. On the left, we added reflection while the cursor was inside the text box. On the right, we clicked the border of the text box and then added reflection.

Figure 6-2:
Reflecting on what's selected.

Having the ability to pick and choose what you want formatted gives you the flexibility to format the contents of a box, or the text box or placeholder itself. We call this thinking inside and about the box at the same time! This flexibility means that you should pay attention while you're working so that you apply the formatting to either the box contents, or to the placeholder or text box, as you intend. This attention ultimately goes back to what you select in the first place.

Also, pay close attention to what's selected when you click the More Options buttons that are in some sections of the Formatting Palette. If the cursor is within the text when you click the More Options button under Quick Styles and Effects, you get the Format Text dialog, as shown in Figure 6-3. Format Text options apply formatting to the text that's inside the text box, but it doesn't affect the surrounding box or placeholder.

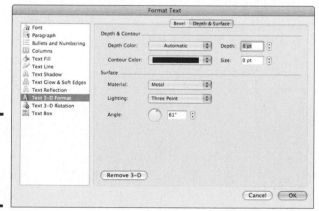

Figure 6-3:
Thinking inside a text box — Format Text.

**Book IV
Chapter 6**

**Adding Text,
Pictures, Tables,
and Charts**

On the other hand, if you click the *border* of that same text box and then click the More Options button under Quick Styles and Effects, you get the Format Shape dialog shown in Figure 6-4. Format Shape options apply formatting to the shape (either the text box or placeholder) that surrounds the text, not the text inside the text box or placeholder. Format Text and Format Shape have one item in common — the Text Box settings.

To make it even easier to see the differences between Format Text and Format Shape, we put the left panes of each of these two wizards next to each other in Figure 6-5.

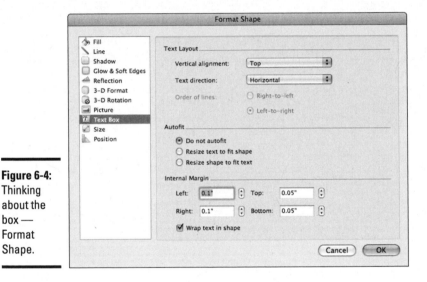

Figure 6-4: Thinking about the box — Format Shape.

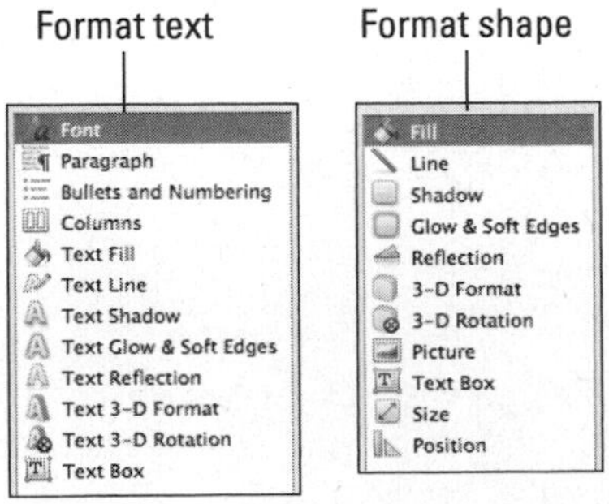

Figure 6-5: Thinking in the box and about the box.

Importing a Batch of Pictures

In PowerPoint 2008, PowerPoint automatically scales pictures when you import them from other sources. To insert a picture on a slide:

1. **Click the Picture button on the Standard toolbar and then select Insert Picture from the pop-up menu.**

   The Choose a Picture dialog appears.

2. **Navigate to any picture or use Spotlight to locate a picture.**

3. **Select a picture file, and then click Insert.**

   The picture appears on your slide.

If your picture is smaller than the size of your PowerPoint slide, the picture is centered on the slide. If the picture is larger than the slide, PowerPoint automatically scales the picture to fit the slide, and it offers a widget to bypass the automatic scaling, as shown in Figure 6-6.

Figure 6-6:
Skipping the automatic scaling of a picture.

We have to admit that we've been frustrated by this topic. While we write this, no one has figured out a way to import a batch of pictures into PowerPoint 2008 for Mac. We know there's a built-in feature in PowerPoint for Windows that does it, but that feature isn't in PowerPoint for Mac. One of the authors of this book has a popular add-in that works in earlier versions of PowerPoint, but without VBA, it just doesn't work in PowerPoint 2008.

While we contemplated what to tell you about this dilemma, we decided to take one last look at AppleScript. Well, we figured it out! Moreover, thanks to Apple's new Automator Actions and Microsoft Office's integration with Automator, we think we can explain how to create your own Automator Action to import a batch of pictures into PowerPoint. It takes just two Automator Actions. The resulting Automator script imports pictures from iPhoto into PowerPoint.

Making an Automator Action

Even if you're new to Automator, we're a bit proud that we figured this out and can share it with you in an easy-to-get-started way. You should be able to do this, even if you've never used Automator. It's a testament to how well

Book IV
Chapter 6

Adding Text, Pictures, Tables, and Charts

things work together on the Mac. Follow these steps to create an Automator action that can import a batch of pictures into PowerPoint:

1. **Open the Automator application.**

   You can find Automator in the Applications folder. The Select a Starting Point to Open a New Workflow dialog appears, as shown in Figure 6-7.

2. **Select the Custom option and then click the Choose button to start a new workflow (see Figure 6-7).**

   The Select a Starting Point to Open a New Workflow dialog closes. Automator launches with the interface that you can see in Figure 6-8. The right side is empty except for a prompt that you can ignore for the moment.

3. **In the left pane, click the disclosure triangle next to Library to display the subheadings shown in Figure 6-8.**

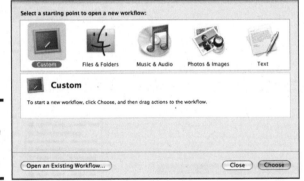

Figure 6-7:
Opening the
Automator
application.

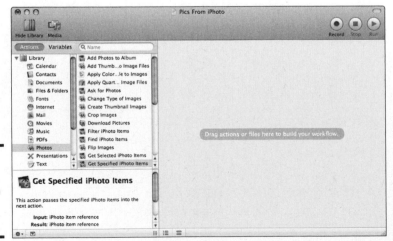

Figure 6-8:
Getting
started with
Mac OS X
Automator.

4. In the list of subheadings, click Photos to select that category.

Again, see Figure 6-8.

5. From the list of actions, drag Get Specified iPhoto Items to the right pane, as shown in Figure 6-9.

The Automator Action should appear in the pane on the right side.

6. In your new Get Specified iPhoto Items box, move the mouse cursor over the word *Options* near the bottom of the action.

Options reveals itself as a button.

7. Click Options.

See Figure 6-9.

8. Select the check box for Show This Action When the Workflow Runs.

9. Go back to the left pane and click the Presentations category.

10. From the list of actions, drag Create PowerPoint Picture Slide Shows to the right pane.

Automator joins the two actions, as shown in Figure 6-9.

11. From Automator's menu, choose File⇨Save as Plug-In. Change the lower pop-up to Plug-In for Script Menu, as shown in Figure 6-10. Give the plug-in an appropriate name, as shown, and then click the Save button.

12. Choose Automator⇨Quit Automator to exit the Automator application.

Congratulations! You've now made the workflow, and you can use it in PowerPoint whenever you want. If Automator asks you to save this workflow again while quitting Automator, do the resave.

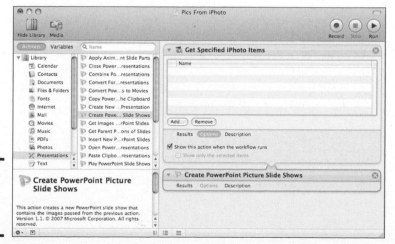

Figure 6-9:
Creating an Automator workflow.

Figure 6-10:
Saving your
Automator
Action as a
plug-in.

Running the Automator Action

After you make an Automator Action (as described in the preceding section), you can use it to import a batch of pictures from iPhoto. When you're ready, run the action by following these steps:

1. **Open PowerPoint to a new, blank presentation.**

2. **Click the rightmost script menu on the menu bar.**

You may see two identical script icons on your menu bar. The rightmost one produces the menu shown in Figure 6-11.

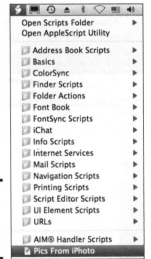

Figure 6-11:
Running the
Automator
script.

3. **At the bottom of the menu, select your Automator script to run it.**

The script is running properly if you see the Get Specified iPhoto Items pane (see Figure 6-12) and a status notification in the menu bar at the top of your screen.

Get Specified iPhoto Items starts off empty. This small pane might be behind the PowerPoint window, so move the window to the side if you don't see the pane shown in Figure 6-12.

Figure 6-12:
Importing
pictures —
Get Specified
iPhoto Items.

4. **In Get Specified iPhoto Items, click the Add button to display the iPhoto chooser pane shown in Figure 6-13.**

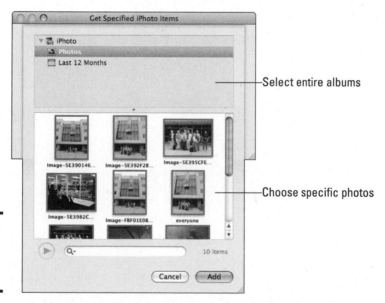

Select entire albums

Choose specific photos

Figure 6-13:
Picking the
pictures to
import.

5. **Use the picture chooser pane to select the pictures that you want to import into PowerPoint.**

This pane has many likable features. Try the following:

- If you select only an album in the top section and then click the Add button, the entire album is imported.

- If you select iPhoto at the top and then click the Add button, your entire iPhoto collection may be imported, so be careful!

- If you click an album and resize the window to be a little larger, you can see previews of your photos. You can select individual photos one at a time and then click the Add button, or hold the Command (⌘) key down and click to select multiple pictures.

- After you click the Add button in the picture chooser, the pane shown in Figure 6-12 reappears. In this pane, you can click the Add button and return to the picture chooser shown in Figure 6-13 to get more pictures. You can go back and forth until you have all the pictures you want imported from your albums.

6. **If you need to remove a picture from the list, click the Remove button, as shown in Figure 6-14.**

7. **When you're done selecting pictures to import into PowerPoint, click the Continue button.**

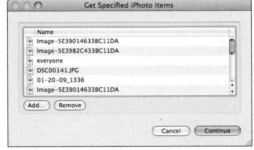

Figure 6-14: Importing pictures — continue after making selections.

Clicking the Continue button may cause iPhoto to come to the front, but you can switch to PowerPoint and watch while the pictures you selected are imported, one picture per slide. Large pictures are automatically sized to fit the slides, and smaller pictures are centered on the slides. Is this great or what?!

It took only two Automator Actions to create the workflow plug-in. You don't need to know any programming. In just a few minutes, you can make a fully functional, useful program that would have taken a professional programmer days to make by using VBA or another programming language. It's worth your while to go back into Automator when you have a chance and explore more actions. You can find out a lot about Automator at this Apple Web site: `www.apple.com/macosx/features/300.html#automator`.

Charting the (New) Way

Microsoft provides an entirely new way to make graphs and charts in Office 2008. In PowerPoint, it takes two clicks to get started with a chart. Because charting is now done the same way in all the Office applications, we cover this topic in Book I, Chapter 5, so head there now for the details. Very little is specific to PowerPoint with regard to charts, except for these steps that you take to insert a chart:

1. **Navigate to the slide where you want to insert a new chart and click the Charts tab of Elements Gallery.**

If Elements Gallery isn't visible, click the Gallery button on the standard toolbar.

2. **Click a chart type, as shown in Figure 6-15.**

Figure 6-15: Picking a chart type.

Tipping the Tables

The Tables feature in PowerPoint 2008 has been updated with table styles. Tables now respond to document themes, and you can choose from a variety of new table styles.

Making a table the new way

Starting with a slide, you can follow these steps to make a table from scratch:

1. **Click the Table Styles tab of Elements Gallery.**

See Figure 6-16.

If Elements Gallery isn't visible, click the Gallery button on the standard toolbar.

All Table Styles

Best Match for Document   Table Styles

Figure 6-16: Creating a new table.

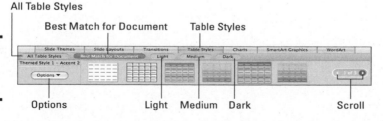

Options   Light   Medium   Dark   Scroll

2. **(Optional) Click Options.**

A pop-up menu appears. Choose from the following formatting options:

• **Header Row:** Formats the top row of the table differently than the other rows to differentiate column headers from the rest of the rows.

- **Total Row:** Adds a white border between the bottom row and the rest of the rows.

- **First Column:** Formats the leftmost column differently from the rest of the columns.

- **Last Column:** Formats the rightmost column differently from the rest of the columns.

- **Banded Rows:** Formats all the rows as alternating light and dark.

- **Banded Columns:** Formats all the columns as alternating light and dark.

3. **Click a table style (see Figure 6-16).**

4. **In the Insert Table dialog that opens (see Figure 6-17), set the number of rows and columns you want to have, and then click the OK button.**

   Your fresh, shiny new table appears instantly!

Figure 6-17: Choosing the number of rows and columns.

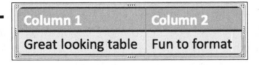

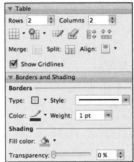

Reformatting a table

After you create a table, you can experiment with variations on how it looks. With the insertion cursor located anywhere in the table, you can click various table styles in Elements Gallery to try them on for size. Click Options to display a pop-up menu from which you can choose formatting options (as described in the preceding section).

The Formatting Palette is also your friend when working with tables. Notice that the new Table section appears when a table is selected, and that the Borders and Shading section becomes available in addition to font formatting. See Figure 6-18. You can also apply a new document theme to a presentation by choosing a theme from the Formatting Palette, resulting in table styles getting changed and updated to styles based on the new theme.

Figure 6-18:
Formatting
tables
with the
Formatting
Palette.

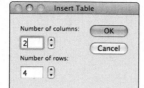

When you're ready to take table formatting to the ultimate level, right-click
the border of your table and select Format Table from the pop-up menu that
appears, which opens the Format Table dialog. In this dialog, you can go
crazy with all the new table-formatting options. You even get to use the new,
fancy, multicolor linear gradient fills, which we discuss in Chapter 3 of this
minibook.

Chapter 7: Applying Animation

*H*ave you ever been "PowerPointed to death?" Chances are good that you have. If you've ever sat through a presentation where every slide had 20 bullets of text, no subtle animations, and no smooth transitions, you can claim to be a victim. Likewise, if you've seen a presentation that had every mesmerizing transition and swooshing animation possible, making you dizzy, you, too, can claim to be a victim.

Both extremes are deadly to presenters. There's no reason to use presentation software to simply display text, especially if there are oodles of text for each slide. If text is all you have, do your audience a favor and consider distributing it as a Word document or PDF file. Your audience will conclude that you're reading to them if your slides are mostly just text. We've heard some people mention a 7-x-7 rule. Use no more than seven words in a bullet point, and use no more than seven bullet points on a slide. And then there's the 10-20-30 rule, which calls for 10 slides to be presented in 20 minutes with text that's at least 30 points in size. Both rules seem reasonable to us — and hopefully to you, as well.

PowerPoint's role is to help you present rich media content that complements the points you make while you give your presentation. Animations and transitions help your presentation flow, just like they do in movies and television programs. In this chapter, we explore how animation — which isn't possible on the printed page or in PDF — plays an expository role. (See Book IV, Chapter 1 for more information on transition effects.)

Classifying Custom Animations

Custom animation effects have four main categories:

✦ **Entrance effects:** Use entrance effects to bring objects into the slide while the show is running.

✦ **Emphasis effects:** You can apply emphasis effects to objects that are already visible on the slide. The object remains on the slide when the effect has completed.

✦ **Exit effects:** Exit effects make objects disappear from the slide while the show is playing.

✦ **Media actions:** These settings affect when and how sound and movies play. We discuss media actions in Chapter 8 of this minibook.

A motion path is another type of PowerPoint animation that's available to users of PowerPoint for Windows. Unfortunately, this option still isn't available on PowerPoint for Mac. However, if you have a presentation that contains a motion path animation created in PowerPoint for Windows, the Mac version of PowerPoint can play that animation.

As this book was going to the press, Microsoft released Service Pack 2 for Microsoft Office 2008, a free update that added motion path animations to PowerPoint 2008. Download Bonus Chapter 2 from this book's Web site at www.dummies.com/go/office2008formacaiofd to learn more!

Animating Text

As you've probably seen with other features in Office, Microsoft provides both simple and elaborate ways to control features. Custom Animation has both a quick method and a detailed method of application. In Project Gallery, you can find a presentation template called Widescreen Presentation. This particular presentation has no custom animation in it, so in the following sections, we use it as an example. To open this presentation so that you can follow along with the examples, follow these steps:

1. **In PowerPoint, choose File➪Project Gallery.**

Project Gallery appears.

2. **In the Category list, select Presentations.**

3. **Double-click Widescreen Presentation.**

PowerPoint opens a new presentation in Normal View based on Widescreen Presentation.

Telling a story with PowerPoint

While you build a presentation, imagine yourself as the editor of a film rather than a presentation. Your job in making your presentation is to present your content in an order that tells your story. You expose the audience to the content you want at just the right moment, in just the right order.

When you're building your slide show, keep in mind how it will look to someone who has never seen it before. Your job as editor can be fun!

Adding an entrance effect quickly

You enable Custom Animation by using the Custom Animation tab in the Toolbox. Refer to Figure 7-1 for this example. Follow these steps to put a text animation in a text box in slide 3 of Widescreen Presentation:

Toolbox

1. **If the Toolbox isn't currently visible, click the Toolbox button on the Standard toolbar.**

2. **Select the text box for Widescreen Advantages.**

3. **Click the green Add Entrance Effect button to activate the pop-up list.**

4. **Select an effect from the list.**

   In our example, we chose the Fade effect.

When you select an effect, PowerPoint plays it for you on the slide. If you missed it, or if you want to see the effect play again, click the Preview Effect button. That's all you have to do to quickly add an entrance effect. If you run the show, PowerPoint waits until you click the mouse button before exposing the text on the slide.

As much as possible, keep animation simple and subtle. Remember, the purpose of animation is to enhance rather than distract, and two animations that work best with this approach are the fades and the wipes.

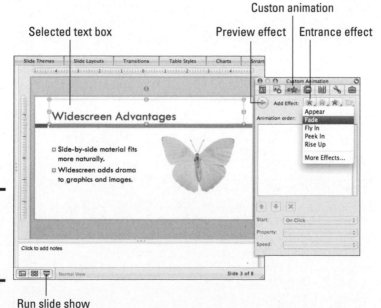

Figure 7-1:
Quickly adding an entrance effect.

Selected text box
Custon animation
Preview effect
Entrance effect
Run slide show

Book IV
Chapter 7

Applying
Animation

Getting a little fancier

You can get a little bit fancier with the next effect. This time, we animate the text box that starts with the words Side-by-Side. We want the text to appear one bullet point at a time, rather than all at the same time, and we want it to appear automatically right after the first animation plays. Refer to Figure 7-2 for this example and follow these steps:

1. **Select the text box that starts with the text Side-by-Side.**

2. **Click the Add Entrance Effect button.**

3. **Select an effect.**

We chose Fade because it doesn't draw too much attention to itself.

The Custom Animation palette gets bigger.

4. **Because we want this effect to play immediately following the previous effect, change the Start property to After Previous.**

After Previous means that the effect is activated as soon as the previous effect finishes.

5. **To make your text to appear one bullet at a time, in the Text Animations section of Custom Animation, change the Group Text box to 2nd Level.**

Only some effects let you choose group levels. Be sure to experiment with combinations of Animate Text and Group Text options.

6. **After looking at the preview, decide which speed setting looks best to you.**

We chose the Medium speed setting in our example.

The number of seconds you should allow appears next to the speed. Your animation's actual time may vary, depending on your computer's hardware and what other applications are running.

7. **Run the slide to see how it looks so far.**

 To run your show by starting with the current slide, click the Slide Show button at the lower-left corner of the window. It's the third button from the left, which looks like a small screen, as shown in the margin.

Start options

You can choose from three start options (we like to call them *animation events*):

✦ **On Click:** This option works just like it sounds. PowerPoint waits for you to click the mouse button before running the animation when the slide show is running. On Click is the default setting when you add a new animation to a slide.

✦ **With Previous:** When With Previous is selected, the animation plays simultaneously with the previous animation in the list in the Animation

Order palette. You can chain many animations together so that they play all at the same time. If you want all the animations to play without having to click the mouse, the first animation in the list should be With Previous or After Previous.

✦ **After Previous:** After Previous tells PowerPoint to wait until the previous animation has completed before automatically starting this animation.

Making a moth fly

In this section we're going to add three animation effects to the image of a moth, and then set each one to play after the previous animation so that they play in sequence. See Figure 7-3 for this example, and get ready to dig through the big list of animations by following these steps:

1. **Select the image.**

We select our moth image.

2. **Click the green Add Entrance Effect button in the Custom Animation toolbox.**

Select More Effects from the pop-up menu every time you add a new effect so that you can choose from the big list of all the effects that are in the Animation Effects palette.

3. **In the Exciting category, select the Boomerang effect and then click the OK button.**

The buttons at the bottom of the palette are now Cancel and OK.

4. **Change the Start setting to After Previous.**

5. **Click the yellow Add Emphasis Effect button.**

6. **In the Moderate category, select Teeter, and then click the OK button.**

7. **Change the Start setting to After Previous.**

8. **Click the red Add Exit Effect button.**

9. **In the Exciting category, select Swivel.**

10. **Change the Start setting to After Previous.**

11. **Click the Animation Preview button to preview the slide and watch while the moth flies in and then flies away from you!**

Entrance effects have a green star, emphasis effects have a yellow star, and exit effects have a red star. If you look closely, you can see that the stars are different. You can delay an effect by using the Timing section of the Animation Effects palette.

**Book IV
Chapter 7**

**Applying
Animation**

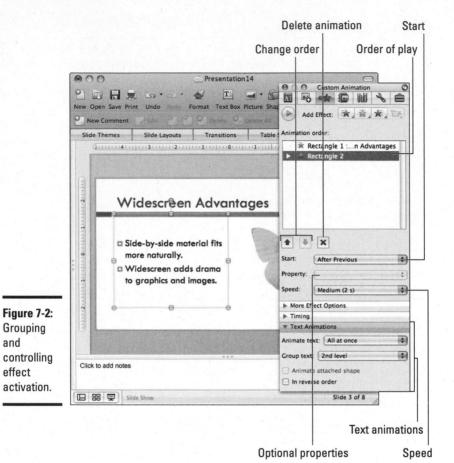

Figure 7-2:
Grouping
and
controlling
effect
activation.

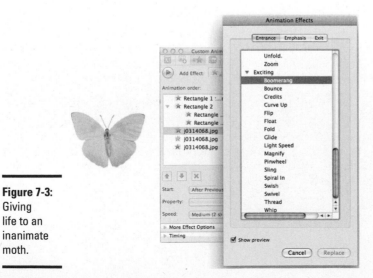

Figure 7-3:
Giving
life to an
inanimate
moth.

Changing your mind

You can easily change an effect. To see which effect you've already applied or to change an effect that's already been applied, double-click the item in the Animation Order palette. PowerPoint shows you which animation has been applied. You can change it right there (see Figure 7-3).

You can easily change the order in which objects enter and play by selecting them in the Animation Order palette and then clicking the Change Order buttons, as shown in Figure 7-2. Animations play in order, starting at the top of the palette.

Animating a Chart

Animating charts adds interest and helps tell the story of your data. The Widescreen Presentation we work with throughout this chapter has a chart. See Figure 7-4. You won't believe how easily you can animate a chart in PowerPoint for Mac. The chart at hand is a bar chart, and we think the Rise Up animation would be a good one for this type of chart. Follow these steps to add animation:

1. **Go to slide 4 and select the chart by clicking its border.**

2. **Click the Add Entrance Effect button in the Custom Animation palette of Toolbox.**

3. **Select the Rise Up animation.**

   A new Chart Animations section appears in the Custom Animation toolbox (see Figure 7-4).

4. **In the Group Graphic pop-up menu, select By Category.**

5. **Click the Preview Effect button (see Figure 7-1) and watch the magic happen!**

   By all means, experiment with other grouping options and animation effects. Some effects have directional options. In Figure 7-4, we captured the last category while it was rising into place.

PowerPoint for Windows includes an animation feature called Triggers, which allows you to click on objects while a presentation is running to make a specific animation occur on the slide. PowerPoint for Mac doesn't have this feature. The Mac version ignores triggers if they're in a presentation created in Windows, so triggers don't fire in PowerPoint for Mac.

Figure 7-4:
Making a
bar chart
dance.

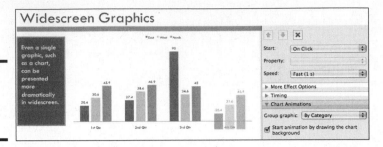

Chapter 8: Presenting Sounds and Movies

In This Chapter

✔ **Rehearsing your presentation**

✔ **Adding music and sound**

✔ **Making a smooth transition**

✔ **Incorporating video**

✔ **Using custom animation**

✔ **Dealing with eccentricities**

Rich media, also known broadly as multimedia, enhances your presentations. You can add music, sounds, movies, and YouTube videos to your PowerPoint presentations. You can also add your own voice narrations to individual slides. PowerPoint may be 25 years old, but it's been keeping up with the times and knows about Web 2.0. This chapter helps you incorporate the rich media that can make your presentations interesting.

For the most part, working with audio in PowerPoint is straightforward. We cover the basics first. At the end of this chapter, we talk about some of the "gotchas" in details about using sounds and music.

Speaking to Your Audience

You may want to create a narrated version of your presentation that you can distribute. You can't be everywhere, and even though your audience won't get the benefit of your physical presence, they'll at least be able to hear you while they enjoy your slide show. We cover a method of adding sounds during our Slide Sorter View discussion in Book IV, Chapter 1, but we don't talk about narrating slides in that chapter.

PowerPoint has two features that are almost the same. Both of them play the slide show while you rehearse it. While you rehearse, both features record how much time you spend on each slide. When you're done, PowerPoint offers to let you use those timings for the slide show. The difference between the two features is as follows:

✦ Rehearse Timings captures only the timings.

✦ Record Narration captures the timings plus your audio narration.

Rehearsing timings

Use Rehearse Timings whenever you want your presentation to advance slides automatically one after the other, after a preset period of time. You turn on this feature by choosing Slide Show➪Rehearse Timings. The slide show runs from the first slide, and PowerPoint keeps track of how much time you take while you rehearse. At the end of the show, or when you press the Escape key, you decide whether to keep the timings. If you opt to save these timings, they're saved as automatic transition timings.

Many users work with the Rehearse Timings option to practice their PowerPoint slides out loud. They can get an idea about how long it'll take to do an actual presentation using these slides. Thereafter, they opt not to save the timings.

Even if you opt to save the timings, you can always fine-tune them later in Slide Sorter View, where you can also remove those timings altogether. (See Book IV, Chapter 1.)

If you need to adhere to strict time limits, timings keep you on track. Timings are also used for self-running presentations in kiosk mode.

Recording narrations

Use the Record Narration feature when you want to make a version of your presentation that has narration included for distribution. Of course, to use this feature, your computer requires a microphone and speakers, or a good-quality audio headset. Record Narration works the same way as Rehearse Timings, but PowerPoint records what you say while you rehearse. At the end of each slide, PowerPoint creates a sound file and adds it to the slide. You can always go back, delete the sound icon from the slide, and rerecord the slide's narration if you're not happy with the audio.

To start the slide show and begin recording, choose Slide Show➪Record Narration. PowerPoint asks your Mac what audio hardware it has, and then asks you which hardware you want to use to record. In the following sections, we discuss the settings shown in Figure 8-1.

Recording options

PowerPoint tells you approximately how much time you can use to record your narration based on the settings you choose. If you have more than one sound input device, click the Sound Input Device pop-up menu and select the option you want to use from the available sound input devices.

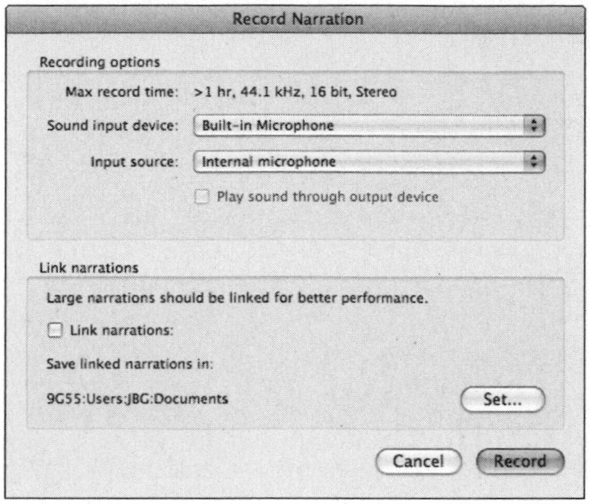

Figure 8-1:
Choosing audio input options for recording narration.

Link narrations

If you select the Link Narrations check box, PowerPoint prompts you to choose a place to store the narrations in your file system. Linking keeps the size of your presentation file small. If you choose to link, you should make a note of this fact in the slide notes of your title slide. To make versions for distribution, use the PowerPoint Package feature so that narrations accompany the distributed presentation. Choose File⇨Save As, click Format in the Save As dialog that appears, and select PowerPoint Package from the pop-up menu.

If you need to share narrated presentations with folks who run PowerPoint for Windows, don't link narrations because PowerPoint for Mac seems to save narrations files without a file extension, and that's something PowerPoint for Windows can't understand!

If you want professional-sounding narrations, get a high-quality headset and record in a silent room. Consider using sound-editing and -recording software so that you can easily delete unwanted parts of your sound track. Using sound-editing software eliminates the worry about making mistakes, and you can kill extraneous noises. Audacity is a free sound-editing and -recording program that you can download from this open-source Web site:

    http://audacity.sourceforge.net

You can much more easily work from a script than try to "wing it." Even with a script, expect to spend 40 minutes or more working on the audio for each 15 minutes' worth of audio that'll finally make it into your presentation. If you're not happy with the sound of your own voice, you may have to pay a professional to record the narrations.

**Book IV
Chapter 8**

Presenting Sounds and Movies

Adding Music and Sounds

Soothing or not so soothing. It depends! Regardless of the kind of music or sound you plan to add to your presentation, you might want to make some noise in three distinct points in a presentation. Each point has some special considerations:

✦ While a slide is playing

✦ During a slide transition

✦ As background throughout a presentation

Our hunch is that most of your audio and video content is in iTunes, so we're going to feature iTunes as a content source. We think that you'll be pleased with the high level of integration among PowerPoint, Mac OS X, and Apple applications. Of course, you can use music, sounds, and movies from almost any sound file anywhere in Finder. We love GarageBand, and we encourage you to use it to create your own music and audio content for PowerPoint, but we're not going to describe GarageBand in this book. For that, we refer you to *GarageBand For Dummies,* by Bob LeVitus (Wiley). Likewise, iMovie, iDVD, and Final Cut are superb for creating video content to use in PowerPoint presentations.

Making audio and video play while a slide plays

You can easily add music, sounds, and video to a slide. Before you add the content, think about when it should start to play. PowerPoint offers several different ways to get your rich content started on a slide:

✦ The easiest way is to have your audio or video content start playing automatically when the slide starts. When you select this option, the music or video plays until it finishes or until you move to the next slide, whichever comes first.

✦ The next easiest way is to have your content play when you click something that's on your slide, such as a sound icon or a video placeholder, while the slide show is running.

✦ A fancier way to use audio or video is as if it's one of the bullet points on your slide. You can actually add sounds and video to the schedule in the Custom Animation dialog of the Toolbox so that animation effects determine when the rich content plays.

✦ The final way is to have your audio play when you move the cursor over something on your slide while the slide show is running.

Adding audio that plays when the slide starts

We recommend that you place your saved presentation in a new folder. Then, copy the media files you want to insert within the presentation in this new folder and launch the presentation file.

You can easily add sounds and music to a slide. Choose either of two ways to activate the Insert Sound dialog:

✦ **The Media button:** Click the Media button on the Standard toolbar and select Insert Sound and Music from the pop-up menu.

When you select this option, the Insert Sound dialog appears. Navigate to a sound file or use Spotlight to search for a file name. Select Music from the Mac OS X Places list in Finder to navigate to your iTunes library.

✦ **Insert:** Choose Insert⇨Sound and Music, and then select one of the three Insert options:

- **From File:** When you select this option, the Insert Sound dialog appears. Navigate to a sound file or use Spotlight to search for a file. Choose Music from the OS X Places list in Finder to navigate to your iTunes library.

- **Play CD Audio Track:** We talk about how to use this option in the section "Adding a CD audio track," later in this chapter.

- **Record Sound:** We cover this option in "Recording a sound directly onto a slide," later in this chapter.

Whether you click the Media button or choose Insert⇨Sound and Music⇨ From File, the Insert Sound dialog opens. Insert Sound not only lets you navigate to any file in Finder, but it also lets you select from your iTunes music library and playlists. In Figure 8-2, we select a song from an iTunes playlist we made for PowerPoint.

When you use the Insert Sound dialog, you get to choose from all the media content anywhere on your computer. You can use sounds, music, and audio podcasts directly from your iTunes collection. The Search feature of Insert Sound is integrated with Mac OS X Spotlight and is amazingly fast. You can enter any part of a title or artist, and Search finds it instantly.

After you select the audio content in the Insert Sound dialog, click the Insert button to bring your audio content onto your slide. PowerPoint then prompts you to start the audio content when the slide starts, as shown in Figure 8-3. If you click the Automatically button, your audio content begins to play when the slide starts during a running slide show. A sound icon is placed on your slide.

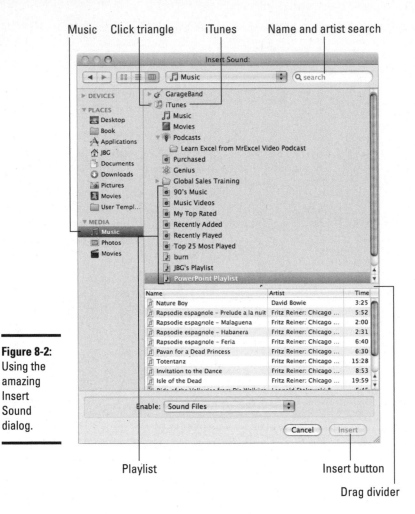

Music   Click triangle   iTunes   Name and artist search

Figure 8-2:
Using the
amazing
Insert
Sound
dialog.

Playlist   Insert button

Drag divider

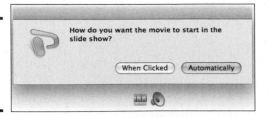

Figure 8-3:
Making
audio play
automat-
ically.

Adding audio that plays when clicked

To add audio that plays when clicked, the steps are the same as those
described in the preceding section, except instead of clicking the

Automatically button, you'll click the When Clicked button (see Figure 8-3). When you click the Insert button, the sound icon appears on your slide.

You're not limited to playing sounds by using the standard icon. You can have a sound play when you click any type of object, such as a picture, clip art, SmartArt, or WordArt (see Figure 8-4). To make an object clickable for sound, follow these steps:

1. **Right-click or Control-click the object.**

2. **Select Action Settings from the pop-up menu that appears to open the Action Settings dialog shown in Figure 8-4.**

3. **In the Play Sound section of the Action Settings dialog, click the pop-up button.**

4. **Select one of the sounds from the list, or scroll all the way down to the bottom and select Other Sound.**

If you select Other Sound, you're presented with a Choose a Sound dialog that lets you navigate Finder to select a sound file. Choose a Sound is almost the same as Insert Sound, so you can use Figure 8-2 as a guide.

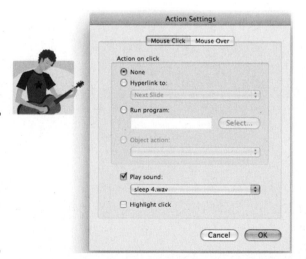

Figure 8-4:
Using an action setting to play a sound when clip art is clicked.

**Book IV
Chapter 8**

Presenting Sounds and Movies

Adding audio that plays when moused over

The Action Settings dialog in Figure 8-4 includes two tabs: Mouse Click and Mouse Over. The default setting is Mouse Click. If you want to change it so that the audio plays on your slide when you move the mouse over a picture or other object (so that you don't even have to click the picture), click the Mouse Over tab before selecting which sound to play. Otherwise, the steps to add an action setting are the same as those described in the preceding section.

Adding a CD audio track

PowerPoint can play audio from an ordinary CD while your presentation runs. To use this feature, slide a regular music CD into your Mac and let the CD's icon appear on the desktop. Then, choose Insert⇨Sound and Music⇨Play CD Audio Track. A simple dialog appears (as shown in Figure 8-5), which lets you select which track or tracks you want to add to the presentation. Although this feature is neat, remember to bring the audio CD with you whenever you give the presentation. If the CD isn't in your Mac before you start the presentation, the audio won't play.

Figure 8-5:
Inserting
the first 2
minutes and
28 seconds
of a song.

Recording a sound directly onto a slide

If you choose Insert⇨Sound and Music⇨Record Sound, the Record Sound dialog, as shown in Figure 8-6, opens. This is a bare-bones tool, and it might do in a pinch. We suggest you download, install, and understand how to use Audacity, instead. If you use Record Sound, the sound is embedded into the current slide; it's not exported as is implied when saving your sound.

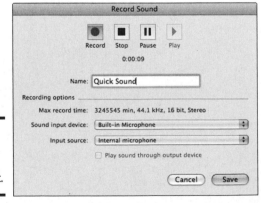

Figure 8-6:
Recording
a sound in
PowerPoint.

Filling the Transition Gap

On rare occasions, you might want to have a sound play during the transition period when one slide ends and the next one starts. Transition sounds add punctuation, bridge the gap from one slide to another (perhaps with humor), and can help with the continuity of a show.

The built-in PowerPoint transition sounds are definitely of the punctuation kind. If you're going to use a slide transition sound, we suggest that you use one of your own making. GarageBand is the perfect tool to use to make music and sounds for this purpose. Our screen shot in Figure 8-7 illustrates the import of a GarageBand loop that we made, after we converted it to AIFF format by using Audacity. Follow these steps to add your own sound to a slide transition:

1. **On the Transitions tab of Elements Gallery, click Options.**

We suggest that you use Slide Sorter View, but you don't have to.

2. **In the Transitions Options dialog, click the Sound pop-up menu.**

A pop-up menu appears.

3. **Scroll down to the bottom of the long list and select Other Sound.**

The Choose a Sound dialog appears.

4. **In the Choose a Sound dialog, navigate or use Spotlight to locate and select the audio file you want to use for the transition sound, and then click the Insert button.**

5. **Click the Apply button in the Transition Options dialog.**

When your presentation runs, the chosen sound plays during the transition from one slide to the next.

Figure 8-7: Importing a GarageBand loop as a transition sound.

Adding Narration and Video to a Slide

So, you bought this fancy Macintosh, and it has all this built-in video capability. Can you use it to make video narrations for your PowerPoint slides? Well, of course you can! We trust that you won't use this capability to just capture your face while you speak to your audience. Instead, be creative.

Creating a video narration

Most Macs come with built-in video capture and an iSight camera. You need some type of video camera to create a video narration. Follow these steps to make a video narration that you can use in PowerPoint:

1. **Open Photo Booth.**

Photo Booth is an application that you can find in your Mac OS X Finder's Applications folder.

2. **(Optional) Select an effect before recording your video by clicking the Effects button on Photo Booth's toolbar (See Figure 8-8) and selecting one of special effects.**

3. **Click the Take a Movie Clip button.**

4. **Click the Start Recording button.**

The Take a Movie Clip button turns into a time-elapsed indicator while you're recording.

5. **Click the Stop Recording button to end the recording.**

Your video appears at the bottom of Photo Booth.

Figure 8-8:
Recording video by using Photo Booth's toolbar.

Take a movie clip   Start/stop recording   Special Effects

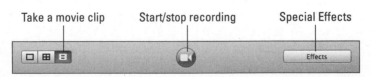

That's all there is to it! PowerPoint knows where to find your Photo Booth narrations, as you can find out in the following section.

Adding video to a slide

You can easily add video to a slide, and you have more than one way to go about it. You can choose any one of the following three ways to activate the Insert Movie dialog:

✦ Click the Media button on the Standard toolbar and select Insert Movie from the pop-up menu that appears (see Figure 8-9).

✦ Choose Insert⇨Movie.

✦ Click the Insert Movie from File button on a media slide layout (see Figure 8-10).

Figure 8-9:
Using the Media button to insert a video.

Figure 8-10:
Using a slide layout button to insert a movie.

The Insert Movie dialog not only lets you navigate to any file in Finder, but it also lets you select from all the places shown in Figure 8-11. Yes, you can even import your Photo Booth narrations. Spotlight search works, too! Follow these steps to insert a movie:

1. **Select a video in the Insert Movie dialog.**

2. **Click the Choose button to bring your video content onto your slide.**

PowerPoint then prompts you whether you want to start the video when the slide starts (see Figure 8-12).

3. **Select an option for How Do You Want the Movie to Start in the Slide Show?:**

• **Automatically:** If you select the Automatically option, your video begins to play automatically when the slide runs.

• **When Clicked:** If you select this option, you click the placeholder on your slide while the presentation is running to play the content.

A frame of your movie is placed on your slide as a placeholder.

Click triangles   Spotlight search

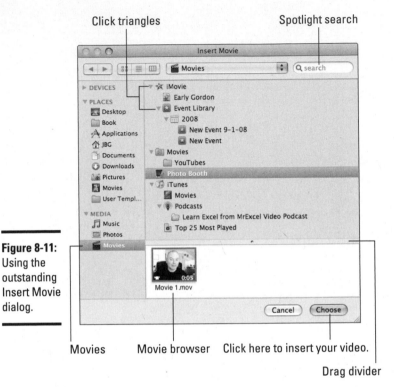

Figure 8-11:
Using the
outstanding
Insert Movie
dialog.

Movies   Movie browser   Click here to insert your video.

Drag divider

If you resize or reposition the placeholder, your movie plays at the specified size and location on the slide. If you use a slide layout placeholder button to insert the movie, your movie fits the size and position of the layout placeholder.

Your movie has a Preview button on it. You can play or *scrub through* (meaning drag the slider to scan) the movie right on the slide without having to run the show.

Preview

Figure 8-12:
Choosing
how your
video will
start.

How do you want the movie to start in the slide show?

(When Clicked) (Automatically)

Using Custom Animation to Control Movies and Audio

In the section "Making audio and video play while a slide plays," earlier in this chapter, we mention that you can treat audio and video just like text bullets and other objects in the Custom Animation dialog of the Toolbox. (Refer to Book IV, Chapter 7 for Custom Animation details.) You can use entrance, emphasis, and exit effects on sound icons and video placeholders, but the key thing to remember when doing this is that you have to use the Play effect at some point to make the audio or movie start playing (see Figure 8-13). You can also use Pause and Stop effects, but the most important one to remember is Play, which gets things rolling.

Figure 8-13: Getting audio and video to play in an animation sequence.

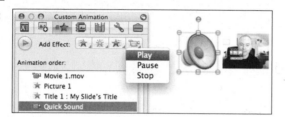

A very practical use of applying animation effects to a sound is to play background music while your slide show plays. The following steps add music so that it plays while your show is running, and we set the number of slides to the max so that the music continues to play, even if you move from slide to slide while your presentation is running. Follow these steps:

1. **Click the Media button on the Standard toolbar.**

2. **Choose Insert Sound and Music from the pop-up menu that appears.**

The Insert Sound dialog appears.

3. **Navigate or use Spotlight to locate your media; then select the music you want to play (see Figure 8-4) and click the Insert button to add the sound to your slide.**

The dialog shown in Figure 8-5 appears.

4. **When prompted, choose to play the sound automatically.**

A sound icon appears on your slide.

5. **Select the Sound icon, and then Control-click or right-click this icon. Choose Custom Animation from the pop-up menu to display the Custom Animation dialog of the Toolbox (see Figure 8-14).**

Figure 8-14:
Setting up
background
music —
adding a
Play action.

6. **In the Custom Animation dialog, for Add Effect, click the Add Media Actions button and select the Play option, as shown in Figure 8-16.**

7. **Go to the bottom of the Custom Animation dialog. In the Media Options section, select the After option and set it to After 999 Slides (see Figure 8-15).**

When you run your slide show, the sound plays throughout the show!

Figure 8-15:
Setting up
background
music —
setting
the media
options.

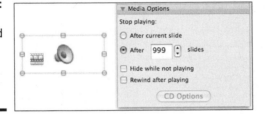

Dealing with Audio and Video Odds and Ends

When you use rich media, give some thought to file sizes if you're planning to distribute your presentation. Audio and video files range from small to large. The larger the audio files, the larger the whole package becomes. For the record, it's difficult to send anything larger than 5 megabytes (5MB) via e-mail. Distribution by other media, such as CD, DVD, and online storage, is now very inexpensive, so most of the time, you don't have to be too concerned with file size. Plus, with new Web-sharing options such as Mesh.com and Office Live, you no longer have to keep file sizes small.

Hiding sound icons

You can position sound icons off the visible portion of the slide layout if you choose to play the sound automatically or if you use animation effects to trigger the sound. Sound icons don't have to be visible onscreen unless you choose to play the sound when clicked. In Figure 8-16, we moved the sound icons off the slide's visible area.

Off-scene

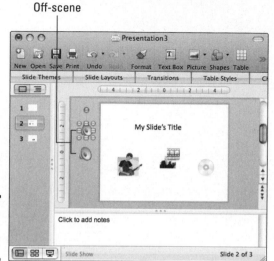

Figure 8-16:
Hiding
sound icons.

Linking and embedding

PowerPoint lets you create links to rich media so that you can keep PowerPoint presentation sizes under control. The alternative method is to embed, which means that PowerPoint makes a copy of the media and includes it as an integral part of the presentation. Table 8-1 shows PowerPoint's default behaviors.

Table 8-1	Linking or Embedding Defaults
Media Type	*Default Behavior*
Pictures	Embed
Sounds	Link if more than 100K; otherwise, embed
Video	Always linked; can't be embedded

If your content is linked, choose Save As⇨PowerPoint Package to create versions of your presentation for distribution or archive. Within a PowerPoint package folder, don't rename or move the audio source files, or change any part of the directory path to those files — otherwise, the links will break.

Discerning a sound difference

In this section, we describe two very similar dialogs. One is called Insert Sound, and the other is called Choose a Sound. You may not even have noticed this difference in the discussion. As you may know, your content may be managed by something known as Digital Rights Management, or DRM. The difference between these two dialogs helps you deal with DRM problems.

Insert Sound

Insert Sound is the dialog shown in Figure 8-2. You can see the Insert Sound dialog when you insert sound by clicking the Media button on the Standard toolbar or by choosing Insert⇨Sound and Music⇨From File. Insert Sound allows you to use all your audio content, even if it has Digital Rights Management (DRM) control to manage how you use your content.

You have no indication about whether the content you're selecting has DRM associated with it. If you use DRM-controlled content, it plays only on your computer. For DRM-protected content to play when you present your slide show, it must be in the same location as it was when you inserted it into PowerPoint. You can restrict your selection to non-DRM content by using action settings.

When you choose File⇨Save As and change the format to PowerPoint Package in the Format pop-up menu, DRM-managed content is *not* added to the package and doesn't play in the package's slide show when distributed to other computers.

Choose a Sound

The Choose a Sound dialog looks and works just like the Insert Sound dialog, except that it lets you choose only from content that's not controlled by DRM. You can see DRM-managed content in the browser, but it's grayed out. The Choose a Sound dialog appears when you insert a sound following our instructions in the section "Adding Music and Sounds," earlier in this chapter, and when adding sounds to slide transitions, as discussed in "Filling the Transition Gap," earlier in this chapter.

When you choose File⇨Save As and select PowerPoint Package in the Format pop-up menu, audio content is added to the package and plays in the package's slide show when distributed to other computers. Use Choose a Sound when you're creating presentations that you plan to distribute as PowerPoint packages.

Making sounds compatible

When it comes to sound files, PowerPoint doesn't support every common sound type. Luckily, you can easily convert sounds to formats that PowerPoint does understand. Sometimes, DRM can cause problems, even with your own content. You can't convert every protected or oddball-format file by using these methods, but these methods might help with many of them.

If you already have Apple's QuickTime Pro, you can use it to do the converting. In this example, we convert one of our own GarageBand loops that we dragged to the desktop from iTunes. We convert iTunes AIF format to AIFF by choosing File⇨Export in QuickTime (see Figure 8-17). Making the conversion allows the loop to work in a PowerPoint package.

Standing on our soapbox

DRM expands ownership rights to content creators over and above that granted by copyright. We've never come across a DRM scheme that properly returns content to the public domain after the copyright time period has expired, nor have we come across a DRM scheme that properly manages Fair Use rights. If DRM is

what's keeping you from getting your content, we don't have a solution. One way to try to get your rights back is to join the Electronic Frontier Foundation. The foundation offers a *Users Guide to DRM in Online Music*. Find out more at `www.eff.org`.

If you don't already have the Pro version of QuickTime, use freeware, such as Audacity (discussed in the section "Link narrations," earlier in this chapter). Either way, you create a file that PowerPoint can use. Figure 8-18 shows the settings that you can use by choosing File➪Export in Audacity.

Figure 8-17: Converting audio format by using QuickTime Pro.

Making video compatible

PowerPoint on Mac doesn't actually play video. It uses Apple's QuickTime as the helper application. Whatever plays in QuickTime plays in PowerPoint on the Mac. As it turns out, QuickTime is a lot more versatile than the player used by PowerPoint for Windows. PowerPoint for Windows chokes when it encounters QuickTime movies, even if the current QuickTime version is installed on the PC. PowerPoint for Windows just doesn't do QuickTime.

Using WMV

If you plan to use video content and distribute it to Windows users, you must convert it to WMV (Windows Media Video) or AVI before you insert it into PowerPoint. We think WMV is the best cross-platform format to use.

It provides high-quality video, and WMV file sizes are very reasonable. Fortunately for Mac users, QuickTime can understand WMV when you install a free program called Flip4Mac. Flip4Mac has other interesting capabilities that you might want if you plan to make a lot of cross-platform video content, but at the very least, we suggest that you install the free player from this Web site:

```
www.telestream.net/flip4mac-wmv/overview.htm
```

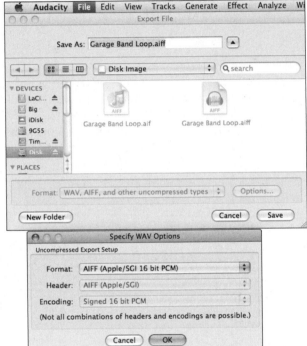

Figure 8-18:
Converting audio format by using Audacity.

You can use several products to convert QuickTime files to WMV. Flip4Mac's Studio products can perform the conversion. If you don't mind spending a little extra time, you can have the conversion done free by one of the many Web sites that offer this service. MediaConverter is one such Web site; it also has a free Firefox add-on that readily converts YouTube videos to QuickTime (.mov) or WMV format, and then saves them on your computer. Visit the following site:

```
www.mediaconverter.org
```

Video DRM

When you choose File↷Save As, and then select PowerPoint Package from the Format pop-up menu, DRM-managed video content isn't added to the package and doesn't play in the package's slide show when distributed to other computers.

Chapter 9: Printing and Sharing Presentations

In This Chapter

✓ **Printing handouts and more**

✓ **Sharing presentations with others**

✓ **Presenting to real, live people**

Sharing presentations with others is an integral part of PowerPoint. Audiences often expect printed handouts and online versions of your presentations as reference materials. This chapter can help you prepare to meet those expectations by showing you a wide variety of printing options and introducing you to new ways to share presentations with others.

Printing Your Presentations

You can print many different sizes with PowerPoint. Although it's most common to print handouts on regular-size paper, you can use PowerPoint to print large-scale versions of slides to use for poster sessions at booths in conferences or for wall mounting. You can also use PowerPoint to print small-scale objects, such as postcards. Your printing output can take a variety of forms, such as PDF, slides, handouts, or even Notes Pages.

Printing to PDF files

We want to encourage you to be earth-friendly. Maybe you don't have to print to paper; instead, you can print to PDF files. Put the PDF file into an Internet sharing service for those who want to download it, and view or print it themselves. All the printing options that we show you offer the PDF file printing option. Just click the PDF button in the lower-left of the Print dialog of PowerPoint (and every other application, for that matter) and choose Save as PDF from the pop-up menu, as shown in Figure 9-1.

Figure 9-1:
Printing to
PDF.

Printing handouts for everyone

If you need to print handouts to give to your attendees, PowerPoint offers many printing options. You can access all these nice options by choosing File⇨Print rather than clicking the Print button on the Standard toolbar. If you click the Print button on the Standard toolbar, PowerPoint prints full-page printouts of the slides, and that might not be what you want.

Printing handouts with note-taking lines

This very popular arrangement prints pictures of three slides on the left, along with lines on the right, on each page so that people can take notes. This handout option is the only one that prints note-taking lines. You can find this option in the Print What field of the Print pane. Click on the field and choose Handouts (3 Slides per Page) from the pop-up menu, as shown in Figure 9-2. The other handout options print pictures of the slides in various arrangements that you can see in the preview when you select them.

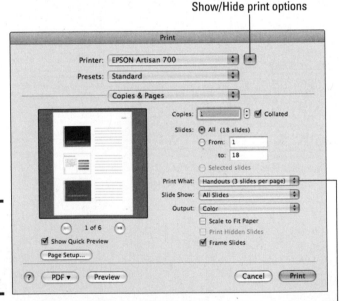

Figure 9-2: Printing handouts with note-taking lines.

Printing handouts with slide notes

Another popular style of printing is to print the Notes View. These printouts include one picture of the slide, plus the slide notes for that slide, as shown in Figure 9-3. You follow the same procedure that we describe in the preceding section, except that in the Print What selection of the Print pane, select Notes.

Figure 9-3:
Printing
Notes View.

Printing the slide outline

The option at the bottom of the Print What selection in the Print pane is
Outline. This option prints the text that appears in the Outline pane of the
Normal View.

Setting headers and footers

When it's time to print those handouts, you might want to have page numbers and other information for your audience. Choosing View➪Header and
Footer opens the Header and Footer pane shown in Figure 9-4.

You might expect them to, but slides don't have headers. Slides just have
footers. Notes and handouts have both headers and footers. That's just a
little trivia.

Slide tab   Notes and Handouts tab

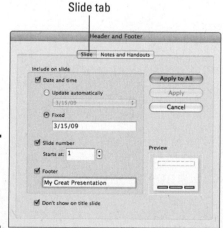
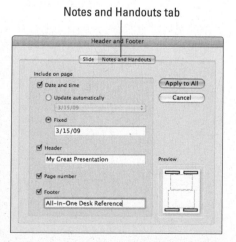

Figure 9-4:
Adjusting
settings for
headers and
footers.

The Header and Foot pane has the following tabs:

+ **Slide:** When you select this tab, the setting choices you make apply to the slides in your presentation.

+ **Notes and Handouts:** Setting choices made on this tab apply to printed handouts, printed notes, and Notes Page View.

When facing the task of printing large and small, choose File⇨Page Setup. In Book II, Chapter 8, we explain how to use Page Setup to create custom paper sizes in Microsoft Word. You use the same procedure in PowerPoint.

If you know you're going to print to a paper size other than PowerPoint's default, choose File⇨Page Setup *before* you create any slides, Slide Masters, or slide layouts in your presentation. If you wait until after you build your presentation, when you change the paper size, it can cause graphic objects and even text to look squished, stretched, or otherwise distorted.

Exploring Sharing Options

You can share PowerPoint presentations in so many different ways that we hardly know where to begin. Each one is best for specific circumstances. Know your audience and choose an appropriate distribution method.

Distributing in PowerPoint format

Microsoft Office is extremely popular with Mac users. It's one of the most widely installed software suites among Mac and Windows users. That means your audience probably already has PowerPoint installed. Distributing in PowerPoint format is the highest-quality option to play your slide show on another computer.

Use the Save as PowerPoint Package feature to create a Package folder, which you then distribute intact so that your media files can play.

Other software that can open and play PowerPoint presentations includes Apple's Keynote, Sun Microsystems's OpenOffice, Planamesa Inc.'s NeoOffice, and Google Docs. Applications other than PowerPoint may substitute fonts and change or fail to play transitions or animations. Graphic objects may be altered. Effects such as soft shadows and 3D effects may look different. Charts may not look the same.

Distributing as a movie

As we mention in Book IV, Chapters 1 and 2, you can easily save a slide show as a QuickTime movie by choosing File⇨Save as Movie, or you can use SnapZPro to record a perfect playback. Remember to set timings by using the Options button on the Slide Transitions tab of Elements Gallery so that your slides advance during the movie (see Figure 9-5). Here are some fun things you can do with these movies:

✦ **Upload your movie to YouTube or another video-sharing site.** The movies created by PowerPoint are in QuickTime format, so you can upload them as-is. Just head to the upload section of your favorite sharing site and follow the directions.

✦ **Import your PowerPoint movie into iMovie.** In iMovie09, choose File⇨Import⇨Movies, as shown in Figure 9-6.

✦ **Turn your PowerPoint movie presentation into a DVD.** One feature of iDVD lets you turn your PowerPoint movie directly into a DVD. Open iDVD and choose File⇨OneStep DVD from Movie, as shown in Figure 9-7. Pop a blank DVD into your Mac and burn!

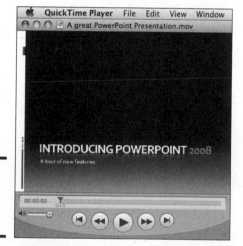

Figure 9-5:
Power-
Pointing in
QuickTime.

Figure 9-6:
Importing a
PowerPoint
movie into
iMovie.

Figure 9-7:
Turning a
presentation
into a DVD
in one step!

Sending directly to iPhoto

This option is especially fun. PowerPoint talks directly with iPhoto. Even if you
don't have a particular reason to do this option, try it just for fun. Following
these steps turns your presentation into a new photo album in iPhoto:

1. **With your presentation open in PowerPoint, choose File⇨Send
   To⇨iPhoto (see Figure 9-8).**

   The Send to iPhoto dialog opens.

2. **Name your new album, decide which picture format you want to use,
   and then click the Send to iPhoto button (see Figure 9-9).**

   PowerPoint prepares your slides and gives them to iPhoto, which creates a new album and presents the slides to you (see Figure 9-10).

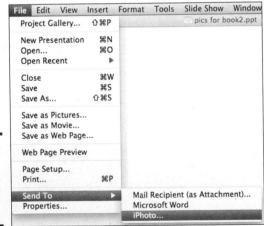

Figure 9-8:
Sending
PowerPoint
to iPhoto —
Step 1.

Figure 9-9:
Naming
your new
album —
Step 2.

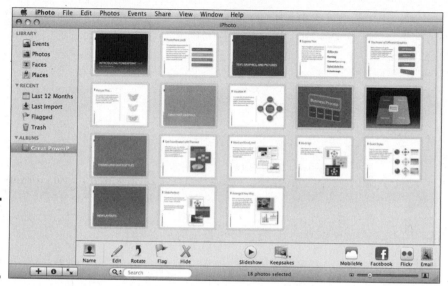

Figure 9-10:
Viewing
your new
album.

Sending by e-mail or MSN Messenger

Take a peek at the Mail Recipient (as Attachment) option in the Send To list
in Figure 9-8. Using this option is okay only if your presentation has no linked
media. But if your presentation has sounds or movies, choose File➪Save
As, click Format in the Save As dialog that appears, and select PowerPoint
Package from the pop-up menu so that you don't lose the media content.

Before you attach a PowerPoint package to an e-mail message, compress the
package folder, as shown in Figure 9-11. Be sure to compress first if you want
to send your presentation by using any of the popular chat services, such
as MSN Messenger, Yahoo!, or AIM. To compress the Package folder, follow
these steps:

1. **Right-click or Control-click the Package folder in Finder.**

2. **Choose Compress or Archive (depending on the version of Mac OS X
   you're using) from the pop-up menu.**

   The compressed file has a ZIP extension, and you can easily unarchive
   (or unzip) these files on both Mac and Windows computers, usually by
   simply double-clicking the files in Finder on the Mac, or in Windows
   Explorer or My Computer in Windows.

Sharing with iChat

You can do amazing things with PowerPoint and iChat, such as share a
presentation with your sister, business associate, or friend. Of course, the
person you want to share with needs to be online at the same time as you are.
We realize that you have several ways to use iChat to share a presentation,

but our testing indicates that sharing your screen is a clear winner in terms of quality. We cover screen sharing in detail in the following section and give a brief explanation of using iChat Theater in "Sharing with iChat Theater," later in this chapter.

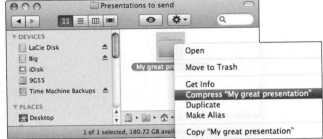

Figure 9-11:
Compressing
before
sending.

Sharing your screen

Assume that you already have a text chat going with someone. Either party can initiate the process, but our example assumes that you're going to start the sharing process. Sharing your presentation involves allowing the other party to see your computer's desktop and even have access to your mouse, so if you're not willing to let this happen, use the iChat Theater method (discussed in the following section), instead. To present, follow these steps:

1. **Open iChat and make sure that you're signed on.**

2. **In iChat, click your buddy in the Buddy list, and then choose Buddies⇨ Share My Screen with [name of buddy], as shown in Figure 9-12.**

Your buddy receives an invitation, and he or she must accept it before the next step can happen.

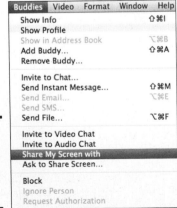

Figure 9-12:
Sharing
your screen
by using
iTunes.

3. **Start your PowerPoint presentation by using any method except Presenter Tools (unless you want to share the presenter's side of the presentation, rather than the slide show in its own window).**

   You can narrate your presentation while you present because the other person can hear what you say, and you can hear the other person, assuming that you both have microphones and speakers turned on.

4. **To stop screen sharing, press Control-Escape.**

Sharing with iChat Theater

When we tried using iChat Theater, we found that the presentation looked good but that it didn't fit the iChat Theater window, so we hesitate to suggest this option. And this size problem seems to be common enough with many users.

Before you use iChat Theater, you must save your presentation as a file on your computer. Then, in iChat, choose File⇨Share a File with iChat Theater. We couldn't find a way to tell iChat Theater to fit the presentation in the window, but you can use this method if you don't want to share your desktop. iChat also lets you share with two other people at the same time, so if you don't experience the window-size glitch, this option is the way to go.

Sharing by using Google Docs

While we're writing this book, Google Docs is beta software, so if you're shy about using beta software, Google Docs might not be for you. However, if you're like us, it's full steam ahead! Google Docs and other online Web-hosting services let you upload your PowerPoint presentations to share with others.

To use this option, you must have a Google (or Gmail) account. In general, you can go to a Web site that supports PowerPoint and follow the directions for uploading your presentation, which you do right from within your Web browser. Most of these services allow you to restrict viewers to ones you prescribe or to share with the entire world. To upload your PowerPoint presentation file to Google Docs, follow these steps:

1. **Save your presentation in the PowerPoint 97 through 2004 (.ppt).**

   It needs to be in this format before you can upload it to Google Docs.

   By the time you read this, PowerPoint (.pptx) format likely will be supported, in which case, you can skip Step 1.

2. **Upload to Google by going to this Web address:**

   `http://docs.google.com`

   After you sign in, Google's file space and toolbar open, as shown in Figure 9-13, unless this setup has changed since we took this screen shot.

Set sharing restrictions

Toolbar   Upload   Click to edit or view

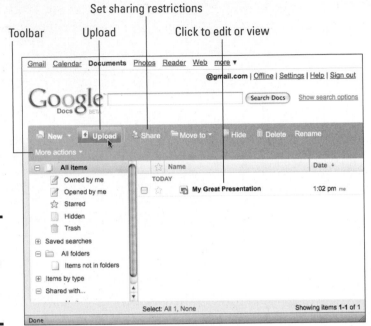

Figure 9-13:
Looking
over Google
Doc's
command
center.

3. **Click the Upload button and navigate to your presentation file in Finder, as shown in Figure 9-14. Click the Upload File button to begin the upload process, which may take some time.**

   After the presentation finishes uploading, the slide-editing screen appears. You can edit your presentation online (see Figure 9-15). This screen is analogous to PowerPoint's Normal View.

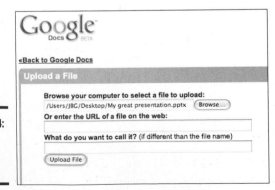

Figure 9-14:
Uploading
to Google
Docs.

4. To run your presentation, click the Start Presentation button.

Now, your presentation is running in a browser window.

We were able to resize the window and easily go through the presentation. The quality of the product was very good. In Figure 9-16, you can see the available options on the Actions menu.

Exploring slide-sharing sites

Sometimes, you want others to see your presentation slides, and you may or may not want them to download the actual PowerPoint file. Whatever you prefer, a new breed of slide-sharing sites puts all these options and more at your disposal. We call this a way to get your slides in the clouds!

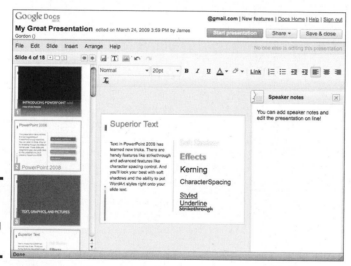

Figure 9-15: Google's slide-editing view.

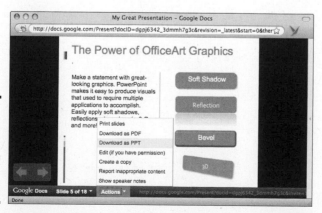

Figure 9-16: Viewing a PowerPoint presentation in Google Docs (beta).

Here's a listing of such slide-sharing sites with their URLs:

✦ **SlideShare:** www.slideshare.net

✦ **authorSTREAM:** www.authorstream.com

✦ **SlideBoom:** www.slideboom.com

Presenting Live

This sharing option brings you full circle to the beginning of Book IV. We have more tips to share with you regarding giving an in-person live presentation. We hope by now that you have the confidence to build a slide show that people will enjoy watching and that you know will do your content justice. If you still have some butterflies, remember that your audience is almost always friendly. Only a few people are unlucky enough to have shoes thrown at them.

Using the letter B (or W)

While a slide show is running, the audience is usually paying some attention to the screen. Some may be texting on a cell phone or e-mailing, but that's the way it goes these days. When you press the letter B, the screen goes black. That means the audience will usually focus its attention on you, which you may want every once in a while. Press just about any other key to resume the presentation.

Similarly, press W to get a white screen. And before you try, R doesn't do red, and G doesn't make it green!

Using Pen tools

If you start a slide show by using a method other than Presenter view, you can draw on a slide by using the Pen tool while the slide show is running. Follow these steps:

1. **While your presentation is running, right-click or Control-click a slide.**

   A pop-up menu appears (see Figure 9-17).

2. **Select Pointer Options➪Pen.**

   The mouse cursor changes to a pen to indicate that when you drag, lines will appear.

3. **Right-click or Control-click a second time and, from the pop-up menu, select Pen Color to select a color for drawing on the slide.**

4. **Hold the (left) mouse button down and drag to draw on the slide.**

5. **When you're done, right-click or Control-click the slide again. From the pop-up menu, select Pointer Options⇨Arrow to restore the normal PowerPoint arrow pointer.**

Figure 9-17:
Writing on a slide.

Navigating while showing

Except when you're using Presenter view to run your slide show, you can navigate from one slide to another by clicking the little triangle that appears in the lower-left portion of each slide while the show is running (see Figure 9-18). From the pop-up menu that appears, choose Go to Slide. You can also get to this menu if you right-click or Control-click the slide while the show is running.

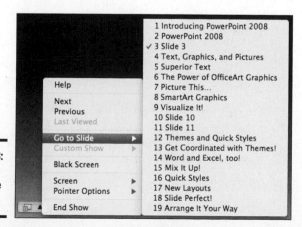

Figure 9-18:
Going to a slide on the fly.

Book V

Entourage 2008

The 5th Wave   By Rich Tennant

"Tell the boss he has more flame mail from you-know-who."

Contents at a Glance

Chapter 1: Introducing Entourage: Seven Applications in One

In This Chapter

✔ Getting to know Entourage

✔ Making the most of Mail

✔ Using Entourage to stay organized

✔ Adding workflows to automate Entourage

✔ Working with the Entourage database

Entourage is the application in the Microsoft Office suite that you're most likely to use. You may not give a hoot about spreadsheets, but you probably do care a lot about your e-mail. E-mail is where many people start their days, and we begin our tour of Entourage in this chapter with e-mail. If that's all you want to know about, that's okay with us. However, e-mail is just one of the Entourage application's many capabilities. And we cover all the things that Entourage does. After you understand how Entourage's features work together, you can use this application to its full extent.

Everything in Entourage revolves around people, communication, time, and organization. Entourage integrates tightly with the other Office applications, as well as with Mac OS X and the Internet.

In this chapter, we provide an overview of Entourage. We organize the chapters in this minibook by using the same order that you find in the Entourage application interface.

Introducing Entourage

For those who are new to Office for Mac but are familiar with the Windows version of Office, Entourage for Mac is the rough equivalent application to Microsoft Outlook in Office for Windows. Microsoft's Macintosh Business Unit (MacBU) has been adding Outlook functionality to Entourage with the goal of having Entourage match Outlook's functionality, especially with regard to providing Microsoft Exchange support on Mac OS X. If you're coming to the Mac from Windows Outlook, we try to help you feel right at home.

You find many new features in Entourage 2008, and the icons shown in Figure 1-1 are just the beginning.

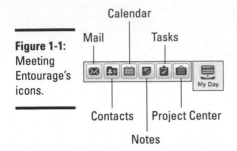

Figure 1-1:
Meeting
Entourage's
icons.

Mail

Calendar

Tasks

Contacts

Notes

Project Center

My Day

Entourage is an application that flows. You read your e-mail and receive contact information from a colleague, friend, or relative, so you add to or modify your contacts. You can receive and send invitations for events. While you're reading an e-mail, you decide to make a note of something. Your boss sends you a text message that requires you to do a task, so you add a task to your calendar. Any one or all the preceding tasks may be related to a project that you're working on, so Project Center is in the mix. All day long, you need to be aware of what's coming up, where you should be, and what you should be doing. My Day brings it all together in an onscreen organizer. If all this talk about Entourage's capabilities dazzles you, don't worry — we touch on each of these features in later sections of this chapter and then cover these items in depth throughout Book V. See Figure 1-2 for a visualization of this concept.

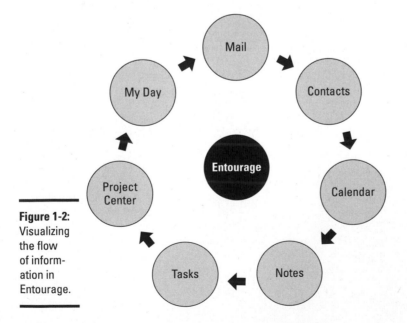

Figure 1-2:
Visualizing
the flow
of inform-
ation in
Entourage.

We cover Project Center extensively in Book VI.

Connecting to the Internet with Entourage's Mail

Looking at e-mail from a distance, we realize it's been around for longer than some of our readers have been alive. To many of you, it's simply a utility. Yet to others, it contains their life. You save your e-mail in archives, and it's your memory. You may store business and personal records in e-mails. Although it's not the newest Internet technology, we can help you understand how to use it most effectively.

Discerning the Exchange difference

Exchange is a messaging and collaborative product from Microsoft that helps create an e-mail infrastructure backend. And the version of Entourage you use affects your ability to connect to an Exchange e-mail server. If you're interested, we explain more about the new Exchange-specific features in the sidebar, "Big news for Exchange," near the end of this chapter.

Three different bundles of Microsoft Office are available. The version of Entourage that ships with the Home and Student edition has different capabilities compared to the version that ships in the regular Office 2008 for Mac and Special Media editions.

The difference involves whether Entourage can connect directly to the Microsoft Exchange e-mail server. If you know that you want to connect to a Microsoft Exchange Server, be aware that the Home and Student package doesn't include Exchange support in Entourage. Regular Office 2008 for Mac and Special Media editions do include Exchange support in Entourage. This capability difference parallels the Office for Windows versions, where Outlook in the Home and Student edition doesn't include Exchange support.

Making connections to the world

Entourage can connect to most e-mail services, and supports all the popular messaging formats, and has easy wizards to help you set up your accounts. In some cases, Entourage can figure out your settings just from your e-mail address! Figure 1-3 shows that Entourage can connect to many different e-mail accounts at the same time.

You can read your Gmail in the same window that you read the mail from your Internet service provider (ISP).

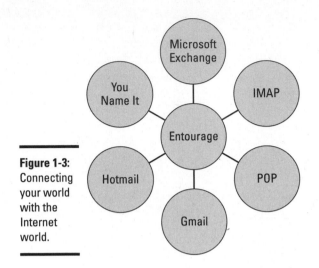

Figure 1-3:
Connecting your world with the Internet world.

Keeping Yourself Organized

Entourage offers multiple ways of keeping your contacts and events straight by using the program's Address Book and Calendar options.

Keeping track of people with your contacts list

Sometimes, keeping track of personal information about your contacts is called *PIM (Personal Information Management)*. Also, a program such as Entourage that helps you keep track of all your contacts' info is called a *Personal Information Manager (PIM,* again!). Managing your contacts involves acquiring and organizing the details you need to know about the people you interact with every day. You may want to include home addresses, business phone numbers, private phone numbers, and birthdays in your contacts list. And you can also add your contacts' Facebook and MySpace details, if you want.

You can send contact information to other people by using e-mail in a special message format called a *v-card.* If you receive a v-card as an e-mail attachment, you can add that person to your Entourage contacts. Many organizations support Entourage-friendly directories by using a standard known as *Lightweight Directory Access Protocol,* or *LDAP.* You can add multiple LDAP directories to Entourage, which has automatic integration to AutoFill e-mail addresses while you type in address text boxes. Figure 1-4 shows this relationship.

Figure 1-4:
Integrating
with
LDAP and
Messenger
technologies.

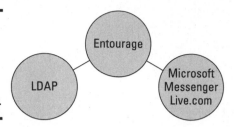

Your contacts list doesn't just sit there. Entourage is always checking to see who's online. Well, that's not exactly true — Entourage can't find out this information, but a companion program called Microsoft Messenger can. Messenger often runs along with Entourage, and it can look at your contact names and provide you with information about who's available to communicate in real-time with you within the Microsoft Messenger instant messaging service.

You can use Microsoft Messenger as a further extension of your online presence on the Microsoft's Live site (`http://download.live.com`). The Live site integrates all Microsoft online services, such as instant messaging, e-mail, photo sharing, and so on.

Keeping track of your events with Calendar

Whether it's a conference agenda, your daily work, or a holiday trip to an exotic island, your life depends on time, and Entourage Calendar is the tool that you can use to wisely allocate your limited time resources. The number of ways you can tag your Calendar events, share them, display them, organize them, and print them in the Calendar is truly amazing.

One of the key features of Microsoft Exchange, a collaborative server platform, is the *Free-Busy schedule,* where you can find out the availability of other people in your circle. The Free-Busy schedule is supported by the Entourage Calendar. Figure 1-5 shows just one of many possible views that you can have of an Entourage Calendar.

Making notes for yourself

Everyone needs a place to keep notes. Entourage's Notes offers a place to keep those notes where you can associate them with your contacts, events, and projects. Not every feature in Entourage is dramatic. This one is simple, good, and convenient.

Figure 1-5:
Getting a
bird's-eye
view of a
month.

Assigning tasks

Closely aligned with the Entourage Calendar is Entourage Tasks. Tasks are time-sensitive, like Calendar events, but are kept separate so that you can check them off when you complete them. Tasks are also tied into the new My Day feature so that you can keep an eye on them during your day. Tasks can trigger notifications so that you get reminders about your tasks. When you use Flag for Follow Up in Word, Excel, or PowerPoint, Entourage Tasks handles the follow-up job.

Making My Day your day

A brand-new feature in Entourage 2008 is the My Day floating reminder and organizer. My Day (see Figure 1-6) is on top and visible all day long to let you see your appointments, events, and tasks when they're coming due so that you can stay on top of things.

Figure 1-6:
Staying on
top of your
day with My
Day.

Organizing a project in the Project Center

The Project Center is a large application within Entourage. Project Center is so large that we devote an entire minibook to it (see Book VI). In many situations, it's sensible to organize things for a project. You may have ongoing projects, such as being a member of a standing committee. You may work on projects that have a specific timeframe, such as organizing or attending a conference, wedding, business project, or remodeling job. Project Center can help you plan, coordinate, execute, and document standalone and multiple projects.

Entourage's Project Center can associate documents and e-mail with particular contacts. Entourage supports advanced linking of anything and everything that has to do with your contacts, tasks, mail, Calendar events, and projects. You can share projects that you create in the Project Center with coworkers, which is especially useful when everyone has Microsoft Entourage. Windows users can share some aspects of Project Center, including documents and Calendar events. We explain how to take advantage of all this in the Project Center minibook.

Customizing Entourage toolbars

A great new feature of Entourage is that now you can customize its toolbars. Entourage has always had a Web-browser feel to it, and now even more so with the ability to drag and drop toolbar icons. Each application within Entourage has its own set of toolbar icons, and you'll see those icons as we discuss some of the individual applications throughout this minibook.

Automating Entourage

AppleScript and Entourage have a great working relationship. *AppleScript* is a scripting language built by Apple into Mac OS X. Entourage's AppleScript dictionary was updated for the 2008 version. Many useful AppleScripts are available, and you can also make your own. The following Web site contains almost everything you need to know about scripting Entourage: www.entourage.mvps.org/script/index.html.

Completely new for Office 2008 are Entourage Automator workflows. Some prebuilt workflows come with the Office 2008 for Mac and Special Media editions, but regardless of which edition of Office 2008 you have, you can build your own Automator workflows. Building workflows is easy. You just drag and drop within the Automator application, which you can find in your Applications folder. You can build workflows from one application to another, as shown in Figure 1-7. And you're not limited to building workflows within Microsoft Office. Workflows can interact with any application that provides Automator support.

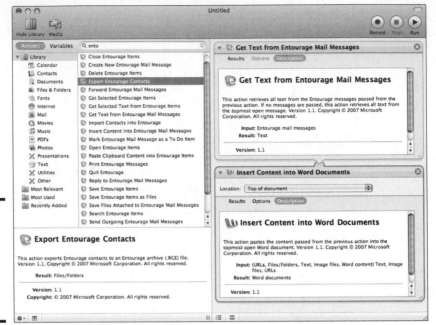

Figure 1-7:
Building an
Automator
workflow
from
Entourage
to Word.

In Book IV, Chapter 6, we have a detailed, step-by-step example that explains how to create your own Automator Actions. If you've never built Automator Actions before, that's a good one to start with. After you get the general idea, we think you'll find experimenting with Automator Actions in Entourage fairly easy. You'll be building useful workflows in no time!

Taking Care of the Entourage Database

Entourage can handle enormous amounts of information — terabytes, if needed. Most Entourage databases are much smaller than that. Everything that Entourage saves is kept in a single database file. You can compress the database if you want to reduce the amount of drive space that Entourage uses.

You can also use a database rebuild utility in the rare case that Entourage requests that you use it. Before using the rebuild utility, be sure that your hard drive is functioning properly by checking it with DiskWarrior, TechTools, Drive Genius, or a similar disk-checking utility. We don't cover these utilities in this book, but a quick online search gets you more details on these products.

Make an archive of your database before rebuilding it. It's always a good idea to have a backup!

Before you attempt to compact or rebuild your Entourage database, be sure to exit not just Entourage, but also all Office applications, as well as Microsoft Messenger. Don't open any Office applications or Microsoft Messenger while you're using this utility. To activate the Database Utility, press and hold the Option key when you start Entourage. Database Utility, as shown in Figure 1-8, opens. Be aware that if your database is large and complex or if your hard drive is nearly filled to capacity, this utility can take a very long time to complete the process.

Figure 1-8:
Maintaining
Entourage
databases.

> **Database Utility**
>
> Select the database you want to maintain.
>
> | Identity | Date Last Modified |
> |----------|-------------------|
> | ForDummies | Today |
> | Home | Fri, 4/10/09 5:48 PM |
> | Hotmail | Yesterday |
> | junk | Sun, 3/29/09 12:03 PM |
>
> Select the maintenance activity to perform.
>
> ● Verify database integrity
>   Check database for corruption. If problems are found, you can choose to rebuild your database. If your database is working properly, no changes will be made.
>
> ○ Compact database
>   Compact and back up the current database files.
>
> ○ Rebuild database
>   Perform repairs, compact database files, and back up current database. If Sync Services are enabled, they will be disabled during the rebuild and must be re-enabled.
>
> ○ Set database preferences
>   Changes database maintenance preferences.
>
> (Quit) (Continue)

Verifying database integrity

You can run the Database Utility to determine whether your Entourage database is functioning correctly. If your database is working correctly, you can safely compress your database. If your database isn't working correctly, you can rebuild your database.

Compacting your database

Running Database Utility can result in disk-space savings. Entourage creates a copy of your existing database and then makes a new, compacted version. So, temporarily, your database needs twice as much room (the original, plus a copy). You can trash the old database after you're convinced that the new one's working properly.

Rebuilding your database

Rebuilding your database is a radical step to take, so use Database Utility only if Entourage's Verify Integrity check advises you to do so, or if you receive a database warning message while using Entourage. Follow the instructions carefully in Entourage's help topic, Verify and Rebuild the Entourage Database, particularly if you use Microsoft Exchange.

Big news for Exchange

Major improvements have been made to the way Microsoft Exchange Server works with applications, such as Outlook, Entourage, and Apple Mail. The result is that programs that connect to exchange servers can offer faster connections and support Exchange features better. Apple and Microsoft's MacBU are revamping their respective e-mail programs to take advantage of the new Exchange features.

Exchange users will soon have three major applications from which to choose: Microsoft Entourage, Apple Mail, and for Windows users, Microsoft Outlook. While we write this chapter, Microsoft is beta-testing a new version of Entourage, and Apple is beta-testing Snow Leopard.

According to Apple's Web site: "Snow Leopard includes out-of-the-box support for Microsoft Exchange 2007 built into Mail, Address Book, and iCal. Mac OS X uses the Exchange Web Services protocol to provide access to Exchange Server 2007. Because Exchange is supported on your Mac and iPhone, you'll be able to use them anywhere with full access to your e-mail, contacts, and Calendar."

Microsoft has been steadily making Entourage a better Exchange application. In the past, Microsoft hasn't waited for major releases of Office to include new and improved functionality for Microsoft Exchange support. Based on Microsoft's history, major updates could come to Entourage before the next full release of Office. IT professionals should keep track of this site: www.microsoft.com/mac/itpros/default.mspx.

Any way you look at it, if your organization uses the current version of Microsoft Exchange, you'll soon (maybe even by the time you read this) be able to choose from several newly available e-mail applications and platforms.

Chapter 2: Welcome to the Setup Assistant

In This Chapter

✔ Getting familiar with the Setup Assistant

✔ Exploring account settings

✔ Perking up preferences

*B*efore you can actually use your e-mail account, Entourage needs to know certain things about how to connect to the mail server. You can get most of this information from your Internet service provider (ISP) or your company's system administrator.

In this chapter, we cover basic e-mail configuration information, followed by a tour of Entourage's preferences. We organized this chapter so that if you already know what kind of connection you're dealing with, or if you have a relatively high skill level, you can go right to the appropriate section. Even if you don't know anything about how to set up Entourage, we go step by step through the basic setup with you. We know the built-in wizard in Entourage is good, so if you already have your e-mail account up and running, feel free to skip the setup information.

Setting Up with the Setup Assistant

The first time you open Entourage, you're greeted by the default e-mail view in the background with the Entourage Setup Assistant on top, as shown in Figure 2-1. Additionally, you may be asked whether you want to choose Entourage to be your Mac's default e-mail application. We recommend that you answer in the affirmative.

If you dismiss Entourage's Setup Assistant when it appears for the first time and it doesn't show itself when you launch Entourage again, you can't do much to get the same initial Setup Assistant screen. But you can get to the screen that follows the initial one (as shown in Figure 2-2). To launch the Setup Assistant manually (so that you can access the second screen), follow these steps:

1. **Choose Tools⇨Accounts to open the tabbed Accounts dialog.**

2. **Click the arrow next to New in the toolbar and choose Mail from the pop-up menu that appears.**

   The Setup Assistant appears.

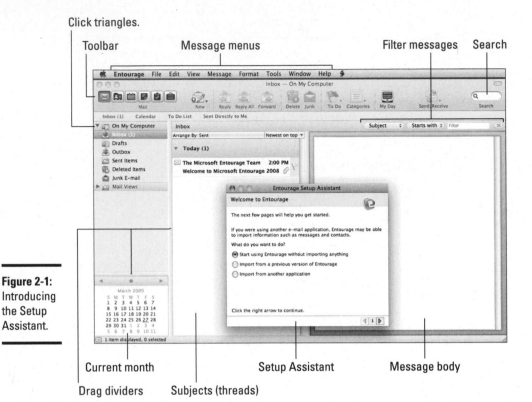

Click triangles.

Toolbar   Message menus   Filter messages   Search

Figure 2-1:
Introducing
the Setup
Assistant.

Current month   Setup Assistant   Message body

Drag dividers   Subjects (threads)

First, we focus on the Entourage Setup Assistant and help you get through
some of the most common scenarios, but take a moment to look over the
other elements of the starting mail interface (see Figure 2-1).

The Entourage Setup Assistant offers three options:

✦ Start using Entourage without importing anything

✦ Import from a previous version of Entourage

✦ Import from another application

Click the small forward-arrow button in the lower-right corner of the Setup
Assistant when you want to advance to the next step.

Starting without importing anything

You can use the Start Using Entourage without Importing Anything option
if you want to set up a new e-mail account and have no files to import from
another e-mail program. Follow these steps:

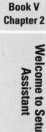
1. **In the Set Up a Mail Account step of the Setup Assistant, no matter what kind of mail host you have, enter your full e-mail address (see Figure 2-2) and then advance to the next step by clicking the right-pointing arrow in the bottom right of the window.**

Figure 2-2:
Telling
Entourage
your e-mail
address.

What you see in the next window depends on what you enter in this one. Entourage attempts to figure out your e-mail settings based on your e-mail address:

- If you entered an e-mail address at Hotmail, Gmail (Google mail), or another well-known e-mail provider, it's clear sailing. You receive a message stating that the configuration settings were successfully determined.

- If you see a different message, Entourage couldn't determine the settings for your e-mail account. Entourage explains the situation and then prompts you to enter the settings supplied to you by your e-mail service provider. If you don't have the settings, you can almost always find them at the Web site of your ISP. Skip ahead to the section "Configuring an e-mail account manually," later in this chapter, if you need to supply this info.

2. **After Entourage successfully finds your e-mail settings, advance to the next window and enter your password.**

3. **Click the arrow to advance to the Verify and Complete Settings window.**

Figure 2-3 shows the proper settings for a Gmail account.

You can change the Incoming Mail server type to IMAP or POP, depending on how it's set up in the dialog shown in Figure 2-3. Figure 2-4 shows the actual pop-up menu that lets you alternate between IMAP and POP.

Figure 2-3:
Confirming
the e-mail
settings.

Figure 2-4:
Choose
between
IMAP and
POP mail
server
types.

Whether you choose IMAP or POP, when you reach the end of the Setup Assistant, the full Entourage e-mail interface appears in the same view, as shown in Figure 2-1.

Figure 2-1 shows the message body displayed on the right side, with a list of the e-mail subjects in the middle. You can change the view setting by using the Entourage View menu. Choose View➪Preview Pane➪Below List to reposition the display so that the message subjects (sometimes called *threads*) appear above the message body, as shown in Figure 2-5. To display the sample message, click the subject.

Inbox   Welcome   Drag to resize.

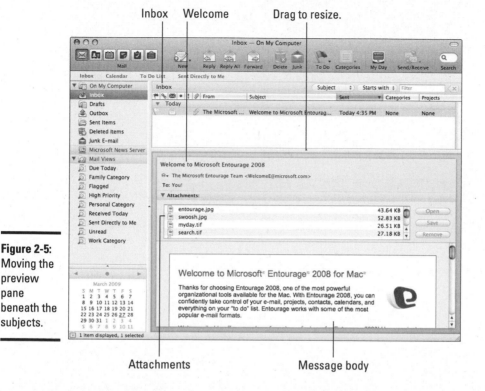

Figure 2-5:
Moving the
preview
pane
beneath the
subjects.

Attachments   Message body

POP or IMAP: Deciding which service to use

Internet service providers usually offer two different kinds of service. One kind is POP; the other kind is IMAP. At one time, POP was the dominant method, but IMAP is what we recommend now if you have a choice. Here's a brief explanation of the difference:

✓ **IMAP:** Configured to keep your mail inbox on the provider's server. You can create subfolders on the server to store mail in folders, such as read mail, deleted messages, junk mail, or any folder you want. The advantage of IMAP is that you can connect to the server from various devices. Your message list appears the same from

any device, such as your iPod or cellphone, your computer at home, or your laptop while you're at a hotel. Your e-mail account has the same messages available, regardless of what device you use, no matter where you connect.

✓ **POP:** Usually configured to download e-mail messages to your local computer and delete them from the server right away. This option is fine if you have only one computer and one location. Although you can set POP to leave the messages on the server, in general, you run the risk of accidentally deleting a wanted message.

Setting up an account for Microsoft Exchange

To set up an account for Microsoft Exchange, go to Step 2 of the Setup Assistant (see Figure 2-2). You find a check box for My Account Is on an Exchange Server, unless you're using the Home and Student edition of Microsoft Office. If you're using an Exchange account, select the check box. You're then prompted to enter the following information:

✦ Domain

✦ Account ID

✦ Password

You can add your password to your Mac OS X keychain, if you want.

Then, you're ready to advance to the next step. If Entourage is successful at connecting to your Exchange account, you proceed to the preview pane (see Figures 2-1 and 2-5). If Entourage isn't successful connecting, a pane appears in which you can manually enter your account information (see Figure 2-6).

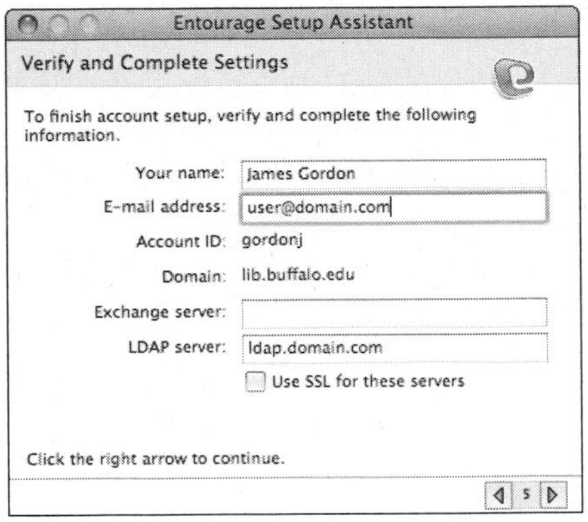

Figure 2-6:
Entering
Exchange
account
information.

Figuring out an IMAP account

When you set up an IMAP account, you might be a little confused because you see two items called Inbox in your list of mailboxes in the left pane of the mail view. The Inbox at the top of the list is actually located on your Internet mail provider's server. The other Inbox is located under the On My Computer category. The purpose of this second Inbox is to allow you to store messages locally, on your own computer's hard drive. You can't access any messages that you copy or move to folders of the Inbox located On My Computer from any other computer.

The default behavior for deleting messages from the first Inbox, the one at the top of the mailboxes list, is a two-step operation (see Figure 2-7). After you delete a message from an IMAP server, you usually can't retrieve it. To delete a mail message from an IMAP Home account, follow these steps:

1. **Mark the message for deletion.**

You can press the Delete key, click the Delete button on the toolbar, or choose Edit⇨Delete Message. Messages marked for deletion show a red X, and the subjects have a line drawn through them.

If you change your mind after you mark a message, choose Edit⇨ Undelete.

2. **Delete the message by clicking the Delete button.**

You can change the settings that determine this behavior, and we explain more about these changes in the section, "Settings for IMAP users," later in this chapter.

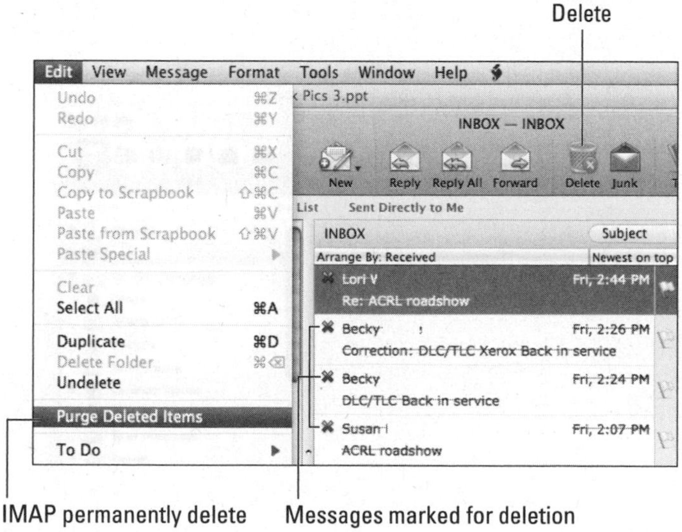

Delete

Figure 2-7:
Deleting
messages
from an
IMAP
account.

IMAP permanently delete   Messages marked for deletion

Importing from a previous version of Entourage

Importing from a previous version of Entourage is safe and easy. Your old identity will be imported but left intact in its current location so that you can always go back to it again later. Follow these steps:

1. **In the Setup Assistant, select the Import from a Previous Version of Entourage option (see Figure 2-1).**

A window appears, asking which version of Entourage created your database, as shown in Figure 2-8.

2. **Specify your version of Entourage.**

Entourage attempts to locate that database. If Entourage can find the database, the identity or identities that you can import appear in a list for you to choose from.

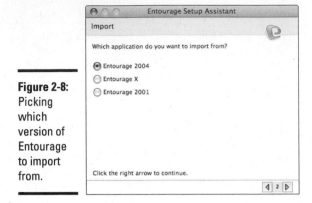

Figure 2-8:
Picking
which
version of
Entourage
to import
from.

If your identities don't show up automatically or if you want to select a
particular database, click the Browse button and direct Entourage 2008
to find your old database, as shown in Figure 2-9.

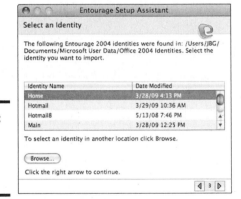

Figure 2-9:
Selecting
which
identity to
import.

3. **Click the right-pointing arrow in the lower-right corner of the window
   to make your database selection.**

   Entourage 2008 imports your entire database, which contains all your
   previous e-mails and other content. You're ready to use your new
   account.

Importing from another e-mail program

Entourage 2008 can help you migrate your accounts from other e-mail
programs. This example shows how to safely create an Entourage account
from Apple Mail without damaging your original Apple Mail account.

1. **Select Import from Another Application when Entourage starts up.**

Entourage asks you from which application you want to import your account (see Figure 2-10). In this example, you import an Apple Mail account.

Figure 2-10:
Choosing
your
Apple Mail
account.

2. **Make your selection and go to the next window where Entourage provides the appropriate steps to take.**

In this case, the Setup Assistant reports that it's ready to import, and it wants to know whether you want to import various aspects of your Apple Mail account (see Figure 2-11).

3. **Make your selections and click the arrow in the lower-right corner of the window.**

Entourage completes the process, and you're ready to use your account.

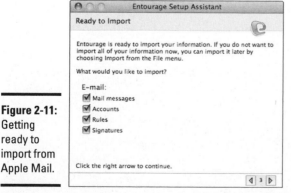

Figure 2-11:
Getting
ready to
import from
Apple Mail.

Adding additional e-mail accounts

You can add additional e-mail accounts to the pane that has your Inbox and mailboxes. Follow these steps:

1. **Choose Tools➪Accounts.**

The Accounts dialog appears.

2. **Click the New button and select Mail.**

The Entourage Setup Assistant, as shown in Figure 2-2, starts.

3. **Enter the settings for the new account by following the steps in the wizard.**

You can add any kind of e-mail account, and the new e-mail account doesn't have to be the same kind as a previous account. Accounts that you add share your Calendar and contacts.

We discuss both the Calendar and contacts in Book V.

If your Mac has multiple users, each user should have her own Mac OS X login so that each e-mail account identity is discreet, secure, and separate. When you set up Entourage e-mail accounts for different Mac OS X users, each one is independent. One Mac OS X user can't see another user's messages or any other aspect of Entourage. Even if you use Mac OS X Fast User Switching, Entourage keeps each user's account properly as its own secure, independent account.

If you manage major events or physical entities (perhaps a meeting room), consider using Mac OS X user accounts, and treat each event or thing as an identity. You can create a new user in Mac OS X by choosing System Preferences➪Accounts. You can use additional accounts for large discreet functions or for those you want to keep separate from your regular activities. Use Mac OS X Fast User Switching to quickly move from one account to another.

Chapter 4 of this minibook discusses newsgroups, for which you can use this feature. Another example is hosting a conference. If you use this strategy, you can give your event its own e-mail address, contacts, and Calendar. You can keep those special things separate from your every day mail.

Configuring an e-mail account manually

You can also configure your Entourage account yourself:

1. **Start Entourage.**

2. **When the Setup Assistant (see Figure 2-2) appears, click the red Close button.**

The Setup Assistant closes.

3. **Choose Tools⇨Accounts.**

   The Accounts pane opens.

4. **Click the New button and then click the Configure Account Manually button.**

5. **Configure your account.**

   For more information on how to configure your e-mail account, see the following section.

Digging Deeper into Account Settings

After you create an e-mail account, you can adjust many settings in the Edit Account Wizard. To get to this wizard, follow these steps:

1. **Choose Tools⇨Accounts.**

   The Accounts pane appears.

   If you have more than one account, you can click the Make Default button to choose a default account that Entourage uses when it opens.

2. **Double-click the account name in the Accounts pane for the account you want to view or edit (see Figure 2-12).**

   The Edit Account Wizard opens.

Double-click to edit account.

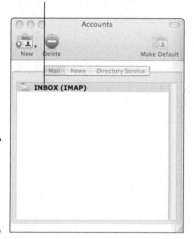

Figure 2-12:
Viewing
your e-mail
account's
settings.

Configuring settings

The first tab of the Edit Account pane is Account Settings, as shown in Figure 2-13. The name that appears in the Name text box of the Personal Information section is the name that appears when people receive e-mail from you.

In most cases, you don't need to change any of the settings on the Account Settings tab, but you should review the other tabs.

If your ISP changes its e-mail server or other account settings, you can make changes in this pane. You have to configure some e-mail accounts manually with special security settings.

Account Settings tab

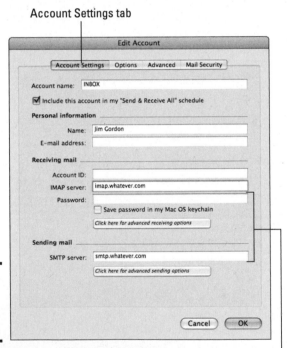

Figure 2-13:
Edit e-mail
account
settings.

Advanced options

In the Receiving Mail category of the Account Settings tab, click the Click Here for Advanced Receiving Options button (or its counterpart, Click Here for Advanced Sending Options in the Sending Mail category). A dialog opens, where you can make specific configuration settings, as shown in Figure 2-14.

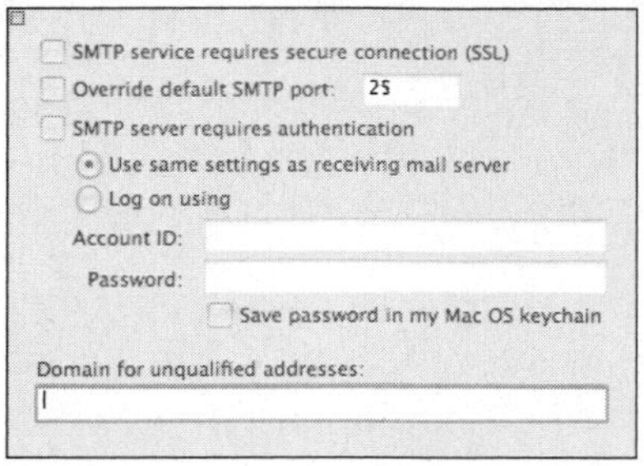

**Book V
Chapter 2**

Welcome to Setup Assistant

Figure 2-14:
Configuring advanced options.

Opting for options

The Options tab of the Edit Account pane is an eclectic collection of settings that just didn't seem to fit anywhere else in Entourage. You can select which message signature to use as your default, among other things (see Figure 2-15).

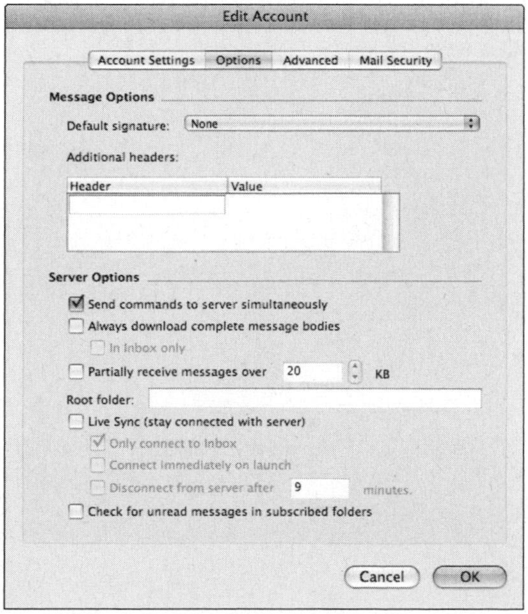

Figure 2-15:
Setting odds and ends.

Most of these settings are for advanced users, so don't worry if they don't make sense to you.

Settings for IMAP users

The Advanced tab (see Figure 2-16) doesn't appear for POP e-mail accounts. Don't let the Advanced label scare you away. This pane lets you decide what happens when you delete messages. Instead of deleting, you might want to save them to a different folder, either on the server or on your own computer. This pane also lets you decide how to automatically deal with draft messages and junk mail.

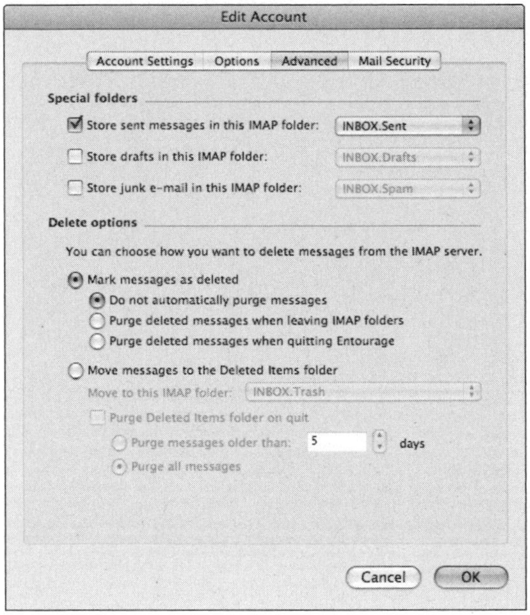

Figure 2-16: Looking over (not very) advanced settings.

Accommodating digital signatures and encryption

Chapter 3 of this minibook covers working with digital signatures and document encryption. In the Mail Security tab of the Edit Account pane, you can deal with digital signatures (see Figure 2-17). If you plan to use digital signatures when sending mail or if you need to add a digital signature you received from someone who sent a digital signature to you, this is the pane you need.

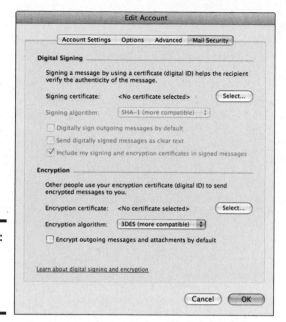

Figure 2-17:
Working
with digital
signature
settings.

Touring the Entourage Preferences

Although it might seem that account settings are preferences, they're not
general preferences that affect the overall behavior of Entourage. Account
settings affect only the specific account they're applied to. In the following
sections, we explore settings that apply to the entire Entourage program.
We're not going to talk about every single setting. You'd die of boredom
if we did that. We highlight particular settings we think you might want to
know about.

All the preferences we discuss are from the upper-left corner of your screen,
where you choose Entourage⇨Preferences, as shown in Figure 2-18.

Figure 2-18:
Finding
Entourage's
preferences.

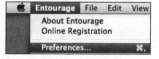

Going with general admission

The first category of the Preferences pane is General. When you select General Preferences, you see the choices offered in Figure 2-19. We want to draw your attention to two settings, in particular:

✦ **Double-Clicking in the Folders List Opens a New Window:** This setting is selected by default. We've seen people accidentally open window on top of identical window without realizing it. To prevent something of this sort, we suggest that you deselect this check box.

✦ **Set Entourage to Be My Default E-Mail Client:** Click this button to change the default e-mail client to Entourage. When you click a Mail To link in a document, PowerPoint presentation, or Web browser, your Mac uses the default e-mail client to send the message.

Figure 2-19: Setting Entourage to be your default e-mail client.

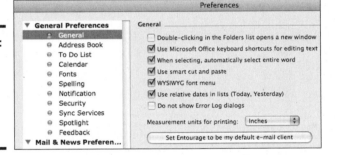

Customizing the Address Book

In the Address Book preferences, near the upper-right corner, is a Customize button. Click it to select an Address Book format or add your own custom address format (see Figure 2-20).

Changing the To Do List

The To Do List preferences are only two. We changed the settings, as shown in Figure 2-21, but that's just our preferences. Do your own thing. Here's some more info on what these options do:

✦ **Default Due Date for To Do Items:** Normally set to Today, but you can set it for anything from Tomorrow to Next Week, or even No Date.

✦ **Default Snooze Time for Reminders:** Reminds you to do something in a given amount of time. You can change that time to anything from 5 minutes to 2 weeks.

Figure 2-20:
Changing
the Address
Book
format.

Figure 2-21:
Doing To
Do List
preferences.

Clarifying the Calendar preferences

Take a peek at the Calendar preference settings, as shown in Figure 2-22.
Even if you don't need to change them, you may want to know where these
settings are, for future reference:

✦ **First Day of the Week:** Everyone knows it's *Sunday,* right? We've heard
rumors that entire countries get this one wrong and think it's Monday.
No matter. Whatever day you want, go ahead and pick it from the pop-up
menu.

✦ **Calendar Work Week:** Entourage's default is Monday through Friday,
but of course, not everyone works the same days. Select the check
boxes to match your own work week.

✦ **Work Hours:** 8:30 a.m. to 5:30 p.m. is a fine schedule, but if this doesn't
match your work hours, you can change this setting.

Fiddling with your fonts

You're not stuck with Entourage's default fonts and font sizes. In the Fonts
category, you can change them (see Figure 2-23). You can assign various
fonts for viewing plain text, HTML, or printed text.

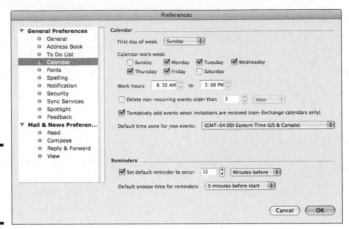

Figure 2-22:
Getting to
work on the
right days.

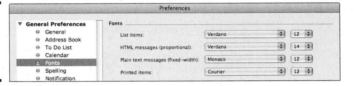

Figure 2-23:
Changing
the default
fonts.

Controlling the spell checker

Like the other Office applications, Entourage uses Microsoft Word's spell
checker, dictionary, and custom dictionaries. We have a great deal of detail
about these tools in Book II, Chapter 4. Generally, Entourage's default settings
are just fine (see Figure 2-24), unless you want more control over your spell
checks. Among other settings, you can opt to not spell check words that
contain numbers, Web URLs, or anything that's typed in ALL CAPS (such as
an acronym). You can also select a check box to tell Entourage to run the
spell checker before it sends each e-mail message.

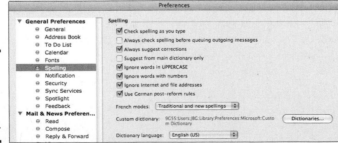

Figure 2-24:
Viewing
the spell-
checking
preferences.

Turning off that little mail notification

If you don't like the little window that appears and then disappears now and then to tell you about new mail while you're working, the Notification section has a check box that lets you turn it off.

Staying slightly more secure

You might want to check out the Security preferences (see Figure 2-25). We have no objections to the default settings. Display Complex HTML in Messages is the default, so don't change that setting unless you have a reason to do so.

Figure 2-25:
Allowing
complex
HTML
messages
to be
displayed.

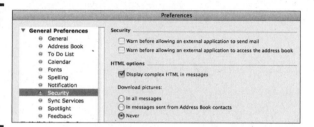

We strongly advise against changing the Download Pictures setting (see Figure 2-25). Leave it at Never. Spammers and other ne'er-do-wells can use pictures to spy on you. Someone might include a picture in an e-mail so that he can determine whether you look at his message. Downloading pictures tells the message sender your IP (Internet Protocol) address, as well as the date and time that you download the picture.

The Never setting causes Entourage to warn you when you receive a message that wants you to download one or more pictures — pictures that can tip off a server somewhere, that is. Figure 2-26 shows the warning that appears at the top of an e-mail message that contains a dangerous picture. It probably wants to tattle on you. Only click the blue Download Pictures link if you don't mind telling the sender who you are, where you are, and when you download the picture. Download Pictures is especially risky when you don't know the sender and when you receive a forwarded e-mail message.

Of course, if you know and trust a sender, you can download the pictures he attaches to an e-mail. Don't get paranoid about displaying vacation pictures your friends send you!

Figure 2-26:
Letting
strangers
into the
house.

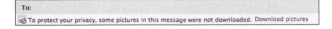

Figure 2-26:
Letting
strangers
into the
house.

Syncing the services

Entourage databases can be synced with your Apple Address Book, Apple iCal, and even your .Mac account. The settings in the Sync Services pane let you turn these sync options on and off (see Figure 2-27).

Figure 2-27:
Syncing
with Apple
applications
and
services.

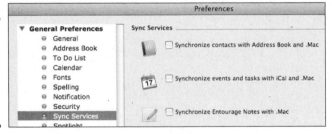

Enjoying the Spotlight

Spotlight is the search technology that Apple included in Mac OS X. Allowing Spotlight to index your Entourage database might slow your computer and/ or cause Spotlight to use considerably more disk space, so the indexing Entourage attachments option is deselected by default. Each Entourage user is unique. Consider the following things before using the Spotlight option to index Entourage attachments:

✦ It might slow Spotlight.

✦ It might use up a lot of hard drive space.

✦ You may find it handy if you use Spotlight a lot and have tons of Entourage attachments.

Feeding MacBU

If you don't object to sending your system profile and other information related to software crashes to Microsoft's Macintosh Business Unit (MacBU), say yes to the Feedback option. Details are in the pane.

Nothing to read

We think the settings in the Read section are benign. You don't have much to worry about here. Of course, if you want your messages to appear unread after being displayed for 20 seconds or your message windows to close automatically after you delete a message, you can spend some time with these options.

Gaining your composure

The Compose settings, as shown in Figure 2-28, do deserve a once-over. You may find a few of interest:

✦ **Mail Format: HTML:** In Entourage 2008, the default setting has changed from Text to HTML. HTML allows formatting more like a word processor but uses a little more bandwidth. If you have friends in remote areas that have slow dialup connections, change this setting to Text. Otherwise, HTML is fine.

✦ **Append File Name Extensions:** Always keep this setting selected — it's actually deselected by default (how bizarre!). If you don't select this option, Windows users may have trouble opening your attachments.

✦ **Display a List of Recently Used Addresses When Addressing Messages:** When this option is selected, Entourage keeps track of the 300 or so most recently sent or received e-mail addresses and uses them to auto-complete e-mail addresses while you type them in address fields.

✦ **Click List button:** If you click this button, Entourage erases those 300 or so addresses from its memory. Removing those addresses might cause a problem if you haven't added someone to your contacts and are used to having his or her address automatically fill in, so don't click this button unless you're sure about it.

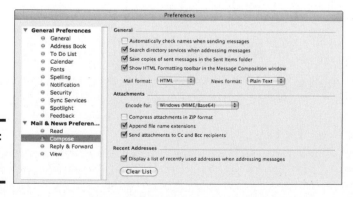

Figure 2-28:
Clearing up
Compose.

Replying and forwarding fun

In the Reply & Forward section, you can tinker with the little message header that gets inserted when you reply to or forward a message (see Figure 2-29).

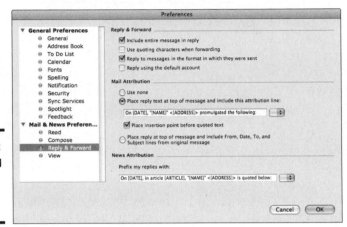

Figure 2-29:
Customizing reply and forwarding tag lines.

Viewing the colors

The Mail & News Preferences pane lets you change the colors of the messages, newsgroup folders, and IMAP folders (see Figure 2-30). We like the defaults, but you might prefer other colors.

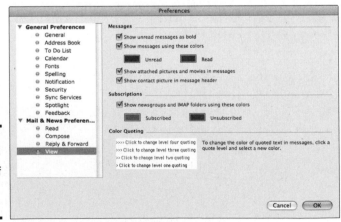

Figure 2-30:
Changing the colors of messages and more.

Chapter 3: Mastering Mail

In This Chapter

🖝 **Arranging the preview pane**

🖝 **Opening, reading, creating, and sending e-mail**

🖝 **Exploring Entourage's menu options**

🖝 **Figuring out your toolbars and panes**

🖝 **Dealing with digital certificates for e-mail**

E-mail is more than just a way of communicating; it's a vital lifeline for businesses and organizations. Socially, text messaging on cellphones may have supplanted e-mail as the dominant form of casual communication for some people. Devices like the Apple iPhone blend text messaging, phone, and e-mail into a single device, extending the utility of all the features of e-mail with the benefit of portability.

E-mail is a staple of everyone's life because it's convenient; and it's easy to save, search, archive, and organize. If you need to have solid evidence that mail was sent or received, you can use digitally signed mail as proof that a particular document was transmitted from one person or entity to another.

We begin this chapter with simple mail basics and then cover mail organization tools. Along the way, we take a detour to mention some nice features of Entourage that you may not be aware of.

Picking a Preview Pane View

By now, you may have your e-mail account set up. After you select your Inbox in the folder list (on the left side of the pane), choose the View menu, and then select one of the following preview pane arrangements:

✦ **On Right:** This is Entourage's initial arrangement, as shown in Figures 3-1 and 3-2. When the preview pane is on the right, message subjects appear in a column in the middle. If you click to highlight a message subject, a preview of your message appears to the right of the list of subjects, as shown with the built-in sample message in Figure 3-2.

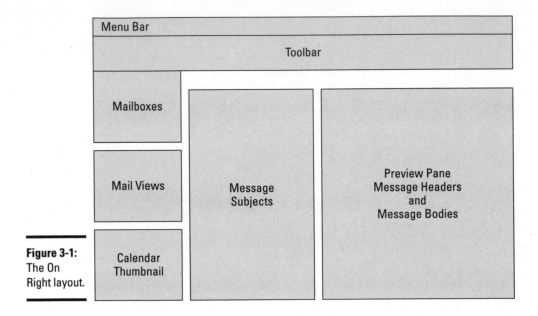

Figure 3-1:
The On
Right layout.

✦ **Below List:** This layout option moves the preview pane to a position below the list of message subjects, as shown Figures 3-3 and 3-4. When you click a message subject, a preview of the message appears below the list of message subjects.

If you compare Figures 3-2 and 3-4, the main difference between them is that the message body now appears below the message list. In the folder list on the left side of each of the screens, we clicked the disclosure triangles to show Microsoft Newsgroups (we show you how to set up newsgroups up in Chapter 4 of this minibook), and we closed the Mail Views triangle. We also widened the left pane to show two months of the Calendar at the same time.

✦ **None:** If you select this option, you don't see a preview pane. The list of message subjects fills a larger area. To read a message, double-click a message subject, and the message opens in its own window.

Local folders

Inbox

Mail Application

Folder list

Create message

Reply options

Delete

Forward

Categorize as junk

Assign a category

To Do list

Search Entourage

Filter e-mail

Open My Day

Get new messages

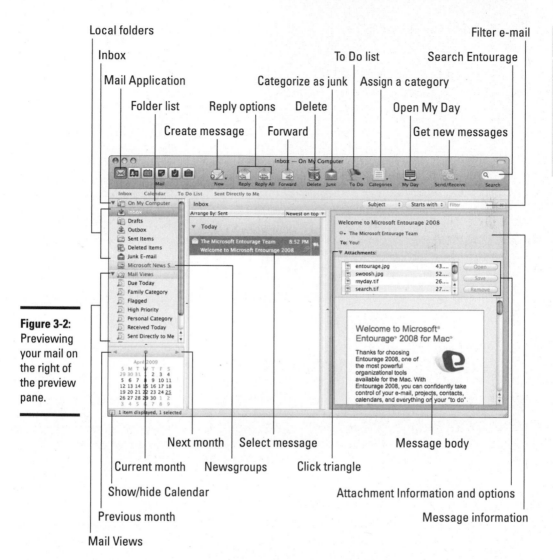

Figure 3-2:
Previewing
your mail on
the right of
the preview
pane.

Next month

Select message

Message body

Current month

Newsgroups

Click triangle

Show/hide Calendar

Previous month

Attachment Information and options

Message information

Mail Views

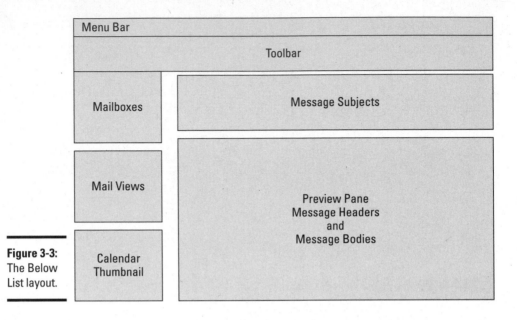

Figure 3-3:
The Below
List layout.

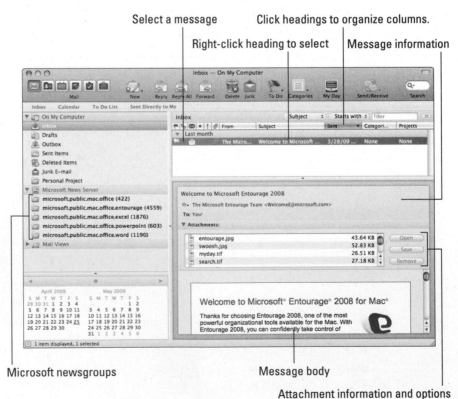

Figure 3-4:
Previewing
mail below
the list of
subjects.

Reading Mail

Entourage makes reading your mail simple, not to mention organizing your e-mail and activities in useful ways.

Regardless of which preview pane view you select, you can double-click a message subject in the message list to open the message in its own window, as shown in Figure 3-4. The Reply, Reply All, Forward, Print, and Delete buttons on the toolbar do just what they say. The following list provides a quick run down of the buttons that do additional things you may not have started to include in your daily routine:

✦ **To Do:** Sometimes, you wind up having to do something as the result of an e-mail message. That's when you should click the tiny triangle just to the right of the big red To Do flag. Of course, make sure that the relevant e-mail is the open e-mail! Select an option from the pop-up menu that appears, and you've just created a To Do task!

✦ **Categories:** Click the Categories button and then tag the message with one or more categories from the list.

✦ **Projects:** Click the Projects button to mark a message as being associated with an existing project, or even start a new project at the same moment. We talk about projects in Book VI.

✦ **Links:** Entourage can automatically link messages to other items so that you can find them more easily and document your activities.

You can find even more options available to you when you right-click or Control-click icons and attachments in the message header, also shown in Figure 3-4. We right-clicked an e-mail address from a sender who wasn't already in our contacts, so Entourage offered to use this e-mail address to start a new contact. Try right-clicking or Control-clicking in the message body, and even try selecting some text first and then right-clicking to see even more options!

When you see the warning that pictures weren't downloaded, only download the pictures if you want a server somewhere to know who you are, where you are, and when you downloaded the picture.

Creating a Message

You can compose e-mail messages in Microsoft Office 2008 in several different ways. Most people use the Entourage message creation window. In the following sections, we discuss how to use this application as well as describe the other ways you can create e-mail.

Creating e-mail in Entourage

Perhaps the most common way to start a new mail message is to click the New button in the Entourage Mail application. The window shown in Figure 3-5 opens. Entourage shows an empty message-body area where you can type your message, just like if you were using a word processor. In fact, you're using Microsoft Word's spell checker in Entourage Mail, and the Tools menu includes the same familiar dictionary, thesaurus, and other editing tools that you can find in Microsoft Word. We right-clicked our misspelled word to select a correction from the pop-up menu that Entourage offered.

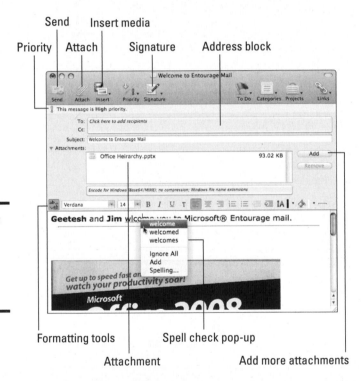

Figure 3-5: Making a message (and spell checking, too).

Formatting tools   Spell check pop-up

Attachment   Add more attachments

Send   Insert media

Priority | Attach   Signature   Address block

Although you can easily include media, such as pictures and movies, in your Entourage e-mails, be careful about file sizes. E-mail servers often have a 5MB limit per message, although some mail servers aren't as picky these days. Even then, some recipients might not be happy with e-mails half that size. You can insert media into an e-mail message by using the Insert button on the toolbar or by dragging the media into the message body. You've inserted media where the cursor is blinking.

Creating e-mail in Microsoft Word

Some people are comfortable with Microsoft Word when they write, and that's just fine. You might prefer to use Word to create your e-mail messages so that you can use the tools and interface you're familiar with, or perhaps you have templates that you want to use. We can think of three ways to send mail from Microsoft Word. In all cases, Entourage actually sends the mail.

Sending in HTML format

If you choose HTML format, your composed message appears in the body of the recipient's e-mail message. We recommend that you compose your e-mail messages by using Web Layout, which you can find on Word's View menu. When you're ready to send your message, choose File⇨Send To⇨Mail Recipient (as HTML). You can't use all of Word's features when you use this method because e-mail programs aren't as robust as Microsoft Word. However, you can still use niceties, such as pictures and tables.

Sending as an attached Word document

If you choose this format, your message appears as an attachment to an e-mail message. You can use all of Word's features when you use this method. When you're ready to send your message, choose File⇨Send To⇨Mail Recipient (as Attachment).

Using Mail Merge

You use Mail Merge while in Microsoft Word. By using Mail Merge, you can send hundreds of similar e-mails to different people. All these e-mails may have the same body content, but all your recipients see a greeting that's addressed specifically to them so that they think you wrote that e-mail only to them! See Book II, Chapter 6 for more details.

Exploring the Entourage Menu Options

Entourage's interface is very context-sensitive. The menu options and toolbars are so varied that we can only urge you to explore them often while you're working in Entourage. We start at the top of the interface and work our way down. Because many of the interface features are based on what you're doing or what you've selected, we can't show you them all.

While you're working in Entourage, you can open a pop-up menu that offers context-sensitive options for whatever you've selected. Right-click or Control-click just about everything in Entourage, and you're rewarded with a pop-up menu that's been tailored specifically for whatever you clicked.

We're so glad that Microsoft retained the menus in Office for Mac just the way we like them. Menus are a sensible, time-tested, and easy way to organize features in an interface. Also, you can access many features only through the menus.

The Entourage menu alone has an explosion of new features because the Mac OS X Services submenu has been added in Entourage 2008 (see Figure 3-6). If you first select something in Entourage's interface and then explore the Services submenu, you can find a lot of amazing new things to try. Just look at them all! You may see different options than the ones in Figure 3-6 because Services integrates Entourage with all the other applications on your computer, and you probably have different applications than we do. One of our favorite services is to have Entourage speak selected text, especially when we're tired. Everyone gets this service because it's part of Mac OS X.

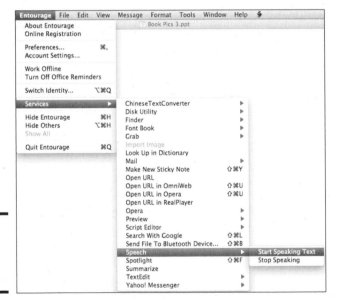

Figure 3-6:
Mining the Entourage menu.

The following list explores some other Entourage options we use frequently:

✦ **Work Offline:** This toggle switch (see the Entourage menu in Figure 3-6) changes the way Entourage handles e-mail messages. When you're not connected to the Internet, select this item. You can work normally in Entourage. Entourage brilliantly keeps track of everything you do while you're not connected. Then, when you're connected to the Internet again, select the Work Offline setting again to toggle it off. Entourage then sends all the messages that it queued and brings itself up to date with your mail server. A check mark next to Work Offline in the menu means that Entourage isn't communicating with the network.

Use this feature when you're on an airplane that's not WiFi-equipped or any time you can't get a network connection.

✦ **Switch Identity:** A long time ago, before Mac OS X fast user switching, Entourage had its own way of handling multiple identities. In Chapter 2 of this minibook, we explain that you should create Mac OS X user accounts to handle multiple identities. Although Entourage 2008 still supports the old-style identities, we don't recommend them because they're not as secure as using Mac OS X user accounts. If you're using the old Entourage identities, we recommend that you migrate your Entourage identities into new Mac OS X identities.

✦ **Search with Google:** Select some text, and then choose Entourage ➪ Search with Google. Google searches for whatever you selected.

✦ **Summarize:** If you have this option in your version of Entourage, you can select text to copy from a Web site and then choose Entourage➪Services➪Summarize. A new window opens displaying a cleaned-up copy of the Web site text with all the extraneous formatting, spacing, and links removed. Then you can copy the text in this new window and put it wherever you like.

Using File menu options

Entourage doesn't have its own document type, so it doesn't have a File➪ Open feature. You can save things from Entourage in various formats, and you can import different sorts of things, such as pictures, into Entourage. Here's some must-have information about the Entourage File menu options:

✦ **Project Gallery:** Opens Project Gallery, which we discuss extensively in Book I.

✦ **New:** Choosing File➪New enables you to make new things in Entourage, such as a new mail message, a new Calendar event, and so on. You can find New buttons in each of the Entourage applications, but choosing File➪New gets at all the new stuff at the same time, as shown in Figure 3-7.

✦ **Import:** This menu option starts a wizard that can bring many different kinds of things into Entourage. You may find it particularly useful when you want to import an Entourage archive file (for example, if you switch computers and need to import all your old e-mails), a list of contacts, or a list of holidays. See Figure 3-8 to see the Import Wizard pane.

✦ **Export:** Export offers two options, export contacts and create an archive, which we talk about in the following sections. Figure 3-9 shows the complete set of exporting options.

You can simply drag almost any item from Entourage and then let it go in Finder. A file of the appropriate type is created instantly.

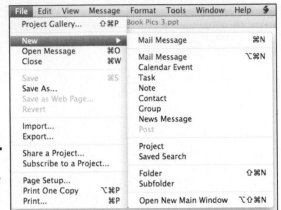

Figure 3-7:
Making new
everything.

Figure 3-8:
Importing
all kinds of
content into
Entourage.

Figure 3-9:
Exporting
Entourage
items.

Export contacts

The first export option, export contacts, lets you save your contacts in a tab-delimited text file. *Tab-delimited text files* are essentially text files in which each record is separated from another by a tab. You can open them in Excel or use them to migrate to another e-mail program (heaven forbid!).

Create an archive

Create an archive, the second Export option, creates an archive file that contains various Entourage contents. An archive files has an .rge file extension. We recommend creating archives as a good way to back up your files.

Time Machine is Apple's backup solution that's built into new versions of Mac OS X. Entourage databases can be very large and fill up a Time Machine backup drive quickly. If your Entourage database is causing problems with Time Machine, exclude it from the Time Machine backup. Instead, you can use AppleScript to create an Entourage archive on a scheduled basis, or you can use some other method, such as a file-synchronizing program, to make sure that the Microsoft User Data folder in your Documents folder is regularly backed up.

Using Edit menu options

Entourage's Edit menu has the expected cut, copy, and paste actions, but it also has some special actions that are unique to Entourage, as shown in Figure 3-10. We don't think you can find yourself in a situation in which every one of the Edit menu items is active at the same time. The Edit menu knows when it should let you do something and when it shouldn't.

The Edit menu contains these options (some of these options may not be available, depending on what you select in your Entourage window):

+ **Purge Deleted Items:** If this option appears, it lets you permanently delete mail messages that you've previously marked for deletion. Some mail programs use *expunge* for their comparable feature. Purge Deleted Items appears only if you're using an IMAP mail account.

+ **Auto Text Cleanup:** Nope, this isn't Word's AutoText feature. Use this feature to clean up quotation marks and other clutter before forwarding an e-mail.

+ **Increase (or Decrease) Font Size:** This handy keyboard shortcut works in many Entourage windows. Press ⌘+ to enlarge a font and ⌘− to make a font smaller.

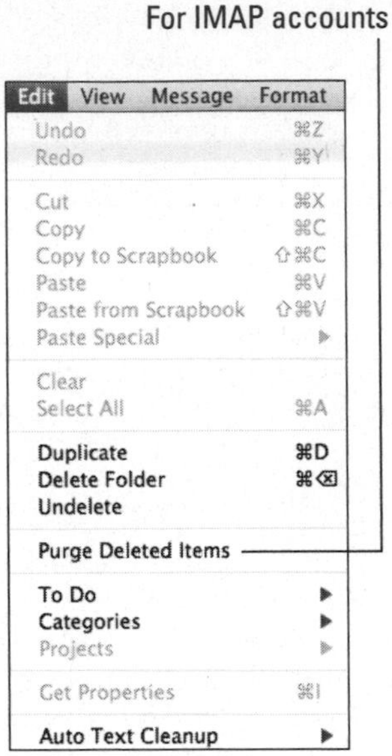

For IMAP accounts

Figure 3-10:
Inspecting
the Edit
menu
options.

Scoping the View menu

The View menu has plenty of interesting options from which to choose, as shown in Figure 3-11. We already discussed the preview pane options in the section, "Picking a Preview Pane View," earlier in this chapter. The following list gives you a closer look at some of the other View menu options:

Figure 3-11:
An overview
of the View
menu.

✦ **Unread Only:** When you turn on this option, only messages that you haven't read appear in the message list. Select this option a second time to view all messages.

✦ **Refresh Message List:** If it seems like Entourage isn't synchronized with the mail server, select your Inbox and then choose this option. Entourage abandons the current message list and replaces it with whatever's on the server.

✦ **Customize Toolbar:** New for Entourage 2008 is the ability to customize Entourage toolbars. See Figure 3-12 for the main Entourage mail toolbar customizations. The Customize Toolbar feature is new, and it works differently from the customizing toolbars in Word, Excel, and PowerPoint. Entourage works like a Web browser, so you use a sheet to drag and drop controls to and from Entourage toolbars. A *sheet* is the pane that appears beneath the toolbar when you select the Customize Toolbar option. The sheet contains the customization buttons. As we mention in Book I, each application within Entourage has its own toolbar customizations. Not only that, but each different kind of Entourage window has its own toolbar customizations. Try the Customize Toolbar feature in different windows while you're working in Entourage.

Figure 3-12: Customizing toolbars in Entourage's main mail window.

Minding the toolbar buttons and palettes

You can find most of the subheadings on the menus, as shown in Figure 3-13, also on the toolbars of message windows and in the Toolbox. As you'd expect, they do the same things.

If you see the Message menu, you know you're in the Mail component of Entourage.

Figure 3-13:
Viewing
menu
subheadings.

| Message | Format | Tools | Window | Help |

Sailing through the Script menu

That little strange-looking figure that appears on the right side of the Help menu is actually a menu (see Figure 3-14) — the Script menu, to be precise. It has some very useful stuff, so click it and have a look, or just peek at Figure 3-14. The options are all self-explanatory. If you have the Home and Student edition of Office, you probably don't see the Sample Automator Workflows option, but you can make your own workflows in Automator.

You can find out more about Automator in Book IV, Chapter 6.

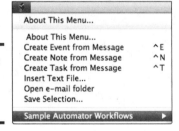

Figure 3-14:
Sizing up
the built-in
scripts.

About This Menu...

About This Menu...
Create Event from Message   ^E
Create Note from Message   ^N
Create Task from Message   ^T
Insert Text File...
Open e-mail folder
Save Selection...

Sample Automator Workflows   ▶

Tooling Down the Toolbar Highway

Like the menus, Entourage toolbars change while you work. Each window has its own set of default toolbar buttons that you can customize, as shown in Figure 3-12. The commands that are available at any given moment depend on whether you've selected a mailbox, a subject, or even the text within a message.

If you want to figure out how you can customize the toolbar in Entourage, head to Book I, Chapter 3.

Picking Apart the Panes

In the following sections, we dig into the panes of the Mail interface. We begin our tour on the left side of the interface and then we talk about the message list and the preview pane.

Living with the folder list

Take a look at Figure 3-15, where we've dissected the left Mail application pane. Microsoft calls this the *folder list*. In the folder list, mailboxes are on top. Below the mailboxes, you find newsgroups (read more about them in Chapter 4 of this minibook), followed by the very handy Mail views. At the bottom, you see a Calendar thumbnail, which you can turn on and off by clicking a little button. If you click a date in the calendar, you're taken to that date in Entourage's Calendar application. We've set the triangles to hide our mailboxes and to show the Mail views, where we chose to show only high-priority messages. Notice that you can see our high-priority messages to the right in the preview pane. Why do we have high-priority messages in the Trash? Uh oh!

Creating a custom Mail view

The Mail Views section comes with a variety of preset views. The default Mail views are handy, but you can create your own custom Mail views, as shown in Figure 3-16.

Before you begin making your custom Mail views, make sure that Entourage is set to show native Entourage search windows, rather than those integrated with the Spotlight search contained within Mac OS X. Follow these steps:

1. **Choose Entourage⇨Preferences.**

2. **In the Preferences dialog that appears, select the Spotlight item in the left pane.**

3. **Click OK to get back to the Entourage Mail window.**

We explain the options in the Preferences dialog in Chapter 2 of this minibook.

Now, you're ready to create custom Mail views in Entourage — just follow these steps:

1. **In the Mail application of Entourage, click the small triangle to the right of the New button on the Standard toolbar.**

Newsgroups

Mailboxes

Shortcut buttons   Scroll bar

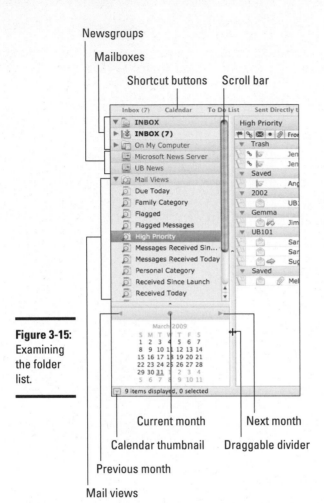

Figure 3-15:
Examining
the folder
list.

Current month   Next month

Calendar thumbnail   Draggable divider

Previous month

Mail views

2. **From the pop-up menu that appears, choose Saved Search.**

   If you opened a new e-mail message instead of getting a pop-up menu,
   you missed the little triangle when you clicked. Try again.

3. **Type a name for your custom view.**

4. **Don't change any of the Item Types options.**

   It should default to Messages if you're in the Entourage Mail application.

5. **Adjust the search criteria.**

   The possibilities are nearly endless. Be sure to check out all the available pop-up menus to see the large number of options available.

6. Click OK.

Your new Mail view appears alphabetically under the Mail Views heading in the left pane of the Entourage Mail application. Click your new view to watch it in action, as shown in Figure 3-17.

Now, you might want to enable Spotlight searches again within Entourage. Reverse the options in the step list earlier in this section.

Messages

Enter a name.

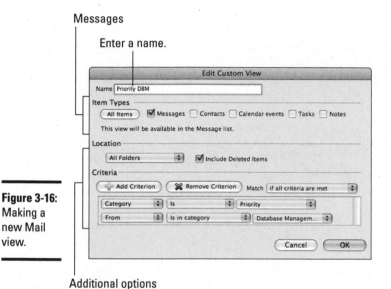

Figure 3-16:
Making a
new Mail
view.

Additional options

Figure 3-17:
Using a new
custom Mail
view.

Now that you know how to make a custom Mail view, you can follow the same steps to add new custom views to other Entourage applications. When you're working in the other applications, just follow the same steps (the Item Types option automatically changes to the application-specific one). You can create new views for any of the following Entourage applications:

✦ Mail

✦ Contacts

✦ Calendar

✦ Tasks

✦ Notes

Manipulating the message list

In the section, "Picking a Preview Pane View," earlier in this chapter, we mention that you can control the placement of the message list by using the Entourage main menu — simply choose View⇨Preview Pane. As it turns out, when you choose to view the preview pane On Right (with the message list in the middle), you can work with some special options.

Pop-up in the middle

When the message list appears in the middle, you can right-click or Control-click the Arrange By header. The pop-up menu, as shown in Figure 3-18, appears. You can choose to show the messages in groups by toggling the Show in Groups setting in the menu.

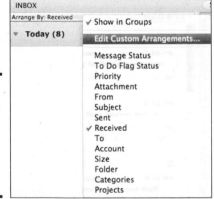

Figure 3-18: Determining how you want to arrange the message list.

In addition, you can place the messages in the list in order by using any of the criteria, or you can create a custom order. Follow these steps to make custom arrangements:

1. **Right-click or Control-click the Arrange By header.**

A pop-up menu appears.

2. **Choose Edit Custom Arrangements from the pop-up menu, as shown in Figure 3-18.**

An empty Custom Arrangements box appears, as shown in Figure 3-19.

Figure 3-19: Using Custom Arrangements for the first time.

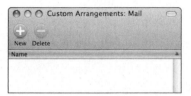

3. **Click the big green New button.**

The Edit Custom Arrangements pane opens, as shown in Figure 3-20.

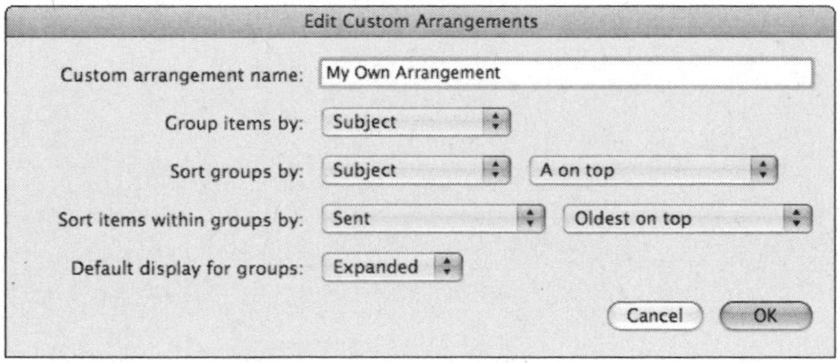

Figure 3-20: Setting up a custom arrangement for the message list.

4. **Make any selections you want in the Edit Custom Arrangements pane.**

Click plenty of the pop-up menus, just to amaze yourself at the many options.

5. **When you finish setting the custom arrangements options, click OK to close the pane.**

The next time you right-click or Control-click the Arrangements header of the message list, your new custom arrangement is ready to use. While you're in the vicinity, immediately to the right of the Arrange By header, you can find a second header labeled Newest on Top. Click that header, which is also a button, to reverse the order to Oldest on Top. Click it again to reverse the order back to Newest on Top.

Other preview options

The two preview pane view options Below List and None put the message list above the preview pane or give the message list the entire space without the preview pane, respectively. (See Figures 3-1 and 3-2.) The following sections discuss the options available to you when you use these two arrangements.

Sorting your messages

Headers appear at the top of each column in the message list. If you click any of the headers, the messages in the list are reordered based on the heading. Click the same header a second time to reverse the sort order. In Figure 3-21, the messages are ordered by the date when they were received.

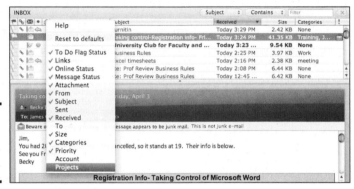

Figure 3-21: Getting just the headers you want.

Picking the column headers

If you right-click or Control-click any of the headers, a pop-up menu appears, as shown in Figure 3-21. You can turn any column header on or off by choosing column names from the pop-up menu.

Assigning a category to a message

Select a message from the message list, and then use the keyboard shortcut ⌘-; (Command and a semicolon). Or you can click the Categories button on Entourage's Standard toolbar. Either method opens the Assign Categories pane, as shown in Figure 3-22. You can select more than one category for a message. Your categories are probably different than ours. You can assign categories to Mail messages, Tasks, Calendar events, and more. We tell you how to create your own categories in the following section.

Creating, changing, and deleting categories

Just about everywhere in Entourage, you can use the keyboard shortcut Shift-⌘-; (Shift plus Command plus semicolon). You can also click the small triangle immediately to the right of the Categories button on the Standard toolbar and choose Edit Categories from the pop-up menu. Either method opens the Categories box, as shown in Figure 3-23. Here's how to set up categories:

Figure 3-22:
Assigning
category
tags to
messages.

✦ **To add a category, click the New button.** A field appears in the list so that you can type a category name. To the left of the name, click the Color rectangle to display the available colors and then select a color. Darker colors work better, although we can't show you how much better they work within the black-and-white Figure 3-23!

✦ **To delete an existing category, select a category and then click the big red Delete button.** Be careful with this option, especially if you're not too sure that you want to delete the category.

✦ **To change the name of an existing category, click the name, wait a second or so, and then click the name again.** Changing a category name works similarly to renaming a file in Mac OS X Finder.

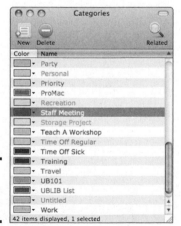

Figure 3-23:
Managing
categories.

You can also assign categories automatically by choosing Tools⇨Rules. Rules are robust, and we explain how to create rules in Book Chapter 4 of this minibook.

Displaying a list of items in a category

You have to wait until after you assign categories to some messages before you can use the feature. When you're ready, use the keyboard shortcut

Shift-⌘-; to open the Categories box, as shown in Figure 3-23. Select a category and then click the Related button to produce a listing of all the messages that are tagged with the category that you selected. The search result window is called Search Results, as shown in Figure 3-24.

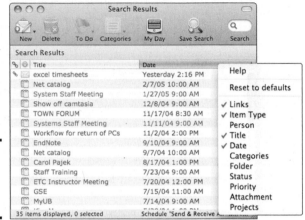

Figure 3-24:
Viewing the items in a category.

Right-click or Control-click a header to change the column header. The pop-up menu shown in Figure 3-24 appears. Of course, you can click the headers to order the columns in the list.

In the Search Results window in Figure 3-24, the Save Search button appears on the toolbar. When you click the Save Search button, the Edit Custom View dialog appears, prompting you to enter a name for your search so that you can make it a custom view. All the Item Types options are selected. If you want a new Mail view, deselect all the check boxes except for Messages, as indicated in Figure 3-25. Now you know another way to create your own custom Mail views!

Enter a name.

Figure 3-25:
Making a custom Mail view of a category.

Edit Custom View
Name: Search Results
Item Types
All Items ☑ Messages ☐ Contacts ☐ Calendar events ☐ Tasks ☐ Notes
This view will be available in the Message list.

Keep checked.   Uncheck these.

Understanding Digital Certificates

Uh-oh. We're getting on our soapbox! Please forgive us. We just want to keep you out of trouble. We've seen people scan signatures and then insert the scanned signatures into documents, especially Microsoft Word documents and Entourage Mail messages. Without sounding too alarmist, if you've done that, we want to scare the wits out of you for having done it. You have our immediate forgiveness, and if no one has stolen the signature or created a forged document with it, you can consider yourself lucky.

If you're accustomed to putting scanned signatures into documents as an indication of authenticity or for any other reason, we have bad news for you. It's incredibly easy for anyone to reuse that signature in a forged document. Remember, all it takes to get that signature is to right-click and choose Save as Picture! Or use a screen shot. Or take a picture of the signature with a camera. You'd have a very hard time refuting the authenticity of a forged document with your signature on it if you relied on this method for authentication. Please don't use pictures of signatures. Period.

Can you find a free or inexpensive easy way to digitally sign documents? The answer is, "No!" You can use a cumbersome, somewhat expensive way — by purchasing real digital signing certificates from certificate-issuing authorities, such as Thawte and VeriSign. Plan to spend about $20 each year for each computer that a person uses. It works best when both the sender and receiver each have his or her own certificate. A digital signing certificate is the only way to be assured of a sender's authenticity and generate a solid accountability record that he or she actually sent documents.

Using digital certificates takes training and setup time. They usually cost too much for casual communication, but you may find them worth the inconvenience for legal, FBI, CIA, NSA, military, security, and law enforcement communications, as well as communications in which you need privacy, such as with HIPAA–compliant medical communications.

You can find digital certificates difficult to work with when you upgrade operating systems or move a user from one computer to another. You can get USB devices that allow you temporary use of certificates on a computer, but if you lose or break the device, you can't get to your documents! You can't forward digitally signed e-mail with the signature intact. Don't expect mobile devices to work well with digitally signed e-mail.

After saying all that, we're happy to tell you that Entourage fully supports real digital certificates, but the mechanics of using them aren't within the scope of this book. We recommend that you get a copy of *Cryptography For Dummies* by Chey Cobb (Wiley), which has a section about digital certificates.

Chapter 4: Your Mail Rules and Newsgroups

*A*utomating Entourage can save you countless hours and make your e-mail workflows manageable. The best part is that you don't have to know any scripting language to take advantage of Entourage's tremendous automation capabilities. Of course, if you do know AppleScript, you can extend these capabilities even further. Regardless, you're sure to be pleasantly surprised by how much you can do easily by using Entourage's automation options.

In this chapter, we also show you how you can become part of, read, and post to the newsgroup communities from within Entourage.

Sandbagging the Flood of Junk Mail

Everyone hates mail that they didn't ask for! Unless you've lived under a rock for the last decade, you know that the electronic version of unsolicited mail is *spam*. Except for the jerks who send it, no one likes spam. Spam makes a lot of money for spammers — at least, until they're caught and sent to jail. The folks at Microsoft hate junk mail, too, so they created a *Junk Mail Filter,* affectionately called the *JMF* by people who deal with it regularly. The Entourage JMF on the Mac is the same JMF that's used in Microsoft Outlook in Windows. The JMF is updated regularly at no additional cost through the Office Automatic Software Update feature.

You can control certain settings in the JMF. To get at the Entourage JMF, in Entourage choose Tools⇨Junk E-Mail Protection. The Junk E-Mail Protection Wizard, as shown in Figure 4-1, opens. You can find three tabs in the JMF Wizard — we explain the options that these tabs offer:

✦ **Levels:** We generally use the High setting and find that we don't lose any valid messages. Of course, review your Junk Mail folder often to see whether some genuine mail has slipped through the filter. As shown in Figure 4-1, we allow ourselves 30 days to review our junk mail before it's permanently deleted.

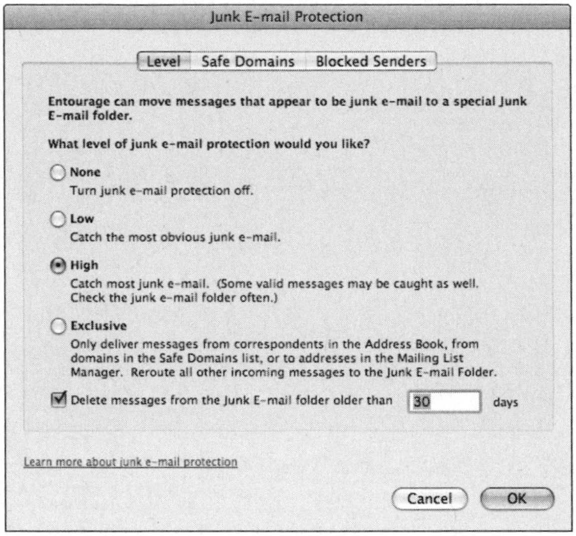

Figure 4-1:
Adjusting the junk mail protection level.

If you need to receive messages from strangers, perhaps the High setting is too aggressive. In that case, you just have to deal with more junk mail. On the other hand, maybe you can be even more selective about what messages you allow to get through. Entourage offers the Exclusive option. Use this setting to be tough on spam. Only messages that you've given clearance can reach you.

✦ **Safe Domains:** Click the Safe Domains tab to enter Internet domains that you consider to be okay so that messages from these domains don't get flagged as junk mail. A domain is the part of the e-mail address after the @ sign, such as `microsoft.com` or `verizon.net`. Enter your trusted domains in the Safe Domains pane and separate them with commas, as shown in Figure 4-2.

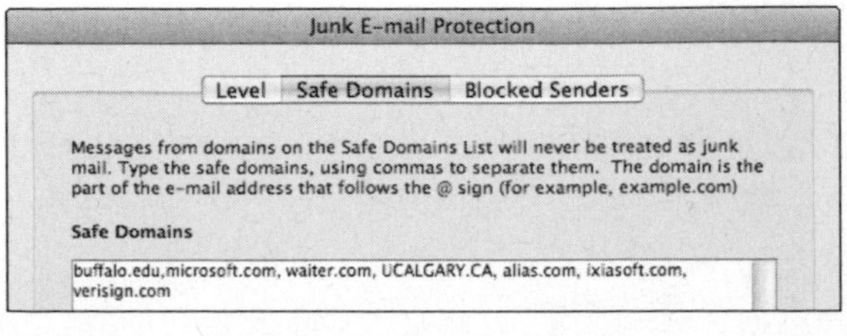

Figure 4-2:
Giving the green light to safe domains.

✦ **Blocked Senders:** The Blocked Senders pane lets you banish messages from the scum and flotsam of the Internet. You enter domains the same way that you do with Safe Domains (see Figure 4-2). The effect, however, is the opposite. The mail from domains that you put into Blocked Senders is automatically flagged as junk.

Building Mailing List Rules

The Exclusive setting of the Junk Mail Filter mentions mailing list rules. Entourage allows you to create specific rules concerning how e-mail will be handled when it arrives from mailing lists. In the preceding section, we mention that we use the High setting for the Junk Mail Filter. But at the High setting, the JMF marks messages as junk that come from a ListServ we subscribe to. To solve this problem, we can create a mailing list rule.

To create a mailing list rule, follow these steps:

1. **Choose Tools⇨Mailing List Manager.**

   An empty Mailing List Manager pane opens the first time you make this choice.

2. **Click the New button to open the Edit Mailing List Rule pane.**

   The Mailing List Manager and the Mailing List tab of the Edit Mailing List Rule pane are shown in Figure 4-3.

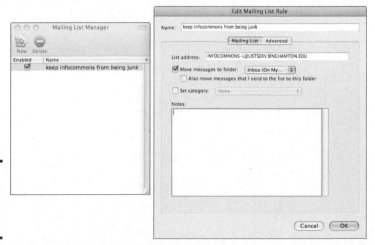

Figure 4-3:
Creating a
new mailing
list rule.

3. **Click either the Mailing List tab or the Advanced tab depending on what you want to do.**

The following two tabs appear on the Edit Mailing List Rule pane:

- *Mailing List:* As shown in Figure 4-3, we want to get the messages from the ListServ to our Inbox before the Junk Mail Filter has a chance to send them to their doom.

- *Advanced:* If you click the Advanced tab, you can get specific about various aspects of messages sent from mailing lists (see Figure 4-4).

Before we forget to mention it, to edit an existing rule, double-click the rule name in the Mailing List Manager. To delete a rule, select its name and then click the big, red Delete button.

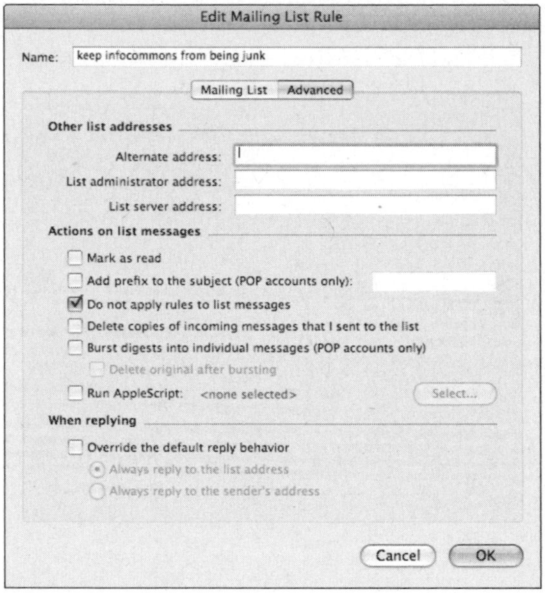

Figure 4-4:
Dealing with advanced mailing list rules.

Ruling the Roost

Among the most powerful features of Entourage is the ability to automatically apply rules to incoming and outbound e-mail messages. These Mail rules are different from the Mailing List rules we explain in the preceding section — these rules apply to regular e-mails that you receive, rather than the ones you receive from mailing list subscriptions.

You can apply rules simply, but you have plenty of power to create complex sets of rules if you want them. We want to help you by explaining the rules about using rules. To get started, we choose Tools⇨Rules. The Rules pane opens, which is where Entourage stores the rules that you make (see Figure 4-5).

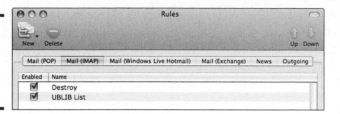

Figure 4-5:
Creating,
storing,
and editing
rules.

Rules about rules

When you first open the Rules pane, it's empty. Figure 4-5 shows two rules, and we show you how to create your rules in just a bit. Before we get to that, you need to look at the six tabs in the Rules pane. Entourage offers different sets of rules to you, depending on which tab you pick. To select the proper tab(s), you need to know what kind e-mail server your e-mail account(s) use.

In the example in Figure 4-5, we show rules that we want to apply to our IMAP e-mail account. Rules that we make on the IMAP tab don't apply to any other e-mail account types — such as POP, Windows Live, Hotmail, or Exchange — that we may have set up. The News tab is for rules that apply to newsgroup messages, a topic we cover in the section, "Connecting to World Communities by Using Newsgroups," later in this chapter. The Outgoing tab lets you apply rules to outbound messages. The rest of the tabs that we mention earlier in this paragraph deal with incoming messages.

Rules are applied first at the top of each list and then in sequence while you go down the list. You can create a lot of rules, but you should think about them thoroughly and carefully. You can change the order in which the rules are applied by selecting a rule and then clicking the up- or down-arrow buttons located toward the right end of the Rules toolbar.

Making rules

You might have heard the old adage about rules being made to be broken. However, Entourage is quite serious about any rules you create — no rules are broken! You can use rules to categorize your mail messages in an orderly fashion. The following steps show a rule that we made, which says anything that comes from a coauthor of this book becomes tagged with a category we call Book.

You can save yourself some typing by knowing this secret. If you're going to make a rule that involves a particular subject or person, start by selecting a message in one of your message lists that contains the subject of interest — or is to or from the person of interest. Entourage prefills some of the fields for you. Keep this tip in mind and use the following steps to make a rule:

1. **In any message list, select a message from the person whom you want to make the rule about.**

   In this case, we click a message from one of the coauthors of this book.

2. **Choose Tools⇨Rules.**

   The Rules pane opens in all its glory (we show you part of that interface in Figure 4-5).

3. **On the Rules toolbar, click the New button.**

   The Edit Rule pane, as shown in Figure 4-6, opens. This pane is divided into two main sections: The top half is the If section that contains criteria; the bottom half is the Then section that contains actions to perform when the criteria are met (again, see Figure 4-6).

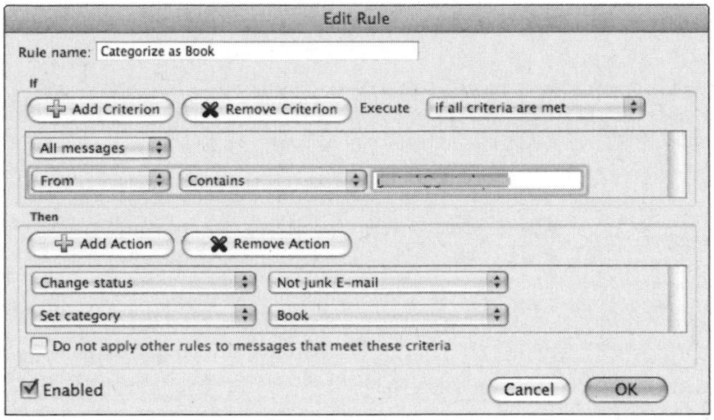

Figure 4-6: Making our first rule.

4. **At the top of the pane, in the Rule Name field, type a name for the new rule.**

   We're calling our example rule Categorize as Book.

   Because you selected a message from the list in Step 1, Entourage prefills the From criterion, so you don't have to change it.

   You can type or paste information into the criteria fields. In Figure 4-6, we've blanked out the coauthor's e-mail address, but you should be able to see the From address of the e-mail you selected if you're following these steps with us.

5. **In the Then section, change the Set Category action to Book.**

   Messages matching the criteria is tagged automatically in the Book category.

6. **Deselect the Do Not Apply Other Rules to Messages That Meet These Criteria check box.**

   We might want to apply additional rules to messages from this coauthor. If we leave the check box selected, Entourage doesn't apply any additional rules to messages from the coauthor.

7. **Make sure that the Enabled check box is selected.**

   If you deselect this box, the rule remains in the list of rules but won't be executed. You may find temporarily disabling a rule handy when you test a sequence of rules. You can run tests to see how your rules are interacting with each other.

You can add and remove criteria from the If section easily with the Add Criterion and Remove Criterion buttons. If you have more than one criterion, be sure to think about the setting you have in the Execute pop-up field. As shown in Figure 4-7, the choices for Execute are

✦ **If Any Criteria Are Met:** The rule executes when one or more criteria are met.

✦ **If All Criteria Are Met:** The rule executes only when all criteria are met.

✦ **Unless Any Criteria Are Met:** The rule executes only when no criteria are met.

✦ **Unless All Criteria Are Met:** The rule executes until all criteria are met.

Figure 4-7:
Triggers for executing a rule.

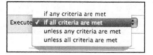

When you make rules, click the pop-up buttons to see what kinds of combinations are possible. Start at the top of the Edit Rule pane and work your way down, moving from left to right in each subsection of the pane. Start with If criteria; then, examine the possible actions. The last action in the pop-up list is to run AppleScript. With that possibility, you can automate anything that's AppleScript-able based on an action from a rule.

While you look at the Edit Rule pane, you can almost read your rule settings as sentences. The rule in Figure 4-6 says, "For the rule named Categorize as Book, if any message is from `mycoauthor@isp.com`, change the message's status so that it's not junk and change the category to Book." Thinking through your rules this way may help you more easily create and manage them.

Keeping on Schedule

Entourage does things all by itself, such as performing send- and receive-mail operations, every so often. If you look in the lower-right corner of the Mail application window, you can even see a message that tells you when the next send-and-receive operation will occur. Although this is the default setting, you can easily change it. Not only that, but you can also create schedules for other Entourage functions.

Choose Tools⇨Schedules to summon a pane similar to what you can see in Figure 4-8. We've scheduled Send & Receive All Mail to run every nine minutes. Naturally, we don't expect you to do the same; we just want to make you aware of how you can adjust these settings.

Figure 4-8:
Viewing existing schedules.

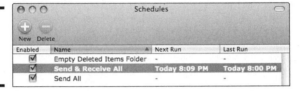

To edit an existing rule, double-click its name, which opens the Edit Schedule pane. You can see our Send & Receive All schedule setting in full detail in Figure 4-9.

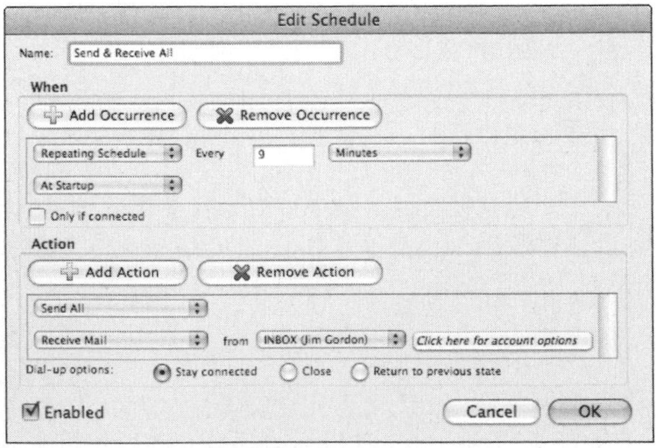

Figure 4-9:
Adjusting the default send-and-receive interval.

Microsoft made the Edit Schedule pane similar in logic and design to the Rules pane: It's divided into When and Action sections. You can have multiple entries in both sections of the pane. Figure 4-10 shows the options for a timed schedule and the actions that are possible. With a timed schedule, you can specify any number of specific times on the quarter-hour. Actions that are available include running AppleScripts and automating publication of Excel Web pages.

Multiple occurrences

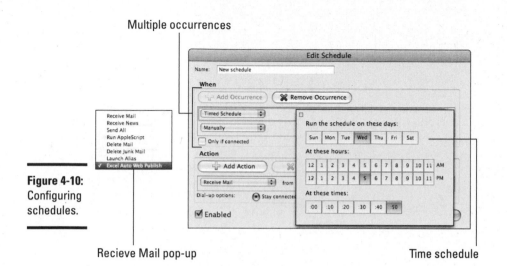

Figure 4-10:
Configuring
schedules.

Recieve Mail pop-up

Time schedule

Connecting to World Communities by Using Newsgroups

Newsgroups are like electronic bulletin boards. Instead of posting paper notes, people can place e-mail messages into public forums that are hosted on newsgroup servers. Microsoft offers free public newsgroups on its newsgroup servers as a service to its customers so that they can communicate with each other regarding topics relating to Microsoft products. You don't have to pay a charge to gain access to these newsgroups, and the support you get is often quick and first-rate.

To protect your e-mail account from getting spam, we recommend that before you post any messages to a newsgroup, you first create a new identity in Mac OS X for the express purpose of connecting to newsgroups. We explain how to create new identities in Chapter 2 of this minibook. If you use a different identity, you can use a From e-mail address that doesn't include your real e-mail address. Unfortunately, spammers scan newsgroups for e-mail addresses, so we highly recommend that you create a fake address to be used with your new identity, as shown in Figure 4-11.

If you want to fetch newsgroups, look for the Microsoft News Server (as shown in Figure 4-12) in the folder list of Entourage's Mail interface. Entourage is preconfigured to connect to the proper server, so you don't have to do any setup.

Figure 4-11:
Protecting
your privacy
in news.

Change e-mail address.

Figure 4-12:
Making the
connection
to Microsoft
News
Server.

Microsoft News Server   Receive

If you don't see the Microsoft News Server option, follow these steps to set up the newsgroups access manually:

1. **Choose Tools⇨Accounts.**

   The Accounts dialog appears.

2. **Select the News tab and click the New button.**

   The Account Setup Assistant, as shown in Figure 4-13, appears.

3. **Select the e-mail identity you want to use for the newsgroups from the Mail Account pop-up menu and type in a descriptive name for this news account in the Organization text box.**

   We typed **Microsoft News Server** (see Figure 4-13).

4. **Click the next arrow button.**

   The Account Setup Assistant screen appears, as shown in Figure 4-14.

5. **Type** msnews.microsoft.com **in the News (NNTP) Server text box and click the next arrow button.**

   The third Account Setup Assistant screen appears.

Figure 4-13:
Creating
a news
account.

Figure 4-14:
Provide
news server
details.

6. **Enter a name for this news account in the text box.**

   We typed **Microsoft News Server** again.

7. **Click the Finish button.**

Now, when you click the Microsoft News Server option in Entourage's folder list, a dialog appears, asking whether you want to receive the list of newsgroups. Click the Receive button. Entourage displays the list of news feeds that are available for Microsoft products. It may take a few minutes if you're using a dialup connection.

After you receive the entire list of newsgroups, you can quickly find the newsgroups directly related to Microsoft Office for Mac (see Figure 4-15). To find them, follow these steps:

1. **Type mac in the Display Newsgroups Containing filter box.**

2. **Highlight the groups, as shown in Figure 4-15, by holding down the ⌘ key while you click each group's name.**

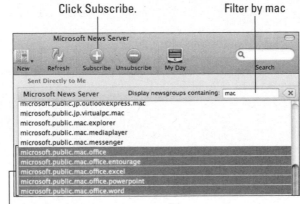

Click Subscribe.

Filter by mac

Figure 4-15:
Selecting
the Office
for Mac
newsgroups.

Select groups.

3. **Click the Subscribe button.**

   A disclosure triangle appears in the left pane next to Microsoft News Server.

4. **Click the disclosure triangle to see the names of the groups to which you've subscribed.**

5. **Click the folder for each group, one by one in succession, as shown in Figure 4-16.**

   While you click, Entourage checks with the news server and downloads the subjects within each news feed. How fast this happens depends on your Internet connection speed. Each group name becomes bold, and the number of unread messages appears. You can see the subjects fill in.

By default, Entourage displays the messages within each group by order of the date and time they were posted to the newsgroup. You may need to change that setting to make sense of the news feed. Follow these steps:

1. **At the top of the column that contains all the subjects, click the header Arrange By: Sent.**

   The pop-up menu, as shown in Figure 4-16, opens.

2. **Choose Edit Custom Arrangements.**

   An empty Custom Arrangements pane appears.

3. **Click the New button, as shown in Figure 4-17.**

Click the triangle.　　　　　Click Arrange By.

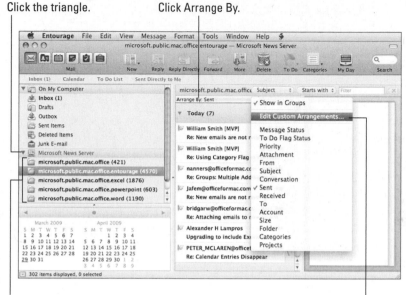

Figure 4-16:
Filling in the
subjects.

Click each group.　　　　　　　Choose Edit Custom Arrangements.

Figure 4-17:
Making
a custom
arrange-
ment
for your
newsgroup
list.

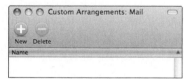

The Edit Custom Arrangements pane appears, as shown in Figure 4-18.

4. **Enter the settings, as shown in Figure 4-18, and then click OK.**

   You want to make a custom arrangement that displays the messages so that they're grouped by topic and ordered with the newest messages appearing at the top of each group.

5. **Click OK to close the Edit Custom Arrangements pane.**

   The normal Entourage interface reappears.

6. **Click the Arrange By: Sent header again.**

   This time, your new custom arrangement appears near the top of the list of choices, as shown in Figure 4-19.

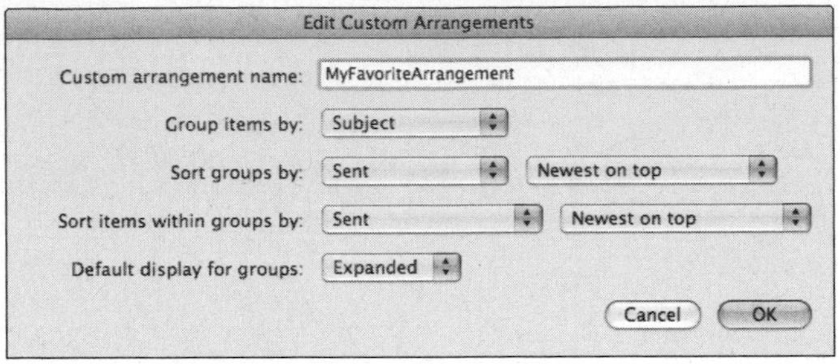

Figure 4-18:
Setting up
a custom
arrangement.

7. **Select your custom arrangement from the list.**

   Entourage then groups and sorts all the messages to follow your custom arrangement, and the column header changes to the name that you gave to your custom arrangement. When you're done, the interface looks similar to Figure 4-20 (we intentionally obscured the e-mail addresses in the figure).

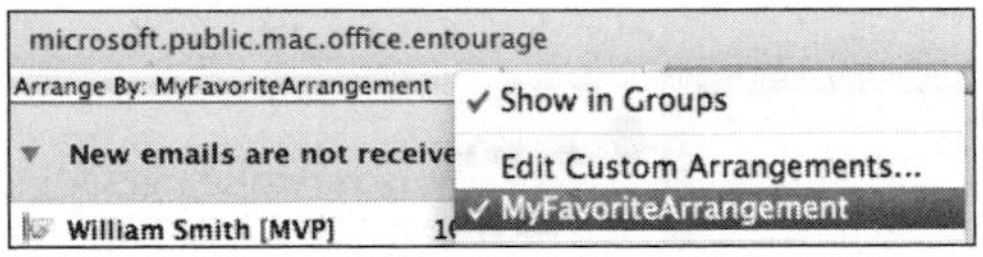

Figure 4-19:
Choosing
your new
custom
arrangement.

8. **To refresh the message lists, click each newsgroup name in succession.**

   Now that you have a fully operational news window, you can follow the message threads, and you can safely post your own replies to answer questions. You can also create your own, new subject threads. Use the Entourage Message menu to mark all messages as read. When you come back to Entourage newsgroups, click the triangle next to Microsoft News Server twice to refresh the contents of the newsgroups. The new messages are highlighted automatically for you. The View menu lets you limit the display to unread messages.

   Before you start a new subject, we suggest that you search Google Groups to make sure that your question hasn't already been answered. You can find Google Groups at http://groups.google.com.

   When you search Google Groups, you can use keywords such as Word, Excel, PowerPoint, and Entourage, coupled with Mac and any search terms you think may help you find information about the topic you're interested in.

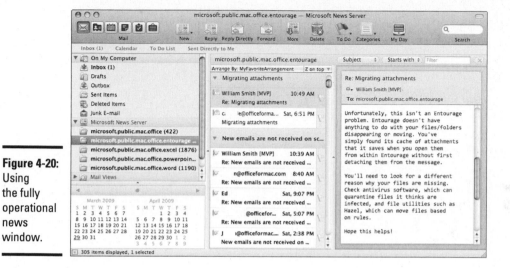

Figure 4-20:
Using
the fully
operational
news
window.

Chapter 5: Personalizing Your PIM

*I*n Entourage, *PIM* stands for *Personal Information Manager.* PIM is the feature that lets you keep track of the people and organizations that are most important in your life. Entourage calls its PIM application the Entourage Address Book. Other programs call it Contacts or Contact Manager. In the Address Book, you keep personal information about people and businesses, and store the kind of private information about contacts that doesn't appear on their Facebook, LinkedIn, or MySpace pages, such as phone numbers and what you gave them on their birthday.

Perusing the Address Book Interface

To get to the Entourage Address Book, just click the Address Book button on the Standard toolbar while you're using any Entourage application. The Address Book layout is similar to the layout of the Entourage Mail application (which we talk about in Chapter 3 of this minibook), as shown in Figure 5-1. Menus appear across the top, and each window has its own toolbar. The main view has a pane on the left that lets you choose from your Address Book, LDAP (we talk about LDAP in the section, "Using LDAP Directory Services," later in this chapter), customized mail views, and the handy little calendar. You can resize the panes by dragging the dividers that separate them.

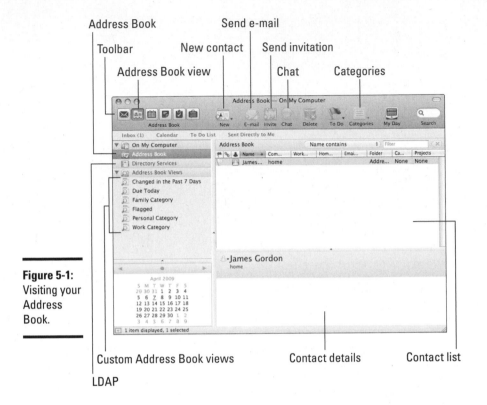

Address Book

Toolbar

Address Book view

Send e-mail

New contact

Send invitation

Chat

Categories

Figure 5-1:
Visiting your
Address
Book.

Custom Address Book views

LDAP

Contact details

Contact list

Meeting Yourself

The first time you open Address Book, only one contact appears in your contacts list. As it turns out, that particular contact is very special. Only one contact can be what Entourage calls the Me contact. You can think of the Me contact as the owner of all the other contacts and groups of contacts in the Address Book.

Filling in the information for the Me contact is a great way to get started building your contact list. The Me contact has a special purple icon. Double-click the Me contact in the list to open the contact (see Figure 5-2). Your Me contact opens on an almost empty Summary tab. You need to go through each of the tabs and fill in the blanks with your own information. (You can skip the Certificates tab until someone sends you a digitally signed message.)

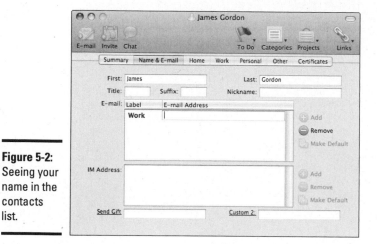

Figure 5-2:
Seeing your
name in the
contacts
list.

Adding Friends and Associates

After you fill in your own contact information for the Me contact (as we describe in the preceding section), start adding contacts. Here are the two most common ways:

✦ **Add a contact from a mail message.** Select a mail message in Entourage Mail and choose Message➪Add to Address Book. Alternatively, you can right-click or Control-click a message and select Add to Address Book from the pop-up menu that appears. The keyboard shortcut to add a contact is Alt-⌘-C. Using any of these three methods adds a new contact so that you can begin filling in the contact's information.

✦ **Add a contact while using the Address Book.** If you click the New button on the Standard toolbar, Entourage gets you started with a new contact by using an abridged Create Contact form for inputting contact information, as shown in Figure 5-3. You can display the full input screen (as shown in Figure 5-2) by clicking the More button at the bottom of the abridged version.

When you get to the Personal tab of the full version of the Create Contact form, you don't necessarily have to add a picture of your contact to the Address Book. You can drag clip art or another picture into the pane. Whatever picture you use appears in the message window whenever you receive a message from that contact.

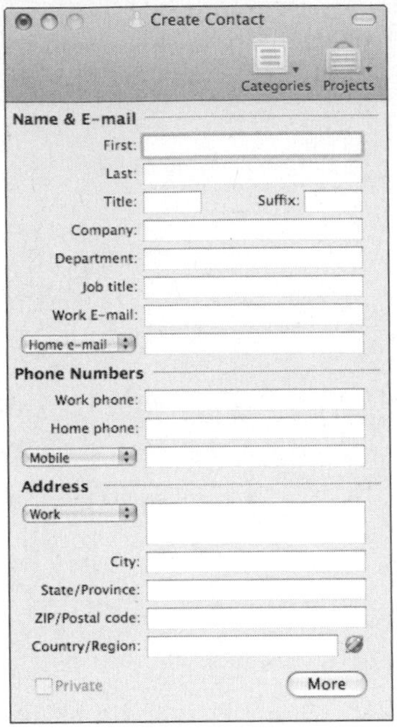

Figure 5-3:
Starting
with basic
contact
information.

Managing Your Contacts

While you add contacts, your contacts list grows (see Figure 5-4). The more contacts you add, the more interesting this feature becomes. You can decide what information to display by right-clicking or Control-clicking any of the column headings. An enormous pop-up menu appears. Selected items appear as headers in the message list. Select a header name in the menu to turn that header on in the message list. Select the same header name a second time in the menu to turn it off in the message list. To place entries in your list in order, click the column header you want to use for ordering the entries. A second click reverses the order. In the Name Contains field, you can enter keywords to filter the list of your contacts. The Name Contains pop-up menu has additional filtering choices.

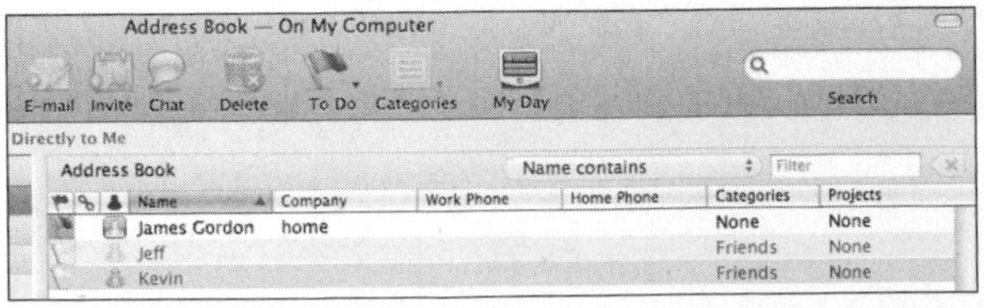

Figure 5-4:
Setting up
the contacts
list.

If you have Microsoft Messenger service running, when a contact is available for chat, his icon turns blue. Select that contact in the list to make the Chat button on the Standard toolbar light up. Click that button to start a messenger chat session, if you want.

Right-click or Control-click a contact to open a pop-up menu that contains many useful options, as shown in Figure 5-5.

Figure 5-5:
Exploring
the right-
click options
of a contact.

Printing contacts

When you right-click or Control-click a contact and choose Print from the pop-up menu that appears (as shown in Figure 5-5), or if you choose File➪Print, a very special Print options screen opens, as shown in Figure 5-6. You have various options available to you.

Fans of Franklin Covey and Day Timers take note! You can print your contacts so that they fit your contact books, complete with marks for the proper holes to punch in the paper.

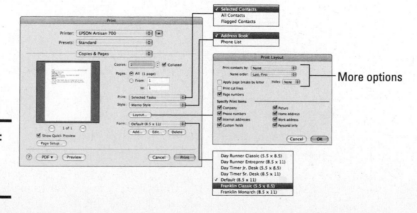

Figure 5-6:
Printing
your
contacts.

Finding contacts

You can search your contacts list in a variety of ways. We think the most efficient is to simply press ⌘-F to open the Find pane, as shown in Figure 5-7. Clicking the More Options button enables you to be a bit more specific about what you want in your search.

If you can't see the dialog that we show in Figure 5-7, Entourage is using *Spotlight* (the search technology built inside Mac OS X), rather than its own search options. To make Entourage use its own search, choose Entourage➪Preferences and select the Spotlight option in the left pane of the Entourage Preferences dialog that appears. Then, deselect both the check boxes and click OK. Want to restore Spotlight as the search engine in Entourage? Just reverse the process!

Figure 5-7: Digging through your contacts list.

Creating a custom view for a contact

When you conduct a contacts search (as we describe in the preceding section), the result of your search is presented in a Search Results pane (see Figure 5-8). Among the buttons on the Search Results toolbar is Save Search. Click this button to open the Edit Custom View pane, also shown in Figure 5-8. Enter a name for the view in the Name field, and then click the OK button. The new view is added to the Custom Views section of the main Address Book window of Entourage.

Grouping contacts

You can easily create groups of contacts. If you create a group, you can send a message to the entire group by entering the name of the group when addressing an e-mail or invitation, instead of having to add people to an address block individually. Follow these steps to create a group of contacts:

1. **Open the Entourage Address Book and click the small triangle to the right of the New button on the Standard toolbar in the main window.**

   The pop-up menu, as shown in Figure 5-9, opens.

2. **Choose Group.**

   The Group Manager opens.

Click to get the Edit Custom View dialog.

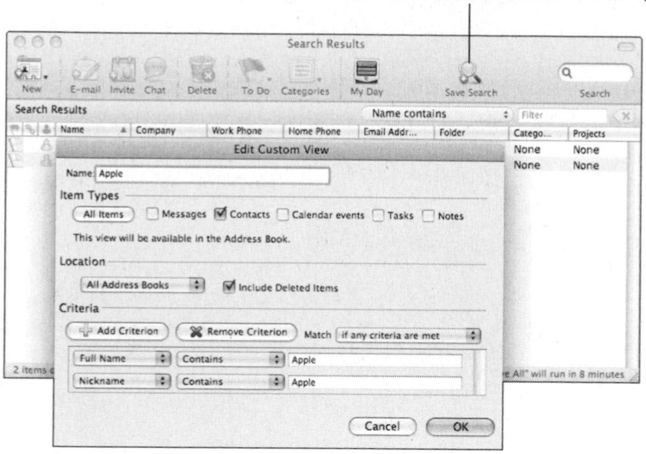

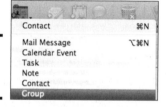

Figure 5-8:
Creating a
custom view
based on
a contact
search.

Figure 5-9:
Starting a
new group.

3. **Type a name for the group in the Group Name field and then start adding members.**

   It's good etiquette to select the Don't Show Addresses When Sending to Group check box (see Figure 5-10). You have two easy ways to add contacts to a group:

   • Click the Add button on the Group Manager's toolbar. Then, type the name of each contact you want to add to the group.

   • Drag contacts from the contacts list into the Group Manager.

Figure 5-10:
Adding
contacts to
a group.

Exporting contacts

In the Export Wizard (which you can access by choosing File⇨Export Wizard), you can click the Save button to save your contacts as a Comma Separated Values (.csv) file, which creates a file that Excel can open (see Figure 5-11). Additionally, you can export individual contacts as vCard files by dragging them from the Address Book into Finder.

Figure 5-11: Exporting contacts as a .csv file.

Mapping contacts

When you have a contact open, look for little buttons to click. For example, you can get directions to a contact, or even instantly get a map of a contact's work or home address, depending on which tab you select. In Figure 5-12, we clicked the button to the right of the address block to open the pop-up menu that lets us accomplish these feats.

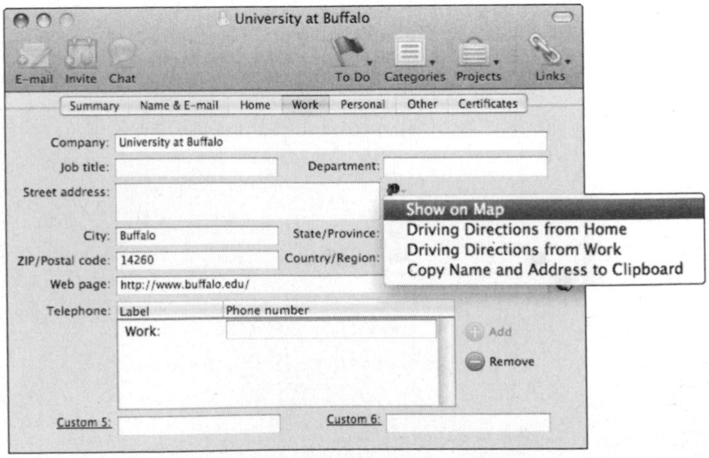

Figure 5-12: Driving to a contact.

Creating custom fields

Scattered throughout each contact, you can find some fields that have custom labels on them. You can rename these fields and use them for any kind of data about your contacts that you want. On the Other tab, you can even customize two fields specifically related to dates for a contact.

To name (or rename) a custom field, just click the existing name. A small Edit Custom Label dialog appears (see Figure 5-13). This dialog allows you to type a new name for the field.

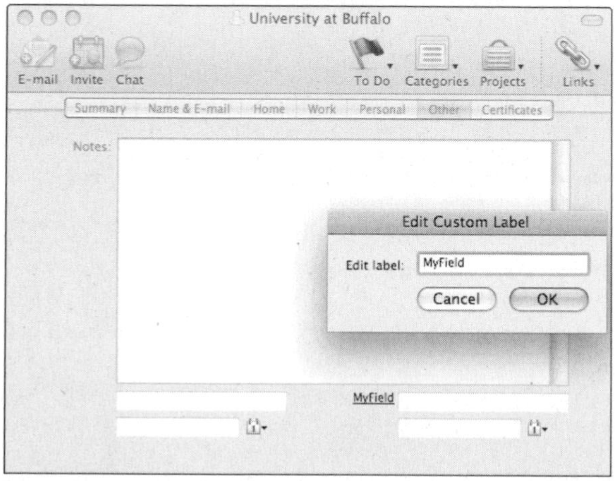

Figure 5-13:
Naming
a custom
field.

Deleting contacts

Sadly, at times, you must delete a contact. To delete an existing contact, simply select the contact in the contacts list, and then click the Delete button on the toolbar or press the Delete key.

Addressing Mail and Invitations

Time to discuss the various ways of entering addresses into address blocks. Keep in mind that Chapters 1 through 4 of this minibook offer additional information on addressing messages.

Sending from the Address Book

All the windows in Address Book that show contacts allow you to select one or more contacts. You can use Mac OS X standard selection methods. Hold down the ⌘ key while you click individual names to send to multiple recipients. After you make your selection(s), click either the E-Mail button or the Invitation button on the toolbar to open a preaddressed message.

Sending a new message or invitation

You can very easily send a message or invitation. Whenever you're in Entourage, you can start a new message or invitation from the File menu and various New buttons in the interface. When you do that, you're presented with a message header that has no addresses in it.

Addressing automatically

Your instinct to start typing either the intended recipient's name or e-mail address into the heading fields is correct. While you type, Entourage searches through all the following options, and it instantly offers to auto-complete the address for you:

✦ Names and addresses stored in your Address Book

✦ The most recent 300 or so sent or received names and addresses

✦ Group names that you've created in your Address Book

✦ Directory services (if you've configured one or more directory services)

✦ Exchange directory (if you're on a Microsoft Exchange server)

Entourage has a lot of e-mail names and addresses to check on the fly, yet it does this check so fast you don't even notice. It's truly amazing. The auto-complete results appear in a special drop-down list that has matching results grouped by their source (see Figure 5-14). The top group shows addresses from your contacts, groups, and recently received and sent e-mail addresses. The lower group shows matches from directory services. Watch while the group results become more focused with each letter that you type.

Contacts from Address Book

Type here.

Figure 5-14: Watching Entourage dazzle you with auto-complete.

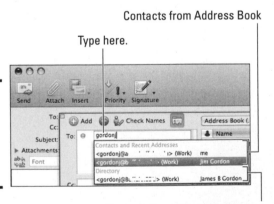

Contacts from Directory Services

But what if you can't remember the name or e-mail address of a contact, even enough for auto-complete? Entourage comes to the rescue! To the right of the input field, you can use the Address Book lookup to search your Address Book right in the same box that you use to address messages. You can even search directory services from the same pane. Not only that; after you find the contact you're looking for, you can simply drag the contact into the address field or double-click names to add them to an address field! Figure 5-15 shows the Address Book lookup in action.

Choose source

Expand/Hide Address Book   Enter search term

Figure 5-15:
Searching
the Address
Book and
directory
while
addressing
a message.

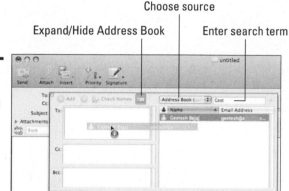

Not only can you drag contacts into the address block, but you can also drag them into the general e-mail message area. If you do, Entourage turns the contact information into a vCard and attaches it to the mail message. A *vCard* is like an electronic calling card. You can send and receive vCards as a method to share contacts. If you receive a message that has a vCard attached, you can add the contact to your Address Book by double-clicking the vCard attachment.

Using address blocks

In every address area, you can choose from three blocks. Find out how each one works so that you don't accidentally violate someone's privacy:

✦ **To:** Every contact added to the To block receives your message, and each recipient can see the name and address of all the To and CC recipients.

✦ **CC (carbon copy):** Every contact added to the CC block receives your message, and each recipient can see the name and address of all the To and CC recipients.

✦ **BCC (blind carbon copy):** Every contact added to the BCC block receives your message. Recipients added to BCC aren't visible to other recipients.

Using LDAP Directory Services

Entourage is very smart when it comes to using an Internet standard called *LDAP* (Lightweight Directory Access Protocol, in case you're curious). Many organizations put their members into LDAP address books, which Entourage can search. Think of LDAP as an online, accessible equivalent of a telephone directory — except that an LDAP can store more information than names and telephone numbers. Of course, large businesses typically use LDAP, not home users.

Before you can use an LDAP service, you need to know what settings to use — your LDAP server administrator supplies those settings. If you don't know whether your organization has LDAP support, contact your help desk or IT department. Setting up LDAP in Entourage is worth the small bother if your organization offers LDAP.

Setting up an LDAP account

To enable a directory service, choose Tools⇨Accounts. In the Accounts pane, click the Directory Service tab, and then click the New button to open the Account Setup Assistant (see Figure 5-16). Usually, you have to click the Configure Account Manually button because LDAP servers often have special settings that need to be entered. See Figure 5-17 for a look at the manual settings.

Figure 5-16: Using the Setup Assistant to create an LDAP account.

Using directory services

After you set up an LDAP directory service, Entourage starts using it automatically to offer address suggestions when you address e-mail messages. You can also search the LDAP directory directly from within Entourage by following these steps (see Figure 5-18):

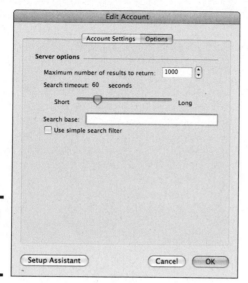

Figure 5-17:
Configuring
LDAP
manually.

1. **In the folder list, click the name of the directory service you want to search.**

2. **Click Search Criteria and select a category of criteria to use for searching the directory database from the pop-up menu that appears.**

3. **Enter a directory search term.**

   If you pause even for a moment, you might find that Entourage may have retrieved too many records, so you may have to type quickly in this field.

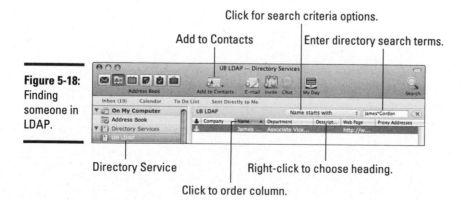

Figure 5-18:
Finding
someone in
LDAP.

Click for search criteria options.

Add to Contacts

Enter directory search terms.

Directory Service

Right-click to choose heading.

Click to order column.

Entourage creates a list of matching entries from the directory server. Like with other windows, you can right-click or Control-click column headers to find options that turn headers on and off. Click a header to order a column based on that header.

Use an asterisk (*) as a wild card when doing directory searches. If you don't know exactly how someone's name was entered into a directory, you can use an asterisk to make your search a little easier. For example, use only parts of a name, such as `FirstName*LastName`. This way, you won't have to worry about not finding names that have middle initials or hyphenated names. You can use the asterisk in the beginning, middle, or end of a search string.

Chapter 6: Crafting Your Calendar

In This Chapter

✔ Peeking at the Calendar interface

✔ Going on a holiday

✔ Working with events

✔ Using Calendar to send and receive invitations

✔ Searching and printing your Calendar

✔ Exchanging Calendars with others

C locks, dates, and calendars are items we almost always take for granted, yet they're amazingly intricate timekeepers that have a significant place in our daily lives. Fortunately, Entourage makes it easy for you to stay organized. Even if you travel, Entourage can keep your appointments straight while you go from one time zone to another. Do you live in a Daylight Saving Time area? No problem; let Entourage take care of those small details!

We start this chapter with a completely blank Calendar, just like you see the first time you open the Entourage Calendar application. Then, you can see how easily you can fill in events and manage your time. Using Entourage Calendar is quick, easy, and logical. In fact, it wouldn't surprise us that after you incorporate using your Entourage Calendar into your everyday activities, you'll be wondering how you got along without it.

Taking a Look at the Interface

When you click the Calendar button on Entourage's Standard toolbar for the first time, your Calendar is a blank slate, ready for you to start filling it. You find plenty of different views to the Calendar. We decided to click the Month button of the Calendar Standard toolbar for Figure 6-1. You can click the Browse buttons to switch from one month to another, and you can click the View Date button to go to any specific date in another month. The views get more interesting after you add some events.

You can modify the way the interface looks considerably by choosing Calendar➪List. The List view shows only your existing Calendar events, so it could be empty if you haven't already made some. Also, you can display the To Do List in the same window as the Calendar by choosing Calendar➪To Do List.

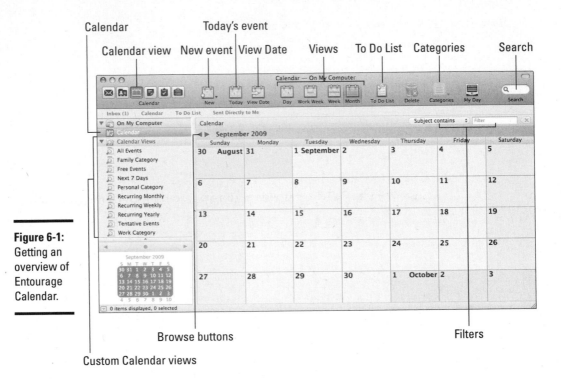

Calendar

Calendar view New event View Date Views To Do List Categories Search

Today's event

Figure 6-1:
Getting an
overview of
Entourage
Calendar.

Browse buttons

Filters

Custom Calendar views

Going on Holiday

Our Calendar definitely needs to have some events added to it. It's so bare!
We put holidays into the Calendar as a way to get started. Entourage has an
Import Wizard that comes to our aid. To use it, follow these steps:

1. **Choose File⇨Import.**

Step 1 of the Import Wizard, as shown in Figure 6-2, opens.

Step 1

Step 2

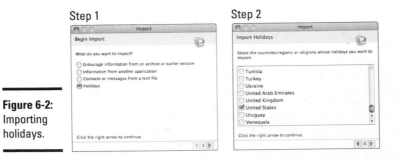

Figure 6-2:
Importing
holidays.

2. **Select the Holidays option.**

3. **Click the right arrow to advance to the next step.**

4. **In Step 2 of the wizard, also shown in Figure 6-2, select one or more countries or religions to add their holidays to the Calendar.**

   In our example, we chose the following groups of holidays:

   - India (for Geetesh)
   - United States (for Jim)
   - Canada (for Jim because he lives 15 minutes from Canada)
   - Christian Religious Holidays (for you, so that we can let you know that it's one of the choices)

5. **Click the right arrow to continue.**

6. **Click OK on the confirmation message and click the Finish button to exit the wizard.**

One of the benefits of having friends in different countries is that you get to celebrate more holidays!

Adding Calendar Events

You can add events to your Calendar by using several options. We start with the ways you can initiate Calendar events. In the section, "Enhancing an Event," later in this chapter, we discuss ways that you can share events with other people.

Say that you have an event that you need to add to your Calendar. For example, if you plan to attend a committee meeting on Friday, November 6 at 9:00 a.m., you can add it to your Calendar. To add events to your Calendar, follow these steps:

1. **For the purpose of this exercise, choose an event date several months in the future.**

   To quickly advance to a future (or past) date, click the View Date button on the Calendar's Standard toolbar.

   If your event is going to occur in the timeframe that already appears in the Calendar window, you can skip directly to Step 3 and start there.

2. **Click the little button next to the input field to choose a date from the pop-up calendar, as shown in Figure 6-3, or type a date into the field. Then, click OK to show that date in the Calendar.**

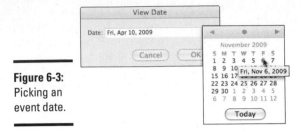

Figure 6-3:
Picking an
event date.

3. **Open the New Event pane (as shown in Figure 6-4).**

To open this pane, do either of the following:

- If you're in Month, Week, or Work Week view, double-click the date of the event.

- If you're in Day view, double-click in the day's view at the time of the event.

Set Reminders

Event details

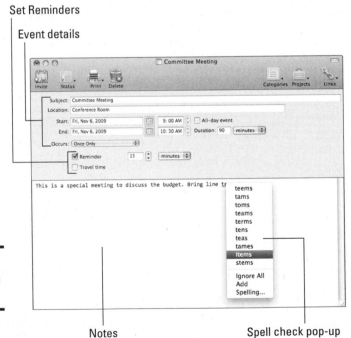

Figure 6-4:
Setting up a
meeting.

Notes   Spell check pop-up

While you add event details, when you type the subject into the New Event pane, the subject becomes the title of the pane. Also, when you enter event dates and times, you can either type your information into the fields or use the buttons to the right of the fields to select from pop-up menus.

If you want a little reminder to appear on your screen before the event, select the Reminder check box and then set the amount of time you want to be reminded prior the event. You can add travel time, if need be. We go into detail about reminders in Chapter 7 of this minibook.

Entering notes about the event is always a good thing. As you can see from Figure 6-4, you can right-click or Control-click words that have red underlines to get the spell checker to offer suggestions in a pop-up menu — just like it does in Word 2008!

When you finish adjusting the event settings and making entries, click the red Close button or use the ⌘-W keyboard shortcut. Closing the window signifies that you're done editing and ready to have Entourage add the event to the Calendar. When you close the New Event window, you receive one of those pesky "Are you sure?" type of prompts, as shown in Figure 6-5. Select the Always Save Changes without Asking check box if you find this sort of prompt annoying. Congratulations! You have now successfully saved the event to your Calendar.

Figure 6-5:
Ending
a pesky
prompt.

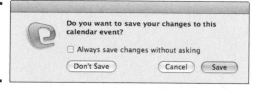

You can add events by simply typing in the Entourage Calendar view. Just click a time and start typing. You can adjust the time of your new event (or any other event) by dragging the event's border in the Calendar. Dragging to move an event seems to work best in Day, Week, and Work Week views. If you have a large monitor, it might work fine in Month view, as well.

Enhancing an Event

As luck would have it, your boss decided that you're now in charge of the budget meeting, and you need to invite the committee members to attend. Not only that; rather than just one meeting, you need to hold a meeting each Friday for three consecutive weeks. Entourage makes this task easy! Simply open the existing event in your Calendar, modify the event, invite the committee, and then save the changes. The following sections detail what you need to do.

Opening an existing event

To edit your event, reopen the event's window — just double-click the event in the Calendar.

Creating a recurring event

When you saved the meeting the first time, you set the event to occur just once, which is Entourage's default setting for Calendar events. Refer to Figure 6-4 — the Occurs setting is Once Only. You need to change that setting. To let Entourage know that this event occurs more than once, click the pop-up button next to the Occurs field. The choices offered by the pop-up menu are shown in Figure 6-6.

Figure 6-6:
Choosing a recurring schedule.

The options offered are intuitive, and you can remember them for the future. If they work for you, that's great. In a situation where none of these options may be exactly what you're looking for, you need more options, so choose Custom on the pop-up menu. The Recurring Event window, as shown in Figure 6-7, opens so that you can establish a customized event schedule.

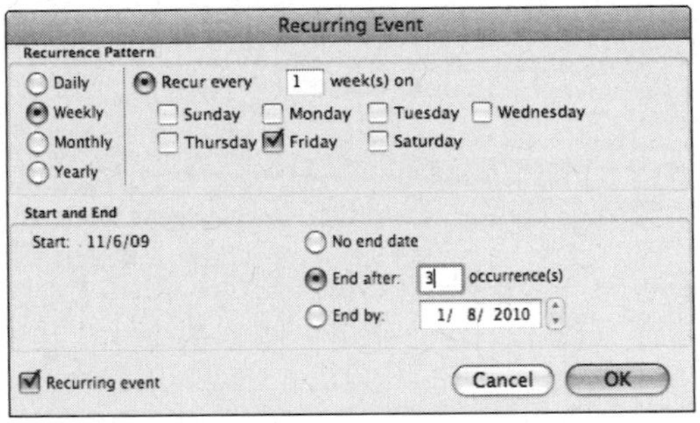

Figure 6-7:
Setting a recurring event.

You can find millions of possible combinations in the Recurring Event pane, but the settings that work for our particular event are illustrated in Figure 6-7. The arrangement is logical from left to right and top to bottom within the Recurring Event pane. When you choose the Daily, Weekly, Monthly, or Yearly options in the Recurrence Pattern section, the entire pane's options are updated to offer appropriate choices for each pattern.

Inviting others to an event

You might not expect this, but Entourage can assist you with your manners. You should follow a certain protocol to be polite when sending invitations. You, as the event organizer, create an event and then invite potential attendees.

Each attendee receives an invitation. If the invitee so desires, she can accept your invitation. What's nice is that all this happens electronically, without a lot of fuss.

It's time to send invitations to the committee members for your budget meetings. To get the invitations rolling, in the New Event pane (refer to Figure 6-4), click the Invite button on the event's toolbar. Entourage opens the Address block field so that you can invite the committee members. In Figure 6-8, we created a Budget Committee group, so we don't have to enter each person individually. If you want to create your own group, instead of adding individual contacts, you can click the Cancel Invite button to cancel the invitation (see Figure 6-8). We explain how to create groups in Chapter 5 of this minibook.

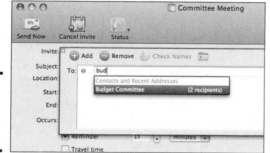

Figure 6-8:
Sending (or canceling) invitations.

After you add invitees to an event, you can then add attachments to the invitation. These can be the same kinds of attachments that you'd send with an e-mail message. In this example, you might want to attach documents that you plan to discuss at the meeting. Before you can add attachments, you need to click the small disclosure triangle next to Attachments in the Calendar event, as shown in Figure 6-9.

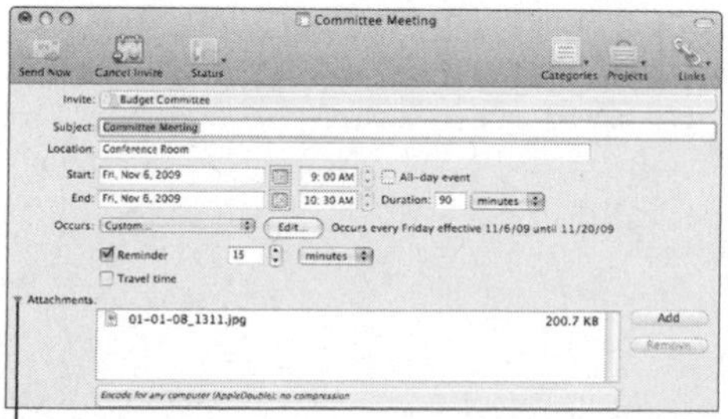

Figure 6-9:
Adding attachments to an invitation.

Click triangle.

Thereafter, click the Add button at the bottom of this pane to include an attachment. Clicking the Send Now button on the toolbar sends your invitations via e-mail to the committee members. We explain what happens after you send the invitations in the section, "Receiving Acceptances and Rejections," later in this chapter. You might want to do some additional things while still in the meeting window.

Changing your status

You can change your status by clicking the Status button on the toolbar. For the time being, if you're not sure whether everyone who was invited can attend, set your status to Tentative. When the plans are finalized, you can change your status to Busy or Out of Office (see Figure 6-10).

Figure 6-10:
Changing
your status.

Assigning categories

When you click the Categories button, you can assign categories to your event. In Chapter 3 of this minibook, we explain how to work with categories. By using the Categories button, when you assign categories to a Calendar event, the category assignments aren't transmitted with invitations.

Linking to other things

Although you usually have a variety of activities going on in Entourage, you don't have much to look at in the Links pane. After you reach a certain level of activity, you'll find some interesting functions when you click the Links button. In this case, you might have a report that you're planning to present at the meeting. You can link the event to that report or to any other existing file, as shown in Figure 6-11. Just click the To Existing button on the Links toolbar.

Figure 6-11:
Linking an
event to a
file.

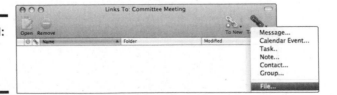

Receiving Invitations

In the section, "Inviting others to an event," earlier in this chapter, you sent event invitations to committee members. Now, you can see what your invitees see in Entourage when they receive invitations. When you receive an invitation in Entourage Mail, you open it the same way that you open any other Mail message. Double-click an invitation to open it in its own window, as shown in Figure 6-12. As you can see from the figure, Entourage is very smart when it comes to handling invitations. Because Entourage knows this message is an invitation, the toolbar offers various options that specifically deal with invitations. Immediately below the toolbar, you can see a notification advising you that you haven't yet acted on this invitation.

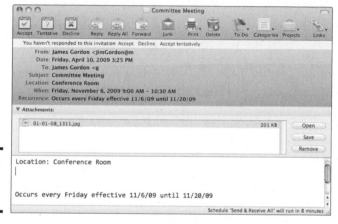

Figure 6-12:
Opening an
invitation.

Accepting an invitation

If a recipient elects to accept the meeting, he clicks the Accept button on the invitation's toolbar. Entourage then offers to alert the sender of the invitation that the invitee plans to attend (see Figure 6-13).

Figure 6-13:
Deciding
on an
acceptance
response
to the
organizer.

Accepting with comments

In this example, we chose to accept the invitation and to send comments along with our acceptance. Because we chose this option, Entourage opens a new window that lets us send additional information in a special Accepted mail message, as shown in Figure 6-14.

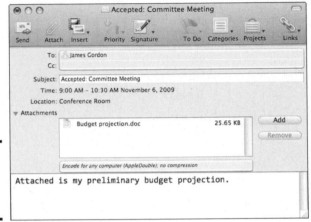

Figure 6-14:
Accepting
with
comments.

Click the Send button to send your reply with comments. When the event's organizer receives this reply, the organizer's copy of Entourage automatically tabulates the replies and builds a list of attendees. Entourage also adds the event to the invitee's Entourage Calendar, and the invitee's status is set to Busy for the period used by the event.

Accepting without comments

This option is basically the same as Accepting with Comments, except you don't send comments along with the reply. If you select this option, a special acceptance e-mail message is sent to the event's organizer indicating you can attend.

Accepting with no response

If an invitee chooses this option, Entourage adds the event to the invitee's Calendar, and the invitee's status for the period is changed to Busy. However, the event organizer receives no response.

Tentatively accepting an invitation

An invitee can accept an invitation tentatively by clicking the Tentative button on the toolbar (refer back to Figure 6-12). The mechanics work the same as with a full acceptance (see the section, "Accepting an invitation," earlier in this chapter), except the invitee's status flag is set to Tentative, rather than Busy, for the event.

Declining an invitation

When an invitee declines an invitation by clicking the Decline button on the toolbar (refer to Figure 6-12), the event isn't added to the invitee's Calendar. Entourage offers the same three response options to those who decline as it does to those who accept (see Figure 6-15), which we talk about in the section, "Accepting an invitation," earlier in this chapter.

Figure 6-15:
Options for
declining an
invitation.

Entourage can work with invites you receive from others who use a program other than Entourage. Outlook for Windows users have the same options available for sending and receiving invites as Entourage users, and generally, you can work similarly with invites from other non-Microsoft programs, such as Apple Mail, and even open source programs, such as Thunderbird and Sunbird.

Receiving Acceptances and Rejections

When the event organizer receives an acceptance or rejection notice, Entourage places a notification below the toolbar of the invitee's response. In this example, we accepted the invitation. As shown in Figure 6-16, the organizer can click the Show Attendee Status link to display a list of the attendees and their responses. The same link also appears in the event's window if the organizer opens it in a Calendar view.

Figure 6-16:
Opening an
invitation
response.

Although the Attendee Status window is on the plain side, it has a little secret. The event organizer has some extra control, so if you're the event organizer, you can use this control in case someone changes her mind — and tells you without using an Accept or Reject Calendar message. People often accept an invitation over the phone, or even in the office corridor! You need to input that acceptance into Entourage. Just click the response from an attendee (even if she hasn't given a response yet), and manually change the response. Even though the responses don't look like buttons, they turn into buttons after you click them (see Figure 6-17).

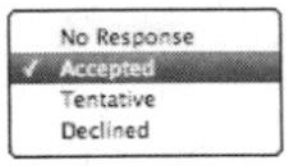

Figure 6-17:
Changing
a response
manually.

Changing Your Mind

Things change. Event invitees and organizers can change their minds about events, and Entourage is very accommodating about these changes. Whether you're the organizer or an invitee, when you double-click an existing event in the Calendar, the event window opens. You can make changes to the event or even delete it.

If the organizer of an event that already has invitees makes changes to that event, when he saves the changes, Entourage asks whether to send an update to the invitees.

When an invitee makes changes to an event in his own Calendar and saves those changes, Entourage cautions the invitee that his changes aren't going to affect the organizer's event. The only thing an invitee can change is his attendance response.

If you change your mind about the date you want to hold an event but all other aspects of the event remain the same, look at your Calendar in Month view, where you can drag events from one day to another. You can drag events in other views to change event times without having to open the event window. You can copy events by holding down the Option key while you drag an event in the interface.

Finding and Searching

After you have several years' worth of Calendar events under your belt, finding specific events might be a challenge. Your events likely accumulate, and at times, you might want to quickly search through all your Calendar events to find some particular piece of information.

Conducting a search

No matter which of the many Calendar views you're using, you can search for Calendar events by taking the following actions:

1. **Enter a broad search term in the Entourage Search field (in the upper-right corner of the Entourage window, as shown in Figure 6-18).**

In this example, search the Holiday category. In a flash, Entourage changes the interface so that you can refine your search.

Figure 6-18:
Beginning a
search.

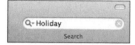

2. **Click the round plus sign (+) next to the Save button if you want to expand the search criteria, as shown in Figure 6-19.**

Click here.

Figure 6-19:
Revealing
additional
search
criteria.

The expanded search feature becomes available, as shown in Figure 6-20, where you can add search criteria and fine-tune your search.

Fine-tune criteria.   Add search criteria.

Figure 6-20:
Fine-tuning
a calendar
search.

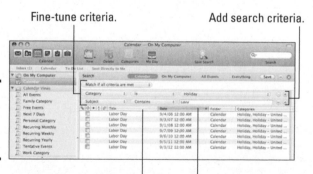

Right-click to select headings.   Click to organize results.

Saving a custom Calendar view

Having gone to all the trouble of setting up this elaborate search, you can save it so that you can have it available instantly as a Calendar view in the folder list of the Calendar window. Saving the search is a cinch. Just click the Save button in the band above your custom search, as shown in Figure 6-21.

Figure 6-21:
Saving a search as a Calendar view.

Entourage prompts you to give your search a name in the Name field. After you enter a name for your search, it appears in the list of Calendar views in the folder list of the Calendar window, as shown in Figure 6-22.

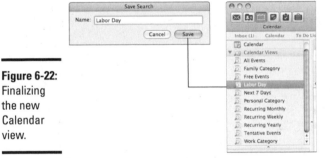

Figure 6-22:
Finalizing the new Calendar view.

Using Special Exchange Features

Entourage has a very special Calendar-sharing capability that Microsoft Exchange users can utilize. Exchange allows users to look at each other's Calendars, which makes scheduling events a whole lot easier. It also enables rumormongers to make guesses about office trysts. Don't assume that just because Tom and Mary have the same time blocked off every day that some hanky-panky is going on! Look for lipstick and other telltale signs. Of course, we're just kidding, but we do want to raise your awareness that privacy issues are involved in sharing Calendars. Entourage Help has a lot of detail about how to take advantage of these special Exchange features — in a responsible way!

Sharing Calendars and other items

You can find step-by-step instructions for sharing your Calendar, address book, and e-mail folder by searching Entourage Help for the *share calendar,* as shown in Figure 6-23.

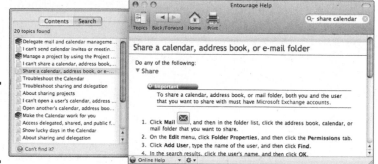

Figure 6-23:
Sharing in
Microsoft
Exchange.

Delegating authority

Microsoft Entourage provides free, comprehensive, online courses to help those who want to use delegation, the global Address Book, and other advanced topics related to using Entourage with Microsoft Exchange. To find the courses, search for *delegate* in Microsoft Help. In the list of results, you can find at least two free courses of interest. We urge you to take these courses if you want to discover more about the following (see Figure 6-24):

✦ Delegating Mail and Calendar management to others

✦ Finding out about Entourage and Exchange as powerful partners

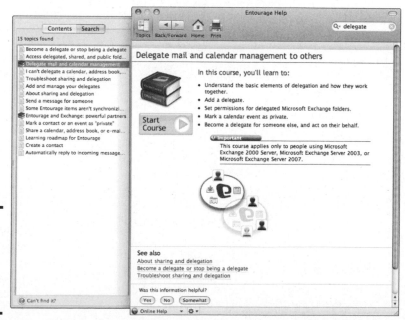

Figure 6-24:
Taking a
free online
course
about
Exchange.

Free Exchange for higher education

For higher-education institutions, at the time of this writing, Microsoft is offering no-charge exchange hosting via its Live@edu program in a head-to-head challenge to Google — and Google's promoting its Gmail product. If you're in higher education, compare the features of these and other in-the-cloud hosted services before switching from your current setup. Consider whether Microsoft and/or Google reserve the right to scan user content within their servers for the purpose of targeting ads either directly or indirectly, such as through DoubleClick or other partners. How secure is the cloud against private and government spying and prying, both foreign and domestic? You have a lot to consider. Here's the Web address for Live@edu: `http://my.liveatedu.com`.

You can get an Exchange account pretty easily. In fact, you or your organization can obtain hosted online Exchange services. At the time this book was written, the retail price for a basic, single-user Exchange account started at $15 per month. A wide variety of options are available at: `www.microsoft.com/online/exchange-hosted-services.mspx`.

Importing an Outlook PST File

Outlook, Microsoft's e-mail program that runs on Windows, saves all its e-mail, contact, and Calendar data in a single PST file. Oddly, Entourage doesn't provide direct support to import an Outlook PST file from Windows.

But Microsoft invested heavily in making Entourage AppleScript-able. So, third-party developers can make a living by selling scripts that extend the capabilities of Entourage.

Entourage MVPs have assembled a collection of methods that you can use to bring Microsoft Outlook PST files into Entourage. You can find them here: `www.entourage.mvps.org/import_export/pst.html`.

Printing Your Calendar

Some pleasant surprises are waiting for you in Entourage's Print pane when you're in the Calendar application. You can find an amazing number of customizations available for printing, as shown in Figure 6-25. Here are some of the printing options you have:

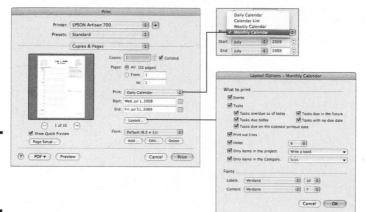

Figure 6-25:
Customizing
Calendar
printouts.

+ **Print:** The pop-up menu for print settings offers four different Calendar views: Daily Calendar, Calendar List, Weekly Calendar, and Monthly Calendar. The Start and End options change, depending on which view of the calendar you decide to print.

+ **Layout options:** Not only can you specify What to Print options, but you can select Fonts options, as well!

+ **Presets for options:** If you click the Presets pop-up menu, you can select the Save As option to save your customizations. If this feature doesn't work for you, you might not have the latest Mac OS X and Office updates installed.

Chapter 7: Keeping Track of Your Day

In This Chapter

✔ Setting reminders

✔ Making a note

✔ Remembering your tasks

✔ Moving through your day with My Day

Keeping your daily life in order involves the kind of organization that was designed into Office 2008. All the Office applications can key into the features we discuss in this chapter. Instead of wondering whether things are going as planned, you can find out exactly how your day is going. You can get things done your way because you prioritize them. In the end, you probably find your days more satisfying because you know you did your best to fulfill your own desires.

In this chapter, we deal with the tools that help you get through your day. We start with using the Reminders feature; then, we discuss making tasks, to-do lists, and notes; and finally, we describe how all this great Office organization comes together in the My Day feature.

Bringing Up Reminders

You can set reminders in various ways throughout Office 2008. In Word, Excel, Entourage, and PowerPoint, you can use the Flag for Follow Up and To Do flags to set reminders about all kinds of different things. When you create an event in Entourage, you can set a reminder.

A *reminder* is a little window that appears on your screen when the event trigger you set for it is met, as shown in Figure 7-1. For example, if you have an 11 o'clock meeting and you want to be reminded 30 minutes ahead of time, you can set up 10:30 as the event trigger for sending you a reminder. Reminders have two buttons: Snooze and Dismiss. The message in the reminder changes while time passes. Figure 7-1 shows various messages each time the reminder popped up while we snoozed.

Click to see Event Trigger.

Figure 7-1:
Being
alerted by a
reminder.

Click and hold for pop-up.

Snoozing

If you want to hide the reminder for about ten minutes, click the Snooze button. When the reminder reappears, you can snooze again. In fact, you get unlimited snooze! You're not obligated to use the default Snooze option. If you hold your mouse button down on the Snooze button for a couple seconds, a pop-up menu of Snooze options appears, as shown in Figure 7-2.

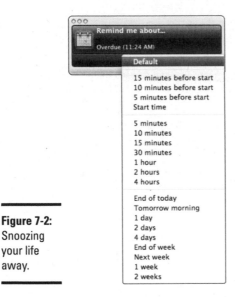

Figure 7-2:
Snoozing
your life
away.

To open the item that triggered the reminder, click the small Calendar icon in the reminder — it's a button!

Fixing an accidental snooze

If you make a mistake and select the wrong option from the pop-up menu, look on your Dock for the application Microsoft Office Reminders, as shown in Figure 7-3. Just give the Dock icon (it's a clock) a click, and the reminder window reappears. The number on the badge tells you how many pending reminders you have.

Figure 7-3:
The
Reminder
Dock icon.

Dismissing forever

When you click the Dismiss button, the reminder goes away permanently. If you have a lot of pending reminders and want to dismiss them all at the same time, click and hold the Dismiss button and choose Dismiss All from the pop-up menu that appears.

Making Notes for Future Reference

When the thought pops into your head, "I should make a note of that," click the Notes button on the Entourage toolbar to display the Notes list, as shown in Figure 7-4. The Notes feature fills the need to make a quick note, and you can use it quickly and simply. Think of Notes as a sticky-notes equivalent within Entourage.

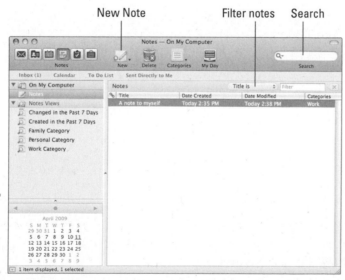

Figure 7-4:
Keeping
track of your
notes.

Looking at the Notes list

The Notes application has a consistent look and feel with the other Entourage applications we discuss throughout this minibook. Filtering, searching, sorting the Notes list, and creating new custom views work the same way in Notes as they do for Calendars, which we discuss in Chapter 6 of this minibook.

Making a note on the spot

When you click the New button in the Notes application, or if you choose File⇨New⇨Note, a New Note window appears. As you might expect, you can type a note. You can also add non-text content to your note by clicking the Insert button on the toolbar. Figure 7-5 shows a new note that has a QuickTime movie inserted.

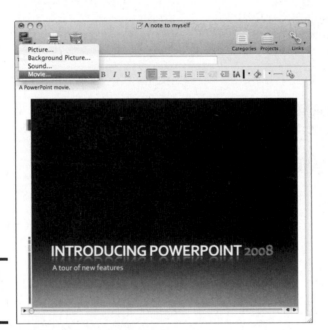

Figure 7-5: Making a new note.

Printing notes

When you print from the Notes application, the full Print panel offers you specialized options, as shown in Figure 7-6.

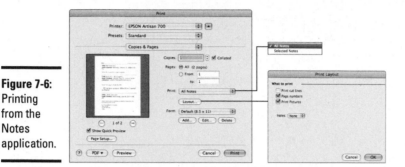

Figure 7-6:
Printing
from the
Notes
application.

Remembering to Do Things

Entourage's Tasks application is similar to Notes (which we discuss in the section, "Making Notes for Future Reference," earlier in this chapter), but Tasks ties in with Reminders (which we talk about in the section, "Bringing Up Reminders," earlier in this chapter). To get to your To Do items, use the Entourage Tasks feature on the Entourage toolbar. (Entourage uses *Task* and *To Do* interchangeably, so we follow suit.)

Checking out the Tasks interface

The Tasks application interface, as shown in Figure 7-7, includes list-filtering buttons on the toolbar, in addition to the collection of standard buttons. Filtering, searching, sorting the Notes list, and creating new custom views work the same way in Tasks as they do for Calendars, which we discuss in Chapter 6 of this minibook.

The Tasks interface has a dual personality. In the folder list's On My Computer category, two options result in different sets of items appearing:

✦ **Tasks:** When you select Tasks, tasks that you created in Entourage by using the Tasks application appear.

✦ **To Do List:** This option displays items that you created by clicking the red To Do flags on various Entourage toolbars. A task can appear in both this list and the Tasks list if you use the red flag to mark the task as a To Do item. This list also displays the Flag for Follow Up items created in Word, Excel, and PowerPoint.

When you're using the Tasks application, be sure to click both Tasks and To Do List in the left pane so that you don't accidentally overlook something.

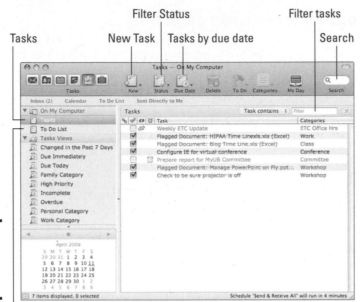

Figure 7-7:
Scoping
the Tasks
application.

To Do List

Creating a new task

When you click the New button on the toolbar within the Tasks application, you open a new, untitled Task window, as shown in Figure 7-8. A new task opens, even if you're in the To Do list. You can also create new tasks from My Day, which we cover in the section, "Making Your Day with My Day," later in this chapter.

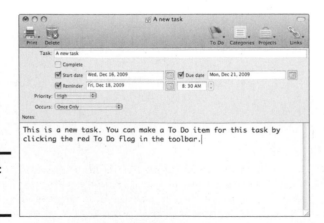

Figure 7-8:
Making a
new task.

Marking a task as completed

When you complete a task, reopen the task by double-clicking it in the Tasks list (refer to Figure 7-7) and then select the Complete check box. The feeling of satisfaction you get each time you select that check box can make your work seem worthwhile.

Creating a new To Do item

In many windows in Entourage, you find red To Do flags on the toolbars, including the new task item, as shown in Figure 7-8. Click the red To Do flag to add a To Do item for the task and/or set a reminder. In Word, Excel, and PowerPoint, use the Flag for Follow Up feature.

Printing tasks and To Do lists

The Print dialog, like this dialog in other Entourage applications, offers special choices for printing tasks and To Do lists, as shown in Figure 7-9.

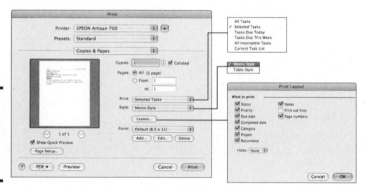

Figure 7-9:
Customizing
task and
To Do print
options.

Making Your Day with My Day

My Day is a completely new, Mac-first, Mac-only feature of Office 2008. The idea behind My Day is to give you a forward-looking window into the immediate future. The My Day window can float on top of your other application windows. You can also use My Day to create new tasks.

Looking at My Day

The My Day interface, as shown in Figure 7-10, is unique — and very purple. The top half of the interface shows upcoming events from your Entourage Calendar. While time passes during the day, the day's events automatically drop off from the top, and upcoming events appear at the bottom. The lower half of the My Day window shows tasks from your Entourage Tasks list. You can reorder your tasks by dragging them up and down in the Tasks list while you go through your day.

Mouse-over   Change time

Go to date   Change date

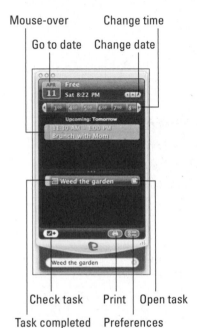

Figure 7-10:
Getting through My Day.

Check task   Print | Open task

Task completed   Preferences

Choosing a different day or time range

At the top of My Day, you can see controls that let you quickly view days or time ranges that are different from the default. The Go to Date button opens a small window that lets you enter a specific date to look at in My Day. To use the other controls, click their buttons.

Creating a new task

If you want to create a new task, you can do it right from within My Day. Just click the Create Task button to expand the hidden sheet, where you can type the name of your task. When you press the Return key, your new task appears in the Tasks portion of My Day, and a new task is added to your Entourage tasks.

To change the details of your new task, double-click the Open Task button to open Entourage (if it's not open already). Double-click the Open Task button a second time to open the task's detail pane in Entourage.

Setting My Day preferences

Yes, you can set some preferences for My Day, as shown in Figure 7-11. Click the My Day preferences button to expose the General preferences. Click the appropriate buttons to work with the remaining preferences.

You can work with more than one calendar at a time if you're using Microsoft Exchange. You even have a customizable keyboard shortcut!

Figure 7-11:
Changing
My Day
preferences.

Watching a My Day movie

Sometimes, a short movie is worth a thousand words, so if you want to see My Day in action, head to Entourage's Help menu. Search Entourage Help for *My Day* and then click the Start Video button to watch the Manage Tasks and Events by Using My Day movie that's right in the Help system (see Figure 7-12).

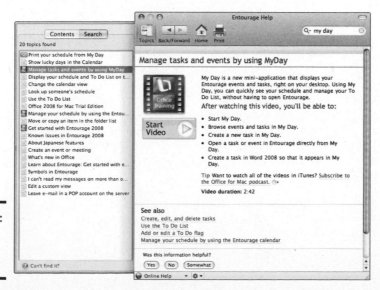

Figure 7-12:
Queuing
a My Day
video.

Book VI

Entourage's Project Center

Project Calendar

Project Center tabs

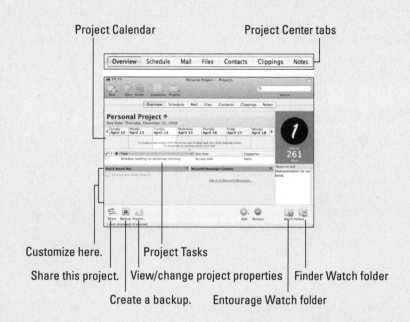

Customize here.

Project Tasks

Share this project.

View/change project properties

Finder Watch folder

Create a backup.

Entourage Watch folder

Contents at a Glance

Chapter 1: Creating New Projects

*E*verybody wants to keep their projects organized and on track. The first step is planning, but no matter how well you plan, you're sure to experience twists and turns along the way. Fortunately, Project Center is flexible — and it's there every step of the way to help you manage your project for optimal results. Don't worry, Project Center doesn't do too much hand-holding, unless you ask it to.

Project Center may be just one of the Entourage applications, in addition to Contacts, Calendar, and so on. But Project Center is extraordinarily powerful software, so we give Project Center an entire minibook of its own! We want to highlight just how important this application can be to Office users and emphasize that Project Center is a distinct application in its own right that isn't limited to working with Entourage alone. Whether in Word, Excel, or PowerPoint, you can use Project Center to help you manage almost any sort of project.

Incidentally, Project Center is available only on the Mac. Windows versions of Office don't have a comparable program.

This chapter starts with a discussion of the kinds of project scenarios in which Project Center is the right application to use. Then, we give you an overview of what you can expect to get out of Project Center, as well as how to make your very first project.

Deciding When to Use Project Center

You may want to consider Project Center when the project you're working on involves more than just one or two tasks. Setting up and managing a project takes a little time, so you probably don't want to use Project Center for every little thing. However, here are some occasions when you could benefit from using Project Center:

✦ Participating in a committee at work or tackling an assignment.

✦ Working on an office or home remodeling project.

✦ Writing a thesis or another major written work.

✦ Preparing a colloquium.

✦ Fulfilling and tracking your job responsibilities.

✦ Running a department.

✦ Managing facilities.

✦ Writing a book like this one!

Of course, after you begin to use Project Center, you'll surely find many other times when it can come in handy. Because Project Center is targeted to fulfill the organizational needs of both office and personal projects, almost everyone who's employed or has a significant home project to work on can appreciate Project Center.

When deciding which project organizing tool to use, you can refer to a hierarchy based on the size and complexity of the project. Here are the three different levels to consider:

✦ **Entourage Tasks:** When you just need an unstructured, casual approach, you can use Entourage Tasks and other regular Entourage features to handle a small project. For example, if you're picking up artwork at the graphics shop as a favor for a coworker, record that activity as an Entourage task. But if you make picking up artwork at the graphics shop for a project, you're working on a Project Center task.

✦ **Entourage Project Center:** A structured, organized approach that enables you to manage a series of tasks, assignments, communications, and shared documents. Your project can be open-ended, or it can have a specific timeframe.

✦ **Microsoft Project:** Used by people who manage projects for a living, Microsoft Project is a Windows-only product designed for large-scale, complex projects. If more than 50 percent of your workday involves managing projects, consider using this or another specialized project management software, such as OmniPlan (www.omnigroup.com/applications/omniplan).

Use Entourage Project Center when working without some sort of formal organization isn't enough but when using something like Microsoft Project is massive overkill.

Understanding How Project Center WorksWhen your project involves other people, you can share documents, contacts, messages, tasks, and files of all kinds. The documents and files aren't limited to Entourage, or even Office. Project Center takes advantage of Mac OS X and Windows file-sharing capabilities, so you can share projects and their contents with others in your organization.

Book V shows how you can tag mail, contacts, tasks, notes, and Calendar events within Entourage by using the Categories feature. Similarly, you can tag these same items, and even files, in Entourage to associate them with projects. Then, you can use the superb project management tools contained in Entourage's Project Center.

Different projects require different levels of involvement from all stakeholders. Depending on the scope of your project and your role in it, here are the three main project scenarios and how Project Center can make your life simpler in each one:

✦ **Doing an independent project:** Project Center can help you manage a one-person project.

✦ **Working as part of a team:** Project Center has sophisticated sharing tools that you can use for any given group project.

✦ **Organizing a group project:** By using Project Center's Share feature, you can share your projects with others, and others can share their projects with you. As far as Project Center is concerned, the person who controls the project is the project organizer.

Determining the Scope

You use Project Center in two general situations: as a single user or in a shared environment (see Figure 1-1). Everyone can make and use single-user projects (designated by the Number 1 icon). We encourage you to use Project Center with a single-user project to get started because single-user projects are simpler than shared projects. Shared projects (designated by the pedestrian-crossing sign) are the way to go when working with others, especially within organizations. Shared projects in Project Center are among the most powerful organizational tools you'll find anywhere.

Single-user projects

Single-user projects limit the scope to just one person — you. Everyone has projects that fall into this category. Office 2008 uses the symbol, as shown in the margin.

Starting out with a single-user project as your first project is a great way to get familiar with Project Center. Here are some examples of single-user projects that you might have:

✦ **Getting hired:** Use Project Center to organize your résumé, applications, appointments, related e-mail, and documents.

✦ **Staying hired:** Manage your resume, curriculum vitae, awards, certifications, and so on.

✦ **Managing finances:** Organize mail and documents related to your IRA (Individual Retirement Account), investments, savings, checking account, and other financial information.

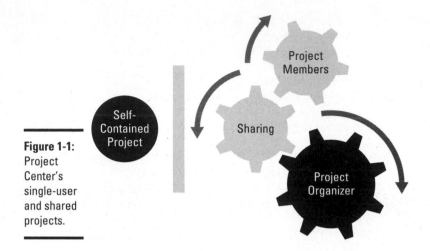

Figure 1-1:
Project
Center's
single-user
and shared
projects.

Sharing projects

Project Center can save individuals and organizations a lot of money. The time savings, efficiency, and convenience of Project Center are almost irresistible. After you use a project or two, you might feel the urge to get everyone in your organization in on this great technology. The symbol that Office 2008 uses to designate aspects of Project Center that relate to sharing projects is shown in the margin.

You shouldn't deploy sharing projects in Project Center on an individual basis, except for testing purposes or for your own personal projects. When you work in an organization, treat Project Center as a mission-critical application. Shared projects can be as important to your organization as your organization's e-mail server and file servers. Project Center isn't like a simple Web service; it's a full-fledged file-server-dependent application. Project Center can scale from individual projects to departmental projects or even organization-wide shared projects.

When you share a project, you allow others to share project-related documents, e-mail, tasks, and Calendar events. Entourage uses a shared file location. People who need to share a particular project have access to a special Watch Folder in the shared directory. (See the section, "Project Watch Folders," later in this chapter, for more on Watch Folders.) However, before you begin, think about two essential considerations before sharing projects: security and consistency.

Thinking about security

Shared projects in Project Center are serious business. The shared folder's security is critical. Choosing a location for sharing projects requires some thought. For starters, you have to acknowledge that your group will almost certainly place sensitive documents in the shared folder. So, you have to make decisions about who has access to that folder — limit access to trusted people only. The physical location of the shared folder is very important. A shared directory shouldn't reside on a person's individual computer; even if that computer is backed up regularly. Use a secure (both from a physical and network perspective) file server that has integrated backup. You may need to use encryption to ensure your shared documents' privacy.

Your shared projects may need a lot of disk space if your organization deals with multimedia files. If you ever wondered whether you have a need for a Mac OS X server, well, now you do! Mac OS X Disk Utility can create encrypted disk images, so you might want to take that approach. However, you can use any file server that supports SMB connections, which means you can use Windows, Unix, and Linux servers to host shared projects. Consult Mac OS X Help for assistance with configuring Finder to mount an SMB directory.

Controlling consistency

Network administrators have power over your shared volumes. They need to be involved in any setup and maintenance of shared project directories. You absolutely need to think about the file directory structure ahead of time. Windows and Linux administrators seem to have a penchant for using symbolic links and then not telling anyone about them. When links change, projects can potentially stop working suddenly. When any part of a file path to a shared Watch Folder changes, projects become inaccessible.

We urge you to involve your network IT people before you start deploying shared projects to any significant degree. Come to an agreement so that the network folks understand that the entire company can face serious costs and consequences if they alter the directory structure. A signed *Service Level Agreement (SLA),* which specifies what the IT department agrees to provide and outlines the rules that govern how the service operates, is certainly in order so that IT understands the importance of not changing the directory structure and knows who has to pay for the costs involved if they do. You need a file directory scheme that remains consistent — or unchanged — essentially forever, or until someone's willing to pay the costs for making a change migration. If you've ever experienced a broken link in a PowerPoint presentation, imagine that frustration and cost times thousands or millions if something goes wrong with your file server.

Your IT network crew can also help you understand the security aspects of their particular network. Work together as a team to deploy Project Center shared projects.

Starting a New Project

You can start a new project from many places in the Office 2008 suite. You may have seen an option to start a project in a menu, a pop-up menu, or in the Toolbox. Regardless of where you begin, you're taken to a wizard that helps you establish a new Project Center project. In this example, we start in Entourage. First, we set up a personal, single-user project. In Chapter 2 of this minibook, we explain how to share a project.

Follow these steps to start a new project:

1. **Open Entourage and, on the Standard toolbar, click the Project Center button, as shown in Figure 1-2.**

Project Center appears — and looks almost empty if this is your first project. The Project Center window now displays the title Projects.

Figure 1-2:
Project
Center
selected
on the
Entourage
Standard
toolbar.

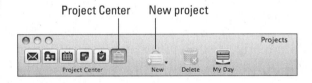

2. **Click the New button on the Standard toolbar to open the New Project Wizard screen, as shown in Figure 1-3.**

At each step in the wizard, be sure to read the Description area, as shown in Figure 1-3. This area has valuable information.

Wizard Step 1 — Setting the framework

Refer to Figure 1-3 or, of course, your own computer's screen while you add the information that the wizard requests, as follows:

✦ **Name:** Initially, this field says Untitled Project. Give your project a suitable name that's descriptive but not too long.

✦ **Due Date:** A due date is optional, depending on the nature of your project. You can always change this setting later, but if your project has limited duration, you may want to set a due date now. A little pop-up calendar button appears to the right of the date input field. Click the button to use a pop-up calendar to select a due date.

✦ **Notes to Self:** You can make a note about the purpose or nature of the project. If you decide to share the project, other members don't see these notes.

✦ **Drag and Drop Image Here:** Drag and drop a picture or clip art from your computer on this area so you have a visual cue that distinguishes this project from others that you create.

✦ **Click to Pick Color:** Click Click to Pick Color to display a pop-up menu. Select a color that you want to use in the header and in Entourage lists to help you distinguish this project from other projects.

When you're finished with this page of the wizard, click the small arrow at the bottom-right corner.

Wizard Step 2 — Deciding where and what

In Step 2, you decide the file location of your project and what existing items, if any, you want to associate with your project. Start at the top of Step 2 of the New Project Wizard, as shown in Figure 1-4.

Drag art here to represent the project.

Pop-up calendar button

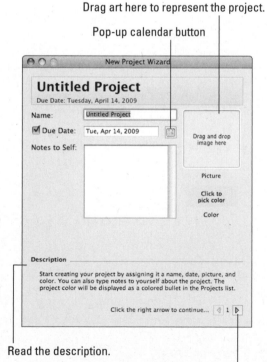

Figure 1-3:
Getting
your first
look at the
New Project
Wizard.

Read the description.

Click to go to the next wizard screen.

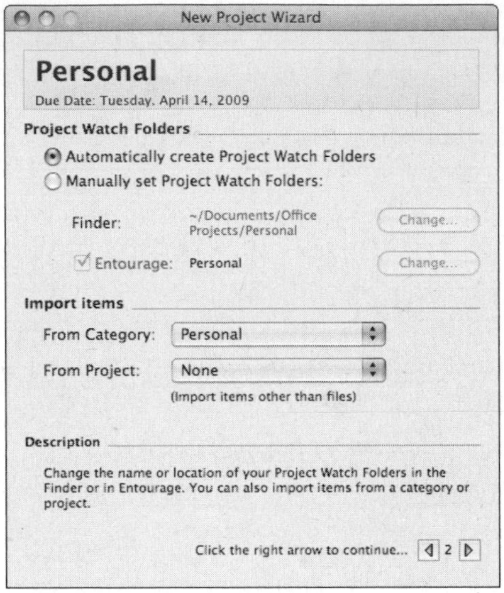

Figure 1-4:
Selecting a
file location
and adding
items.

Project Watch Folders

Of course, the most obvious question that you need to answer is, "What's a project Watch Folder?" One nifty feature of Project Center is that your projects can contain any sort of file. You store the files that are associated with your project in a *Watch Folder*. You have two choices:

✦ **Automatically Create Watch Folders:** For this example, we accept the default, which is Automatically Create Project Watch Folders. We suggest this option for a single-user project.

✦ **Manually Set Project Watch Folders:** This option allows you to select any file location for the Finder Watch Folder and designate any folder inside Entourage to store project e-mail. Select this option if you want to locate a Watch Folder on a shared directory, such as a network drive, or perhaps a Microsoft Mesh.com free file-sharing volume. If you put the Watch Folder on a network drive, you can share project files.

Import Items

This option takes into consideration three different situations that you may face:

✦ **Default options:** From Category and From Project are set to None. Use these settings if you're starting fresh and you don't have an existing category or project that you can use as a basis for your new project.

✦ **From Category:** The need to create a project doesn't always manifest itself right off the bat. You may have created a category in Entourage (see Book V, Chapter 3) and at some point realized that a simple category isn't enough — you're ready to convert the category into a project. Use this option to associate items that you already have in a category with your project. The category doesn't go away.

✦ **From Project:** Projects sometimes spawn additional sub-projects. This option enables you to import items from an existing project as the basis of a new one.

When you're finished with this page of the wizard, click the small arrow at the bottom-right corner.

Wizard Step 3 — Applying rules and tools

As shown in Figure 1-5, Step 3 helps you automatically populate your new project. If you're familiar with Entourage mail rules, this step of the wizard makes sense to you. If you have no experience with Entourage mail rules (see Book V, Chapter 4), the following section gives you a good introduction because these rules aren't very complex.

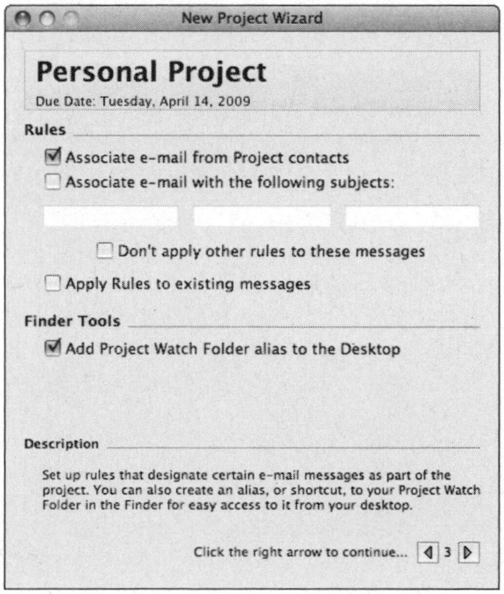

Figure 1-5: Applying rules and choosing tools.

New Project Wizard

Personal Project
Due Date: Tuesday, April 14, 2009

Rules

☑ Associate e-mail from Project contacts

☐ Associate e-mail with the following subjects:

☐ Don't apply other rules to these messages

☐ Apply Rules to existing messages

Finder Tools

☑ Add Project Watch Folder alias to the Desktop

Description

Set up rules that designate certain e-mail messages as part of the project. You can also create an alias, or shortcut, to your Project Watch Folder in the Finder for easy access to it from your desktop.

Click the right arrow to continue... ◀ 3 ▶

Rules

The rules you decide on in this section are simple, yet powerful. Be thoughtful in applying these rules because they might put more items into your project than you might expect at first blush:

✦ **Associate E-mail from Project Contacts:** If you select this option, when you finish the New Project Wizard, you can associate Entourage contacts with your project so that all e-mail to and from the contact automatically associates with your project.

To associate a contact with your project, in your Entourage Address Book, right-click or Control-click the contact's name. From the resulting pop-up menu, choose Projects⇨*[Project Name]*. All messages from project-associated contacts are associated automatically with your project.

This rule can be very convenient if you have someone in your contact list exclusively for your project. On the other hand, if you also receive non-project-related messages from a contact, the following method is better.

✦ **Associate E-mail with the Following Subjects:** This option is a good way to ensure that Entourage tags project-related e-mail as belonging to your project. Tell project members to use a unique, agreed-on (or specified) uncommon word, phrase, or nonsense character combination so that Entourage mail rules properly tag incoming mail messages and associate them with your project.

✦ **Don't Apply Other Rules to These Messages:** Selecting this option prevents existing rules from affecting incoming messages that are associated with your project.

✦ **Apply (These) Rules to Existing Messages:** Be careful with this one. If you select this check box and someone you associated with your project already has thousands of messages in your mailbox, all those messages become tagged as related to your project. On the other hand, if you already have a bunch of messages with a keyword in the subject, you can bring them into the project all at the same time, very easily.

Finder Tools

The Finder Tools area has one option. If you select the Add Project Watch Folder Alias to the Desktop check box, you put a shortcut to the shared files folder onto your Desktop.

When you're finished with this page of the wizard, click the small arrow at the bottom-right corner.

Wizard Step 4 — Summary

The final step in the wizard is perhaps the most thoughtful. (Maybe that's why we like this wizard so much.) Here, the wizard presents a summary of the choices you made. Read the information provided. If you need to change anything, click the left arrow buttons to return to any step in the wizard. When you approve the summary, click the right arrow to create your project. Your project shows up in Project Center. Incidentally, you always have the opportunity in Project Center to change your project's settings, so if you made a mistake or aren't sure you made the right choices, you can relax!

Chapter 2: Overviewing and Sharing Projects

In This Chapter

✔ Working in the Projects list

✔ Clicking the tabs

✔ Customizing the Overview tab

✔ Sharing your project

✔ Using a shortcut

As you might expect, Project Center has a place where you can view all your projects at the same time and then switch easily from one to another. That place is the Overview tab, which we talk about in this chapter. The Overview tab is also where you get an overview (makes sense, right?) of individual projects with customizable blocks that let you choose which aspects of your project you want to view. In this chapter, we also discuss how you can share a project by using Project Center's sharing capabilities.

The windows and layout of Entourage's Project Center are similar to the other Entourage applications. For more on Entourage, see Book V, which covers topics such as ordering the lists in the interface, right-clicking and Control-clicking to get pop-up menus, and using Search to create custom views. If you haven't created a project yet, turn to Chapter 1 of this minibook.

Lurking in the Projects List

When you first get into Project Center from the New Project Wizard (see Chapter 1 in this minibook for more on this wizard), the Projects window appears, featuring a list of projects, as shown in Figure 2-1.

The Projects list is a bit like a fork in the road: You can continue in two different ways, and the route you choose depends on what you want to see in Project Center's interface. You can open a project

✦ Within the Project Center window

✦ In its own window

We explain each option in the following sections.

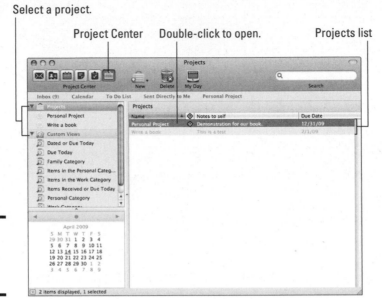

Figure 2-1:
Peeking at
the list of
projects.

Opening a project within the Project Center window

When you view a project within the Project Center window, you can have access to the Favorites bar, the mini-calendar, and custom views. Before you can open your project within the Project Center window, you need to toggle the disclosure triangle (next to the Projects folder) so the triangle is pointing down in the folder list. See Figure 2-2.

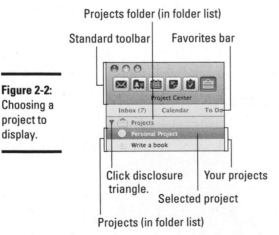

Figure 2-2:
Choosing a
project to
display.

Within the Project Center window, you can view a list of all your projects, or you can view everything about one of the projects:

✦ **To view a list of all your projects:** Select the Projects folder at the top of the folder list (it has the disclosure triangle next to it). A list of all your projects appears in the pane to the right. You can see the list of all projects only when you have the Projects folder (which appears at the top of the folder list) selected.

✦ **To view everything about one of your projects:** Select a project from the projects that appear below the Projects folder in the folder list. A series of project tabs appears for the selected project in the pane to the right, along with project details, as shown in Figure 2-3.

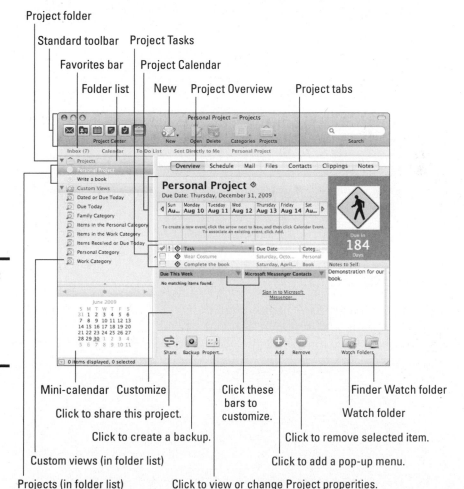

Figure 2-3: Viewing a project in a Project Center window.

You can show or hide the folder list by using any of the following methods:

✦ Choose View⊅Hide Folder List.

✦ Drag the divider to hide the folder list.

✦ Press ⌘-B to toggle the folder list on and off.

We explain the remaining interface options in the section, "Touching the Tabs," later in this chapter.

Opening a project in its own window

With the Projects folder selected in the folder list, right-click or Control-click the project name to see a pop-up menu, as shown in Figure 2-4. If you choose Open Project from the pop-up menu, the project opens in its own window. Opening a project in its own window gives you more screen space to work in. The trade-off is that you can't access the folder list, including all the views and custom views; you don't see the mini-calendar; and you can't use the Favorites bar (which we describe in the section, "Taking a Shortcut," later in this chapter).

Figure 2-4:
Opening
a project
it its own
window
from the
default
view.

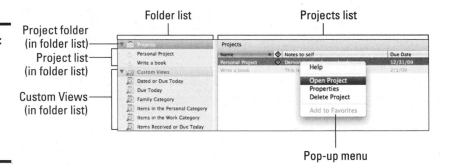

Pop-up menu

If you prefer opening a project in its own window all the time, consider changing one of Entourage's preferences so that you can simply double-click a project name to open it in its own window. Follow these steps:

1. **Choose Entourage⊅Preferences.**

The Preferences dialog appears.

2. **In the General Preferences list, select General.**

The General Preferences dialog appears.

3. **Select the Double-Clicking in the Folders List Opens a New Window check box.**

4. **Click OK to close the General Preferences dialog.**

   Now, when you double-click a project in the folder list or the Projects list, your project opens in its own window. You can double-click more than one project so that you can have multiple projects open at the same time and still have access to the Projects list.

Touching the Tabs

Figure 2-3 shows the result of opening a project in its own window. The window has no folder list on the left side, so custom views aren't available. We use the Personal Project example in this section, and as shown in Figure 2-5, it opened in the Overview tab. If your project doesn't open on the Overview tab, just click the Overview tab in the project tabs.

Project Tasks

Project Calendar

New button

Standard toolbar

Projects tabs

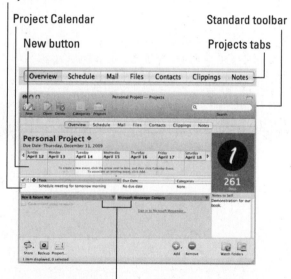

Figure 2-5:
Opening a project in its own window.

Click these bars to customize.

Here are the seven different tabs in Project Center, as shown in Figure 2-5 (we discuss many of these tabs in Chapter 4 of this minibook):

✦ **Overview:** Presents a snapshot of your project with customizable viewing boxes (see the following section for details).

✦ **Schedule:** Allows you to view all Calendar events and tasks associated with your project. See Chapter 3 of this minibook.

✦ **Mail:** Displays mail associated with your project. You can also create new project-associated mail in this tab.

✦ **Files:** Displays a list of the files that are associated with your project. You can add and delete files from this tab.

✦ **Contacts:** Allows you to manage the list of contacts who are involved in your project.

✦ **Clippings:** Displays Scrapbook contents associated with your project.

✦ **Notes:** Allows you to create and display notes to yourself about your project.

Surveying the Overview

The Overview tab has an executive summary of your project. Overview lets you use many features on the Project Center tabs, but it's less robust than each of the individual tabs for each feature. For example, you can work with a view of your project's Calendar in Overview without having to switch to the Schedule tab.

Trying out the toolbars

Project Center is a bit unusual in that project windows have two toolbars: one at the top and another not so conspicuously at the bottom. In Project Center windows, you can customize the top toolbar by choosing View⇨Customize Toolbar to display the Toolbar Options dialog. (See Book V, Chapter 3 for how to customize Entourage toolbars.) You can't customize the toolbar on the bottom of the window.

Each of the tabs we mention in the preceding section has its own set of default toolbar buttons on both the top and bottom of the window. In Figures 2-3 and 2-5, you can see the default toolbar buttons for the Overview tab. Here are the most important Overview toolbar buttons (the rest are explained in Chapters 3 and 4 of this minibook):

✦ **New:** When you click the New toolbar button on the Overview tab, a new, blank e-mail message opens, ready to be addressed and filled in. Because you're working in a project, the new e-mail message is associated automatically with this project.

✦ **Share:** When you want to turn a project from a single-user project into a shared project, click this button. The Share button is on every tab within Project Center. Read more about this button in the section, "Sharing a Project," later in this chapter.

✦ **Backup:** Click this button to start the Entourage Export Wizard. See Book V, Chapter 3 for more on exporting Entourage items.

✦ **Add:** When you select an Add option, the new item is associated with your project. Figure 2-6 shows the choices in the Add pop-up menu:

- *Event:* Create a new Calendar event.

- *Task:* Create a new task.

- *Message:* Create a new e-mail message.

- *File:* Open the Add a File dialog, where you can navigate or use Spotlight to select files to add to your project.

- *Contact:* Add a new contact to your Entourage contacts. The contact is associated with your project.

- *Clipping:* Open the Add Clipping dialog, where you can add clippings to your project from Scrapbook.

- *Note:* Add a project-related note.

Figure 2-6: Adding an item to your project.

✦ **Remove:** Removes the selected item from the project.

✦ **Watch Folders:** You have two Watch Folders:

- *Entourage Watch Folder:* Clicking this button displays a custom view of the mail associated with your project.

- *Finder Watch Folder:* Clicking this button displays the folder that contains all the documents and files that are in your project.

Don't create subfolders in the Finder Watch Folder. Finder allows you to create subfolders, but the Office interface can't always display them.

Peeking at the Calendar and Tasks

This mini-view of your project's Calendar allows you to see your project's Calendar events. When you add an event, it appears in your Entourage Calendar, marked as associated with your project. Here's more info on working with events:

✦ You can add events by double-clicking in the Calendar, or you can use the Add button to associate Calendar events with a project.

✦ You can open Calendar events and tasks by double-clicking them.

✦ You can mark tasks as completed by selecting the check box next to a task's name.

Customizing the customizable areas

The Customize area in Figures 2-3 and 2-5 has two gray bars anchored to the top of a gray shaded block. (In Figure 2-5, these bars are labeled New and Recent Mail, and Microsoft Messenger contacts.) Click either bar to open a pop-up menu, as shown in Figure 2-7, and then select a menu item to preview various aspects of your project. The same menu choices appear for the bar on the left and the bar on the right. What appears under each bar changes considerably, depending on which elements you select. The Overview tab does indeed allow you to check each aspect of a project, although not in as much detail, as we explain in Chapters 3 and 4 of this minibook.

Figure 2-7: Customizing the Overview.

Sharing a Project

 The steps you follow to turn a single-user project into a shared project are simple. The hard part is having a secure place to locate the shared folder, as we emphasize heavily in the Chapter 1 of this minibook. But you may find deciding whether you're ready to upgrade the project from single user to shared even harder. Whatever you decide, be kind to yourself and share the first few projects with colleagues and friends, not your boss or competitors!

You need a location on a shared directory that's accessible to your project members so that those other people can join your project, as we describe in Chapter 1 of this minibook.

Share

When you're ready to turn on sharing, click the Share button on the bottom toolbar in Project Center. From the pop-up menu, select the only option that's offered for your first project: Start Sharing Project.

Step 1 — Start the Assistant

When you select Start Sharing Project from the Share pop-up menu, the Project Sharing Assistant, as shown in Figure 2-8, opens. Step 1 is informational only.

When you're done with this step in the Project Sharing Assistant, click the right arrow in the lower-right corner to proceed to the next step.

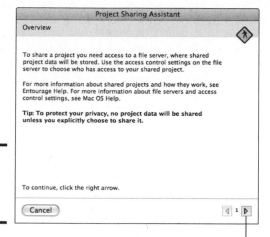

Figure 2-8:
Step 1 of sharing a project.

Click here to go to the next step.

**Book VI
Chapter 2**

Overviewing and
Sharing Projects

Step 2 — Select which project to share

After a while, you'll probably have more than one project. In Step 2, you simply select from a pop-up menu so that you can tell Entourage which of the available projects you want to share (see Figure 2-9). Entourage uses the cute little pedestrian-crossing icon (in the top-right of the Assistant) to signify shared projects.

When you're done with this step in the Project Sharing Assistant, click the right arrow in the lower-right corner to proceed to the next step.

Step 3 — Choose the file location for the shared folder

This third step requires more than just one mouse click. In this step, select the location in Finder for your project's Watch Folder. Usually, you place the Watch Folder on a shared network volume.

Shared Project icon

Choose the subject you want to share.

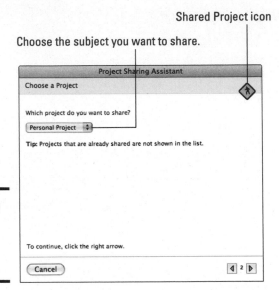

Figure 2-9:
Choosing
which
project to
share.

Yes, we know you can turn on Mac OS X file sharing and use a shared folder. That's okay for testing and demonstrating Project Center's sharing features, but it's definitely not okay for using at work in your organization for daily project activities. Having said that, if you just want to test the waters for project sharing with a colleague at the office, Mac OS X file sharing is a good way to get started. Personal file sharing is inappropriate for daily use of Project Center.

Follow these steps to set your project's Watch Folder:

1. **In the Project Sharing Assistant, as shown in Figure 2-10, click the Choose button.**

 The Choose a Location on a File Server dialog opens (see Figure 2-11). Everyone you're sharing your project with needs to have read and write access to this folder. Usually, you select a shared folder on a network for the Watch Folder.

2. **Navigate to the folder on the shared directory in which you want to store the project's files.**

 This location is the around-the-clock secure, consistent location for your project (see Figure 2-11).

3. **Select New Folder or the folder you want to use, and then click the Choose button.**

 You return to the Project Sharing Assistant, which displays the file path to your project's shared folder, as shown in Figure 2-12.

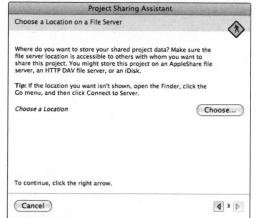

Figure 2-10:
Choosing
the project's
Watch
Folder
location.

Figure 2-11:
Using Finder
to locate
the project's
shared
folder.

When you're done with this step in the Project Sharing Assistant, click the right arrow in the lower-right corner to proceed to the next step.

Step 4 — Share existing items

In many cases, you share a project that you've been using for a while on your own, so you have existing items already in your project. You can decide whether you want to include the existing items or just items that are added after you convert your single-user project to a shared project (see Figure 2-13).

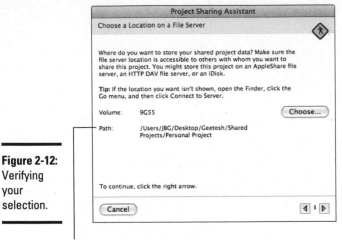

Figure 2-12:
Verifying your selection.

Where your project files are stored.

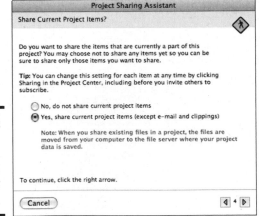

Figure 2-13:
Deciding whether to share what you already have.

Pay attention to the big red notice that advises you that if you select Yes, the existing project items, including all related files, will be moved to the shared location and will no longer be where they were when you created the project.

When you're done with this step in the Project Sharing Assistant, click the right arrow in the lower-right corner to proceed to the next step.

Step 5 — Decide how to manage new items

You have two ways to share items within a project (see Figure 2-14). The simple way is to share everything with everyone all the time. However, you can share only the items that you mark individually for sharing. So, you can put all sorts of things into your project without having to share each and every one of them. You can always change an item's sharing status at any time.

When you're done with this step in the Project Sharing Assistant, click the right arrow in the lower-right corner to proceed to the next step.

**Book VI
Chapter 2**

Overviewing and
Sharing Projects

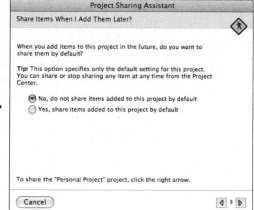

Figure 2-14:
Choosing
automatic
or individual
item
sharing.

Step 6 — Close the Project Sharing Assistant

This step has only one option, as shown in Figure 2-15. Click the Close button after you review your settings. Now, your project is being shared in Project Center.

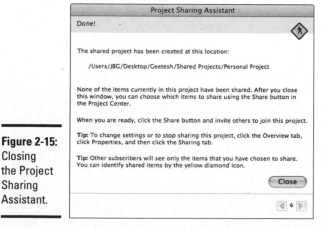

Figure 2-15:
Closing
the Project
Sharing
Assistant.

Changing Project settings

To change the settings you made in the Project Sharing Assistant or to stop sharing a project entirely, click the Project Center Overview tab. Click the Properties button on the bottom toolbar and then click the Sharing tab. The Project Properties dialog appears, which has tabs that replicate steps of the Project Sharing assistant, as shown in Figure 2-16:

✦ **To stop sharing:** Click the Stop Sharing button.

✦ **To save your Project Sharing setting changes:** Click the Save button, which also dismisses the Project Properties dialog.

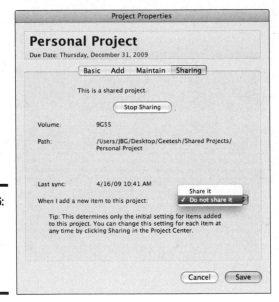

Figure 2-16:
Changing your project's sharing settings.

If the path to your project changes, visit the Project Properties dialog to reset it. Everyone who's sharing projects has to change this setting in their copy of Entourage for each project's location. If hundreds or thousands of projects exist, this process can be time-consuming and inconvenient, which is why we advise you to choose a safe, consistent place to store your projects.

Taking a Shortcut

Perhaps you noticed the shortcuts directly beneath the Standard toolbar in many Entourage windows. You can add your project to the shortcuts by right-clicking or Control-clicking the project name in the folder list, and then choosing Add to Favorites Bar, as shown in Figure 2-17. If your project is already in the Favorites bar, the same pop-up menu offers Remove from Favorites Bar. Figure 2-18 shows our Personal Project after we added it to the Favorites bar. The Favorites bar isn't visible in projects that are opened in their own windows.

Figure 2-17:
Adding and removing toolbar shortcuts.

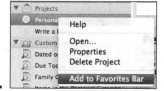

Favorites bar   Personal Project

Figure 2-18:
Seeing our favorites.

Chapter 3: Keeping on Schedule

In This Chapter

✓ **Managing Calendar events and tasks**

✓ **Making the most of the lower toolbar**

✓ **Gadding about with Gantt charts**

Managing the time aspects of your project is one of the most important activities that you can do to meet your project's deadlines. Because Entourage offers advanced calendar- and task-management capabilities, you can take advantage of them as they apply specifically to your individual projects.

For those who seek that elusive project-management tool — a *Gantt chart* — we show you how to make these helpful charts and include them in your project.

Before you can use the features in this chapter, you must first open a project in its own window or in the Project Center window, which we explain how to do in Chapter 2 of this minibook.

Keeping Track of Events and Tasks

When you click Project Center's Schedule tab, a detailed and robust application appears that focuses on your project's Calendar and Tasks. In this combination window, as shown in Figure 3-1, you have all the tools of Entourage's regular Calendar and Tasks applications. In Project Center, the events and tasks that you've associated with the selected project in the folder list at the left or with the project you opened in its own window from the Projects list (see Chapter 2 of this minibook).

Working with the Calendar

The Calendar portion of the Schedule tab looks and works intuitively. The toolbar buttons are the same as the regular Entourage Calendar view, and you can right-click or Control-click in the interface to use pop-up menus, as shown in Figure 3-1.

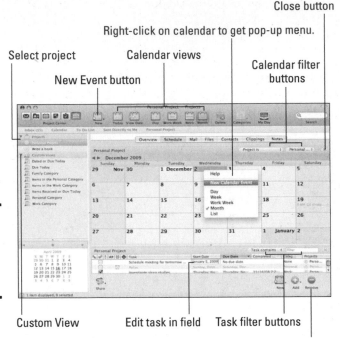

Close button

Right-click on calendar to get pop-up menu.

Select project   Calendar views

New Event button

Calendar filter
buttons

Figure 3-1:
Project
Center's
Schedule
tab.

Custom View   Edit task in field   Task filter buttons

Click to remove from project.

When you create a new event, it's automatically tagged for the selected project, no matter which interface option you use, such as clicking the New button, using the File menu, double-clicking the Calendar, or selecting New Calendar Event from the context-sensitive pop-up menu.

Double-click an event to open the event in its own window.

If you right-click or Control-click an event and choose Delete Event from the pop-up menu, the event is deleted from all Entourage Calendars. If you select an event and then press the Delete key on the keyboard or choose Edit⇨Delete to delete an event, it's also deleted from all Calendars. You may not be able to undo this action, so be careful with Delete.

If you select an event and then click the Remove button from the bottom toolbar, the event is still in your main Entourage Calendar. Click the Remove button to disassociate the event from your project but not delete it.

Filtering and making overlays

Because you probably have more than one project underway at any given time, the Schedule tab allows you to easily switch your Calendar view from one project to another, without leaving the current project.

The Schedule tab also allows you to filter and overlay the Calendar events of a single project and overlay all your projects in a live view within the Schedule Calendar view. The more projects you have, the more useful the Schedule tab becomes!

Beneath the Project Center tabs, off to the right side is a combination of pop-up menus (and sometimes an input field) that together comprise the Calendar Filter:

+ **Menu 1:** Click the arrow to see a pop-up menu where you can filter based on project, category, or subject. In Figure 3-1, this menu is the left-most pop-up menu.

+ **Menu 2:** The Personal menu appears to the right of pop-up Menu 1. Pop-up Menu 2 changes depending on what you select in Menu 1. Table 3-1 summarizes your options.

+ **Search field:** At times, you may see a blank search field (which Figure 3-1 *doesn't* show) when Subject Contains is chosen in Menu 1.

+ **X (Clear) button:** On the far right, you can see an X (Clear) button that clears the Calendar Filter. When you click the X (Clear) button, pop-up Menu 2 switches to All.

    Although this behavior may seem strange, when pop-up Menu 1 displays Subject Contains, nothing happens to the input field when you click the X (Clear) button.

The Calendar Filter affects only the Calendar, not the Tasks associated with it.

Table 3-1	Calendar Filter Buttons in Project Center
Menu 1 Option	*Corresponding Menu 2 Options*
Project Is	All, None, and a listing of your projects.
Category Is	All, None, and a listing of your categories.
Subject Contains	A blank search field appears, rather than a pop-up menu.

You may find the Schedule tab indispensable. While your responsibilities increase, you can use the Schedule tab to make sure your meetings, tasks, and events don't overlap or conflict with each other from one project to another.

In the Schedule tab, the project you work with is selected in the top portion of the left panel, the folder view (see Chapter 2 of this minibook), which you can turn on and off by pressing ⌘-B when viewing your project in a Project Center window. (You don't have this option if your project is in its own window.)

To copy an event, press and hold the Option key while you drag your event in the Calendar.

Changing Calendar views

When you use the Schedule tab, Calendar View buttons appear on the Standard toolbar. Choose from these options:

+ **Today:** Displays today's date in the current view.

+ **View Date:** Displays a small dialog in which you can enter a date or select a date from a pop-up calendar.

+ **Day:** Displays one day's calendar.

+ **Work Week:** Displays one week of your calendar. You can set the work week in Entourage Preferences (see Book V, Chapter 2 to find out how).

+ **Week:** Displays one week's calendar.

+ **Month:** Displays one month's calendar.

Working with Tasks

The Tasks portion of the Schedule tab, as shown in Figure 3-1, shows a Tasks list that's associated with your project. You have the same interface features that you do for Calendar events, as we discuss in the section, "Working with the Calendar," earlier in this chapter, plus some additional options:

+ **Edit task in field:** Click the fields in the Task list and edit the field right in the window.

+ **Completed check box:** Mark a task as completed by clicking this check box.

+ **Order tasks:** Click the column headers to order tasks.

+ **Drag and drop:** You can drag a task to the Desktop to create a standard Calendar event file with an `.ics` extension that you can send as an e-mail attachment.

Right-clicking or Control-clicking a task produces a handy pop-up menu that's definitely worth investigating, as shown in Figure 3-2.

Like with the Calendar Filter in the upper part of the Schedule tab, you can filter and/or compare tasks with all your projects in an overlay. The Task Filter's pop-up menus look and work the same way as the Calendar Filter, which we discuss in the section, "Filtering and making overlays," earlier in this chapter.

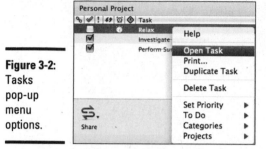

Figure 3-2:
Tasks
pop-up
menu
options.

Exploring the Lower Toolbar

The toolbar at the bottom of the Schedule tab starts with the Share button and then features a New button, which works a little differently from the New button in the Standard toolbar. We explore the bottom toolbar's buttons in the following sections.

Sharing your project with others

In Chapter 2 of this minibook, we explain how to share a project. (If you haven't already, start there to find out about how to share a project.) After you start a shared project, you might want to invite a colleague, a relative, or a friend to join in the shared project. The person you invite becomes a project member after he accepts your invitation. If your invitee has Entourage, he can add the same project to his Project Center and share all the documents, Calendar events, notes, and tasks that you've designated to share with project members.

To invite someone to become a project member, follow these steps:

1. **Click the Share button in the bottom toolbar.**

   A pop-up menu, as shown in Figure 3-3, appears.

Figure 3-3:
Step 1 of
sending an
invitation.

2. **Choose Invite People to Join Project from the pop-up menu.**

   A prompt, like the one shown in Figure 3-4, appears.

3. **Click the Create E-Mail Invitation button in the confirmation dialog.**

   A special invitation mail message, as shown in Figure 3-5, opens. When an invitee receives the invitation, she can click the yellow bar that has the Click Here to Subscribe to the Shared Project *[Project Name]* link. Clicking this link allows your invitee to associate her Entourage Project Center with your shared project.

Figure 3-4:
Confirming
your action
request.

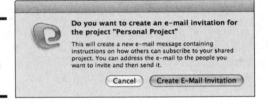

Figure 3-5:
Crafting
a special
invitation.

You can send invitations to people who don't have Entourage, but they can't subscribe fully to a project. They can only share project documents with their file system by manually using the project Watch Folder.

New button

The New button on the lower toolbar has a pop-up menu, as shown in Figure 3-6. Automatically associate a new item with your project by choosing from these options:

✦ **Event:** Create a new Calendar event.

✦ **Task:** Create a new task.

✦ **Message:** Create a new e-mail message.

✦ **File:** Open the Add a File dialog, in which you can navigate or use Spotlight to select files to add to your project.

✦ **Contact:** Add a new contact to your Entourage contacts. The contact is associated with your project.

✦ **Note:** Add a project-related note.

Add button

When you click the Add button on the lower toolbar, a pop-up menu appears, offering the same choices as the New button's pop-up menu (which we discuss in the preceding section). The difference is that instead of creating a new item, you're presented with a mini-viewer that displays all your existing items that fit into the option you choose from the pop-up menu (see Figure 3-6). By clicking the Add button, you can add an existing item to your project.

Say that you recently received an e-mail that you want to add to your project. To do so, click the Add button and then choose Message from the pop-up menu that appears. The Add Mail dialog appears and enables you to select messages from your entire Mail list, as shown in Figure 3-6.

Figure 3-6:
Adding mail
messages to
a project.

Creating a Gantt Chart

While we're on the topic of scheduling, one of the popular tools that project-oriented people like to use is a *Gantt chart,* which is a visual representation of the timelines associated with various aspects of your project. You can even use a Gantt chart to compare timelines of one or more projects. Although large-scale project management software generally can generate Gantt charts, you can create excellent Gantt charts in Microsoft Excel.

Making a very simple Gantt chart

A simple Gantt chart consists of colored cells. If you use Excel to create a Gantt chart, you can take advantage of the Fill color picker, which you can float anywhere on the screen, as shown in Figure 3-7. Follow these steps to float the Fill color picker:

1. **Open Excel**

   A new, blank worksheet appears.

2. **In the Formatting Palette, click the disclosure triangle next to the Borders and Shading section to display it.**

   If the Formatting Palette isn't visible, click the Toolbox button on the Standard toolbar.

3. **In the Shading area, click the Color button, and at the top of the Fill color picker that appears, click the dotted lines.**

4. **Type column names and row labels, as shown in Figure 3-8.**

   Column names in a Gantt chart are usually dates, and row labels are usually project tasks.

   In Figure 3-8, the grid lines are turned off. To hide gridlines, in the Formatting Palette's Page Setup section, deselect the Gridlines check boxes.

5. **Drag your mouse over cells and click different colors on the Fill color picker under the dates appropriate for each task.**

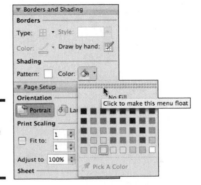

Figure 3-7:
Floating the
Fill color
picker.

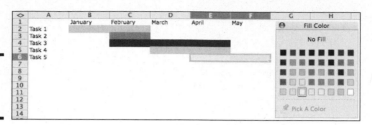

Figure 3-8:
Making a
Gantt chart.

Making a more robust Gantt chart

Unfortunately, Excel 2008 doesn't support Visual Basic for Applications. Many excellent add-ins can make Gantt charts, but none of them work in Office 2008. But now you have something to look forward to in the next version of Office for Mac. Meanwhile, you can manually create detailed Gantt charts by following the instructions given on Jon Peltier's Web site. Although the instructions are Windows-centric, you can follow the steps that Excel MVP Jon Peltier outlines on this Web page and adapt them to work for you in Excel 2008 for Mac: www.peltiertech.com/Excel/Charts/GanttChart.html.

Chapter 4: Managing More Project Details

In This Chapter

✔ Mining project mail

✔ Following your project files

✔ Speeding up Project Center

✔ Finding files in Project Gallery

✔ Chilling with project contacts

✔ Avoiding Clippings

✔ Taking notes

✔ Working with the amazing Project Palette

A ctivities related to project e-mail and contacts are easy to watch over in Project Center. Managing the files that are associated with a project doesn't require a lot of work because Project Center keeps tabs on everything for you. In this chapter, you see that Project Center's e-mail, contacts, and notes work very similarly to the regular Entourage interface. But we point out the special differences that Project Center offers. We try to satisfy your curiosity about Clippings, and then show off the Project Center's crowning achievement: the Project Palette.

Viewing Project Mail

Take a peek at Project Center's Mail tab, as shown in Figure 4-1. You see hardly any difference at all between this tab and the Entourage Mail application, except for the lack of mailboxes!

The messages that you see in the messages list have been previously associated with the project you're currently working with. If messages reside in different folders, they still show up on Project Center's Mail tab as long as you associate these messages with your project.

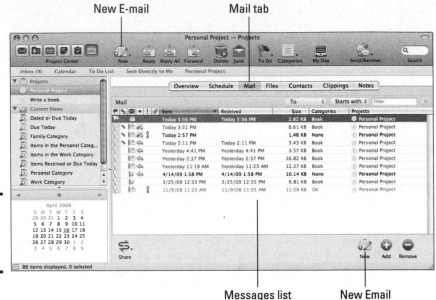

New E-mail   Mail tab

Messages list   New Email

Figure 4-1:
Making use
of Project
Mail.

New

On the Mail tab, the New buttons on the Standard toolbar and bottom tool-bar do the same thing: They open a new e-mail message that's associated with your project. In Figure 4-1, we chose to view the messages list without a Preview pane, but you can select a different Preview setting from the View menu on the menu bar, if you want. To change the column headings, right-click or Control-click the column names.

Watching your Project's Files

Project Center's Files tab is a nifty file browser. The Files tab, as shown in Figure 4-2, displays all the files in the Finder Watch Folder — shared files first, followed by files in your hard drive's local project file folder (which aren't shared). The local (not-shared) folder was created when you designated your project as a place to store your project's files. You also have the option of moving those files to the Finder Watch Folder when you begin sharing your project. Even if you choose to move all your files to the shared Finder Watch Folder, the local folder still exists. Of course, if a folder's empty, you don't see any files for that folder.

Refresh ▸ If you aren't logged in to your network, a dialog may appear, prompting you to enter user authentication information when you click Project Center's Files tab. In the Project Center Files title bar, you see a Refresh button that you rarely, if ever, need to use to refresh the list of files. The list refreshes automatically whenever you do anything on the Files tab, so you probably don't ever need to click Refresh.

Open selected file

Create E-Mail   Files tab   Refresh

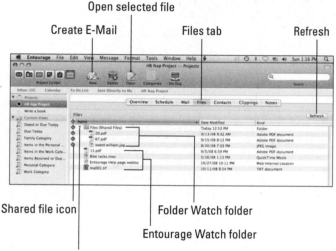

Figure 4-2:
Project
Center's
Files tab.

Shared file icon   Folder Watch folder

Entourage Watch folder

Click triangle to see file names.

A disclosure triangle appears just to the left of the Entourage Watch Folder icon in the Files list. Click the disclosure triangle to see a list of the files contained in the Finder Watch Folder. In the Files list, you see a directory of all files currently associated with the project you selected. If you're sharing this project, the files listed under the Finder Watch Folder are in the shared folder on the file server (refer to Figure 4-2).

 Files that are located in the local file folder for your project don't have the orange Shared icon. If you don't have a shared Finder Watch Folder in the project, all the files listed are located in the local file folder for your project.

If you do have a shared Finder Watch Folder in your project, you see a Shared folder icon in the list with a small orange icon indicating that it's a shared item. The orange icon appears by the filenames of shared items.

 Besides Office file formats, Project Center's Files tab can handle any file type. You're not limited to Office files. You can manage PDF, Quark Express, CAD (Computer Aided Design) files — you name it! When you work with files in the Files list, you can work with more than one file at a time. Select multiple files by holding down the ⌘ key while you click filenames.

 The Files tab doesn't work with subfolders. If you create subfolders in your Finder Watch Folder with Mac OS X Finder or Windows Explorer, the Files tab ignores the subfolders and all files contained in them. Mac OS X Finder does allow subfolders and their files to be shared with others, but they don't appear in Project Center's Files tab. To avoid confusion, don't use subfolders in Finder Watch Folders.

Adding files to the Files list

When you add a file to the Files list, it appears in the shared Finder Watch Folder. You can add to the Files list by using any of the following methods:

+ Drag files into the Files list from any Finder window.

+ Drag files into the Files list from the Desktop.

+ Click the green Add button, as shown in the margin. The Add a File dialog appears. Navigate or use Spotlight to select a file that you want to add, and then click the Open button to add your file to the project.

Project Center asks your permission before moving a file into the shared Finder Watch Folder.

Sharing a file

To share a file that's currently not shared, you first must set up a shared Finder Watch Folder. We discuss how to share a project and create a Finder Watch Folder in Chapter 1 of this minibook. You can find files that you're not sharing located in your project's local file folder, which was created when you created your project. If you add files to your project before you start sharing and opt not to share those files already present when you turn sharing on, the files remain in the local folder and appear without the sharing icon in the Files tab's Files list.

You can take one of two approaches to share a file. Taking either approach moves the selected file from the local project file folder (not shared) into the Finder Watch Folder (shared). The shared file icon (as shown in the margin) appears next to the file when the operation is complete. We outline the two ways that you can share a file in the following sections.

Sharing a file — Method 1

1. **Select the file you want to share and then click the Share button in the bottom toolbar.**

2. **Choose Share from the pop-up menu that appears.**

Sharing a file — Method 2

1. **Right-click or Control-click the file you want to share.**

2. **From the pop-up menu that appears, choose Share.**

Stop sharing a file

To stop sharing a file, follow these steps:

1. **On the Files tab, right-click or Control-click the filename in the Files list.**

2. **From the pop-up menu that appears, choose Do Not Share File.**

The file is moved to the local file folder for your project and appears in the Files list below the shared files.

Opening a file

To open a file, do any of the following actions in the Files list:

Book VI
Chapter 4

◆ Double-click a file in the list.

◆ Right-click or Control-click a file in the list, and then select Open from the pop-up menu that appears.

◆ Select a file and then click the Open button on the Standard toolbar.

◆ Select a file and then choose File⇨Open.

◆ Select a file and then press ⌘O.

Removing a file from a project

When you remove a file from a project, the file isn't deleted. The file is removed from the Watch Folder, and either placed on your computer's Desktop or returned to the unshared local file folder for your project.

To remove files from a project, follow these steps:

1. **Select a file in the list and then click the red Remove button in the bottom toolbar.**

A Remove Files from Project dialog appears.

2. **Select Yes.**

The Remove Files from Project dialog closes.

3. **Select the Overview tab of Project Center.**

4. **Select the Finder Watch Folder.**

The Finder Watch Folder opens. In this folder, you can use Mac OS X Finder to drag the file to the Desktop or other Finder location.

Sending files via e-mail or Microsoft Messenger

You can easily send files to anyone by using e-mail or Microsoft Messenger. You have to open Messenger before you can use it with this Files tab feature. You can send multiple files via a single e-mail, but only one file at a time via Messenger. You can send a file in one of two ways, which we talk about in the following sections.

Send

Sending a file — Method 1

1. **Click the file in the Files list to select it and then click the Send button on the lower toolbar.**

   A pop-up menu appears.

2. **Choose either E-Mail or Messenger from the pop-up menu.**

Sending a file — Method 2

1. **Right-click or Control-click a file, as shown in Figure 4-3.**

   A pop-up menu appears.

2. **From the pop-up menu, select the option you want to use.**

   You can choose from these two options:

   • *Send as Mail Attachment*

   • *Send to Microsoft Messenger Contact*

3. **Select a contact from the pop-up's submenu.**

Figure 4-3:
Sending
files from
Project
Center.

Speeding Up Things

If you have your Finder Watch Folder on a network drive and your network connection isn't gigabit speed, expect delays, called *latency,* when you use Project Center's Files tab. If you connect to a server with a virtual private network (VPN) on a DSL or cable connection, expect quite a bit of delay because these connections are slow. Unfortunately, we haven't found a way to tell Entourage to not refresh the list so often. It seems that no matter what you do, while you have the Files tab open, the Files list refreshes, which can take time. We chose Help⇨Send Feedback about Entourage and requested Microsoft change this behavior. If you also send feedback, chances are good Microsoft will improve the overall speed of the Files tab considerably.

Finding Files in Project Gallery

From any application, you can visit Project Gallery by choosing File⇨Project Gallery. On Project Gallery's Project Center tab, you can open any documents that are associated with projects, as shown in Figure 4-4.

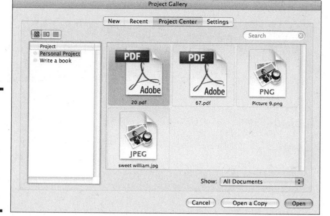

Figure 4-4: Using Project Gallery to open Project Center files.

Associating with Project Contacts

Independent of the list of people that you currently share a project with is the list of contacts from your Entourage Address Book that you designate as associated with your project. Select a contact to display that contact's information in the Files tab window. You have the following buttons at your disposal:

✦ **Add:** To associate contacts with a project, simply click the Add button on the bottom toolbar. Figure 4-5 shows the Contacts tab of the Project Center window. We describe the Add button in Chapter 3 of this mini-book.

✦ **New:** The New buttons on both the Standard and bottom toolbars do the same thing — they open the New Contact input form. (See Book V, Chapter 3 for more about managing contacts.)

✦ **Messenger:** The Messenger button on the bottom toolbar is a fast, easy way to create and manage a group of contacts in MSN Messenger. If you aren't signed in already, you can click the Messenger button to sign into MSN Messenger. To create a new MSN Messenger group from the contacts associated with your project, click the Messenger button and then choose Create Messenger Group (see Figure 4-6). After you create an MSN Messenger group for your project, the other two actions — Remove Messenger Group and Update Messenger Group — become available.

New Contact   Contact tab

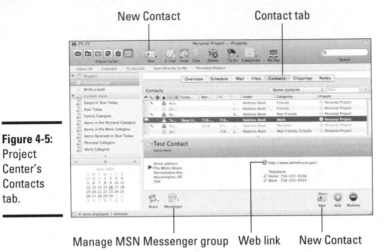

Figure 4-5:
Project
Center's
Contacts
tab.

Manage MSN Messenger group   Web link   New Contact

Figure 4-6:
Creating a
new MSN
Messenger
group.

Storing and Using Clippings

When you open Project Center's Clippings tab, you're presented with an interesting interface. The Clippings interface looks like you can permanently store anything you want from the Scrapbook in your project. Unfortunately, that's not the case. When you add a clipping to your project, it's not actually added to your project. The clipping stays within the Toolbox's Scrapbook. If you remove something from the Scrapbook, you also remove it from Clippings.

You can be in Word, Excel, or PowerPoint, working on something that's not related to your project in any way — yet, you can delete something from the Scrapbook that you had stored in one of your project's Clippings collections and not even realize that you deleted a project clipping. Worse, you might decide to clear the Scrapbook by clicking the readily accessible Delete button and choosing Delete All from the pop-up menu that appears. Clearing the Scrapbook deletes all the clippings from all your projects, and you might not even know you did it! We recommend that you avoid the Clippings tab.

Using Notes in Project Center

The Notes tab in Project Center works like the Notes application in Entourage. Figure 4-7 shows the Notes tab. In this section, we highlight features from the Share and New buttons.

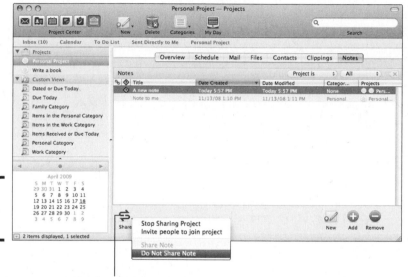

Figure 4-7:
Sharing
a note.

The Share button

To share a note, follow these steps:

1. **Select the note in the Notes list and then click the Share button, as shown in Figure 4-7.**

A pop-up menu appears.

2. **Choose Share Note from the pop-up menu.**

If you want to stop sharing a note, follow these steps:

1. **Select a shared note in the list and then click the Share button.**

A pop-up menu appears.

2. **Select Do Not Share Note from the pop-up menu, as shown in Figure 4-7.**

To open a new note in its own window, click the New button on either the Standard or bottom toolbar.

Working with the Project Palette

In Book I, Chapter 4, we discuss the dazzling Project Palette (see Figure 4-8). Here, we want to showcase one of the most incredible pieces of screen real estate that we know about. You can open the Project Palette in several ways:

✦ Choose View➪Toolbox➪Project Palette to open the Project Palette in Word, Excel, or PowerPoint.

✦ Under the Toolbox subheading, select Project Palette.

✦ Click the Toolbox button on the Standard toolbar and then click the Projects button (see Figure 4-9).

This amazing palette (as shown in Figure 4-8) enables you to manage your projects with almost every tool we mention in this minibook.

Figure 4-8:
The entire
Project
Palette.

Because this book is, after all, an easy go-to reference manual, the most helpful thing we can do is to break the palette into sections so that you can see what each of the incredible array of features available does. Starting from the top . . .

Right-click or Control-click the Project Palette heading area to switch from one project to another, or even start a brand-new project, as shown in Figure 4-9.

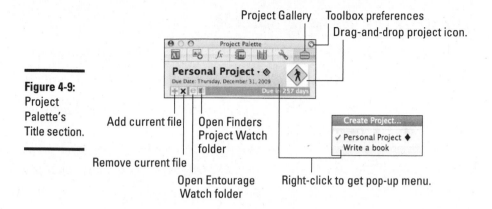

Figure 4-9:
Project Palette's Title section.

The Project Palette's Schedule section (see Figure 4-10) is like My Day for projects. (We talk about My Day in Book V, Chapter 7.) You can see the events that are scheduled for the day, and you can change the Notes to Self without going to your project's properties. To open an event or a task in its own window, just click it.

Figure 4-10:
The Schedule section.

The Tasks section, as shown in Figure 4-11, allows you to select check boxes to check off tasks after you complete them. You can create new tasks in their own windows by clicking the New Task button.

The Project Palette's Recent Items section is another handy area. The Recent Items section has a More link that takes you to Entourage. However, you can also customize this block of the palette. If you click the gray bar near the top of this section of the palette, you can switch the view instantly to any of the options shown in the pop-up menu in Figure 4-12. You can click the Go to Project Center button to jump to Project Center.

Book VI Chapter 4

Managing More Project Details

Click to mark task completed.   Change list order

New Task button

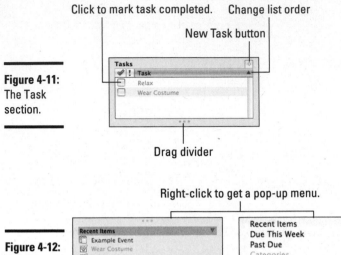

Figure 4-11:
The Task
section.

Drag divider

Right-click to get a pop-up menu.

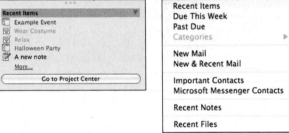

Figure 4-12:
The Recent
Items
section.

Index

C

D

N

O

S

T

W

Notes